COMPARATIVE POLITICAL DYNAMICS

HarperCollins Series in Comparative Politics

Series Editors:

Gabriel A. Almond
Lucian W. Pye

COMPARATIVE POLITICAL DYNAMICS:

Global Research Perspectives

Edited by

Dankwart A. Rustow

City University of New York
Graduate School and University Center

Kenneth Paul Erickson

Hunter College and City University of New York
Graduate School and University Center

HarperCollins *Publishers*

Sponsoring Editor: Lauren Silverman/Catherine Woods
Project Editor: Robert Cooper
Design and Cover Coordinator: Mary Archondes
Text Design: North 7 Atelier Ltd.
Cover Design: Edward Smith Design, Inc.
Production: Willie Lane/Sunaina Sehwani
Compositor: House of Equations Inc.
Printer/Binder: Courier Companies Inc.
Cover Printer: New England Book Components, Inc.

Comparative Political Dynamics: Global Research Perspectives
Copyright © 1991 by HarperCollins Publishers Inc.

Library of Congress Cataloging-in-Publication Data

Comparative political dynamics : global research perspectives / edited
   by Dankwart A. Rustow and Kenneth Paul Erickson.
      p. cm.
   Includes bibliographical references and index.
   ISBN 0–06–045673–6
   1. Comparative government. I. Rustow, Dankwart A. II. Erickson,
Kenneth Paul.
JF51.C6144   1991   90–44800
320.3—dc2090-44800   CIP

92 93   9 8 7 6 5 4 3 2

Contents

Preface

Most of the chapters assembled in this volume were first presented as papers at a conference held September 7–9, 1988, at the Graduate School of the City University of New York (CUNY). The meeting marked the twentieth anniversary of the publication of the quarterly journal *Comparative Politics*, sponsored by the CUNY Ph.D. Program in Political Science. A concluding reception honored Gabriel A. Almond, Professor Emeritus of Political Science at Stanford University, for his singular contribution since the 1950s in guiding the discipline of comparative politics from its narrow American and European focus toward a truly global perspective.

In planning the conference and the present volume, the editors received valuable advice from members of the *Comparative Politics* Editorial Board and other colleagues, notably Asher Arian, Bernard E. Brown, Sumit Ganguly, Irving Leonard Markovitz, and Sharon Zukin, all of the CUNY Graduate School; James C. Scott, Yale University; and Ezra N. Suleiman, Princeton University. The preparation of the present volume also benefited from the input of other conference participants including Maria Helena Moreira Alves, Universidade Estadual do Rio de Janeiro; Nancy Bermeo, Princeton University; Forrest D. Colburn, Princeton University; Stephen D. Krasner, Stanford University; Robert Legvold, Columbia University; Juan J. Linz, Yale University; Roy C. Macridis, Brandeis University; Guillermo O'Donnell, CEBRAP, Brazil, and Notre Dame University; A.F.K. Organski, University of Michigan; Giovanni Sartori, Columbia University; Theda Skocpol and Jeff Goodwin, Harvard University; Marie-France Toinet, University of Paris; and Christa Altenstetter, Frank Bonilla, John Bowman, John Harbeson, and Donald S. Zagoria of CUNY.

Generous funding for the conference and for the preparation of the book was provided by the International Affairs Program of the Ford Foundation, the German Marshall Fund of the United States, and the CUNY Chancellor's Special Projects Fund. We particularly wish to thank Stanley J. Heginbotham of the Ford Foundation, Peter R. Weitz

of the German Marshall Fund, and Chancellor Joseph S. Murphy of the
City University of New York for their encouragement and support. Dr.
Larry N. Peterson, Managing Editor of *Comparative Politics*, and Dr.
Marie A. Manca of the CUNY Ph.D. Program assisted with energy,
imagination, and an eye for detail in the preparation both of the conference and the present volume, as did Judianne LoCasto in the voIumi-
nous correspondence and preparation of the manuscript.

From conference to book, the editing process involved a good deal
of collaborative exchange between editors and authors. We gratefully
acknowledge the authors' responsiveness and perseverance as they
addressed our critiques through several rounds of revision. In the final
publication phase, it was a pleasure to work with Bob Cooper, Donna
DeBenedictis, and Lauren Silverman at HarperCollins.

The discipline of comparative politics, after expanding its geographic scope in the 1950s and 1960s, began an extensive search in the
1970s and 1980s for new conceptual parameters and methodological
tools. Meanwhile, in recent years the world has witnessed a breathtak-
ing spectacle of political transformation, as civilian governments have
replaced military dictatorships from the Philippines to Turkey and
Chile, *apartheid* has come into question in South Africa, and communist regimes have yielded to competitive elections throughout Eastern
Europe and in parts of the Soviet Union.

It is the hope of the editors and contributors that this volume will
make a contribution to the understanding and interpretation of such
dynamic global developments—and thus help prepare the discipline for
the new tasks it will be facing in the twenty-first century.

Dankwart A. Rustow

Kenneth Paul Erickson

Contributors

Douglas E. Ashford is Andrew W. Mellon Professor of Comparative Politics at the University of Pittsburgh. He has published many books and articles on politics and policy making in Western Europe and in the Third World. His most recent book, *The Emergence of the Welfare States* (1986), compares the development of the welfare state in the late nineteenth and early twentieth century in European countries and the United States. A sequel on the postwar politics of democratic welfare states will appear shortly.

David G. Becker is Associate Professor of Government at Dartmouth College. He has written extensively on Peruvian development and on issues of development theory, with particular emphasis on the idea of postimperialist capitalism in Latin America. He is the author of *The New Bourgeoisie and the Limits of Dependency* (1983) and coauthor of *Postimperialism: International Capitalism and Development in the Late Twentieth Century* (1987). He is currently at work on a book that will comparatively treat Bolivian, Peruvian, and Venezuelan democracy.

Henry Bienen is James S. McDonnell Distinguished Professor of Politics and International Affairs and Director of the Center of International Studies at Princeton University. He is the author of the forthcoming *Of Time and Power* and of many books, including *Political Conflict and Economic Change in Nigeria* (1985), and most recently, *Armed Forces, Conflict and Change in Africa* (1989). Bienen is also editor of *World Politics*.

Ronald H. Chilcote is Professor of Political Science at the University of California at Riverside. He is the author or editor of nine books, including *Protest and Resistance in Angola and Brazil* (1972), *The Brazilian Communist Party: Conflict and Integration, 1922–1972* (1974), *Theories of Comparative Politics* (1981), *Theories of Development and Under-development* (1984), and *Power and the Ruling Classes in Northeast Brazil* (1990). He is founder and managing editor of *Latin American Perspectives*.

David Collier is Professor of Political Science and department chair at the University of California at Berkeley. He has also held appointments at the universities of Chicago, Stanford, Princeton, and Notre Dame and at the Institute for Advanced Study. He is the author of *Squatters and Oligarchs: Authoritarian Rule and Policy Change in Peru* (1976), editor of *The New Authoritarianism in Latin America* (1979), and coauthor of *Shaping the Political Arena: Critical Junctures, the Labor Movement, and Regime Dynamics in Latin America* (1991).

Bruce Dickson is a doctoral candidate in the Political Science Department of the University of Michigan. He is the coauthor of *A Research Guide to Central Party and Government Meetings in China, 1949–1986* (1988), and editor or coeditor of *The Emerging Pacific Community: A Regional Perspective* (1984), and *Economic Relations in the Asian-Pacific Region* (1987).

Susan Eckstein is Professor of Sociology at Boston University. She is the author of *The Poverty of Revolution: The State and Urban Poor in Mexico* (2d ed., 1989), *The Impact of Revolution: A Comparative Analysis of Mexico and Bolivia* (1976), and numerous articles in professional journals. She is editor of *Power and Popular Protest: Latin American Social Movements* (1989). Currently she is writing a book on the impact of Cuba's revolution.

S. N. Eisenstadt is Professor of Sociology at the Hebrew University, Jerusalem, and the author of, among many other writings, *From Generation to Generation* (1956), *The Political Systems of Empires* (1963), *Modernization: Protest and Change* (1966), *Tradition, Change, and Modernity* (1973), *Revolution and the Transformation of Societies* (1978), and *A Sociological Approach to Comparative Civilizations: The Development and Directions of a Research Program* (1986).

Kenneth Paul Erickson is Professor of Political Science at Hunter College and the Graduate School of the City University of New York and a member of the editorial committee of *Comparative Politics*. He is the author of *The Brazilian Corporative State and Working-Class Politics* (1977) and articles on corporatism, the state, working-class politics, energy policy, and dependency in Latin America.

Jack Hayward is Professor of Politics at the University of Hull (England). He is the author of *The State and the Market Economy: Industrial Patriotism and Economic Intervention in France* (1986) and articles on economic interest groups, the state, and the policy process. He is currently editor of *Political Studies*.

Metin Heper is Professor of Political Science and Public Administration at Bilkent University, Ankara, Turkey. He is the author of *The State Tradition in Turkey* (1985) and editor of and contributor to *Islam and Politics in the Modern Middle East* (1984), *The State and Public Bureaucracies: A Comparative Perspective* (1987), *Local Government in Turkey: Governing Greater Istanbul* (1989), and coeditor and contributor to *State, Democracy and the Military: Turkey in the 1980s* (1988) and *Political Parties and Democracy in Turkey* (1991).

Jeffrey Herbst is Assistant Professor of Politics and International Affairs at the Woodrow Wilson School of Princeton University. He is the author of *State Politics in Zimbabwe* (1990) and articles on the political economy of Africa.

Terry Lynn Karl is Associate Professor of Political Science and Director of the Center for Latin American Studies at Stanford University. She is the author of *The Paradox of Plenty: Oil Booms and Petro-States* (1991) and has written extensively on democratization, United States policy toward Latin America, and the Central American crisis.

Nikki R. Keddie is Professor of History at the University of California at Los Angeles and past president of the Middle East Studies Association. Her writings include *An Islamic Response to Imperialism* (1968), *Sayyid Jamal ad-Din "al Afghani": A Political Biography* (1972), *Roots of Revolution: An Interpretive History of Modern Iran* (1981), and *Religion and Politics in Iran: Shi'ism from Quietism to Revolution* (1983).

Edmond J. Keller is Professor of Political Science at the University of California at Los Angeles. He is the author of *Revolutionary Ethiopia: From Empire to People's Republic* (1988) and editor of *Afromarxist Regimes: Ideology and Public Policy* (1987), and *South Africa in Southern Africa: Domestic Change and International Conflict* (1989).

Michel Oksenberg is Professor of Political Science and Research Associate at the Center for Chinese Studies at the University of Michigan. He is author of *Bureaucratic Politics and Chinese Energy Development* (1986), *Policy Making in China: Leaders, Structures, and Processes* (1988), and *China's Entry into the IMF, World Bank, and GATT: Toward a Global Economy* (1990).

T. J. Pempel is Professor of Government at Cornell University. His recent works include *Policy and Politics in Japan: Creative Conserva-*

tism (1981), *Japan: The Dilemmas of Success* (1986), and the edited volume, *Uncommon Democracies: The One-Party Dominant Regimes* (1990). He is currently working on a study of the contemporary Japanese state.

Dankwart A. Rustow is Distinguished Professor of Political Science at the Graduate School of the City University of New York, editor of *Comparative Politics*, chairman of *The Energy Forum*, and cochairman of the U.S.-Soviet Symposium on the Contemporary Middle East. Earlier he served at Princeton, Columbia, and Brookings and as vice-president of the Middle East Studies Association and the American Political Science Association. His many publications include *Turkey: America's Forgotten Ally* (1987), *Oil and Turmoil: America Faces OPEC and the Middle East* (1982), and *A World of Nations: Problems of Political Modernization* (1967).

Klaus von Beyme is Professor of Political Science and Director of the Institute of Political Science at the University of Heidelberg. From 1982 to 1985 he was president of the International Political Science Association. His publications include *Economics and Politics Within Socialist Systems* (1982), *Political Parties in Western Democracies* (1985), and *The Soviet Union in World Politics* (1987).

Howard J. Wiarda is Professor of Political Science at the University of Massachusetts, Amherst; Research Associate of the Center for International Affairs, Harvard University; Adjunct Scholar at the American Enterprise Institute for Public Policy Research in Washington, D.C.; and Associate of the Foreign Policy Research Institute in Philadelphia. His most recent books include *New Directions in Comparative Politics* (2d edition, 1990), *The Democratic Revolution in Latin America* (1990), *The Transitions to Democracy in Spain and Portugal* (1989), *Latin American Politics and Development* (3rd edition, 1990), and *Foreign Policy without Illusion* (1990).

Chapter

1

Introduction

Dankwart A. Rustow and Kenneth Paul Erickson

Comparative analysis of political institutions and processes emerged as a distinct subfield of political science in the decades between the two world wars, when political scientists in the United States began systematically studying the political systems of European countries. Analytic concerns of the era focused on such themes as presidential versus parliamentary systems; federal versus unitary organization; the structure of political parties; and the origins, nature, and impact of democratic, socialist, and fascist regimes.

Following the Second World War, the discipline again responded to a changed world. Countries of Asia and Africa were moving from colonialism to independence, and a successful revolution in Cuba challenged United States hegemony in the Western hemisphere. Experts in Washington and at the United Nations were formulating programs for development assistance, and major universities were initiating area-study programs on Eastern Europe, the Middle East, Latin America, Asia, and Africa.

Responding to such stimuli, social scientists were searching for concepts that would provide a coherent perspective for their expanding horizons. Walt W. Rostow and Seymour Martin Lipset saw democracy as the culmination of a process of economic growth and social development. Borrowing from Talcott Parsons's model of social systems, Gabriel Almond proposed a set of functions that would allow systematic comparison of nations at different levels of development. David E. Apter and Dankwart A. Rustow preferred the historian's concept of modernization. Samuel P. Huntington advanced a theory of political development and decay. Within these and other frameworks, impressive amounts of empirical research were undertaken on the politics of Third World countries and of communist regimes. Comparative politics, once and for all, had transcended its earlier European-North American confines.

By the late 1960s, with global politics frozen into the Cold War and social scientists in the United States now interacting with intellectuals of the Third World, the discipline presented a rather less coherent picture. The earlier liberal theories of economic and political development were challenged by social scientists who, drawing insights from Marxist scholarship, attributed the social and economic ills of Third World countries to their dependence upon the dominant industrial, capitalist nations. Amid such sharpening ideological battles, a compulsive search for new paradigms precipitated a flood of confusing neologisms. Far from systematically comparing political processes in Western and Third World countries, political scientists began to fan out into their separate regional specialties; and research on communist countries became, in practice, a separate discipline. Nonetheless, many scholars continued to seek the basis of a new consensus, and a number of newly founded journals (*Comparative Political Studies*, 1967; *Comparative Politics*, 1968) began to provide a forum for testing concepts and presenting empirical research.

As we approach the end of the twentieth century, political realities are undergoing yet another transformation of truly global dimensions. Nations from Chile and Brazil to South Korea and the Philippines are struggling to consolidate political democracy. Contested elections in the Soviet Union, efforts to build democracy in Eastern Europe, and moves toward a market economy there and in China are dismantling the barriers that once separated the study of politics in the West from that in communist countries.

This volume, with its contributions from leading political scientists, historians, and sociologists, systematically reviews the problems of scope and method that face comparative politics because of this global transformation. It addresses five aspects of contemporary comparative political analysis: (1) conceptual and methodological advances, (2) the institutional framework of politics and its international setting, (3) the dynamic process of the search for democracy, (4) revolution and reform in communist and noncommunist societies, and (5) the process of policy making in stable political systems.

Specifically, Part One presents some basic Dimensions of Comparison. David Collier surveys research approaches in the field: comparative, case study, statistical, and experimental. Highlighting recent conceptual and methodological advances in each of these, he suggests that such innovations provide us with a set of research tools of unprecedented potential. Howard J. Wiarda discusses challenges to the early political development paradigm from rival approaches such as dependency, bureaucratic-authoritarianism, and corporatism. He concludes that the recent global movement from authoritarianism toward democracy in countries from Latin America to East Asia invites us to take a fresh look at the earlier developmental theories of Almond, Lipset, Rostow, and others. S. N. Eisenstadt argues for reintroducing into the study of politics a cultural and "civilizational" dimension that can account for the process of revolution in the history of England, the United States, France, Russia, and China and its absence in such countries as Japan.

Part Two seeks to resolve some of the past controversies over State, Class, and Dependency. Ronald H. Chilcote, in a sweeping survey of writings by both Marxist and non-Marxist scholars, finds that new labels, such as postliberalism, post-Marxism, and postimperialism, sometimes obscure the fact that scholars are most creatively addressing contemporary issues by redirecting their empirical and conceptual energies into such classic issues of political science as the state, social class, political participation, and political economy. David G. Becker argues that, in the context of today's international capitalism, development results from the interplay of international and domestic social and political forces and that analysis of development must include those of a non-deterministic class analysis that examines bourgeois social movements. Edmond J. Keller, turning to tropical Africa, presents recent methodological and ideological controversies about state, class, and ethnicity and concludes that we need new concepts and far more empirical research to resolve the controversies satisfactorily.

Part Three addresses the worldwide Search for Democracy. Terry Lynn Karl, focusing on Latin American cases, proposes a path-dependent approach to the study of transitions to democracy, with the major initiative coming either from the political elite or from the masses, and the actors seeking either to impose the change by force or to negotiate it through compromise or "foundational pacts." Metin Heper, taking as his examples Mediterranean and Latin American countries, suggests that we seek the explanation for different patterns of transition to democracy not in the tactical decisions of particular political leaders, but rather in each nation's historical processes, antecedent regime types, and recent patterns of political institutionalization. Henry Bienen and Jeffrey Herbst, noting that democracy is not on the near-term agenda of most African countries, urge that research on Africa's authoritarian regimes pay attention to some of the prerequisites of democratization such as the emergence of a sense of national identity.

Part Four addresses The Dynamics of Reform and Revolution. Michel Oksenberg and Bruce Dickson distinguish between revolution and great reform, noting that scholars have devoted little attention to the latter and that the absence of a well-developed theoretical or conceptual framework on great reform has seriously handicapped analysts of contemporary events in China and the Soviet Union. They caution, in particular, against imputing to great reformers any preconceived ideological blueprints of the sort that have inspired the leaders of great revolutions. Similarly, Klaus von Beyme reminds us that great reformers must devote much of their effort to coping with unintended consequences. For Mikhail Gorbachev, in particular, these include the massive revival of the nationality problem, dormant since Lenin's days, and the danger that too much *glasnost* may destroy *perestroika*. Nikki R. Keddie argues that in the Islamic world, the Khomeini revolution in Iran is unlikely to be repeated elsewhere, because Iran's historical evolution, social structure, religious institutions, and specific relations with foreign powers are distinctive. She demonstrates that the contemporary Iranian revolution combines traditional and innovative aspects, and she traces them historically from the birth of Islam itself in social revolution through more recent conflicts between modernizers and Islamists. Finally, Susan Eckstein develops a methodology for evaluating the impact of revolution on economic and social welfare. Applying this approach to five twentieth-century Latin American cases (Mexico, Bolivia, Cuba, Peru, and Nicaragua), she not only measures their postrevolutionary performance against that of their own prerevolutionary past and that of their contemporary nonrevolutionary neighbors, but also compares the nations with one another to assess the relative impact of revolution from above and revolution from below and of commitment to a socialist as opposed to a capitalist mode of production.

The book's concluding section presents a number of new approaches to the study of Policy Making in Industrial Welfare States. Douglas E. Ashford emphasizes the contrasting ideological assumptions and political motivations that led Great Britain, France, and Sweden to their respective welfare states. Jack Hayward proposes a policy-community approach to analyze national industrial policy making and uses the approach to trace the networks of communication among industrialists, administrators, and trade union officials in advanced democracies. T. J. Pempel, singling out two of those democracies, finds something of a mirror-image pattern in the economic policies of Japan under the aegis of the conservative Liberal-Democratic party and Sweden under Social Democratic dominance. The unexpected symmetry derives from the fact that each party, secure in its solid support from, respectively, business and labor, can formulate economic policies that are generous to the other side.

In sum, along with some constructive disagreements, there is a strong consensus among the scholars who have joined in writing this volume that we must pay careful attention to historical context, recurring patterns of interaction, and processes of change. They are confident that in so doing we can overcome the ideological controversies and methodological impasses of the past so as to move into a constructive era of truly global research on comparative political dynamics. The conclusion elaborates some of the challenges on the global research agenda of the discipline of comparative politics into the twenty-first century.

DIMENSIONS OF COMPARISON

Chapter
2

The Comparative Method: Two Decades of Change

David Collier

"And what should they know of England who only England know?" Rudyard Kipling[1]

"Nations can be understood only in comparative perspective." Seymour Martin Lipset[2]

The idea that comparison is a "good thing" is built into our intuitive sense of how we understand the world. Comparison sharpens our powers of description and can be an invaluable stimulus to concept formation. It provides criteria for testing hypotheses and contributes to the inductive discovery of new hypotheses and to theory building. Harold D. Lasswell, in the lead article of the first issue in 1968 of the journal *Comparative Politics*, argued that comparison is so central to good analysis that the scientific method is unavoidably comparative.[3]

Within the political science subfield of comparative politics, a concern with techniques of comparison is very much alive and well, and the expression "comparative method" is often used to refer to the partially distinctive methodological issues that arise in the systematic analysis of a small number of cases, or a "small-N." This concern with analyzing few cases appears to derive in part from the types of large-scale political phenomena commonly studied by scholars of comparative politics—such as revolutions, national political regimes, and the evolution of nation-states. A small number of cases is studied either because these phenomena occur relatively infrequently or because, even if they are more common, it is believed that they are best understood through the close analysis of relatively few observations.[4] The practice of focusing on few cases has been reinforced during the past decade with the rise of the school of "comparative historical analysis," in which countries are studied over long periods. This intensive scrutiny of each case limits the number of cases a scholar can consider.[5]

Choosing to study relatively few cases confronts the analyst with the problem of having more variables to analyze than cases to observe, or the quandary of "many variables, small-N," as Arend Lijphart put it.[6] The quandary has stimulated much writing on how to analyze relatively few cases most productively. Such writing extends well beyond the subfield of comparative politics, drawing on insights from and being applicable to a broad spectrum of work in the disciplines of political science, sociology, economics, psychology, and statistics.

The late 1960s and early 1970s saw a boom in writing on comparative method as it applies to international studies.[7] This literature established a set of norms and practices for small-N research, drew attention to questions of how to conduct such analyses, and created a baseline of understanding that has played an important role in the ongoing practice of comparative politics. In a book such as this prepared for the twentieth anniversary of the journal *Comparative Politics*, it is appropriate to assess issues of comparative method that have been debated since the journal first appeared and to consider their implications for future research. This chapter takes as a point of departure Arend Lijphart's "Comparative Politics and Comparative Method," published in 1971.[8] Among the studies of that period, Lijphart's piece stands out for its imaginative synthesis of basic issues of comparison and of the relationship between comparative method and other branches of methodology. The present discussion reviews Lijphart's perspective and uses it as a point of departure for exploring new developments in the intervening two decades.

A central theme which emerges is that the small-N comparativist is pulled in two directions. On the one hand, in important respects the value of quantitative and statistical approaches in addressing the substantive problems of comparative politics is more in doubt today than it was two decades ago, and the growing interest in "interpretive social science" reflects the conviction that the close, qualitative analysis of few cases is the most fruitful approach. On the other hand, innovations in the research designs and statistical techniques available for small-N analysis have created new opportunities for doing quantitative research with relatively few cases. The lesson drawn from these contrasting trends is that the most fruitful approach to the field of comparative politics is eclectic, one in which scholars are willing and able to build upon both sets of developments.

SYNOPSIS OF LIJPHART

Lijphart defines the comparative method as the analysis of a small number of cases, entailing at least two observations, but less than about twenty. A central goal of his article[9] is to assess the comparative method in relation to three other methods—experimental, statistical, and case study—and to evaluate these different approaches by two criteria: (1) how well they achieve the goal of testing theory through adjudicating among rival explanations, and (2) how difficult it is to acquire the data needed to employ each method (see Figure 1).

The experimental method has the great merit of providing strong criteria for eliminating rival explanations through experimental control, but unfortunately it is impossible to generate appropriate experimental data for most topics relevant to international studies. The statistical

Figure 1. Situating the Comparative Method as of 1971: Lijphart's Scheme

Case Study Method	**Comparative Method**	**Experimental Method**
Merit: Permits intensive examination of cases even with limited resources	**Defined as**: Systematic analysis of small number of cases ("small-N" analysis)	**Merit**: Eliminates rival explanations through experimental control
Inherent Problem: Contributes less to building theory than studies with more cases	**Merit**: "Given inevitable scarcity of time, energy, and financial resources, the intensive analysis of a few cases may be more promising than the superficial statistical analysis of many cases" (Lijphart, p. 685)	**Inherent Problem**: Experimental control is impossible for many or most topics of relevance to field of comparative politics
Types of Case Studies: 1. Atheoretical 2. Interpretive 3. Hypothesis-generating 4. Theory-confirming 5. Theory-infirming (i.e., case studies that weaken a theory marginally) 6. Deviant case studies	**Inherent Problem**: Weak capacity to sort out rival explanations, specifically, the problem of "many variables, few cases"	**Statistical Method**
	Potential Solutions: 1. Increase number of cases 2. Focus on comparable cases 3. Reduce number of variables a. Combine variables b. Employ more parsimonious theory	**Merit**: Assesses rival explanations through statistical control **Inherent Problem**: Difficult to collect adequate information in a sufficient number of cases, due to limited time and resources

method has the merit of assessing rival explanations through the weaker but still valuable procedure of statistical control, but it is often not feasible to collect a sufficiently large set of reliable data to do this form of analysis. The case study method has the merit of allowing the scholar with relatively modest time and resources to assess at least one case with care, but the opportunities for systematically testing hypotheses are far more limited than with the other methods. Yet case studies do make a contribution, and Lijphart offers a suggestive typology of the different ways case studies can be used in forming and testing theories.

The comparative method, as defined by Lijphart, has an intermediate status on both of his criteria. It provides a weaker basis than the experimental or statistical method for evaluating hypotheses, specifically because of the many variables, small-N problem. Yet it offers a stronger basis for evaluating hypotheses than do case studies. Even with the problem of having more variables than cases, the comparative method allows systematic comparison which, if appropriately utilized, can contribute to the assessment of alternative explanations.

Although the data requirements of the comparative method are much greater than for case studies, they are far less demanding than for experimental or statistical research. Lijphart therefore views the comparative method as suitable in research based on modest resources, and he suggests that studies using the comparative method might often serve as a first step toward statistical analysis. Lijphart states that:

> If at all possible one should generally use the statistical (or perhaps even the experimental) method instead of the weaker comparative method. But often, given the inevitable scarcity of time, energy, and financial resources, the intensive comparative analysis of a few cases may be more promising than a more superficial statistical analysis of many cases. In such a situation, the most fruitful approach would be to regard the comparative analysis as the first stage of research, in which hypotheses are carefully formulated, and the statistical analysis as the second stage, in which these hypotheses are tested in as large a sample as possible.[10]

In addition to triangulating among these different approaches, Lijphart proposes solutions to both sides of the dilemma of many variables, small-N entailed in the comparative method.[11] With regard to the small number of cases, even if researchers stop short of a statistical study, they can nonetheless increase the number of cases and thereby enlarge the scope of comparison that can be used to assess hypotheses. With regard to the large number of variables, he suggests two approaches. First, analysts can focus on "comparable cases," that is, on cases that (1) are matched on many variables that are not central to the study, thus in effect "controlling" for these variables, and (2) differ in terms of the key variables that are the focus of analysis, thereby allowing a more adequate assessment of their influence. Hence, the selection of cases acts as a partial substitute for statistical or experimental control.[12] Second, analysts can reduce the number of variables either by combining variables or through theoretical parsimony, that is, through the careful elaboration of a theory that focuses on a smaller number of explanatory factors.

Thus, Lijphart provides a compact formulation of the relationship between the comparative method and other methodologies and offers possible solutions to problems posed by the small-N analysis entailed in the comparative method.

INNOVATIONS RELEVANT TO THE COMPARATIVE METHOD

The two decades following Lijphart's study have seen a number of innovations in the comparative method, as well as a renewed focus on methodological alternatives already available before he wrote his article. Though many of these innovations appeared in work concerned with small-N comparison, others appeared in writing on the experimental, statistical, and case study methods. The result has been an intellectual cross-fertilization of great benefit to the comparative method. Figure 2 provides an overview of these innovations. The arrows in Figure 2 suggest the potential contributions of work in other methodologies to the comparative method.

Innovations in the Comparative Method

Innovations in the methodology of small-N comparison can be discussed in terms of the issues introduced above, encompassing the goals of comparison, justifications for focusing on few cases, and the problem of many variables, few cases.

Different Uses of Comparison   A criterion in evaluating any methodology is how good a job it does in assessing rival explanations. One direction that discussions of the comparative method have taken is toward broadening the criteria of assessment. Perhaps the most striking formulation is Skocpol and Somers's discussion of three types of comparative analysis.[13] The first is concerned with the systematic examination of covariation among cases for the purpose of the *generation and testing of hypotheses*.[14] The second is the examination of a number of cases with the goal of showing that a particular set of concepts or a particular model usefully illuminates many cases. No real test of the theory

Figure 2. Innovations Relevant to the Comparative Method

Comparative Method

Broadened Understanding of Types of Comparative Studies

1. Emphasis on interpretive understanding
2. Idea of a "research cycle" among the types (Skocpol and Somers)

Further Justifications for Focus on a Small-N

1. To pursue "disciplined configurative approach" (Verba, reinforced by Almond and Genco)
2. To avoid problem of "conceptual stretching" (Sartori)
3. To facilitate "thick description" and other forms of interpretive understanding (Geertz and many others)
4. To achieve analytic depth of case-oriented approach (Ragin)

Debates on Solutions to Problem of Many Variables, Small-N

1. Value of increasing number of cases
2. Comparable cases versus contrasting cases (Lijphart versus Przeworski and Teune)
3. Reducing number of variables in conjunction with using stronger theory

Case Study Method

New Perspectives on Case Studies

1. New defense of the case study method (Campbell)
2. Refinements in Lijphart's typology of case studies (Eckstein, George)
3. Improvement of causal analysis in case studies through "process tracing" (George and McKeown)
4. Critique of value of case studies in assessing rational choice theory (Achen and Snidal)

Experimental Method

Diffusion of Older Ideas and Introduction of New Ideas on Quasi-Experimental Design

1. Methodology of quasi-experiments and interrupted time-series design becomes more widely known
2. Analysis of the Connecticut crackdown on speeding as exemplar of interrupted time-series analysis (Campbell and Ross)
3. Diffusion of ideas about quasi-experiments encouraged by codification of evaluation research
4. Proposed statistical solution to problem of selection bias in quasi-experiments (Achen)

Statistical Method

New Warnings and New Solutions

1. Criticism of standard statistical practice in the social sciences (Freedman)
2. New statistical techniques relevant to small-N analysis
3. Effort to refine statistical analysis of a small-N in the debate on corporatism and economic growth in Western Europe (Lange-Garrett-Jackman-Hicks-Patterson)

12

occurs, but rather the goal is the *parallel demonstration of theory*. This use of comparison plays an important role in the process through which theories are elaborated in international studies. The third type of comparison is the examination of two or more cases in order to highlight how different they are, thus setting the framework for interpreting the way different processes of change play out within each context. This *contrast of contexts* is central to the more interpretive side of the social sciences and reflects yet another way that comparison is, in fact, frequently used.

In addition to providing a more multifaceted account of the goals of comparison, Skocpol and Somers suggest the intriguing idea of a "research cycle" among these different approaches. This cycle occurs because the inherent weakness of each approach may stimulate work that employs the other approaches. Thus, a "parallel demonstration" scholar may introduce a new theory and show how it applies to many cases. A "hypothesis-testing" scholar, seeing that the theory does *not* fit certain cases, may go on to formulate and test hypotheses about where it fits and where it does not. In turn, a hypothesis-testing study that too brashly compares disparate contexts may stimulate a "contrast of contexts" scholar to examine more carefully the meaning of the difference in context. It is thus useful to move beyond an exclusive focus on the role of comparison in testing explanations to a broader understanding that encompasses the different elements in this research cycle. This is not to say that assessing hypotheses does not remain a paramount goal of comparison, and many scholars insist that it is *the* paramount goal. Yet this broader perspective offers a valuable account of how comparative work proceeds within a larger research community, pointing usefully to the interaction between hypothesis-testing studies and those with a more interpretive emphasis.

Justification for Small-*N*   A second trend is toward a more elaborate justification of a focus on relatively few cases. Lijphart's rationale, though incisively stated, seems in retrospect rather modest, in that it emphasizes only the problem of inadequate resources and treats the small-*N* comparison as a way-station on the route to more sophisticated statistical analysis.

A very different defense of working either with a small-*N* or with case studies had previously been available in arguments favoring a "configurative" approach,[15] and this perspective was expressed in a more interesting form a couple of years before the publication of Lijphart's analysis in Sidney Verba's advocacy of the "disciplined configurative approach."[16] In evaluating Robert A. Dahl's *Political Oppositions in Western Democracies*,[17] Verba points both to the sophistication of the hypotheses entertained in the book and to the difficulty of assessing them adequately, except through a close command of the cases, leading him to advocate this disciplined configurative mode of research. Verba's formulation is appealing because he is concerned with systematic hypothesis testing and theory building, and yet he links this priority with a more explicit appreciation of how hard it is to test hypotheses adequately and how useful properly executed case studies can be in providing subtle assessments of hypotheses.

It could be claimed that this issue of adequately testing hypotheses ultimately derives from the problem of limited resources. If enough talented researchers worked long enough, they could do a *Political Oppositions* study for many dozens of countries. Yet the problem is somewhat different from the one emphasized in Lijphart's initial formulation. It is not so much that resources are limited, but that research problems have proved more intractable than had often been thought in the 1960s and early 1970s in the initial days of enthusiasm for comparative statistical research. Among these problems, that of creating indicators that validly and reliably measure important concepts across diverse contexts of analysis has proved especially vexing.

Another key step in elucidating these problems of validity and in justifying a small-N focus is Giovanni Sartori's article on "Concept Misformation in Comparative Politics," the major ideas of which are greatly elaborated in his later book *Social Science Concepts*.[17] Sartori suggests that the temptation to apply concepts to a broader range of cases can readily lead to conceptual "stretching," as the meanings associated with the original concept fail to fit the reality of the new cases. The concepts that can most easily be applied to a broad range of cases are often less interesting, highly abstract, and less worthy of scholarly attention. Thus research employing the most interesting concepts may do well to focus on relatively few cases.

Since 1970 the growing interest in interpretive social science, which is concerned with deciphering the meaning of behavior and institutions,[19] has strengthened the justification for advancing cautiously with relatively few cases. In his term "thick description," Clifford Geertz provides a brilliant label for the concern with unraveling the underlying meaning of political phenomena and with seeing how this meaning is rooted in particular contexts.[20] This focus has appeared in many guises relevant to the practice of comparative politics, including Almond and Genco's[21] analysis of "Clouds and Clocks" and Skocpol and Somers's category of contrast of contexts, encompassing studies that use comparison to richly contextualize research findings. Charles Ragin's *The Comparative Method*[22] explores another facet of these concerns in his analysis of the holistic orientation of what he calls case-oriented research and the complex problems of "conjunctural causation," that is, causal patterns that vary according to context—to which configuratively oriented scholars are typically far more sensitive.

Finally the great intellectual success in recent years of the school of comparative historical analysis has played an important role in legitimizing a focus on a small-N. This approach was pioneered by Reinhard Bendix[23] and Barrington Moore,[24] and it has been extended by such writers as Jeffrey Paige,[25] Theda Skocpol, [26] and Gregory M. Luebbert.[27] The particular form of analysis in these studies varies considerably, as suggested by the typology of Skocpol and Somers noted above, ranging from systematic hypothesis testing to carefully contextualized interpretation that is placed within a comparative framework. Overall, however, these studies have in common a commitment to *systematic* qualitative comparison that often involves a number of nations and evaluates each national case over a number of time periods. This tradition of research thus combines carefully thought-out comparison with an appreciation of historical context, thereby successfully responding to a broader concern with finding new ways to "historicize the social sciences."

Indeed, this tradition has made a major contribution in terms of demonstrating the viability of comparative analysis based on relatively few cases. These studies have shown that truly comparative work can be sensitive to diverse contexts of analysis, and that systematic procedures of small-N comparison can be used to very good effect. Efforts to codify these procedures, such as that in Ragin's *Comparative Method*, have further reinforced the plausibility of insisting on the viability of small-N analysis as a middle ground between case studies and statistical studies.

Solutions to the Problem of Many Variables, Small-N   Proposed solutions to the problem of many variables, small-N are increasing the number of cases, focusing on matched cases, and reducing the number of variables. Important debates and innovations have emerged under each of these headings.

Increasing the Number of Cases   One of Lijphart's original suggestions for addressing the small-N problem was to increase the number of cases. Given the several new justifications for analyzing relatively few cases, how should this recommendation now be evaluated? In part due to the changed intellectual climate already discussed, analysts have not tended to move on to ever larger case bases. Correspondingly, more recent research has not met the earlier expectation that studies employing quantitative data on large numbers of countries would become a more predominant mode of analysis. Robert Jackman[28] has usefully insisted that comparative statistical research has had more success than is recognized, and Lijphart's own recent work has indeed moved in this direction.[29] Yet there can be no question that, for better or worse, quantitative cross-national research within the field of comparative politics and quantitative international politics, or QIP, within the field of international relations have not come to occupy as dominant a position in their respective subfields as many had expected.

As commonly occurs, the reaction may have gone too far. Comparative politics specialists may be less well trained to do quantitative analysis today than they were twenty years ago, and the quantitative approach was doubtless set back as many scholars discovered how extraordinarily time-consuming it is to construct appropriate data sets, often far out of proportion to the professional rewards that seem to be forthcoming. In addition, the quantitative comparative approach was hurt by the publication of too many studies in which concepts were operationalized with dubious validity and which employed causal tests that were weak, unconvincing, or inappropriate.[30]

However, the failure to seize good opportunities to do quantitative research could certainly be viewed as being as much of a mistake as premature quantification. The outstanding debate on corporatism and economic growth in Western Europe discussed below is an example of how statistical methods can effectively address major analytic issues. Further, the availability of new statistical techniques (also discussed below) has made it far more productive to do quantitative analyses with as few as twelve to fifteen cases. Consequently, the option of increasing the N to that level is still worth pursuing, and it probably should be pursued more often.

Focus on Comparable Cases The recommendation that analysts focus on carefully matched cases has been both reinforced and challenged. In the mid 1970s Lijphart explored further the trade-off he had noted in 1971 between the goal of increasing the number of cases and the goal of matching cases as a substitute for statistical control.[31] Obviously if a researcher is to select cases that are "really" similar, however that similarity is defined, the number of appropriate cases is likely to become limited. In the face of this trade-off, Lijphart opts in favor of the more careful matching of fewer cases, and he goes so far as to restrict the application of the term comparative method to analyses that focus on a small number of carefully matched cases. This emphasis parallels a much earlier perspective on the comparative method referred to as the method of "controlled comparison."[32] More recently, Arthur Stinchcombe's advocacy of the method of "deep analogy,"[33] that is, the comparative analysis of very few, extremely closely matched cases, has pushed this approach even further.

The opposite strategy has been advocated by Przeworski and Teune.[34] They suggest that even with careful matching in a "most similar" systems design, there remains a problem of "overdetermination" in that this design will fail to eliminate many rival explanations, leaving the researcher with no criteria for choosing among them. They prefer instead a "most different" systems design, based on a set of cases as diverse as possible in which the analyst traces similar processes of change.[35] Przeworski has more recently suggested[36] that the strength of this design is in part responsible for the great success of the recent literature on democratization, such as the work of O'Donnell, Schmitter, and Whitehead.[37] Przeworski maintains that this literature addresses such a broad range of cases that analysts were forced to distill out of that diversity a set of common elements with great explanatory power.

This debate can be placed in perspective by recognizing that notions of "similar" and "different" are relative. Two cases which from one perspective are closely matched may contrast sharply from another perspective. My own recent work[38] combines the two strategies by starting with a set of eight Latin American countries that are roughly matched on a number of variables. Among the eight countries, I proceed to analyze pairs of countries that are as different as possible. The overall matching assures at least partially similar contexts of analysis, and the paired comparison places parallel processes of change in sharp relief because they are operating in contexts that are in many respects quite different.

The debate on most similar versus most different systems designs has major implications for the status of area studies, and here again the debate pulls in two directions. Dankwart Rustow[39] argued some time ago in favor of moving beyond an area studies approach, and many scholars agree that cases should be selected in response to the specific analytic requirements of particular research projects, rather than on the basis of geographic proximity.

However, for a variety of reasons area studies are a booming business today. Important analytic issues do present themselves in countries that cluster together within a region, as with the experience of successful export-led growth in East Asia and of the bureaucratic-authoritarian states of Latin America, and work on these issues can reinforce an area studies emphasis. An important and legitimate role is played by the demands of language preparation and by the intellectual leverage gained when individual scholars develop, over many years, a cumulative and well contextualized understanding of a particular region. The impressive funding by U.S. foundations of area studies in the late 1970s and 1980s has certainly played a role, as does institutional momentum. In any case, the debate over area studies versus comparative studies continues, and attention to the issue of most similar versus most different systems designs could usefully sharpen the debate.

Reduce the Number of Variables   The last solution to the small-N problem is to reduce the number of variables, either through combining variables in the spirit of "data reduction" or through using stronger theory that focuses the analyst on a more parsimonious set of explanatory factors. In the quest for theoretical parsimony, perhaps the most interesting development is the emergence of a variety of rational choice and strategic interaction models that have precisely this purpose: To use strong theory that serves to reduce the number of explanatory factors that must be considered.

Interestingly, the availability of stronger theory may help address not only problems of small-N analysis, but also problems of quantitative statistical work. Statistical models of complex phenomena such as reciprocal causation may require assumptions that are sufficiently precarious that analysts might well prefer instead to invest more in new assumptions on the side of theory. They may thus be able to provide a theoretical basis for simpler causal models that do not strain the statistical techniques as much.[40] If this is in fact productive in quantitative studies, there is reason to hope that it might be helpful in small-N comparative studies as well.

A related need is for more work on concept formation. Apart from the major, sustained contribution of Giovanni Sartori, older work by McKinney and Kalleberg, and a more recent article by DeFelice,[41] this is a relatively neglected topic. Comparative politics specialists do not devote enough attention to thinking through how well or poorly concepts and categories are serving them and therefore may have insufficient ground for knowing if they are making appropriate choices to achieve theoretical parsimony.

Fortunately, the field of cognitive science has recently provided insights into processes of categorization and model formation that may be useful in refining analytic techniques in the field of comparative politics. An important source of such insights is George Lakoff's massive synthesis of recent developments in cognitive science.[42] An example of how they may be applied is the challenge to "classical categorization" of the kind used in Sartori's work on categories and concepts. Sartori frames his discussion in terms of the defining properties of concepts and the trade-off between a concept's "intension" (meaning) and "extension" (range of cases referred to).[43] Cognitive science suggests that this form of concept analysis fails to capture how concepts actually function and that the analysis of concepts is more effective when it focuses on: the cognitive model underlying the concept; the tendency for concepts to be "graded," rather than having sharply defined boundaries; and the closely related role of "exemplar" cases in anchoring concepts. More effective modes of concept analysis will almost certainly entail a synthesis of these two approaches, and that synthesis remains to be worked out.

Innovations Suggested by Work on Other Methods

Innovations in the Experimental Method   The experimental method is a superb set of procedures for adjudicating among rival explanations, yet these procedures seem of little relevance to most research in the field of comparative politics. However, writing on variants of the experimental method contain important new ideas that may improve small-N comparative analysis. Certainly the most influential work has been Campbell and Stanley's [44] classic discussion of how the logic of experimental design can be applied to "quasi-experiments," that is, to "observational" studies that include some event or choice that has a form analogous to an experimental intervention, but that occurs in a "natural" setting. An example would be the initiation of a new public policy whose impact one wishes to assess—an analytic task that entails many pitfalls.

Campbell and Stanley underline the great value in quasi-experiments of the interrupted time series design, in which the analyst looks at a long series of observations over time, so that the values of the observed variables are examined not only immediately before and after the policy change or other innovation, but also well before and well after. They present a remarkable figure[45] that shows the large number of different situations in which observations at two proximate points within a long series may appear to indicate an ordered pattern of change. Yet if one looks at the full time series, it becomes clear that the pattern of change suggested by the two observations is extremely misleading. Causal inferences about the impact of discrete events can be risky if one does not have an extended series of observations.

The continuing widespread use over many years of Campbell and Stanley's book in methodology courses has played an important role in diffusing their sensible advice. Their influence has been important to specialists in small-N analysis in comparative politics, who continually ask questions about the impact of discrete events, ranging from wars, revolutions, and military coups to specific public policies.

Two developments further diffused these ideas. Campbell and Ross's[46] subsequent analysis of the impact on traffic fatalities of the Connecticut crackdown on speeding in the 1950s provided a stunning exemplar of the imaginative application of a quasi-experimental design to a problem of public policy analysis. Indeed, Przeworski has argued that the practice of research is influenced far more by exemplars than by formal attempts to "legislate" correct methodology.[47] The reprinting of Campbell and Ross's article in a reader on social science methodology[48] made it widely available to political scientists.

The case considered by Campbell and Ross appears to be a simple one: When the State of Connecticut initiated strict enforcement of the vehicular speed limit in the 1950s and traffic deaths dropped sharply, the cause and effect relationship seemed obvious. Yet Campbell and Ross do an impressive analysis of the potential threats to the "internal validity" (was that really the cause in Connecticut?) and the "external validity" (can the finding be generalized?) of this study. No sensitive analyst can read this article without acquiring a more sober view of the problem of determining the impact of a policy innovation.

A second development that encouraged the diffusion of ideas about quasi-experimental and interrupted time series design was the emergence of a large body of writing on evaluation research. This includes work on political development which usefully codified procedures for using "experiment-like" designs in natural settings.[49]

Although much writing on quasi-experiments appears to offer helpful guidance and practical advice to small-N analysts, Christopher H. Achen's excellent *The Statistical Analysis of Quasi-Experiments*[50] may leave them feeling that the methodological challenges posed by quasi-experiments are simply too great to deal with. A core problem is the lack of randomization in who gets the "treatment" and who does not, which may be referred to as "selection bias." For example, it rarely occurs that a new public policy is applied at random to some citizens and not to others. Rather, it is applied according to criteria that may be correlated with some of the hypothesized impacts of the policy, which are the central object of analysis. This causal riddle is best solved by constructing a model of how citizens got "into" the category of being recipients of the policy. This model then becomes a building block in the analysis of what impact the policy really has, in that these prior considerations can be "factored out" of the assessment of the impact. Achen shows that this type of analysis requires what is called two-stage least-squares regression analysis. Without this technique, the riddle is hard to solve.

The implications of Achen's book might seem discouraging. It may be an interesting exercise to think about these research problems as quasi-experiments, but when one gets down to serious solutions to the lack of randomization, one is forced back into a form of statistical analysis which—although straightforward for the scholar who has the appropriate data—is hard to carry out with a small data set. However, a somewhat more hopeful view might be that the literature on experiments and quasi-experiments at least provides valuable warnings about the perils of analyzing discrete events as if they were true experiments.

In the absence of sophisticated data sets, the researcher must exercise as much common sense as possible in making causal claims. There are no easy solutions.

Innovations in Statistics   Recent work on statistical analysis has provided both new warnings about the risks of statistical studies and new opportunities for doing meaningful statistical work with relatively modest case bases. The statistician David Freedman has launched a major assault on the use of multivariate quantitative analysis in the social sciences, which he claims fails because the underlying research design is generally inadequate and because the data employed fail to meet the assumptions of the statistical techniques.[51] His criticism may bring considerable satisfaction to those who have been skeptical about statistics all along and who take comfort in the greater "control" of the material they feel derives from analyzing relatively few cases through more qualitative techniques. Further, it is realistic to expect that we may go through a period of greater questioning of the use of statistics in the social sciences. However, as with the rejection of quantitative cross-national research discussed above, it would be unfortunate if a reaction against quantitative studies went too far.

The emergence of new statistical techniques that are helpful in the analysis of relatively few cases makes such a blanket rejection particularly unfortunate. One example is the development of the "bootstrap" and "jackknife," sometimes referred to as "resampling strategies."[52] These techniques use computer simulation to take a small initial sample and artificially create a large sample on which statistical tests are conducted. The tests of statistical significance that result are not as vulnerable to violations of distributional assumptions as are more conventional tests, and hence they are less prone to some forms of error that can be a problem in small-N analysis. They may be especially useful for providing better estimates in cross-national comparisons where there is great heterogeneity among units.

The development of "robust" and "resistant" statistical measures[53] is promising in much the same way. These are measures that are relatively unaffected by extreme or deviant values and can therefore help overcome the problem in small-N analysis that findings may be seriously distorted by a single observation that is greatly in error.

Another set of techniques concerned with this same problem is "regression diagnostics."[54] These are tests used in conjunction with conventional regression analysis to assess whether unusual values on particular observations, called influential cases, have distorted the findings. The advantage of regression diagnostics over robust and resistant statistics is that one can employ them with the familiar coefficients associated with regression analysis.

The use of regression diagnostics is nicely illustrated in the recent Lange-Garrett-Jackman-Hicks-Patterson debate on the relationship between corporatism and economic growth in Western Europe.[55] The starting point of this debate is an inventive article by Lange and Garrett—whose model, based on small-N analysis, includes an interesting "interaction term" intended to capture the interplay between the organizational strength of the labor movement in the labor market and the political strength of the left in the electoral and governmental arenas. In an analysis of their article, Robert W. Jackman employs regression diagnostics to examine certain influential cases that he believes distort their findings.[56] An ongoing scholarly debate in a series of journal articles by these authors brings together an important substantive problem, a high level of area expertise and knowledge of specific cases, the interesting use of a relatively straightforward statistical model, constructive criticism based on regression diagnostics, and a sustained process of cumulative knowledge generation through the scrutiny of a shared data set. Just as the Campbell and Ross article on the Connecticut speeding crackdown is an exemplar of a quasi-experimental design, this debate should stand as an exemplar of a methodologically sophisticated effort by several scholars to solve an important problem within the framework of small-N quantitative analysis.

Another example of solutions to a complex problem, within the framework of small-N studies, is seen in relation to the issue of "average effects" in regression analysis. The results of regression analysis, the most widely employed multivariate statistical technique, represent an average of the strength of causal relations across the cases being studied. For the coefficients produced by regression analysis to be meaningful, it is necessary that these causal relations be the same, or at least similar, among the cases. Yet Charles Ragin,[57] among others, has argued that, given the complex forms of conjunctural causation often encountered in comparative politics and comparative sociology, this assumption commonly does not hold.

However, solutions to this problem are available. John E. Jackson[58] addresses this issue by suggesting a statistical technique for detecting the presence of varying effects. A study by Ruth Berins Collier[59] provides a straightforward example of how one can estimate varying causal effects by using two separate regression equations even in the context of a relatively small number of cases. In her study of the relationship between voter turnout and the degree of electoral dominance of a leading party in the new states of tropical Africa, although there was no statistical relationship between these two variables among twenty-six countries, this average effect concealed positive and negative relationships among subsets of cases that corresponded to former colonial groupings. The separate analysis of the subsets thus produced a very different result from that derived from the analysis of all twenty-six cases.

Innovations in the Case Study Method   When Lijphart wrote his 1971 article, he apparently felt some hesitation about including a discussion of case studies in an assessment of the comparative method,[60] but it is fortunate that he did. His helpful typology of the uses of case studies in hypothesis testing and theory building set the stage for further efforts to show how case studies can and should be integrated into comparative research.

The most engaging subsequent analysis of this topic is perhaps that of Donald Campbell.[61] Campbell dramatically recants the bold assertion he made in his 1963 book with Stanley that "one shot" case studies are "of no scientific value." He shows instead that case studies are in fact the basis of most comparative research, that they offer many more opportunities than people realize for falsifying the researcher's main hypotheses, and that much can be learned from making explicit the important comparisons that are often implicitly built into case studies. In addition, any given hypothesis about a case has implications for many facets of the case. By using the procedure of "pattern matching" to discover if these implications are realized, the analyst can multiply the opportunities, within what may initially have been viewed as a "single" case, to test hypotheses.

Harry Eckstein[62] and Alexander George[63] have refined the typology of how case studies can be linked to broader comparison and theory testing. George and McKeown's[64] thoughtful discussion of the procedure of "process tracing," which is related to Campbell's notion of pattern matching, provides a much clearer intellectual rationale for one of the most important approaches to case study analysis: that which supplements hypothesis testing based on the overall evaluation of the case with a close processual analysis of the unfolding of events over time within the case. The scholar thus assesses whether the dynamics of change within each case plausibly reflect the same causal pattern suggested by the broader appraisal of the case in relation to other cases.

Overall, these articles, along with works such as Robert K. Yin's *Case Study Research*,[65] offer a new systematization of case study procedures that provides a valuable point of reference for scholars concerned with small-N analysis. At the same time, the debate continues on the proper role of case studies in assessing and building theory. An interesting recent phase of this debate, published as a special issue of the journal *World Politics*, focuses on the contribution of case studies to evaluating a branch of rational choice analysis, that is, rational deterrence theory in international relations. The opening article by Achen and Snidal[66] argues that the case studies employed by many international relations specialists do not adequately address the central ideas of this body of theory, thereby raising an issue perhaps not often enough considered in discussions of the comparative method: How can the methodological concern with executing good comparisons be linked to the key analytic issues posed by the particular theories that are to be evaluated? Achen and Snidal also note the problem of selection bias in case studies of deterrence theory, that is, the problem that case studies usually focus on deterrence failure, whereas much or most of the time deterrence in fact works. The issue of the journal includes a series of articles by scholars closer to the case study tradition who debate the questions raised by Achen and Snidal. Although the articles do not offer a decisive resolution of the debate, they constitute an excellent attempt to do something that needs to be done much more: to think through how case studies have functioned in relation to the assessment of a particular body of theory. In this debate on deterrence theory, the intellectual tension recurs that has been noted throughout this article, that is, the tension between analyses that seek to achieve a general understanding, based on relatively few variables and encompassing many cases, as opposed to analyses that seek to draw out the complexities of particular cases.

CONCLUSION

This discussion points in two directions. On the one hand, the inclination of many comparativists to stick to relatively few cases has been reinforced by several developments: the rise of interpretive social science, the success of comparative historical analysis, the systematization of case study procedures, the continuing intellectual and institutional strength of area studies, and skepticism about quantitative and statistical analysis among small-N specialists and among some statisticians. The earlier contention that insufficient resources were a major constraint on the number of cases has been replaced or supplemented by the belief that the analytic problems are more intractable than originally thought by some scholars. For many scholars, the idea that small-N analysis is a step toward studies based on more sophisticated statistical analysis is thus unconvincing or irrelevant.

On the other hand, quantitative techniques employing a moderate number of cases can successfully address important substantive questions. This approach merits revitalization in light of the new statistical tests suitable to small-N analysis and the success of such exemplary efforts as the Lange-Garrett-Jackman-Hicks-Patterson debate. If scholars use these new techniques in conjunction with good quantitative analysis, area studies skills, and sensitivity to context, then they may well succeed in showing that insights derived from case studies and from more qualitative comparative work can, after all, serve as a stepping-stone on the path toward statistical analysis.

Both of these intellectual tendencies will persist, and perhaps the key question is how well they can be linked. The tradition of research on Western Europe provides an encouraging model in that the findings of quantitative comparative scholars (Cameron, Hibbs, Lange and Garrett, Schmitter, Wilensky, and others) are routinely taken seriously and cited by those who do other kinds of research on Western Europe. In research on Latin America, by contrast, quantitative comparative work often receives considerably less attention from mainstream scholars. Yet it is precisely the kind of two-way pressure found in the West European field that may ultimately produce the best research. With good communication, country specialists and experts in qualitative small-*N* comparison will push the comparative quantifiers toward more carefully contextualized analysis; and the comparative quantifiers will push the country specialists and experts in qualitative comparison toward more systematic measurement and hypothesis testing. A central goal in the field of comparative method must be to sustain such communication.

The implications for graduate training are clear. New Ph.D.s in the field of comparative politics should have enough training in statistical methods to evaluate quantitative studies that employ old—and new—methods of statistical analysis and to use such analysis when appropriate. Those more oriented toward statistical analysis should have enough background in other methods of small-*N* comparison to understand not only these methods but also the reasoned critique of statistical studies contained within that tradition of research. Compared to current graduate training, both groups should have more exposure to basic writings on the philosophy of science and logic of inquiry that provide the framework in which choices about methodological alternatives must be made. In this way, the foundation could be laid for an eclectic practice of comparative politics that takes advantage of opportunities that present themselves on both sides of what could otherwise be a major intellectual divide.

The other major choice faced by comparativists, which again is best understood in terms of complementarity, is confronted within the set of scholars who do qualitative analysis of few cases. One alternative, the case study tradition, has seen a major advance in terms of the codification of procedures, and the view is widely accepted that case studies remain the cornerstone of comparative research.

The other alternative, the systematic analysis of relatively few cases, is of course precisely where Lijphart began the debate twenty years ago. Lijphart then seemed to suggest that this alternative was simply a way-station on the route to more sophisticated analysis. In the intervening years, by contrast, this alternative has been greatly strengthened, and the systematic comparison of roughly three to ten cases (or occasionally a few more) is an important and routine form of analysis in the field of comparative politics. Thus, today the comparative method, in the sense of small-*N* analysis, plays an important role within the field, though the viability of this form of analysis is increased to the extent that scholars develop the kind of links with other methodologies that have been explored in this paper.

NOTES

Kenneth Paul Erickson provided many valuable suggestions for revising and improving this article. Other helpful comments were made by Ruth Berins Collier, James Fearon, Leonardo Morlino, and Deborah L. Norden. Numerous conversations with Christopher Achen and Merrill Shanks have played a role in shaping my thinking about comparative method, and Achen also provided helpful comments on this article. This research has been supported by a Guggenheim Fellowship, the Social Science Research Council, and the Institute of Governmental Studies at Berkeley.

1. From *Kipling*, James Cochrane, ed. (Harmondsworth, England: Penguin Books, 1977), 95.
2. *Continental Divide: The Values and Institutions of the United States and Canada* (New York and London: Routledge, 1990), xiii.
3. Harold D. Lasswell, "The Future of the Comparative Method," *Comparative Politics* 1, no. 1 (October 1968): 3.
4. Many other domains of analysis are also fruitfully pursued through focusing on few cases.
5. References to work in this tradition are presented below. To the extent that a study is longitudinal, the number of cases can be increased through comparison over time. However, since the goal of many of these comparative historical analysts is to explain overall configurations of national outcomes as they are manifested over long periods, these outcomes often cannot be disaggregated into a series of longitudinal observations. Hence the case base may remain small.
6. Arend Lijphart, "Comparative Politics and Comparative Method," *American Political Science Review* 65, no. 3 (September 1971): 686.
7. For example, Richard Merritt and Stein Rokkan, eds., *Comparing Nations* (New Haven: Yale University Press, 1966); Arthur L. Kalleberg, "The Logic of Comparison: A Methodological Note on the Comparative Study of Political Systems," *World Politics* 19, no. 1 (October 1966): 69–82; Sidney Verba, "Some Dilemmas in Comparative Research," *World Politics* 20, no. 1 (October 1967): 111–127; Neil Smelser, "The Methodology of Comparative Analysis of Economic Activity," in Smelser, ed., *Essays in Sociological Interpretation* (Englewood Cliffs, N.J.: Prentice-Hall, 1968); Lasswell, "Future of the Comparative Method"; Adam Przeworski and Henry Teune, *The Logic of Comparative Social Inquiry* (New York: Wiley, 1970); Giovanni Sartori, "Concept Misformation in Com-

parative Politics," *American Political Science Review* 64, no. 4 (December 1970): 1033–1053; Richard L. Merritt, *Systematic Approaches to Comparative Politics* (Chicago: Rand McNally, 1970); Amitai Etzioni and Frederic L. Dubow, eds., *Comparative Perspectives: Theories and Methods* (Boston: Little, Brown, 1970); Lijphart, "Comparative Politics and Comparative Method"; Ival Vallier, ed., *Comparative Methods in Sociology: Essays on Trends and Applications* (Berkeley: University of California Press, 1971); Morris Zelditch, Jr., "Intelligible Comparisons," in Vallier, *Comparative Methods in Sociology*; Michael Armer and Allen Grimshaw, eds., *Comparative Social Research* (New York: Wiley, 1973).

8. In the context of this discussion, the parallels between Lijphart's analysis and Smelser's excellent earlier article should be noted. See Smelser, "Methodology of Comparative Analysis of Economic Activity." Smelser elaborated this analysis in *Comparative Methods in the Social Sciences* (Englewood Cliffs, N.J.: Prentice-Hall, 1976).

9. Lijphart, "Comparative Politics and Comparative Method," 683–85, 691–693.

10. Ibid., 685.

11. Ibid., 686 ff.

12. In the present volume, Susan Eckstein's analysis of Latin American revolutions (Chapter 14) is an example of this approach.

13. Theda Skocpol and Margaret Somers, "The Uses of Comparative History in Macrosocial Inquiry," *Comparative Studies in Society and History* 22, no. 2 (April 1980): 174–197. This perspective was elaborated by Skocpol in the concluding chapter of *Vision and Method in Historical Sociology* (New York: Cambridge University Press, 1984), and a parallel formulation is found in Charles Tilly, *Big Structures, Large Processes, Huge Comparisons* (New York: Russell Sage, 1984), chap. 4.

14. Skocpol and Somers refer to this as "macro-causal analysis." Yet comparative historical studies generate and test hypotheses with both a macro and a micro focus, and it does not seem productive to exclude those with a microfocus from this category. Hence this alternative label is used.

15. Gunnar Heckscher, *The Study of Comparative Government and Politics* (London: George Allen and Unwin, 1957), 46–51, 85–107.

16. Verba, "Some Dilemmas in Comparative Research."

17. (New Haven: Yale University Press, 1966).

18. Giovanni Sartori, ed., *Social Science Concepts: A Systematic Analysis* (Beverly Hills, Calif.: Sage, 1984).

19. A helpful overview is provided in Paul Rabinow and William M. Sullivan, *Interpretive Social Science: A Reader* (Berkeley: Univer-

sity of California Press, 1979). A revised and updated edition was published in 1987 as *Interpretive Social Science: A Second Look*.

20. "Thick Description: Toward an Interpretive Theory of Culture," in Clifford Geertz, *The Interpretation of Cultures* (New York: Basic Books, 1973). "Thick description" is sometimes mistakenly understood to refer simply to "detailed description," which is not what Geertz intends.

21. Gabriel A. Almond and Stephen J. Genco, "Clouds, Clocks, and the Study of Politics," *World Politics* 29, no. 4 (July 1977): 489–522.

22. Charles C. Ragin, *The Comparative Method: Moving Beyond Qualitative and Quantitative Strategies* (Berkeley: University of California Press, 1987).

23. Reinhard Bendix, *Nation-Building and Citizenship* (New York: Wiley, 1964).

24. Barrington Moore, Jr., *Social Origins of Dictatorship and Democracy* (Boston: Beacon Press, 1966).

25. Jeffrey Paige, *Agrarian Revolution: Social Movements and Export Agriculture in the Underdeveloped World* (New York: Free Press, 1975).

26. Theda Skocpol, *States and Social Revolutions: A Comparative Analysis of France, Russia, and China* (Cambridge: Cambridge University Press, 1979). This analytic perspective is creatively synthesized in Skocpol, *Vision and Method in Historical Sociology*. A recent example is Ruth Berins Collier and David Collier, *Shaping the Political Arena: Critical Junctures, the Labor Movement, and Regime Dynamics in Latin America* (Princeton, N.J.: Princeton University Press, forthcoming).

27. Gregory M. Luebbert, *Liberalism, Fascism, and Social Democracy: Social Classes and the Political Origins of Regimes in Interwar Europe* (New York: Oxford University Press, forthcoming).

28. Robert W. Jackman, "Cross-National Statistical Research and the Study of Comparative Politics," *American Journal of Political Science* 29, no. 1 (February 1985): 161–182.

29. Arend Lijphart, "The Political Consequences of Electoral Laws, 1945–1985," *American Political Science Review* 84, no. 2 (June, 1990): 481–496.

30. See Ragin, *Comparative Method*, chap. 4.

31. Arend Lijphart, "The Comparable Cases Strategy in Comparative Research," *Comparative Political Studies* 8, no. 2 (July 1975): 158–177.

32. Fred Eggan, "Social Anthropology and the Method of Controlled Comparison," *American Anthropologist* 56, no. 5, part 1 (October 1954): 743–763.

33. Arthur L. Stinchcombe, *Theoretical Methods in Social History* (New York: Academic Press, 1978).

34. Przeworski and Teune, *The Logic of Comparative Social Inquiry*; and Adam Przeworski, "Methods of Cross-National Research, 1970–1983: An Overview," in Meinolf Dierkes, Hans N. Weiler, and Ariane Berthoin Antal, eds., *Comparative Policy Research: Learning from Experience* (Aldershot, England: Gower, 1987).

35. These two types of designs correspond, respectively, to John Stuart Mill's method of difference and method of agreement. See John Stuart Mill, "Of the Four Methods of Experimental Inquiry," in Mill, *A System of Logic* [1843] (Toronto: University of Toronto Press, 1974).

36. Personal communication from Adam Przeworski.

37. Guillermo O'Donnell, Philippe C. Schmitter, and Lawrence Whitehead, eds., *Transitions from Authoritarian Rule* (Baltimore: Johns Hopkins University Press, 1986).

38. R. B. Collier and D. Collier, *Shaping the Political Arena*.

39. Dankwart Rustow, "Modernization and Comparative Politics: Prospects in Research and Theory," *Comparative Politics* 1, no. 1 (October 1968): 37–51.

40. I acknowledge conversations with Merrill Shanks on this issue.

41. Sartori, "Concept Misformation in Comparative Politics"; Sartori, *Social Science Concepts*; and Giovanni Sartori, Fred W. Riggs, and Henry Teune, *Tower of Babel: On the Definition and Analysis of Concepts in the Social Sciences*, International Studies Association, Occasional Paper no. 6 (Pittsburgh: University of Pittsburgh, 1975); John C. McKinney, *Constructive Typology and Social Theory* (New York: Meredith, 1966); Kalleberg, "Logic of Comparison"; and E. Gene DeFelice, "Comparison Misconceived: Common Nonsense in Comparative Politics," *Comparative Politics* 13, no. 1 (October 1980), 119–126.

42. George Lakoff, *Women, Fire, and Dangerous Things: What Categories Reveal about the Mind* (Chicago: University of Chicago Press, 1986).

43. Sartori, "Concept Misformation in Comparative Politics," and *Social Science Concepts*.

44. Donald T. Campbell and Julian C. Stanley, *Experimental and Quasi-Experimental Designs for Research* (Chicago: Rand McNally, 1963).

45. Ibid., 38.

46. Donald T. Campbell and H. Laurence Ross, "The Connecticut Crackdown on Speeding," *Law and Society Review* 3 (August 1968): 33–53.

47. Przeworski, "Methods of Cross-National Research."
48. Edward R. Tufte, *The Quantitative Analysis of Social Problems* (Reading, Mass.: Addison-Wesley, 1970).
49. See Francis W. Hoole, *Evaluation Research and Development Activities* (Beverly Hills, Calif.: Sage, 1978). For an excellent treatment of experimental design and evaluation research in an introductory textbook on social science methodology, see Earl Babbie, *The Practice of Social Research*, 4th ed. (Belmont, Calif.: Wadsworth, 1986), chaps. 8, 12.
50. Christopher H. Achen, *The Statistical Analysis of Quasi-Experiments* (Berkeley: University of California Press, 1986).
51. David A. Freedman, "As Others See Us: A Case Study in Path Analysis," *Journal of Educational Statistics* 12, no. 2 (Summer 1987): 101–128.
52. Persi Diaconis and Bradley Efron, "Computer-Intensive Methods in Statistics," *Scientific American* 248, no. 5 (May 1983): 116–130.
53. See Frank R. Hampel et al., *Robust Statistics: The Approach Based on Influence Functions* (New York: Wiley, 1987); Frederick Hartwig, with Brian E. Dearing, *Exploratory Data Analysis*, Sage University Paper, Series no. 07-016 (Beverly Hills, Calif.: Sage, 1979); Frederick Mosteller and John W. Tukey, "Robust and Resistant Measures," in Mosteller and Tukey, *Data Analysis and Regression* (Reading, Mass.: Addison-Wesley, 1977).
54. Kenneth A. Bollen and Robert W. Jackman, "Regression Diagnostics: An Expository Treatment of Outliers and Influential Cases," *Sociological Methods and Research* 13 (1985): 510–542; Robert W. Jackman, "The Politics of Economic Growth in Industrial Democracies, 1974–1980: Leftist Strength or North Sea Oil?" *Journal of Politics* 49, no. 1 (February 1987): 242–256.
55. Peter Lange and Geoffrey Garrett, "The Politics of Growth: Strategic Interaction and Economic Performance in Advanced Industrial Democracies, 1974–1980," *Journal of Politics* 47, no. 3 (August 1985): 792–827; Jackman, "The Politics of Economic Growth"; Peter Lange and Geoffrey Garrett, "The Politics of Growth Reconsidered," *Journal of Politics* 49, no. 1 (February 1987): 257–274; Alexander Hicks, "Social Democratic Corporatism and Economic Growth," *Journal of Politics* 50, no. 3 (August 1988): 677–704; Alexander Hicks and William David Patterson, "On the Robustness of the Left Corporatist Model of Economic Growth" (unpublished paper, 1988); Robert W. Jackman "The Politics of Economic Growth, Once Again," *Journal of Politics* 51, no. 3 (August 1989): 646–661; and Geoffrey Garrett and Peter Lange, "Government Partisanship and Economic Performance: When and How Does 'Who Governs' Matter?" (unpublished paper, 1989).

56. Jackman, "Politics of Economic Growth."
57. *Comparative Method*, chap. 4.
58. John E. Jackson, "Estimation of Models with Variable Coefficients," paper presented to the Third Annual Political Methodology Conference, 1986.
59. Ruth Berins Collier, *Regimes in Tropical Africa: Changing Forms of Supremacy* (Berkeley: University of California Press, 1982): 63–64, 76–80.
60. Personal communication from Arend Lijphart.
61. Donald Campbell, " 'Degrees of Freedom' and the Case Study," *Comparative Political Studies* 8, no. 2 (July 1975): 178–193.
62. Harry Eckstein, "Case Studies and Theory in Political Science," in Fred Greenstein and Nelson W. Polsby, eds., *Handbook of Political Science*, vol. 7 (Reading, Mass.: Addison-Wesley, 1975).
63. Alexander L. George, "Case Studies and Theory Development: The Method of Structured, Focused Comparison," in Paul Gordon Lauren, ed., *Diplomacy: New Approaches in History, Theory, and Policy* (New York: Free Press, 1979).
64. Alexander L. George and Timothy J. McKeown, "Case Studies and Theories of Organizational Decision Making," *Advances in Information Processing in Organizations*, vol. 2 (Santa Barbara, Calif.: JAI Press, 1985).
65. Robert K. Yin, *Case Study Research: Design and Methods*. Applied Social Research Methods Series, vol. 5 (Beverly Hills, Calif.: Sage, 1984).
66. Christopher H. Achen and Duncan Snidal, "Rational Deterrence Theory and Comparative Case Studies," *World Politics* 41, no. 2 (January 1989): 143–169.

Chapter
3

Concepts and Models in Comparative Politics

Political Development Reconsidered—and Its Alternatives

Howard J. Wiarda

Looking back over the last twenty or thirty years in comparative politics, one is struck by how closely the dominant concepts and models in the subfield are related to actual events and the broad currents sweeping the world of nations, to attitudinal and mood changes in the United States itself (where most, but by no means all, of the comparative politics literature is written), and to intellectual and methodological innovations within the larger field of political science. It is not that comparative politics exactly follows the headlines (although it may do that too), with their almost daily and often fickle flights from one dramatic crisis or area to the next; but it does tend to reflect the long-term trends in public and/or elite opinion that help determine which geographic area or issue or which intellectual approach will receive priority. Such fluctuations in our attention and priorities have also affected the field of comparative politics and its changing emphases, research priorities, and conceptual perspectives over the last several decades.

  The purpose of this chapter is to trace in broad terms these developments and interrelations over the last thirty years, to show how comparative politics developed from its earlier formal-legal approach to a more vigorous and genuinely *comparative* discipline, to trace the rise and decline of the political development school, to examine the approaches that supplanted it, to analyze the fragmentation of the field, and to assess its current condition— most particularly, the comeback of the political development approach. We seek to show how the field interacts with and is part of a larger national, international, cultural, and political environment. As United States (and maybe global) politics and policy making have become increasingly divided, fragmented, and in disarray in recent years, comparative politics has seemed to follow these same trends. We ask is this new ferment, lack of coherence, and fragmentation a pathetic sign of the state of the field or is it an indication of intellectual health and vigor?[1]

THE ASCENDANCE AND DECLINE OF THE POLITICAL DEVELOPMENT APPROACH

Traditional comparative politics is universally thought to have been a parochial, formal-legal, and institutional approach. That is the charge that Roy Macridis, in a tub-thumping, flagwaving, and influential little book, raised against it in 1955.[2] Macridis, representing a new generation of comparativists, who were more influenced by the recent approaches in political science than by the older approach that had been heavily dominated by lawyers and legalists, wanted a comparative politics that concentrated on informal and dynamic aspects: public opinion, interest groups, political parties, process variables, input functions, decision making, and the processes of change. His proposed approach, which soon became the prevailing one, corresponded to other factors that we might call global. For our purposes, the most important of these were the Cold War in the 1940s and 1950s and the sudden emergence onto the world scene in the late 1950s and early 1960s of a host of new nations.

The interrelations among these three events—a more dynamic comparative politics, the Cold War, and the emerging nations—have yet to be analyzed adequately, in my view.[3] Some U.S. officials, and doubtless a few scholars as well, saw the fashioning of a body of literature dealing with the emerging nations purely as a means by which U.S. foreign policy could control and dominate these countries for Cold War purposes. Other scholars saw the constructs of development theory as purely an intellectual approach, a way of understanding and perhaps of encouraging development, but not a means of manipulation. Still others, a majority I would guess, saw varying degrees of interrelations between U.S. Cold War strategies and a theory to analyze and help shape the politics of the developing nations, saw no incompatibility between the two, perhaps thought of them as complementary, or thought both goals were worthy of pursuing at once.

By the 1960s the political development approach had become dominant in comparative politics. Some scholars continued to labor in the vineyards of the more traditional institutional approaches and others continued to write first-rate books on Western Europe. But the developing nations were clearly where the action was, particularly so with the election of John F. Kennedy; the creation of the Peace Corps, whose mood was carried over into the effort to bring development to the emerging nations and not just to analyze it; the growth of the U.S. Agency for International Development, which sought to put development into concrete, realizable programs; the Cuban revolution; and the Alliance for Progress, which focused attention on Latin America and the Third World and reemphasized powerfully the Cold War considerations that undergirded the U.S. government's development efforts.[4]

Considerable variation existed among the leading writers and approaches to development—differences that have blurred in our memories over the years or that have been purposely subordinated to the goal of lumping all "developmentalists" together for the sake of more easily criticizing or discrediting them. There are the disciplinary differences: the more deterministic approaches of economists such as Rostow[5] and Heilbroner[6]; and the more sociological, but in their own ways also deterministic, approaches of Deutsch,[7] Levy,[8] and Lipset[9]; and to my mind the more sophisticated and subtle, political science approaches of Pye,[10] Apter,[11] Weiner,[12] and others.

Among the political scientists, considerable and important differences also existed. Gabriel Almond, who employed the structural-functionalism and pattern variables of Talcott Science Research Council Committee in Comparative Politics; his and James S. Coleman's 1960 book, *The Politics of the Developing Areas*,[14] was a pathbreaker in the field and perhaps the most influential of this approach. The SSRC/CCP was the dominant group in the comparative politics field,[15] producing during the 1960s a series of volumes through Princeton University Press that charted new ground in such areas as political culture, political parties, and other areas.[16]

But not all development-oriented political scientists shared Almond's views or his approach, and even within the SSRC/CCP not everyone was as enamored as Almond was of structural-functionalism and pattern variables. In addition, many area specialists believed at that early time that Almond was comparing apples and oranges and that the effort to stuff all the world's culturally diverse political systems into one overarching scheme was artificial and false. They also read the area-specific chapters, which followed Almond's long and theoretical introduction in *The Politics of the Developing Areas*, as an attempt to impose supposedly universal categories on areas where they didn't fit well and thus did a disservice to a better understanding of these regions.

At the same time that there was sniping from afar, in graduate seminars and other less public forums, some members of the SSRC/CCP were pursuing their own research agendas in ways that did not seem to owe so much to the Parsonian-Almondian approach. Still others—and one thinks particularly of Guy Pauker in this regard—began the study of developing nations as committed Parsonians, but after actually spending time in those countries came back convinced that the pattern variables were not useful. Some members of the SSRC/CCP have said that to their recollection Almond was the only one of their group who really accepted and was enthusiastic about the pattern variables.[17]

Nor should one discount the possibilities for change, growth, modification, and amendment within the developmentalist approach. For example, the Cambridge scholars who were members of the Joint (Harvard-MIT) Seminar on Political Development (JOSPOD) continued to explore new development-related topics every year for over twenty-five years and to develop new concepts or refine old ones in the process.[18] Other members of the SSRC/CCP continued to expand their understanding of development as well.[19] In addition, a whole new generation of graduate students, armed with the developmentalist ideas and concepts, went out to the Third World in the early-to-mid 1960s and came back with dissertations that often obliged their mentors to modify their views. Finally, critics from within the establishment such as Samuel P. Huntington (though not a member of the SSRC/CCP) published a devastating critique of the earlier developmentalist approach, challenging the view that socioeconomic modernization and political development went hand in hand, were mutually supportive, and that the latter was somehow automatically produced by the former.[20]

What is required first of all, therefore, is a considerable sorting out of earlier development theory. There is a rich body of literature that deserves to be read and considered anew. It is not a monolithic "school" and its principal advocates were not all of one mind on the issues. Rather, right from the beginning there were nuances, diverse views and approaches, and a wealth of scholarship and ideas. Far too often the developmentalist approach has been dismissed with a blanket condemnation and its principal figures have been lumped together in one amorphous category. While certain of its intellectual thrusts seem in retrospect to have taken us in some wrong directions, this early focus on the developing areas yielded rich insights and a vast literature. It is a shame that this literature is not paid more attention than it is at present because the information contained therein is still a marvelously fertile ground for the student of developing nations.

The second, related, factor to remember is that the criticisms of development theory (analyzed in the next section) were not necessarily applicable to the whole body of thought and research, but only some of its (I would say) most vulnerable published work. The criticisms have been most strongly leveled against the writings of Almond, Lipset, and

Rostow, who are taken as the paradigm writers in the developmentalist school. But it seems to me their works are, in some of their particulars, the easiest works to set up as strawmen and to criticize; further, I am not sure that their writings are representative of the entire development approach. The field is far too rich and diverse for us to dismiss an entire body of work because a few of its leading writers went too far, said some things that can easily be criticized, or exaggerated the universality of their model.

CRITICISMS OF DEVELOPMENTALISM

During most of the 1960s the developmentalist approach was dominant in comparative politics. Although other comparative politics scholars continued to write from other points of view, the political development paradigm became the prevailing one. It appeared at the time to be the most intellectually stimulating approach; that was where the money was, in the form of research grants and opportunities; that was where the most prestigious publication outlets were (*World Politics*, Princeton University Press); and, since political development had also been accepted as a major goal of U.S. foreign policy toward the Third World, that was where the opportunity to influence policy was.

But eventually criticisms of developmentalism began to come from diverse directions[21]; their cumulative impact was devastating—so much so that today's graduate students are acquainted with the criticisms, but hardly know the original literature, no longer read it, and tend to treat it (if at all) dismissively in their seminars in one brief session. A listing of some of the main criticisms follows:

First, the political development literature is criticized as biased and ethnocentric, derived from the Western experience of development, and of doubtful utility in non-Western areas and only limited utility in the incompletely Western ones. For societies lacking the sociopolitical precepts of Greece, Rome, and the Bible, without the same experience of feudalism and capitalism, and not having experienced the cultural history of the West, the argument is, the Western developmental model is either irrelevant or of meager usefulness.[22]

Second, it has been argued that the timing, sequences, and stages of development in the West may not be replicable in today's developing nations. With regard to timing, it can be said that countries whose development is occurring in the late twentieth century face different kinds of problems from those whose development began in the nineteenth century; with regards to sequences, it appears, for example, that rapid urbanization may precede industrialization in the Third World whereas in the West just the reverse occurred. With regard to stages, whereas capitalism followed feudalism in the West, the two have most often been fused in the Third World. Almost all our interpretations based on the Western developmental experience—the political behavior of the middle class, the presumed professionalization of the armed forces, the demographic transition, and other key indicators of modernity or the transition thereto—need to be rethought and reconceptualized when applied to the Third World.[23]

Third, the international context of today's developing nations is quite different from that of the earlier developers. That factor was ignored in most of the development literature, which in the 1960s focused almost exclusively on domestic social and political change. Few countries have ever developed autonomously and in complete isolation; but it is plain that today's developing nations are caught up in a much more complex web of dependency relations, international conflicts, alliances and blocs, transnational activities, and the "world culture" (Lucian Pye's term) of tastes, communications, and travel than was the case of the early modernizers. These international connections need to be factored into any theory of political development.[24]

Fourth, the critics argue, the political development literature often misrepresented the role of traditional institutions. In much of the literature traditional institutions were treated as anachronisms, fated earlier to fade away or be destroyed as modernization went forward. But in most modernizing nations, traditional institutions have proved durable, flexible, and long lasting, adapting to change rather than being overwhelmed by it. They have served as filters of modernization and even as agents of modernization. A much more complex understanding of the relation between tradition and modernity is required.[25]

Fifth, in the developing nations, the sense is strong that the early political development literature raised false expectations and created unrealistic goals for these societies. Almond's original functional categories seemed reasonable and nonethnocentric enough, but in actual practice "rule adjudication" was taken to mean an independent judiciary, political parties and an independent legislature were required, and countries that lacked these institutions were too often labeled "dysfunctional." Hence the development literature frequently skewed, biased, and distorted the political processes working in the developing nations, forced them to create Potemkin village-like institutions (such as political parties) that looked wonderful on paper but proved to be ephemeral, or that obliged them to destroy traditional institutions that might have been viable within their own contexts.[26]

A sixth criticism is that political development was part of a larger Cold War strategy fomented by the United States to keep the Third World depressed and "in chains." Two distinctions need to be pointed out here. The first is between those who did have such a blatantly Cold

War strategy in mind[27] and those who more simply wanted to analyze development and, often in addition, wanted to help the emerging nations to achieve it. Frankly, most of the scholars who wrote on political development had both goals and saw no contradiction between them; they favored development and thought that in the same process both U.S. and Third World aspirations and interests could be achieved.

And that leads us directly to the second distinction. Many of those who wrote the early development literature shared the general U.S. attitude of that time of the need to contain the Soviet Union and prevent the developing nations from going communist. But the way to do that, they all but universally agreed, was not to keep the developing nations depressed and in chains, but to help stimulate their development, help make them viable, promote economic growth and political institutionalization by which they could themselves resist communist appeals. There was clearly a Cold War motive behind much of the early development analysis, but its goal was emphatically not to keep the Third World depressed but rather to build it up socially, economically, and politically.[28]

Seventh, the political development perspective has been criticized as wreaking downright harm on the developing nations. The focus on political development sometimes had the effect of helping to destroy or undermine indigenous institutions within the Third World that were often quite viable, provided some cultural or social "cement," and might have helped these nations bridge some transitions to modern forms. Instead, because many intellectuals and government leaders within the Third World themselves accepted the developmental perspective and the seemingly inevitable progression from "traditional" to "modern," these traditional institutions (family and patronage networks, clan and tribal groups, and so forth) had to be eliminated in order for development to occur. The result in many developing nations is the worst of all possible worlds: Their traditional institutions have been largely destroyed, their modern ones remain inchoate and incompletely established, and they are hence left not with development but with a political and institutional vacuum.[29]

One final criticism of the political development approach is that its early leaders were themselves not always sufficiently adept politically. There were rivalries for leadership within the political development movement and resentment among members of the SSRC/CCP against the leadership; some of these rivalries and bitterness are still strongly felt even after thirty years. More important from the point of view of the receptivity of the political development approach was that the SSRC/CCP, which dominated the field for at least a decade, failed to broaden its base sufficiently to bring in adequate numbers of new members and to incorporate the research findings and concepts of comparativists other than themselves. Year after year throughout the 1960s the SSRC/CCP volumes had the same editors and the same contributors. The fact that little fresh blood and few fresh ideas were introduced created resentment among many other comparativists who also had important and worthwhile things to say, and many of these persons turned out to be among the foremost critics of the developmentalist approach.

These criticisms of the literature of political development were powerful and quite devastating. By the end of the 1960s not only were these criticisms widespread, but other factors were operating as well. So many case studies of developing nations had now been written in which the developmental approach was found wanting that the assumptions of the approach were questioned. Samuel Huntington weighed in with his powerful critique, suggesting that socioeconomic modernization and political development, instead of going forward hand in hand, might well work at cross purposes. The Vietnam war provided another blow since in some quarters the war was presented as what a misplaced emphasis on political development can get the United States into with disastrous consequences; in addition, some of the early writers on development were viewed as supporters of the war or even its "architects."

A generational factor was also involved: the political development literature was largely fashioned by one generation of scholars and by the end of the 1960s there was a new generation of scholars who were critical of their predecessors or who simply had other ideas. And that gets us to the final reason for political development's demise: fad and fancy. Political development was in part a product of the early 1960s, of the enthusiasms of the Kennedy administration, the Alliance for Progress, and "the Peace Corps mood of the times" (Almond's phrase). But by the late 1960s both that spirit and that body of literature had largely come and gone. By then other approaches had come into existence: dependency theory, corporatism, political-economy, bureaucratic-authoritarianism, revived Marxism, and others.

NEW AND ALTERNATIVE MODELS

The decline in the consensus undergirding the political development approach brought a variety of other approaches to the fore. In part these changes were related to logical and methodological flaws within the development approach; in part they were due to broader changes in the larger society. One is tempted to draw parallels between the decline of the development approach in the 1960s and the decline of the societal and foreign policy consensus in the United States and to relate the rise of multiple approaches in comparative politics in the decade that followed to increasing division, even fragmentation, in the society as a whole. But it may be that such larger conclusions are not justified at the present time.

The decline of the older consensus in the field need not necessarily be lamented. There *are* major problems with the political development approach, and the new approaches, for the most part, made a contribution to the discipline. However, as with development theory, there are "vulgar" as well as more sophisticated versions of most of these newer approaches which need to be sorted out. Furthermore, many of these newer approaches had run their courses by the 1980s and had begun to be supplanted. What is taking their place? What is the future of the field?

Dependency Theory

Dependency theory grew directly out of general dissatisfaction with the development approach and specifically out of the criticism that development theory ignored international or "dependency" variables, such as international market forces over which the Third World had little control, multinational corporations, and the machinations of U.S. embassies abroad.[30] Now of course there are dependency relations in the world as well as complex relations of interdependence, and I think we all recognize that the embassies of the United States and other nations and various transnational actors such as multinational corporations (MNCs) do sometimes muck around in the internal affairs of other nations. The trick in utilizing dependency theory, therefore, is to distinguish between those writers who use the theory pragmatically to shed light on the role of international actors operating within the borders of Third World nations or otherwise controlling their destinies[31] and those who would use the theory as an ideological weapon, usually from a Marxist or Marxist-Leninist perspective, to flagellate the United States.[32] A sophisticated dependency theory can be a useful tool of analysis, but the more vulgar ideological kind should be viewed as purely a political instrument.

Corporatism

The corporatist approach similarly arose out of discontent with development theory and was meant to shed light on political phenomena which both development and dependency theory only inadequately explained. Two schools of thought within corporatism emerged early on. One viewed corporatism as a general pattern of political cognition like liberalism and Marxism. It seemed to have had an especially strong impact on the nations of the Iberic-Latin (including the Philippines) culture area,[33] because of that area's particular history and traditions. A second view took corporatism as a general model of the political system, without particular regional or cultural affinities, implying a certain kind of relationship between societal structures and the state and therefore present in a wide variety of regimes.[34] These views need not be seen as incompatible; indeed the two perspectives can be used fruitfully in conjunction with each other rather than as polarized approaches.[35]

Corporatist features have now been found to be present in different forms and in varying degrees in virtually all political regimes. Their very ubiquitousness, however, has diminished the utility of corporatism as an explanatory device. The result is that the corporatist approach has suffered a different fate than dependency theory. The corporatist approach has been accepted in the literature as a contributing but not a complete or sufficient explanation; and the field has gone on to other things. The corporatist approach has been superseded not out of controversy (although some still goes on from time to time), but out of acceptance and, hence, a certain boredom.[36]

Political Economy

The early writings on political development largely ignored political economy variables. In part that was because in the 1950s, when the theory was first formulated, the barriers between the social science disciplines were sharper and interdisciplinary work less appreciated than is the case today. In part, also, it was because development studies had previously been dominated by economists and sociologists, and the new development literature made a conscious effort to emphasize the autonomy of the political variables. It further seems likely that, given the Cold War origins of some of this literature (recall Rostow subtitling his classic 1960 book "A Non-Communist Manifesto"), the development approach made a conscious effort to stay away from political economy explanations that could too easily be confused with Marxism.

And, like dependency theory, that is still the problem with the political economy approach. In subtle, sophisticated hands,[37] the political economy perspective can be useful and insightful. In less sophisticated hands or among those who consciously wish to use it that way, the political economy approach has a tendency to tail off into a Marxian interpretation with, again, greatly varying levels of sophistication as opposed to vulgarity.

Bureaucratic-Authoritarianism

Bureaucratic-authoritarianism arose out of the same disillusionment with the development approach as did a number of these other approaches, and was particularly aimed at explaining the rash of military coups that occurred in Latin America in the 1960s and early 1970s. The term *bureaucratic*-authoritarianism was used to distinguish the newer, more institutionalized military regimes in Argentina, Brazil, Chile, Peru, and Uruguay from the older, more personal or *caudillo*-dominated military regimes of the past.[38]

Bureaucratic-authoritarianism is a good term, for in fact the newer Latin American authoritarian regimes were more bureaucratic, more institutionalized, more "developed" than those in the past. The trouble was that this useful contribution was accompanied by an attempt to explain the bureaucratic-authoritarian phenomenon through a convoluted argument that pointed to the crisis of Latin America's growth strategy of import substitution as *the* cause of bureaucratic-authoritarianism and thus shaded off into a kind of economic determinism that the evidence could not sustain.[39] Like so many of the approaches examined here, bureaucratic-authoritarianism made a significant contribution shorn of its ideological baggage and as long as it was considered a useful but partial explanation and not elevated to the status of a single, all-encompassing one.

Revived Marxism

I know of few scholars who do not find that the general Marxian paradigm is useful in providing a broad-gauged explanation for the transition from feudalism to capitalism. The Marxian explanation has been popular intellectually in the developing nations because that is precisely the transition through which they are presently going. The trouble with this approach comes when it is used to explain the transition from capitalism to the next stage, when it is applied to specific groups where it does not fit very well (the Church and the armed forces, for instance), and when it is used as a rigid, ideological formula rather than as a flexible tool of analysis.[40] In addition, the socialist countries have found that Marxism is not a useful guide in providing for an efficient and productive economy, their intellectuals have abandoned Marxism almost to a person, and many of the developing nations—once enamored of Marxism—are no longer so attracted to it. In the present era Marxism and especially Marxism-Leninism appears to be valued as a formula for gaining, consolidating, and hanging onto power; but it is no longer valued as a way to achieve either political freedom or economic efficiency.

Many of these newer explanations have provided useful contributions to comparative politics. Quite a number have by now been successfully integrated into, and are widely accepted in, the broader field.

It should be remembered that they provide partial explanations, not complete ones, and that they, like the political development approach, have gone through a life cycle of birth, growth, cooption, and assimilation or a gradual fading away.

In another work,[41] I suggested that the disappearance of the consensus that used to exist about the political development approach and the rise of these other, competing, approaches is not necessarily an unhealthy sign for the discipline. The existence of a variety of approaches has stimulated a healthy discussion and ferment and reflects the methodological and political realities in which we and the discipline live. In that earlier work, therefore, I suggest three priorities of research: continued refining of these several separate approaches, efforts at building connecting bridges among these "islands of theory," and continued attempts to fashion larger syntheses incorporating elements from these several theories. To these three I would now add a fourth task: grappling with the revival of the political development approach and comprehending the newer political phenomena emerging around us which may also point back to a revival of developmentalism.

POLITICAL DEVELOPMENT REVISITED

In the early 1960s, when the last major experiment in democratic development in Latin America took place, great hope existed that democracy, development, peace, and security would be closely correlated. Intellectual justification for such correlations were provided in the development literature of that period, and most particularly in the writings of Walt Rostow, Seymour Lipset, and Karl Deutsch. Using his famous aeronautical metaphor of the several stages of "take-off," Rostow demonstrated, based on the European and U.S. experiences, that as countries developed economically, they also tended to become middle class, pluralistic, democratic, stable, socially just, and peaceful.[42] Lipset and Deutsch in pathbreaking articles[43] at that time showed the close correlations between literacy, social mobilization, economic development, and democracy. An obvious foreign policy lesson also followed from this research: If we can help developing countries to be more literate, affluent, and middle class, they will consequently become more democratic and more able to resist the appeals of communism.

But correlations do not imply causal relationships, and in Latin America as well as many other developing areas in the 1960s a wave of military coups swept the civilian democratic governments out of power. Greater literacy and social mobilization did not lead to democracy and stability but to upheaval and, ultimately, under military governments, to repression. The middle class proved to be not a bastion of stability and democracy but deeply divided and very conservative, often goading the military to seize power from the civilian democrats. By the late 1970s, none of the correlations was correlating very well. Democracy had collapsed, seventeen of the twenty Latin American nations were under military-authoritarian rule, the developmentalist literature was rejected and in shambles, and the new, postdevelopmentalist interpretations (dependency theory, corporatism, Marxist explanations, bureaucratic-authoritarianism) were in their heyday.[44]

But since the late 1970s nations as diverse as South Korea, the Philippines, and the Republic of China have embarked on some remarkable transitions to democracy. In Latin America the figures of a decade ago have been almost exactly reversed: Eighteen of the twenty-one countries and over 90 percent of the population are either democracies or en route to democracy. This transition in so short a time has been nothing less than amazing. Not only has this given rise to a whole new approach and body of literature ("Transitions to Democracy")[45] in comparative politics, but it also forces us to reconsider and maybe resurrect the older, discredited developmentalist approach. At least six factors at work here demand our attention.

What Works in Development

By now we have some thirty years experience with development. We no longer need to limit our discussions to the conceptual and theoretical level, as we did to a large extent in the 1960s. We now know, with the proper qualifications, what works in development. We have abundant case histories and sophisticated comparative studies. We know what are unsuccessful development strategies and what are successful ones. Overwhelmingly, the evidence now points to the conclusion that what works in development is democracy, representative institutions, personal and group security, open markets, social modernization, stable governments, and peaceful, moderate change[46]—all the elements that Lipset, Rostow, and the early development writers posited as necessary.

A World Political Culture in Favor of Democracy

The concept of a "world political culture," first articulated by Lucian Pye,[47] is and always will be imprecise and difficult to verify empirically. Nevertheless there can be no doubt that in the last decade a remarkable transformation that can be called cosmic has occurred. No one wants corporatist, bureaucratic-authoritarian, organic-statist, or Marxist-Leninist regimes anymore. In Asia, the Soviet Union and Eastern

Europe, and in Latin America the sentiment in favor of democracy is overwhelming. Public opinion surveys in Latin America indicate that over 90 percent of the population in almost every country favors democracy. *Glasnost* and *perestroika* may have ushered in one of the most fundamental transformations of the late twentieth century: political opening and democracy within communist regimes. A host of authoritarian regimes in diverse parts of the world—"friendly tyrants," as one research report labels them[48]—have been swept from power. Though the measures are inexact, few of us can doubt that a revolution in favor of democracy of very profound dimensions has begun to sweep the world.

U.S. Foreign Policy

Most of the transitions to democracy that have occurred have been the products of indigenous forces and only secondarily of external ones. Nevertheless in some key countries at critical times a U.S. policy in favor of democracy has also been important. The United States has traditionally expressed strong support for democracy and human rights for ethical and moral reasons and for the practical reason that it is in our interests to do so. The most recent campaign for democracy and human rights began under President Carter, who emphasized human rights, and continued under President Reagan, who focused more on democracy and the belief that human rights tend to flow from American strength, not American weakness. A foreign policy agenda of human rights and democracy has acquired bipartisan support and it is inconceivable that any future U.S. administration could have a successful foreign policy without these components.[49]

The Decline of the Other Models

Not only have the major explanatory models (corporatism, Marxism-Leninism, bureaucratic-authoritarianism) largely run their course (some have, in part, been incorporated into the discipline), but the regimes based upon these models have either been discredited or overthrown as well. Cuba, Nicaragua, and the Soviet Union are no longer viewed as viable models by many people; the "Nasserist" (progressive, nationalistic) military of Peru, the generals in Brazil, and the corporatist regimes of Portugal and Spain are no longer with us. The demise or discrediting of the older "models" and the resurgence of democracy have given rise to the sentiment that perhaps the development paradigm had (and has) something to recommend it after all.[50]

Changed Political Attitudes in the United States

After Vietnam, Watergate, the relative decline of the United States in the 1970s, and Jimmy Carter's "malaise," the sense was strong in the United States that we had nothing to offer the world. Our self-confidence had been eroded by events both at home and abroad. But during the 1980s, as the economy recovered and then flourished, American self-confidence began to recover. The sense grew that maybe the United States was not such a bad place after all—at least compared with most others—and that it still had a great deal to offer the rest of the world. There are many criticisms that can be raised against it but undoubtedly Allan Bloom's book that emphasized the democratic and civilizing values in the Western cultural tradition and pointedly suggested, in contrast to much of the prevailing cultural relativism and the earlier criticism of developmentalist ethnocentrism, that some cultures (the Western one) are in fact more democratic, more humane, and more civilized than others (let us say, the Iranian one) undoubtedly struck a responsive chord.[51]

Development in the Short and Long Run

The democratization, development, and modernization that have occurred in many Third World areas in the last decade force us to reassess the Lipsetonian and Rostowian theories in the light of these new circumstances. Lipset, Rostow, and the entire development approach and school were thoroughly discredited in the 1960s and 1970s—and often for good reasons as we have said. They and their followers, as well as many U.S. government officials, tended to portray development in ways that proved far too simple, implying a causative relationship between development and democracy that did not exist, basing their theories of development too heavily on the Western and European experiences, and thus helping to misdirect development theory and the policies that flowed from it.

But we now need to consider that while Lipset and Rostow (and their schools) were wrong in the short run, they may still prove to have been correct in the long run. That is, although there is no necessary, automatic, or causative connection between development and democracy (as some of the early developmentalists themselves pointed out), there are tendencies, correlations, and long-term relationships that cannot be denied. It is therefore necessary, I believe, to begin a serious reexamination of the earlier development literature to see what should be saved and what jettisoned. There may well be more worth saving than we might have guessed ten years ago.[52]

For example, we learned in the 1960s that there was no necessary correlation between democracy and the size of the middle class; indeed in many countries it was the middle class that plotted to overthrow democracy. But in the 1980s it was the middle class that led the opposition to military authoritarianism and became convinced, having tried other models, that democracy is much to be preferred. Employing other indexes yields further correlations. The armed forces have become both more professionalized and more in favor of democracy than they were in the 1960s. Literacy has increased and so has the spread of democracy. Despite the depressing circumstances of many Third World countries today, economic development over three decades has gone forward and in many others the desire for democracy has increased. The correlations that did not correlate in the 1960s now seem to be correlating very well indeed.[53]

These strong correlations raise the possibility that while Lipset, Rostow, and others were too optimistic and hence mistaken in the short run, in the longer term their correlations (and the predictions that went with them) may yet prove to be correct. One decade (the 1960s) was simply too short a period for the developmentalist propositions to be tested adequately. The more sophisticated theories of development recognized that these were long-term processes, that the transitional period was almost by definition likely to be chaotic, and that there were bound to be many setbacks on the road to development. By the 1990s, with a longer period of observation and considerable experience with development, the correlations and assumptions of the development approach have begun to look better and better.

The fact is that the base for democracy in Latin America as well as in Asia is bigger, more solid, and more promising now than it was in the 1960s. The middle class is larger, there is far greater affluence, bureaucracies are better trained and more experienced with development, the associational and institutional life has grown and become better consolidated, literacy is far higher, vast social changes have led to pluralism, the military is better educated and more professional, per capita income is higher, more persons are better educated, the private sectors are larger and more active, and so on.[54] These changes may well mean that the current openings to democracy in much of the developing world may prove more than just cyclical, popular now but subject when the next crisis comes to a new round of coups. When civil society was weak and the process of development just beginning for many countries in the 1960s, an authoritarian regime might have seemed to some a possible alternative; but as development and pluralism have gone forward, a new wave of military coups seems increasingly unlikely, at least in the better institutionalized and more economically advanced countries. It may be that the developmental changes of the last three decades have been sufficiently profound that not only can many countries look forward to a more stable future based on development and democracy, but the processes involved force us to reconsider the main premises of the development approach in a newer and more positive light.

CONCLUSIONS AND IMPLICATIONS

Since the decline, discrediting, and demise of the development approach in the 1960s, the field of comparative politics has become increasingly fragmented. There is no one approach that dominates the field nor is there an approved body of theoretical knowledge on which all or even most scholars can agree. Perhaps this is a reflection of the increasing fragmentation within the discipline of political science more generally and in the United States itself, or perhaps in the world. Whatever the ultimate answers to those questions, it is clear that within comparative politics there are separate subsections, each with its own apostles, theory, and research work. There are "islands" of research work and theory, with limited attempts to construct causeways and linkages among these diverse subsections, and almost no central structure or theory that would provide unity to the field as a whole.[55]

It seems unlikely that the unity that reigned in the 1960s in the comparative politics field as a whole will be restored in the near future. But I am not at all certain that such unity is desirable. The unity that centered around political development in the 1960s may have contributed valuable new insights and approaches, but it also led us down some wrong trails and blinded us to phenomena and approaches that did not seem to fit comfortably in the development approach. My own view is that the field has been greatly enriched by the variety of approaches and perspectives that came to the fore in the 1970s.

But those approaches have also largely had their day and their useful contributions have been incorporated into the field. We are in a new era of vast social and political changes and of remarkable transitions to democracy. These changes have made the once all but moribund developmentalist approach look better and better and deserving of a second consideration. It looks far better from a long-term perspective than it looked in the late 1960s and 1970s. Shorn of its ethnocentrism, its biases, and its blindnesses, the development approach and paradigm contain a rich body of sophisticated literature and a large storehouse of theory and insight from which we can still, and again, profitably learn. The developmentalist approach is not likely to recapture the central place in the field that it enjoyed in the 1960s (too much has changed and so have we and the field), but it certainly can retake its place as one of the major approaches here surveyed—another one of the "islands of theory" from which the painstaking task of constructing drawbridges to other islands and to the mainland can now take place.

NOTES

An earlier version of this chapter was presented at the Fourteenth World Congress of the International Political Science Association, Washington, D.C., August 28–September 1, 1988. That version was published in *Studies in International Development*, 24 (Winter-Spring, 1990): 65–82.

1. For an earlier discussion of some of these themes see Howard J. Wiarda, ed., *New Directions in Comparative Politics* (Boulder, Colo.: Westview Press, 1985; new edition, 1991).
2. Roy Macridis, *The Study of Comparative Government* (New York: Random House, 1955).
3. A useful but still incomplete effort is Irene I. Gendzier, *Managing Political Change; Social Scientists and the Third World* (Boulder, Colo.: Westview Press, 1985).
4. For some reflections on the "political culture" in which political development studies began and flourished see Gabriel A. Almond, *Political Development: Essays in Heuristic Theory* (Boston: Little, Brown, 1970), Introduction.
5. Walt W. Rostow, *The Stages of Economic Growth: A Non-Communist Manifesto* (Cambridge: Cambridge University Press, 1960).
6. Robert Heilbroner, *The Great Ascent* (New York: Harper & Row, 1963).
7. Karl W. Deutsch, "Social Mobilization and Political Development," *American Political Science Review* 55 (September 1961): 493–514.
8. Marion Levy, *The Structure of Society* (Princeton, N.J.: Princeton University Press, 1952).
9. Seymour Martin Lipset, "Some Social Requisites of Democracy: Economic Development and Political Legitimacy," *American Political Science Review* 53 (March 1959): 69–105.
10. Lucian W. Pye, *Aspects of Political Development* (Boston: Little, Brown, 1966).
11. David E. Apter, *The Politics of Modernization* (Chicago: University of Chicago Press, 1965).
12. Myron Weiner, ed., *Modernization* (New York: Basic Books, 1966).
13. Talcott Parsons, *The Social System* (Glencoe, Ill.: Free Press, 1951); Parsons and Edward A. Shils, eds., *Toward a General Theory of Action* (Cambridge, Mass.: Harvard University Press, 1951).
14. Gabriel A. Almond and James S. Coleman, eds., *The Politics of the*

Developing Areas (Princeton, N.J.: Princeton University Press, 1960).

15. For a brief history see Committee on Comparative Politics, "A Report of the Activities of the Committee, 1954–1970" (Social Science Research Council, New York, 1970). Mimeographed.

16. Social Science Research Council series, Studies in Political Development: Almond and Coleman, *Politics of Developing Areas;* Lucian W. Pye, ed., *Communications and Political Development* (Princeton, N.J.: Princeton University Press, 1963); Joseph LaPalombara, ed., *Bureaucracy and Political Development* (Princeton, N.J.: Princeton University Press, 1963); Robert E. Ward and Dankwart A. Rustow, eds., *Political Modernization in Japan and Turkey* (Princeton, N.J.: Princeton University Press, 1964); James S. Coleman ed., *Education and Political Development* (Princeton, N.J.: Princeton University Press, 1965); Lucian W. Pye and Sidney Verba, eds., *Political Culture and Political Development* (Princeton, N.J.: Princeton University Press, 1965); Joseph LaPalombara and Myron Weiner, eds., *Political Parties and Political Development* (Princeton, N.J.: Princeton University Press, 1966); Leonard Binder, James S. Coleman, Joseph LaPalombara, Lucian W. Pye, Sidney Verba, and Myron Weiner, eds., *Crisis and Sequences in Political Development* (Princeton, N.J.: Princeton University Press, 1971); Charles Tilly, ed., *The Formation of the National States in Western Europe* (Princeton, N.J.: Princeton University Press, 1975).

17. Almond, "Introduction," *Political Development.*

18. For a twenty-year assessment and appreciation of this work, see Myron Weiner and Samuel P. Huntington, eds., *Understanding Political Development* (Boston: Little, Brown, 1987).

19. An especially brilliant collection was the inaugural issue of *Comparative Politics* in 1968.

20. Samuel P. Huntington, *Political Order in Changing Societies* (New Haven, Conn.: Yale University Press, 1968).

21. See, among other, Sidney Verba, "Some Dilemmas in Comparative Research," *World Politics* 20 (October 1967): 111–127; Mark Kesselman, "Order or Movement: The Literature of Political Development as Ideology," *World Politics* 26 (October 1973): 139–153; Philip H. Melanson and Lauriston R. King, "Theory in Comparative Politics: A Critical Appraisal," *Comparative Political Studies* 4 (July 1971): 205–231; Geoffrey K. Roberts, "Comparative Politics Today," *Government and Opposition* 7 (Winter 1972): 38–55; Sally A. Merrill, "On the Logic of Comparative Analysis," *Comparative Political Studies* 3 (January 1971): 489–500; Robert T. Holt and John E. Turner, "Crises and Sequences in Collective Theory Development," *American Political Science Review* 69 (Sep-

tember 1975): 979–995; R. S. Milne, "The Overdeveloped Study of Political Development," *Canadian Journal of Political Science* 5 (December 1972): 560–568; Philip Coulter, "Political Development and Political Theory: Methodological and Technological Problems in the Comparative Study of Political Development," *Policy* 5 (Winter 1972); 233–242; Geoffrey K. Roberts, "Comparative Politics Today," *Government and Opposition* 7 (Winter 1972): 38–55; Ignany Sachs, "The Logic of Development," *International Social Science Journal* 24, no. 1 (1972): 37–43.

22. A. H. Somjee, *Parallels and Actuals of Political Development* (London: Macmillan, 1986); Howard J. Wiarda, *Ethnocentrism in Foreign Policy: Can We Understand the Third World?* (Washington, D.C.: American Enterprise Institute for Public Policy Research, 1985).

23. Reinhard Bendix, "Tradition and Modernity Reconsidered," *Comparative Studies in Society and History* 9 (April 1967): 292–346; S.N. Eisenstadt, *Post-Traditional Societies* (New York: Norton, 1974).

24. Fernando Enrique Cardoso and Enzo Faletto, *Dependency and Developments in Latin America* (Berkeley: University of California Press, 1978).

25. See Lloyd I. Rudolph and Susanne Hoeber Rudolph, *The Modernity of Tradition* (Chicago: University of Chicago Press, 1967).

26. Somjee, *Parallels;* Wiarda, *Ethnocentrism.*

27. Max M. Millikan and Walt W. Rostow, *A Proposal: Key to an Effective Foreign Policy* (New York: Harper & Row, 1957); Gendzier, *Managing Political Change.*

28. This interpretation is quite different from that of the radical critics.

29. Huntington, *Political Order;* A. H. Somjee, *Political Capacity in Developing Societies* (New York: St. Martin's Press, 1982).

30. Cardoso and Faletto, *Dependency and Development.*

31. Among the better examples would be Theodore H. Moran, *Multinational Corporations and the Politics of Dependence* (Princeton, N.J.: Princeton University Press, 1974).

32. See André Gunder Frank, *Capitalism and Underdevelopment in Latin America* (New York: Monthly Review Press, 1967).

33. Charles W. Anderson, Review in *American Political Science Review* 72, no. 4 (December 1978): 1478; also Howard J. Wiarda, "Toward a Framework for the Study of Political Change in the Iberic-Latin Tradition: The Corporative Model," *World Politics* 25 (January 1973): 206–35.

34. Philippe C. Schmitter, "Still the Century of Corporatism?" *The Review of Politics* 36 (January 1974): 85–131.

35. Howard J. Wiarda, *Corporatism and National Development in*

Latin America (Boulder, Colo.: Westview Press, 1981).

36. A solid, balanced treatment is Douglas Chalmers, "Corporatism and Comparative Politics," in Wiarda, *New Directions*.

37. David Cameron, "The Expansion of the Public Economy: A Comparative Analysis," *American Political Science Review* 72 (December 1978): 1243–61; Douglas A. Hibbs and Heino Fassbender, eds., *Contemporary Political Economy* (Amsterdam and New York: North Holland, 1961).

38. Guillermo O'Donnell, *Modernization and Bureaucratic-Authoritarianism: Studies in South American Politics* (Berkeley: Institute of International Studies, University of California, 1973).

39. David Collier, ed., *The New Authoritarianism in Latin America* (Princeton, N.J.: Princeton University Press, 1979).

40. Among the better approaches is Ronald Chilcote, *Theories of Comparative Politics: The Search for a Paradigm* (Boulder, Colo.: Westview Press, 1981).

41. Wiarda, *New Directions*, Conclusion.

42. Rostow, *Stages of Economic Growth*.

43. Lipset, "Some Social Requisites"; Deutsch, "Social Mobilization."

44. Howard J. Wiarda, ed., *The Continuing Struggle for Democracy in Latin America* (Boulder, Colo.: Westview Press, 1979).

45. Enrique A. Baloyra, ed., *Comparing New Democracies: Transition and Consolidation in Mediterranean Europe and the Southern Cone* (Boulder, Colo.: Westview Press, 1987); Guillermo O'Donnell, Philippe C. Schmitter, and Laurence Whitehead, eds., *Transitions from Authoritarian Rule* (Baltimore: Johns Hopkins University Press, 1986); Larry Diamond, Juan J. Linz, and Seymour Martin Lipset, eds., *Democracy in Developing Countries*, 4 vols. (Boulder, Colo.: Lynne Rienner, 1988–1990).

46. See Peter Berger, *The Capitalist Revolution* (New York: Basic Books, 1986); also Howard J. Wiarda, ed., *The Relations Between Democracy, Development, and Security: Implications for Policy* (New York: Global Economic Action Institute, 1988).

47. Pye, *Aspects of Political Development*.

48. See the series of reports edited by Daniel Pipes and Adam Garfinkle, *Friendly Tyrants* (Philadelphia: Foreign Policy Research Institute, forthcoming).

49. Howard J. Wiarda, *The Democratic Revolution in Latin America: Implications for Policy* (New York: Twentieth Century Fund, Holmes and Meier, 1990).

50. For a discussion of the discrediting and demise of the older, more radical, left and right wing models in Latin America, see Howard J. Wiarda, *Latin America at the Crossroads: Debt, Development and the Future* (Boulder, Colo.: Westview Press for the Inter-American Development Bank, 1987).

51. Allan Bloom, *The Closing of the American Mind: How Higher Education Has Failed Democracy and Impoverished the Souls of Today's Students* (New York: Simon & Schuster, 1987).

52. Ronald Scheman, ed., *The Alliance for Progress—Twenty-Five Years After* (New York: Praeger, 1988); also Howard J. Wiarda, "Development and Democracy: Their Relationship to Peace and Security," Paper presented at the Conference on Regional Cooperation for Development and the Peaceful Settlement of Disputes in Latin America, International Peace Academy and the Peruvian Center for International Studies, Lima, October 27–29, 1986. But see also, for an earlier statement, Apter, *Politics of Modernization*.

53. The outstanding study is Diamond, Linz, and Lipset, *Democracy in Developing Countries*.

54. The most substantial report is *Democracy in Latin America: The Promise and The Challenge* Special Report no. 158 (Washington, D.C.: Bureau of Public Affairs, U.S. Department of State, 1987).

55. Wiarda, *New Directions in Comparative Politics*, Conclusion.

Chapter
4

The Civilizational Dimension of Politics

Some Indications for Comparative Analysis

S. N. Eisenstadt

THEORETICAL BACKGROUND

The major purpose of this chapter is to emphasize and illustrate the importance of the civilizational dimension in the analysis of political institutions and dynamics. This dimension is strongly emphasized in some classic works, especially Max Weber, and in some major works of the late 1940s and 1950s, but it is rather neglected in later writings.

I would like to explore the importance of the civilizational dimension against the background of some of the recent developments in political sociology and then to illustrate such importance on the basis of some of the research undertaken within the Program on Comparative Civilizations during the last ten or so years at the Department of Sociology and Social Anthropology and the Truman Research Institute of the Hebrew University in Jerusalem.[1]

An appropriate starting point for the analysis of recent developments in political sociology is the trend in the 1980s that stressed the "rediscovery of the state" as an autonomous and distinct sphere or agent. This trend developed as a reaction against the tendency in the late 1950s and early 1960s (itself at least partly a reaction against the then dominant structural-functional approach and studies of modernization) which was characterized by a growing dissociation between studies emphasizing structural and organizational variables and those emphasizing more cultural variables.[2]

In sociology and political science the prevalent trend during the late 1950s and 1960s was toward behavioral and organizational studies. Many of these studies tended also, at least initially, to limit the political sphere and political activities to the status of epiphenomena of various social forces. The political sphere and the state were seen as using their power and control functions in the service of these forces. Some of the most important among these studies saw politics as the representation of group interest in terms of "who governs" or of different Marxist approaches.

Anthropology, as in the work of Geertz and his followers and to some extent in Louis Dumont's work on India,[3] emphasized the symbolic dimensions of politics, mostly through hermeneutical interpretation and "thick description." The contrary tendency— to analyze political formations exclusively in terms of structural, demographic, or power forces— developed mainly among students of the early state (chiefly anthropologists). New ways to combine the symbolic and structural dimensions of politics were attempted almost only in the works of S. J. Tambiah, C. Keyes, and other students of South and Southeast Asia.[4]

This situation represented a change from the classical period of sociology, especially the work of Durkheim and Max Weber,[5] as well as from the period of the 1950s and early 1960s, especially the works of Parsons, Lipset, Rokkan, Almond, and Eisenstadt[6] and the many studies of modernization and political culture.

In the 1970s and 1980s many studies displayed a shift back to a recognition of the autonomy of the state. This shift was most obvious in the analysis of contemporary societies, but it could also be identified in the analysis of premodern states, such as in the analysis of the preconditions for revolutions, and particularly for "revolutions from above" (for example, in Japan or Turkey), in the renewed interest in early states, and to some degree in the analysis of some major historical political formations.[7]

This growing recognition of the autonomy and distinctness of politics and the state developed in several directions, such as the emphasis on the autonomy of political agents and especially civil servants in the formulation and execution of policy,[8] and on the development of corporative practices,[9] or on the various "objective" (especially structural) characteristics of the state and particularly its relation to other social groups and the ways in which these characteristics and relations tend to influence the development of different modes of economic conflict,[10] class formation, and social movement, especially revolutions;[11] and the analysis of different forms of modern states, defined not in constitutional terms but in terms of their strength and modes of activity, both in Europe and beyond it.[12]

Yet another approach, of special interest from the point of view of our analysis, represented above all in the work of John Meyer and his colleagues,[13] saw the modern state as an autonomous ideological and institutional entity, continally expanding the scope of its activities, both internally and internationally.

This renewed emphasis on the state signaled a return to the conception of the state as a relatively autonomous subsystem of the society, dealing with the exercise of power through political, administrative, and juridical actors and agencies. At the same time a marked shift occurred in the definition of the state, in line with some of the major trends in the social sciences that took place in the 1960s and 1970s. The concept of state tended on the whole to be reified; the state was defined as a real actor, a sort of ontological entity, and not as the major arena of the political process in society, as it was defined in the work of Weber, to some extent of Marx (especially in his historical writings), and the structural-functional school. Although the various scholars who "brought the state back" differed with respect to the identity of this actor—the government, the bureaucracy, or some other agency—most of them seemed to share this perception of the state, or of its agents, as a real actor or actors.

These works provided a more extensive analysis of the relations between political control and types of social processes and also of the formation of economic and social policies, the structure of social movements of classes, modes of conflict resolutions, and the like. Yet the reification of the state led to a rather limited conception of the political process, which was seen chiefly in terms of a struggle among real actors over distributive resources, with scant attention either to the symbolism and ideology of this process or to the framework of rules within which such struggle takes place.

At the same time the basic conception of the state, especially the modern state, predominant in many of these works was couched in terms of the European experience; the structural characteristics of this experience were taken as common to all states. Thus, for instance, the variations among different states were often conceived in terms of "the relations between state and civil society" (to use Michael Mann's expression) and were expressed in terms based at least implicitly on this historical experience.

The major types of modern regimes—authoritarian, totalitarian, one-party, military, and the like—were often seen as variations on this basic model. Their success or failure in Europe and elsewhere was often explained in terms of the specific pattern of economic development, class structure, or the relative strength of different strata of the societies within which these states developed. This combination of the reification of the state with the predominance of the European model of the state was connected with a failure to consider the importance of the cultural dimension in the political process and in the formation of the state. Thus these works ignored several important developments in closely related fields, such as the criticisms of modernization studies that emphasized the importance of tradition, or some of the anthropological literature mentioned above, and much of the literature dealing with modern Japan,[15] which emphasizes that several crucial aspects of the political process and struggle, particularly of non-European or non-Western societies, can be fully understood only by considering what may be called the cultural, or rather civilizational, dimension of these societies.

Even when the importance of the cultural dimension began to be recognized (for example, by John Meyer and his collaborators), the emphasis was more on the specific ideological dimension of the modern state system as it developed in the West and expanded throughout the world. Even these important suggestions about the importance of the specific ideological dimension of the modern state have not been fully explored in analytic and comparative terms in most works that emphasize the autonomy of the state.

Most of these analyses have failed to consider the possibility that many variations in the political process and in the structure of political power are related to the combination of several factors: first, to the relative strength of the state vis-à-vis various social, especially class, forces; second, to the basic ideologies of the ruling elites, whether authoritarian or totalitarian, corporatist or competitive, and so forth; third, to the interaction between such forces and the basic cultural or civilizational premises of the political realm and of the state that are prevalent in the different societies, and to the concomitant different sets of rules governing political action. Because of this neglect, these developments in political sociology have been associated with a narrow definition of the political process and a consequent neglect of some central aspects of this process and the analytical concepts that bear upon it.

This impoverished conception of the political process can perhaps best be seen in the analysis of one central aspect of this process, emphasized by many of these scholars: protest. Most of these analyses focused on protest and on patterns of distribution and allocation of resources, but paid little attention to the symbolism of protest as a relatively autonomous dimension of such movements or to the possibility that such symbolism may be important in the impact of such movements on the political process, particularly in democratic societies, chiefly by effecting changes in the basic rules that regulate political struggle and conflict.[16]

The same neglect could be found in many works in comparative historical sociology, such as those of John Hall, Michael Mann, and Jean

Baechler,[17] which have taken up again the problem of the origins of the West in a broad comparative framework. Most of these works have analyzed, often in a very sophisticated way, various structural factors, such as power relations between different groups, various political-ecological conditions, and above all intersocietal relations. They have, however, almost entirely neglected to analyze one type of social group, namely, heterodoxies (so strongly stressed by Weber and to some extent also by Marx and some of the early Marxists), in the political dynamics of the civilizations.[18]

As indicated above, the importance of the civilizational dimension in the formation of political institutions and political dynamics has been analyzed in several research projects within the framework of the Program on Comparative Civilizations. These studies have addressed themselves to such problems as the origins and diversity of axial-age civilizations; comparative analysis of the political dynamics of some of these civilizations;[20] as well as processes of center formation and protest in selected modern societies,[21] civilizational frameworks of modern revolutions,[22] crystallization of different types of early states in Africa,[23] and comparative study of cities and urban hierarchies in the major historic civilizations.[24]

THE CIVILIZATIONAL FRAMEWORK OF THE GREAT (MODERN) REVOLUTIONS

These researches emphasize the analysis of interweaving between "cultural" and "institutional" dimensions in the crystallizations and dynamics of societies and civilizations. We shall illustrate this approach by analyzing the civilizational framework and conditions of the "Great Revolutions" that ushered in the modern era in Europe and the world: the Great Rebellion in England, the American and the French revolutions, and the revolutions in China and Russia. The Turkish and Vietnamese revolutions can probably also be included in this category.[25]

On the ideological level these revolutions were characterized by the intensification, transformation, and combination of several themes found separately in most axial-age civilizations. The most important of these are a highly articulated ideology of social protest, especially in a utopian emancipatory vein, that is, ideologies based on symbols of equality, progress, and freedom, presumably leading to the creation of a better social order; a strong emphasis on violence, novelty, and totality of change; and a strong universalistic missionary zeal oriented to creating a new type of human being and ushering in a new historical era.

On the organizational level they were characterized by bringing together several components of social movements and political struggle articulated and organized by counterelites, central political struggle, and religious (or intellectual) heterodoxies. While the tendency to such a combination of different symbolic and organizational components, as well as of these two sets of components can be found in all axial-age civilizations, only in these revolutions was this combination accomplished.

The combination of these ideological and organizational aspects of these revolutions shaped their outcomes and distinguished them from other changes of regimes in history. They interwove "cultural" and institutional dimensions in a way not to be found in other processes of change, generating a simultaneous change in central aspects of the ontological conceptions prevalent in a civilization alongside changes in the basic rules regulating the political arena and the center.

These revolutions were characterized by the overthrow of existing political regimes; by changes in the basic premises and constitutional arrangements of the regimes and in the bases and symbols of their legitimation; by a radical break with the past; by the displacement of the incumbent political elite or ruling class in favour of another one; and by the concomitant development of significant changes in all major institutions of society, above all in economic and class relations.

How can these revolutions be explained? In broad terms, two types of explanations of the "causes" of revolutions have been predominant in the literature—one dealing with different types of structural conditions and the other with specific historical circumstances. Among the structural conditions singled out are interelite struggles in combination with other forces, such as class struggle; the dislocation, social mobilization, and political articulation of newly emerging social groups; and the weakening of the state, often under the impact of international forces. Yet a closer look at the historical evidence reveals that most of these conditions are found in many human societies, especially in the more differentiated ones, within both axial-age and non–axial-age civilizations.[26]

It may of course be claimed that these revolutions occurred only in special historical conditions and that such conditions can be seen as necessary, if not sufficient, causes of the revolutions. The condition mentioned as most important in the literature is a relatively early state of transition to a modern setting, in which three major aspects of the breakthrough from a traditional to a modern setting occur together.

Although there is no doubt that these revolutions occurred only in such conditions, there remains the crucial problem of how we can explain that such revolutions did not occur in all societies where the types of conflict analyzed above could be identified or in all societies making this transition to modernity (for example, Japan and India).

Our analysis begins from a simple yet basic historical fact: The first revolutions (in Europe and America) occurred in the decentralized setting of Europe in what can be designated imperial-feudal societies, while the later revolutions occurred in centralized imperial societies. No such revolutions have occurred in patrimonial societies, whether centralized or decentralized, such as India, Buddhist societies (Southeast Asia), Islamic countries (with the partial exception of the Ottoman Empire and much later in Iran), or in centralized feudal-patrimonial ones such as Japan. Thus, it was only in some special types of societies that these different movements, conflicts, and protest movements came together and coalesced in the revolutionary patterns and transition to modernity analyzed above.

How can this fact be explained? The conditions that account for the major differences in the patterns of change between the imperial and imperial-feudal societies on the one hand and the other various patrimonial regimes on the other cannot be identified in terms of the variables often stressed in recent approaches that tend to reify the concept of the state or of social structure. Such sociological literature or literature on the state stresses such factors as the type of social division of labor and the degree of economic development.

The imperial and imperial-feudal societies developed within the framework of some great civilizations or traditions of the axial-age civilizations, analyzed above, and they shared some of the basic cultural orientations and institutional premises that developed in these civilizations. These characteristics included, as we have seen, a highly distinct center perceived as an autonomous symbolic and organizational entity, with continuous interaction between center and periphery. Another characteristic important for our present discussion is the development of distinct collectivities, especially cultural and religious, with a high symbolic component in their construction as well as ideological structuring of social hierarchies. A third characteristic was the development of relatively autonomous primary and secondary elites, especially cultural, intellectual, and religious ones, which continually struggled with one another and with the political elites. Many of these elites, particularly the religious and intellectual, were also carriers of strong utopian visions with universalistic orientations. They constituted the crucial elements in the development of heterodoxies and in activating the connection between them and different political struggles and protest movements.

A fourth characteristic was the perception of worldly arenas in general, and the political one in particular, as the major arenas in which to institutionalize the attempt to bridge the transcendental and mundane realms, that is, in which salvation could be achieved.

The combination of all these characteristics gave rise in the imperial and imperial-feudal regimes to a tendency toward a high degree of coalescence between protest movements, institution building, levels of articulation, and ideologization of the political struggle and changes in the political system, that is, processes of change containing at least some kernels of the revolutionary processes analyzed above.

The basic cultural premises inspired utopian and universalistic visions of new social orders, while the organizational and structural characteristics provided the framework to institutionalize some aspects of these visions. The two were combined by the activities of the different types of elites analyzed above.

Given the combination and interaction between these structural and cultural characteristics, the different conditions singled out in the literature as causes of revolutions, such as interelite and interclass conflict, could, in the appropriate historical situations attendant on the breakthrough to modernity, engender the form of the modern revolutions. When these characteristics were not combined, the transition to modernity, however far-reaching and dramatic, tended to develop in different and nonrevolutionary patterns.[27]

In Japan, which did not experience an axial-age breakthrough, the transcendental and utopian orientations and the autonomous intellectual and religious heterodoxies did not develop or play a strong role. Many of the structural outcomes of the Meiji restoration most closely related to the process of modernization—urbanization, industrialization, the development of a modern administrative state, and even the deposition of an existing ruling class—are indeed comparable to those of the Great Revolutions and in some aspects even more far-reaching.[28]

Yet the symbolism of the Meiji restoration was quite different from that of the Great Revolutions. True, a regime that had not previously existed was established. Yet the labeling of the change as a "restoration" underlined its emphasis on the crystallization of a neotraditional polity that seemingly emphasized the ultimate nonaccountability of the new rulers to the population and the legitimation of the new regime in terms of the inviolable emperor. This ideology did not contain universalistic missionary orientations, but rather emphasized the reconstruction, in seemingly modern terms, of the specifically Japanese collectivity.

This outcome of the Meiji revolution is related to a characteristic of the revolution that distinguished it from the Great Revolutions, namely, the absence of autonomous religious and intellectual heterodoxies. Similarly, the processes of change in India and in Buddhist countries, especially after the onset of modernization, and in most Latin American countries, where other-worldly premises were predominant or very strong, were also different from those of the Great Revolutions.[29]

Thus it was in Western and Central Europe, and later in Russia, China, and to a smaller extent the Ottoman Empire, that the development of sects and heterodoxies and their combination with secondary political elites proved to have the most far-reaching impact on the restructuring of ontological reality, and on the ground rules regulating the major arenas of social life and cultural creativity.

The distinction between the "first" European (and American) revolutions and the later ones, especially the Russian, Chinese, and to some extent Vietnamese, brings out the importance of political-ecological and economic conditions.[30] It was no accident that the first revolutions, which had no other revolutionary model before them, developed in relatively centralized, absolutist, or semiabsolutist regimes that grew out of the imperial-feudal background with the many autonomous elites and subelites characteristic of these types of regimes.

The later revolutions had different revolutionary models before them and did not have to invent one, although needless to say they changed the models greatly. They erupted in highly centralized imperial regimes in which the secondary elites were closely supervised and segregated. They also occurred, to a much greater extent than their predecessors, under the impact of international political, economic, and ideological forces.

Significantly enough, the first revolutions can be seen as continuing the processes of reconstructing centers and the boundaries of collectivities that had been taking place in Europe throughout the Middle Ages, although they gave rise to the most radical of such reconstructions. Moreover, the postrevolutionary regimes evinced a relatively smaller discontinuity from the prerevolutionary ones, although the break from the past constituted at least one important component in their ideologies. The later revolutions constituted much more radical breaks within their respective societies and were characterized by greater symbolic and institutional discontinuity from their preceding regimes.

The combination of civilizational and structural conditions and historical contingencies that generated the Great Revolutions has been rather rare in history. In many ways, its occurrence, and the later institutionalization of postrevolutionary regimes, is similar to the crystallization of the axial-age civilizations, even though the revolutionary process and the crystallization of revolutionary regimes were much shorter. But however rare such a combination may be, it may still recur in "propitious" circumstances, albeit in a different format from the two types of revolution discussed here.

Perhaps the closest approximation to such an occurrence has been the Iranian revolution led by the Ayatollah Khomeini.[31] As many scholars have shown, the disenchantment with an autocratic, modernizing regime and the attack on it by a combination of religious, intellectual, and popular elites with a strong missionary and universalistic, semiutopian vision were of crucial importance in spawning this revolution. Needless to say, the "basic cosmology" of this revolution (to use Said Arjomand's term) differed radically from the antitraditional cosmology of earlier revolutions. In many ways this cosmology was oriented against the premises of modernity, but it was a universalistic-missionary one. It constituted the central symbolic element in this revolution, while the intellectual elites that articulated it constituted a central organizational element.

SOME ANALYTICAL CONCLUSIONS: CENTER FORMATIONS AND ELITE COALITIONS

The preceding analysis of the framework of the Great Revolutions has not only brought out the importance of the civilizational dimension in all these cases. It has also pointed out the importance of several dimensions of the political process that have often been neglected by many recent studies and that are, in my mind, of crucial importance for comparative political analysis.

These dimensions are the different definitions of the political arena that can be found in different societies or civilizations; the concept of center and the existence of different types of centers that develop in different societies; and the great importance of different coalitions of elites and the cultural visions they articulate as they are related to the structure and dynamics of such centers.

It is important to analyze the definitions and evaluations of the political arena in the broader context of the civilizations in which they develop, as they crystallize and change in the historical experience of various civilizations. These definitions are related to the basic premises of such civilizations; the basic conceptions and rules concerning authority, justice, and the place of the political arena in the totality of humanity and cosmos; and to the concomitant rules that regulate this arena and are prevalent in the respective civilizations.

In this context we have found the concept of center—originated by Edward Shils[32] and later elaborated by other scholars—wherein the center or centers are seen as the arena in which the cultural and organizational dimensions of social life meet, to be of special importance. Centers cannot be viewed only in terms of the relative specialization of political roles and organizations and of the regulation of different aspects of the social division of labor and group conflicts derived from it. The center or centers of a society deal not only with the organizational aspects of the social division of labor in general and of the political sphere in particular, but also with the connection of such activities to the charismatic dimension of the social order—the construction of trust, the regulation of power, and the provision of meaning. Furthermore, within different centers each dimension may be articulated to a different degree, leading to different modes of control. These are in turn closely related to the nature of the coalitions of elites predominant in a particular center and to the cultural orientations they articulate. As a result, different centers exhibit diverse structures and dynamics.

Our analysis of the centers of different axial-age civilizations and other societies indicates that centers can be distinguished according to their structural and symbolic autonomy and distinctness; the nature and types of activities undertaken by them; their relationship to the periphery; the patterns of elite coalitions predominant in them; and the nature of the systematic tendencies and capacity for change that develop within the societal and political dynamics.

The autonomy of the center manifests itself in the degree to which the center is organizationally distinct, not structurally embedded in the existing social division of labor (specifically not in various ascriptive units based on territory or kinship), and develops symbolic autonomy. In addition, the nature of center activities and dynamics can be identified in several ways. One way is the areas of social life or order on which the activities of the center focus. These can be distinguished according to the major aspects of the charismatic dimension of social order mentioned above: the articulation of values and models of cultural and social order; the articulation of solidarity and collective identity; the regulation of power relations; and the regulation of the social division of labor in the narrow sense, that is, economic activities. Another distinction, cutting across the former, is the degree to which the different activities of the center regulate and possibly exploit existing social arrangements in the periphery or construct new types of activities and structure there.

Closely related to the preceding distinction, yet also cutting across it, is the degree to which centers tend to expand their activities beyond their original territorial or symbolic boundaries. Different centers can be distinguished according to the types of activities they undertake. The constellation of such activities, and the degree of distinctness of the centers, elicit different types of institutional formations and dynamics.

The distinction between different centers is important for all types of political regimes and all "stages" of political development from the "earliest" to the most highly "developed." The role of such differences in the political dynamics of different political regimes has been analyzed with respect to so-called early states, especially in Africa. Contrary to the usual assumption, that distinction was found in two developmental stages of early states in Africa and even more in the analysis of the political dynamics of axial-age civilizations and of the civilizational frameworks of the modern revolutions.

The analysis of different types of centers has indicated the close relationship between the structure and dynamics of centers, the basic civilizational premises, and the different coalitions predominant in the center and the countercoalitions that oppose them. We have shown that a society may possess many centers, both political and sociocultural, which stress different types of activities (regulation, maintaining the boundaries of different collectivities, and so forth) and which represent different conceptions of cosmic order. These different conceptions significantly affect the political dynamism of the societies. Recognition of these facets of centers leads to an appreciation of the importance for the political process of types of actors other than those envisaged in most of the works mentioned at the beginning of this chapter, namely, the political and administrative actors found in all political formations. But the structure and activities of such elites may vary greatly between centers in societies with relatively similar levels of structural differentiation, economic types, and the like.

These differences in the dominant elite coalitions are closely connected with the different emphases placed by different centers on such activities and the consequent dynamics of the centers. They are closely related to the cosmological visions (basic perceptions of the relations between the cosmic and the mundane order) and civilizational and cultural premises (particularly the rules of the political sphere and power and the conception of authority, justice, and hierarchy) that prevail in a society or sector thereof.

This analysis has also thrown some light on yet another concept, structural differentiation, which has emphasized the structural dimension of social organization and the social division of labor and which was important in some evolutionary approaches that analyzed the conditions of emergence of the early states.

Our analysis indicated first that, on all levels and in all types of technological and economic development and structural differentiation, it is the interaction between these aspects of the social division of labor and major elites that generates the different patterns and dynamics of centers and institutional formations. Second, at any given level or in any given type of differentiation or social division of labor there may have developed, in different circumstances, a wide variety of such patterns. Third, the differences in such dynamics are shaped above all by the crystallization of different coalitions of elites who exercise different processes of control.

The most important of these elites and influentials are the political ones, who deal most directly with the regulation of power in society; the articulators of the models of the cultural order, whose activities are oriented to the construction of meaning; and the articulators of the solidarity of the major groups, who address themselves to the construction of trust.

Such processes of control are not activated only by representatives of class relations or "modes of production." Rather, they are activated by the major coalitions of elites in a society, who carry different cultural visions and represent different types of "ideal" and "material" interests and shape class relations and the modes of production.

The structure of these elites is closely related to the basic cultural orientations prevalent in a society. In other words, different types of elites carry different types of visions. On the other hand, and in connection with the types of cultural orientations and their respective transformation into basic premises of the social order, these elites tend to exercise different modes of control over the allocation of basic resources in the society or sectors thereof.

The processes and mechanisms of control, as effected by the activities of the major elites and influentials in their interaction with broader groups and strata, are not limited to the exercise of power in the specific "narrow" political or coercive sense. They are much more pervasive—as indeed even the more sophisticated Marxists have stressed—and include many autonomous symbolic aspects. Such structuring of the symbolic dimensions of human and social life and the attempts to control information pertaining to it are closely related to Gramsci's concept of intellectual hegemony, although not necessarily identical with it.

The different coalitions of the major elites and the modes of control they exercise shape, through varied processes of "structuration," the major characteristics and boundaries of the respective social systems, of the political system, the economic one, the system of social stratification and class formation, the major collectivities, and the overall macro-societal framework(s), however conceived.

At the same time such different coalitions of elites and the modes of control activated by them generate strong countertendencies, giving rise to procesess of change and movements of protest. The very institutionalization of such cultural visions, through the various social processes and mechanisms of control mentioned above, as well as their "reproduction" through space and time, entails continuous reactivation of the social processes of control through which the basic premises are institutionalized. That reactivation necessarily generates tensions and conflicts, movements of protest, and processes of change that entail some possibility of reconstruction of these very premises. While propensities to change and protest are universal to all societies, their specific locations, ideologies, and outcomes vary greatly among societies, and such variations are greatly influenced by the conditions specified above.

But different new types of civilizational settings and social organization, whether the Great Civilizations, those that ushered in capitalism in the West, or the Great Revolutions, are not "naturally" caused by the basic tenets of religion. Rather, they arise out of a variety of economic, political, and ecological conditions, all in interrelation with religious beliefs, with basic civilizational premises, and with specific institutions.

Such visions give rise to some of the potential developments of the societies or civilizations in which they become institutionalized. But the types of social organization that develop in different civilizations were not merely a result of the basic inherent tendencies of any culture or located in its basic premises.

Many such historical changes and constructions of new institutional formations were probably the outcome of the factors listed by J. B.

March and Johann Olsen[33] in their analysis of changes in organization. These factors are the combination of basic institutional and normative forms; processes of learning and accommodation and different types of decision making by individuals in appropriate arenas of action who respond to a great variety of historical events. But relatively similar types of contingent forces could have different impact in different civilizations, even if these shared many concrete institutional or political-ecological settings, because of the differences in their premises.

The crystallization of any pattern of change is the reset of history, structure and structure—with human agency bringing them together.

NOTES

1. See S. N. Eisenstadt, *A Sociological Approach to Comparative Civilizations: The Development and Directions of a Research Program* (Jerusalem: Hebrew University, 1986).
2. See S. N. Eisenstadt, *Culture and Social Structure: A Comparative Analysis of Civilizations.* Forthcoming.
3. See, for instance, Clifford Geertz, *Negara: The Theatre State in Nineteenth-Century Bali* (Princeton N.J.: Princeton University Press, 1980); Louis Dumont, *Homo Hierarchicus* (London: Weidenfeld & Nicholson, 1970); Dumont, *Religion, Politics and History in India* (The Hague: Mouton, 1970).
4. See S. J. Tambiah, *World Conqueror and World Renouncer* (Cambridge: Cambridge University Press, 1976), and "The Renouncer, His Individuality and His Community," *Numen* 23 no. 2 (1981); G. Obeyskere, "The Rebirth Eschatology and Its Transformation: A Contribution to the Sociology of Early Buddhism," in W. O. Flaherty, ed., *Karma and Rebirth in Classical Indian Tradition* (Berkeley: University of California Press, 1980), 137–165, and *The Cult of the Goddess Pattini* (Chicago: University of Chicago Press, 1984); C. F. Keyes, *The Golden Peninsula*; and C. F. Keyes, ed., *Karma* (Berkeley: University of California Press, 1983).
5. Emil Durkheim, *The Elementary Forms of Religious Life* (London: Allen & Unwin, 1976); W. S. Pickering, ed., *Durkheim on Religion* (London: Routledge & Kegan Paul, 1975); Max Weber, *Economy and Society*, 3 vols., ed. Guenther Roth and Claus Wittich (New York: Bedminster Press, 1968), esp. vol. 2, chap IX, and vol. 3; Weber, *The Religion of China* (New York: Free Press, 1951); Weber, *Ancient Judaism* (New York : Free Press, 1952); *The Religion of India* (New York: Free Press, 1958).
6. Talcott Parsons, *Politics and Social Structure* (New York: Free Press, 1969); Seymour Martin Lipset, *Political Man: The Social*

Bases of Politics (Garden City: Doubleday, 1960); Lipset, *Politics and the Social Sciences* (New York: Oxford University Press, 1969); Lipset and Rokkan, eds., *Party Systems and Voter Alignments, Cross-National Perspectives* (New York: Free Press, 1967); Gabriel A. Almond, *Comparative Politics, a World View* (Boston: Little, Brown, 1974); S. N. Eisenstadt, *The Political Systems of Empires* (New York: Free Press, 1963).

7. See, for instance, E. K. Trimberger, *Revolutions from Above, Military Bureaucrats and Development in Japan, Turkey and Peru* (New Brunswick, N.J.: Transaction Books, 1978).

8. Eric A. Nordlinger, *On the Autonomy of the Democratic State* (Cambridge, Mass.: Harvard University Press, 1981).

9. See, for example, Gerhard Lehmbruch and Philippe C. Schmitter, eds., *Trends Towards Corporatist Intermediation*, vol. 1 (Beverly Hills, Calif.: Sage, 1981).

10. Theda Skocpol, *States and Social Revolutions: A Comparative Analysis of France, Russia and China* (Cambridge: Cambridge University Press, 1979); Peter B. Evans, Dietrich Rueschemeyer, and Theda Skocpol, eds., *Bringing the State Back In* (Cambridge: Cambridge University Press, 1985).

11. Bertrand Badie and Pierre Birnbaum, *The Sociology of the State* (Chicago: University of Chicago Press, 1983); Metin Heper, "The State and Public Bureaucracies—A Comparative and Historical Perspective," *Comparative Studies in Society and History* 27, no. 19 (January 1985): 86–110.

12. Alfred Stepan, ed., *Authoritarian Brazil* (New Haven, Conn.: Yale University Press, 1973); Stepan, *The State and Society: Peru in Comparative Perspective* (Princeton, N.J.: Princeton University Press, 1978); S. Schwartzman, *São Paulo e o Estado nacional* (São Paulo: Difel, 1975); Fernando Henrique Cardoso, *O modelo político brasileiro* (São Paulo: Difusao Europeia do Livro, 1972); J. L. Reyna and R. S. Weinert, eds., *Authoritarianism in Mexico* (Philadelphia: Institute for the Study of Human Issues, 1977).

13. John M. Meyer, "The World Polity and the Authority of the Nation-State," in John M. Meyer et al., *Institutional Structure—Constitutional State, Society and the Individual* (Beverly Hills, Calif.: Sage, 1987): 41–71; G. M. Thomas and J. M. Meyers, "The Expansion of the State," *Annual Review of Sociology* 10 (1984): 461–482.

14. Michael P. Mann, "States, Ancient and Modern," *Archives Européennes de Sociologie* 18, no. 2 (1977): 262–298.

15. See, for instance, Geertz, *Negara*: Tambiah, *World Conqueror and World Renouncer*.

16. P. Burstein, Review of *Bringing the State Back*, In *American Journal of Sociology* 92, no. 5 (1987) 1268–1270.

17. Jean Baechler, "Aux origines de la modernité: castes et feodalités (Europe, Inde, Japon)," *Archives Européennes de Sociologie* 27, no. 1, (1986): 31–57; John A. Hall, *Powers and Liberties* (Berkeley: University of California Press, 1985); Hall, "Religion and the Rise of Capitalism," *Archives Européennes de Sociologie* 26, no. 2 (1985): 193–223; Michael Mann, *The Source of Social Power*, vol. 1 (Cambridge: Cambridge University Press, 1986).

18. See S. N. Eisenstadt, "Macrosociology and Sociological Theory: Some New Directions," *Contemporary Sociology* 16, no. 5, (September 1987): 602–609.

19. Axial-age civilizations was a term coined by Karl Jaspers to designate those "Great Civilizations"—the Greek and Hellenistic, the monotheistic ones, Hinduism, Buddhism, and Confucianism, especially neo-Confucianism—all of which were characterized by the development and institutionalization of conceptions of a sharp chasm between the transcendental and the mundane orders and by the development of autonomous cultural elite groups. S. N. Eisenstadt ed., *The Origins and Diversity of Axial-Age Civilizations*, (Albany, N.Y.: SUNY Press, 1986).

20. Eisenstadt, *Culture and Social Structure*.

21. S. N. Eisenstadt, L. Roniger, and A. Seligman, *Centre Formation, Protest Movements, and Class Structure in Europe and the United States* (London: Frances Printer, 1987).

22. S. N. Eisenstadt, *Revolutions and the Transformation of Societies* (New York: Free Press, 1978).

23. S. N. Eisenstadt, M. Abitbol, and N. Chazan, "The Origins of the State Reconsidered" and "State Formation in Africa, Conclusions," in *The Early State in African Perspective: Culture, Power and Division of Labor*, Eisenstadt, Abitbol, and Chazan, eds., (Leiden, The Netherlands: Brill, 1988).

24. S. N. Eisenstadt and A. Shachar, *Society, Culture and Urbanization* (Beverly Hills Calif.: Sage, 1987).

25. See Eisenstadt, *Revolution and the Transformation of Societies;* E. Kamenka, ed., *A World in Revolution* (Canberra: Australian National University Press, 1970); Kamenka, "The Concept of a Political Revolution", in C. J. Friedrich, ed., *Revolution: Yearbook of the American Society for Political and Legal Philosophy*, Nomos 8 (New York: Atherton, 1967), 122–138; B. Mazlish, A. D. Kaledin, and D. R. Baloton, eds., *Revolution* (New York: Macmillan, 1971); Jean Baechler, *Revolutions* (Oxford: Blackwell, 1976).

26. S. N. Eisenstadt, *The Political Systems of Empires* (New York: Free

Press, 1963), chap. 12; Eisenstadt, ed., *The Decline of Empires* (Englewood Cliffs, N.J.: Prentice-Hall, 1966).

27. These comparative indications are worked out in greater detail in Eisenstadt, *Revolutions and the Transformation of Societies.*

28. On Japanese premodern society, see E. O. Reischauer, J. K. Fairbank, and A. M. Craig, *A History of East Asian Civilization, vol. 1* (Boston: Houghton Mifflin, 1965); J. W. Hall, *Japan from Prehistory to Modern Times* (London: Weidenfeld & Nicolson, 1970); C. Nakane, *Japanese Society* (London: Weidenfeld & Nicolson, 1970); H. Passin, "Japanese Society", in D. L. Sills, ed., *The International Encyclopedia of the Social Sciences, vol. 8* (New York: Macmillan and Free Press, 1968), 236–249; R. N. Bellah, "Japan's Cultural Identity," *Journal of Asian Studies* 24, no. 4 (1965): 573–594.

29. See W. G. Beasley, *Meiji Japan Thought* (Tokyo: Center for East Asian Cultural Studies, 1969); Beasley, *Modern History of Japan* (London: Weidenfeld and Nicolson, 1981).

30. On the first phase of the Chinese revolution, see especially F. Wakeman, Jr., *The Fall of Imperial China* (New York: Free Press, 1975); F. Schurmann and O. Schell, eds., *Imperial China: The Decline of the Last Dynasty and the Origins of Modern China, the Eighteenth and Nineteenth Centuries* (New York: Random House, Vintage, 1967); Schurmann and Schell, *Republican China: Nationalism, War and the Rise of Communism, 1911–1949* (New York: Random House, Vintage, 1968); M. C. Wright, ed., *China in Revolution: The First Phase, 1900–1913* (New Haven: Yale University Press, 1968); Fairbank, Reischauer, Fairbank, and Craig, *A History of East Asian Civilization*, chaps. 5, 8; and M. B. Rankin, *Early Chinese Revolution: Radical Intellectuals in Shanghai and Chekiang, 1902–1911* (Cambridge, Mass.: Harvard University Press, 1971). On the whole cycle of Chinese Revolution see, in addition to the above, Ping-ti Ho and Hange Tsou, eds., *China's Heritage and the Communist Political System: China in Crisis*, 2 vols. (Chicago: University of Chicago Press, 1968).

31. On the Khomeini revolution see Said A. Arjomand, *The Shadow of God and the Hidden Imam: Religion, Political Order and Societal Change in Shi'ite Iran from the Beginning to 1890* (Chicago: University of Chicago Press, 1984); Arjomand, "Iran's Islamic Revolution in Comparative Perspective," *World Politics* 38, no. 3 (1986); S. Bakhash, "Islam and Social Justice in Iran," in M. Kramer, ed., *Shi'ism, Resistance and Revolution* (Boulder, Colorado: Westview Press, 1987); R. K. Ramazani, *Revolutionary Iran: Challenge and Response in the Middle East* (Baltimore: Johns Hopkins University Press, 1986); S. Bakhash, *The Reign of the Ayatollahs: Iran and the Islamic Revolution* (New York: Basic Books, 1984).

32. Edward Shils, *Center and Periphery* (Chicago: University of Chicago Press, 1975).
33. J. B. March and Johann P. Olsen, "The New Institutionalism: Organizational Factors in Political Life," *American Political Science Review* 78, no. 3 (1984): 734–749.

Two

THE STATE, CLASS, AND DEPENDENCY

Chapter
5

The Search for a Class Theory of the State and Democracy

Capitalist and Socialist Perspectives

Ronald H. Chilcote

Years ago I asserted that no matter what the difficulties of conceptualizing a science of politics or political science, the study of politics is essentially comparative whether we are Americanists, Europeanists, Asianists, Africanists, Latin Americanists, Middle Easternists, or whatever. I continue to feel strongly about this and believe that our discipline has suffered from both parochialism in its emphasis on the U.S. polity and from lack of vision in its concern with empiricism to the neglect of theoretical considerations. At the heart of this malaise is an underlying defense of political democracy in its indirect representative form and of capitalism as the basis of our economy. Our idealism and myths about U.S. politics have been undermined by Watergate and the Iran-Contra scandals. Our confidence in capitalism has been challenged by the decline of the U.S. economy in a world context[1] and the pervasiveness of the international political economy. Thus the crisis of contemporary political science reflects both national and international dimensions. The struggle to transcend the crisis, in my view, has involved redirection rather than new direction, attention to traditional issues of politics and society, and some provocative thinking and conceptualization around themes of historical examples in their political and economic setting. This in turn has led to a return to theories of the state, a focus on capitalist and socialist development and their respective transitions, and a serious look at democracy in both its indirect and representative forms, and its direct and participatory forms. In this chapter I argue that these themes are significant to contemporary comparative study, and I reflect upon them after assessing a tendency to obscure them with pseudo and idealistic theories of a new society.[2]

POST-FORMS OF SOCIETY

Since about 1960 intellectuals have conjured up labels to suggest that the past has been transcended as we advance toward a new society. Traditional notions of bourgeois order, the dilemmas of capitalism and socialism, and class struggle became blurred as futuristic thought established itself in academic circles. Daniel Bell's advocacy of an end of ideology foreshadowed concern with the cultural contradictions of capitalism and his thesis of the "postindustrial society."[3] This view envisioned an improvement of living standards, a closing of gaps between classes through mass education, mass production, and mass consumption, and a diminishing of ethnic, linguistic, regional, and religious loyalties along with a marginalization of total ideologies. In variants of this thought "Amitai Etzioni speaks of 'the post-modern era,' George Lichtheim of 'the post-bourgeois society', Herman Kahn of 'post-economic society,' Murray Bookchin of 'the post-scarcity society,' Kenneth Boulding of 'post-civilized society.' "[4] Inglehart and Bakvis and Nevitte write of "post-materialism," and the latter extend their analysis to the search for "postbourgeois man."[5] Many of these ideas have been criticized as idealistic or manifestations in defense of the capitalist order.[6]

Radical criticisms or conservative and liberal views of postindustrial society did not deter some left theories from seriously assimilating this notion into their efforts to move beyond capitalism, as Frankel suggests. He dates the term to Arthur Penty, a nineteenth-century follower of William Morris, and to ideas of craft socialism based on decentralization and artisan society. Frankel suggests that therein lies a basis for contemporary postindustrial and utopian socialism, as represented by Rudolf Bahro, André Gorz, Barry Jones, and Alvin Toffler, whose anticapitalism and support for a more egalitarian and democratic world could not be ignored, even by Marxists.[7] The utopians moved beyond the national industrial society to a more globally linked society. Some favored mixed economy societies, while Gorz advocated a combination of socialist state planning and decentralized production. Most of them emphasized self-sufficiency and opposition to growth that damages the environment and gives power to transnational corporations.[8]

Their discussion of alternative decentralized and cooperative economies and welfare services, guaranteed income schemes, disarmament, and other ideas contributed to the search for a new politics—a politics of transition in an era of capitalist national and international reorganization, introduction of new technology and change in labor processes, erosion of planning, and increase in alienation and dissent. They tended to focus on state institutions as political and administrative apparatuses that are distinguishable from civil society, a view that did not account for workers employed within state institutions who manifest opposition to the state in the name of civil society, as was the case of the Solidarity movement in Poland. Their rejection of Marxist class theory in favor of a theory of new social movements or a conception of a bureaucratized technostructure where nobody holds power did not prove convincing:

> The post-industrial theorists seriously neglect some vital questions concerning transitional politics and alternative forms of representation and participation . . . [they] have failed to address adequately the vital issue of state power, as well as the related strategic issue of how class-dominated and bureaucratized state institutions can be transformed . . . While policies and practices developed by feminists, environmentalists and other movements can never all be reduced back to class politics, the post-industrial theorists conspicuously fail to explain how working class organizations fit into their transitional scenarios. . . . [They] are either openly hostile to workers' organizations, or regard them as irrelevant to the shaping of the future.[9]

Fred Block adopts postindustrialism to suggest a basic change in the relationship between the state and economy. He sees the state as comprising less traditional hierarchies characterized by less supervision and authority and expanded decision making. This "debureaucratization" is the consequence of the need for postbureaucratic organization that faces the continuous need to adjust to rapidly changing conditions: "debureaucratization of the state depends on the renewal of political participation in which the citizenry plays a more active role in the regulation of social life."[10] Despite their deficiencies, postindustrial perspectives were incorporated into the recent debate around postliberalism, postimperialism, and post-Marxism.

Postliberalism

Bowles and Gintis criticize contemporary liberal and Marxian political theory and seek space for a radical democratic synthesis. Capitalism and democracy are incompatible, they argue; the welfare state does not give citizens the power to make democratic decisions in the economic sphere, and democratic theory is in disarray. "Liberalism, moreover, has justly enshrined the democratic tenet that choice and agency are the keystones of freedom, whereas Marxism has shown us that individual choice and agency are but false freedoms in the absence of collective action."[11] They believe that neither liberalism nor Marxism has given priority to democracy; whereas liberalism creates liberties, it "shelters the citadels of domination," while Marxism obscures "nonclass and noneconomic forms of domination."[12] They advocate a postliberalism, a synthesis of "both the Jeffersonian commitment to decentralized control of the productive apparatus and the Marxian recognition that because production is social its decentralization cannot take the form of individual property ownership." Democratic personal rights must displace property rights because "neither the Jeffersonian universalization of individual property nor the Marxian collectivization of private property is acceptable."[13]

Four propositions constitute the postliberalism:

> First, the capitalist economy . . . is a public arena whose structure regulates the distributional, appropriative, political, cultural, and other projects. . . . Second, lack of secure access to one's livelihood is a form of dependency, one that confers power on those who control the means of life [and] arbitrarily limits individual choices and erodes democratic accountability. . . . Third, . . . a commitment to democracy entails the advocacy of institutions that promote rather than impede the development of a democratic culture. . . . Fourth, . . . democratic decision making in production units will replace unaccountable hierarchy with democratic participation and commitment.[14]

Thus, they believe, the promise of a postliberal democracy would be the expansion of personal rights through the affirmation of traditional political forms of representative democracy and individual liberty while ensuring the establishment of innovative and democratically accountable economic freedoms in community and work.

Postimperialism

In an effort to move beyond neoimperialist and dependency explanations of capitalist underdevelopment or associated capitalist development,[15] Becker, Frieden, Schatz, and Sklar argue that global institutions tend to promote the integration of diverse national interests on a new international basis by offering access to capital resources and technologies.[16] This necessitates the location of both foreign labor and management in the dependent country as well as local participation in the ownership of the corporation. In such a situation two segments of a new social class appear. The first segment consists of privileged nationals or a managerial bourgeoisie made up of managers of firms, senior state functionaries, leading politicians, members of professional associations, and other persons of prominence; the second segment consists of the foreign nationals who manage the businesses and transnational organizations. This coalescing of dominant class elements across national boundaries suggests the rise of an international oligarchy. A theory of postimperialism serves as an alternative to a determinist Leninist understanding of imperialism and to dependency orthodoxy, according to Becker. The theory postulates a national bourgeoisie in the less developed countries as part of a nascent transitional bourgeoisie linked by ties of foreign capital. Frieden calls it "a major theoretical advance and a refreshing example of how class analysis, once freed from doctrine, can enlighten our understanding of social life."

Post-Marxism

This most articulated of the post-forms has evolved from Eurocommunist and Eurosocialist trends of the 1970s and 1980s. Its roots are found in the thought of European Marxists and former Marxists, including Fernando Claudín, Nicos Poulantzas, and Ernesto Laclau. Claudín, a Spanish Marxist, writes of Eurocommunism in terms of historical conjuncture, the last being the economic crisis of overproduction and recession and democratic transitions in Southern Europe during the mid 1970s when the international workers' movement was unable to move the capitalist crisis to a socialist transition. Meeting in the midst of the crisis in Rome during November 1975, the French and Italian Communist parties resolved that socialism would constitute a higher phase of democracy; there must be continual democratization of economic, political, and social life; the socialist transition would involve public control over the principal means of production while small and medium agrarian and industrial producers participate in the building of socialism; and democratization of the state must increasingly provide a role for local and regional government, for a plurality of parties, and for freedom and autonomy of trade unions.[17]

Poulantzas, a Greek Marxist who lived in exile for many years in Paris, published a comparative study of the democratic opening made possible by the crisis and fall of dictatorships in Spain, Portugal, and Greece.[18] Influenced especially by the emphasis of Antonio Gramsci[19] on bourgeois hegemony in civil society and of Louis Althusser[20] on structural levels of society, including a political-legal and ideological superstructure, Poulantzas applies a class analysis to a structural theory of the state. His case studies, and especially that of the revolutionary period in Portugal during 1974 and 1975, prompted him to shift from a Marxist-Leninist position that emphasized dual power and an assault upon the state by workers and popular forces who had built their revolutionary base outside the state apparatuses to the possibility of a bloodless revolution through penetration and occupation of key state apparatuses. The argument that struggle within the state apparatuses was necessary to disrupt the balance of forces and bring about a transition to socialism appeared more explicitly in his last work, *State, Power, and Socialism* (1978) and may have inspired some left intellectuals in the early 1980s to move beyond structural interpretations and evolve theory within a post-Marxist terrain.

The extension of many of these ideas into an explicitly expressed framework of post-Marxism is evident in the recent work of Laclau, an Argentine political sociologist now teaching in England and influential in left circles. Together with Chantal Mouffe, he argues that "it is no longer possible to maintain the conception of subjectivity and classes elaborated by Marxism, nor its vision of the historical course of capitalist development."[21] Their ideas relate to the English experience, in particular the moderation of a Marxist position among some intellectuals through the journals *Marxism Today* (the theoretical journal of British Eurocommunism), *New Socialist,* and *The New Statesman* and their withdrawal from some basic socialist positions.

Ralph Miliband calls a group of theorists "the new revisionists"[22] and Ellen Meiksens Wood labels them "the new true socialists."[23] Their ranks include Gareth Steadman Jones of the History Workshop group at Oxford, Barry Hindess and Paul Hirst who recanted their earlier orthodox interpretation of mode of production,[24] and Laclau himself who is perhaps best known for his attack on André Gunder Frank's underdevelopment thesis.[25] While these intellectuals differ in many respects, they appear to agree that the primacy of organized labor should be repudiated because the working class in capitalist countries has failed to live up to its revolutionary expectations[26] and the model of struggle should now incorporate a multitude of interests emanating from various strata, groups, and social movements. Some of them believe that post-Marxism is a way of expressing commitment to build on as well as go beyond Marxism: "the questions that Marx posed remain central for understanding and transforming our social world. However, the answers that Marx offered no longer suffice, and just as Marx sought to transcend Hegel, so too, those who pursue the Post-Marxist project seek to transcend Marx."[27]

Laclau and Mouffe outline a new politics for the left based on a project of radical democracy. Their retreat from class and what Wood characterizes as the declassing of the socialist project can be synthesized into a number of propositions: The working class has not evolved into a revolutionary movement; economic class interests are relatively autonomous from ideology and politics; the working class holds no basic position within socialism; a socialist movement may evolve independent of class; a political force may form out of "popular" political and ideo-logical elements, independent from class ties; the objectives of socialism transcend class interests; and the struggle for socialism comprises a plurality of resistances to inequality and oppression.[28]

Critical Examination of Post-Forms

These three post-forms of theoretical understanding move away from traditional ideologies and theoretical frameworks, in particular Marxism and class analysis, and in the direction of a technological economic development and an apolitical democracy. A critical examination of each post-form reveals its deficiencies.

The radical democratic synthesis of Bowles and Gintis attempts to relate democracy to both private property and the patriarchal family, which are viewed as political, and, in addition, suggests that people act not merely to satisfy needs as individuals but to work in concert with other persons. Their synthesis rejects many ideas of Marxism, in particular a view of class consciousness and direct democracy (ignoring Marx's advocacy of representative democracy in certain instances or his association of democracy with direct participatory activities). Their argument that Marxism reduces institutions to class terms leads to an emphasis on conflictual pluralism while obscuring class interests, diminishing the role of the state, and playing down the internal contradictions of capitalism which affect relations of production and often lead to class struggle. Thus, they do not examine reactionary democracy (illustrative of the Reagan and Thatcher governments) or ways the dominated may unite to overcome oppression.[29] The postimperialism of Becker, Frieden, Schatz, and Sklar attempts to build a theory of international political economy devoid of Leninist determinism and dependency orthodoxy. While Frieden acknowledges its usefulness, he offers three criticisms. First, there is a contradiction between national and international capital; historically, international capital has dominated Third World situations, and there is little evidence to affirm that a managerial national bourgeoisie will emerge as hegemonic and other classes will decline. Second, the postimperialist position relies more on relations of power than relations of production: "It would be self-contradictory if an approach that began with an unabashed call for class analysis were to fall back upon arguments that do not rely on the self-interested actions of social classes." Finally, the postimperialist thesis is "inherently oligarchic," and it is not clear if the national bourgeoisie favors democracy or authoritarianism.[30] Their theory ignores the important Marxist literature on internationalization of capital, the work of Palloix[31] being a representative early example, yet it would appear that the two theories reflect similar characteristics and tendencies. One problem with postimperialism is its implication that imperialism is dead and that neither capitalism nor socialism need be decisive in the development of the Third World.

The post-Marxism of Laclau and Mouffe reflects intellectual thinking that has accompanied political discourse on social democracy and democratic socialism where socialist parties have come to power (especially France and Italy, Spain, Portugal, and Greece since the mid 1970s). This discourse has focused on the transition to socialism, the necessity of blocs of left-center political forces to ensure a political majority within a fragmented multiparty setting, popular reforms to mitigate demands of the popular classes (workers and peasants), and tolerance to promote and develop the forces of production in the present capitalist stage. Mainstream politics appear to have mitigated the revolutionary rhetoric so that terms like class struggle, working class, dictatorship of the proletariat, and even Marxism itself are dropped from left dialogue.

The new thinking not only excises classes from a socialist perspective but differs from the traditional Marxist view that the working class is essential for its revolutionary potential because of its structural position as the class that produces capital. The post-Marxists generally avoid analysis of the exploitative relations between capital and labor. Further, their emphasis on politics and ideology as autonomous from economics undermines the attention to political economy which has been of interest to classical and contemporary Marxists. Debate on the nature of the capitalist mode of production no longer appears as important. Consequently, classes and class struggle are displaced by an emphasis on political pluralism, political organizations, and interest groups. Analysis of the state may stress differences between the power bloc and the people while overlooking opposition between capital and labor. There may also be a tendency to focus on a single or a few political institutions; the segmenting of political forces may limit prospects for a societal overview. Political movements attempting to penetrate the mainstream may be isolated; populist strategies designed to challenge the establishment may be diffused and weakened by the separation of particular interests.

These paradigmatic post-forms and conceptions of society suggest a fundamental thesis about contemporary comparative political theory and analysis. *However innovative and useful the revisions may be, they appear to reflect what is fashionable and temporarily appealing, perhaps reflective of the parameters of our profession, in particular, and constraints of the polity, in general, and therefore probably are unable to shape a new paradigm for the future.* Support for this assertion may be associated with the pressures upon intellectuals for reasons of age and status, the need of academics to find recognition, and the impact of a conservative political environment that prompts an escape from revolutionary ideas. Norman Geras characterizes this dilemma: "In the mid-1960s a generation of intellectuals was radicalized and won for Marxism. Many of them were disappointed in the hopes they formed and for a good while now we have been witnessing a procession of erstwhile Marxists . . . in the business of finding their way 'out' and away. This exit is always presented, naturally, in the guise of an intellectual advance."[32] Geras sees a diminishing of political commitment, yet at the same time the intellectual seeks to advance new thinking. Miliband understands the retreat from Marxism as reflecting the crisis of confusion and despair that has affected left intellectuals in recent years: "the phenomenon is not confined to Britain and has assumed much more virulent and destructive forms in other countries, most notably in France, where it has constituted not a 'new revisionism,' but a wholesale retreat into anti-communist hysteria and obscurantism."[33] James Petras observes a similar pattern among the major academic centers where intellectuals are shifting from Marxism and embracing liberal and conservative beliefs and views on the basis of newly discovered "truth." He attributes this shift in thinking to the financial support and influence the state and educational foundations provide intellectuals.[34]

REPRODUCING OLD THEMES

The mystique of the post-forms, the retreat from Marxism, and the declassing of the socialist project, I believe, are manifestations of ideas and practices prevalent in mainstream social science, including comparative politics over the past thirty years. The legacy of the contributions of the 1960s carries to the present; and the breadth of the field and our inadequacies in comprehending the diverse nation-states beyond the familiar Anglo-American systems have contributed to uncertainties on how to proceed and what paradigms allow for useful comparative inquiry. My personal experiences suggest a strategy for solving this problem. First, we should consciously relate theory to practice so as to frame our thinking in critical fashion and reassess our thought in accordance with real experiences. I have discovered in my teaching and writing that critical thinking is stimulated through dichotomies of ideas, for example, in comparative politics juxtaposing of a liberal mainstream paradigm and a radical alternative paradigm to show a diversity of views, interpretations, and questions; or in the development field contrasting reformist capitalist theories and revolutionary socialist theories; or in Latin America contrasting capitalist (diffusionist) development and capitalist (dependency) underdevelopment. Second, as comparativists, it seems essential that we constantly carry out field research. This can, of course, be frustrating. I initiated personal research during the colonial period and carried it beyond independence in Portuguese-speaking Africa and during dictatorial and authoritarian regimes into periods of democratic openings in Brazil and Portugal. Not only have these situations revealed the complexity of rapidly moving events, but they have also exposed me to the poverty and repression suffered by peoples outside the advanced world and sensitized me to respect revolutionary changes. At the same time, it seems to me important to comprehend the complexity of the advanced capitalist political economies in which most of us reside and to realize how slowly the problems of people are resolved.

During the late 1960s and early 1970s the emergence of the new left in the United States brought new perspectives on dealing with societal problems and a deep interest in socialism. Differences appeared within the academic disciplines, and alternative and radical professional associations formed. Through the Nixon, Ford, and Carter administrations, Watergate, and the end of the war in Vietnam, radical academics offered significant critiques and analyses of the U.S. and international political economy. While their presence in American political science was not substantial, alternative and radical ideas did challenge and eventually found roots within the mainstream. Three themes promise to hold our attention for some time to come: capitalist and socialist development, class theories of the state, and socialism and democracy. The remainder of this chapter examines these as major themes of past, present, and future.

Capitalist Versus Socialist Development

I have distinguished between capitalist and socialist perspectives of development elsewhere.[35] Conservative and liberal ideological interpretations of development permeated the early political development literature, which emphasized a model of Anglo-American civic culture and pluralism. Accordingly, the diffusion of capital and technology from advanced to less developed nations presumably would lead to modernization and industrialization along lines of the Western experience. Progress would occur through predetermined stages of development as nation-states emerged in the Third World through a process of independence, nationalism, and capitalist consolidation. Ultimately, democracy in its representative form appears as a sign of political development. The intellectual sources for this thinking stem from the thought of Max Weber (authority), James Madison (interests), and Adam Smith (invisible hand). The Western worldview of capitalist development contrasted with the left-wing sectarianism of the Soviet Communist party and its international network of parties around the world. The Soviet thinking also envisioned linear progress, with economic development through a stage of capitalism that would advance the forces of production and inevitably evolve to socialism and communism, while political development would occur through a national democratic stage prior to the socialization of the means of production and consolidation of power under a vanguard party and the working class.

In the aftermath of the Cuban revolution, intellectuals in the Third World reacted both to the diffusionist prescriptions of the Anglo-American model as well as the reductionist formulas of the traditional Communist parties, but this radical response evolved along two paths. One set of views advocated a mixture of nationalism and autonomy in defense of reforms and the implementation of a capitalist infrastructure; Latin American economists such as Raúl Prebisch and Osvaldo Sunkel defended this position, while Cardoso and Faletto argued that a combination of domestic and international capital, aligned with state-influenced policies and actions, could promote capitalism within a country despite its dependent ties to the international system.[36] From a left stance Bill Warren insisted on expansion of imperialism as the necessary means of developing capitalism and the forces of production so that underdevelopment in the Third World could be overcome.[37] While their respective positions were ideologically quite different, all these writers appear to converge around issues of autonomy and the immediate need to reform and overcome backwardness through capitalist development.

A second set of views rejected this reformist capitalist perspective in favor of achieving an immediate transition to socialism through a revolution; its proponents included Frank,[38] who argued that capitalism promotes underdevelopment in the Third World; Dos Santos,[39] who interpreted the new dependency in terms of multinationals who exploit the less dependent nations; and Marini,[40] who identified subimperialism as a means whereby some dependent Third World nations could exploit others.

Although diffusionist and modernization theories were discredited long ago,[41] their influences remain strong in comparative politics today. Curiously, radical, even some Marxist, scholars within the Third World assimilate modernization terminology into their analysis of emerging capitalism; their vision of socialism assumes the development of the capitalist forces of production.[42] Similarly there is no doubt that dependency interpretations enjoy a place in the mainstream of comparative politics, as the essays in Weiner and Huntington make abundantly clear,[43] although their survey of development theory overlooks important research on modes of production theory[44] and a theory of internationalization of capital.[45]

Class Theory of the State

David Easton reminds us that political science owes much to Marx's conception of the state: "In part, political science could emerge as a discipline separate from the other social sciences because of the impetus Marx had given to the idea of the difference between state and society, an idea virtually unheard of before his time."[46] Yet a generation ago Gabriel Almond and colleagues urged us to drop the concept altogether: "instead of the concept of the 'state,' limited as it is by legal and institutional meanings, we prefer 'political systems.'"[47] Only recently have Evans, Rueschemeyer, and Skocpol[48] pushed for bringing the state back into political analysis in spite of the strong objections of Almond.[49] While assessing the contributions of Poulantzas to a theory of the state, Easton also urged us to back his own emphasis on political system.[50] Although differences persist over whether system or state is more relevant to comparative analysis, I believe comparative politics has become deeply interested in state theory. At issue is the linkage between state and class.

In his systematic criticism of Hegel in 1843, Marx distinguished between state and civil society; and together with Engels in *The German Ideology* (1845–1846) and the *Manifesto* (1848), he conceptualized the state briefly, while the complexity of a class theory of the state was apparent in *Class Struggles in France, 1848–1850* (1850) and *The Eighteenth Brumaire* (1852). Among the theoretical ideas in these works, the economic base is distinguishable from a political superstructure; under the state class interests coalesce in the social formation; and in exceptional periods of dictatorship and strong authority the state may function autonomously. In *On the Origins of the Family, Private Property and the State* (1884), Engels shows that the state legitimates the right of individuals to pursue particular interests through the possession of private property which promotes inequality and disunity among people. In *State and Revolution* (1918), Lenin argued that the state does not mediate class conflict but facilitates the repression of one class by another; only through the building of a parallel power structure can the working class destroy the state through violent revolution. Gramsci conceptualized the state as coordinating complex activities which the ruling class uses to ensure its dominance and to win consent of those over whom it rules.[51] With its dominance intact, the ruling class exercises hegemony by establishing its view and shaping the interests and needs of other classes.

Contemporary Marxists draw various theories of the state from these ideas, including the state as an instrument of the dominant class which influences policies through its control over the means of production[52]; the state as autonomous and not the passive tool of the ruling class in "exceptional" periods of rule such as that of Louis Napoleon Bonaparte from 1852 to 1870[53]; the state as a matrix of institutional apparatuses and bureaucratic organizations, norms, and rules to legitimate authority[54]; the state as intervener in the polity to build and ensure capital accumulation[55]; and the state as a means to ensure bourgeois democracy and mystify administrative actions.[56]

All of these theories of the state make use of class categories. Marx referred to three big classes (landowners, industrial capitalists, and workers) in the brief last chapter of volume three of *Capital*, but he incorporated other classes, including the petty bourgeoisie and peasantry in his studies of mid-nineteenth century France. Contemporary Marxist thinkers, however, elaborate different and conflicting theories of class from the analysis of Marx. The class position of salaried intermediary workers and their potential role in class struggle, for example, has provoked debate, including Poulantzas's theory of the new petty bourgeoisie, Erik Olin Wright's theory of class structures and exploitation, Guglielmo Carchedi's theory of the new middle class, and Barbara and John Ehrenreich's theory of a professional-managerial class.[57]

Another controversy involves the issue of deterministic and reductionist class analysis. While adhering to Marxism, Poulantzas revised his class theory of the state,[58] based on his experience and interpretation of the transition to democracy in Southern Europe and especially in Portugal, where workers and popular forces were able to penetrate the state apparatuses during 1974–1975. This revision of Poulantzas's thinking, together with the impact of ecological, peace, feminist, and other popular movements and with the docility or ineffectiveness of organized labor in advanced capitalist countries, led some theorists away from a class analysis. Laclau and Mouffe best exemplify this "retreat from class" as Wood has characterized their polemic, and the ensuing debate reveals the depth of the differences between proponents and opponents of a class analysis.[59] Baudrillard levels his attack against both structuralism and historical materialism; in his deconstruction of Marxism, he argues that "all the fundamental concepts of Marxist analysis must be questioned."[60] Jon Elster, another critic concerned with reconceptualizing Marxism, acknowledges that "Marx's theory of class consciousness, class struggle, and politics is vibrantly alive," but believes that interest groups must also be taken into account: "one simply cannot defend the traditional Marxist view, that these nonclass interest groups will lose in importance as classes increasingly acquire class consciousness and organization."[61]

John Roemer focuses on exploitation and class consciousness but discounts the Marxist labor theory of value. Property relations, he believes, determine class income and welfare. People have a rational choice: "a person acquires membership in a certain class by virtue of rational activity on her part, by virtue of choosing the best option available subject to the constraints she faces, which are determined by the value of the property she owns."[62] James O'Connor argues, to the contrary, that American individualism has outlived its usefulness: "In the regime of consumer capitalism, individualist ideologies became very expensive economically. . . . In the interest-group liberal state, individualism became a political extravagance."[63] While confronting critics, Michael Burawoy offers a penetrating analysis of the production process in an effort at "bringing workers back in." He posits the thesis that "the process of production decisively shapes the development of working-class struggles," and he shows that as people "transform raw materials into useful things, they also reproduce particular social relations."[64] He argues that through self-conscious interventions the working class has established its important role in history.

Essentially these criticisms rebut the structural theories of Althusser, Poulantzas, and other French writers who were influential in the 1960s. Althusser argued that we are indebted to Marx for understanding our history as a history of class struggle and that "Marx conceived the structure of every society as constituted by 'levels' or 'instances' articulated by a specific determination: the infrastructure or the economic base (the 'unity' of the productive forces and the relations of production) and the superstructure, which itself contains two 'levels' or 'instances': the politico-legal (law and the state) and ideology (the different ideologies, religious, ethical, legal, political, etc.)."[65]

Indebted to this understanding of structuralism, yet desirous of reviving a Marxist class theory of the state, Wolff and Resnick recast the debate by distinguishing between Marxian and neoclassical theory: "what differentiates Marxists is their view that theories and explanations are all partial, their own included, while neoclassical theorists presume that final causes of events exist and that their theory can and will disclose them in a finished and completed explanation." They insist that Marxian theory is class theory in terms of "overdetermination," a concept derived from Freud and Althusser: "The Marxian view assigns no priority to economic over noneconomic aspects of society as determinants to one another. All the different aspects shape and are shaped by all others. No one part of a society, neither the economy nor any other part, determines the whole society. Every aspect of society, including the economic, is overdetermined by all the others."[66] They emphasize the centrality of class as process in Marxian theory and the need to focus on class in order to understand Marx's method of analysis of exploitation.

The search for a class theory of the state should benefit from the approach of Wolff and Resnick who are sensitive to criticisms of simplistic and reductionist theories. It would seem useful to focus on the forms of the state that evolve from relations of production in a capitalist society where the state is considered to be both the political expression of the class structure and the contradiction of capitalist accumulation inherent in production.[67] Political economists wish to avoid overemphasis of political concepts such as the state and its apparatuses, ideology, and so on without turning to a materialist critique. Concentration on political institutions may lead to static analysis, for example, as the appearance of political parties and interest groups divert attention from the locus of power in the state and economy. Likewise, political economists are wary of economistic analysis that concentrates on the economic base of society in isolation from class relations of production.

Some of the issues that might be addressed by a balanced approach are the extent the form and function of the state are determined by relations of class within the capitalist mode of production; whether the capitalist class mobilizes the state as a counterforce to the crisis of capitalism; how the state bureaucracy operates separately from the interests of the capitalist class or, conversely, how the bourgeoisie in certain instances delegates power to the bureaucracy to act on its behalf; and finally, what contradictions appear between the constraints of an autonomous state and a bourgeoisie that no longer is content with Bonapartist rule in "exceptional" periods or a restless proletariat that threatens revolution.

Socialism and Democracy

The interest of political scientist in the United States in democracy has concentrated on the Anglo-American system. Robert Dahl, who contributed to this trend in his early work, later modified his conception of pluralism to embrace democratic socialism and to suggest comparisons, for example, with the socialist governments in Southern Europe and workers' councils in Yugoslavia.[68] Cohen and Rogers explore these issues in their search for a transformation of American society.[69] We also have been fascinated by revolutionary experiences that accompany expectations for democracy and socialism. In Latin America, Cuba (1959), Chile (1970), and Nicaragua (1979) caught our attention as social scientists wrote about conditions favorable to socialism and democracy.[70]

In Europe the May 1968 demonstrations were preceded and followed by a break with orthodoxy on the left, and new thinking (for example, Althusser and Sartre) appeared in the space opened in the traditional socialist and communist movements. Nearly a decade later Poulantzas explored the confrontation of popular movements with exceptional capitalist regimes and contributed an insightful comparative

analysis of regime transition in Southern Europe.[71] Influenced by Eurocommunist developments, Poulantzas and others began to reconceptual-
ize these experiences in terms of an array of groups and class interests.
Norberto Bobbio, an Italian socialist deeply conscious of the pitfalls and
obstacles to democracy, wrote of the need for a transition, not from
representative to direct democracy, but from political to social democracy through the spread of power to various spheres of civil society.[72]

The problem for left intellectuals is how to achieve a transition to a
better society through democracy and socialism. In the cases of Spain,
Portugal, and Greece, a transition to representative democracy occurred
in the mid 1970s, and the rhetoric of the times suggested some sort of a
political transition that would combine the fall of traditional dictatorships with democracy and an illusion of a socialist possibility. Yet no
true social transition of the political economy took place because the
private means of production were not all socialized, and popular classes
did not emerge to power with or without the vanguard of a workers'
movement or proletarian party. In the end capitalism and bourgeois
economic interests were decisive in stemming the tide toward socialism,
while the new regimes evolved from radical possibilities to bourgeois
parliamentary and social democratic forms, and political parties
overshadowed the popular and revolutionary movements. Attempts at
direct participatory democracy were undermined by indirect representative forms. An essential question was whether solutions could be found
for the economic and political crises without more direct and participatory democracy. The rise to power of socialist and social democratic
governments in France, Greece, Italy, Portugal, and Spain did not
mean an end to their crises; communist movements splintered and
weakened (especially in France and Spain) and the intellectual left fell
into disarray (especially in France and England but also in Portugal
where, due to a half century of dictatorship, the left had not established
any profound roots outside the Communist party and a moderate democratic opposition).

As bourgeois political forces insist on the parliamentary process and
the dominance of political parties, democracy and socialism may succumb to modest reform and incremental change rather than lead to a
radical transformation. Further, if pluralism is premised on individual
choice, bargaining, and compromise, whither the prospects for alliances
and coalitions of popular movements outside the political party system
and what are the prospects for declassing the socialist project altogether? Bobbio argues for a socialist pluralism and a broader distribution of power that leads to democratization of civil society, which in
turn eventually extends and integrates political democracy. He affirms
that democracy is "a set of rules . . . for the solution of conflicts without
bloodshed."[73] Bobbio thus attempts to reconcile the demands of social

justice, common to Marxists, with civil and political liberties, essential to liberalism. He discounts arguments, based on Marx and Lenin, that the abolition of class differences through repression of private property will mitigate the need for bourgeois liberties of the individual. He identifies with the tradition of socialist thought that discredits the Marxist solution of identifying individual interests with communal interests. At the same time he acknowledges the Marxist preoccupation with democratic accountability in the face of inequalities of wealth and influence and the growing complexity of bureaucratic society.

The transition to democracy and the goal of socialism may relate to revolutionary strategy. I have emphasized the role of class and class struggle in the search of a theory of the transformation, but other observers differ over whether the working class should be the agency that leads the revolution. Boyte argues for a synthesis of two approaches in the search for a democratic radicalism, on the one hand, through the actions of the working class, and, on the other, through the demands of people or populism.[74] Wood favors the view that the working class has objective interests and beliefs and that as the producing and exploited class it has a special place in capitalism. Laclau and Mouffe, however, argue that the struggle of workers is a democratic and not a class struggle; it represents an extension of democracy rather than the emancipation of a class; they turn to E. Bernstein because he "clearly understood that future advances in the democratization of the state and of society would depend on autonomous initiative.... Since rising labor productivity and successful workers' struggles were having the combined effect that workers ceased to be 'proletarian' and 'became citizens.'" They emphasize the need not to attack the state apparatuses but to consolidate and democratically reform the liberal state and its division of powers, universal suffrage, multiparty systems, civil rights, and so on; the transcendence of capitalism involves locating capitalism in the democratic revolution "founded on the plurality of social agents and of their struggles."[75]

Norman Geras finds that this view "brings together virtually all the key positions of a sector of the European left moving rightwards." He rejects their position as presenting "both a theoretical and a normative void, with some very old viewpoints, prejudices and caricatures around it." He shows that their concern with gender, ethnicity, ecology, nuclear power, war, and peace is also shared by Marxism's opposition, not just to exploitation of the working class but to all forms of capitalist oppression, and he concludes that these "prejudicial attitudes" lead to "the warmest possible view of liberalism."[76]

Whatever the form of democracy, the road to socialism will be difficult whether an evolutionary or revolutionary course is taken. The prospects for rapid change, envisioned in France in 1968 and in Portugal in 1974–1975, are lessened in the evolving and consolidating capitalism of Western Europe so that the process of building socialism will be incremental. In the Third World the level of the productive forces and the seemingly insurmountable problems of external and internal debt, inflation, unemployment, and so on appear to stifle progress toward socialism and democracy. In revolutionary Nicaragua, for example, the state in a transitional society must, in the perspective of Orlando Núñez Soto, combine dictatorship and democracy: "intransigent towards those who oppose or endanger the proletarian project, but democratic in implementing that project."[77] While the conditions for a transition to democracy and socialism are identifiable in Third World revolutionary experiences, Richard Harris has synthesized them into a general framework to understand the process of a transition to socialism. First, a resolution at the political level involves seizure of power by a bloc of popular forces, including the working class; the destruction of the bourgeois state apparatus; the establishment of a regime that functions as a democracy for the popular masses and as a dictatorship for those who resist the regime. Second, a revolution in the relations of production involves work for everyone, eliminating private property in large industry and agriculture; economic planning to satisfy human needs and develop the forces of production; worker participation in production; and pay according to work performed. Third, a revolution in the cultural and ideological sphere involves struggle against bourgeois ideology; popular education and vocational training for workers; and combining work with study.[78]

The diversity in perspectives just reviewed reveals that the achievement of a socialist transition may necessitate an intermediary stage, involving indirect representative forms of democracy in the political sphere and development of capitalist forces of production in the economy. I assume that some intellectuals have disguised this reality with post-Marxist conceptions as one means of acknowledging the difficulty of implanting socialism because of the persistence of capitalism and its pervasive impact. Their reluctance to employ a structural interpretation of society implies an effort to avoid deterministic and reductionist analysis and to favor a broadly conceived pluralism extending beyond the working class to such other social movements as feminists, ecologists, and pacifists. A more preferable approach might account for these social movements as well as the working class.

My examination of old themes further suggests that intellectuals differ over development once questions become of fundamental preference for capitalism or socialism; over questions of the state because of their use of either class or non-class analyses; and over the question of socialism and democracy because of their inclination to favor either indirect or direct forms of participation in the political process. Thus, I conclude with the proposition that *the preference for one system or another (capitalism or socialism) may shape ideals and distort realities and that production of new ideas may be nothing other than the reproduction of old ideas in a new guise.*

REFERENCES

1. See, for example, the best-selling work by Paul Kennedy, *The Rise and Fall of Great Powers: Economic Change and Military Conflict from 1500 to 2000* (New York: Random House, 1988).

2. I should like to thank Kenneth Erickson and Sheryl Lutjens for comments and suggestions that have been incorporated into my paper.

3. See Daniel Bell, *The End of Ideology: On the Exhaustion of Political Ideas in the Fifties*, rev. ed. (New York: Free Press, 1960); *The Coming of Post-Industrial Society* (Harmondsworth: Penguin, 1976); and *Cultural Contradictions of Capitalism* (New York: Basic Books, 1976).

4. See Krishan Kumar, *Prophecy and Progress* (Harmondsworth: Penguin, 1978), 193–194, quoted in Boris Frankel, *The Post-Industrial Utopians* (Madison: University of Wisconsin Press, 1987), 2.

5. Ronald Inglehart, "The Persistence of Materialist and Postmaterialist Value Orientations: Comments on Van Deth's Analysis," *European Journal of Political Research* 11 (March 1983): 81–91; Herman Bakvis and Neil Nevitte, "In Pursuit of Postbourgeois Man: Postmaterialism and Intergenerational Change in Canada," *Comparative Political Studies* 20 (October 1987): 357–389.

6. Frederic Jameson, "Postmodernism or the Cultural Logic of Late Capital," *New Left Review*, no. 146 (1984): 53–90; Michael S. Miller, "Notes on Neo-Capitalism," *Theory and Society* 2, no. 1 (1975): 1–35; B. S. Page, "Anatomy of a Theory: The Post Industrial Theory," *Critical Anthropology* 2, no. 2 (1972): 29–57; T. Schroyer, "Review of the Coming of Post-Industrial Society," *Telos* 19 (1974): 162–176.

7. Rudolf Bahro, *From Red to Green* (London: Verso, 1984); André Gorz, *Farewell to the Working Class* (London: Pluto Press, 1980); Barry Jones, *Sleepers Wake!* (Melbourne: Oxford University Press, 1982); Alvin Toffler, *The Third Wave* (London: Pan Books, 1981).

8. See Frankel, *Post-Industrial Utopians*, 24–32.

9. Ibid., 241–242.

10. Fred Block, *Revising State Theory: Essays in Politics and Postindustrialism* (Philadelphia: Temple University Press, 1987), 32.

11. Samuel Bowles and Herbert Gintis, *Democracy and Capitalism: Property, Community, and the Contradictions of Modern Social Thought* (New York; Basic Books, 1986), 13.
12. Ibid., 17–18.
13. Ibid., 178.
14. Ibid., 204–205.
15. André Gunder Frank, "The Development of Underdevelopment," *Monthly Review* 18 (September 1966): 17–31; Fernando Henrique Cardoso and Enzo Falleto, *Dependency and Development in Latin America*, trans. Marjorie Mattingly Urquidi (Berkeley: University of California Press, 1979).
16. David G. Becker, Jeff Frieden, Sayre P. Schatz, and Richard L. Sklar, *Postimperialism, International Capitalism, and Development in the Twentieth Century* (Boulder, Colo.: Lynne Rienner, 1987).
17. Fernando Claudín, *Eurocommunism and Socialism* (London: New Left Books, 1978), 65–66.
18. Nicos Poulantzas, *Crisis of the Dictatorships* (London: New Left Books, 1976).
19. Antonio Gramsci, *The Modern Prince and Other Writings* (New York: New York University Press, 1957).
20. Louis Althusser, *Lenin and Philosophy and Other Essays* (New York: New Left Books, 1971).
21. Ernesto Laclau and Chantal Mouffe, *Hegemony and Socialist Strategy: Towards a Radical Democratic Politics* (London: Verso, 1985), 4.
22. Ralph Miliband, "The New Revisionists in Britain," *New Left Review*, no. 150 (March-April 1985): 5–26.
23. Ellen Meiksins Wood, *The Retreat from Class: A New "True" Socialism* (London: Verso, 1986).
24. Barry Hindess and Paul Q. Hirst, *Pre-Capitalist Modes of Production* (London: Routledge and Kegan Paul, 1975); *Mode of Production and Social Formation: An Auto-Critique of Pre-Capitalist Modes of Production* (New York: Macmillan, 1977).
25. Ernesto Laclau, "Feudalism and Capitalism in Latin America," *New Left Review*, no. 67 (May-June 1971): 19–38.
26. See Gorz, *Farewell to the Working Class*, for example.
27. Block, *Revising State Theory*, 35.
28. Paraphrased from Wood, *Retreat from Class*, 3–4.
29. These criticisms are elaborated by James N. Devine in a book review in *Science and Society* 51 (Fall 1987): 362–364; and by Michael Burawoy in "Should We Give Up on Socialism?" *Socialist Review* 19 (January-March 1989): 57–74.
30. Becker et al., *Postimperialism*, 182–184.

31. Christian Palloix, *L'économie des jeunes nations, industrialization et groupements des nations* (Paris, n.p., 1975).
32. Norman Geras, "Post-Marxism?" *New Left Review*, no. 163 (May-June 1987): 41.
33. Miliband, "New Revisionists in Britain", 6.
34. James Petras, "Intellectuals' Cop-Out Hinders Development of a New Left," *In These Times* (November 4–10, 1987), 16.
35. Ronald H. Chilcote, *Theories of Comparative Politics: The Search for a Paradigm* (Boulder, Colo.: Westview, Press 1981); and *Theories of Development and Underdevelopment* (Boulder, Colo.: Westview Press, 1984).
36. Osvaldo Sunkel, "Big Business and 'Dependencia,'" *Foreign Affairs* 50 (April 1972): 517–531.
37. Bill Warren, *Imperialism: Pioneer of Capitalism* (London: New Left Books, 1980).
38. Frank, "The Development of Underdevelopment," 17–31.
39. Theotonio dos Santos, "The Structure of Dependence," *American Economic Review* 60 (May 1970): 231–236.
40. Ruy Mauro Marini, "World Capitalist Accumulation and Sub-imperialism," *Two Thirds* 1 (Fall 1978): 29–39.
41. See Susanne Bodenheimer, "The Ideology of Developmentalism: American Political Science's Paradigm-surrogate for Latin American Studies," *Berkeley Journal of Sociology* (1970): 95–137; André Gunder Frank, "Sociology of Development and Underdevelopment of Sociology," *Catalyst* 3 (Summer 1968): 20–73; and Henry Bernstein, "Sociology of Underdevelopment vs. Sociology of Development?," in David Lehmann, ed., *Development Theory: Four Critical Studies* (London: Frank Cass, 1979).
42. José F. Graziano da Silva, "Capitalist 'Modernization' and Employment in Brazilian Agriculture, 1960–1975: The Case of São Paulo," *Latin American Perspectives* 11 (Winter 1984): 117–136.
43. Myron Weiner and Samuel P. Huntington, eds., *Understanding Political Development* (Boston: Little, Brown, 1987).
44. For a synthesis of these trends, see Aiden Foster-Carter, "The Modes of Production Controversy," *New Left Review*, no. 107 (January-February 1978): 47–77.
45. Palloix, *L'économie des jeunes nations*, for example.
46. David Easton, "Political Science," *International Encyclopedia of the Social Sciences* 12 (1968): 295.
47. Gabriel A. Almond, "Introduction: A Functional Approach to Comparative Politics," in Gabriel A. Almond and James S. Coleman, eds., *The Politics of the Developing Areas* (Princeton, N.J.: Princeton University Press, 1960), 4.

48. Peter B. Evans, Dietrich Rueschemeyer, and Theda Skocpol, eds., *Bringing the State Back In* (Cambridge: Cambridge University Press, 1985).

49. Gabriel A. Almond's essay in Weiner and Huntington, *Understanding Political Development*.

50. David Easton, "The Political System Besieged by the State," *Political Theory* 9 (August 1981): 303–325.

51. Gramsci, *Modern Prince*.

52. Ralph Miliband, *The State in Capitalist Society* (New York: Basic Books, 1969).

53. Nicos Poulantzas, *Classes in Contemporary Capitalism*, trans. David Fernbach (London: New Left Books, 1975).

54. Claus Offe, *Disorganized Capitalism* (Cambridge, Mass.: MIT Press, 1985).

55. See Joaquim Hirsch's essay in John Holloway and Sol Picciotto, eds., *State and Capital: A Marxist Debate* (London: Edward Arnold, 1978).

56. See Martin Carnoy, *The State and Political Theory* (Princeton N.J.: Princeton University Press, 1984), for elaboration of these and other perspectives.

57. Val Burris provides a useful synthesis of these various theories in "Class Structure and Political Ideology," *Insurgent Sociologist* 14 (Summer 1987): 5–46.

58. Nicos Poulantzas, *State, Power, Socialism* (London, New Left Books, 1978).

59. See Geras, "Post-Marxism?" and the reply by Laclau and Mouffe, "Post-Marxism Without Apologies," *New Left Review*, no. 166 (November-December 1987): 79–106; the initial debate is in Laclau and Mouffe, *Hegemony and Socialist Strategy*, and in Wood, *Retreat from Class*.

60. Jean Baudrillard, *The Mirror of Production* (St. Louis: Telos Press, 1975), 21.

61. Jon Elster, *An Introduction to Karl Marx* (Cambridge: Cambridge University Press, 1987), 196–197; see also *Making Sense of Marx* (Cambridge: Cambridge University Press, 1985).

62. See John D. Roemer, *Free to Lose: An Introduction to Marxist Economic Philosophy* (Cambridge: Cambridge University Press, 1988), 10; see also Adam Przeworski, *Capitalism and Social Democracy* (Cambridge: Cambridge University Press, 1985); and Alan Carling, "Rational Choice Marxism," *New Left Review*, no. 90 (November-December 1986): 24–62, for a review and critique of rational choice Marxism.

63. James O'Connor, *Accumulation Crisis* (Oxford: Basil Blackwell, 1984), 4.

64. Michael Burawoy, *The Politics of Production: Factory Regimes Under Capitalism and Socialism* (London: Verso, 1985), 7.

65. Althusser, *Lenin and Philosophy*, 134.

66. Richard D. Wolff and Stephen Resnick, *Economics: Marxian Versus Neoclassical* (Baltimore: Johns Hopkins Press, 1987), 21, 134. See also Stephen Resnick and Richard D. Wolff, *Knowledge and Class: A Marxian Critique of Political Economy* (Chicago: University of Chicago Press, 1987).

67. See Christian Anglade and Carlos Fortín, *The State and Capital Formation in Latin America* (Pittsburgh: University of Pittsburgh Press, 1985), for a useful application of such a model of the experiences of Brazil, Chile, and Mexico.

68. Robert Dahl, "Pluralism Revisited," *Comparative Politics* 10 (January 1978): 191–203.

69. Joshua Cohen and Joel Rogers, *On Democracy: Toward a Transformation of American Society* (Harmondsworth: Penguin Books, 1986).

70. On Cuba, see Marta Harnecker, *Cuba: Dictatorship or Democracy?* (Westport, Conn.: Lawrence Hill, 1980); on Chile, see Barbara Stallings, *Class Conflict, and Economic Development in Chile, 1958–1973* (Stanford: Stanford University Press, 1978); on Nicaragua, see Richard Fagen, Carmen Diana Deere, and José Luis Coraggio, eds., *Transition and Development* (New York: Monthly Review Press, 1986).

71. Poulantzas, *Crisis of the Dictatorships*.

72. Norberto Bobbio, *The Future of Democracy* (Minneapolis: University of Minnesota Press, 1987).

73. Ibid., 156.

74. Harry C. Boyte, "Populism and the Left," *Democracy* 1 (April 1981): 53–66.

75. Laclau and Mouffe, "Post-Marxism Without Apologies," 105–106.

76. Geras, "Post-Marxism?" 43, 45, 82; see also Milton Fisk, "Why the Anti-Marxists Are Wrong," *Monthly Review* 38 (March 1987):7–17, with subsequent debate in vol. 39 (December 1987): 41–55.

77. In Fagen, Deere, and Corragio, *Transition and Development*, 247.

78. Richard Harris, "Marxism and the Transition to Socialism in Latin America," *Latin American Perspectives* 15 (Winter 1988): 16.

Chapter
6

Beyond Dependency

Development and Democracy in The Era of International Capitalism

David G. Becker

Defined as improvement in the quality of human life, development has a political aspect. The quality of life is bound up with the social order, inasmuch as the political, social, and economic relationships which constitute that order determine the nature and distribution of social goods. This system of determinations is ordinarily defended by those who wield political power and exercise social control; it changes when and as the prospective beneficiaries of change either overwhelm it or, far more frequently, compel it through their contestation to accommodate to their demands. The study of development is the study of this fundamental conflict.

By defining development humanistically we also link it with progressive values. Values shape the conceptual content of development itself, and they are embedded in the consciousness that motivates the behavior of social actors. Since the study of development aims not just at acquiring knowledge but at bettering the human condition, values also affect developmentalists' theoretical paradigms and research programs.

Until recently the reigning paradigms of development studies were organized around versions of the dependency concept. Dependency paradigms presented themselves as progressive and critical. Heavily indebted to the Marxist view of class and state and to the Leninist notion of capitalist imperialism, they interpreted development as a conflict among social forces with unambiguous national identifications. The shortcomings of existing development patterns were laid at the door of an exploitative world economic order whose domination over the newly developing countries was secured by bonds of mutual interest with certain local bourgeois elites. Some dependency research, it is true, sought to locate practical measures by which nationalistically inclined state managers might influence the process in favor of the needs of the majority. But the implications of even these "moderate" dependency approaches went much further. For if the international economic system were imperialist and exploitative, then, barring an unlikely wholesale overhaul of the system, the Third World's popular majorities would fare better if their countries' linkages to it were weakened or broken.

My argument in this essay challenges all of these conclusions. Today's international capitalism is not imperialist,[1] although it remains a system of class domination with oligarchic implications for the distribution of political power. Bourgeois groups with links to international capital often are the most progressive elements of the Third World's national bourgeoisies; their preference for constitutional governance and political pluralism, as well as their ability to accommodate to subordinate-class political organization and action, stems directly from their class interests and from the ideological views they have imbibed from their metropolitan partners. Their current effort to transform their societies is hardly altruistic; but the transformations they contemplate will, if implemented, make it easier for popular groups to engage in democratic political action.

To criticize the dependency approach and advocate its transcendence is not to denigrate its contribution in its day. It may be credited with having opened some eyes to the hidden flaws and subtle ideological biases of the preceding "modernization" paradigms; and the experience ensures that its passing will not result in a relapse into old errors, provided we are clear about the sources of its own defects. There are two such sources. The first is Marxist orthodoxy, which has contributed its deficient theory of politics and institutions, its economistic comprehension of class, and its dogmatic insistence on capitalism-as-imperialism. The second source is the Left's ingrained suspicion of concentrated economic power, a populist ideological tendency that impedes an understanding of the business corporation as a political institution.

Fortunately, development theory is itself developing. A confluence of new ideas—the postimperialist paradigm of world capitalism, "post-Marxist" thinking about language and epistemology, the neo-Gramscian concern with ideology, and novel perspectives on social movements—enables us to adumbrate a postdependency research agenda which promises significant advances without sacrifice of our progressive values.

DEPENDENCY: A BRIEF HISTORY OF AN IDEA

Dependency is a paradigmatic conception that stresses the role of external forces in conditioning processes of development. Numerous variations on the dependency theme have appeared in the literature. All, however, share two fundamental postulates that distinguish them from notions of asymmetrical interdependence[2] and give them a distinctly radical thrust. First, international capitalism is conceived as a system whose structures and institutions are organized around the imperialist domination and exploitation of the less industrialized national economies by those of the highly industrialized West. Second, imperialism is regarded as a system-maintenance requisite of the capitalist world economy rather than a contingent outcome of past history or of the West's military might.

Although these claims were debated by Hobson, Lenin, and others at the beginning of this century,[3] today's dependency theorists confront a different world. Lenin had to explain why the contradictions of metropolitan capitalism, which should have taken political form as ever more intense *class* struggle, had assumed the guise of *national* conflict over colonies; then he had to demonstrate why anticolonialist struggles were progressive regardless of their class character. His intellectual heirs, in contrast, must explain how international domination and exploitation are maintained in a world system organized around the coexistence of a global capitalist economy with universal statehood and intolerance of territorial conquest; then they must demonstrate why capitalist development is not progressive despite the worldwide attainment of political sovereignty.

The resultant effort to explicate systemic mechanisms which enforce dependency relations has taught us much about economic processes, institutions, and effects that we did not know a decade or two ago. But in spite of considerable effort, no one has managed to build a consensus within the discipline (even one restricted to those who sympathize with the dependency approach and share its value premises) in behalf of a systematic analysis of dependency.[4]

In order to establish that capitalist development is regressive, researchers have addressed the character of the social and political relationship it engenders. New forms of class analysis have gone beyond Marx's dichotomous scheme and attempted to theorize the full complexity of interacting groups, subclasses, and institutions to which he was so sensitive in his political writings. The traditional view of the state as a bourgeois cat's-paw has been challenged by the concept of "relative state autonomy" (to which I will return later). The results again are uncertain, however. While the revival of concern with social structure and its linkages to political institutions has raised development theory to new heights of sophistication and made it one of the most dynamic subfields of our discipline, we still lack confidence that dependency accounts for extreme class privilege and inequality.[5]

Does the difficulty reside in the way that advocates of dependency have designed their research and interpreted their observations, or does it stem from flaws in the dependency concept itself? Let us test the latter possibility by reexamining what is widely regarded as the most sophisticated formulation of the dependency idea: Fernando Henrique Cardoso's class-centered dependency analysis.[6]

The Cardosian Analysis of Dependency

Cardoso's approach did not disavow the tradition of Marxist-imperialist thought,[7] but it represented a noteworthy advance over earlier efforts at analyzing the structures of "dependent" societies. His predecessors, who treated political institutions as superstructures determined by economic relationships, had reasoned thus: "Dependent" economies are by definition under the effective control of metropolitan bourgeoisies; hence, Third World states must be the latter's handmaidens; such states cannot pursue truly national objectives and therefore exist in order to secure dependency relations by force.[8] Although Cardoso agreed that every newly industrializing country's relations with international capital incorporate domination and exploitation, he rejected this kind of deterministic argument. Having done so, he was compelled to reject as well the validity of any "general theory of dependency" based on abstract systemic mechanisms. Rather, relations of dependency would assume different forms, involve different groups in the "dependent" society, and have different outcomes, in accordance with the particularities of the country and the historical moment.

Cardoso described his approach as a "method," not a "theory," of dependency analysis.[9] It rested on the following principles.

1. Classes are composed of distinct subgroups ("fractions"). The identities of the various "fractions" are determined objectively by their economic roles and functions, from which their particular interests are derived.
2. Certain bourgeois fractions in each newly industrializing country are linked by objective commonalities of interest to foreign capital; they are the internal embodiment of dependency relations. Inasmuch as dependency relations are embedded inside the society, they can be studied within its confines, provided that the external linkages are kept ever in mind.

3. The newly industrializing country's state apparatus is "relatively autonomous." It does not minister blindly to the interests of either the entire bourgeois class or the leading fraction thereof. Rather, state authorities have considerable leeway, so long as they respect fundamental property rights and accumulation requisites, to respond to the demands of other classes and fractions.

Dependency is, for Cardoso, a dynamic condition that plays itself out historically through shifting relations of alliance and conflict among various class fractions. (In general, bourgeois, middle-class, and popular fractions with interests confined to the domestic economy will ally with one another against fractions with international interests.[10]) This unstable configuration of class conflict, together with the state's relative autonomy, sometimes leads to situations where political action to alter dependency relations becomes feasible. Such action may enable the dependent economy to register considerable improvement in output per hour worked, gross product, or technological level.[11] It cannot, however, overcome dependency itself or the many inequities and "distortions" characteristic of "dependent development"; only a socialist transformation can do so.

Cardoso's portrait of Latin American dependency in the current era is by now familiar. "[B]oth capital flow and economic decisions are controlled from abroad" by the parent firms of transnational corporations, whose decisions "only partly reflect the domestic market situation" and which often prefer to export their profits rather than reinvest them. The heights of the domestic economy are organized around close cooperation among "the public sector, the multinational corporation, and the modern capitalist sector." Economic life centers on the production and exchange of producer goods and high-priced consumption goods; redistribution of wealth would be counterproductive in such an economy and is avoided. Popular unrest, resulting from the absence of redistribution, leads to political instability; when instability causes a slowdown in the rate of foreign investment, authoritarian rule is imposed. Owing to the absence of redistribution as well as to the capital-intensive nature of the production methods employed, this sort of capitalism does not have the capacity to modernize the economy as a whole.[12] For that reason it cannot play the historically progressive role that Marx assigned to early capitalism in Europe and North America.

In summary, Cardoso has abandoned his precursors' identification of dependency with neocolonialism ("the development of underdevelopment") and has focused his critique on the way that dependency "distorts" *internal* capitalist development by fostering greater economic inequality and structural tendencies toward political authoritarianism. He also has rejected the very idea of dependency "theory" (in the systemic Marxist sense) in favor of a concrete, empirical-historical analysis of class "fractions" and their interests and actions, arguing that only by uncovering the "correlation of forces" at any moment can we comprehend the opportunities and limits of progressive structural transformation in the Third World.

The first departure is unquestionably a step forward: The most cursory observation suffices to falsify "the development of underdevelopment" in Latin America. Let us therefore probe the second and consider its implications.

The Cardosian Paradigm   To begin with, Cardoso cannot do without *some* theory of international capitalism—a paradigm or model of the system which has not been deduced solely from observations of class relations and defective development in newly industrializing countries—if he hopes to avoid circularity of argument. That is, he cannot use the locally dominant class's association with international capital to explain the nature of the development he observes, and simultaneously use the latter observation to explain the nature of the international capital with which the class is associated. He is aware of the problem, however, for he argues that the newly industrializing country's economy is "not strong enough to ensure continuous advance of the system, in financial as well as in technological and organizational terms." Owing to this weakness, "rules of domination are enforced" upon the country when it approaches transnational corporations and banks to acquire what it desperately needs but cannot create for itself.[13] In other words, domination and exploitation derive from the asymmetry of the relationship.

Obviously, not every economic exchange between unequal parties automatically entails domination and exploitation (if it did, capitalism would be highly improbable at best); so we need to know why that result obtains in the kinds of exchanges that concern Cardoso. As he does not provide the reasons, we must find them ourselves.[14]

Now Cardoso wants above all to explain how dependency affects his native Brazil, whose economy is the largest, the most diverse, and one of the most industrialized in Latin America. He cannot rest his claim on empirical observation of this or that transnational enterprise or group of enterprises or even all the firms of a given industry, for the impact of any one of these on Brazilian society cannot possibly be so great as to determine its structure or the nature of its political institutions. The claim therefore must pertain to a generalized feature of the relationship between international capital and newly industrializing countries. In fact, he apparently is thinking in parallel with Marx's "unmasking" of the capitalist wage contract, whose appearance of equity *does* conceal generalized relations of domination and exploitation. How close is this parallel?

For Marx the inequitable character of the wage contract (which has the *appearance* of a contract between equals) stems not only from the fact that the individual proletarian needs the wage payment more than the capitalist needs to hire her, but also from two other features of capitalist labor relations: the bourgeois monopoly of control over the means of production, meaning that the proletarian has nothing to exchange but labor-power; and the presence of an "industrial reserve army" of unemployed, meaning that the proleterian is unable to bargain up the price of labor-power. Neither is replicated in relations between international capitalists and newly industrializing countries. There is no vast "reserve army" of Third World countries in need of investment; the number of such countries is small and becomes smaller still when the poorest of them are ruled out because of their lack of market potential. What is more, in every newly industrializing country the state controls foreigners' access to the national market, which gives it real bargaining power. Transnational corporations and banks, for their part, do not have unlimited freedom to forgo investment unless they can dictate the terms. The corporations are exposed to competitive pressures, and their failure to enter a national market when competitors do so would mean a loss of worldwide market share and declining profitability. As for the banks, nothing drives them to failure more rapidly than an accumulation of interest-bearing deposits which is greater than their loan portfolio—exactly the situation they faced in the 1970s when many OPEC countries placed enormous sums of dollars on deposit.

Lenin understood well the nature of the theoretical problem, and his discussion of capitalist imperialism meets it forthrightly. In the Leninist analysis, the fully industrialized countries' need for investment outlets *cannot* be met through the establishment of unequal economic relationships with other sovereign entities; thus coercion must be brought to bear, and sovereign states must be transformed forcibly into colonial dependencies. Cardoso, though, is arguing against those who contend that international capitalism remains overtly coercive. He reminds us, to be sure, that the existing economic structures of Latin America evolved out of earlier relations which were in many cases coercively imposed. Even so, an international capitalism which no longer relies on diplomatic pressure and military force should leave ample openings for local dominant classes to redress inequities in their own favor.

What Cardoso's paradigm comes down to, then, is the "little person's" (or country's) populist mistrust of concentrated economic power. It is not difficult to see whose interests are served by such populism: those of the newly industrializing country's small businesspeople, who want to fend off competition that they cannot meet.[15] It is no reflection on the sincerity of small-business perceptions and beliefs to point out that this class's economic and political record—its reliance on low wages, its extreme hostility toward working-class organization and toward the political empowerment of the propertyless poor—hardly qualifies it as progressive. In the particular case of Latin America, moreover, the petty bourgeoisie's chief political-ideological achievement has been to gain widespread acceptance for the belief that all development strategies which are not inward-looking are perforce "anti-national." The disastrous consequences include the construction of monopolistic, inefficient industrial systems which are bound to produce the very inequities that Cardoso and all progressives rightly deplore.

An Assessment of Cardoso's Contribution Cardoso's work will be remembered as a landmark in the evolution of development theory long after the dependency idea has been forgotten. He did not originate the idea; indeed, Cardoso's may be the last of many efforts to refine it. But in creating a form of dependency analysis that moved away from unsupportable and manifestly inaccurate generalizations such as "the development of underdevelopment," he defended much more effectively the notion of a critical approach to development against attacks from the Right.

Our brief exploration of Cardoso's thought has taught us, however, that not even a concrete, empirically based structural analysis of newly industrializing societies can dispense with a well-developed theory or paradigm of international capitalism. Progressives, because they hold anti-corporate values, need to be particularly on guard against populism; and the best way of avoiding that trap is to be sure that we have reasoned through all the implications of the systematic mechanisms we postulate when we put forward a structuralist conception of social forces in the present age.

Cardoso's empirical class analysis helped our discipline cast off the blinders of orthodox economism.[16] Unfortunately, his break with orthodoxy is insufficiently radical. Although he is sensitive to the ideological determinants of class *action*, he has not recognized that class *formation* has institutional and ideological as well as economic bases. A proper understanding of the nature and bases of class formation is absolutely necessary if class analysis is to account for the relative progressiveness (briefly noted in the introductory section of this essay) of externally linked bourgeois elements and explain what this signifies for the evolution of the social and political order in newly industrializing societies.

The Eclipse of Dependency

By the late 1970s the Cardosian formulation of the dependency idea had achieved near-hegemonic status among Latin American students of capitalist development. One reason for its popularity was that it was not contaminated by North Americans' ideologically questionable interest in homeostatic systems theory and quantitative hypothesis testing, both of which Cardoso regarded with suspicion.[17] Instead, its intellectual roots lay mostly within the region: in ECLA structuralism,[18] in the cultural-nationalist tradition,[19] and, above all, in the Marxism of José Carlos Mariátegui (1894–1930) and the young Víctor Raúl Haya de la Torre (1895–1979).[20] This wholly indigenous current of Marxist thought is anything but deterministic; it is voluntaristic and empirically grounded. One of its major preoccupations, given the minority status of the region's proletariat, always has been that of locating class alliances that might permit an early transition to socialism. From this ideological standpoint, Cardoso's class analysis and his suspicion of sweeping theoretical dicta made his work seem sophisticated, realistic, and yet capable not only of establishing a positive role for human agency but also of suggesting viable political strategies for overcoming dependency.

Meanwhile, U.S. political science was transcending the conformism of the Cold War years. The civil rights struggle and the Vietnam war encouraged a critical rethinking from an increasingly "Third Worldist" perspective of "free enterprise" at home and of U.S. policy abroad. Revisionist scholarship laid bare the imperialistic component of U.S. policy in Latin America. A surge of interest in Marxism and a revival of anticorporate populism led to a spate of writings that attempted to link U.S. imperialism to the enormous postwar expansion of foreign investment in newly developing areas of the world.[21]

After the failure of the 1968 "revolutions," many progressives in the United States and Europe became deeply pessimistic about the prospect of an early transcendence of capitalism in the West; for Western working classes, as in 1914, appeared satisfied with a status quo that had brought them unprecedented material benefits (the mutual incomprehension of U.S. workers and intellectuals over the latter's "antipatriotic" opposition to the Vietnam war was symptomatic). But dependency held out a new hope, aside from the prospect of reducing the human costs of development. If its arguments proved strong enough to withstand vigorous counterattack, as seemed to be true of Cardoso's; if they could persuade the newly developing countries to weaken or rupture their linkages with international capital; and if the international capitalist system could not survive without imperialist domination, then the Third World might prove to be the midwife of socialism in the first.

In other words, the appeal of the dependency idea was and is in some part ideological—which is why the idea has been resistant to positivist efforts to refute it with contrary data. For anyone who holds these views sincerely, it is more comforting to imagine our discipline moving forward "in the tradition of the dependency approach but without the dependency label"[22] than to conceive that more must be left behind than merely a name.

Still, there comes a time when ideology has no choice but to bend before reality. Postwar Latin America has undergone basic structural transformations, the most salient examples of which are the disappearance or modernization of hacienda systems, the acquisition of national control over natural resources, and the rise of "informal" entrepreneurship. These transformations can be neither ignored nor attributed to capitalist imperialism, even if one judges them to have had a negative impact on the lives of ordinary people. The conduct of many "associated" bourgeois sectors during and since the transition to constitutional governance has not conformed to dependency predictions. And a glance at recent world and regional affairs turns up a truth that should prove fatal to all conceptions of capitalist imperialism. Whereas "national interests" (that is, the interests defined and pursued by governments in their foreign relations) and the interests of dominant classes are increasingly congruent throughout Latin America and the rest of the Third World, the two sets of interests are increasingly divergent from each other in the metropolitan capitalist countries.[23]

Cardoso's later writings on the possibilities for redemocratization in Brazil testify to the flexibility and usefulness of a class analysis liberated from economic determinism.[24] I remain convinced, however, that the full potential of this approach, and of the praiseworthy renewal of interest in constitutionalism, requires us to rid our theoretical paradigms and research agendas of the last vestiges of populist nationalism. A sounder theory of development will still be critical; it will continue to "look 'behind' corporations and governments to the group and class bases of their actions."[25] But, having incorporated the values of limited government and democracy, it will concern itself less with the distribution of wealth and more with the distribution of political power.

POSTIMPERIALISM: AN ALTERNATIVE PARADIGM OF CAPITALIST DEVELOPMENT

A central but seldom voiced axiom of the capitalism-as-imperialism standpoint is that "[c]apital without a state is . . . unthinkable."[26] Nowadays only a handful of doctrinaire ultraliberals disregard the key role played by the state in the development of every *national* capitalism. Equally unproblematic is the expansion of that role in the prewar era of capitalist imperialism: even if imperialism is explained by deterministic "necessity" originating from the structure of the economy, colonial domination could not have been established or maintained without the military and political power of the state.

And yet. . . . Modern capitalism has spawned a "nonstatist political institution"—the business corporation—which has assumed many of the macroeconomic regulatory and management functions that theorists customarily assign to the state.[27] The ambit of corporate action has surpassed state frontiers and become global; transnational firms are such powerful international actors that no state, whether alone or with the participation of local nonstate entities, can control its society's economic course without reference to them. Thus it seems appropriate to ask: Are the nonstatist corporate institutions of international capital assuming statelike functions of regulation and management of the world economic system?[28] If so, what are the implications for Third World development of this significant change in the nature of world order?

These considerations led Richard L. Sklar to put forth a new paradigm of capitalist development, *postimperialism.* Sklar answered the first question in the affirmative and concluded that international capitalism was evolving into a new stage in which the use of state power to dominate other peoples ceases to be necessary for the expanded reproduction of capital on a world scale. Sklar's answer to the second question entails a consideration of how the new institutions are affecting global processes of class formation and, thereby, class action.[29] A central and irreconcilable difference between postimperialism and dependency is that for postimperialism *class is the basic unit of analysis*, whereas for dependency—even those forms which take into account the class-structural concomitants of dependent economic relationships—the basic unit of analysis is the *nation*.

The Class Analysis of Postimperialist Capitalism

Class formation means the evolution of a social group whose members "tend to act and think as an entity"[30] and whose fundamental basis of cohesion is common interest. The orthodox criterion for defining classes and assigning membership in them—control over the means of production, distribution, and exchange—is not adequate for an age in which the boundary between the state ("political society") and the private institutions of civil society is becoming ever more diffuse.[31] Certainly, the economic foundations of political power retain their importance in capitalist society; but the political foundations of economic power are important as well—and nowhere more so than in the Third World, where most states are involved directly in the accumulation process. Sklar therefore broadens the criterion: He defines the dominant class as the subject of political power and social control and the subordinate classes as the object. The subordinate classes are differentiated from one another by the nature of the social control mechanisms to which they are subjected (the working class to the wage and factory systems, the peasantry to the institutions of land tenure and marketing) and by the character and effectiveness of whatever autonomous power resources they may command (for example, middle-class possession of small productive property or educational credentials).

At the world level a true international bourgeoisie is forming; the "condensation nuclei" of the new class are the transnational corporations and the public and quasi-public institutions (the World Bank, IMF, GATT, OECD, and the like) that help regulate the international economy. The class's leading sector consists of the managers and directors of the transnationals' parent firms, together with the top officials of the regulatory institutions. Sklar calls this sector the *corporate international bourgeoisie*; the managers of transnational subsidiaries domiciled in newly developing countries may be thought of as the corporate international bourgeoisie's "local representatives."[32]

In each newly developing country that plays host to subsidiaries of transnational capitalist institutions, the leading stratum of the local dominant class maintains intimate associations with the "local representatives" of the corporate international bourgeoisie. The leading local class stratum is aptly described as a "corporate national bourgeoisie" (Becker) or a "managerial bourgeoisie" (Sklar). The first designation applies where industrialization is relatively advanced, where the "commanding heights" of the economy are occupied by the corporate form of enterprise, and where, in consequence, corporate interests and ideologies carry great political weight. Included within the leading stratum are the directors and managers of large parastatal and private national firms, high state officials, the commanding officers of the military, and important politicians. The second designation applies where industrialization is slight and the state is economically paramount. Here the membership balance within the class stratum is somewhat different. There is little private-sector representation, state and parastatal officials are relatively more important, and members of the learned professions are included because of their relative wealth, high status, and small numbers. The qualifier "managerial" signifies that the members of the group are more concerned with managing wealth originally created by others (ex-colonists, one-time foreign owners) than with creating new wealth.

The corporate international bourgeoisie's "local representatives" are the main channels of communication between it and the corporate national or managerial bourgeoisie.

In the advanced countries the corporate international bourgeoisie is also the leading sector of a much larger corporate bourgeoisie, from which it is scarcely distinguishable. In the newly developing countries the corporate national or managerial bourgeoisie is, similarly, the leading sector of a larger national bourgeoisie with predominantly local interests. In both instances, then, the bourgeoisie is a diverse class containing subgroups with different, sometimes competing immediate interests; yet the whole class has an identity for the analyst, based on class members' common interest in capital accumulation and the preservation of a capitalist economic system.[33]

The relationship between the corporate international bourgeoisie and the corporate national or managerial bourgeoisie may be conceptualized as a "partnership" or "marriage" based on complementarity of interest. Both share an interest in capitalism as such; the first wishes to enlarge its ambit of action, while the second wishes to take advantage of this expansive drive in order to enhance its own economic base and, thereby, to make the "partnership" a more equal one. Like any partnership or marriage, this one embodies tensions and conflicts over power, control, and the sharing out of rewards. Systemic and institutional pressures shape, but do not determine, how such tensions and conflicts are worked out. Although international class formation draws the Third World countries more tightly into the capitalist system, the process is a dialectical one that simultaneously alters the system itself— sometimes, perhaps, to the Third World's net advantage.

But Sklar does not confine himself to enunciating an abstract schema for specifying classes. Instead he confronts orthodoxy head-on by insisting that class action must be comprehended as the action of ideological groups whose members share a common world view, a common set of values and beliefs. While agreeing that ideological world views serve as justifications of interests, he rejects the dictum that the former are determined by the latter. The requisite justifications, he suggests, might be provided by a range of possible beliefs, each with different ramifications for political action; the operative system of belief must therefore be detected through an empirical investigation of the case at hand. The investigation, moreover, cannot treat ideology either as static or as the product of a unidirectional, top-down flow, especially not when the flow of ideas links "partners" within the same class:

> It would be innocent and illusory to suppose that partnership agreements with transnational corporations and banks . . . are ideologically or politically neutral. These partnerships transmit capitalist values to the host countries through the alliances that are cemented with the local wing of the managerial bourgeoisie. . . . Even so, traffic in ideas and attitudes does not pass between the partners of a dominant-class alliance on a one-way street. Members of the corporate international bourgeoisie are as likely to be sensitized to the developmental values of their host country partners as the other way around.[34]

With these qualifications in mind, we can roughly characterize the ideologies of the bourgeois class sectors as follows.

First, owing largely to the fact that the earliest transnational corporations were of North American and British origin, the corporate international bourgeoisie partakes of a "corporate-liberal" world view. Among the components of its ideology are a belief in limited government and the rule of law, an inclination to regard politics and economics as separate realms, a sincere conviction that the corporate order works to the benefit of all the world's peoples, and an understanding that the realization of those benefits is fostered by cooperation between private business and a welfarist state.[35] These beliefs dispose transnational managers to defer to the policy-making powers of each local state where their subsidiaries operate (provided that official policies do not threaten essential corporate prerogatives) and to have each subsidiary behave like a "good corporate citizen" of the host country—a disposition which amounts to an ideological *doctrine of domicile*.[36] They also dispose managers to make significant accommodations to the local subordinate classes' urgent demands (for example, for union recognition and higher wages) that do not challenge the capitalist order. Lastly, they cause managers to view constitutionalism, not authoritarianism, as the most "natural" form of governance and the best form for business interests.[37] Sklar cautions, though, that the liberal notion of the separateness of economics and politics, combined with the pressures of economic interest, conduces toward tolerant acceptance of authoritarian local regimes (as opposed to corporate action aimed at weakening them), especially if the perceived alternative is social disorder.[38]

Second, the world view of the corporate national or managerial bourgeoisie, strongly influenced by its "senior partner," is becoming more receptive to corporate-liberal ideas about political and socioeconomic organization. But those who belong to this group are also intensely nationalist. They have an interest in attaining a more equal "partnership" with the international class sector, which requires not only a stronger national economy but political action to redress inequities in the international order. In addition, their belief in the "public service" aspect of corporate liberalism leads them to take seriously their national society's problems of poverty and social justice (defined in the liberal way, that is, as equality under the law, equality of opportunity, and freedom from want). They therefore prefer a local state that is nationalistically assertive in international forums and economically activist at home.[39] Both preferences are sources of tension between them and the members of the corporate international bourgeoisie.

Third, the ideological dispositions of national (noncorporate) bourgeoisies around the world require further study. I offer two tentative hypotheses for investigation: (1) Metropolitan national bourgeoisies, lacking easy access to overseas markets and mistrusting corporate regulation of the economy, favor a combination of internal laissez-faire and external neomercantilist activism—import protection, export subsidization, sometimes the use of force to keep overseas markets open. Owing to their weak economic position and dependence on individual property, they worry about taxation (especially on incomes and inheritances) and have no use for domestic policies aimed at a wider sharing of wealth and power. They are the chief supporters of the "New Right." (2) Third World national bourgeoisies also are antagonistic to market regulation and welfarism. They, too, favor an externally dynamic neomercantilist state, since they need tariff protection and restrictions on competition from transnational corporations. Because they are less able to bear the costs of accommodating the subordinate classes, they are intolerant of labor unions and accepting of authoritarian solutions to social unrest. But they are readier than their metropolitan counterparts to support state activity in two areas: industrial promotion, through means that do not infringe upon private prerogatives, and education, since they believe that access to low-cost schooling best assures their children's chances for upward mobility.

Implications and Behavioral Concomitants

The interests and ideological dispositions of the principal bourgeois class elements are embodied in the behavior of institutions controlled by these groups. We anticipate, for instance, that transnational subsidiaries will work out their inevitable conflicts with local governments alone or in cooperation with local firms and institutions and that when all else fails, they will submit rather than call upon the political assistance of home governments.[40] If a country finds itself in an international conflict, a local subsidiary of a transnational firm should act so as to promote (or, at any rate, so as not to undercut) the host country's "national interests"—a behavioral maxim that remains operative even if another subsidiary (or the headquarters) of this transnational in the adversary country, guided by the selfsame maxim, is simultaneously promoting *its* host country's interests.[41] Local dominant classes, though approving of foreign investment in principle, should not hesitate at times to challenge their foreign "partners" and should prove adept at building nationalist coalitions around their interests. When intraclass conflict within newly developing countries results in the replacement of traditional (landed or agro-export) bourgeois dominance by that of corporate national or managerial bourgeoisies, the political consequences for the subordinate classes should be progressive. Such a transformation in the nature of class dominance should eventuate in the substitution of constitutionalism for authoritarianism, as in Latin America since 1980, unless the only alternative to authoritarianism is populist chaos.

Case studies of relations between international capitalism and Third World societies have developed, and are still developing, much evidence tending to support these propositions, all of which run counter to the dependency view.[42] Sklar did not work out his paradigmatic conception of world capitalism with the intent of mounting a critique of dependency. I would suggest, rather, that postimperialism has evolved into such a critique and is replacing dependency owing to a better fit between its implications and the case study data.

More abstractly, the idea of postimperialism implies that international capitalism is still developmentally dynamic. Otherwise stated, capitalism on a world scale has proved capable of transforming itself and of bringing about significant material advances in the Third World—which is not to claim that capitalist development is, or will be, everywhere uniform, equitable, and permanent. What is more, the world view of its leading class sectors, together with the margin for compromise made possible by continuing advances in productive (organizational as well as material) technologies, conduces to accommodative strategies for dealing with class conflict.

Postimperialism posits constraints on the powers of the sovereign state but not its disappearance. In a world whose political institutions are based on the anarchy of the state system, all state officials regardless of ideology perceive a need to build up their societies' economic power in order to preserve the immunities of sovereignty. As long as this is so, the task of enlarging a society's material base and expanding its productivity takes precedence over goals of social justice whenever the two are in conflict—precisely the lesson to be learned from the history of "really existing socialism." Capitalism will retain its primacy for years to come because its lack of a theory of social justice is less significant to the "real world of development" than is socialism's lack of a theory of incentive.[43]

Three conclusions follow. First, if capitalism is destined to remain with us for a time, and if the dialectics of intraclass conflict enable the capitalist system to transform itself up to a point, then analysts must give as much attention to this form of conflict as they do to Marxian class struggle. One of the great strengths of postimperialist class analysis is that its attention to subclass interests and world views lays bare the nature and sources of intraclass conflict and relates both directly to political outcomes. Yet the analysis does not ignore the role of class struggle, for there is no claim that the bourgeoisie accommodates to other groups out of altruism. Much to the contrary, accommodation is a response to political pressure from below, when other solutions seem more costly (ideologically or materially) from a capitalist point of view. Since the requirement for periodic accommodations and adjustments also explains transformation in capitalist society, any claim that postimperialism ignores class struggle is without foundation.

Second, the question of development turns not on capitalism versus socialism but on dictatorship versus democracy and the contrasting processes of class formation to which each gives rise.[44] The postimperialist view attributes considerable importance to the fact that most of the world's "really existing socialisms" are class societies whose dominant classes are "bourgeoisoid" in terms of the privileges they seek and the values they uphold, even if their power stems from control of state and party apparatuses, rather than from civil society.[45]

Third, postimperialism is not uncritical. The experience of the developed countries leads one to expect that insofar as the corporate form of international capital continues to expand and entrench itself, the political future points toward oligarchy rather than toward substantive democracy. Postimperialists have no quarrel with the proposition that institutions of corporate power and the private ownership of industry cast a long shadow over corporate liberalism's democratic claims. Liberal constitutionalism may be vastly superior from a progressive standpoint to any form of dictatorship, for the reason that if offers the popular classes a larger theater and greater freedom for autonomous political action; but it is not the final answer to the democratic aspirations of the people at large.

In short, postimperialism is a dialectical theory that portrays international capitalism as a historically evolving system and explains its evolution by probing a series of tensions and contradictions: oligarchy versus democracy, corporate internationalism versus nationalism, the competing aspirations of nation-states at different levels of development, and, by no means least, the class struggle.

TAKING THE STATE BACK OUT?

The compilers of a recent volume of essays, hoping to advance an already evident tendency, exhort us to "bring the state back in" to the study of capitalist development.[46] Liberalism and Marxism alike, it can be argued, have been so absorbed with the dynamics of civil society that they have overlooked the importance of the "pure" political power based upon, and condensed in, state institutions. "Bringing the state back in" means taking account of two facts: that state institutions exert a powerful, sometimes determinant influence on all national and international political interaction, and that state officials hold and act upon specific interests which derive from their institutional positions and which are not neatly reducible to the economic interests associated with dominant classes.

This renewed interest in the state as an independent variable in the analysis of development is closely connected to the popularity of Cardoso's "method" of dependency analysis, for the reasons I have discussed. Since the notion of relative state autonomy is central both to Cardoso's approach and to the wider call for "bringing the state back in," let us briefly explore this concept.

For orthodox Marxists the state in a capitalist order can only be a "capitalist state," that is, a state constrained by the requisites of maintaining the capitalist system and bound to the class interests of the bourgeoisie. The rise of corporate capitalism, however, along with the growing role of the state in managing conflict and thereby heading off the "sharpening of contradictions" which was supposed to bring about the transition to socialism, meant that the state could no longer be conceptualized as an "executive committee for the management of the affairs of the whole [dominant] bourgeoisie"[47]; instead it had to be capable of acting on behalf of other class interests. According to the doctrine of relative state autonomy, the capitalist state is economically constrained to serve the long-term interests of the system's dominant class. Yet maintenance of the system demands that conflicts be resolved (when they arise among different bourgeois "fractions") or be papered over and held at bay (when they involve the bourgeoisie versus the working class), and only the state is institutionally positioned to arrange or oversee the necessary compromises. To do so the capitalist state must have room for maneuver and cannot, therefore, be utterly beholden to the bourgeoisie's immediate interests. Indeed, the state must enjoy a degree of independence from all classes in order to fulfill this function.[48]

The relative autonomy of the state thus gives its officials some freedom (its extent depending on the balance of forces among classes and "fractions" at a particular historical moment) to act in behalf of their own interests and those entailed by interstate competition: to enhance their institutional privileges, say; to enlarge the state's military capabilities; and even, when international power considerations so advise, to impose modernizing ("organizational") revolutions on their societies. The development literature has been enriched by studies of state-guided "revolutions from above"—which serve in the Third World, it is held, to substitute "dependent development" for backwardness.[49]

Reassessing the State and Development

From a progressive standpoint, development studies are a prelude to problem solving; they are not undertaken to acquire "pure" knowledge about an eternal order of things. To shift the state to the focal point of analysis is to imply that the state is centrally bound up with dependency and its "distortion" of the development process. Given such a focus, the remedies suggested by the analysis are likely to be statist. (When *dependencistas* call for a transition to socialism, it is plain that their reference is to state-socialism, that is, to full state control of the economy.) In Latin America, however, statist strategies are falling out of favor with progressives, many of whom are joining their voices to the bourgeois chorus that has been calling for *desburocratización* and *desestatización*.

Latin American political thought was never much affected by Anglo-American liberalism and has remained faithful to the conception of the positive state.[50] Even in those Latin American countries where conservative political forces hold sway, economic planning and welfarism are enshrined in constitutions and statutes. It is no longer possible to ignore, however, that neither planning nor welfarism has touched the condition of the vast majority: the urban masses above all (most of whom are self-employed participants in the "informal economy") and the peasantry. Economic statism's principal beneficiaries are those groups which depend directly on state employment: bureaucrats, teachers, medical doctors, and employees of large parastatal firms.[51]

The new Latin American antistatism, then, is not synonymous with Manchesterian economic liberalism (which has been swiftly rejected wherever it has been tried). A skeptical view of the size and functions of the state is but another legacy of bureaucratic-authoritarianism, whose bureaucratic component was always as prominent as the authoritarian. In addition, a renewed concern with democratic decision making has focused critical attention on the way in which Latin American state bureaucracies churn out reams of regulations and other administrative acts with no input whatever from the public or its elected representatives. The "informal economy" itself has come to be understood as a symptom of rampant statism rather than as a failure of capitalism.[52]

Other developments, too, have contributed to the reassessment by diminishing the concern over state weakness vis-à-vis external forces. Regulating the transnationals is no longer the contentious issue it was a decade or two ago, thanks to better knowledge and mutual understanding.[53] The vexatious problem of the debt remains, but it has not produced the degree of external imposition that was feared. On almost any criterion it is clear that the actions of Latin American states in foreign affairs are decided locally rather than in Washington.[54]

To the above must be added Latin Americans' far more critical attitude toward "really existing socialism." Even though Fidel Castro is still esteemed for his successful defiance of the Colossus of the North, the Cuban model is no longer regarded as worthy of imitation elsewhere; too much is known about the descent of its postrevolutionary economy into a new form of dependence, the disaffection of many of its ordinary citizens, and its persistent violations of basic political and human rights. The deficiencies of the Soviet and Chinese models are equally well understood, and "African socialism" always has seemed irrelevant to Latin American conditions. In contrast, the region's Marxists have been powerfully affected by the democratic currents of Western (especially Italian) Marxism. Under its influence Latin American social thinkers are now beginning to reformulate the socialist project along antistatist lines, with emphasis on further democratization and on the continuing value to a socialist society of small property and market mechanisms.

Toward a Nonstatist Approach to the State

Postimperialism, we have seen, puts forth a class analysis of development that draws attention to the actions of ideological groups. What is more, its treatment of the bourgeoisie comprehends without difficulty the class positions of civilian and military state officials and makes room in the analysis for their particularistic interests. Relative state autonomy thus becomes a redundant concept; it begins to look suspiciously like another Ptolemaic epicycle patched in to "save the appearances" of orthodox Marxism and avoid a needed revision of theory.

In order for development studies to take democratic values seriously, we must admit realistically that all power expands until it encounters countervailing power. This ancient wisdom should redirect our attention toward the constitutionalist principle of checks and balances. We need a better understanding of how, in the newly industrializing countries as well as in our own, conflicts of interest within civil society, within the state, and between the two can limit both the ability of any one social force to use the state for its own exclusive ends and the ability of the state to impose its will undemocratically on the social order. By searching for that understanding we replace the image of the state as monolith—the "capitalist state"—with a more finely detailed picture in which the state is seen for what it is: a set of institutions united by a common structural position in society, yet divided within itself and from the rest of society by particularities of interest and corresponding belief.

Once we establish ideology as a variable which is not fully determined by the economy, we should be able to combine the foregoing approach with a due appreciation of the state's function in promoting national cohesivess. The keys to such an endeavor, I feel, are found in the new linguistic studies of signification and ideological propagation.

OTHER NEW DEPARTURES IN DEVELOPMENTAL THEORY

Besides postimperialism, two other theoretical currents hold promise for future research on development. The first is the "post-Marxist" turn taken by Ernesto Laclau and Chantal Mouffe, whose studies of Gramsci and modern discourse theory have led them to a blunt rejection of economic determinism in all its forms. The second is the rediscovery of the social movement, implying a political conceptualization of action in everyday life.

Post-Marxism Without Apologies   Political discourse theory is concerned with the process of creation of meaning. Its underlying postulates are that meaning is established and communicated through the social construct we call language and that all language is indefinite owing to its very structure. From these postulates the theory deduces that:

1. Since social orders have no physical existence which can be perceived directly with the senses, they must be interpreted—given meaning—in order for any form of social action to be possible.
2. Since language is indefinite, meaning always is uncertain. Hence, the systems of meaning incorporated within social orders are constantly in flux.
3. Systems of social action are based in part on linguistic mediations. Through such mediations social action continually reproduces and alters meaning.

These theoretical conclusions are important for our understanding of the formation of political groups, the nature and role of interests, and the relation of domination to ideology and social conflict.[55]

The Constitution of Political Subjects Social groups constitute themselves and interact with one another via practices which create or manipulate meanings. When a group creates or manipulates meanings it becomes a political subject, and as such it embodies and reflects a specific element of identity or being which its members ascribe to themselves.[56] There are as many potential subjects as there are elements of being, but only some of them are actualized (that is, are a basis for action). Every actualized subject is associated with a constellation of meanings and referents which together set up both its self-identity and its comprehension of its relationships with other subjects and the physical world. When social agents establish their subjectivity, their members ratify their personal existence, their belonging to a collectivity of people like themselves, and the creativity of being and meaning which marks them as human[57]; figuratively speaking, they *create their world.*

These political subjects are the same as the ideological groups to which postimperialist theory refers. Classes remain theoretically valid as analytical constructs, but they no longer can be regarded as "real" social actors.

The Nature and Significance of Interests Social agents do not have interests of which they are unaware; their interests are "meaning-ful" to them and have been constructed over time through the workings of various social processes. Because interests are bound up with the relations among agents, they are themselves social products and have no existence apart from the consciousness of an agent which holds them.[58]

It follows that "objective interests," too, are nothing more than analytical constructs. They can be used to *interpret* social action in class terms but cannot be held, as orthodoxy does, to be the *cause* of action.

Domination, Ideology, and Social Conflict   Dominant groups use their considerable influence over a society's discourses to articulate the practices of other subjects around their own. They thereby construct an ideological hegemony, that is, they secure their dominance on the basis of voluntary acceptance rather than force.[59] But hegemonic groups stand within the society, not above it, and are immersed in the same discourses as everyone else[60]; their hegemony must be based on their practices and cannot be just a maneuver designed to hoodwink subordinate groups.

If dominance is based on social practices that are effectively shared by subordinate in addition to dominant subjects, and if dominance may rest on a form of consent, only empirical research can disclose whether or not the differential social positions set up by relations of domination have been construed as signifying oppression. Generally they will be so construed only up to a point, and only after the subordinate subjects' internal systems of meaning have incorporated relevant concepts of rights and entitlements.[61]

Studies of development cannot be based on a priori assumptions that social conflicts must take specific forms in accordance with the "objective" character of the groups involved in them. Our research must examine directly the democratic practices and beliefs which convert abstract relations of domination and subordination into relations of felt injustice or oppression.

Social Movements and Everyday Life

Had Marx been a thoroughgoing determinist, it is hard to imagine that he would have devoted so much time to educating workers and helping them organize themselves. In fact, some of the most powerful radical writings are those which detail the drama of resistance to oppression.[62] Such writings teach us that resistance takes place in daily life as well as in the headline-grabbing discourses and actions of formalized groups; they appeal not just to our political sympathies but also to our "commonsensical" appreciation, born of experience and needing no confirmation from theory, that there is no progress unless those who object to the existing social arrangements raise their voices against them.

Curiously, this appreciation of human activity has rarely been extended to the defenders of the existing order—the bourgeoisie. That class is portrayed either as acting out of the crudest, most egocentric kind of self-interest or as the hapless "bearer-victim" of market forces beyond its members' control. Martin J. Sklar asks us to set aside such prejudices and comprehend bourgeois classes

> as social formations changing in time.... [C]apitalists... should be studied ... like, say, workers and farmers, as a social movement.... No less than other classes, the capitalist class consists of associated people with goals, values, ideas, and principles, as well as interests. They are people with a way of life to develop, defend, and extend, based on a definite type of property ownership and labor exploitation, the characteristics of which undergo historical change.[63]

On the one hand, changes in social and economic structures are produced by the action of social movements wrought by people in interaction with each other and their environment. On the other hand, capitalists are "a social class to which social movements pertain as an attribute, just as with any other social class." If we assume that all bourgeois social action is ancillary to the class's activity in the market, we obtain a distorted picture of that social action as a narrow interest-group activity serving instrumentally to protect and legitimize the class's activity in the market. "The effect is to maintain the dichotomy between 'economics' and social movements and politics, or to reduce politics to interest-group pressure activity."[64]

A further complication intrudes. We also cannot assume that bourgeois social movements struggle to maintain an unchanging status quo while popular movements do so to overthrow capitalism. All social movements, irrespective of their class "belonging," act on the basis of beliefs about what is just, actual, and possible.[65] Each movement, even one conducted by subordinate groups in a hegemonic order, draws to some extent on autonomous sources of meaning (the group's customs and traditions, the significance its members give to their past history and current experience) for these beliefs. We therefore have no choice but to seek an empathetic understanding of them as best we can. Close observation of how the group behaves on a daily basis is probably the only way to gain such an understanding, albeit with the difficulty that some of what we observe is also what we hope to explain. That problem, I suspect, is irremediable.

BEYOND DEPENDENCY: A RESEARCH AGENDA

The above considerations suggest that more attention be devoted to specific, often self-identified groups: workers in a particular factory or city, peasants in a particular kind of natural environment, business executives in a particular industry. In parts of Latin America the turn away from sweeping determinism has meant a new attention to studies of just such groups.[66] Latin American academics have told me of their amazement at discovering, as the new research advances, how little they really knew about other members of their own societies.

Richard Sklar's effort to build what he calls "a theory *for* development" concentrates on indigenous, often small-scale institutions that the common people erect as vehicles for their political action. These institutions, he argues, are as important for comprehending the evolution of constitutionalism as is, say, the New England town meeting in the case of the United States; he is convinced that their study will be more fruitful under Third World conditions than descriptions of large-scale social institutions or efforts to rank whole societies as "more" or "less" democratic.[67] Local unions, peasant cooperatives, neighborhood associations, women's clubs, professional guilds, even sports teams are grist for the political analyst's mill.

Among large-scale institutions, political parties merit closer examination than they have tended to receive in recent years. They are among the principal institutions which self-consciously create and propagate hegemonic discourses. But the hegemonic influence of political parties is affected by their leadership, internal organization, and mode of campaigning, not just by their platforms and pronouncements. Such practices, too, bear additional investigation.

Bourgeoisies create many institutions that warrant attention when we study these classes as social movements. To date the inner workings of trade associations have been given relatively short shrift; too often their publications and pronouncements have merely been laid against a set of "objective" interests in hopes of deducing which bourgeois "fraction" can be said to control them. Informal bourgeois institutions—networks encompassing social clubs, regular dinner engagements, *compadrazgo* (godparentage), and the like—are important for class cohesion and the propagation of class ideology; many of them have never been approached by a political analyst. Lastly, increasingly self-confident Latin American bourgeoisies are beginning to set up formal institutions to address larger social questions; here is yet another area that calls out for research.

Given the centrality to capitalism of law, without which contracts and property rights cannot exist, it is surprising that there are so few studies of the development of legal institutions in the Third World. In Latin America, to be sure, laws and lawlike administrative acts often have an arbitrary character under formally democratic regimes as well as under openly authoritarian ones. Yet Latin America's political culture is highly legalistic, and even dictators take pains to cover their actions by referring them to some constitutional provision or piece of legislation.

In every part of the world where they take root, capitalist market systems introduce

> a government subject to law—constitutionalism, written or unwritten—and a government administering the law . . . , without regard to person, in the marketplace. . . . The rise, development, and stability of the capitalist order go hand in hand with the rise of a suitable legal order, which . . . is characterized by public legislation, open courts, universally accessible judicial process. . . .

Consequently,

> [t]here is no society more "political" than . . . capitalist society. The more economic a society becomes, the more political it is bound to be. The more producers are drawn into the market, the more they are drawn into politics. By the same token, . . . legalism . . . rise[s] and develop[s] with the bourgeoisie and capitalist society. A legalistic mentality . . . represents a characteristic mode of consciousness of a . . . capitalist society.[68]

Development research faces promising opportunities in the years ahead. "Modes of consciousness" could well become our watchword as we proceed to explore them.

NOTES

I am profoundly grateful to Frank Bonilla, John Bowman, David Collier, Richard L. Sklar, Virginia E. Swain, and, most of all, Kenneth P. Erickson for their comments on earlier drafts of this essay. It goes without saying that they bear no responsibility for any errors of commission or omission it may still contain.

1. Throughout this essay imperialism means the domination of one national collectivity by another. Any attempt to define imperialism as the outward expansion of capitalism is ideological and prejudges one of the most important questions facing the study of development.

2. It is a tribute to the ideological power of the term that dependency is presented in some of the literature as equivalent to asymmetrical interdependence. This is so whenever "dependency" refers to forms of external domination and exploitation which, because they are not reflected in the social structure, can be overcome through more adroit policy choices, institutional reforms, or comparable means.

3. J. A. Hobson, *Imperialism* (New York: Pott, 1902); V. I. Lenin, *Imperialism, the Highest Stage of Capitalism* (1917), rev. trans. (New York: International, 1933); Rudolf Hilferding, *Finanz Kapital* (Vienna, 1910); Rosa Luxembourg, *Die Akkumulation des Kapitals* (Berlin: Buchhandlung Vorwärts Paul Singer, 1913).

4. So numerous are the publications that attempt to verify or falsify systemic dependency arguments that bibliographic essays have been written in hopes of sorting them out. The following is merely a sampling of works that cast doubt upon systemic dependency claims; omission from the list implies no judgment on my part, nor does inclusion signify my agreement. On a variety of such claims: Raymond Vernon, *Storm over the Multinationals* (Cambridge, Mass.: Harvard University Press, 1977); also Robert R. Kaufman, Harry I. Chernotsky, and Daniel S. Geller, "A Preliminary Test of the Theory of Dependency," *Comparative Politics* 7, no. 3 (1975): 303–30. On the supposed metropolitan interest in preventing industrialization elsewhere: Bill Warren, "Imperialism and Capitalist Industrialization," *New Left Review*, 81 (1973): 3–44. On "unequal exchange": Jacques Delacroix, "The Export of Raw Materials and Economic Growth: A Cross-National Study," *American Sociological Review* 42, no. 4 (1977): 795–808. On claims that foreign investors are uninterested in export development: José de la Torre, "Foreign Investment and Export Dependency," *Economic Development and Cultural Change* 23, no. 1 (1974): 133–50. On a number of arguments that integration with the world economy weakens local economic actors: Charles Ragin and Jacques Delacroix, "Comparative Advantage, the World Division of Labor, and Underdevelopment," in Robert F. Tomasson, ed., *Comparative Social Research* vol. 2 (Greenwich, Conn.: JAI Press, 1979), 181–214.

5. We know that everywhere and in every era capitalist development brings increased inequality of income and wealth in its early stages. What we don't know is whether inequality is worse today. Some authorities who have examined the available data doubt that such is the case: Giuseppi C. Ruggeri and Chris A. Jecchinis, "Economic Growth and Living Standards in the Americas," *Review of Social Economy* 32, no. 2 (1974): 148–161; Felix Paukert, "Income Distribution at Different Levels of Development: A Survey of Evidence," *International Labour Review* 108, no. 2–3 (1973): 97–105. Sanjaya Lall, "Is 'Dependence' a Useful Concept in Analysing Underdevelopment?" *World Development* 3, no. 11–12 (1975): 799–810, properly criticizes dependency writers for overlooking this issue.

6. Fernando Henrique Cardoso and Enzo Faletto, *Dependency and Development in Latin America*, trans. Majority Mattingly Urquidi (Berkeley: University of California Press, 1979). Also Cardoso, *Ideologías de la burguesía industrial en sociedades dependientes* (México, D.F.: Siglo XXI, 1971); and "Associated-Dependent Development: Theoretical and Practical Implications," in Alfred Stepan, ed., *Authoritarian Brazil* (New Haven, Conn.: Yale University Press, 1973), 142–76.

7. Gabriel Palma, "Dependency: A Formal Theory of Underdevelopment or a Methodology for the Analysis of Concrete Situations of Underdevelopment?" *World Development* 6, no. 7–8 (1978): 881–924, related Cardoso's work to the same concerns and assumptions that already were present in the debates among Lenin, Luxemburg, Hilferding, Kautsky, and others.

8. Paul A. Baran, *The Political Economy of Growth* (New York: Monthly Review Press, 1957); André Gunder Frank, *Capitalism and Underdevelopment in Latin America*, rev. ed. (New York: Monthly Review Press, 1969); Frank, *Lumpenbourgeoisie: Lumpendevelopment: Dependence, Class, and Politics in Latin America* (New York: Monthly Review Press, 1973).

9. Fernando Henrique Cardoso, "The Consumption of Dependency Theory in the United States," *Latin American Research Review* 12, no. 3 (1977): 7–24.

10. For example, working-class fractions that depend on employment with foreign-owned firms (their members usually receive wages much higher than the national average) may "become dissociated from the mass popular pressures" against dependency, and this dissociation may "to some extent cushion the pressure from below" (Cardoso and Faletto, *Dependency and Development*, 164–165). Meanwhile, bourgeois "fractions" in the domestic economy may be among the most vociferous opponents of dependent relations.

11. Cardoso thus anticipated the devastating critique of dependency theory offered by Bill Warren, "Imperialism and Capitalist Industrialization" and *Imperialism, Pioneer of Capitalism* (London: New Left Books, 1980). Warren accepted that international capitalism is imperialist and differed only in his assessment of the consequences for the newly industrializing countries.

12. Cardoso and Faletto, *Dependency and Development*, 154–165.

13. Ibid., xx–xxii.

14. Philip J. O'Brien, "A Critique of Latin American Theories of Dependency," in Ivar Oxaal, Tony Barnett, and David Booth, eds., *Beyond the Sociology of Development* (London: Routledge & Kegan Paul, 1975), 7–27, also complains that Cardoso and Faletto (whom he otherwise praises) fail to spell out the mechanisms which produce and reproduce dependency. His criticism differs from mine in that he holds them guilty of circularity, whereas I maintain (see below) that they avoid circularity but at unacceptable cost.

15. The same position is argued more directly by Osvaldo Sunkel, "Big Business and 'Dependencia': A Latin American View," *Foreign Affairs* 50, no. 3 (1972): 517–531.

16. That is, the insistence that classes are defined by relation to ownership and control of the means of production. Cardoso sometimes

considers consumption patterns as a fundamental class interest, especially in the case of the middle class.

17. Cardoso, "Consumption of Dependency Theory." I am grateful to Kenneth P. Erickson for reminding me that Cardoso nonetheless employed quantitative methods on occasion when they suited his purposes; see Cardoso, *Ideologías*.

18. Raúl Prebisch, *Towards a Dynamic Development Policy for Latin America* (New York: United Nations, 1963).

19. For example, Manuel González Prada, *Anarquía* (Santiago de Chile: Ediciones Ercilla, 1936) and *Horas de lucha* (Callao: Tipografía "Lux," 1924); José Martí, *Los Estados Unidos* (Madrid: Sociedad Española de Librería, 1915) and *Martí y la primera revolución cubana* (Buenos Aires: Centro Editor de América Latina, 1971); also José Vasconcelos, *La raza cósmica* (Paris: Agencia Mundial de Librería, n.d. [192?] and *Hispanoamérica frente a los nacionalismos agresivos de Europa y Norteamérica* (La Plata: Universidad de Buenos Aires, 1934).

20. José Carlos Mariátegui, *Siete ensayos de interpretación de la realidad peruana*, 2d ed. (Lima: Editorial Librería Peruana, 1934) and *La escena contemporánea* (Lima: Editorial Minerva, 1925); Víctor Raúl Haya de la Torre, *Por la emancipación de América Latina* (Buenos Aires: M. Gleizer, 1927) and *El antimperialismo y el Apra*, 2d ed. (Santiago de Chile: Ediciones Ercilla, 1936).

21. In the United States prior to 1970, the "Monthly Review school" stood virtually alone in offering a sustained radical critique of capitalist development; see Baran, *Political Economy of Growth*; also Harry Magdoff, *The Age of Imperialism* (New York: Monthly Review Press, 1969). By 1979 critical works by U.S. authors were far too numerous for listing in a single footnote. The following bibliographic essays will serve as a guide to the later literature: James A. Caporaso and Behrouz Zare, "An Interpretation and Evaluation of Dependency Theory," in Heraldo Muñoz, ed., *From Dependency to Development* (Boulder, Colo.: Westview Press, 1981), 43–56; Ronald H. Chilcote, "Dependency: A Critical Synthesis of the Literature," *Latin American Perspectives* 1, no. 1 (1974): 4–29; H. Jeffrey Leonard, "Multinational Corporations and Politics in Developing Countries," *World Politics* 32, no. 3 (1980): 454–83; and Theodore H. Moran, "Multinational Corporations and Dependency: A Dialogue for Dependentistas and Non-Dependentistas," *International Organization* 32, no. 1 (1978): 79–100. A sign of the times was the extended presence on the national best-seller lists of Richard J. Barnet and Ronald E. Müller, *Global Reach* (New York: Simon & Schuster, 1974).

22. Peter Evans, "After Dependency: Recent Studies of Class, State,

and Industrialization," *Latin American Research Review* 20, no. 2 (1985): 149–160.

23. From the preface by myself and Richard L. Sklar to David G. Becker, Jeff Frieden, Sayre P. Schatz, and Richard L. Sklar, *Postimperialism: International Capitalism and Development in the Late Twentieth Century* (Boulder, Colo.: Lynne Rienner Publishers, 1987), ix. Only a few systemic-dependency advocates dispute nowadays the first of these claims (congruence in the Third World between "national interests" and the interests of locally dominant bourgeois groups), but the second claim encounters greater resistance. Some randomly selected evidence which supports it: widespread U.S. business opposition to the Soviet grain embargo; the discomfiture of many large U.S. corporations over pre-*glasnost* efforts to limit technology exports to the Soviet Union; the banking establishment's lack of cooperation with the Baker Plan; the departure of U.S. investors from El Salvador at a time when the United States was trying to shore up that country's conservative regime; and the unanimous opposition of transnational firms with subsidiaries in Nicaragua to Reagan administration policy toward that country. For this last piece of evidence see John F. H. Purcell, "The Perceptions and Interests of U.S. Business in Relation to the Political Crisis in Central America," in Richard E. Feinberg, ed., *Central America: International Dimensions of the Crisis* (New York: York: Holmes & Meier, 1982), 103–123.

24. See the discussion in Kenneth P. Erickson, *The Brazilian Corporative State and Working-Class Politics* (Berkeley: University of California Press, 1977), 188–90. An even more dramatic turn away from economism in favor of a direct concern with political variables is apparent in the latest works of Guillermo O'Donnell, e.g., O'Donnell and Philippe C. Schmitter, *Transitions from Authoritarian Rule: Tentative Conclusions About Uncertain Democracies* (Baltimore: Johns Hopkins University Press, 1986). Cf. O'Donnell, *Modernization and Bureaucratic-Authoritarianism*, Politics of Modernization Series, no. 9 (Berkeley: Institute of International Studies, University of California, 1973), where the explanation for the onset of authoritarian rule in Argentina and Brazil follows exactly the Cardosian argument on dependency.

25. Richard L. Sklar, foreword to David G. Becker, *The New Bourgeoisie and the Limits of Dependency* (Princeton, N.J.: Princeton University Press, 1983), xix.

26. Paul M. Sweezy and Harry Magdoff, "Notes on the Multinational Corporation, *Monthly Review* 21, no. 5 (1969): 5.

27. The term "nonstatist political institution" was coined by Adolph A. Berle, Jr., *The Twentieth Century Capitalist Revolution* (New

York: Harcourt Brace Janovich, 1954), 60; also see Berle, *Power Without Property* (New York: Harcourt Brace Janovich, 1959), 17–24. For an illustrative case study of U.S. corporations' assumption of statelike regulatory functions in the early years of this century, see Martin J. Sklar, *The Corporate Reconstruction of American Capitalism, 1890–1916* (Cambridge: Cambridge University Press, 1988). Chief among these statelike functions is market regulation to avoid crises of overproduction and enforce product standards; such regulation arguably serves the public interest even as it protects oligopoly. To be sure, the apportionment of responsibilities between the state and the network of private corporations varies from one society to the next.

28. The question can be answered positively, and the implications of that answer can be explored, without taking the issue to extremes: *either* the state *or* the corporation. It is entirely possible to conceive a world order in which a system of sovereign states retains its primacy with respect to certain issue areas (such as those involving territorial aggrandizement and defense, and the movement of people), while new, nonstatist institutions attain primacy with respect to other issue areas (such as those involving the movement of capital and goods).

29. Richard L. Sklar, "Postimperialism: A Class Analysis of Multinational Corporate Expansion," *Comparative Politics* 9, no. 1 (1976): 75–92.

30. Richard L. Sklar, "Socialism at Bay: Class Domination in Africa," paper presented at the Joint Meeting of the African Studies Association and the Latin American Studies Association, Houston, November 2–5, 1977 (mimeographed).

31. The point is proven by the complexity and inconclusiveness of the debate within orthodoxy over the class situation of the technicians, professionals, and white-collar employees who depend on private and public bureaucracy. See Eric Olin Wright, *Class, Crisis and the State* (London: Verso, 1979); Val Burris, "The Neo-Marxist Synthesis of Marx and Weber on Class," in Norbert Wiley, ed., *The Marx-Weber Debate* (Newbury Park, Calif.: Sage, 1987), 67–90 (esp. 85–87); and, for a critical appraisal, Jean L. Cohen, *Class and Civil Society* (Amherst: University of Massachusetts Press, 1982), 9–14.

32. A class or class element requires institutional mechanism that create and maintain its cohesion. The corporate international bourgeoisie's transcultural cohesion is maintained by, *inter alia*, the increasingly international composition of transnational corporate managements; the trend toward listing shares of large corporations on several exchanges (New York, London, Hong Kong) in order to encourage

internationalization of ownership; the high lateral mobility between the executive offices of business corporations and those of the other institutions mentioned above; and, as will be seen, the common ideological outlook of corporate liberalism.

33. R. L. Sklar, "Postimperialism," for the overall schema outlined above and for an explication of the corporate international and managerial bourgeoisies; Becker, *New Bourgeoisie*, 330–336, for a discussion of the corporate national bourgeoisie. See also David G. Becker and Richard L. Sklar, "Why Postimperialism?" in Becker et al., *Postimperialism*, 1–18 (esp. 6–8). In a recent private communication Sklar stresses that the relationships among all these bourgeois sectors, or strata, are fluid and do not mark off a rigid hierarchy; to assume in advance a hierarchical ranking on the basis of economic power alone would be to return to economism. He concludes: "For all its diversity, the bourgeoisie—from top to bottom—does have an analytical class identity."

34. Becker and Sklar, "Why Postimperialism?" 11.

35. Neil J. Mitchell, *The Generous Corporation: A Political Analysis of Economic Power* (New Haven, Conn.: Yale University Press, 1989).

36. Richard L. Sklar, *Corporate Power in an African State: The Political Impact of Multinational Mining Companies in Zambia* (Berkeley: Unversity of California Press, 1975), 182–88; also R. L. Sklar, "Postimperialism."

37. Authoritarian regimes by their very nature cannot be kept from economic-statist impositions upon civil society if the rulers decide that this is their best (or only) alternative at a given political juncture; the actions of authoritarian regimes in Argentina, Brazil, Chile, and elsewhere prove the point and further indicate that the regime's proclaimed ideological preferences will be of little import when such a situation arises. Constitutionalism, in contrast, formally guarantees the autonomy that corporate managers insist upon. The latter are not naive; they know how much value to place on a dictatorship's promises.

38. This tolerance extends to "really existing socialism" of the Third World kind, whose true objective is the rapid development of the society's material base rather than the transformation of the world's economic order. "Socialist" Third World states are as eager as their "capitalist" counterparts to gain access to the capital, technology, and market outlets that transnational corporations can provide. Frequently, they offer a "business climate" better than that of unstable capitalist regimes, thanks to greater continuity of political leadership or to the success of their ideology or policies in enhancing social stability. Social stability, in turn, reduces the probability that

the state will need to infringe upon the transnationals' corporate autonomy (see n. 36). Verification comes from the case of Nicaragua during the early years of the Sandinista government; see Purcell "Perceptions and Interests of U.S. Business."

39. The desire for economic activism does not always extend to out-and-out dirigism. In the more industrialized countries of the Third World, a powerful and self-confident corporate national bourgeoisie is beginning to demand that some parastatal enterprises be turned over to private control and that the private sector be given a greater role in economic planning. David G. Becker, "Business Associations in Latin America: The Venezuelan Case," *Comparative Political Studies* 23, no. 1 (1990): 114–138; also Alfred Stepan, "State Power and the Strength of Civil Society in the Southern Cone of Latin America," in Peter B. Evans, Dietrich Rueschemeyer, and Theda Skocpol, eds., *Bringing the State Back In* (Cambridge: Cambridge University Press, 1985), 317–343.

40. "Good corporate citizenship" means obedience to local law and business custom. Transnational subsidiaries attempt to influence the political process in behalf of their interests, but they limit themselves to the same tools that local firms use (and often act through the same political institutions). Sometimes the subsidiaries violate certain local laws (e.g., tax and currency-exchange regulations) if local businesses do so and go unpunished, although the subsidiaries' greater visibility usually makes them more cautious. The point is that subsidiaries behave neither better nor worse than comparable locally owned firms and, allowing for local differences, do the same in their home countries.

41. The apparent incoherence actually serves overall corporate interests by legitimizing the firm's presence in each host country and is justified by the ideological separation of "politics" from "economics."

42. R. L. Sklar, *Corporate Power*; Becker, *New Bourgeoisie*; David G. Becker, "Development, Democracy, and Dependency in Latin America: A Post-imperialist View," *Third World Quarterly* 6, no. 2 (1984): 411–431; Henricus J. Stander III and David G. Becker, "Postimperialism Revisited: The Venezuelan Wheat Import Controversy of 1986," *World Development* 18, no. 2 (1990): 197–213; Rhys Payne, "Transnational Capitalism and Structural Adjustment in North Africa," paper presented at the Fourteenth World Congress of the International Political Science Association, Washington, D.C., September 1, 1988 (mimeographed). Furthermore, it appears that the findings of some studies which have been said to confirm Cardosian dependency propositions can be interpreted

equally well or better within a postimperialist context. One example is the fine study of Brazilian development since 1964 by Peter Evans, *Dependent Development* (Princeton, N.J.: Princeton University Press, 1979); see my comments in David G. Becker, "Postimperialism: A First Quarterly Report," in Becker et al., *Postimperialism*, 203–225 (esp. 209).

43. Richard L. Sklar, "Beyond Capitalism and Socialism in Africa," *Journal of Modern African Studies* 25, no. 1 (1988): 1–21. Welfarism is not a theory of social justice because it was not and cannot be derived from basic capitalist principles of markets and property rights. It is an ad hoc accommodation to class pressures which the theory of capitalism does not recognize.

44. The notion that development is a "great competition" between capitalism and socialism is put forward by Sayre P. Schatz, "Postimperialism and the Great Competition," in Becker et al., *Postimperialism*, 193–201. His argument is countered by R. L. Sklar, "Beyond Capitalism and Socialism."

45. Richard L. Sklar, "Developmental Democracy," *Comparative Studies in Society and History* 29, no. 4 (1987): 686–714.

46. Evans, Rueschmeyer, and Skocpol, *Bringing the State Back In*.

47. Karl Marx and Friedrich Engels, *Manifesto of the Communist Party*, trans. Samuel Moore (New York: International, 1932).

48. An instrumentalist version of the doctrine was put forward by Ralph Miliband, *The State in Capitalist Society* (New York: Basic Books, 1969). Nicos Poulantzas countered with a structuralist version which he explicated in "The Problem of the Capitalist State," *New Left Review*, 58 (1969): 67–78; *Political Power and Social Classes*, trans. Timothy O'Hagan (London: New Left Books, 1973); and *Classes in Contemporary Capitalism*, trans. David Fernbach (London: New Left Books, 1975). The debate between the two was carried on in Ralph Miliband, "Poulantzas and the Capitalist State," *New Left Review*, 82 (1973): 83–92, and in Nicos Poulantzas, "The Capitalist State: A Reply to Miliband and Laclau," *New Left Review*, 95 (1976): 63–83.

49. Ellen Kay Trimberger, "A Theory of Elite Revolutions," *Studies in Comparative International Development* 7, no. 3 (1972): 191–207; Trimberger, *Revolution from Above* (New Brunswick, N.J.: Transaction Books, 1978); Theda Skocpol, *States and Social Revolutions* (Cambridge: Cambridge University Press, 1979); and Evans, *Dependent Development*. Much of the theory of "revolution from above" is prefigured (albeit without reference to "relative state autonomy") in Barrington Moore, Jr., *Social Origins of Dictator-*

ship and Democracy: Lord and Peasant in the Making of the Modern World (Boston: Beacon Press, 1966).

50. Bill Jordan, *The State: Authority and Autonomy* (Oxford: Basil Blackwell, 1985), 105–107.

51. In Peru, for example, the most militantly statist political institution is SUTEP, the union of public school teachers. It is followed closely by CITE, the union of state employees, and by the guild of state-employed physicians. Only by an ideological manipulation or language can such groups (whose grievances are nonetheless real) be labeled "popular" or "proletarian."

52. In the sense that "informality" is largely a response to the overly burdensome regulations which are imposed on "formal" businesses.

53. Sayre P. Schatz, "Assertive Pragmatism and the Multinational Enterprise," *World Development* 9, no. 1 (1981): 93–105; also Barbara C. Samuels II, *Managing Risk in Developing Countries: National Demands and Multinational Response* (Princeton, N.J.: Princeton University Press, 1990). Admittedly, changing economic conditions are relevant here as well: the postwar boom of U.S. overseas investment being well behind us, it is now plain that no Latin American economy has suffered, or is threatened by, "denationalization."

54. Which is not to claim that the Latin Americans can freely ignore U.S. concerns. Because the United States looms so large in the external environment with which the makers of Latin American foreign policies have to deal, its presence inevitably affects the decisions that are taken. The same has been true since the dawn of international relations, however, of small states located close to powerful neighbors; the small states' problem is not a product of capitalism and, for that reason, would not be solved or mitigated by a more radical nationalism. Besides, Latin American states, irrespective of political complexion, have shown in recent years a growing willingness openly to defy the United States when their national interests so require. The examples include Brazil's sales of military equipment to Libya; Argentina's decisions to sell grain to the USSR during the Carter boycott and to go to war against Britain over the Malvinas; and, most dramatic of all, the ability of such truly weak states as Honduras, Costa Rica, and Panama to frustrate thoroughly U.S. policy toward Central America.

55. Ernesto Laclau and Chantal Mouffe, *Hegemony and Socialist Strategy: Towards a Radical Democratic Politics* (London: Verso, 1985); Laclau and Mouffe, "Post-Marxism Without Apologies," *New Left Review*, 166 (1987): 79–106; Carlos Franco, "Los sujetos

sociales y el movimiento por el socialismo," *Socialismo y Participación*, 20 (1982): 81–103.

56. "Element of being" describes any of those aspects of our existence which may conceivably serve as a basis of identification with (or differentiation from) others.

57. Mikhail Bakhtin, *Problems of Dostoevski's Poetics*, ed. and trans. Caryl Emerson (Minneapolis: University of Minnesota Press, 1984), esp. 287–293; Bakhtin, "The Problem of Speech Genres," in his *Speech Genres and Other Late Essays*, ed. Caryl Emerson and Michael Holquist, trans. Vern McGee (Austin: University of Texas Press, 1986), 94.

58. Laclau and Mouffe, "Post-Marxism," 96–97.

59. Joseph V. Femia, *Gramsci's Political Thought* (Oxford: Clarendon Press, Oxford University Press, 1981), 24–45. Femia also makes the important point that most hegemonic practices are not planned for the purpose but are undertaken for other ends; such practices acquire a hegemonic content when they happen to interact with the social system of meaning at a particular time and place in a way that generates consent. In its discursive aspect, the production of hegemony depends on the ideological content of the "second-order" (symbolic) meanings made possible by linguistic mechanisms such as polysemy and figures of speech; see Laclau and Mouffe, "Post-Marxism," 100–101.

60. Gramsci used expressions like "popular religion" and "collective will" to express this idea. See Antonio Gramsci, *The Modern Prince and Other Writings* (New York: International, 1957), esp. "The Southern Question," 28–51 and, "The Modern Prince," 135–88; Gramsci, *Selections from the Prison Notebooks*, trans. and ed. Quintin Hoare and Geoffrey Nowell Smith (New York: International, 1971); Femia, *Gramsci's Political Thought*, esp. 192–95; Chantal Mouffe, "Hegemony and Ideology in Gramsci," in Mouffe, ed., *Gramsci and Marxist Theory* (London: Routledge & Kegan Paul, 1979), 168–204.

61. Laclau and Mouffe, *Hegemony*, 153–156.

62. For example, Eric J. Hobsbawm, *Primitive Rebels* (New York: Norton, 1959); E. P. Thompson, *The Making of the English Working Class* (London: Gollancz, 1963); James C. Scott, *Weapons of the Weak* (New Haven, Conn.: Yale University Press, 1985).

63. M. J. Sklar, *Corporate Reconstruction*, 2–3.

64. Ibid., 11–12, 13–14.

65. For instance, a Peruvian study of working-class militancy shows that militants' demands, even when expressed through radical politics, may be motivated by nothing more than desires for respectful human treatment on the job and a living wage; and that militancy

may disappear without the demands being met if other options, such as self-employment, are available. The study also demonstrates that many workers believe in individual advancement through effort and that their "common sense" of justice allows for inequality if merited through hard work or education. See Jorge Parodi, *"Ser obrero es algo relativo..."*: *Obreros, clasismo y política* (Lima: Instituto de Estudios Peruanos, 1986).

66. The trend is well advanced in Peruvian studies, the area of the discipline I know best. The following works are representative: On the peasantry, Marisol de la Cadena, "Cooperación y mercado en la organización comunal andina," Documentos de Trabajo, Serie Antropología, no. 1 (Lima: Instituto de Estudios Peruanos, 1985). On the working class: Parodi, *"Ser obrero es algo relativo..."*. On urban migrants: Susan B. Lobo, *Tengo casa propia* (Lima: Instituto de Estudios Peruanos and Instituto Indigenista Americano, 1984); José Matos Mar, *Desborde popular y crisis del Estado* (Lima: Instituto de Estudios Peruanos, 1984); Teresa Tovar Samanez, "Vecinos pobladores en la crisis (1980–1984)," in Eduardo Ballón ed., *Movimientos sociales y crisis* (Lima: DESCO, 1986), 115–164; and Anthony Leeds and Elizabeth Leeds, "Accounting for Behavioral Differences: Three Political Systems and the Responses of Squatters in Brazil, Peru, and Chile," in John Walton and Louis H. Masotti eds., *The City in Comparative Perspective* (New York: Halsted Press, Wiley, 1976), 193–248. On women: Albert O. Hirschman, *Getting Ahead Collectively* (New York: Pergamon Press, 1984), 13–18.

67. R. L. Sklar, "Developmental Democracy."

68. M. J. Sklar, *Corporate Reconstruction*, 86–88.

Chapter

7

The State in Contemporary Africa

A Critical Assessment of Theory and Practice

Edmond J. Keller

In the past decade political scientists have rediscovered the concept of the state as a key to understanding the dynamics of politics. Like so many conceptual schemes in an academic discipline, it has seen its "star" rise and fall as the discipline moved through periods in which one paradigm or another assumed temporary predominance.[1] Today studies of the state are back in style and are the subject of lively debates among scholars of various intellectual and methodological persuasions.[2] The most critical points of debate center on the nature of the state, its actual or potential autonomy, and its capacity and performance in policy making. Nowhere is the debate over the state and state-centered research more vigorous than among Africanists.[3]

The current concern of Africanists with the role of the state in contemporary politics is largely a by-product of the emergence of political economy as the dominant paradigm in the study of development. Marxists, neo-Marxists, and pluralists alike have begun to focus on the state as a central actor in the processes of political and economic change.[4] Whereas the state had previously been considered nothing more than an epiphenomenon, an arena of political competition and conflict, it is now being widely viewed as managed by a self-interested class that acts not only on behalf of the common good, but also for self-preservation, self-aggrandizement, and hegemonic power.

Africanists are now asking questions such as: Do states exist in Africa? If they do, how did they emerge? What do they look like? What are their respective goals? How are they organized? How do they perform and with what effect? Are they autonomous or dependent? How do they relate to their domestic and external environments? Are the personal predilections of African leaders or their ideological preferences important determinants of their political behavior?

Some scholars caution against too heavy an emphasis on the state and state-centered research. Robert Fatton argues that the focus on the African state as a catalyst for change is misplaced and that at this time class analysis is more relevant.[5] Rothchild and Chazan call for a more balanced perspective centered not solely on the state but on the state's relations with society.[6] Jackson and Rosberg doubt whether African states can meet the empirical definition of the state based on its ability to exercise control over the citizenry under its jurisdiction. For them, African states exist more as juridically defined entities than anything else.[7] Ayoade argues that some African states have so little vitality that they can best be described as "bedridden," "comatose," or "expired." [8] While not denying the importance of the state in political and economic analysis, Claude Ake questions whether we can properly speak of the state in postcolonial Africa, since it possesses only limited autonomy or hegemony. What we have in Africa today, he suggests, are "states in formation."[9]

This chapter attempts to evaluate and to place in some perspective the current Africanist focus on the state. We need to cut through the confusion and take stock of what we know and don't know about how African states are organized and how they function. Although there is now a wealth of literature claiming to help us understand the African state and its role, there is no clear-cut model or theory of the African state. We are still at the pre-theory stage of development in our thinking. Critical analyses and case studies of the literature may yield some broad generalizations that could form the basis for some middle-range theories.

This chapter is divided into two main parts. The first identifies and assesses the most common themes deriving from the literature on political economy that relate to the concept of the state in modern Africa, its origins, its organization, and its performance. The second outlines a descriptive model of the African state of the future. The discussion concludes with suggestions for further research.

THE MODERN AFRICAN STATE

In the lexicon of political science there is no consensus on a definition of the "state." In fact, over a hundred different meanings have been suggested.[10] However, with the resurgence of state-centered research, scholars of various ideological and epistemological persuasions have attempted to come up with refined conceptualizations of the state. Steven Krasner identifies four main elements in a concept of the state: government, administrative apparatus and institutionalized legal order, ruling class, and normative order.[11] Otwin Marenin identifies four different themes: manager, provider of fundamental societal needs, unitary actor, and part of society.[12] Rothchild and Olorunsola reduce the African state to two primary functional elements: manager and controller.[13] The list goes on. For instance, Howard Lentner has countered Krasner's scheme with his own ten-element scheme.[14] Rather than clarifying matters, the proliferation of efforts to streamline the conceptualization of the state in general and the African state in particular could result in even further confusion.

However, despite occasional confusion, there appears now to be widespread agreement among scholars that the state is more than just "government" and that it exists at two fundamental levels: the concrete and the abstract.[15] At the concrete level it is represented in a juridically defined, sovereign territory, in governmental institutions, and in the political organizations used by those who govern to achieve the goals of the regime. At the abstract level the state is represented in its ideology. That ideology is articulated in a regime's political rhetoric, in the language of the rules governing relations between state and society, and among citizens.

In the 1950s and 1960s, when the structural-functionalist and systems theory paradigms were in their heyday among comparativists, the state was seen as nothing more than a mechanism for processing societal demands by turning them into policies and as a mechanism for managing, regulating, and adjudicating the behavior of the citizenry.[16] This approach has been described by Lemarchand as "antistatist."[17] It assumed that variants of Western democratic and capitalist organization could be effectively grafted onto African and other developing societies and that the legacy of colonialism would be of no enduring consequence.[18] These scholars recognized the fragility of the new African states and their new political and economic institutions, but they assumed that Africa could follow the West and build strong, new nations from artificially created colonial states. The role of government or the state, then, was merely to pursue policies intended to result in the political, social, and economic integration of disparate, constituent groups.[19] Despite the neatness of the structural-functional paradigm as a conceptual scheme, scholars quickly realized that it was seriously flawed, being static and ethnocentric. The model was of little help in understanding the dynamics of change in the Third World.

By the early 1970s, the structural-functional and systems theory perspectives were being vigorously challenged, mostly by the intellectual left. Some of the challengers questioned the ahistorical, ethnocentric orientation of these approaches and their failure to recognize the profound effect of the "weight of history" and the impact of colonial domination in the contemporary Third World. The initial assault was led by neo-Marxist adherents of the *dependencia*, underdevelopment theory and world systems schools of thought.[20] Despite their frequent dogmatism and bias toward economic determinism, these approaches highlighted the importance of history in determining the character of the political economy of underdeveloped societies, thus avoiding a serious pitfall of the structural-functional and systems theory approaches. Colonialism was found to have laid the foundation not only for the character of the relations of new states with the world community, but also for the broad outlines of their domestic political economies.

Africanists borrowed the conceptual framework of dependency theory from radical structuralist students of Latin America.[21] They portrayed the neocolonial state in Africa as devoid of an indigenous ruling class and controlled and manipulated by the metropolitan bourgeoisie. A local dominant class facilitated the continued exploitation of the domestic economy by the neocolonial, peripheral state apparatus.[22] These states were extremely vulnerable and dependent upon the persistence of close relationships with external interests. The primary weakness of many studies that use the dependency theory approach is their lack of empirical grounding. They tend to assert, rather than prove, the points that they make and therefore are limited in their utility as analytic tools.[23]

Although dependency theory must be given credit for recognizing the importance of history in structuring contemporary political economy, it was generally weak on historical analysis. This weakness is somewhat circumvented in the world systems approach, but the limitation of the latter perspective for the student of African politics is that it focuses mostly on the dynamics of the *international* political economy. Underdevelopment theory persuasively established "how Europe underdeveloped Africa" and how the structure of the neocolonial African state was created.[24] Students of neo-Marxian class analysts, such as Markovitz and Ake,[25] and developmental policy analysis, such as Rothchild and Curry and Bates,[26] however, have done the most to broaden and refine our understanding of the modern African state and how it relates to its domestic environment and the international environment.

Borrowing from Hamza Alavi's theory on the emergence of the postcolonial state in Pakistan and Bangladesh,[27] John Saul suggests three defining characteristics of the contemporary African state. First, the postcolonial African state was created by the metropolitan bourgeoisie because that class needed an administrative apparatus it could control while the local administrative state in turn controlled the indigenous population. Second, the postcolonial state has a special role in promoting and manipulating the indigenous economy. Third, in post-colonial societies capitalist hegemony must be maintained by the African state once it assumes political power.[28] Claude Ake furthers this argument, claiming that the modern African state is a creature of the capitalist mode of production and as such is a specific modality of class domination.[29] Acceptance into the dominant political class is conceived as a reward to those who hold power because of the role they play in commodity exchange.

Saul, Ake, and other neo-Marxist Africanists conceive of the state as being controlled and manipulated by a dominant (if not ruling) class. The notion of a self-interested "state class" that staffs the central bureaucratic and political apparatus and autonomously pursues various goals and objectives has sparked lively scholarly debate. Such an idea stands in sharp contrast to the views of functionalist scholars who see the state as nothing more than an arena of political competition and conflict or "government," an action agency whose only mission is pursuit of the common good.[30] Radical structuralists have made us sensitive to the fact that the state is more than just government. This is particularly evident when we consider the context in which modern African states emerged and continue to function.

Modern African states are syncretic phenomena at both the concrete and abstract levels. They inherited many of their organizational structures and institutions from their former colonizers, and their ideological foundations are blends of traditional, foreign, and recently derived indigenous value systems.[31] Several recent case studies employing what may be termed a historical sociology or political economy approach have greatly enhanced our understanding of how the historical experience and contemporary context bear upon the states' character and behavior.[32]

At a fundamental level the modern African state appears to be a top-heavy administrative state.[33] It has been variously described as "overdeveloped,"[34] "swollen,"[35] "superimposed,"[36] and "absolutist."[37] However, it is now clear that throughout Africa, the heavy-handed, authoritative image projected by the state is more evidence of weakness than of power. Crawford Young notes that "there is a prime contradiction of the contemporary state, it is at once hard and distant, soft and permeable. In its habits and operating modes, the state reflects the inertial perpetuation of the colonial past; in its command style, the domination that gave it birth still persists.[38]

Rather than being born with power, authority, and legitimacy, the contemporary African state, with few exceptions (Swaziland, Botswana, Mauritius) has been consumed with attempting to establish its hegemony and right to rule. The administrative norms that guided the colonial state quickly proved insufficient to enhance the effectiveness of rulership in the new states. In its quest for hegemony and "hardness," the tendency has been for the state to suppress or ignore Weberian bureaucratic norms.[39]

In a context where it has few political and economic resources that could allow it to purchase legitimacy, the tendency has been for the African state—no matter what its ideology —to be preoccupied with trying to establish its security, control, and autonomy. Consequently, the personalization of rulership has become the rule.[40] Thomas Callaghy terms this the emergence of the "patrimonial administrative state."[41] African leaders have patrimonialized the states bequeathed to them by their colonial predecessors, and corruption has become a defining feature of contemporary politics. Politics has become more like business. Political power is the vehicle to economic power, and political resources tend to be reduced to economic ones. Under such circumstances political power is not sought for its own sake but for the material advantage it promises.[42] Although Zaire is often characterized as the quintessential "cleptocracy,"[43] patrimonialism and corruption are used as political resources throughout Africa. Richard Joseph, in his important book on democracy in Nigeria, identifies what he terms "prebendalism" at the center of that country's politics.[44] In general usage, the term "prebend" refers to offices of feudal states that could be obtained in recognition of services rendered to a noble person, or through outright purchase, and then utilized to generate income for the holders of such offices. As used by Joseph, the term refers to patterns of political behavior based upon the assumption that the offices of the existing state may be competed for and then used for the personal benefit of the officeholders and their supporters. This condition is characterized by the intense struggle among various segments of society to control and exploit offices of the state. Graft and corruption are part and parcel of everyday political life at all levels.

Such patterns reveal the vulnerability and weakness of the state in most of Africa. In terms of its monopoly over the means of coercion, the African state tends to be strong relative to other segments of society, but in terms of its ability to ensure voluntary and regular compliance to rules and policies, it tends to be "soft."

Borrowing from Gunnar Myrdal, Goren Hyden has suggested three main features of the "soft state": "the circumvention of laws and regulations by officials and the inconsistent application of policies and laws; secret collusion between civil servants and politicians whose task it is to supervise the implementation of policies; use of corruption to secure objectives other than those officially stated."[45] The soft state operates in the context of resource scarcity, with persistent claims emanating from ethnically based and other corporate groups in the domestic environment. It tends to lack the reservoir of resources that are essential to enable it to respond effectively to uncertainties during the processes of change and modernization.

Naomi Caiden and Aaron Wildavsky have noted that what distinguishes poor countries from rich ones is the formers' lack of "resource redundancy."[46] Poor countries like the ones we find in Africa generally lack reserves of the types of resources needed to guard against uncertainty in policymaking such as hard currency, skilled work force, and appropriate technology. The policies these soft states pursue are usually sufficient only to ensure the survival of the regime. Even when the state is able to engage in rational planning, it often cannot ensure citizen compliance. Under such conditions it is common for significant segments of the populace, particularly in areas outside the capital city, to exercise their "exit option" and to become disengaged from the state.[47] They ignore the regime's policy directives, rules, and regulations and turn inward, preferring to deal with the state through political patrons, if at all.

Another common occurrence is for large segments of the general population to engage in parallel or informal economies based upon smuggling, unregulated manufacturing enterprises, and forms of corruption.[48] Perhaps more importantly, it is common for public servants, from the lowest to the highest echelons, to be engaged in such practices as petty entrepreneurs. Chazan holds that,

> The initial capital for these activities is frequently provided by monies siphoned off from the formal economy. Corruption, bribery and embezzlement are essential features of the parallel market. However, as informal structures are solidified and reproduced, capital is also being accumulated and reinvested in this sector independently. . . . The informal economy is a complex response to either opportunities presented by state engagement in the market or the inadequacies and frailties of state economic structures.[49]

The limited resource capacity of most African states moves them toward varying degrees of authoritarian control. In some instances, such as in Ethiopia, regimes attempt to legitimate their authoritarian rule by introducing new ideological forms that emphasize national and class unity. In others, such as Amin's Uganda or Bokassa's Central African Empire, control is valued above all else.[50]

The efforts of regimes aimed at state consolidation, national political integration, and social and economic development all are designed to reinforce state authority. A facade of democracy is in some cases maintained through one-party systems, but there are few instances of unfettered democratic interparty or intraparty competition. The party is used merely as an instrument for state control and for the reward of political patrons.[51] In other instances military dictatorships obtain, and they rule with a combination of raw force and patrimonialism. In 1990 at least twenty-seven of Africa's fifty-five states were governed by regimes which had their origins in a military coup.

Potential opponents of the state are often coopted into what might be called the "state class" and allowed to enrich themselves through public office. In other words, public office is seen as a quasi-legitimate vehicle to personal economic benefits. This tendency is reflected in the dramatic growth in African public bureaucracies. Young notes that by 1982 the average fraction of the gross domestic product commanded by the public sector in many African countries was more than 30 percent, and in places like Zaire it was as much as 59 percent.[52] African regimes are prone to overstaffing their central bureaucracies in hopes of enhancing both their administrative efficiency and statist control over society. The employees of those bureaucracies tend to be better paid than most other members of society and are accorded the best housing, medical care, and other social amenities to be offered.[53]

African societies are generally characterized by weak, monoculture economies based upon commodity production for export. The industrial manufacturing sector is poorly developed because of its historic emphasis on import substitution and represents a huge drain on scarce foreign exchange because of current attempts to diversify and modernize it. Moreover, the tax bases of African states are extremely limited, and tax collection inefficient. Consequently they rely inordinately on foreign assistance, commodity trade, and international borrowing to supply the necessary capital to satisfy the appetite of members of the state class for the trappings of modern privilege and power, to finance the activities of the public bureaucracy and the military, and to pursue developmental objectives. Indebted industrialization, neglect of agricultural development, failure to diversify the economy, expensive social reforms, cleptocracy, developmental "gigantomania," and indebted militarization all add up to economic crisis.[54] Most African states are mired in debt, and this compounds the soft state syndrome.

No matter what their political or economic ideological orientation, African states are generally more involved in their economies than is common in Western societies. They have been variously described as "neomercantilist"[55] or "mercantilist states in the making."[56] Callaghy cogently notes that "In the basic mercantilist equation of African state formation, the key element in the search for sovereignty and unification is power, the basis of power is wealth, and the foundations of wealth are foreign exchange and economic development. The crucial link between foreign exchange and economic development is external trade."[57]

The extensive involvement of African governments in the economy through parastatal bodies also contributes to the bloating of the budget and size of the public sector. After independence, it was common for leaders of African states, no matter what their ideological persuasion, to choose to involve the state in promoting, manipulating, and leading development. The vehicles for achieving this end were public enterprises. Larry Diamond, for example, notes that "Zambia had 134 parastatal bodies in 1970, Nigeria 250 by 1973, Tanzania about 400 by 1981."[58] It is estimated that between 1970 and 1980 at least twenty sub-Saharan African countries had an average of 100 parastatal bodies each.

In the African political arena the most significant class is the state class. The state class is composed of the reigning political authorities, the central bureaucracy and its regional functionaries, the top echelons of the military, and members of, where it exists, the dominant political party. For the most part African class systems are only in the process of formation. Kinship and ethnic affinities continue to be extremely significant in determining political dynamics. Yet ethnicity and "tribalism" are not what Western scholars once thought them to be.

Three decades ago many people assumed that "tribalism" could explain the political motivations and behavior of Africans. Initially scholars, such as Clifford Geertz, Leo Kuper, and M. G. Smith, argued that ethnic affinities were primordially based and that ethnic groups tended to be locked in hard and fast categories based on factors such as language, religion, race and/or assumed blood ties.[59] It was thought that constituent ethnic groups were made to cohere by the coercive authority of the colonial state. Intergroup conflicts, when they occurred, were conveniently labeled "tribal conflicts," without much attention being given to understanding the fundamental origins of the conflicts. There is no doubt that the political attitudes and behavior of some ethnic struggles we find in Africa today are primordially based, but such instances are rare.

A revisionist school of thought on the political saliency of the ethnic factor in Africa, while acknowledging the significance of ethnicity, suggests new interpretations of the fundamental forces underpinning contemporary incidents of ethnic conflict.[60] The argument made is that instead of being based on primordial sentiments, the politicizing of ethnicity is often based on the competition among various groups over the scarce resources of the modernizing sectors. I refer to this phenomenon as the "new ethnicity."[61] Although kith and kin in rural areas continue to be important reference groups for urban-based relatives, ethnic competition occurs most frequently in the cities and towns and involves friction over economic resources, such as jobs, patronage, education, and so forth. Furthermore, revisionists argue that ethnicity, when found to be a factor affecting individual and group political behavior, is fluid, intermittent, and experiential.[62]

Traditionally, in most parts of Africa people organized themselves along clan and not tribal lines. The clan was considered the terminal community. But with the advent of colonialism, it became common for groups to be identified (and eventually for them to identify themselves) in terms of an expanded ethnic community that came to be known as the tribe.[63] First the colonial state and then the independent state in Africa contributed greatly to the emergence of a modern, expanded conception of ethnic identity. However, revisionists appreciate the fact that the new ethnicity is not always the primary determinant of political action. Often, competition is based on clan identities and results in intraethnic rather than interethnic or tribal conflict. What seems to determine the scope of the individual's ethnic reference group at a given time are the nature of the stakes involved and the nature of the existing political climate. For example, the various clans of the Kikuyu in Kenya regularly compete through political patrons and communally based organizations over the delivery of social services from the central government. But when, for one reason or another, the political climate begins to emit cues that force individuals from various clans of a larger ethnolinguistic group to identify more closely with one another, the change in fundamental allegiance has been dramatic. For instance, in 1968 when Tom Mboya, a prominent Luo politician was killed by a Kikuyu, the Kikuyu clans, as a group, felt threatened and began to organize for possible collective action as an expanded ethnic community.[64]

Ethnically based political action today is clearly intermittent. Individuals and groups may act on the basis of individual preferences at one time, make choices based on clan considerations at another, and even decide to base behavior on class considerations at still another time. The scope and intensity of political competition based on ethnic identification is most often determined by how ethnic patrons active in the modern political arena define political situations with national implications. It is important to note, however, that the new ethnicity is not always politically relevant.

Revisionists acknowledge that social class as well as ethnicity could form the basis for political action in modern Africa; but it is neo-Marxist students of class analysis who have done most to try to factor social class into the context of political relations.[65] Some scholars, such as Archie Mafeje, see ethnic affinities as nothing more than "false consciousness" and a hindrance to class formation.[66] It is clear that throughout Africa class consciousness is not widespread. At the same time, there is no doubt that classes are being formed. To the extent that politically relevant class consciousness exists, it is found mainly among members of the state class and, to a limited degree, among members of the incipient

African working class. The latter is generally suppressed by the state, but in places like South Africa its potential political power is clearly evident because of its size and critical role in the most industrialized economy on the continent. The important point to note here is that the political significance of social class, like ethnicity, is intermittent and experiential. A great deal depends upon the idiosyncratic features of given societies, the political stakes involved, and the character and intensity of political tensions. Together, however, ethnicity and class are at the base of much of African politics today.

The holders of state power constitute a governing class and may often, but not always, be correctly referred to as the "ruling class." Some dependency theorists, such as André Gunder Frank and John Saul, assumed that the ruling class resided in the metropole, but it is now generally agreed that they overstated their case, as there is evidence of at least occasional autonomy on the part of peripheral states in their dealings with external patrons.[67] In fact, rather than being puppets of external or domestic class interests, the rulers of African states have proved themselves adept at manipulating various interests in order to assert and further their autonomy.[68] Ethiopia, for example, despite being heavily dependent upon the Soviet Union for military assistance, resisted pressure from its superpower patron to form a civilian vanguard party for almost a decade. When the party was formed, it was largely the design of the indigenous state class rather than of Soviet ideologues.[69]

The two primary goals of African states are survival and socioeconomic development. One objective cannot be guaranteed without the other. Embedded in the concept of state survival are the maintenance of the juridically defined state and the governmental apparatus of the regime and the consolidation of the hegemony of the state class. In its quest for survival, the state class must constantly attend to the tasks of ensuring domestic order and competing with other states for power, prestige, and respect. Rather than always being compelled to serve the common good or to adhere to the dictates of external or domestic class interests, the state class often acts in a self-interested manner and comes into conflict with nonstate interests.

The state class employs public policies as instruments for achieving a wide range of purposes. Without the capability to use public resources to mobilize or control the general population, the state class would not be able to act instrumentally on its own behalf or to achieve the political and developmental goals it pursues. Because they are resource-poor and soft, African states must usually rely upon external sources for needed inputs such as economic and military assistance and on coercion to establish a semblance of hegemony. Richard Higgott has correctly noted that "there is a clear link between dependence and the authoritarian nature of most African regimes. . . . The desire of the ruling elites to achieve stability, more often than not perceived simply as the absence of open conflict, will see African leaders continue to rely on the former colonial power, or the broader international system, for economic and military support."[70]

The autonomy of African states is not universal and absolute. In fact, what exists is a state in relative autonomy that varies from society to society and from context to context.[71] Leonard Binder contends that since 1952 the Egyptian rural middle class has had a profound influence on the state's ability to rule in an autonomous fashion. He argues that it is a class that does not rule, but the state cannot rule without its support.[72] Focusing partly on the same period in Egypt's political history, Waterbury finds that the state possessed a good deal of autonomy from indigenous classes.[73] Springborg, on the other hand, focusing on Egyptian politician and wealthy landowner Sayed Marei and his extended family, demonstrates how traditional elites adapt their patron-client networks to exercise continuing leverage on the changing national political scene.[74] He suggests that in Egypt certain families are cohesive and adaptive enough to outlive almost any changes in the national political system. In other places such as Ethiopia, the state has at times been able to exercise considerable autonomy from both domestic and external interests in domestic policy matters, while being heavily dependent on external sources of economic and military aid. This has particularly been the case over the past decade or so since the USSR became Ethiopia's superpower patron.[75]

In addition to utilizing public policies and coercion to establish their autonomy and hegemony, some African states have developed ideologies intended to enhance their control while laying the foundations for their legitimacy. Afro-Marxist states such as Ethiopia, Mozambique, and Angola, for example, for most of the 1980s tried to use varieties of the Marxist-Leninist ideology and modes of political organization to restructure their respective societies and to create a new socialist ethic.[76] They sought to neutralize the potentially divisive effects of ethnicity and other forms of cultural pluralism and to introduce a new, unifying, egalitarian value system. The same could be said of populist socialist regimes. History has shown, however, that ideology is not magic. It cannot absolutely compensate for state softness, vulnerability, and limited resource capacities, but it can tell us much about a regime's policy preferences.[77] Pragmatism more often than not determines the reality of a state's political economy. Of course, this might be different if the dependency and soft state syndromes did not prevail.

More African states (40 percent) claim to be socialist than actually are socialist or probably will ever be. Few claim to be explicitly capitalist, but most are characterized more by capitalist tendencies (free market, private enterprise, private ownership of the means of production) than by state control over the means of production, distribution, and exchange or by central planning. Richard Sklar has noted that outside South Africa it is erroneous to speak of a competition between capitalism and socialism.[78] States that lean in the capitalist direction and publicly favor the free market appear as compelled to regulate their economies closely as are Afro-Marxist states. The form and extent of state involvement in the economy vary, but the results are generally the same. The legacy of colonialism, the international and domestic environments in which they operate, their generally low resource levels, and their limited legitimacy all combine to make most African states politically authoritarian and largely statist in their economic modes of operation.

THE AFRICAN STATE IN THE MAKING

What will the African state of the future look like? How will it function? Will we be more able to generalize about the African state twenty years from now than we could twenty years ago?

African states will continue to be heavily influenced by their colonial past in the foreseeable future. It was during the colonial era that the bases of economic and political dependence were laid and the foundations of the bureaucratic, autocratic welfare state were established. Democratic norms and institutions were quickly eroded or suppressed throughout Africa after independence, and there are no signs that this will change dramatically in the near future.

Martin Carnoy argues that the Third World state's failure to establish its legitimacy or hegemony can be traced to the fact that colonial capitalism inhibited the development of indigenous middle classes that might have had the capacity and legitimacy required to lead development.[79] This fact has contributed to the emergence of coercive, corporatist-authoritarian regimes in Africa and other parts of the Third World. The creation of the authoritarian regimes of the Third World, Carnoy warns, may foreshadow the institutionalization of militarism in the periphery.[80] Certainly, there is evidence that this is the direction in which many African states are headed. In few places is democratic or quasi-democratic presidential succession a norm. Rigged elections and military coups are more common. Lip service is paid to democratic and egalitarian principles by leaders throughout Africa, but in practice the tendency is toward centralized, authoritarian control. Centralized political control is likely to continue to be valued more than liberal democracy by African leaders, no matter what their ideological orientations, because of fragility of the state's position of authority. Many African leaders appear to assume that over time improvements in the quality of life or the application of a correct ideology will allow even autocratic regimes to secure popular legitimacy. Indeed, as is proven by the case of the Soviet Union just after World War II, this is a possibility. However, such a scenario seems unlikely in the near future in most of Africa.

In some African states new rounds of constitutional development will be employed to encourage the citizenry to accept regimes' efforts to impose their own views of political, institutional, organizational, and social relations. In 1987, for example, Afro-Marxist Ethiopia introduced a constitution that spelled out the rights and obligations of the state and civil society in the language of scientific socialism.[81] Since the inauguration of the constitution, the regime has been trying with difficulty to have the vision it represents accepted by the population.

Sklar suggests that, in spite of flaws and inherent contradictions, Nigeria's current phase of constitution building holds some promise of succeeding.[82] His optimism is founded not on the projected democratic-socialist character of the new constitution, but on the fact that it promises to enshrine a constitutional form of government. This, according to Sklar, will "open the door to movements for democracy and social justice."[83] Yet, as Nigeria's history has shown, a constitutional form of government is no guarantee of a rapid movement toward democracy and social justice. In fact, I would argue that, as in the past, progress in this direction is likely to be fraught with false starts and setbacks of indeterminate magnitude and duration.

The leadership that guided African states to independence is gradually fading from the scene. Its legacy to the next generation of holders of state power is in most cases likely to be statist, authoritarian organization and modes of operation. This is as much true where there has been uninterrupted civilian rule as it is where military rule has predominated. It is also as true in places where the economic ideology is capitalist as it is where the hope is to build a socialist economy.

What seem to be emerging in Africa are the initial manifestations of the corporatist mode of political organization, or proto-corporatism. Corporatist ideology serves to justify authoritarian rule, and corporatist practices provide governing elites with mechanisms for controlling key socioeconomic sectors. Contemporary corporatist ideology derives from natural law doctrine and grounds its political prescriptions upon the organic view of the state. Early corporatist writers reasoned that if human beings are hierarchically ordered, specialized components of an organic whole that serve by performing specific functions, each component part of society should accept its place and serve the common good by performing the functions assigned to it.

This hierarchical vision of society easily serves to justify an authoritarian political order. Kenneth Erickson, discussing the organic view in the Brazilian context, observed, "In organic-state thought, the ruler or rulers take the role of the brain and are supposed to see that the *general will* or national interest prevails over the specific interests of which society is composed. This view, then, holds that a discernible general will exists—greater than the sum of the desires and demands of the individuals who make up the society—and that a nation's rulers are capable of identifying it."[84] Benevolent rule by enlightened elites, therefore, is vastly superior to individualist liberal democracy, a system believed to allow rapacious special interests to pursue their own selfish ends at the expense of the common good.

Treating corporatism in practice, Philippe Schmitter said, "Corporatism can be defined as a system of interest representation in which the constituent units are organized into a limited number of singular, compulsory, noncompetitive, hierarchically ordered and functionally differentiated categories, recognized or licensed (if not created) by the state and granted a deliberate representational monopoly within their respective categories of leaders and articulation of demands and supports."[85] The state thus controls the very existence of sectoral interest groups and sets the bounds of legitimate representation, so that rulers can pursue the common national interest, defined in today's Africa in terms of economic development.

Schmitter has identified two forms of corporatism: societal corporatism and state corporatism.[86] Societal corporatism is a pattern of institutional relationships in which the officially sanctioned sectoral interest organizations, while collaborating with each other and state policymaking elites in the pursuit of a commonly accepted national interest, speak quite autonomously for their socioeconomic sectors and actively engage the state in the defense of their constituents. In countries characterized by societal corporatism, such as the Scandanavian ones, and the Netherlands, state and peak-level interest groups therefore work in rather close interdependence.

State corporatism is an institutional arrangement in which the state seeks to co-opt or control major sectoral interest organizations, usually by establishing rules that govern their very creation as well as their behavior. Where practiced in Latin American countries such as Brazil and Mexico, state elites have sought to define the boundaries of legitimate politics and to use their control to structure and foster a process of economic development.

Corporatist tendencies exist in Africa, and what is likely to result in the years to come is a peculiarly African variant of this organizational form.[87] It will most likely be closer to the state corporatism found in parts of Latin America than to the societal corporatism that predominates in Europe. Power will be centered on the state, which will preside over and be involved in a mixed economy. The degree of capitalism and privatization and the degree of central economic planning will vary from country to country. Legitimate political participation is likely to be closely controlled. This trend is already evident in countries as diverse as Zaire, Ethiopia, and Kenya. In each of these cases, there is a strong tendency for the state to overcontrol politics and to be unable to exercise sufficient control over the economy. In Zaire Mobutu has created an organic statist regime with corporatist tendencies. It possesses what Callaghy has termed "the pseudo-modern ideological and structural forms of a single party," and the state is seen as essential in the systematic regulation of politics.[88] The state class maintains a tight grip over political expression and suppresses the emergence of independent political as well as economic interests. By the early 1990s, Mobutu claimed to be entertaining a multiparty system, but there was no evidence that such a system, if it were ever established, would be completely open. What is more, the state continued to be a cleptocracy mired in debt, with an economy dominated by an informal market, virtually immune from effective regulation.

The Afro-Marxist regime in Ethiopia by 1987 had constitutionally enshrined a Marxist-Leninist party designed to neutralize ethnic and class affinities, to legitimize its rule, and to force selected members of the populace to form corporate groups for the purpose of participating in a pseudo-democratic vanguard party and in regional and national assemblies. The party and mass organizations defined by the state class were the only vehicles through which legitimate political discourse could take place. Efforts to create a centrally planned economy stalled, and large numbers of rural producers disengaged from the state.[89]

In Kenya, after the death of President Jomo Kenyatta in 1978, the regime of Daniel arap Moi systematically erected an increasingly authoritarian and less democratic regime. The secret ballot, parliamentary primary election was replaced by a requirement to "queue behind your candidate." The de facto one-party system became de jure. The constitution was amended to give the president greater control over the judiciary and to broaden police arrest powers. Corporate entities such as labor unions are allowed to exist, but they are highly regulated. Local business interests are known to favor a liberalization of government policies, but they have been unwilling to press vigorously for reform. After brief consideration in 1990 of creating a multiparty system, President Moi ordered that deliberations on the topic be ended at once. However, pressure from civil society forced the Kenya African National Union (KANU), the only legitimate political party, to hold hearings on ways the party might be made more accountable and democratic. It was clear that KANU and Moi preferred liberalization somewhat short of true liberal democracy. The economy continues to be characterized by the coexistence of active formal and informal markets, despite the governments efforts to supress the latter.

Throughout Africa the past two decades have witnessed an erosion of democratic tendencies rather than further democratization, but the erosion in many nations need not be permanent. Countries in other parts of the world, such as Brazil, have gone through several phases where limited popular democracy and authoritarian corporatism have alternated.[90]

Even in African countries where liberalization may take place in the near future, it is likely that the reigning regimes will continue to adhere to some variant of authoritarian-corporatism. Beneath the facade of fewer political prisoners, a freer press, more religious tolerance, and a more open economy, the centralized control of African states seem likely to continue and indeed become stronger. Richard Higgott has noted that "Liberalization would not necessarily mean an end to the corporatist pattern of relationships between the state and a body of functional, non-competitive and officially sanctioned interest groups in a way in which redemocratization inevitably would."[91]

African corporatism will persist as long as African states are soft and economically dependent, and perhaps even beyond.[92] These deficiencies force the state toward authoritarianism and militarization. States that possess the economic resources to meet the social demands of the populace and are governmentally strong and efficient enough to project an image of legitimacy and authority experience the most success in being able to build on that legitimacy and to tolerate free and open political expression. Only Botswana currently seems to meet these criteria. Sparsely populated and relatively homogeneous ethnically, Botswana has used assets acquired from the sale of its high-quality diamonds on the international market to improve the general quality of life. In the past decade the per capita income has gone from $290 to $1680 per year. Almost half of government expenditures are allocated for development. Despite a recent seven-year drought, the multiparty Botswana political system remains stable.

Current trends seem to suggest that the ideologies of African states will continue either to be latent or to reflect the political preferences of the state class rather than the state's actual economic policy. Most African leaders will continue to disdain or caution against the excesses of capitalism. However, some variant of capitalism will be unavoidable in all African states because of their vulnerable positions in the world economy and because of their poverty and underdevelopment.

Even if socialism takes hold in Africa, it will have to be preceded by capital accumulation.[93] Sklar argues, "Socialism needs capital and lacks a theory of incentive; capitalism needs the state and lacks a theory of social responsibility."[94] He calls for a judicious mixture of capitalism and socialism in Africa and suggests that this is the only way that African societies will progress from their current state of decay.

In the foreseeable future the state class will likely continue to be guided in most cases by patrimonial considerations rather than by economic or political rationality. It seems likely to continue to equate its hegemony more with power and control rather than with legitimacy. The best that can be hoped for is an abatement in the economic crisis which would allow the state to create incentives in the form of favorable market prices for both producers and consumers and social development policies sufficient to reengage significant numbers of the populace. This, however, is beyond the control of most African states.

DIRECTIONS FOR FURTHER RESEARCH

This essay has attempted to take stock of what we know about the modern African state in theory and in practice and to speculate about its future. In the process numerous avenues for further research have surfaced.

First, there presently exists a cumulative body of knowledge about how individual African states were built and how they currently function. What we need now is more comparative studies of how African states formulate and execute domestic public policies. The studies should entail not simply an analysis of state bureaucratic agencies, but an examination of how the governing class mobilizes the state apparatus to achieve certain ends and the manner in which the central bureaucracy interacts with society at the level of implementation. There currently exists a wealth of country case studies on particular policy issues. However, there are far too few cross-sectoral and cross-national policy studies. Such studies would greatly improve our understanding of the policy-making process in Africa. Despite the difficulty of doing rigorous policy analysis in Africa because of the political sensitivity of that kind of research, initial efforts must be made.

Second, the domestic context in which African states must function is rapidly changing. Ethnicity, class, and patron-clientelism continue to be extremely significant determinants of individual and group political behavior. However, it seems reasonable to expect that as the habit of national citizenship becomes the norm; as the state penetrates to the far reaches of society, and as African economies become more diversified, ethnicity and clientelism will become generally less important than social class in explaining political behavior. This would be particularly likely if the state class continues to practice an exclusionary form of proto-corporatism, preferring to recognize and deal with some groups and not others. Armed opposition movements throughout the continent (for example, Sudan, Ethiopia, Somalia, South Africa) are inspired by the fact that large segments of these respective polities have been shut out of legitimate politics and are involved in what they perceive to be struggles for social justice if not revolution.

Third, we need a better understanding of the peculiar nature of the African state as a generic phenomenon. A form of authoritarianism (not of totalitarianism) exists to varying degrees throughout the continent. This phenomenon has corporatist traits, but there have been few case studies that have revealed the true essence of what I have called African proto-corporatism. The various forms of this phenomenon need to be identified and understood. The question remains: Will civil society in Africa accept as legitimate some form of authoritarian corporatism or will the coming decade see the emergence of movements pressing for democratization as has been recently witnessed in Algeria, Camaroon, Benin, and other parts of the non-Western world.

Fourth, the implications of state and societal decay in Africa have yet to be assessed systematically. Numerous studies have established the fact that large segments of the African populace have become disengaged from the state and spend more time trying to evade it than doing its bidding. Moreover, debt, economic stagnation, disease, lawlessness, environmental degradation, and natural calamity are common in many countries. This is not to say that most African states are on the verge of dismantlement, but only that in many places common citizens passively resist or ignore what are perceived to be the repressive and sometimes oppressive policies of the state. In other words, they "tune the state out" and focus on their most immediate needs. As pervasive as this tendency is, few studies have considered the permanency of this condition or the methods being employed by African states to reengage the populace.

Fifth, the prospects for revolution in Black Africa should not be minimized. As the rulers of certain states lose support among the nascent intellectual class because of repressive and nonprogressive policies, and as they continue to accumulate wealth and power in an excessive way, the foundations of revolutionary sentiment may be laid. This is particularly so with the growing availability of modern arms on the continent. The possibility of social revolution in contemporary Black Africa might also be fueled by the fact that throughout most of the continent domestic economies are increasingly unable to absorb the expanded pool of high school and university educated youth. These young people are increasingly cynical about the corruption and ineptness of their political leaders and are suggesting less repressive and more equitable alternatives in the application of social and economic policies. This is the kind of sentiment that led to the overthrow of Haile Salassie and is now inspiring clandestine groups that hope to challenge the regime of Daniel arap Moi in Kenya. Military coups are almost certain to continue in Africa, but scholars should also consider the possibility of genuine social revolution. Critical assessments of revolutionary pressures in Africa are long overdue. We need to answer the questions: What are root causes of social revolution? To what extent (and where) are they to be found in Africa?

Lastly, African states tend to be heavily dependent upon external sources for critically needed economic inputs. Yet, there are times when African regimes exercise considerable autonomy from both domestic and international interests. As was demonstrated above, the state class sometimes acts in its own interest rather than being manipulated by other internal or external interests. The dependency syndrome needs to be examined so that we can better understand how the leaders of African states exercise leverage and autonomy in certain situations. Indeed, in some cases, interdependence would seem a more apt characterization of how some African states deal with their external patrons.

Despite growing scholarly efforts among Africanists to identify patterns of democratization on the continent and tendencies toward societal leverage against the state, the state is likely to remain at the center of African politics for the foreseeable future. The state's access to substantial amounts of scarce economic resources that can be used as patronage and its virtual monopoly over the means of coercion seem likely to dictate in the future the consolidation of varieties of state corporatism in Africa.

NOTES

Thanks are due to Ruth Iyob, my research assistant, for her work on this project, and to my colleagues, Ruth and David Collier, for their valuable comments and suggestions.

1. See Martin Staniland, *What is Political Economy?* (New Haven, Conn.: Yale University Press, 1985).

2. See, for example, Theda Skocpol, "Bringing the State Back In: Strategies of Analysis in Current Research," in Peter B. Evans, Dietrich Rueschmeyer, and Theda Skocpol, eds., *Bringing the State Back In* (Cambridge: Cambridge University Press, 1985); Martin Carnoy, *The State and Political Theory* (Princeton, N.J.: Princeton University Press, 1984).

3. See John Lonsdale, "States and Social Processes in Africa: A Historiographical Survey," *The African Studies Review*, 24, no. 2–3, (June–September 1981): 139–225; Richard A. Higgott, "The State in Africa: Some Thoughts on the Future Drawn from the Past," in

Timothy Shaw, ed., *Africa Projected: From Dependence to Self-Reliance by the Year 2000* (London: Macmillan, 1982); Nelson Kasfir, "Relating Class to State in Arica," *Journal of Commonwealth and Comparative Politics*, 21, no. 3 (November 1983): 1–20; Zaki Ergas, ed., *The African State in Transition* (Basingstoke: Macmillan, 1987); and Donald Rothchild and Naomi Chazan, eds., *The Precarious Balance: State and Society in Africa* (Boulder, Colo.: Westview, 1988).

4. See Nicos Poulantzas, *Political Power and Social Classes* (London: New Left Books, 1973); Ralph Miliband, *The State in Capitalist Society* (New York: Basic Books, 1979); and Eric A. Nordlinger, *On the Autonomy of the Democratic State* (Cambridge, Mass.: Harvard University Press, 1981).

5. See Robert Fatton, Jr., "Bringing the Ruling Class Back in: Class, State, and Hegemony in Africa." *Comparative Politics* 20, no. 3 (April 1988): 253–264; and Irving Leonard Markovitz, ed., *Studies in Power and Class in Africa* (New York: Oxford University Press, 1987).

6. Rothchild and Chazan, *Precarious Balance*.

7. Robert H. Jackson and Carl G. Rosberg, Jr., "Why Africa's Weak States Persist: The Empirical and the Juridical in Statehood," *World Politics* 35, no. 1 (October 1982): 1–6.

8. John A. A. Ayoade, "States without Citizens: An Emerging African Phenomenon," in Rothchild and Chazan, eds., *Precarious Balance*.

9. Claude Ake, *The Political Economy of Africa* (New York: Longman, 1982), 3.

10. David Easton, "The Political System Besieged by the State," *Political Theory* 9, no. 3 (August 1981): 307.

11. Stephen D. Krasner, "Approaches to the State: Alternative Conceptions and Historical Dynamics," *Comparative Politics* 16, no. 2 (January 1984): 223–246.

12. Otwin Marenin, "The Nigerian State as Process and Manager: A Conceptualization." *Comparative Politics* 20, no. 2 (1988): 215–232.

13. Donald Rothchild and Victor Olorunsola, eds., *State Versus Ethnic Claims: African Policy Dilemmas* (Boulder, Colo.: Westview Press, 1983).

14. Howard H. Lentner, "The Concept of the State: A Response to Stephen Krasner," *Comparative Politics* 16, no. 3 (April 1984): 367–377.

15. Crawford Young, "Patterns of Social Conflict: State, Class and Ethnicity," *Daedalus* 3, no. 2 (Spring 1982).

16. See, for example, Gabriel A. Almond and G. Bingham Powell,

Comparative Politics: A Developmental Approach (Boston: Little, Brown, 1966).

17. René Lemarchand, "The State and Society in Africa: Ethnic Stratification and Restratification in Historical and Comparative Perspective," in Rothchild and Olorunsola, *State versus Ethnic Claims*.

18. Typical of this Africanist view in the early 1960s is David E. Apter, *Ghana in Transition* (New York: Atheneum, 1963).

19. See, for example, Karl Deutsch and William Foltz, eds., *Nation-Building* (New York: Atherton Press, 1963).

20. See, for example, Walter Rodney, *How Europe Underdeveloped Africa* (London: Bogle L'Ouverture, 1972); Samir Amin, *Neocolonialism in West Africa* (New York: Monthly Review Press, 1973); André Gunder Frank, *Capitalism and Underdevelopment in Latin America*, rev. ed. (New York: Monthly Review Press, 1969); Colin Leys, *Underdevelopment in Kenya: The Political Economy of Neocolonialism* (Berkeley: University of California Press, 1975); Immanuel Wallerstein, *The Modern World System* (New York: Academic Press, 1974).

21. For a critical assessment of Africanist efforts to apply the model to Africa, see Patrick J. McGowan, and D. L. Smith, "Economic Dependency in Black Africa: A Causal Analysis of Competing Theories," *International Organization* 32 (1978): 179–235.

22. For a useful application of this approach to Africa, see Ivring Leornard Markovitz, *Power and Class in Africa* (Englewood Cliffs, N.J.: Prentice-Hall, 1977), and Markovitz, *Studies in Power and Class in Africa*.

23. For a valuable critique of the approach, see Staniland, *What Is Political Economy?* 126–132. For exceptions to this weakness, see Kenneth P. Erickson and Patrick V. Peppe, "Dependent Capitalist Development, U.S. Foreign Policy, and Repression of the Working Class in Chile and Brazil," *Latin American Perspectives* 3, no. 1 (Winter 1976): 10–13; Peter B. Evans, *Dependent Development: The Alliance of Multinational, State and Local Capital in Brazil* (Princeton, N.J.: Princeton University Press, 1979).

24. See, for example, Rodney, *How Europe Underdeveloped Africa*.

25. See Markovitz, *Power and Class in Africa*; Ake, *Political Economy of Africa*.

26. See Donald Rothchild and Robert L. Curry, Jr., *Scarcity, Choice and Public Policy in Middle Africa* (Berkeley: University of California Press, 1978); and Robert H. Bates, *Markets and States in Tropical Africa* (Berkeley: University of California Press, 1981).

27. Hamza Alavi, "The State in Post-Colonial Societies: Pakistan and

Bangladesh," *New Left Review* 74 (July-August 1972).

28. John Saul, *State and Revolution in Eastern Africa* (London: Heinemann, 1979).

29. Claude Ake, "The State in Contemporary Africa," in Claude Ake, ed., *Political Economy of Nigeria* (London: Longman, 1985), 1–3.

30. See Rothchild and Curry, *Scarcity, Choice and Public Policy*.

31. Crawford Young, "The African Colonial State and Its Political Legacy," in Rothchild and Chazan, *Precarious Balance*, 28.

32. See, for example, Thomas M. Callaghy, *The State-Society Struggle: Zaire in Comparative Perspective* (New York: Columbia University Press, 1984); Edmond J. Keller, *Revolutionary Ethiopia: From Empire to People's Republic* (Bloomington: Indiana University Press, 1989).

33. Aristide Zolberg, "Tribalism through Corrective Lenses," *Foreign Affairs* 51, no. 4 (July 1973).

34. Colin Leys, "The 'Overdeveloped' Post-Colonial State: A Reevaluation," *Review of African Political Economy* 5 (January-April 1976).

35. Larry Diamond, "Class Formation in the Swollen African State," *Journal of Modern African Studies* 25, no. 4 (December 1987): 567–596.

36. Goren Hyden, *Beyond Ujamaa: Underdevelopment and the Uncaptured Peasantry* (Berkeley: University of California Press, 1980), 16.

37. Callaghy, *State-Society Struggle*, 5.

38. Young, "Patterns of Social Conflict," 94.

39. This point is nicely made by Young, "African Colonial State," and Joshua B. Forrest, "The Quest for State 'Hardness' in Africa," *Comparative Politics* 20, no. 4 (July 1988): 423–442.

40. See Robert H. Jackson and Carl G. Rosberg, Jr., *Personal Rule in Black Africa* (Berkeley: University of California Press, 1982).

41. Thomas M. Callaghy, "The State and the Devlopment of Capitalism in Africa: Theoretical, Historical, and Comparative Reflections," in Rothchild and Chazan, *Precarious Balance*, 80–88.

42. Jean-François Médard, "The Underdeveloped State in Tropical Africa: Political Clientelism or Neopatrimonialism," in Christopher Clapham, ed., *Private Patronage and Public Power: Political Clientelism in the Modern State* (London: Frances Pinter, 1982), 180–181.

43. Crawford Young, "The African Colonial State and Its Political Legacy," in Rothchild and Chazan, *Precarious Balance*, 25.

44. Richard A. Joseph, *Democracy and Prebendal Politics in Nigeria: The Rise and Fall of the Second Republic* (Cambridge: Cambridge University Press, 1987), 1–11.

45. Hyden, *Beyond Ujamaa*, 63.

46. Naomi Caiden and Aaron Wildavsky, *Planning and Budgeting in Poor Countries* (New York: Wiley, 1974).

47. See Albert O. Hirschman, "Exit, Voice, and the State," *World Politics* 31, no. 1 (October 1978); Rothchild and Chazan, *Precarious Balance*.

48. Naomi Chazan, "Patterns of State-Society Incorporation and Disengagement in Africa," in Rothchild and Chazan, *Precarious Balance*, 126.

49. Ibid.

50. For a useful discussion of the problem of establishing legitimacy faced by authoritarian regimes, see Juan Linz, "The Future of an Authoritarian Situation or the Institutionalization of an Authoritarian Regime: The Case of Brazil," in Alfred Stepan, ed., *Authoritarian Brazil: Origins, Policies, and Future* (New Haven, Conn.: Yale University Press, 1973), 233–254.

51. See Henry Bienen, *Kenya: The Politics of Participation and Control* (Princeton, N.J.: Princeton University Press, 1974).

52. Young, "African Colonial State," 26.

53. Michael A. Cohen, *Urban Policy and Political Conflict in Africa: A Study of the Ivory Coast* (Chicago: University of Chicago Press, 1974).

54. Peter Korner, Gero Maass, Thomas Siebold, and Rainer Tetzlaff, eds., *The IMF and the Debt Crisis* (London: Zed Press Ltd., 1986).

55. Diamond, "Class Formation," 572.

56. Callaghy, "State and the Development of Capitalism " 83.

57. Ibid.

58. Diamond, "Class Formation," 572.

59. See Clifford Geertz, "The Integrative Revolution: Primordial Sentiments and Civil Politics in New States," in Clifford Geertz, ed., *Old Societies and New States* (New York: Free Press, 1963); Leo Kuper and M. G. Smith, eds., *Pluralism in Africa* (Berkeley: University of California Press, 1969).

60. See Crawford Young, *The Politics of Cultural Pluralism* (Madison, Wisc.: University of Wisconsin Press, 1976); Robert Melson and Howard Wolpe, "Modernization and the Politics of Communalism," *American Political Science Review* 64 (1970), 1112–1130.

61. See Edmond J. Keller, "Ethiopia: Revolution, Class and the National Question," *African Affairs* 80, no. 321 (October 1981): 519–550.

62. See Nelson Kasfir, "Explaining Ethnic Political Participation," *World Politics* 31 (1978–79): 365–388.

63. See Young, *Politics of Cultural Pluralism*, 23–37.

64. See Bienen, *Kenya*.

65. See, for example, Gavin Kitching. *Class and Economic Change in Kenya* (New Haven, Conn.: Yale University Press, 1980); Markovitz, *Power and Class in Africa*; Nzongola-Ntalaja, *Revolution and Counter-Revolution in Africa* (London: Zed Press Ltd., 1987); Issa G. Shivji, *Class Struggles in Tanzania* (London: Heinemann, 1975); John Saul, *State and Revolution*.

66. See, for example, Archie Mafeje, "The Ideology of Tribalism," *Journal of Modern African Studies* 9 (1971): 253–62.

67. Frank, *Capitalism and Underdevelopment*; John Saul, *State and Revolution*.

68. See Edmond J. Keller, "The State, Public Policy and the Mediation of Ethnic Conflict in Africa," in Rothchild and Olorunsola, *State versus Ethnic Claims*.

69. See Edmond J. Keller, "State, Party and Revolution in Ethiopia," *African Studies Review* 28, no. 1 (March 1985).

70. See Higgott, "State in Africa," 24–25.

71. See Edmond J. Keller, "Revolutionary Ethiopia: Ideology, Capacity and the Limits of State Autonomy," *Journal of Commonwealth and Comparative Politics* 23, no. 2 (July 1985): 112–39.

72. Leonard Binder, *In a Moment of Enthusiasm: Political Power and the Second Stratum in Egypt* (Chicago: University of Chicago Press, 1978).

73. John Waterbury, *The Egypt of Nasser and Sadat: The Political Economy of Two Regimes* (Princeton, N.J.: Princeton University Press, 1983).

74. Robert Springborg, *Family, Power, and Politics in Egypt: Sayyed Beg Marei—His Clan, Clients, and Cohorts* (Philadelphia: University of Pennsylvania Press, 1982).

75. See Keller, *Revolutionary Ethiopia*.

76. See Edmond J. Keller and Donald Rothchild, eds., *Afro-Marxist Regimes: Ideology and Public Policy* (Boulder, Colo.: Lynne Rienner, 1987); Crawford Young, *Ideology and Development in Africa* (New Haven, Conn.: Yale University Press, 1982).

77. See Harvey Glickman, "Reflections on Ideology and the State in Africa," in Ergas, *African State in Transition*.

78. Richard L. Sklar, "Beyond Capitalism and Socialism in Africa," *Journal of Modern African Studies* 26, no. 1 (March 1988): 1–22.

79. Carnoy, *State and Political Theory*, 7.

80. Ibid., 192.

81. See Keller, *Revolutionary Ethiopia*.

82. Sklar, "Beyond Capitalism," 8.

83. Ibid., 9.

84. Kenneth P. Erickson, "Brazil: Corporative Authoritarianism, Democratization and Dependency," in Howard J. Wiarda and Har-

vey F. Kline, eds., *Latin American Politics and Development*, 2d ed. (Boulder, Colo.: Westview Press, 1985), 162; see also Erickson, *The Brazilian Corporative State and Working-Class Politics* (Berkeley: University of California Press, 1977).

85. Philippe C. Schmitter, "Still the Century of Corporatism?" *Review of Politics* 36, no. 1 (January 1974): 93–94; also Alfred Stepan, *The State and Society: Peru in Comparative Perspective* (Princeton N.J.: Princeton University Press, 1978).

86. Ibid., 102–105.

87. See Julius E. Nyang'oro and Timothy M. Shaw, eds., *Corporatism in Africa: Comparative Analysis and Practice* (Boulder, Colo.: Westview Press, 1989).

88. Callaghy, *State-Society Struggle*, 14.

89. See Keller, *Revolutionary Ethiopia*.

90. See Erickson, "Brazil."

91. Higgott, "State in Africa," 30.

92. In Latin America some of the strongest states have continued to be organized according to corporatist principles. This "strength," however, is relative and at least in terms of the world economic system, it is shallow. Theoretically, states that are strong and secure in economic terms are more likely to tolerate and even to promote liberal democracy with success.

93. Goren Hyden, *No Shortcuts to Progress: African Development Management in Perspective* (Berkeley: University of California Press, 1983).

94. Sklar, "Beyond Capitalism," 18.

Chapter

8

Dilemmas of Democratization in Latin America

Terry Lynn Karl

The demise of authoritarian rule in Argentina, Bolivia, Brazil, Chile, Ecuador, Peru, and Uruguay; efforts at political liberalization in Mexico; and the recent election of civilian presidents in Guatemala, El Salvador, Honduras, and Nicaragua, taken together, represent a political watershed in Latin America. This wave of regime changes in the 1980s places a number of questions on the intellectual and political agenda for the continent: Will these newly emergent and fragile democracies in South America be able to survive, especially in the context of the worst economic recession since the 1930s? Can the liberalization of authoritarian rule in Central America and the possibility of honest competitive elections in Mexico be transformed into genuine democratic transitions? Will previously consolidated political democracies in Venezuela and Costa Rica be able to extend the basic principles of citizenship into economic and social realms, or will they be "deconsolidated" by this challenge and revert to a sole preoccupation with survival?[1]

Behind such questions lies a central concern expressed by Dankwart A. Rustow almost twenty years ago: "What conditions make democracy possible and what conditions make it thrive?"[2] This chapter addresses Rustow's query by arguing the following. First, the manner in which theorists of comparative politics have sought to understand democracy in developing countries has changed as the once-dominant search for prerequisites to democracy has given way to a more process-oriented emphasis on contingent choice. Having undergone this evolution, it is now important to develop an interactive approach that can relate structural constraints to the shaping of contingent choice. Second, it is no longer adequate to examine regime transitions writ large, that is, from the general category of authoritarian rule to that of democracy. Such broad-gauged efforts must be complemented by the identification of different types of democracy that emerge from distinctive modes of regime transition and by the analysis of their potential political, economic, and social consequences. Before these issues and their implications for the study of Latin America can be addressed, however, a definition of democracy must be established.

DEFINING DEMOCRACY

Defining democracy is no simple task because the resolution of a number of disputes over both its prospects and evaluation rests on how the term itself is operationalized. If democracy is defined in a Schumpeterian manner as a polity that permits the choice between elites by citizens voting in regular and competitive elections, the militarized countries of Central America could be classified as political democracies by many scholars—just as they are (with the exception of Sandinista Nicaragua) by U.S. policy makers.[3] But if the definition is expanded to include a wider range of political conditions—lack of restrictions on citizen expression, absence of discrimination against particular political parties, freedom of association for all interests, civilian control over the military—these same countries (with the exception of Costa Rica and Nicaragua in 1990) could scarcely be classified under this rubric.

The problem is compounded when a number of substantive properties—such as the predominance of institutions that faithfully translate individual preferences into public policy through majoritarian rule, the incorporation of an ever-increasing proportion of the population into the process of decision-making, or the continuous improvement of economic equity through the actions of governing institutions—are included either as components or empirical correlates of democratic rule.[4] Approaches that stipulate socioeconomic advances for the majority of the population and active involvement by subordinate classes united in autonomous popular organizations as defining conditions of democracy are hard-pressed to find "actual" democratic regimes to study. Often they are incapable of identifying significant, if incomplete, changes toward democratization in the political realm. Moreover, they are cut off from investigating empirically the hypothetical relationship between competitive political forms and progressive economic outcomes because this important issue is assumed away by the very definition of regime type. While these substantive properties are ethically desirable to most democrats, such conceptual breadth renders the definition of democracy virtually meaningless for practical application.[5]

For these reasons I will settle for a middle-range definition of democracy as a set of institutions that permits the entire adult population to act as citizens by choosing their leading decision-makers in competitive, fair, and regularly scheduled elections that are held in the context of the rule of law, guarantees for political freedom, and limited military prerogatives. Specified in this manner, democracy is a political concept with several dimensions: (1) *contestation* over policy and *competition* for office; (2) *participation* of the citizenry through partisan, associational, and other forms of collective action; (3) *accountability* of rulers to the ruled through mechanisms of representation and the rule of law; and (4) *civilian control over the military.* This last dimension, so important in the Latin American context, sets this definition apart from Robert Dahl's classic notion of a "procedural minimum."[6] A middle-range definition of this sort avoids the Scylla of an overly narrow reliance on the mere presence of elections without concomitant changes in civil-military relations and the Charybdis of an overly broad assumption of social and economic equality. While perhaps less than fully satisfactory from a normative perspective, it has the advantage of permitting a systematic and objective investigation of the relationship between democratic political forms and the long-range pursuit of equity.

THE FUTILE SEARCH FOR DEMOCRATIC PRECONDITIONS

If the questions raised by democratization remain relatively unchanged from the past, the answers that are offered today come from a different direction. This becomes evident in a brief comparison of the divergent theories about the origins of democratic regimes that have dominated the study of Latin America. The scholarship that preceded the new wave of democratization in the 1980s argued that a number of preconditions were necessary for the emergence of a stable democratic polity.

First, a certain degree of wealth or, better said, level of capitalist development was considered a prerequisite to democracy. Market economies in themselves were not enough; a country had to cross (and remain beyond) a minimum threshold of economic performance before political competition could be institutionalized. "The more well-to-do a nation," Seymour Martin Lipset claimed, "the greater the chances that it will sustain democracy."[7] A wealthy economy makes possible higher levels of literacy, education, urbanization, and mass media exposure, or so the logic went, while also providing resources to mitigate the tensions produced by political conflict.[8]

A second set of preconditions was derived from the concept of political culture, that is, the system of beliefs and values in which political action is embedded and given meaning. The prevalence of certain values and beliefs over others was said to be more conducive to the emergence of democracy. Thus, for example, Protestantism allegedly enhanced the prospects for democracy in Europe, while Catholicism, with its tradition of hierarchy and intolerance, was posited to have the opposite effect in Latin America.[9] Although arguments based only on the link between different religious systems and experiences with democracy have been dismissed by most scholars, more sophisticated claims sought to identify political cultures characterized by a high degree of mutual trust among members of society, a willingness to tolerate diversity, and a tradition of accommodation or compromise because such cultures were considered necessary to the subsequent development of democratic institutions. That a "civic culture" of this sort necessarily rested on a widely differentiated and articulated social structure with relatively autonomous social classes, occupational sectors, and ethnic, religious, or regional groups was an unspoken assumption. In other words, a pro-democratic consensus and set of values was considered the main prerequisite to political democracy.[10]

Third, specific domestic historical conditions and configurations were said to be prerequisites for democracy. Theorists of "crises and sequences" argued that the order in which various crises of modernization appeared and were settled determined whether economic and social transformations were conducive to the development of democracy. Democratic regimes were more likely to emerge if problems of national identity were resolved before the establishment of a central government and if both of these events preceded the formation of mass parties.[11]

In a different, yet still historical vein, Barrington Moore, Jr., contended that democracies were more likely to appear where the social and economic power of the landed aristocracy was in decline relative to that of the bourgeoisie and where labor-repressive agriculture was not the dominant mode of production. When this occurred as a result of the commercialization of agriculture that transformed a traditional peasantry into either a class of small farmers or a rural proletariat, the prognosis for democracy was strong indeed.[12] A version of Moore's approach has been used to explain the different political trajectories in Central America. Specifically, democracy is said to have emerged in Costa Rica due to the creation of a yeoman farmer class, while the persistence of authoritarian rule in Guatemala and El Salvador is attributed to the continued dominance of the landed aristocracy.[13]

Finally, some scholars treated external influences as another set of preconditions on the grounds that these could be decisive for determining whether a polity became democratic or authoritarian. Dependency theorists in Latin America and the United States contended that the continent's particular insertion into the international market made democratization especially problematic at more advanced stages of import-substituting capitalist development and even enhanced the necessity for authoritarian rule under specific circumstances. In a logic that ran counter to Lipset's "optimistic equation," both Guillermo O'Donnell and Fernando Henrique Cardoso argued that as dependent economies became more complex, more penetrated by foreign capital and technology, and more reliant upon low wages to maintain their competitive advantage in the international economy, professional militaries, technocrats, and state managers moved to the forefront of the decision-making process, forcibly replacing unruly, "populist" parties and trade unions in order to establish a supposedly more efficient form of rule.[14]

Inversely, using an argument based on external influences of a different sort, proponents of an aggressive U.S. foreign policy toward the region declared that the rise and decline of democracy was directly related to the rise and decline of the global power of the United States rather than to market mechanisms or accumulation processes. In Samuel Huntington's view, the dramatic increase in authoritarian rule during the 1960s and 1970s was a direct reflection of the waning of U.S. influence. Specifically, it was due to the decreased effectiveness of efforts by U.S. officials to promote democracy as a successful model of development. Concomitantly, he argued, the spate of democratic transitions in the 1980s could be credited to the Reagan administration's renewed effort to "restore American power" through the rollback of revolutions and the promotion of electoral reforms. This position, so ideologically convenient for policy makers, located the roots of democracy outside Latin America.[15]

The experience of Latin American countries in the 1980s challenged all of these presumptions about preconditions. The hypothetical association between wealth and democracy might be called upon to "explain" the transition to democracy in Brazil after a protracted economic boom, but it could hardly account for the case of Peru, whose transition was characterized by stagnant growth rates, extreme foreign debt, persistent balance of payments problems, and a regressive distribution of income. Nor could it explain the anomaly of Argentina, where relatively high levels of per capita gross domestic product were persistently accompanied by authoritarian rule. If the political cultures of Argentina, Uruguay, and Brazil all tolerated, admittedly to varying degrees, the practice of official state terror and widespread violations of human rights, how could they suddenly become sufficiently "civic" and "tolerant" to support a democratic outcome? As the Catholic church took an increasingly active role in opposing authoritarian rule, especially in Brazil, Chile, Peru, and Central America, the argument about the antidemocratic bias of Catholicism became increasingly implausible.[16]

Prediction of a democratic outcome based on international influence fared little better. Although the manner of a country's insertion into the world capitalist economy is now considered essential for explaining its subsequent political and economic development, as dependency theorists claimed, criticisms by other scholars plus the democratic transitions in Brazil and Chile demonstrated that there was no direct or inevitable correlation between capital deepening and authoritarian rule.[17] The general trends toward recession in export earnings, debt crises, diminishing U.S. support for human rights, and the frequent resort to military instruments under the foreign policy of the Reagan administration boded ill for the emergence of democracies in the 1980s, yet emerge they did. The pattern of their appearance undeniably challenged Huntington's thesis linking democratization and the rise of U.S. power. In the Southern Cone, where influence from the North is not especially high, military rulers generally made way for civilian authority. In Central America, Panama, and Haiti, where the overriding historical role of the United States is indisputable, militaries either permitted elections to occur without limiting their own prerogatives or refused to leave power altogether. Indeed, democracy seemed to appear where the decline in U.S. hegemony was greatest, and where dictatorship "should" have been the more appropriate response!

These anomalies suggest the pressing need for important revisions, even reversals, in the way democratization in contemporary Latin America is understood. First, *there may be no single precondition for the emergence of a democratic polity*, and there surely is no single precondition that is sufficient to produce such an outcome. Identifying a single cause rooted in economic, social, cultural-psychological, or international factors has not yielded a general law of democratization, nor is it likely to do so in the near future despite the proliferation of new cases.[18] Thus, the search for a set of identical conditions that can account for the presence or absence of democratic regimes should probably be abandoned and replaced by more modest efforts to derive a contextual approach to the study of democratization.

Second, what the literature in the past considered to be *the preconditions for democracy may be better conceived as the outcomes of democracy*. Patterns of greater economic growth and more equitable income distribution, higher levels of literacy and education, and increases in social communication and media exposure may be better treated as the products of stable democratic processes, rather than as the prerequisites for their existence. A civic culture characterized by high levels of mutual trust, a tolerance of diversity, and a propensity for accommodation and compromise could be the result of the protracted functioning of democratic institutions that generate appropriate values and beliefs rather than a set of cultural norms that must be present before these institutions can emerge. There is evidence for this contention in the fact that most democracies in Europe and Latin America's oldest democracy, Costa Rica, have emerged from quite "uncivic" warfare. In other words, what have been emphasized as independent variables in the past might be more fruitfully conceived as dependent variables in the future.

FROM CONTINGENT CHOICE TO STRUCTURED CONTINGENCY

The failure to identify clear preconditions and the hunch that what once had been thought to produce democracy should be considered as its product have caused theorists of comparative politics to shift their attention to the strategic calculations, processes, and sequential patterns that are involved in moving from one type of political regime to another, especially under conditions of nonviolence, gradualism, and social continuity. For Guillermo O'Donnell and Philippe Schmitter, democratization is understood as a historical process with analytically distinct, if empirically overlapping, stages of transition, consolidation, persistence, and eventual deconsolidation.[19] A variety of actors with different followings, preferences, calculations, resources, and time horizons come to the fore during these successive stages. For example, elite factions and social movements seem to play the key roles in bringing about the demise of authoritarian rule; political parties move to center stage during the transition itself; while business associations, trade unions, and state agencies become major determinants of the type of democracy that is eventually consolidated.[20]

What differentiates these stages above all, as Adam Przeworski points out, is the degree of uncertainty that prevails at each moment. During regime transition all political calculations and interactions are highly uncertain. Actors find it difficult to know what their interests are and which groups and individuals will be their allies or opponents. The armed forces and the civilian supporters of an incumbent authoritarian regime are characteristically divided between "hardline" and "softline" factions. Political parties emerge as privileged in this context because, despite their divisions over strategies and their uncertainties about partisan identities, the logic of electoral competition focuses public attention on them and compels them to appeal to the widest possible clientele. The only certainty is that "founding elections" will eliminate those who make important miscalculations.

The absence of predictable "rules of the game" during a regime transition expands the boundaries of contingent choice. Indeed, the dynamics of the transition revolve around strategic interactions and tentative arrangements between actors with uncertain power resources aimed at defining who will legitimately be entitled to play in the political game, what criteria will determine the winners and losers, and what limits will be placed on the issues at stake. From this perspective, regime consolidation occurs when contending social classes and political groups come to accept some set of formal rules or informal understandings that determine "who gets what, where, when, and how" from politics. In so doing, they settle into predictable positions and legitimate behaviors by competing according to mutually acceptable rules. Electoral outcomes may still be uncertain with regard to person or party, but in consolidated democracies they are firmly surrounded by normative limits and established patterns of power distribution.

The notion of contingency (meaning that outcomes depend less on objective conditions than subjective rules surrounding a strategic choice) has the advantage of stressing collective decisions and political interactions that have largely been underemphasized in the search for preconditions. But this understanding of democracy has the danger of descending into excessive voluntarism if it is not explicitly placed within a framework of structural-historical constraints. Even in the midst of the tremendous uncertainty provoked by a regime transition, where constraints appear to be most relaxed and where a wide range of outcomes appear to be possible, the decisions made by various actors respond to and are conditioned by the types of socioeconomic structures and political institutions already present. These can be decisive in that they may either restrict or enhance the options available to different political actors attempting to construct democracy.

For example, certain social structures do seem to make the emergence of political democracy highly improbable; inversely, it is reasonable to presume that their absence may make accommodative strategies more viable and reinforce the position of democratic actors. Political democracies have lasted only in countries where the landed class (generally the most recalcitrant of interests) has played a secondary role in the export economy, for example, Venezuela and Chile, or where non–labor-repressive agriculture has predominated, for example, Costa Rica, Argentina, and Uruguay. Thus the ability of political democracy to survive does seem to depend on a structural space defined in part by the absence of a strong landowner elite engaged in labor-repressive agriculture or the subordination of that elite to interests tied to other economic activities.[21]

The cases of Venezuela and Chile make the point. In Venezuela dependence upon petroleum as the leading source of foreign exchange had the unintended effect of hastening the decline of that country's already stagnant agriculture and with it the landowner elite. Faced with overvalued exchange rates that hurt agricultural exports and abundant foreign reserves for importing cheap foodstuffs, landowners sold their property to oil companies and converted themselves into a commercial and financial urban bourgeoisie. This largely voluntary self-liquidation removed the incentive for them to commercialize rural areas, to subordinate the peasantry through repressive means, and, eventually, to maintain authoritarian rule. It also removed the social base for an anti-system party of the right, thus actors designing pact-making strategies in Venezuela during the regime transition in 1958 did not face powerfullyorganized antidemocratic rural elites.[22]

Social dynamics in Chile were different, but had the same effect. Conservative elements based in a system of labor-repressive agriculture supported the expansion of suffrage in the nineteenth century as a means of combating the rising power of industrialists and *capas medias*, who were tied to the state and supported by revenues from copper.[23] In effect, the social impact of the dominant presence of mineral exports meant that, when compared to the cases of Central America, both Venezuela and Chile were able to institutionalize democratic agreements with relative ease.

These cases illustrate the limits, as well as the opportunities, that social structures place upon contingent choice. If the focus in explaining the emergence of democracy had been solely on the forging of institutional compromises, that is, conceptualizing the establishment of democracy as only the product of strategic interactions, the pact-making that characterized the Venezuelan transition and the gradual expansion of the suffrage in Chile would appear to be simply the result of skillful bargaining by astute political leaders.[24] Instead, by focusing on the internal social dynamics produced by a mineral-based insertion into the international economy, it becomes evident how oil- or copper-induced structural change makes such "statecraft" possible. This is not to argue that individual decisions made at particular times or all observable political outcomes can be specifically and neatly linked to pre-existing structures, but it is to claim that historical structures, while not determining which one of a limited set of alternatives political actors may choose, are "confining conditions" that restrict or in some cases enhance the choices available to them. In other words, structural and institutional constraints determine the range of options available to decision makers and may even predispose them to choose a specific option.

What is called for, then, is a path-dependent approach which clarifies how broad structural changes shape particular regime transitions in ways that may be especially conducive (or especially obstructive) to democratization. This needs to be combined with an analysis of how such structural changes become embodied in political institutions and rules which subsequently mold the preferences and capacities of individuals during and after regime changes. This approach should make it possible to demonstrate how the range of options available to decision makers at any time is a function of structures put in place in the past and, concomitantly, how decisions are conditioned by institutions established in the past. The advantages of this approach are evident when compared to a structural approach alone, which leads to excessively deterministic conclusions about the origins and prospects of democracy, or to a sole focus on contingency, which produces overly voluntaristic interpretations.[25]

MODES OF TRANSITION TO DEMOCRACY

Once the links between structures, institutions, and contingent choice are articulated, it becomes apparent that the arrangements made by key political actors during a regime transition establish new rules, roles, and behavioral patterns which may or may not represent an important rupture from the past. These, in turn, eventually become the institutions shaping the prospects for regime consolidation in the future. Electoral laws, once adopted, encourage some interests to enter the political arena and discourage others. Certain models of economic development, once initiated through some form of compromise between capital and labor, systematically favor some groups over others in patterns that become difficult to change. Accords between political parties and the armed forces set out the initial boundaries of civilian and military spheres. Thus, what at the time may appear to be temporary agreements often become persistent barriers to change, barriers that can even scar a new regime with a permanent "birth defect."

These observations have important implications for studying democracy in Latin America. They suggest that rather than engage in a what may be a futile search for new preconditions, scholars would do well to concentrate on several tasks: (1) clarifying how the mode of regime transition (itself conditioned by the breakdown of authoritarian rule) sets the context within which strategic interactions can take place; (2) examining how these interactions, in turn, help to determine whether political democracy will emerge and survive; and (3) analyzing what type of democracy will eventually be institutionalized.

Thus it is important to begin to distinguish among possible modes of transition to democracy. First, we can distinguish between transitions in which democracies are the outcome of a strategy of overt force and transitions in which democracies are the outcome of a strategy of compromise (see the horizontal axis in Table 8.1). Second, we can distinguish between transitions in which incumbent ruling groups, no matter how weakened, are still ascendant in relation to mass actors and those in which mass actors have gained the upper hand, even temporarily, vis-à-vis those dominant elites (vertical axis in Table 8.1). The

Table 8.1   MODES OF TRANSITION TO DEMOCRACY

Relative strength of actors	Strategies of transition	
	Compromise	**Force**
Elite ascendant	Pact	Imposition
Mass ascendant	Reform	Revolution

cross tabulation of these distinctions produces four ideal types of democratic transition: reform, revolution, imposition, and pact. Actual transitions in practice combine elements of these ideal types.

Latin America, at one time or another, has experienced all four modes of transition. To date, however, no stable political democracy has resulted from regime transitions in which mass actors have gained control, even momentarily, over traditional ruling classes. Efforts at reform from below, which have been characterized by unrestricted contestation and participation, have met with subversive opposition from unsuppressed traditional elites, often aided by the United States, as the cases of Argentina (1946–1951), Guatemala (1946–1954), and Chile (1970–1973)[26] demonstrate. Revolutions generally produce stable forms of governance (Bolivia is an obvious exception), but such forms have not yet evolved into democratic patterns of fair competition, unrestricted contestation, rotation in power, and freedom of association, although recent developments in Nicaragua may soon challenge this assertion.[27]

Thus far, the most frequently encountered types of transition and the ones which have most often resulted in implantation of a political democracy are "transitions from above," or elite-ascendant transitions. Here traditional rulers remain in control, even if pressured from below, and successfully use strategies of compromise (pact) or force (imposition) or some mix of the two to retain at least part of their power.

Of these two modes of transition, democratization by pure imposition is the less common in Latin America, unless we include cases in which force or the threat of force was applied by foreign as well as domestic actors. This is not the case in Europe and Asia, where democratization through imposition often followed in several cases in the wake of World War II. In Table 8.2, the cell labeled imposition includes Brazil and Ecuador (where the military used its dominant position to establish unilaterally the rules for civilian governance). Cases on the margin include Costa Rica (where in 1948 an opposition party militarily defeated the governing party but then participated in pact-

Table 8.2   MODES OF TRANSITION TO DEMOCRACY IN LATIN AMERICA

PACT Venezuela (1958–) Colombia (1958–) Uruguay (1984–)		Costa Rica (1948–)		**IMPOSITION** Brazil (1974–) Ecuador (1976–)	
Chile (1932–1970)		Chile (1988–)		Guatemala (1984–)* El Salvador (1979)* Peru (1978–) Venezuela (1945–48)	
		Argentina (1983–)			
REFORM Argentina (1946–1951), Guatemala (1946–1954) Chile (1970–1973)†				**REVOLUTION** Mexico (1910–)* Bolivia (1952–) Nicaragua (1979–)**	

Elite Ascendant ↑ Mass Ascendant

Compromise ————————→ Force

*These cases cannot be considered democracies according to the definition used here. They are included because they are in periods of transformation and thus illustrate possible modes of transition in the future.

†See n. 26.

**See n. 27.

making to lay the foundation for stable democratic rule), Venezuela (1945–48) and contemporary Peru (where the military's control over the timing and shape of the transition was strongly influenced by a mass popular movement),[28] and Chile (where the military's unilateralism was curbed somewhat by its defeat in the 1988 plebiscite).[29]

Democracies that have endured for a respectable length of time appear to cluster in the cell labeled pact, indicating relatively strong elite actors who engage in strategies of compromise. This cell includes Venezuela (1958–), Colombia (1958–), the recent redemocratization in Uruguay (1984–), and Chile (1932–1970).[30] What unites these diverse cases, except Chile, is the presence of foundational pacts, that is, explicit (though not always public) agreements between contending actors, which define the rules of governance on the basis of mutual guarantees for the "vital interests" of those involved. Chile is an exception because there was no explicit pact among elites in 1932 when the democratic regime was simply "restored" on the basis of constitutional rules left over from the first democratic transition in 1874. Although the Chilean case suggests that elite-ascendant democracies can be established in the absence of foundational pacts, this may be more difficult in the contemporary period which is characterized by more developed organized interests, mass politics, stronger military capabilities, and a tighter integration into the international market. Under such conditions, *pactismo* may prove to be essential.[31]

Foundational pacts are well exemplified by the case of Venezuela (1958–). Here a series of agreements negotiated by the military, economic, and party leaders rested on explicit institutional arrangements.[32] The military agreed to leave power and to accept a new role as an "apolitical, obedient and non-deliberative body" in exchange for an amnesty for abuses committed during authoritarian rule and a guaranteed improvement of the economic situation of officers. Political parties agreed to respect the electoral process and share power in a manner commensurate with the voting results. They also accepted a "prolonged political truce" aimed at depersonalizing debate and facilitating consultation and coalitions. Capitalists agreed to accept legal trade unions and collective bargaining in exchange for significant state subsidies, guarantees against expropriation or socialization of property, and promises of labor peace from workers' representatives. This arrangement changed what could have become potentially explosive issues of national debate into established parameters by removing them from the electoral arena.

The foundational pacts underlying some new democracies have several essential components. First, they are inclusive and comprehensive. Indeed, because pacts are negotiated compromises in which contending forces agree to forego their capacity to harm each other by guaranteeing not to threaten each other's vital interests, they are successful only when they include all significant threatening forces and cover many areas of interest. The typical foundational pact is actually a series of interlocking and dependent agreements. It necessarily includes an agreement between the military and civilian elites over the conditions for establishing civilian rule, an agreement among political parties to compete under the new rules of governance, and a "social contract" involving state agencies, business associations, and trade unions regarding property rights, market arrangements, and the distribution of benefits.

Second, while such pacts are both substantive (concerned with the main tenets of policy) and procedural (concerned with the rules of policy making), they initially emphasize rule-making because "bargaining about bargaining" is the first and most important stage in the process of compromise. Only after all contending forces have agreed to bargain over their differences can the power sharing that leads to consensual governance result. This initial bargain can lay the basis for mutual trust if only by building familiarity among opposing groups. The very decision to enter into a pact can start a habit of pact making and an accommodative political style.

Such foundational pacts must be differentiated from smaller "managerial" accords.[33] These include the neofunctional arrangements frequently found in social democratic polities in Europe, for example, the annual corporatist negotiations between capital, labor, and the state in postwar Austria for setting wages and social policy, and the frequent accords hammered out between political opponents in Latin America. Unlike foundational pacts, managerial accords are partial rather than comprehensive, exclusive rather than inclusive, and oriented toward substance rather than rule making in content. Comprehensiveness, inclusiveness, and rule-making orientation are the identifying characteristics of a foundational pact. They help distinguish between basic agreements, such as those made in Venezuela in 1958, and more transitory political deals, such as the Pact of Apaneca which was forged between the Christian Democratic Party and ARENA in El Salvador in 1983.[34]

Finally, these pacts help ensure survival of the regime by reassuring traditional dominant classes that their vital interests will be respected. Although they include all the contending power holders, they simultaneously restrict the scope of representation. In essence, they are antidemocratic mechanisms, bargained by elites, which seek to create a deliberate socioeconomic and political contract that demobilizes emerging mass actors and delineates the extent to which all actors can participate or wield power in the future. They may accomplish this task by restricting contestation (as Colombian parties did in 1958 by agreeing to alternate in power regardless of the outcome of elections), by restricting the policy agenda (as Venezuelan parties did in 1958 by agreeing to implement the same economic program), or by restricting the franchise (as Chilean elites did beginning with the electoral law of 1874). Regardless of the strategic option chosen, the net effect is the same: The nature and extent of the initial democracy that results is markedly circumscribed.

TYPES OF DEMOCRACIES AND THEIR PROSPECTS IN THE CONTEMPORARY PERIOD

What are the implications of this discussion of preconditions and modes of transition for the prospects for democratization in contemporary Latin America? To begin with, the notion of process and sequence from regime breakdown to transition to consolidation and persistence is fundamental to understanding the two concurrent realities of democratization in Latin America today. On the one hand, most of the new civilian or militarized-civilian regimes—Argentina, Chile, Peru, Ecuador, Guatemala, Honduras, El Salvador, and Nicaragua—face an overwhelming problem of sheer survivability. What threatens their survival is the omnipresent specter of a military coup—a coup that may be provoked by intense partisan political disagreements, by the inability of political parties to manage the current profound economic crisis of the region, by the actions of antisystem elites, by a mass mobilization of labor, peasants, or the urban poor that escapes the control of traditional dominant classes, by the actions of a foreign power, or by threats to the vital corporate interests of the military itself. Significant uncertainty over the rules of the game still prevail in these fragile democracies.

What becomes important for maintaining civilian rule to find mechanisms—other than rigged or unpredictable elections—that can limit this uncertainty, especially by reducing incentives for civilians on the losing end to appeal to the military for salvation. This suggests two critical tasks initially facing Latin American democracies: first, to arrive at a sufficiently strong consensus about the rules of the game (including institutional formalities guaranteeing respect for certain crucial but minority concerns) such that no major elite is tempted to call upon the military to protect its vital interests and, second, to begin to design conscious strategies for the establishment of new civilian-military relations appropriate to future stable civilian rule. This is probably easier to accomplish in the more developed regions of the continent, where the armed forces have learned the importance of cooperating with capitalist and managerial elites, than in the less developed ones (Bolivia, Central America, and the Caribbean), where the military is still relatively confident about its ability to manage the economy and polity or is simply too corrupt to worry about such matters.[35]

On the other hand, other types of democracies in the region— Venezuela, Costa Rica, and, more recently, Brazil and Uruguay—are relatively consolidated in that actors are not preoccupied by an overriding concern with survival. Rather, the challenge that confronts most of these polities (and that will certainly confront others as preoccupation with mere survival recedes) is providing some new and better resolution to the ancient question of *cui bono*. This issue of "who benefits" from democracy is singularly problematic in Latin America, where dependent capitalist development has been especially ruthless in its historic patterns of exploitation.[36] This means that the extension of citizenship and equal political rights must take place in a context of extreme inequality, unparalleled even in Africa or Asia.[37] It must also take place during *la decada perdida*, that is to say, in the midst of the most severe and prolonged economic crisis since the Depression.[38]

The relationship between survival and cui bono may well be the central dilemma of democratization in Latin America. Choices made by key political actors to ensure the survival of a fragile democracy—the compromises they make, the agreements they enter—will necessarily and even irrevocably affect who gains and who loses during the consolidation of a new regime. Subsequent "populist" decisions to redistribute gains without regard for losses may affect the durability of the regime itself—regardless of how consolidated it may appear to be. At the same time, decisions not to redistribute or inaction on this front may also influence the regime durability because the commitment to democracy in part rests on the widely held (if sometimes inaccurate) conviction that economic benefits will be more fairly distributed or the welfare of the general population improved under this type of polity. Hence, the current concern with both survival and "who benefits" merely underlines the significance of choices made during the founding moments of democracies and highlights some potential relationships between political democracy and economic outcomes for future research. It also produces some not-so-promising scenarios for the emergence of different types of democracies.

First, political democracy in Latin America may be rooted in a fundamental paradox: The very modes of transition that appear to enhance initial survival by limiting unpredictability may preclude the future democratic self-transformation of the economy or polity further down the road. In other words, the conditions that permit democracies to persist in the short run may limit their potential for resolving the enormous problems of poverty and inequality that continue to characterize the continent. Indeed, it is reasonable to hypothesize that what occurs in the phase of transition or early consolidation may involve a significant trade-off between having some form of political democracy and achieving equity. Thus, even as these democracies guarantee a greater respect for law and human dignity when compared to their authoritarian predecessors, they may be unable to carry out substantive reforms that address the lot of their poorest citizens. If this scenario should occur, they would become the victims of their successful consolidation, and the democratic transitions of the 1980s that survive could prove to be the "frozen" democracies of the 1990s.

Second, while this may be the central dilemma of elite-ascendant processes of democratization, there may be important differences between countries such as Uruguay, which underwent a pact transition, and Brazil, which underwent an imposed transition. Pact democracies, whatever their defects, have been honed through compromise between at least two powerful contending elites. Thus their institutions should reflect some flexibility for future bargaining and the revision of existing rules. In Uruguay, even though the agreed-upon rules made it difficult to challenge agreements between the military and the parties on the issue of amnesty for atrocities committed during authoritarian rule, the left opposition, excluded from the agreement, was still able to force the convocation of a plebiscite on this major issue (which it subsequently lost). It is difficult to imagine that anything similar could occur in Brazil. Because the military exerted almost complete control over the transition, it never curtailed its own prerogatives nor fully agreed to the principle of civilian control, and it has not been compelled to adopt institutional rules reflecting the need for compromise.

The contrast between Uruguay and Brazil raises a hypothesis that merits investigation: To the extent that transitions are unilaterally imposed by armed forces who are not compelled to enter into compromises, the new regimes are likely to evolve into civilian governments controlled by authoritarian elements who are unlikely to push for greater participation, accountability, or equity for the majority of their citizens. In other words, the heritage left by "successful" authoritarian experiences, that is, those characterized by relatively moderate levels of repression and economic success which have left the military establishment relatively intact, may prove to be the major obstacle to future democratic self-transformation.[39] This danger also exists, albeit to a lesser extent, in civilian-directed unilateral transitions, for example, Mexico, because institutional rules that are imposed are likely to favor incumbents and allow less scope for contestation.

Third, the attempt to assess possible consequences of various modes of transition is most difficult where strong elements of imposition, compromise, and reform are simultaneously present, that is to say, where neither incumbent elites nor newly ascendant contenders for power are clearly in control and where the armed forces are relatively intact. This is currently the case in Argentina and Peru (as Table 8.2 demonstrates). Given the Argentinean military's defeat in the Falklands/Malvinas war, the high level of mass mobilization during the transition, and the absence of pacts between civilian authority and the armed forces and between trade unions and employers, Argentina combines elements of several modes of transition. Such a mixed scenario, while perhaps holding out the greatest hope for political democracy and economic equity, may render a consistent strategy of any type ineffectual and thus lead to the repetition of Argentina's persistent failure to consolidate any type of regime. The prospects for failure are even greater in Peru. Given the absence of explicit agreements between the leading political parties, the possibility of mass mobilizations in the midst of economic depression, the presence of an armed insurgency confronting a unified military, Peru is currently the most fragile democracy in South America.

Fourth, because political democracies generally arise from a compromise between contending organized elites that are unable to impose their will unilaterally or the unilateral action of one dominant

Table 8.3   MODES OF TRANSITION AND TYPES OF DEMOCRACY

Modes of Transition (Conditions of Demise of Authoritarian rule)	Regime Type (Variations in Regime Outcomes)
IMPOSITION ⟶	CONSERVATIVE DEMOCRACY
External ⟶	Electoral Authoritarian Rule
Internal ⟶	Conservative Democracy
PACT ⟶	CORPORATIST DEMOCRACY
	Multi-Party (Collusive)
REFORM ⟶	COMPETITIVE DEMOCRACY
	Multi-Party (Competitive)
REVOLUTION ⟶	ONE-PARTY DOMINANT REGIME

group, usually the armed forces, this does not bode well for democratization in situations in which the armed forces are inextricably tied to the interests of a dominant (and antidemocratic) agrarian class. Guatemala and El Salvador in particular are characterized by a landowning elite whose privileged position is based on labor-repressive agriculture and on a partnership with the armed forces, thereby, making it unlikely that their militaries (as currently constituted) will tolerate comprehensive political competition, civil liberties, or accountability. Regardless of the profound differences between these two Central American countries, in both cases democratization depends on a restructuring of the military and a transformation of its direct links to economic elites. Short of these changes, the extraordinary pressure of U.S. intervention as well as international diffusion means that, at minimum, they can be expected to adhere to "electoralism," meaning the regularized holding of elections even as they continue to restrict the other political rights and opportunities of their citizens. This hybrid mix of electoral form and authoritarianism, which has been dubbed "electocratic rule" by one observer,[40] is likely to emerge in other developing areas wherever the spread of elections under foreign inspiration either precedes or is intended to coopt strong domestic pressures for democratization.

These observations can be distilled into types of democracies, which, at least initially, are largely shaped by the mode of transition, as Table 8.3 illustrates. They suggest that democratization by imposition is likely to yield conservative democracies that cannot or will not address equity issues. To the extent that imposition originates from outside, the result is likely to be some form of electoral authoritarian rule, which cannot be considered democracy at all. Transition through pact is likely to produce corporatist or consociational democracies in which party competition is regulated to varying degrees by the nature of foundational bargains. Transition through reform is likely to bring about competitive democracies, whose political fragility paves the way for an eventual return to authoritarianism. Finally, a revolutionary transition, should it result in democracy at all, will tend to result in one-party dominant democracies, where competition is also regulated. These types are characterized by different mixes and varying degrees of the chief dimensions of democracy: contestation, participation, accountability, and civilian control over the military.

Such predictions are discouraging, but they may be offset by more hopeful observations that affect the contingent choices of contemporary democratizers. On the one hand, the Cold War features of the international system have changed remarkably, and this may offer new opportunities to the reformist mode of transition in Latin America. The failure of two of the three cases cited in this category, Guatemala (1946–1954) and Chile (1970–1973), was profoundly affected by U.S. intervention, motivated in large part by the ideological identification of mass-based reforms with the spread of Soviet influence on the continent. U.S. intervention against peasant-based movements in Central America has been justified in the same manner. To the extent that the global state system loses its "bipolarity," the credibility of such accusations becomes increasingly difficult to sustain, thus potentially creating more space for mass-ascendant political movements. The fact that this mode of transition failed in the past in Latin America does not mean that it will not succeed in the future.[41]

On the other hand, this discussion of modes of transition and varying probabilities for survival has not presumed that democracies will benefit from superior economic performance, which is fortunate given the state of contemporary Latin American economies. Most observers assume that crises in growth, employment, foreign exchange earnings, debt repayments, and so forth necessarily bode ill for the consolidation of democratic rule, and few would question the long-run value of an increasing resource base for stability. But austerity may have some perverse advantages—at least, for initial survival. In the context of the terrible economic conditions of the 1980s, the exhaustion of utopian ideologies and even of rival policy prescriptions has become painfully evident. Neither the extreme right nor the extreme left has a plausible alternative system to offer—to themselves or to the public. Though populism, driven by diffuse popular expectations and *desencanto* with the rewards of compromised democracy, is always a possibility—witness the experience of Peru and the recent elections in Argentina —it cannot deliver the immediate rewards that have been its sustenance in the past.

To the extent that this situation diminishes both the expected benefits and rewards from antisystem activity, it enhances the likelihood that democracies will endure. This suggests a possible hypothesis for future exploration: The relationship between democratization and economic performance, rather than rising or falling in tandem, may be parabolic. Conditions to strike bargains may be most favorable in the midst of protracted austerity, as well as in the midst of sustained plenty. They may be worse when the economy is going through stop-and-go cycles or being hit with sudden windfalls or scarcities. If true, this provides a ray of hope for the otherwise unpromising decade ahead.

Finally, there is no a priori reason why one type of democracy cannot be transformed into another, that is to say, why electoral authoritarian regimes, for example, cannot change into conservative or competitive democracies, or corporatist democracies into more competitive ones. Given the frequency of *pactismo* and the gravity of the equity problem in Latin America, the latter scenario is especially important. While transitions through pacts do establish an improvisational institutional framework of governance that may become a semipermanent barrier to change, this framework can be further modified. Such modification may be brought about preemptively when some ruling groups, having experienced the advantages of democratic rule, become more inclined over time to seek accommodation to potential pressures from below rather than repression or it may occur through the direct pressure of organized social groups.[42] In either case democratization can prove to be an ongoing process of renewal.

The notion that one type of democracy may gradually change into a different type suggests that the dynamics of democratic consolidation must differ in important ways from the transition if "freezing" is to be avoided. Because the overriding goal of the transition is to reach some broad social consensus about the goals of society and the acceptable means to achieve them, successful transitions are necessarily characterized by accommodation and compromise. But if this emphasis on caution becomes an overriding political norm during consolidation, democracies may find it difficult to demonstrate that they are better than their predecessors at resolving fundamental social and economic problems. Thus consolidation, if it is to be successful, should require skills and commitments from leading actors that are different from those exhibited during the transition. In consolidation, actors must demonstrate the ability to differentiate political forces rather than to draw them all into a grand coalition, the capacity to define and channel competing political projects rather than to keep potentially divisive reforms off the agenda, and the willingness to tackle incremental reforms, especially in the domains of the economy and civil-military relations rather than defer them to some later date. If the cycle of regime change that has plagued Latin America is to be broken and replaced by an era of protracted democratic rule, democratizers must learn to divide as well as to unite and to raise hopes as well as to dampen expectations.

NOTES

A version of this essay which appeared in *Comparative Politics*, was originally presented at the Conference on Latin America at the Threshold of the 1990s, Beijing, June 8–16, sponsored by the Institute of Latin America of the Chinese Academy of Social Sciences and the Ford Foundation. The author wishes to thank David G. Becker, Ken Erickson, Richard Fagen, Samuel Valenzuela, and, most especially, Phillippe Schmitter.

1. These questions underlie a number of new studies on democracy, for example, Guillermo O'Donnell, Philippe Schmitter and Lawrence Whitehead, eds., *Transitions from Authoritarian Rule*, 4 vols. (Baltimore: Johns Hopkins University Press, 1986); Paul W. Drake and Eduardo Silva, eds., *Elections and Democratization in Latin America. 1980–1985* (San Diego: Center for Iberian and Latin American Studies, University of California, 1986); Enrique A. Baloyra, *Comparing New Democracies: Transition and Consolidation in Mediterranean Europe and the Southern Cone* (Boulder, Colo.: Westview Press, 1987); Carlos Huneeus, *Para Vivir La Democracia* (Santiago: Editorial Andante, 1987); Larry Diamond, Juan J. Linz, and Seymour Martin Lipset, eds., *Democracy in Developing Countries*, 4 vols. (Boulder, Colo.: Lynne Rienner Publishers, 1988–1990).

2. Dankwart A. Rustow "Transitions to Democracy: Towards a Dynamic Model," *Comparative Politics* 2, no. 3 (April 1970).

3. This statement requires some qualification. J. A. Schumpeter defines democracy as "that institutional arrangement for arriving at political decisions in which individuals acquire the power to decide by means of a competitive struggle for the people's vote" in his classic study, *Capitalism. Socialism and Democracy* (London: Allen and Unwin, 1943), 269. Under this definition the competition for leadership through free elections is the distinctive feature of democracy. But Schumpeter, unlike Jeane Kirkpatrick or other U.S. policymakers in the 1980s, considered civil liberties a necessary condition for the operation of democracy. Thus it cannot be assumed that he would have shared the current emphasis on the mere presence of elections, which I have elsewhere referred to as "electoral-

ism," that is, "the faith that merely holding elections will channel political action into peaceful contests among elites and accord public legitimacy to the winners in these contests." See "Imposing Consent? Electoralism Versus Democratization in El Salvador," in Drake and Silva, eds., *Elections and Democratization*, 34.

4. For an example of this approach, see Suzanne Jonas, "Elections and Transitions: The Guatemalan and Nicaraguan Case," in John Booth and Mitchell A. Seligson, eds., *Elections and Democracy in Central America* (Chapel Hill: University of North Carolina Press, 1989). In "Democracy in Nicaragua," by Jonas and Nancy Stein, the authors argue against separating political democracy from socioeconomic equity; they support "a broader view that meaningful 'transitions to democracy' [in Central America] involve more sweeping social change on the scale of the major bourgeois and socialist revolutions historically." See Suzanne Jonas and Nancy Stein, eds., *Democracy in Latin America* (New York: Bergin and Garvey, 1990), 43.

5. In examining the problem of constructing institutions that can translate the preferences of majorities into public policy, for example, social choice theorists have demonstrated the difficulty of designing decision-making procedures that give equal weight to the preferences of all citizens and that permit the aggregation of these preferences into governmental policies without violating any of the other basic tenets of democratic theory. See, for example, William H. Riker, *Liberalism Versus Populism: A Confrontation Between the Theory of Democracy and the Theory of Social Choice* (San Francisco: Freeman, 1982); Jules Coleman and John Ferejohn, "Democracy and Social Choice," *Ethics* 97, no. 1 (October 1986). Theorists of democracy have long grappled with other dilemmas involving notions of social justice and equity. See, for example, Peter Bachrach, *The Theory of Democratic Elitism: A Critique* (Washington, D.C.: University Press of America, 1980); or Carole Pateman, *Participation and Democratic Theory* (Cambridge: Cambridge University Press. 1970).

6. I have drawn the first two dimensions and, to some extent, the third from Robert A. Dahl's *Polyarchy: Participation and Opposition* (New Haven, Conn.: Yale University Press, 1971). But Dahl, like other democratic theorists, does not emphasize the establishment of civilian control over the military through the limitation of military prerogatives. Indeed, this element often appears to be an assumed condition or even an unstated prerequisite in other definitions of democracy. Alfred Stepan, whose book *Rethinking Military Politics: Brazil and the Southern Cone* (Princeton, N.J.: Princeton University Press, 1988) is an important corrective in this regard, defines the military's institutional prerogatives as "those areas where,

whether challenged or not, the military as an institution assumes they have an acquired right or privilege, formal or informal, to exercise effective control over its internal governance, to play a role within extramilitary areas within the state apparatus, or even to structure relationships between the state and political or civil society" (p. 93). The clear determination and limitation of these areas is a measure of civilian control and, in my view, is also a measure of democratization.

7. This formulation originally appeared in Lipset's classic essay "Some Social Requisites of Democracy: Economic Development and Political Legitimacy," *American Political Science Review* 53, no. 1 (March 1959).

8. Some proponents of this view often measured the prospects for democracy by per capita gross domestic product, leading the occasional political observer to await the moment when a particular country would cross "the threshold" into democracy. This supposed threshold has varied from country to country. Spain's Lopez Redo once predicted that his country would not become democratic until it reached a per capita income of $2,000. More recently, Mitchell Seligson has argued that Central America needs to approach a per capita income of $250 (in 1957 dollars) and a literacy rate of over 50 percent as a necessary precondition for democratization. See James M. Malloy and Mitchell A. Seligson, eds., *Authoritarians and Democrats: Regime Transition in Latin America* (Pittsburgh: University of Pittsburgh Press, 1987), 7–9.

9. Howard J. Wiarda, for example, argued in "Toward a Framework for the Study of Political Change in the Iberic-Latin Tradition: The Corporative Model" in his edited *Corporatism and National Development in Latin America* (Boulder, Colo.: Westview Press, 1981) that Latin America possessed "a political culture and a sociopolitical order that at its core is essentially two-class, authoritarian, traditional, elitist, patrimonial, Catholic, stratified, hierarchical and corporate." A similar argument can be found in Richard N. Morse, "The Heritage of Latin America" in Howard Wiarda, ed., *Politics and Social Change in Latin America: The Distinct Tradition*, (Amherst: University of Massachusetts Press, 1974).

10. The notion of "civic culture," first introduced by Gabriel Almond and Sidney Verba in *The Civic Culture* (Princeton, N.J.: Princeton University Press, 1963), sought to analyze the relationship between the political attitudes of a population and the nature of its political system. It was the forerunner to the works on Latin America cited above.

11. This was the basic argument put forward by Leonard Binder et al., eds., *Crises and Sequences in Political Development* (Princeton,

N.J.: Princeton University Press, 1971) and by Eric Nordlinger, "Political Development, Time Sequences and Rates of Change," in Jason L. Finkle and Robert W. Gable, eds., Political *Development and Social Change*, 2d ed. (New York: Wiley, 1971). See Barrington Moore, Jr., *Social Origins of Dictatorship and Democracy: Lord and Peasant in the Making of the Modern World* (Boston: Beacon Press, 1966).

13. See John Weeks, "An Interpretation of the Central American Past," *Latin American Research Review* 21, no. 3 (1986); Enrique Baloyra-Herp, "Reactionary Despotism in Central America," *Journal of Latin American Studies* 15, no. 2 (1983); Jeffrey Paige, "Coffee and Politics in Central America" in Richard Tardanico, ed., *Crisis in the Caribbean Basin* (Beverly Hills, Calif.: Sage, 1987).

    In a more recent work, Paige seeks to differentiate his argument from that of Moore; see "The Social Origins of Dictatorship, Democracy and Socialist Revolution in Central America," paper presented at the Annual Meeting of the American Sociological Association, San Francisco, August 8, 1989. He correctly contends that there is no collision between an industrial bourgeoisie and a landed class in Costa Rica, El Salvador, and Nicaragua and that the agrarian aristocracy has successfully transformed itself into a modern capitalist class—both conditions that belie Moore's argument. Nonetheless, in Guatemala and El Salvador a landed class continues to exercise domination and the commercialization of agriculture has not replaced a labor-repressive mode of production, thus providing some important confirmation of Moore.

14. Guillermo O'Donnell, *Modernization and Bureaucratic Authoritarianism* (Berkeley: University of California, Institute for International Studies, 1973) and Fernando Henrique Cardoso, "Associated-Dependent Development: Theoretical and Practical Implications" in Alfred Stepan, ed., *Authoritarian Brazil* (New Haven, Conn.: Yale University Press, 1973), 142–178.

15. Samuel P. Huntington, "Will More Countries Become Democratic?" *Political Science Quarterly* 99, no. 2 (1984).

16. Furthermore, through the Church's active promotion of "base communities," it could even be argued that contemporary Catholicism contributes to the creation of a uniquely democratic culture by encouraging participation among previously unorganized groups of the urban and rural poor. See Philip Oxhorn, "Bringing the Base Back In: The Democratization of Civil Society Under the Chilean Authoritarian Regime" (Ph.D. dissertation, Harvard University, 1989).

17. For criticism of the O'Donnell hypothesis linking capital deepening to authoritarian rule, see David Collier, ed., *The New Authoritarianism in Latin America* (Princeton, N.J.: Princeton University Press, 1979) and Karen Remmer and Gilbert Merkx, "Bureaucratic-Authoritarianism Revisited," *Latin American Research Review* 17 (1982).

18. Albert Hirschman has even claimed that this search can be pernicious. In his view, to lay down strict preconditions for democracy, such as "dynamic growth *must* be resumed, income distribution must be improved, ... political parties *must* show a cooperative spirit" may actually encourage the deconsolidation of existing democracies. Hirschman argues that this will almost certainly obstruct constructive thinking about the ways in which democracies may be formed, survive, and even become stronger in the face of and in spite of continuing adversity; "Dilemmas of Democratic Consolidation in Latin America," unpublished notes for the São Paulo Meeting on Democratic Consolidation in Latin America and Southern Europe, 1986.

19. See especially in O'Donnell, Schmitter, and Whitehead, *Transitions*, the work by O'Donnell and Schmitter, *Tentative Conclusions about Uncertain Transitions*, vol. 4, and by Adam Przeworski, "Some Problems in the Study of the Transition to Democracy," vol. 3, and his "Democracy as a Contingent Outcome of Conflicts" in Rune Slagsted and Jon Elster, eds., *Constitutionalism and Democracy* (New York: Cambridge University Press, 1989).

20. Philippe C. Schmitter, "Democratic Consolidation of Southern Europe," unpublished manuscript.

21. Evelyne Huber Stephens makes a similar observation in "Economic Development, Social Change and Political Contestation and Inclusion in South America," paper prepared for the Latin American Studies Association, New Orleans, 1988.

22. See Terry Lynn Karl, *The Paradox of Plenty: Oil Booms and Petro-States* (Berkeley: University of California Press, 1991), and "Petroleum and Political Pacts: The Transition to Democracy in Venezuela," *Latin American Research Review* 22, no.1 (1986).

23. See Arturo Valenzuela and Samuel Valenzuela, "Los Origines de la Democracia: Reflexiones Teóricas sobre el Caso de Chile," *Estudios Públicos*, no. 12 (Primavera) 1983.

24. This is the general thrust of Daniel Levine's analysis of Venezuela, which attributes the emergence of a democratic regime primarily to statecraft and the ability of political actors to compromise. See his "Venezuela Since 1958: The Consolidation of Democratic Politics," in Juan J. Linz and Alfred Stepan, eds., *The Breakdown of Demo-*

cratic Regimes: Latin America (Baltimore: Johns Hopkins University Press, 1978).

25. An approach of this sort treats regime changes as critical junctures and carries an implicit assumption of patterns of political change characterized by gradualism punctuated by sharp discontinuities. It has a long tradition in the study of politics, but it is especially important in recent work on the "new institutionalism." See, for example, J. G. March and J. P. Olson, "The New Institutionalism: Organizational Factors in Political Life," *American Political Science Review* 78 (September 1984): 734–749; Stephen D. Krasner, "Sovereignty: An Institutional Perspective," *Comparative Political Studies* 21, no.1 (April 1988): 66–94. Krasner, though emphasizing political institutions alone rather than the combination of social structures and institutions, also argues that institutions established in the past constrain present choices, that the preferences of individual actors are conditioned by institutional structures, and that historical trajectories are path-dependent. The most recent comparative analysis of patterns of South American and Mexican development adopts a similar framework. Ruth Berins Collier and David Collier's *Shaping the Political Arena: Critical Junctures. the Labor Movement and Regime Dynamics in Latin America* (Princeton, N.J.: Princeton University Press, 1991) is the most ambitious effort to utilize this sort of path-dependent approach. In their comparative analysis they examine the different trajectories that result from the initial patterns of incorporation of the labor movement into political life.

26. Strictly speaking, the case of Chile from 1970 to 1973 is not an effort of regime transition from authoritarian rule in the sense considered here. Rather, it is better understood as an attempt to move from one type of democracy to another, that is, a move down the vertical scale of the classification scheme in Table 8.1 toward a reform democracy.

27. Nicaragua is the first revolutionary regime on the continent to hold national elections in which a number of political parties have been able to compete. In 1984 the traditional Liberal and Conservative parties and several small leftist parties competed with the FSLN and won almost 35 percent of the vote. In 1990 the UNO, a coalition of fourteen anti-Sandinista parties, defeated the Sandinistas, who promised to respect the mandate of the electorate. This apparent evolution from a one-party dominant system to a competitive one is the result of a transition characterized by foreign imposition and some degree of pacting as well as by revolution.

28. There is little information on the dynamics of regime transition in Costa Rica. See Jacobo Schifter, *La fase oculta de la guerra civil en*

Costa Rica (San Jose: EDUCA, 1979). Fabrice Edouard Lehoucq, "Explaining the Origins of Democratic Regimes: Costa Rica in Theoretical Perspective" (Ph.D. dissertation, Duke University, forthcoming), applies the notion of democracy as a contingent institutional compromise to this case. On the transition in Peru, see Cynthia Sanborn, "Social Democracy and the Persistence of Populism in Peru" (Ph.D. dissertation, Harvard University, forthcoming).

29. Even where the military retained control over the transition, however, it systematically engaged in a process of consultation with civilian parties. See Anita Isaacs, "The Obstacles to Democratic Consolidation in Ecuador," paper presented to the Latin American Studies Association, San Juan, Puerto Rico, September 21–23, 1989; Francis Hagopian and Scott Mainwaring, "Democracy in Brazil: Origins, Problems and Prospects," *World Policy Journal* (Summer 1987): 485–514; and Manuel Antonio Garreton, "El Plebiscito de 1988 y la transición a la democracia" (Santiago: FLACSO, 1988).

30. On these cases, see Charles G. Gillespie, "Uruguay's Transition from Collegial Military-Technocratic Rule" in O'Donnell, Schmitter, and Whitehead, *Transtions in Latin America*; Jonathan Hartlyn, "Democracy in Colombia: The Politics of Violence and Accommodation," in Diamond, Linz, and Lipset, *Democracy in Developing Countries: vol. 4, Latin America*; Alexander W. Wilde, "Conversations Among Gentlemen: Oligarchical Democracy in Colombia" in Linz and Stepan, *Breakdown of Democratic Regimes: vol. 4, Latin America*; Karl, "Petroleum and Political Pacts."

31. I am grateful to Samuel Valenzuela for this point. See his *Democratizacion Via Reforma: La Expansion del Sufraaio en Chile* (Buenos Aires: Ediciones IDES, 1985).

32. The roots of these arrangements can be found in the *Pacto de Punto Fijo* and the *Declaración de Principios y Programa Mínimo de Gobierno*, which were signed prior to the country's first elections by all contending presidential candidates. These agreements bound all signatories to the same basic political and economic program regardless of the electoral outcome. These pacts are described more fully in Karl, "Petroleum and Political Pacts."

33. This distinction was originally drawn by Philippe Schmitter in a conference on Microfoundations of Democracy, University of Chicago, March 1988.

34. This agreement served primarily as a mechanism for partitioning state offices and establishing other temporary forms of power sharing. Because it excluded powerful, well-organized forces on the left and was never aimed at establishing permanent rules of the game, it does not meet the criteria for a foundational pact.

35. I am grateful to David G. Becker for this observation.

36. Most observers locate the roots of this exploitation in colonial and postcolonial landholding patterns that, slowly or abruptly, concentrated property ownership and dispossessed the majority. Specific social processes not conducive to democratization accompanied these land-holding patterns. For example, unlike the reciprocal forms of feudalism that developed in Europe and may have eventually contributed to widespread norms of reciprocity and community at the local level, the penetration of capitalism altered traditional clientelist relations between landlords and peasants in Latin America from a two-way to a one-way affair. As Paul Harrison remarks in *Inside the Third World: The Anatomy of Poverty* (London: Penguin Books, 1979), 105, "In Latin America the peasant has only duties, the landowner rights." Such social relations have left little residue of notions of mutual obligation or reciprocity between the rich and the poor.

37. I am referring to indicators of inequality here, not absolute poverty. While most of southern Asia and Africa is far poorer than Latin America, their colonial past, patterns of land tenure, and relations of production are quite different. Parts of Asia that have experienced capitalist commercialization of agriculture are now beginning to approximate these same indicators of inequality, but Asia in general has not reached the regional scale of inequality that marks Latin America.

38. One statistic eloquently demonstrates the depth of the crisis. By 1987, Latin America's debt represented 46 percent of the region's gross national product and more than *four times* the value of its exports. See *Economic and Social Progress in Latin America: 1988 Report* (Washington, D.C.: Inter-American Development Bank, 1988), 541.

39. The notion that especially "successful" authoritarian regimes may pose important obstacles for democratization can be found in Anita Isaacs, "Dancing with the People: The Politics of Military Rule in Ecuador, 1972–1979" (Ph.D. dissertation, Oxford University, 1986), and Guillermo O'Donnell, "Challenges to Democratization in Brazil," *World Policy Journal* 5, no.2 (Spring 1988): 281–300.

40. I am grateful to Charles Call, Ph.D. candidate in the Department of Political Science, Stanford University, for this label.

41. There are important differences here, however, between South America and the Caribbean basin. Military interventions, which have been confined to the latter region in the past, predated the Cold War and are likely to continue after its demise. As the case of Panama shows, the rationale may simply change.

42. Paul Cammack has argued that a ruling coalition might make strategic concessions in its own long-term interest to help sustain democracy, especially after having experienced the failure of militaries to act as reliable allies. See his "Democratization: A Review of the Issues," *Bulletin of Latin American Research* 4, no. 2 (1985): 39–46. There seems to be little evidence for this predicted behavior in the current period, however, and further democratization through mass pressure seems to be more likely.

Chapter
9

Transitions to Democracy Reconsidered

A Historical Perspective

Metin Heper

PRESENT STATE OF THE ART

During the 1950s and a good part of the 1960s, with some notable exceptions (for example, Huntington[1]), social scientific thought was dominated by the convergence theory. It was assumed that all societies would inevitably progress from a *Gemeinschaft* to a *Gesellschaft* type of structure and in the process would come to have a plural democracy, not unlike the political regimes in the industrialized countries.[2] In accordance with this assumption of unilinear evolution research about democracy centered on determining the "prerequisites" of this particular type of regime. At this stage the researchers considered the difficulties that democracies faced to be signs of "political immaturity"; they assumed that such "growing pains" would be alleviated and the developing polities would catch up with the developed ones.

With the reemergence in the 1960s of authoritarian regimes in many Latin American countries, the earlier optimism began to fade. One strand of thought attributed these events in Latin America to the inherently authoritarian and corporatist nature of society in that region.[3] A second approach took "structural constraints produced by dependent capitalism" as the guilty party.[4] Both approaches paid attention to the dynamics of the political systems in the Third World countries themselves, which the functionalist paradigm based on the convergence theory had neglected, but both, not unlike the functionalist approach, were characterized by an unmistakable determinism.

A third approach not only also addressed itself to the issue of establishing democracy in the countries in question, but also avoided determinism. The so-called genetic approach proposed by Dankwart A. Rustow explored from a diachronic perspective the stages through which democracy could be installed and consolidated.[5] Looking at the Swedish and the Turkish experiences, Rustow suggested that, given the single precondition of national unity, a viable democracy would be established through a process of polarization, crisis, and compromise. He offered the view that in the last analysis a smoothly functioning democracy would be the handiwork of politicians skilled in bargaining techniques and the politicians in question would not see politics as a zero-sum game.

The pattern of conflict resolution deemed critical by Rustow had an affinity to, but what was somewhat different from, the *problematique* Huntington had posed earlier. Huntington considered most important the process of political instutionalization, that is, the emergence of an autonomous political center with its own values and norms, rather than individual political actors adept at bargaining and compromise. A smoothly functioning democracy, according to Huntington, needed political institutions that would moderate and redirect the relative power of the social forces.[6] Robert A. Dahl concurred in this idea when he pointed out that while political organizations should be controlled, they should also have their own autonomy.[7] Earlier Otto Kirchheimer, too, had tied the consolidation of democracy to the instutionalization of the norms and structures of the regime itself.[8]

A more recent approach, which resembles the genetic one but differs from it in one important aspect, has informed the mainstream studies of the transitions to democracy as well as of the breakdowns of democratic regimes.[9] While Rustow drew attention to the fact that the consolidation of democracy depended on factors other than the particular strategies of the principal actors, for example, the nature of the cleavages in the polity,[10] the more recent studies of the transitions to democracy have focused on relatively short-run developments and the reactions of the political actors to those developments. A prominent example is the "Transitions" project of Guillermo O'Donnell, Philippe Schmitter, and Laurence Whitehead.[11] Although the authors in this project were careful to qualify their conclusions as "tentative" and the democracies they studied as "uncertain," they nevertheless came up with a specific scenario of successful transition to democracy, which emphasized gradual and controlled regime change. The authors seemed to suggest that if the political actors in the unsuccessful cases had been sophisticated enough they, too, could have led their countries toward stable democracies.

Given the enormous differences in the fortunes of democracy in the different clusters of countries studied (countries in Latin America and Southern Europe, including Turkey), taking the resourcefulness of the political actors as the crucial independent variable does not seem to be a tenable research strategy. While most of the Latin American countries experienced regime oscillation, moving back and forth between authoritarianism and democracy, most of the countries in Southern Europe experienced long-lasting authoritarian regimes which in time evolved into democracies that were on the whole considered much more stable than their Latin American counterparts. Individual countries within each region, too, evinced significantly different patterns. In Latin America, Brazil made a transition to democracy that was much more closely monitored by the preceding authoritarian regime than elsewhere on that continent. In Southern Europe, the authoritarian regime in Greece was dominated by the military; the authoritarian regimes in Italy, Spain, and Portugal, particularly after they had been installed, were controlled by the civilians. There were also important regional differences and similarities. Not unlike the situation in most Latin American cases, but unlike other Southern European examples, the authoritarian regime in Greece showed a greater degree of oscillation. Then there were two cases that were each almost a type in itself— Mexico in Latin America and Turkey in Southern Europe. Although Salvador Giner noted that political dynamics in Turkey were "perhaps unique"[12] and elsewhere they were described as "exceptional," "ambiguous," or "strange,"[13] Turkey, along with Mexico, was included in this project through which the authors expected to generalize on the dynamics of regime transitions to democracy.

As the authors in this project themselves pointed out, at the end they did not have "a 'theory' to test or apply to the case studies and thematic essays" that were produced.[14] They adopted an inductive method and indiscriminately drew upon the experiences of countries different from each other in rather important respects. In this author's estimation, it was for this reason they ended up finding some phenomena paradoxical and some developments surprising. For instance, O'Donnell and Schmitter noted: "Ironically, the more episodic and incoherent authoritarian experiences of Latin America, as well as that of Greece, seem to have done more to undermine the institutions of the more-or-less democratic regimes which preceded them than the longer-lived and ideologically stronger authoritarianisms of Italy, Spain and Portugal."[15]

If this particular development had been looked at from a theoretical rather than a purely empiricist perspective, it might not have seemed ironic. As will be elaborated below, in Latin America there had been on the whole a lesser degree of political institutionalization than in

Southern Europe. It was this fact, and not the duration or the strength of the authoritarian regimes, that posed difficulties for the consolidation of democracy in most countries on that continent.

It should also be noted that the authors attempted to account for different fortunes of democracy in the clusters of countries in question, among other things, but particularly by the "greater resiliency of civil society in Southern Europe" and indicated that in this respect Brazil resembled Southern Europe.[16] Elsewhere in this project, too, Brazil emerged as quite different from most other Latin American countries, yet the implications of this crucial difference were not systematically analyzed.

As already noted, the orientation to the installation and consolidation of democracy adopted in the Transitions project led the authors to a search for skillful manipulation of the situation so that an enduring "opening" *(apertura)* could be brought about. By endless cataloging of differences and similarities in the authoritarian and democratic experiences of the countries concerned, they arrived at a formula for a successful transition to democracy—a gradual and controlled passage. This particular scenario did work in some countries, but there is no reason to expect that it would also take place in other countries with different historical traditions. The authors' otherwise laudable normative (that is, democratic) stance, as explicated by Abraham F. Lowenthal,[17] led them to produce an essentially prescriptive work, but it was not backed up by a theoretically based analysis.

AN ALTERNATIVE APPROACH

This particular approach to the installation and consolidation of democracy should be replaced by a more theoretical version, along the lines implied in Rustow's essay.[18] There is first of all a need to trace the historical antecedents of the present regimes. For instance, if the Transitions project had addressed itself to the question of why in the first place the Latin American authoritarian experience had become "a more episodic and incoherent phenomenon," its authors might not have reached the conclusion that the authoritarian regimes in Southern Europe did more harm to the political institutions than the ones in Latin America.

A study of the history of the regimes is necessary not only in the analyses of "Western states,"[19] but also in the present endeavors. As James M. Malloy suggested, such an approach would reveal the underlying forces that generated the alternation between authoritarianism and democracy in most Latin American polities.[20] It follows that there is a need to study the imprint left on the present political systems by their particular paths of development. We can assume after S. N. Eisenstadt that variations arising from the different paths may persist in some crucial structural areas such as the rules of the political game.[21] Such continuing orientations may lead different polities to produce different responses to the same set of exigencies. An overly empiricist approach uninformed by an appropriate theoretical framework would miss the various meanings attributed to the same problems and, therefore, would not capture the particular logic behind different solutions adopted to deal with those problems. For instance, democracy may be taken in some contexts as an end in itself, for example, Turkey,[22] but in other contexts as a means to other goals, for example, Latin America and Southern Europe, a crucial distinction made by Huntington.[23]

This detour through history should not, of course, lead us back to determinism. While exploring the effect of the past on the present phenomena, we should remain aware that political actors are engaged in an ongoing learning process. The Transitions project did pay attention to this process, but because its theoretical weakness prevented its authors from exploring satisfactorily what was "learned," they failed to differentiate what may be called a "superficial learning" (understanding the immediate causes of political instability, that is, the success and failure of the short-term strategies of the various elites) from "genuine learning" (identifying the enduring underlying causes of that instability, that is, realizing the need for political institutionalization). The causes of the precariousness of democracies in Latin America on the whole and the considerable stability of democracies in Southern Europe can be better appreciated if we distinguish between these two types of learning.

The approach suggested here also needs guidelines concerning which dimensions of political regimes should be examined. If one assumes, after Dahl, that the consolidation of democracy depends on striking a delicate balance between autonomy and control,[24] the critical aspects of the polities that should be investigated are: (1) the kind and degree of institutionalization of politics; (2) the historical antecedents that have an important impact on the institutionalization patterns.

As already noted, Huntington addressed himself to the need for political institutions that would moderate and redirect the relative power of social forces,[25] but he did not deal with the different kinds and degrees of political institutionalization one may find in different contexts, as Mark Kesselman and Gabriel Ben-Dor have shown.[26] Political institutions may be too weak or too strong, and such institutionalization patterns would create problems. A too-strong institutionalization may emerge in polities where it is brought about by nonpolitical entities, for example, the bureaucratic or the military elite. Thus institutionalization may come not in the form of regularly achieving a *modus vivendi*

among the competing interests (as Huntington assumed), but, to use
Kenneth H. F. Dyson's term, in the form of a generalizing, integrating,
and legitimating state, the agents of which identify by themselves
(without reference to the "interests") the leading values of the polity in
terms of which political authority is to be exercised.[27]

Such a generalizing, integrating, and legitimating state is sometimes embodied in the political party, as in the Federal Republic of Germany,[28] most often in the bureaucracy as in France,[29] and in some rare
cases in the office of the president, as in post-1980 Turkey.[30] As will be
elaborated below, these distinctions between too-weak, neither too-
weak nor too-strong, and too-strong institutionalization patterns shed
considerable light on the stability of democracy in many Latin American countries, some Southern European countries, and in Turkey,
respectively.

Turning to the historical antecedents of different patterns of political institutionalization, it is apparent that we need more abstract and
general categories than those provided by Huntington, for institutionalization, or virtual lack thereof, has taken many different forms. For a
study of the underlying and enduring problems of political regimes from
this perspective, a categorization of antecedent regime types developed
by S. N. Eisenstadt seems quite useful. Eisenstadt distinguished between
the imperial-bureaucratic, imperial-feudal, and patrimonial regimes.

A major feature of the imperial-bureaucratic and imperial-feudal
regimes was a high level of distinctness of the center and a perception of
this center by the actors concerned as a separate symbolic and
organizational entity. The distinctness and autonomy of the center in
imperial-bureaucratic and imperial-feudal regimes were evident in the
cultural rift between it and its periphery. This state of affairs was the
consequence of its ability to develop and maintain its own specific symbols and criteria of recruitment and organization. However, the
imperial-feudal regime contained intermediary structures that could act
as effective countervailing powers vis-à-vis the central authority. Thus
the potential for the impingement of at least part of the periphery on
the center developed in the imperial-feudal regime, but was absent in
the imperial-bureaucratic regime. In contrast to both imperial-
bureaucratic and imperial-feudal regimes the patrimonial regime did
not have a distinct symbolic and organizational center. Its center had
neither specific norms and symbols nor distinct criteria of recruitment
and organization.[31]

It is obvious that, to the extent that antecedent regime types have
persisted, the degree of political institutionalization would be greater in
polities with an imperial-bureaucratic or imperial-feudal heritage than
in polities with a patrimonial heritage. It is also apparent that, again if

the above assumption holds, political institutionalization would be stronger in polities with an imperial-bureaucratic heritage than in polities with an imperial-feudal heritage.

If looked at from this vantage point some of the differences noted but often not satisfactorily accounted for by the Transitions project would begin to be explained. The experience of many countries in Latin America, Greece, and to a lesser extent Portugal may be put in perspective if we remember that these polities came historically and presently closest to patrimonialism and evinced weak institutionalization patterns. Southern Europe, in particular Spain, historically and presently best approximated imperial-feudalism and manifested neither too-weak nor too-strong institutionalization patterns (although weak as compared to Northern Europe).[32] Turkey, with its imperial-bureaucratic heritage, had a too-strong institutionalization pattern.

In sum, it is here proposed that regime transitions can be placed in perspective if the kind and degree of political institutionalization in these countries are examined and the historical background of the present political structure is appreciated. The analysis should also pay attention to the ongoing learning process on the part of the political actors. Over time their values and attitudes may change, although the original impulses never completely disappear and, from time to time, resurface.

ANTECEDENT INSTITUTIONALIZATION PATTERNS

Space does not permit us to illustrate satisfactorily let alone fully document the usefulness of the approach suggested here. We can consider briefly, however, some aspects of the antecedent regime types, recent institutionalization patterns, and differences in regime transitions in a number of countries or cluster of countries.

In all the regions and countries in question the polities as they originally emerged excluded (not unexpectedly) the popular sectors. As the centralized state emerged in the Ottoman-Turkish polity, neither the estates nor the religious establishment faced it as rivals.[33] Once the central authority was more or less intact, the old Turkic idea of supreme law was adopted. The ruler in general enforced the law with a view to equity and justice, regardless of his personal wishes.[34] His rule was to be informed by the norm of reason. The bureaucratic elites assimilated the ideals and values in question through formal training and organizational socialization.[35] In the process an imperial-bureaucratic center developed.

The Southern European state did not have as much autonomy and was not as isolated from civil society. It is true that the eighteenth-century Spanish Bourbon monarchy created a unified state, and not unlike the Ottoman, French, and Austrian states, the Spanish state bolstered its legitimacy through its early military glories.[36] The Spanish church, however, then and later, always provided an alternative basis of legitimacy. The estates in Spain, too, were a more potent countervailing force against the central authority than the local notables in the Ottoman Empire.[37] Historically, Southern Europe, but in particular Spain, best resembled imperial-feudalism.

The Spanish state faced a greater threat to its authority in its colonies in the Americas than it faced at home. In fact, the Spanish crown was not able to subdue to its satisfaction the *encomendero* class consisting of the former *conquistadores*, or the leading civilian colonists, and other privileged Spaniards. Most of its directives to regulate the functioning of the formal grant of *encomienda* under which the Spanish colonists exacted both commodity tribute and labor service from the Indians, remained on paper. The Spanish state in the Americas placed emphasis on entering, for purely commercial purposes, into cooperative arrangements with the emerging oligarchical classes. For the Spanish viceroys, captains-general, and governors, office holding in the Americas provided the occasions for rapid self-enrichment, and the members of the oligarchical class in the Americas became the plunderers of their own societies.[38]

After independence rule was embodied in the person of caudillos. A more developed form was oligarchical praetorianism, a coalition of cliques and groups with solely particularistic interests.[39] Thus, when Spain withdrew from the Americas, the primary components of the society were "the clan, the tribe, the hacienda, the village or town and the armed band."[40] Historically, the distinguishing characteristic of most regimes in the Americas was patrimonialism.

Portuguese Brazil constituted an interesting contrast to most of Hispanic America. Unlike the Spaniards, the Portuguese did not face a highly settled and organized indigenous society. Because of the scarcity of human and most other resources, the Portuguese did not settle there in great numbers. Lisbon was thus left with a freer hand[41] and could transfer to Brazil a hierarchical and authoritarian model of polity and the idea of an "organic" representation of community, which further weakened the validity of a status structure made up of independent groups. Thus, the liberal principles eventually adopted by the Brazilians were Lockean, or predemocratic, and not democratic. The Napoleonic invasion of Portugal precipitated the transfer of the Portuguese monarchy and court to Brazil in 1808 and this, too, facilitated the emergence of a distinct center there.[42]

It was not surprising that during their struggle for independence, the Brazilian rebels did not split over the issue of republicanism because, with a few exceptions, they opted for a monarchy.[43] Thus, during his tenure the legitimacy of Pedro II (1840–1889) was unquestioningly recognized by the people, while he in turn felt morally, if not "constitutionally," responsible to them.[44] In state building, Brazil stood far apart from most of its Hispanic-American neighbors.

Conversely, in most of Hispanic America patrimonialism reigned supreme. In the nineteenth century the road to political power tended to be a supporting coalition of allied patrons and their clients. A ruler protected himself from violent resistance or from an unfavorable outcome in elections by installing his entourage in all significant positions of power and patronage. In some countries, such as Bolivia, the rulers did not even go through a charade of constituent assembly. Where a constituent assembly was convened, it was often a docile one that drafted a constitution along the lines desired by the leader. The leader then assured an alternation in the leadership position between himself and his supporters until such time as disgruntled supporters coalesced with opposition elements to overthrow him.[45]

This state of affairs was the upshot of the fact that the social structure was basically composed of personal rulers (caudillos) and an "inchoate, inarticulate populace."[46] Among various political groups there was an irreconcilable division and a lack of shared norms regarding political activity.[47] There were virtually no procedural restraints on power struggles.[48]

During the same century one witnessed in Southern Europe the transformation of the earlier oligarchical social structure into a class (bourgeois) hegemony.[49] The phenomenon of class was bound to bring with it the idea of common (as against individual) interests, the expression of these interests in the form of ideologies, the development of coherent policies, and the need for legal-rational bureaucracies to implement those policies. Also, if it was going to look respectable, the ideology had to make some, even if rhetorical and symbolic, concessions to the common interest, which it mostly did.[50] There also began to emerge class coalitions not only against other "interests," but also against, to use Linz's terms, the disloyal opposition. A case in point was the "realistic" policies of the Cavourian coalition in Italy of Liberal aristocrats and middle-class lawyers that aimed at not allowing revolutionaries and radical reformers to gain a real share of power.[51] Furthermore, the phenomenon of a legal-rational bureaucracy brought with it the Weberian notion of formal legality, the institutionalization of which was facilitated by the growing political influence of the middle classes.[52] Formal legality became the basis of legitimacy of the center first in Italy and later in Spain.[53]

In nineteenth-century Turkey, following three centuries of degeneration of the earlier institutionalization pattern, the state was reconsolidated along bureaucratic lines. During the *Tanzimat* (Reform) period of 1839–1876 the civil bureaucratic elites came to embody the idea of a state isolated from civil society. The bureaucratic elites were "devoted to the secular interests of the state,"[54] which came before their own interests.[55] Influenced by the Enlightenment in Europe, they saw the salvation of the Ottoman Empire in the institutionalization of a rational decision-making process which they themselves had to impose and enforce. Theirs had to be a substantive rather than an instrumental rationality; they were interested in formulating policies rather than putting into effect policies developed by others.[56] In the absence of a bourgeois revolution, a bureaucratic version of imperial tradition reached its zenith. Thus emerged in Turkey a too-strong institutionalization pattern that later posed difficulties for transition to democracy.

On the whole, the countries in Southern Europe did not face such a prospect. The earlier ruling coalitions became differentiated in time into a network of interest group associations and political parties linked to different sectors of economy. Particularly significant for the present purposes was the establishment of fairly pragmatic parties[57]—a development crucial for political institutionalization.[58] Here Italy took the lead. After 1948 Italian politics came to be dominated by such highly organized mass parties.[59] Spain followed suit some three decades later. In Spain, as in Italy, political life began to be monopolized by the party elites, and political conflict was reoriented toward the parliamentary arena.[60] These developments facilitated compromises following longlasting authoritarian regimes in both countries and contributed to the establishment of relatively stable democracies. In Portugal, on the other hand, after 1976 a "truce . . . muted but did not resolve the hostilities."[61] This must be partly the result of the fact that in that country the compromise that resulted was based on "two contradictory views of social and political organizations, each rooted in its own powerful but polarized social base."[62]

It should also be noted that in Italy preceding the political institutionalization around relatively pragmatic, bargaining mass political parties, the resistance movement during World War II helped to create and strengthen a core of central values common to the major political forces. Most of these values found an almost immediate translation into the constitution.[63] Before the 1970s no similar and effective impulse to the development of common values emerged in Spain. This must be why democracy was consolidated in Italy earlier than in Spain.

Greece, on the other hand, has come to have neither relatively pragmatic, bargaining mass political parties nor, with two crises that the irredentist nationalism going back to the nineteenth century faced in

1922 and 1974, an effective integrating value system. These two factors should be responsible for the relative precariousness of Greek democracy.

TRANSITIONS TO DEMOCRACY

As compared to the situation in Latin America, in Southern Europe in general and in Italy and Spain in particular a "new consensus" began to emerge.[64] In these basically inclusionary regimes all groups except the disloyal ones came to be incorporated. The post-World War II economic miracles did help, but, unlike the situation in many Latin American countries, the legitimacy of the governments was not entirely dependent on economic performance. In any case there also emerged a commitment to welfare state policies (in Latin America, lip service was paid to such policies in the larger countries, but adequate resources were not made available).

In most Latin American countries no such political institutionalization took place. As compared to social structures in Southern Europe, diffuse, vertical hierarchies of patron-client networks continued to characterize most Latin American societies. The formal clash between parties and programs continued to be less relevant than a "pragmatic" struggle between ins and outs defined in terms of factional coalitions that often crossed the party lines.[65] This situation led to a pattern of direct, one-to-one interaction with the governments.[66] The objective has been getting into the distributional game through direct access to the executive branch without the mediation of the political parties.[67] Those in government had no way of moderating the demands and were obliged to resort to a strategy of cooptive incorporation. This strategy could only buy time; the "additive" nature of the approach eventually ran up against the distributional capacity of the governments.[68]

The relatively inclusionary authoritarian regimes, such as the one in Peru, only added fuel to the fire. Despite the fact that they emphasized regressive distribution[69] the exclusionary authoritarian regimes had a wider breathing space because of the exclusion of popular sectors. But they, too, soon exhausted their resources. In the absence of political institutionalization and, therefore, of legitimacy, the only alternative was greater repression. As the Transitions project has well documented, greater repression led to a conflict between the soft-liners and the hard-liners. Greater repression only delayed, but did not prevent, the fall of these authoritarian regimes. However, as the above analysis makes clear, any account of the Latin American "openings" should start with a study of the degrees of prior institutionalization patterns and not with the recent events leading to the falling out among themselves of the authoritarian rulers.

It should also be noted that despite the fact that the Latin American authoritarian regimes have been more repressive and therefore costlier than the Southern European ones, because of the lack of prior political institutionalization a gradual and controlled transition to democracy proved to be more difficult in Latin America than in Southern Europe. In Latin America only in Brazil did the transitional governments manage to exercise a firm and enduring control on the process,[70] and their "success" in this regard can to a great extent be explained primarily by the historically higher degree of prior political institutionalization. Eduardo Viola and Scott Mainwaring's conclusion that "whereas in the Brazilian case a marginalization of authoritarian actors seems highly unlikely in the foreseeable future, in Argentina a more fully democratic outcome remains possible as does an authoritarian involution"[71] also becomes meaningful in terms of the perspective suggested here. In fact, all Latin American transitions have faced an extraordinarily high uncertainty,[72] and not all redemocratizations in that region are likely to prove irreversible.[73]

As compared to the other countries in Southern Europe, let alone those in Latin America, Turkey has continued to be a type in itself. A state isolated from civil society has been a datum of the Turkish republic, too.[74] Theda Skocpol suggests that state norms are derived from (1) the exigencies of interstate relations, (2) the critical problems of development and modernization, (3) the need for control and order, and (4) increased specialization in public organizations.[75] The norms that gave the Ottoman-Turkish state its distinctive characteristics had been an emphasis on law and order, the exigencies of interstate relations, and modernization, and not development or increased specialization in public organizations. Thus in the absence in Turkey of social groups with political clout a so-called defensive modernization was initiated and realized by the state elites. For them modernization included democracy, but their version of democracy was a rationalistic one. They were interested in doing away with the hold of Islam on society and replacing it with "reason." Democracy was necessary because what was best for society could be ascertained only through an enlightened debate.

This particular orientation on the part of the state elites in Turkey gave a peculiar twist to the fortunes of democracy in that country. As already noted, these state elites took democracy as an end in itself that would define and promote the best interests of the country, rather than as a means to fulfill the goals of a particular class or interest group. Consequently, as compared to many other countries, the transition to multiparty politics in Turkey began (in 1945) basically as an intraelite conflict over substantive norms behind public policies, not just over procedural rules of democracy, and has continued thus confined.

In Turkey the state was confronted by a party-centered polity that was isolated from the social groups. No network of institutionalized linkages was developed between the political parties and the social groups, and the groups could hardly impinge upon government through voluntary organizations. The relationship between the government and the social groups had been clientelistic.[76] Given the rift not only between the state and society, but also between the political parties and social groups in Turkey, the cooptive incorporation of the social groups could be controlled.

Thus, in Turkey cultural cleavages turned out to be more important than functional ones. The primary conflict was between the state and political elites and not between the left and the right, as has been the case in Southern Europe. Whenever the state elites concluded that the political strife threatened the best interests of the country, the military intervened.[77]

This particular nonpolitical and too strong institutionalization pattern had implications for regime transitions in Turkey, which have been far different from those in other countries. Because democracy was taken as an end in itself and not as a means to other goals, the military interventions (1960–1961, 1971–1973, 1980–1983) did not take as their target the democracy itself; always politicians were the guilty party. For this reason the soldiers withdrew fairly quickly to their barracks after each intervention. Turkey did not have *regime* instability as all other countries under investigation had, but continued to have *political* instability because it was, of course, impossible to reconcile the approaches of the state and the political elites. The countries in Southern Europe had the relatively easier task of reconciling different class interests. Class differences are easier to resolve than conflicts between state and political elites, but only relatively so. Critical here is whether the members of each class accept the system and exercise self-restraint so that each group grants legitimacy to others and refrains from trying to exclude them from the political process. In Latin America interests have not developed their coherent ideologies, thus the continuing precariousness of regime stability there.

The constitutions in Turkey made after each intervention were not primarily a means for gradual and controlled passage, but were essentially guidelines for "proper" political behavior. Once the interregnum was over (there have been no genuine "transitions" in Turkey), the tensions have not arisen essentially between the old authoritarians and the new democrats or between the traditional right and the popular sectors, but between the politicians and the Constitutional Court. For instance, the Constitutional Court reversed in the late 1970s the decision of the National Assembly on such a critical issue as political amnesty, basing its decision on a procedural point of law.[78] The constitutions in Southern Europe, particularly in Italy and Spain, differ from the Turkish constitutions because they did not embody values imposed by the state elites upon the political elites; rather these constitutions turned out to be the handiwork of the political elites themselves, who had arrived at a "new consensus." In Latin America it was difficult even to formulate broadly based value systems, let alone translate them into binding documents.

As Turkey has not drifted into long-lasting authoritarianisms of any variety, let alone highly repressive ones, virtually no learning on the part of the Turkish political elites (either superficial or genuine) took place. In Southern Europe and Latin America learning did take place. Because of their prior intellectual baggage and the institutional usages, Southern European learning was a genuine one; they came to appreciate the virtues of political institutionalization. In the absence of such a tradition the learning on the part of the Latin Americans remained essentially superficial; they missed the significance of political institutionalization, but preoccupied themselves with the more immediate causes of regime oscillation.

NOTES

1. Samuel P. Huntington, "Political Development and Political Decay," *World Politics* 17 (1965): 386–430.
2. A transition from the *Gemeinschaft* to the *Gesellschaft* type of social structure implies a change from the corporate and communal to the individualistic and rational, from ascribed status to contract, and from the sacred-communal to the secular-associational. This typology was developed by Ferdinand Tönnies in his *Gemeinschaft und Gesellschaft*, 1887. An English translation of this work is *Community and Society*, trans. and ed. by Charles Loomis (New York: Harper & Row, 1963).
3. See, among others, Peter H. Smith, "Political Legitimacy in Spanish America", in Richard Graham and Peter H. Smith, eds., *New Approaches to Latin American History* (Austin: University of Texas Press, 1974).
4. See, among others, Paul Cammack, "The Political Economy of Contemporary Military Regimes in Latin America: From Bureaucratic Authoritarianism to Restructuring," in Phillip O'Brien and Paul Cammack, eds., *Generals in Retreat: The Crisis of Military Rule in Latin America* (Manchester, England: Manchester University Press, 1985).
5. Dankwart A. Rustow, "Transitions to Democracy: Toward a Dynamic Model," *Comparative Politics* 2 (1970): 337–363.

6. Samuel P. Huntington, *Political Order in Changing Societies* (New Haven, Conn.: Yale University Press, 1968).

7. Robert A. Dahl, *Dilemmas of Pluralist Democracy: Autonomy vs. Control* (New Haven and London: Yale University Press, 1982).

8. Otto Kirchheimer, "Confining Conditions and Revolutionary Breakthroughs," *American Political Science Review* 59 (1965): 964–974.

9. On the breakdowns of democratic regimes, see Juan J. Linz, *The Breakdown of Democratic Regimes: Crisis, Breakdowns and Reequilibration* (Baltimore: Johns Hopkins University Press, 1978).

10. Rustow, "Transitions to Democracy," 362.

11. Guillermo O'Donnell, Philippe C. Schmitter, and Laurence Whitehead, eds., *Transitions from Authoritarian Rule: Comparative Perspectives* (Baltimore: Johns Hopkins University Press, 1986); Guillermo O'Donnell, Philippe C. Schmitter, and Laurence Whitehead, eds., *Transitions from Authoritarian Rule: Southern Europe* (Baltimore: Johns Hopkins University Press, 1986); Guillermo O'Donnell, Philippe C. Schmitter, and Whitehead, eds., *Transitions from Authoritarian Rule: Latin America* (Baltimore: Johns Hopkins University Press, 1986); Guillermo O'Donnell and Philippe C. Schmitter, *Transitions from Authoritarian Rule: Tentative Conclusions About Uncertain Democracies* (Baltimore and London: Johns Hopkins University Press, 1986).

12. Salvador Giner, "Political Economy, Legitimation and the State in Southern Europe," in O'Donnell, Schmitter, and Whitehead, *Transitions from Authoritarian Rule: Southern Europe*, 38.

13. Laurence Whitehead, "International Aspects of Democratization," in O'Donnell, Schmitter, and Whitehead, *Transition from Authoritarian Rule: Comparative Perspectives*, 4; Philippe Schmitter, "An Introduction to Southern European Transitions from Authoritarian Rule: Italy, Greece, Portugal, Spain and Turkey," in O'Donnell, Schmitter, and Whitehead, *Transitions from Authoritarian Rule: Southern Europe*, 3; Giner, "Political Economy," 38.

14. O'Donnell and Schmitter, *Transitions from Authoritarian Rule: Tentative Conclusions About Uncertain Democracies*, 3.

15. Ibid., 22.

16. Ibid.

17. Laurence F. Lowenthal, "Foreword," in Ibid., viii.

18. Rustow, "Transitions to Democracy."

19. Charles Tilly, "Reflections on the History of European State-Making," in Charles Tilly, ed., *The Formation of National States in Western Europe* (Princeton, N.J.: Princeton University Press, 1975), 12.

20. James M. Malloy, "The Politics of Transition in Latin America," in James M. Malloy and Mitchell A. Seligson, eds., *Authoritarians and Democrats: Regime Transitions in Latin America* (Pittsburgh: Pittsburgh University Press, 1987).

21. S. N. Eisenstadt, "Varieties of Political Development: The Theoretical Challenge," in S. N. Eisenstadt and Stein Rokken, eds., *Building States and Nations: Models and Data Resources*, vol. 1 (Beverly Hills, Calif.: Sage, 1973), 45.

22. Metin Heper, "Extremely 'Strong State' and Democracy: Turkey in Comparative and Historical Perspective," in Deborah Grenium, ed., *Democracy and Modernity* (Leiden: Brill, in press).

23. Samuel P. Huntington, "Will More Countries Become Democratic?" *Political Science Quarterly*, 99 (1984): 193–218.

24. Robert A. Dahl, *Dilemmas of Pluralist Democracy, Autonomy vs. Control* (New Haven, Conn.: Yale University Press, 1982).

25. Huntington, *Political Order in Changing Societies*.

26. Mark Kesselman, "Over Institutionalization and Political Constraint: The Case of France," *Comparative Politics*, 2 (1970): 21–44; Gabriel Ben-Dor, "Institutionalization and Political Development: A Conceptual and Theoretical Analysis," *Comparative Studies in Society and History* 17 (1975): 309–325.

27. Kenneth H. F. Dyson, *The State Tradition in Western Europe. The Study of an Idea and Institution* (Oxford: Martin Robertson, 1980), 206.

28. Gordon Smith, *Democracy in Western Germany: Parties and Politics in the Federal Republic* (London: Heinemann, 1979).

29. Pierre Birnbaum, "State, Centre and Bureaucracy," *Government and Opposition* 16 (1981): 58–77; Birnbaum, "France: Polity with a Strong State," in Metin Heper, ed., *The State and Public Bureaucracies: A Comparative Perspective* (New York: Greenwood Press, 1987).

30. Metin Heper, *The State Tradition in Turkey* (Walkington, England: Eothen Press, 1985).

31. S. N. Eisenstadt, "Strong and Weak States: Some Reconsiderations," in Heper, *The State and Public Bureaucracies*.

32. Historically, Italy does not fit the description of an imperial-feudal regime. It did not have a political center until 1870–1871. Its national political institutions were only partially developed before 1922. Regional and patrimonial traditions remained strong and the center weak when compared to other European countries. In Italy, however, from very early on, the political party made possible a neither too weak nor too strong political institutionalization. See Raymond Grew, "Italy," in Raymond Grew, ed., *Crises of Political*

Development in Europe and the United States (Princeton, N.J.: Princeton University Press, 1978).

33. Metin Heper, "Center and Periphery in the Ottoman Empire with Special Reference to the Nineteenth Century," *International Political Science Review* 1 (1980): 81–105.

34. Stanford J. Shaw, *History of the Ottoman Empire and Modern Turkey. vol. 1, Empire of the Gazis: The Rise and Decline of the Ottoman Empire* (Cambridge: Cambridge University Press, 1976).

35. Carter V. Findley, "The Advent of Ideology in the Islamic Middle East, Part I," *Studia Islamica*, ex fasciculo 60 (1982): 143–169; Metin Heper and Ersin Kalaycioğlu, "Organizational Socialization as Reality Testing. The Case of the Turkish Higher Civil Servants," *International Journal of Political Education* 6 (1982): 175–198.

36. Raymond Grew, "Italy," 279–280.

37. Stanley G. Payne, "Spain and Portugal," in Grew, *Crises of Political Development*, 199–202; Juan J. Linz, "Europe's Southern Frontier: Evolving Trends Toward What?" *Daedalus* 108 (1979): 205.

38. Charles Gibson, *Spain in America* (New York: Harper & Row, 1966), 48–67, 90–111.

39. Huntington, *Political Order in Changing Societies*, 198–199, 201.

40. Ronald C. Newton, "On 'Functional Groups,' 'Fragmentation,' and 'Pluralism' in Spanish American Political Society," *Hispanic American Historical Review* 5 (1978): 27.

41. Thomas E. Skidmore and Peter H. Smith, *Modern Latin America* (New York: Oxford University Press, 1984), 25–6.

42. Fernando Uricoechea, *The Patrimonial Foundations of the Brazilian Bureaucratic State* (Berkeley: University of California Press, 1980), 35–36.

43. Skidmore and Smith, *Modern Latin America*, 38–9.

44. Richard M. Morse, "Toward a Theory of Spanish American Government," *Journal of the History of Ideas* 15 (1954): 89–91.

45. John A. Peeler, *Latin American Democracies: Colombia, Costa Rica and Venezuela* (Chapel Hill: University of North Carolina Press, 1985), 50.

46. Morse, "Toward a Theory of Spanish American Government," 81.

47. Gino Germani and Kalman Silvert, "Politics, Social Structure and Military Intervention in Latin America," *Archives Européennes Sociologie* 2 (1961): 77.

48. Glen Dealy, "Prolegomena on the Spanish American Political Tradition," *Hispanic American Historical Review* 48 (1968): 146.

49. Giner, "Political Economy," 13.

50. Ibid., 27.

51. Grew, "Italy," 276.

52. John A. Armstrong, *The European Administrative Elite* (Princeton, N.J.: Princeton University Press, 1973), particularly chap. 4.

53. Linz, "Europe's Southern Frontier?" 183.

54. Halil İnalcik, "The Nature of Traditional Society: Turkey," in Robert E. Ward and Dankwart A. Rustow, eds., *Political Modernization in Japan and Turkey* (Princeton, N.J.: Princeton University Press, 1964), 55.

55. Niyazi Berkes, *The Development of Secularism in Turkey* (Montreal: McGill University Press, 1964), 62.

56. Metin Heper, "Political Modernization as Reflected in Bureaucratic Change: The Turkish Bureaucracy and a 'Historical Bureaucratic Empire' Tradition," *International Journal of Middle East Studies* 7 (1976): 507–521.

57. Giner, "Political Economy," 37–38.

58. Huntington, "Will More Countries Become Democratic?" 408–412.

59. Grew, "Italy," 285.

60. José María Maravall and Julian Santamaría, "Political Change in Spain and the Prospects for Democracy," in O'Donnell, Schmitter, and Whitehead, *Transitions from Authoritarian Rule: Southern Europe*, 90–91.

61. Kenneth Maxwell, "Regime Overthrow and the Prospects for Democratic Transition in Portugal," in O'Donnell, Schmitter, and Whitehead, *Transitions from Authoritarian Rule: Southern Europe*, 135.

62. Ibid.

63. Gianfranco Pasquino, "The Demise of the First Fascist Regime and Italy's Transition to Democracy," in O'Donnell, Schmitter, and Whitehead, *Transitions from Authoritarian Rule: Southern Europe*, 69. It is true that Italy's transition to democracy came in the 1940s because of the defeat of the fascist regime in World War II; consequently the contrast with Spain, which did not participate in the war, may at first sight seem inappropriate. Here, however, the comparison is not the way democracy was installed but how the transition to democracy later took place in these two countries.

64. Giner, "Political Economy," 14.

65. Malloy, "Politics of Transition," 241–242.

66. Newton, "On 'Functional Groups,' 'Fragmentation,' and 'Pluralism,'" 28–29.

67. Malloy, "Politics of Transition," 243; Douglas A. Chalmers, "Parties and Society in Latin America," *Studies in Comparative International Development* 7 (1972): 102–130.

68. Malloy, "Politics of Transition," 243.

69. On Brazil, for instance, see, Kenneth Paul Erickson, "Brazil: Cor-

porative Authoritarianism, Democratization and Dependency," in Howard J. Wiarda and Harvey Kline, eds., *Latin American Politics and Development*, 2d ed. (Boulder, Colo.: Westview, 1985), 201–205.

70. O'Donnell and Schmitter, *Transitions from Authoritarian Rule: Tentative Conclusions About Uncertain Democracies*, 45.
71. Eduardo Viola and Scott Mainwaring, "Transitions to Democracy: Brazil and Argentina in the 1980s," *Journal of International Affairs* 38 (1985): 219.
72. O'Donnell and Schmitter, *Transitions from Authoritarian Rule: Tentative Conclusions About Uncertain Democracies*, 3.
73. Whitehead, "International Aspects of Democratizations," 31.
74. Metin Heper, "State, Democracy and Bureaucracy in Turkey," in Heper, *The State and Public Bureaucracies*, 131–145; and Heper, "The State, Political Party and Society in Post-1983 Turkey," *Government and Opposition*, 25 (1990): 1–13.
75. Theda Skocpol, "Bringing the State Back In: Strategies of Analysis in Current Research," in Peter Evans, Dietrich Rueschmeyer, and Theda Skocpol, eds., *Bringing the State Back In* (Cambridge: Cambridge University Press, 1985), 9.
76. Metin Heper, "Interest Group Politics in Post-1980 Turkey," paper prepared for submission at the international conference on Government and Organized Interests, Zurich, September 27–30, 1989.
77. Metin Heper, "Conclusion," in Martin Heper and Ahmet Evin, eds., *State, Democracy and the Military. Turkey in the 1980s* (Berlin: de Gruyter, 1988), 249–257.
78. C. H. Dodd, *The Crisis of Turkish Democracy* (Walkington, England: Eothen Press, 1983), pp. 25–26.

Chapter
10

Authoritarianism and Democracy in Africa

Henry Bienen and Jeffrey Herbst

While many analysts of Latin America and Southern Europe have been exploring transitions to democracy, Africanists must ask why there have been so few transitions to democracy in Black Africa.[1] In the last few years Latin Americanists have been reassessing O'Donnell's theories of bureaucratic authoritarianism in the light of the emergence of elected regimes in parts of the Southern Cone.[2] Similarly, students of Spain, Portugal, and Greece now engage in full-scale electoral studies.[3] Yet Africanists must concern themselves with analysis of the continuation of military regimes, the dominance of single-party systems (where parties exist at all), and the vagaries of personal leadership, if not those of aberrant personalities. Indeed, while the 1980s have witnessed the birth or rebirth of democracy on almost every continent and startling increases in the possibilities of political participation in as authoritarian a polity as the Soviet Union, democracy seems far from the grasp of most African countries.

Of course, students of Africa are concerned with many of the same issues that dominate discussion of Latin America even while those discussions take place in the context of authoritarianism and transitions to democracy. Studies of continuity and change in Africa frequently revolve around issues of the emergence (or not) of classes, the relationship of the state to society, the degree of autonomy of the state, the relationship of domestic change to international trade and capital movements (that is, the dependency debate), and the politics of structural adjustment. There may be some clues to the distinctiveness of Africa in that even these analyses of dependency, structural adjustment and stabilization, and autonomy of the state tend to dwell on problems of colonial legacies and state formation, where for South America and Southern Europe, if not Central America, state formation is mostly taken for granted.[4] And while no observer of Spanish- and Portuguese- speaking countries in Europe or the Americas would deny the relevance of leaders and their styles for transitions to democracy, most would not stress the political and psychological makeup of particular rulers to the extent that Africanists do.[5] Similarly, for students of Africa there continues to be at least some focus on ethnic variables and the fragility of nation-states under pressure from ethnic diversity.

Africa also has been differentiated by public officials in their expectations concerning democracy across the Third World. For instance, the Carter administration did not have the same kind of public expectations concerning the prospects for democracy in Africa that it did in Latin America. More generally, there has been far less pressure on African countries to establish democratic-political systems. Instead, international pressure has centered on concerns for the rights of individuals or decreases in the oppression of ethnic minorities. Zimbabwe's unification of the two major parties in 1988 was actually hailed in places as an advance in state consolidation rather than mourned as a loss of a potential democracy.

There are now countless conceptions of what democracy means and what it requires of citizens and leaders. Given that there is not a wide variety of democratic regimes already existing in Africa, Robert Dahl's basic definition of polyarchy still seems to be most useful to understanding what are the minimum characteristics of a democracy. Dahl argues that all polyarchies allow a high percentage of their population to participate in the political system (inclusion) and are characterized by a high degree of public contestation (liberalization).[6] The clearest indication of democracy using Dahl's definition would be a transfer of power to the opposition after a democratic election. Strikingly, such transitions have rarely occurred in Africa over the last twenty-five years. In Mauritius in 1982, the prime minister of the Labour party, Sir Seewoosagur Ramgoolam, who had led the country to independence in 1968 and was questionably the father of the country, was defeated in an upset election by Mr. Aneerood Jugnauth, chairman of the Mauritian Militant Movement. Indeed, the Mauritian Militant Movement won all sixty of the directly contested seats for the new legislative house. In Sierra Leone a competitive party election transferred power in 1967, but a military coup occurred almost immediately. All other peaceful transitions that have occurred in Africa have been within the ruling party and usually at the behest of the leader to his hand-picked successor (for example, Jomo Kenyatta to Daniel arap Moi in Kenya). There have also been staged military transfers of power through competitive elections in Nigeria in 1979, in Ghana in 1969 and 1979, and in Sudan in 1986.

There have been few instances of party competition, much less actual transfers of power. Senegal has allowed a proliferation of parties and even has mandated them by law. And while the ruling party has dominated under two leaders, its electoral system has, for Africa, a degree of openness. However, even in Senegal the integrity of this system was sorely tested when, after the March 1988 presidential elections, the major opposition figure and many of his colleagues were placed in jail. Botswana continues to have a multiparty electoral system, but it, too, has been dominated by one party. Zimbabwe has maintained since independence a parliamentary system where votes have counted, although the major opposition party has now merged with the ruling party and it appears that all opposition parties will be eliminated by the next election in 1995. Gambia also allowed the formation of opposition parties in 1986. Even these partly democratic African states have been exceptionally fragile and the few other states that had democratic ambitions, including Ghana, Sierra Leone, Kenya, and Zambia, have only intermittently held competitive party elections since independence.

The precedent for regimes reverting back to formal democracies is also limited. Nigeria returned to competitive elections in 1979 only to succumb to another military coup at the end of 1983. Its leaders are once again moving toward a civilian regime but it cannot be counted yet as a system with public contestation. The Sudan, after the overthrow of Gaafar Nimeiri in 1985 and a brief military interregnum, did elect a regime formed through a parliamentary majority. However, Sadiq al-Mahdi was, in turn, overthrown by a coup. In general, military regimes in Africa have not been transformed to democratic ones, although some military governments have been less authoritarian than others. For instance, the Buhari government in Nigeria limited the role of the courts to a far greater degree than had previous Nigerian military regimes in the 1960s and 1970s. The successor Babangida military regime has been much less repressive. Thus there has been as much variation in degrees of authoritarianism in Nigerian military regimes as in civilian regimes.[7]

Other than these exceptional cases, there have been few instances of democratic practice south of the Sahara. Most African states had an election at independence that determined a winner, and subsequently either military coups propelled new leaders to power or regimes were installed partially or totally by outside intervention. Jockeying for power within a dominant single party also sometimes brought a leadership succession. Even where one-party systems have existed with electoral mechanisms to change leaders at middle and upper-middle levels, and these mechanisms have allowed significant turnover in Tanzania, Kenya, and the Ivory Coast, among others, in none of the ruling single-party systems have open primaries led to a change in rulers.[8]

How have analysts accounted for the persistent absence of democracy? Have their accounts changed over time? If we go back to the period of promise after independence when prospects seemed bright for African development, there was a debate as to whether African one-party systems could be democratic. African leaders asserted that Africa had democratic traditions and patterns of rule that had been interrupted by colonialism.[9] They argued that the violence of colonial rule had disrupted African societies and that the enforced centralization and authoritarianism of the colonial period had been inimical to further democratic development. One influential participant-observer went so far as to argue that only violent anticolonialism could purge Africa of feelings of subservience and inferiority and create new men.[10]

Julius Nyerere, for one, argued that African traditions were essentially democratic ones and could be reestablished after independence. He asserted that party politics and conflict were antidemocratic. His image of a democratic society was one essentially devoid of politics.[11] Tanzania's first leader argued that a one-party system could be democratic, but that an operating democracy was one without factions. For him, the two essentials of a democracy are freedom of the individual and free choice of the government of a country. According to Nyerere, the national interest could not be separated from the interests of the individuals who formed the nation and there should therefore be no division between the rulers and the ruled. Individuals could have differences of views, but the differences should not have organized expression.[12] Similar views were enunciated across the continent but often for the reason that an ideology that explicitly disapproved of open political conflict was convenient for weak elites dedicated to securing power for themselves irrespective of the democratic institutions present at independence.

It is interesting to go back to this debate now when it seems so far removed from the evolution of African politics over the last three decades. It was a debate about the relationship of individuals to a general will and whether differences of opinion could be maintained without organized parties and factions. It was also one over whether or not African local and precolonial traditions were democratic. However, the debate was aborted by the upsurge of military coups across the continent, the decay of political parties that did not face the challenge of an opposition, and the demobilization of the population after the heady early days of independence. After the mid 1960s most attempts by Africans to develop the intellectual foundations for democratic practices amounted to nothing more than hagiographies of the paramount ruler and his style of leadership.

At the time of African independence Western scholars were concerned with the relationship between levels of economic and social development and political democracy. A literature, following Lipset, was spawned on "the correlates of democracy."[13] Indeed, much of the early "new nations" literature was concerned with the potential for national integration at low levels of development. This literature explored problems of territorial unity in societies where the colonial grid had been thrown over people who were divided by language, religion, and lineage.[14] It was concerned with the issue of political culture or, more accurately, the lack of a shared culture. It was also worried about rural and urban differentials. The development theorists were concerned with the status and economic gaps between elites and the population at large. However, relatively little of the political development and new nations literature of the 1960s focused explicitly on class conflict and democracy.

African countries were late comers to independence and thus the question of how much time is required to build new societies and national institutions seemed critical. The issues of time and institution building were fused with the concern that the demands resulting from growing political participation would overwhelm weak institutions. Various analysts asked if either strong single parties or militaries could channel demands and create an institutional grid in which expanded political participation might occur without destabilizing societies.[15] In the African context the analysts were preoccupied with trying to understand whether the particular qualities of a leader who was the "father of his country" might be transferred to the institutions of the state in such a way that order and progress could go hand in hand.[16]

As the development literature unfolded, from the mid to late 1960s, militaries intervened in a host of African countries. In the Congo, the military intervened before a civilian government could even be established when the planned transfer of power from the Belgians derailed. Even a successful transition from colonialism was not a guarantee that civilian rule would continue for long. Militaries intervened where ethnic struggles overwhelmed civilian authorities, and they sometimes exacerbated the ethnic conflicts when tensions spilled over from within the armed forces themselves, as in Nigeria. They also intervened where one party systems seemed reasonably popular and responsive and where the leader had not become repressive as in Tanganyika. Finally, they intervened where labor began to make demands and where they feared the undermining of their own fragile prerogatives.

The actions of the armed forces in Africa from the mid 1960s onward spawned a large literature on the causes and consequences of the military's entry into politics and the undermining of civilian regimes. For example, Morris Janowitz focused on variables that pertained to the armed forces themselves: rank, service branch rivalry, recruitment procedures.[17] Huntington concentrated on social conflict in society, that is, ethnic and class conflict unmediated by strong institutions.[18] After some military leaders began to develop their own styles of rule, Decalo examined the personal and idiosyncratic features of African armies.[19] Since that time most analysts of African armed forces and society have used a combination of factors to explain military intervention.[20]

In the 1970s arguments about the colonial inheritance were used more frequently to account for authoritarianism in Africa. Observers noted that colonial rule itself had been bureaucratic and undemocratic, centralized and quixotic, and that African leaders had therefore inherited ruling patterns that were undemocratic. Of course, observers of Africa were not arguing that the colonial state was precisely the same as the independent state.[21] Indeed, they often stressed that the colonial state had been more bureaucratic and less patrimonial or personalistic than its successors.

The foreign factor was seen in terms of fishing in troubled waters. The large and middle powers were able to keep their clients in power if they acted decisively. Their interventions could be surgical and sometimes covert. For instance, some attributed the existence of Mobutu's authoritarian regime in Zaire to the support given by Americans, French, Moroccans, and Israelis.[22] Others saw a Soviet hand not only in the former Portuguese territories and in Ethiopia where Soviet support was large, but also earlier on in Ghana, Guinea, Congo-Brazzaville, and other places at various times.[23] The continued support of the French in Ivory Coast and Senegal and the support of the United States and Britain for an increasingly authoritarian Kenyatta regime in Kenya and then its successor, the Moi government, could also be seen as examples of the maintenance of regimes for the convenience of the great powers and the excolonial ones. There were also newcomers to African intervention such as the Chinese, Israelis, Saudis, and Indians, who seemed to care little about democracy. A regime had to become so incredibly repressive and maniacal, such as that of Macia in Equatorial Guinea and Amin in Uganda, before outsiders would turn away. And then the Libyans might even try to shore up such a regime as they did Amin's.

The rise of deviant leaders who seemed erratic and poorly suited to rule and whose leadership styles were consequential for their societies spawned a literature that focused on personal rule.[24] After Weber, many development theorists began to see the African state in patrimonial terms and went back to European states' formation for ideas about the dynamics of political systems when institutions are not strong.[25] The problem was that although the state was weak, it ambitiously tried to extract a variety of resources from society, and interest groups were poorly developed except for ethnic ones. Thus the state was largely unconstrained by organized countervailing power. Private property itself was weakly developed except for peasant small-holders who were scattered and poorly organized. And these peasant small-holders would exit rather than fight by withdrawing from markets and trying to deal locally with the representatives of the state who coerced them.[26] Most African leaders also did not have to worry about strong unions or strong judiciaries which might constrain their behavior. Thus, even in a system where the leader had prevailed for decades, a great deal of political instability could exist, as in Zaire or in Ethiopia both before and after the emperor's fall.[27] The coexistence of long leadership duration in some countries and rapid leader turnover among others gave rise to puzzles concerning leadership longevity.[28]

The questions persisted. Why was personal rule common? How do leaders such as Amin come to rule states? Why does the military not withdraw? Why do inefficient and repressive states continue to exist? Who do they represent? How do they keep going? In other words, why is there no transition to democracy?

Before trying to provide some answers, we note again that many of the writers of the 1960s and 1970s anticipated the questions and the answers. Low levels of development, fragmented societies, and poorly structured but overbearing states which gave free play to erratic leaders were all cited in the conventional literature. However, another set of arguments, to which we have not yet alluded, perhaps provided the most comprehensive answers to the questions of why democracy had failed or had not been tried and why transitions away from authoritarian government would be hard in Africa.

This major set of arguments can loosely be grouped under the label "dependency theories." The theories originated in Latin America and were exported to Africa.[29] The "dependentistas" argued that because of the nature of international capitalist relations with peripheral countries, low levels of development made the failure of democratic institutions inevitable. As primitive accumulation gave way to capitalist accumulation, the need for direct colonial rule declined and "independent" governments representing local strata and classes sustained the colonial economic relationships.[30] It was claimed that a class of "compradors" developed who were intermediaries between their society and foreign firms or foreign countries. In Leys's words, "comprador regimes are apt to be authoritarian" because their only orientation is toward serving the capitalist powers through the promotion of capitalism in the periphery.[31] Thus Europe underdeveloped Africa and held some responsibility for the failure of democracy to take hold there.[32]

Scholars in Africa, as they did elsewhere, soon grew wary of dependency's mechanistic representation of the state itself. Leys, for instance, had declared the African state to be no more than "a sort of subcommittee" of the international bourgeoisie.[33] However, when presented with evidence that many African states did have substantial autonomy, Leys and many other observers of African political economy came more and more to try, in the words of Skocpol and her colleagues, to "bring the state back in" so as to account for the political manifestations of underdevelopment and to locate the mechanisms for control of particular countries.[34]

A number of analysts repaired to the Marx of the *Eighteenth Brumaire of Louis Bonaparte* because they were conscious of the weakness of class development in Africa and the importance of the state apparatus. The postcolonial state was termed "overdeveloped" because it was imposed on all classes in the colony by the metropole in a completely artificial process. The state was therefore assigned some degree of autonomy because it could mediate between local and international capital interests.[35] However, these scholars could not quite bring themselves to see this state apparatus as a situational elite, that is, an elite whose interests were driven by the functional concerns of rank and place in a bureaucracy. But they did try to come to grips with the state bureaucracy in the context of a society of weakly organized peasant small-holders.

As the 1970s progressed, several scholars also began to apply corporatist conceptions, first developed in Latin America, to Africa. Corporatist models were attractive to many scholars because of the creation of one-party states with one trade union organization, one womens' organization, and one youth association and because of the corresponding rhetoric from Africa's leaders that denied any kind of division—class or ethnic—among Africans.[36] However, it was never clear if African leaders actually had real pretensions toward a corporate ordering of society or if the rhetoric which stressed the unity of the population was simply an excuse to continue authoritarian practices and accept no legitimate opposition.

Interestingly, the growing concern with the state and its autonomy in Africa has not been linked to the large and continuing literature on armed forces and society. In Latin America, this link has been made, particularly in the explanation of military withdrawal from rule and the transition to democracy in the Southern Cone.[37] Some authors do take note explicitly of state-society relationships when they examine the prospects for transitions to democracy in Africa, but they do not bring this discussion back to the armed forces.[38] This failure to explain African militaries in terms of state-society relationships may stem from an unwillingness to explore the social base and recruitment of African armed forces.

One promising line of analysis that has been pursued in Latin America but less so in Africa focuses on the strong ties between civil service elites and the armed forces. The role of the civil service expanded greatly under military rule in the 1960s and 1970s. While armed forces have sometimes attacked the civil service, as the Murtala Mohammed regime did in 1975 in Nigeria and the populist military regimes in Ghana and Burkina Faso did fitfully in the 1980s, on the whole the military and civil service have supported each other in Africa.[39]

The alliance between military and civil service in Africa has narrowed the space for democratic transitions. Neither elite of the state has had a strong commitment to democracy. Both have been able to protect their interests under civilian regimes as well as military ones. Military withdrawal has therefore not led to sustained democratic transitions. Certainly, Africa has not witnessed the kind of military collapse that characterized the Argentine military after the Falklands/Malvinas War. Even when militaries have felt great pressures to withdraw from rule as in the Sudan in 1964 and again in 1985 and in Nigeria in the late 1970s, the armed forces have preserved their strong role in government.

The failure of authoritarian regimes to be transformed from above has caused some to ask whether authoritarian regimes can be transformed by pressures from below.[40] Especially with the success of guerrilla movements against settler colonial regimes and the advent of self-consciously Marxist regimes in Southern and West Africa beginning in the mid 1970s, arguments were made to the effect that Africa could develop revolutionary socialist and democratic regimes. At least for a short period of time it was thought that a "bona fide" socialist state could be built in Angola, and if not there, then in Mozambique or Guinea-Bissau.[41] And if the Afro-Marxist regimes in these countries were not yet democracies, it was because they were not revolutionary enough or operated in an international environment that made it difficult to carry through their revolutions, especially in light of South African aggression. Of course, some observers also argued that conditions had not ripened because they were still presocialist societies.[42]

The would-be Afro-Marxist or would-be Marxist-Leninist regimes may, indeed, be different from their African socialist predecessors. Organizationally and ideologically there may be significant differences.[43] Certainly their concept of democracy bears little resemblance to that of a liberal democracy where competition or contestation matters. But they look in many other ways not that much different from other African regimes and have features of regimes characterized by the politics of thuggery. As it was in Uganda, who could shoot first was a key determinant of political struggles in Ethiopia, despite the very different social and economic policies of the Mengistu regime. Ethnic conflict has also been severe in Angola and Ethiopia. Mozambique as well as Ethiopia and Angola have been unable to put down armed insurgencies even with large-scale outside aid (which their opponents have also received). It is hard to find overwhelming support on the part of their populations for any of these regimes.[44]

At the very time that prospects for democracy in Africa seemed weakest, scholars began to look for democratic aspects of the governmental system. Richard Sklar, for instance, argued that Africa retains fragments of democracy and that patterns of accountability and economic and social pluralism exist.[45] Sklar's work reminded us that the lack of competitive democratic elections does not mean that a political system is entirely lacking in democratic procedures and norms. However, except in the most authoritarian regimes, there are fragments of pluralism and perhaps accountability in almost every political system.

In a research agenda for the future, the most obvious requirement for a better understanding of democratic prospects in Africa is for more analysis that is directly relevant to the African experience. Except for the initial theorizing on African democracy by such writers as Nyerere, Africa has been essentially a theory taker for the last twenty-five years. Most of the theories that have been applied to Africa—modernization, dependency, bureaucratic authoritarianism, and corporatism—were developed in other areas of the world and then applied to Africa by people who believed that these theories could explain political phenomena anywhere in the world. However, after initial bursts of enthusiasm that a newly imported theory could "work," the very different circumstances in which leaders and governments operate in Africa have repeatedly caused disillusionment. There are many reasons why Africa has been a theory taker—the underdevelopment of African universities, the need to spend a large amount of time gathering data on polities that have not been previously investigated, the daunting diversity of the continent—but the last thirty years suggests that the prospects for successfully importing theories to explain political phenomena in Africa are poor. Thus, the research agenda for Africa has as its highest priority formulating more directly relevant theory rather than continually coveting eloquent analytic concepts developed for other types of polities.

As we look to the future, there are also several assumptions within the body of work on democracy in Africa that should be clarified and made explicit if we are better to examine the dynamics of authoritarianism and democracy. One is the assumption about the time required to build democratic societies. European states evolved slowly over hundreds of years. Long periods of state consolidation were interrupted by significant periods when the state fragmented again and much of the earlier consolidation disappeared. Such a pattern of consolidation and dissolution occurred in France and elsewhere.[46]

A related question is the time required to establish trends. Despite the fact that many African states have been independent for only thirty years, scholars of different analytical schools and ideological stripes frequently have felt confident enough to be able to pronounce on the future of the continent. Given this short period of time, we do not know if current antidemocratic trends are simply aberrations or if the last three decades are really the beginning of the future. The problem of reaching conclusions without an adequate amount of time to observe becomes especially important because scholars have often been wrong about issues of state consolidation and democracy not only in Africa (where they were often too optimistic) but elsewhere where they were too pessimistic. For example, few, if any, analysts would have predicted in 1955 that South Korea would be able to evolve politically and economically in the manner that it has. Similarly, few predicted in the 1970s the pace of change in the Soviet Union and Eastern Europe.

Scholars telescope time because many believe, even if they explicitly deny it, that if democracy is to come to Africa, it will happen fairly quickly. Indeed, the variety of theories that we outlined above suggests that scholars have been extremely responsive to developments on the continent over what is, in light of Europe's experience, a very short period of time. Few have taken the position that the evidence is not yet in, although those who stressed that Africa has not yet achieved the necessary "correlates of democracy" have some reason to be pessimistic due to the continent's development performance during the last two decades. In development terms, however, the 1970s and 1980s add up to a short time.

The second major assumption concerning democracy in Africa that abounds in the literature is that democracy is almost uniformly consistent with state consolidation and state strength and that many of the undemocratic practices occurring in Africa are caused by the very weakness of African states. For instance, Callaghy argues that African states are "lame Leviathans" because elites must constantly try to consolidate their extraordinarily insecure position by expanding the state into all spheres of life at the expense of the citizens.[47] However, European history suggests a much more complex phenomenon. As Charles Tilly makes clear, the creation of political rights resulted from the interaction of political mobilization and state making. The creation of stronger states, by itself, did not lead to greater rights. Indeed, as Tilly notes, "For a long time after then [the fourteenth century], the builders of states worked to stamp out or absorb existing rights, not to extend them."[48] Only when mobilization of demands was strong enough to impress political entrepreneurs did the process of state consolidation lead to an institutionalization of political rights. Looking at mobilization and state building as two forces leading to democracy also seems legitimate given Dahl's stress on inclusion and public contestation as the basic ingredients of polyarchy.

The dangers of premature judgments given the short time that African states have existed and the deceptiveness of linking democracy with a single variable such as state consolidation suggest a different agenda for looking at the development of democracy in Africa. We are led back to the new nations' literature and to a literature that examined conditions for democracy.

Processes of citizenship orientation, loyalty, and institution building are not linear. Attachments rise and fall. Nonetheless, a basic process that must begin if there is eventually to be anything in Africa close to what is known as democracy is a reorientation of the population's loyalty toward the state. As Dankwart A. Rustow noted, the most basic precondition for democracy is national unity, not some minimum economic level.[49] Dahl also notes that some degree of common identity is a basic condition for polyarchy. While there will always be factions within any polity (indeed, the presence of factions generates healthy political competition), the political opposition must be constrained within limits so that everyone agrees that it is the government, rather than the institution of the state itself, that people oppose.

In few, if any, African countries does this type of basic agreement on loyalty to state institutions exist. Most countries are riven with ethnic, regional, and religious conflicts that seemingly overwhelm any loyalty to the state itself. The most basic indicator that current political strife in Africa is not kept within the basic framework of an allegiance to the state is the fact that elites in Africa do not view opposition as legitimate. Few African leaders are able to accept opposition to a leader or to a policy as anything less than calling into question the legitimacy of the state itself.[50]

Furthermore, in Africa the dominant models for national integration have been assimilationist ones. There has been a lack of congruity between the diversity of African societies and the highly centralized mechanisms and formulas that exist to channel that diversity. The administrative and political formulas for encompassing ethnic diversity are highly consequential because conflict arises over the core values expressed by elites and the institutions that are designed to integrate societies.[51] African states are new creations; even the present boundaries have existed for only a century and there have been serious attempts to have the population identify with the state only in the last thirty years. In Europe the process of unifying the population behind a conception of a state center took far longer.[52] The presence of a multitude of ethnic identities which politicians can draw upon to gain support has only made the problem of creating a basic orientation to the state that much more difficult.

Yet there are hopeful signs that, over a longer period of time, a national identity can be created in at least some African states. Certainly, the passage of time does not guarantee that citizenship. However, if nothing else, a majority of the population in almost all African countries has been born since independence and they have more of an orientation to the modern state.

More importantly, it has now been made clear that attempts to break away from the existing African states and to create new political communities will usually fail. The international community has not supported secessionist movements; governments have been able to turn to allies for the necessary military resources to turn back the creation of new states. True, rebellions have continued for lengthy periods in the Sudan, Ethiopia, Angola, and Mozambique, but even weak African states have so far been able to assemble enough military means to maintain their national boundaries, if not total control of national territory. The possibilities of domestic groups creating "new states" is doubtful. The norms of sovereignty and the international institutions that accept African countries as legitimate states no matter what the nature of their internal support have solidified the African state system.[53] Therefore, African states seem to have created at least the minimum necessary condition for citizens to begin to develop a united orientation to the state: There are no realistic alternative arrangements to the existing states. This is not a sufficient condition, as shown by continuing rebellions, but clearly it is an important first step for many nations.

Indicators of democracy can be grouped under the two broad categories of factors promoting mobilization for democracy and factors promoting state building. Certainly, economic development, which is among the factors that might promote polyarchy, has been virtually absent in Africa over the last decade. Dahl argues that, among other conditions, a relatively rich and decentralized economy with free farmers and low levels of inequality are factors favoring polyarchy.[54] Unfortunately, African countries are among the poorest in the world and have centralized economies (at least in the formal sector) with a large peasant base. Further, the trend on most of these factors is negative as African countries are becoming poorer.

Dahl also stresses that regional identities should be low with crosscutting identities, such as class, limiting the power of any one identity.[55] Once again, conditions in Africa are unfavorable as ethnic identities are the most salient cleavage in almost all societies, and potential crosscutting identities are much less important.[56]

Perhaps more fundamentally, the sequence of Africa's mobilization is unfavorable. Dahl stresses that the most favorable sequence for polyarchy is one in which political competition occurs before the population is highly mobilized.[57] Africa is developing in a dramatically opposed manner as there is little political competition, but attempts are made to mobilize the entire population. Few, if any, elites are trying to increase public contestation of political power. Indeed, despite the obvious failures of one-party states to achieve many of the goals of their designers (for example, funneling political participation constructively, extending the influence of the party, reducing factionalism), African leaders show little desire to reform their current political arrangements.

This contrasts with at least some willingness of African leaders to consider reforming economic structures and policies (for example, state marketing boards, overvalued currencies) that have led to exceptionally poor economic performance over the last twenty years.

Nor are there many positive signs in the general area of popular mobilization that would suggest that African countries are developing in a manner that would allow for more democracies at a future date. Failure to promote mobilization for democracy will be consequential because, as Tilly makes clear, without significant mobilization, attempts at state building are likely to lead to less democratic structures rather than greater political participation and democracy.[58]

Recently, there have been attempts in many African countries to implement structural adjustment programs in order to end the current economic crisis and to promote future growth. These reforms, promoted by the International Monetary Fund, the World Bank, and bilateral donors, attempt to lessen the state's influence on the market by reducing tariffs in favor of resource allocation by market-driven exchange rates, limiting the ability of state marketing boards to tax farmers through low food prices, and reducing the number of state-owned enterprises.[59] If the reforms were fully implemented, there is at least a chance that African countries might become more democratic because the economy would be less centralized. A decrease in centralization is potentially important to the prospects for democracy because: "The likelihood that a government will tolerate an opposition increases with a reduction in the capacity of the government to use violence or socioeconomic sanctions to suppress an opposition."[60]

Structural adjustments could also redistribute resources by restoring the urban-rural terms of trade so that wealth can be redirected to the majority who live in the rural areas and by providing incentives for the peasantry to produce more for the formal economy.

However, it is at this point doubtful if the structural adjustment programs will be implemented in a way that will advance the preconditions for democracy in Africa. Implementation has been at best haphazard with countries agreeing to IMF policy reforms but then only sometimes meeting the proposed targets.[61] Countries such as Zambia and Tanzania have consistently failed to implement agreed-upon reforms because of internal political opposition. In areas of economic decentralization such as privatization there has been very little actual reform despite promises in many countries to begin limiting the size of the public sector.[62] Also, many of the policy reforms have come about only because of the pressure of the IMF, the World Bank, and bilateral donors. It is doubtful that many countries would continue with their structural reform programs once the immediate economic crisis has passed.[63]

Finally, even if the structural adjustment reforms are adopted, the state will still play a major economic role in all African countries. These countries will remain poor and without a significant private sector for a long period of time. Many resources from the outside, including most of the foreign aid flow, go through the state. As a result, there are very real limits to how far African countries will decentralize and therefore improve the prospects for democracy.

The failure to decentralize and to allow for popular and organized mobilization over economic issues to be channeled back to central decision-making levels has been consequential in Africa. Soon after independence came to West African countries, W. Arthur Lewis argued that decentralization was necessary both for democracy and development.[64] Lewis understood well the severe costs of taxation with little representation. Problems were exacerbated when central authorities were recruited from a different ethnic group than the ones providing sources of revenues through taxation, such as Ashanti and Yoruba cocoa farmers in Ghana and Nigeria.

David Apter, another commentator in the 1960s, noted that as the use of coercion increased, the flow of information from local to central levels decreased.[65] African leaders have always had a difficult time acquiring good information; statistics are poor as are communication systems. Anything that reduces the flow of information is likely to prove harmful to governance and to development. There is evidence that when African governments have tried to explain structural adjustment programs and especially have tried to mobilize rural support for cutting urban subsidies or for devaluation, they have avoided severe riots in response to these programs and garnered additional support. For example, Zimbabwe was able to slash consumer subsidies on basic foodstuffs in 1983 and 1984 because a government widely viewed as legitimate had recently been elected and it had fully explained its policies. In Sudan, on the other hand, when an unpopular leader, Nimeiri, personally announced an IMF-supported program in March 1985 and two days later left for abroad, riots followed.[66]

So far there is relatively little evidence to suggest that African elites have considered the costs and benefits of trying to implement new economic programs while opening up their political systems. The Nigerian military government of General Babangida was determined to have a debate on whether or not to accept a conditionality program under the auspices of the IMF in 1985. When sentiment against the fund proved to be great, the Nigerian government implemented an austerity package without the ostensible support of the IMF. This was a rare example of opening major economic issues to national debate. It has been asserted that it is more difficult for democratic regimes than for authoritarian ones to implement structural adjustment programs because pluralist democracies find it harder to dismantle politically popular programs, which are useful in elections. Authoritarian political systems, it is said, have to worry less about political patronage because popular opinion is less consequential to the rulers' maintenance of power.[67]

The evidence seems mixed. The dichotomy between democratic and authoritarian systems seems too stark to explain the successes or failures that have existed in implementing structural adjustment programs. However, the issue cannot be fully joined here. All that can be said is that in Africa the record of economic performance by pluralist democracies is too limited to draw firm conclusions. The Nigerian debate in the mid 1980s took place under a military regime, not a democratic one.[68] Indeed, the debate over whether authoritarian or democratic regimes can best implement economic change has taken place with reference to Asia and Latin America and has all but ignored Africa.

There is at this point considerable dismay at the political evolution of Africa and few guideposts that would suggest a definite direction for greater democratization. Julius Nyerere, once an advocate of the widely adopted one-party system, advised the Zimbabwean leaders in 1980 not to duplicate his mistakes by eliminating political competition. However, Nyerere did not suggest an alternative, and Zimbabwe's rulers found it politically convenient and ideologically comforting to eliminate the major rival political parties.[69]

The failure to develop new thinking on democracy in Africa is hardly surprising because any new institutional arrangement can have only a limited impact given the perilous socioeconomic situation in most African countries. It is unlikely that new African democracies will be created in the coming years. The question then becomes if new institutional arrangements and government operating procedures can be adopted to soften authoritarian systems and make them more sensitive to human rights. Scholars have yet to fully address the problem of how to ameliorate authoritarian regimes. Given the realities, this may be the most pressing problem for Africanists to examine.

NOTES

Henry Bienen wishes to thank the Leon Lowenstein Foundation and the Ford Foundation which have provided support for research during 1988–1989.

1. We will refer to Black Africa throughout, excluding North African countries and South Africa, but including the Sudan.

2. Guillermo O'Donnell, Phillipe C. Schmitter, Laurence Whitehead, eds., *Transitions from Authoritarian Rule*, 4 vols. (Baltimore: Johns Hopkins Press, 1986). For an important critique of this work and an argument that it says more about transitions than about democracy, see Daniel Levine, "Paradigm Lost: Dependence to Democracy," *World Politics* 40, no. 3 (April 1988): 377–394.

3. Kevin Fetherstone and Dimitrios K. Kassoudas, eds., *Political Change in Greece* (London: Croom Helm, 1986); Nancy Bermeo; "Redemocratization and Transition Elections: A Comparison of Spain and Portugal," *Comparative Politics*, January 1987, 213–231.

4. Crawford Young and Thomas Turner, *The Rise and Decline of the Zairian State* (Madison: University of Wisconsin Press, 1985); Thomas M. Callaghy, *The State-Society Struggle: Zaire in Comparative Perspective* (New York: Columbia University Press, 1984); Donald Rothchild and Naomi Chazan, eds., *The Precarious Balance: State and Society in Africa* (Boulder, Colo.: Westview Press, 1988).

5. Robert H. Jackson and Carl G. Rosberg, Jr., *Personal Rule in Black Africa* (Berkeley: University of California Press, 1982).

6. Robert A. Dahl, *Polyarchy: Participation and Opposition* (New Haven, Conn.: Yale University Press, 1971), 7–8.

7. So-called populist military regimes in Ghana and Upper Volta for a time opened up political participation, attacked entrenched elites, and even implemented some reform policies in the economic and social sphere. There has been a radical military experiment in Ethiopia. See Henry Bienen, "Populist Military Regimes in West Africa," *Armed Forces and Society* 11, no. 3 (Spring 1985): 357–378.

8. For a recent review, see Larry Diamond and Dennis Galvan, "Sub-Saharan Africa," in Robert Wesson, ed., *Democracy World Survey, 1987* (Boulder, Colo.: Lynne Rienner, 1987), 63–103.

9. See, for instance, Kwame Nkrumah's "Nation of Destiny," which launched the Gold Coast toward independence in 1953, reprinted in *Revolutionary Path* (New York: International, 1973), 108–109. Kenneth Kaunda made the same type of argument in his "The Future of Democracy in Africa," reprinted in *Zambia: Independence and Beyond* (London: Nelson, 1966).

10. See Frantz Fanon, *The Wretched of the Earth* (New York: Grove Press, 1963).

11. Julius Nyerere, *Democracy and the Party System* (Dar es Salaam: Tanganyika Standard, 1963).

12. Julius Nyerere, "Will Democracy Survive in Africa?" *Africa Special Report*, February 1960, 3–4.

13. Seymour Martin Lipset, *Political Man* (Garden City, N.Y.: Doubleday Anchor, 1963) and "Some Social Requisites of Democracy,"

American Political Science Review 53, no. 1 (March 1959): 69–105; Phillips Cutright, "National Political Development: Measurement and Analysis," *American Sociological Review* 28 (April 1963): 253–264; Walt Rostow, *Stages of Economic Growth* (Cambridge: Cambridge University Press, 1960).

14. There are so many reviews of this literature by now that we need only cite a few works: Edward Shils, *Political Development in the New States* (The Hague: Mouton, 1962); Leonard Binder, "National Integration and Political Development," *American Political Science Review* 57 (September 1964): 662–631; Gabriel Almond and James S. Coleman, eds., *The Politics of Developing Areas* (Princeton, N.J.: Princeton University Press, 1960); Clifford Geertz, ed., *Old Societies and New States* (Glencoe, Ill.: Free Press, 1963).

15. Samuel P. Huntington, *Political Order in Changing Societies* (New Haven, Conn.: Yale University Press, 1968); Samuel P. Huntington and Clement Moore, eds., *Authoritarian Politics in Modern Society: The Dynamics of Established One-Party Systems* (New York: Basic Books, 1970).

16. David Apter, *Ghana in Transition* (Princeton, N.J.: Princeton University Press, 1959).

17. Morris Janowitz, *The Military in the Political Development of New Nations* (Chicago: University of Chicago Press, 1964).

18. Huntington, *Political Order in Changing Societies.*

19. Samuel Decalo, *Coups and Army Rule in Africa* (New Haven, Conn.: Yale University Press, 1976).

20. Claude Welch, Jr., ed., *Soldier and State in Africa* (Evanston, Ill.: Northwestern University Press, 1970); Henry Bienen, *Armies and Parties in Africa* (New York: Africana, 1978); J. M. Lee, *African Armies and Civil Order* (London: Chatto and Windus, 1969); Robin Luckham, *The Nigerian Military* (Cambridge: Cambridge University Press, 1971).

21. For a good discussion of this point see Young and Turner, *Rise and Decline of the Zairian State*, 27.

22. D. Fogel, *Africa in Struggle: National Liberation and Revolution* (Seattle: Ism Press, 1982), 127–145. On intervention generally, see Timothy M. Shaw, "The Future of the Great Powers in Africa: Towards a Political Economy of Intervention," *Journal of Modern African Studies* 21, no. 4 (December 1983).

23. See Walter F. Hahn and Alvin J. Cottrell, *Soviet Shadow over Africa* (Miami: Center for Advanced International Studies, 1976); Robert F. Gorman, *Political Conflict on the Horn of Africa* (New York: Praeger, 1981).

24. Jackson and Rosberg, *Personal Rule in Black Africa.* See also John Cartwright, *Political Leadership in Africa* (London: Croom Helm,

1983); Samuel Decalo, "African Personal Dictatorships," *Journal of Modern African Studies* 23, no. 2 (June 1985).

25. Callaghy, *State-Society Struggle;* and Richard A. Joseph, *Democracy and Prebendal Politics in Nigeria: The Rise and Fall of the Second Republic* (Cambridge: Cambridge University Press, 1987).

26. Goran Hyden, *Beyond Ujamaa: Underdevelopment and an Uncaptured Peasantry* (Berkeley: University of California Press, 1980).

27. In "Dead Dictators and Rioting Mobs: Does the Demise of Authoritarian Rule Lead to Political Instability?" *International Security* 10, no. 3 (Winter 1985–1986): 112–143, Richard K. Betts and Samuel P. Huntington explore the prospects for stability after the death of leaders who have been in power a long time. On Ethiopia, see Ryzard Kapuscinski, *The Emperor: Downfall of an Autocrat* (New York: Harcourt Brace Jovanovich, 1983); Marina Ottoway and David Ottaway, *Ethiopia: Empire in Revolution* (New York: Africana, 1978).

28. See Henry Bienen and Nicolas van de Walle, "Of Time and Power in Africa," *American Political Science Review* 83, no. 1 (March 1989), 19–34.

29. Fernando Henrique Cardoso and Enzo Faletto, *Dependency and Development in Latin America*, trans. Marjorie Mattingly Urquidi. (Berkeley: University of California Press, 1979); André Gunder Frank, *Capitalism and Underdevelopment in Latin America*, rev. ed. (New York: Monthly Review Press, 1969). T. Dos Santos, "La Crise de la Théorie de Dependence Developpement et les Relations et la Societé en Americane Latino," *L'Homme*, no. 12 (April–May 1969).

30. Colin Leys, *Underdevelopment in Kenya* (Berkeley and Los Angeles: University of California, 1974), 9–10.

31. Ibid., 23.

32. Walter Rodney, *How Europe Underdeveloped Africa* (London: Bogel Ouverture, 1972).

33. Leys, *Underdevelopment in Kenya*, 10.

34. Leys's criticism of his earlier dependency writings can be found in his "Capital Accumulation, Class Formation and Dependency— The Significance of the Kenyan Case," in Ralph Miliband and John Saville, eds., *The Socialist Register 1978* (London: Merlin Press, 1978). The argument for more emphasis on the state is found in Peter B. Evans, Dietrich Rueschemeyer, and Theda Skocpol, eds., *Bringing the State Back In* (Cambridge: Cambridge University Press, 1985).

35. See, for instance, John Saul, "The State in Post-Colonial Societies: Tanzania" in his *The State and Revolution in Eastern Africa* (New York: Monthly Review Press, 1979), 173; Joel Samoff, "Class, Class

Conflict and the State in Africa," *Political Science Quarterly* 97 (1982): 126.

36. Timothy M. Shaw, "Varieties of Corporatism in Africa," *Journal of Modern African Studies* 20 (1982): 255; Callaghy, *State-Society Struggle*, 32.

37. Philip O'Brien and Paul Cammack, eds., *Generals in Retreat: The Crisis of Military Rule in Latin America* (Manchester, England: Manchester University Press, 1985); Alain Roquié, *The Military and the State in Latin America* (Berkeley: University of California Press, 1987); Alfred Stepan, *Rethinking Military Politics: Brazil and the Southern Cone* (Princeton, N.J.: Princeton University press, 1988).

38. See Larry Diamond's analysis of Nigeria in Larry Diamond, Juan Linz, and Seymour Martin Lipset, eds., *Democracy in Developing Countries: Africa*, vol. 2 (Boulder, Colo.: Lynne Rienner, 1988), 82–85. Also see Claude Welch, *No Farewell to Arms: Military Disengagement in Africa and Latin America* (Boulder, Colo.: Westview Press, 1987).

39. On military-civil service relations in Africa, see Edward Feit, "Military Coups and Political Development: Some Lessons from Ghana and Nigeria," *World Politics* 20, no. 2 (January 1968): 179–193; Edward Feit, "The Rule of the 'Iron Surgeons': Military Government in Spain and Ghana," *Comparative Politics* 1, no. 4 (July 1969): 485–497; William Gutteridge, *Military Regimes in Africa* (London: Methuen, 1975), 76–77; Henry Bienen, "Military Rule and Political Process; Nigerian Examples," *Comparative Politics*, (January 1978): 205–226. For military attacks on the civil service, see Bienen, "Populist Military Regimes in West Africa."

40. Samuel Huntington raises this question more generally in "Will More Countries Become Democratic?" *Political Science Quarterly* 99 (1984): 201. He points to the possibilities of regime transformation from within when rulers undertake a democratic transition and also examines the collapse of regimes and their replacement.

41. For Angola, see MaKidi-Ku-Ntima, "Class Struggle and the Making of the Revolution in Angola," in Bernard Magubane and Nzongola-Ntalaja, eds., *Proletarianization and Class Struggle in Africa* (San Francisco: Synthesis, 1983). On Mozambique, see Allen Isaacman and Barbara Isaacman, *Mozambique: From Colonization to Revolution* (Boulder, Colo.: Westview Press, 1983), 124. Democratic prospects for Guinea-Bissau were examined by Basil Davidson, *No Fist Is Big Enough to Hide the Sky: The Liberation of Guinea-Bissau and Cape Verde* (London: Zed Press, 1976), 176.

42. Hyden, *op. cit.*, p. 204, for one, made the presocialist societies argument.

43. For a discussion by someone who took ideological differences seriously and also saw important performance distinctions of Marxist-Leninist regimes in Africa, see Crawford Young, *Ideology and Development in Africa* (New Haven, Conn.: Yale University Press, 1982). Also see Edmond J. Keller and Donald Rothchild, eds., *Afro-Marxist Regimes: Ideology and Public Policy* (Boulder, Colo.: Lynne Rienner, 1987); David Ottaway and Marina Ottaway, *Afro-communism* (New York: Africana, 1981).

44. In "The State and Economic Stagnation in Tropical Africa," *World Development* 14, no. 3 (March 1986): 323, Richard Sandbrook wrote of "sizeable pockets of popular support" for them.

45. Richard L. Sklar, "Developmental Democracy," *Comparative Studies in Society and History* (1987): 686–714.

46. Samuel E. Finer, "State-Building, State Boundaries and Border Control," *Social Science Information* 13 (1974): 98–114.

47. Thomas Callaghy, "Politics and Vision: The Interplay of Domination, Equality and Liberty," in Patrick Chabal, ed., *Political Domination in Africa* (Cambridge: Cambridge University Press, 1986), 30–51.

48. Charles Tilly, "Reflections on the History of European State-Making," in Charles Tilly, ed., *The Formation of National States in Western Europe* (Princeton, N.J.: Princeton University Press, 1975), 38.

49. Dankwart Rustow, "Transitions to Democracy: Toward a Dynamic Model," *Comparative Politics* 2, no. 3 (April 1970): 337–364.

50. William J. Foltz, "Popular Opposition in Single-Party States of Tropical Africa," in Robert A. Dahl, ed., *Regimes and Oppositions* (New Haven, Conn.: Yale University Press, 1973), 169.

51. Henry Bienen, "The State and Ethnicity: Integrative Formulas in Africa," in Donald Rothchild and Victor Olorunsola, eds., *State Versus Ethnic Claims: African Policy Dilemmas* (Boulder, Colo.: Westview Press, 1983), 100–126.

52. See Arthur Waldron, "Theories of Nationalism and Historical Explanation," *World Politics* 37 (April 1985): 416–433.

53. Robert H. Jackson and Carl G. Rosberg, Jr., "Why Africa's Weak States Persist: The Empirical and Juridical in Statehood," *World Politics* 35 (October 1982): 1–24.

54. Dahl, *Polyarchy*, 203.

55. Ibid.

56. Henry Bienen, "The Politics of Income Distribution: Institutions, Class and Ethnicity," in his *Political Conflict and Economic Change in Nigeria* (London: Frank Cass, 1985), 64–115. Opposing views are presented by Irving Leonard Markovitz, ed., *Studies in*

Power and Class in Africa (New York: Oxford University Press, 1987); James Mittelman, *Underdevelopment and the Transition to Socialism: Mozambique and Tanzania* (New York: Academic Press, 1981); Dennis Cohen and John Daniels, eds., *Political Economy of Africa* (London: Longman Group, 1981).

57. Dahl, *Polyarchy*, 203. See also Leonard Binder et al., *Crises and Sequences in Political Development* (Princeton, N.J.: Princeton University Press, 1971).

58. Tilly, "Reflections on the History of European State-Making."

59. Many of these reforms are documented in Organization of African Unity, *Africa's Submission to the Special Session of the United Nations General Assembly on Africa's Economic and Social Crisis* (Addis Ababa: OAU, 1986), 19.

60. Dahl, *Polyarchy*, 49.

61. Henry Bienen and Mark Gersovitz, "Economic Stabilization, Conditionality and Political Stabillty," *International Organization* 39 (1985): 729–754.

62. Elliot Berg and Mary M. Shirley, *Divestiture in Developing Countries*, World Bank Discussion Paper no. 11 (Washington, D.C.: World Bank, 1987).

63. John Nellis, *Public Enterprise in Sub-Saharan Africa*, World Bank Discussion Paper no. 1 (Washington, D.C.: World Bank, 1986).

64. W. Arthur Lewis, *Politics in West Africa* (New York: Oxford University Press, 1965).

65. David E. Apter, *The Politics of Modernization* (Chicago: University of Chicago Press, 1965).

66. Henry Bienen and Mark Gersovitz, "Consumer Subsidy Cuts, Violence and Political Stability," *Comparative Politics* 19, no. 1 (October 1986): 25–44.

67. Jagdish Bhagwati, "Rethinking Trade Strategy," in John P. Lewis and Valeriana Kallab, eds., *Development Strategies Reconsidered* (New Brunswick, N.J.: Transaction Books, 1986), 92–93, 101.

68. The Babangida regime did develop support for its austerity programs through debate and by utilizing economic commissions, but this was hardly an exercise in democratic government.

69. *Herald* [Harare], July 15, 1988, 7.

PART Four

DYNAMICS OF REFORM
AND REVOLUTION

Chapter

11

The Origins, Processes, and Outcomes of Great Political Reform*

A Framework of Analysis

Michel Oksenberg and Bruce J. Dickson

Social theorists have devoted great attention to revolution as a form of political and social change. Spurred on by the French Revolution, its aftermath, and subsequent revolutions, historians and social theorists as well as political activists have developed numerous interpretations of that cataclysmic event. Chief among them, of course, was Karl Marx, whose various disciples and their protagonists and antagonists have kept the issue of revolution alive to the present day. The field of comparative politics has been enlivened by several major works that focus on revolution. Barrington Moore's *The Social Origins of Democracy and Dictatorship*, Samuel Huntington's *Political Order in Changing Societies*, Theda Skocpol's *States and Social Revolutions*, and Chalmers Johnson's *Revolutionary Change* come immediately to mind.[1] This emphasis upon the origins, processes, and outcomes of revolutionary change is certainly understandable in light of the significance of the Cromwellian, French, Russian, Nazi, Chinese communist, Cuban, Vietnamese, Iranian Shi'ite, and other revolutions. Curiously, however, another form of sweeping political change has received much less attention from students of society and politics, namely, great political reform. Theoretical writings on the origins, processes, and outcomes of great reform are rather scarce despite the fact that historical monographs describing and analyzing the numerous instances of peaceful and extensive political transformations are available to sustain comparisons and theory building. Among the few works that approach the subject are Samuel Huntington's *Political Order*, the one notable work that analyzes both great revolutions and great reforms in an overarching framework, and several of the essays in Almond, Flanagan, and Mundt's *Crisis, Choice, and Change: Historical Studies of Political Development*.[2]

The relative paucity of comparative and theoretical writings on great reform is all the more surprising when one considers the numerous significant instances of such change: Russia under Peter the Great and Alexander II, Britain of the 1830s to 1840s and the 1860s, the United States from a confederation to a federation, the United States under Andrew Jackson and Franklin Roosevelt, Germany under Bismarck, Mexico under Càrdenas, Japan during the Meiji, Turkey under Ataturk, Spain after Franco, and Portugal after Salazar, the Soviet Union under Gorbachev, and China under Deng Xiaoping.[3] Instances also exist of failed or aborted reform, notably China in 1898, Russia under Stolypin, and, some might argue, the Soviet Union under Khrushchev or (according to David Stockman) the United States under Ronald Reagan.

This is not the place to analyze why political sociologists have devoted more attention to developing theories about revolution than about great reform, though that is an interesting issue. But the paucity of theories about great reform is particularly unfortunate at this juncture in world affairs. Reform seems to have replaced revolution in most regions of the world as the preferred mode of political activists for effecting change. Further, China and the Soviet Union are in the midst of change, and analysts of those reforms proceed relatively uninformed by theories or hypotheses to guide and organize their inquiries. Some might argue that this lack of encumbrance is a blessing, in light of the many dead ends that theories of revolution have produced. But in the absence of theories, explicit hypotheses, or formal analytical frameworks, many of the analyses of the Chinese reforms under Deng Xiaoping or of the Soviet reforms under Mikhail Gorbachev seem to be ad hoc and partial.

Further, many observers of the Deng and Gorbachev reforms seem implicitly to be guided by theories of revolution, and as a result focus on some analytical issues that seem more suited to the study of revolutionary change. For example, many observers painstakingly search for the coherent ideology guiding the Chinese and Soviet reforms, and they find its absence disconcerting. They seem unaware that while revolutionaries characteristically are guided by an ideology (the Mexican revolution of 1911 is an important exception), no great reformer has ever adhered to a formal, explicit, and all-encompassing belief system with action consequences. Nor has any great reform been launched with a clear strategy for effecting change. Thus, the absence of a detailed blueprint to guide the reforms of Deng and Gorbachev is an inherent characteristic of great reform and is not a sign that Deng or Gorbachev's reforms are deficient.

Theories of revolution can be useful to analysis of reform, if they are drawn up explicitly and discriminately. Revolution and reform are both instances of politically induced change brought on by a perceived crisis. To draw on Chalmers Johnson's language, both are responses to a disequilibrium, that is, a situation in which the values, perceptions, or beliefs of the leaders and the populace, the political institutions, and the economic system (the division of labor in society) are not synchronized and do not reinforce one another. The disequilibrium, according to Johnson, results from changes in any of these realms—values, political institutions, or the division of labor—arising from domestic or external factors. As we note below, revolutionaries and reformers differ in the way they seek to establish a new integration of values, institutions, and economic systems. Johnson's notions are helpful in thinking about the nature of the perceived crisis on the eve of reform. Similarly, Skocpol's emphasis upon the role of foreign powers in shaping the course of revolution is useful in thinking about great reform. But the processes of revolutionary and reformist change are sufficiently different and the personalities and outlooks of revolutionaries and reformers are sufficiently different that the same theory or analytical framework is unlikely to illuminate equally both types of change.

In short, the time has come to think more systematically about great reforms: what causes them, what processes they tend to share, what their outcomes are, and what explains the variations in the processes and outcomes. This essay draws upon the existing theoretical writings about reform, revolution, and political change and upon empirical material from primarily the Chinese and also other historical cases. It offers a few systematic observations about the process of great political reforms and seeks to contribute to a richer understanding of that form of change. Rather than offering firm conclusions or even tentative hypotheses, much less a uniform "model" of the reform process— an effort that would be misplaced in any case due to the idiosyncratic aspects of each great reform—the essay primarily presents a series of observations on the defining characteristics of great reform, origins, the beliefs of great reformers, the structuring of reformers' choices, the strategies of great reform, and the outcomes.

DEFINING CHARACTERISTICS OF GREAT POLITICAL REFORM

What defines a great political reform? What distinguishes it from other forms of political change, particularly revolution? We define great political reform as a massive but peaceful and gradual change of political institutions and the roles they play in managing or regulating the society, culture, or economy. We use the word "great" to distinguish this form of change from two other types of "reform." We do not have in mind administrative changes designed to terminate corruption or make the existing system more efficient. That is how the phrase "political reform" is frequently employed in urban politics in the United States. Nor do we have in mind what might be called "lesser reforms," that is, limited changes in political institutions, in the relationship between the state and the economy or society, or in a nation's external relations.

"Great political reforms" involve more than improving the administration of the state; they fundamentally transform the political system. This transformation affects four aspects of a political system: (1) the relationship between the state and society, especially the basis upon which the state elicits response to its commands from the populace, that is, the basis of legitimacy and support; (2) the relationship between the state and the economy; (3) the distribution of power and authority among and within the constituent institutions of the state (head of state, the military, the judiciary, interest groups, political parties, the central, provincial, and local bureaucracies, and so on); and (4) the relationship between the country's political and economic systems and the external world. Put more simply, great political reforms alter the basis of legitimacy of the political system, redistribute power and authority in the constituent elements of the state, significantly alter the tasks of governance, and change the country's foreign relations.

Great reforms differ as to the actual changes affected: centralization or decentralization, expansion or diminution of the prerogatives of the head of state, extension or contraction of state control over the economy, increased involvement in or isolation from world affairs. But they all entail extensive, peaceful, and gradual change.

As already indicated, it is important to maintain a clear conceptual distinction between revolution and great reform. Revolutions by definition are the rapid and violent change of elites and institutions. They differ from great reforms in four important ways. First, revolutions entail extensive violence or the use of force and are massive social upheavals. Reforms occur largely peacefully. This critical difference helps explain the importance of coercion and the continued power of the military and police in postrevolutionary regimes, in contrast to the usual outcome of Great Reform.

Second, revolutions involve the immediate and forceful replacement of one ruling elite by another and usually an effort to inculcate a new value system among the populace. As Chalmers Johnson and Crane Brinton in particular noted, prior to a revolution, antagonistic contending elites emerge in society, each with a different set of beliefs. Many intellectuals cease adhering to the values of the ancien régime and propagate a new set of beliefs. Revolution occurs when a new elite replaces an old one. Reform, in contrast, does not involve the replacement of one elite by another. In fact, it is usually led by a portion of the existing elite, with no prior polarization of contending elites that hold deeply conflicting value systems. Nor do intellectuals abandon old values. Again drawing on Chalmers Johnson, revolution is necessarily preceded by an erosion in the authority of the ancien régime. The existing elite confronts a crisis in its legitimacy, and revolutionaries aim to create a totally new system of authority. While an erosion in popular confidence in the rulers or the political system may precede great reform, the situation has not typically reached the same point of crisis. To the contrary, reformers seek to use and build upon the existing structures of authority.

Third, revolutions entail a rapid change of political institutions in the national capital. Political life in Moscow in 1917, Beijing in 1949, and Paris in 1793 was dramatically transformed. The effect of great reforms on political institutions and political life in the capital is a more protracted and gradual process.

Fourth, the outcome of revolution and reform are different. All great revolutions to date have increased the power of the state and have drawn new portions of the populace into politics. Great reforms do not have any uniform, common outcomes, though most have resulted in expanded political participation. Conventional wisdom holds that revolutions produce greater social change than do reforms, with a redistribution of power among conflicting classes. Closer examination reveals that over the long run great reforms tend to produce at least as enduring and penetrating changes as revolutions. To be sure, during the early stages when the revolutionary elite and ideological purists vigorously pursue their utopia and enforce their ideology, the revolutionary change appears great. But, to use Brinton's metaphor, as the fever subsides, as thermidor sets in, and as the revolutionaries yield to their bureaucratic successors, many qualities of the ancien régime reassert themselves. The extremism and dogmatism of revolution, in case after case, produce a reaction, while the moderation and experimentalism of reform, in many instances, enable the forging of a coalition with interests in sustaining the reform program.

What is the distinction between great and lesser reform? Lesser reforms entail less sweeping, partial, or marginal adjustments to the political system and its functions. We are tempted to assert that great reforms have significant effects on the four aspects of a political system mentioned above (political institutions, state-economy relations, state-society relations, and foreign relations), while lesser reforms affect only one or two of these.

The boundary between great and lesser is not easily drawn. Should the changes wrought by Theodore Roosevelt and Woodrow Wilson be added to the list of great reforms? Were the changes effected in the

United States during Lyndon Johnson's Great Society, in Britain during Clement Atlee's Labour government, and in France from the Fourth to the Fifth Republic, sufficiently sweeping to be considered great reforms? Any typology inevitably generates such questions of classification. However, at this stage such questions are not particularly crucial. The unambiguous cases of great reform are well known, and their common defining characteristics sufficiently differentiate them from other types of political change—revolution and lesser reform—that our analysis can proceed.

ORIGINS OF REFORM: PERCEPTION OF A CRISIS

Until the impetus from below for great reform that swept Eastern Europe in 1989, great political reforms typically had been triggered by a single preeminent leader or a group of leaders. Either the leaders were already in power or near the apex of power, or they were some distance from power but used the issue of reform to propel themselves to power, as with Meiji Japan. No matter what their location or position on the eve of the reform era, political leaders of great reforms had a similar perception: Their state and/or nation confronted a set of problems that threatened its cherished traditions and core institutions.

Great reforms differ in the nature of the crisis that the leaders perceived. In many instances, as with Peter the Great, Alexander II, and Meiji Japan, the immediate crisis was seen as emanating from abroad. Defeat in battle or the sense of encirclement by strong and hostile forces provided a powerful stimulus to undertaking reform. In other instances, as with the New Deal, severe economic problems— widespread unemployment, stagnating or declining growth rates, difficulties in the rural sector—gripped the nation, and the leaders concluded these problems could not be resolved without fundamental changes in the role of the state in regulating the economy and possibly in the structure of the state itself. In yet other instances, a portion of the political elite concluded that the political system confronted an impending legitimacy crisis and that massive changes were required in state-society relations, particularly broadening the basis of political participation. This was obviously a central concern in the British Reform Act of 1832 and in Spain after Franco.

In most instances of great reform, the reformers eventually concluded that the crisis was deep and widespread in its origins, that a few remedial measures would not suffice, that the manifest problems— whether external, economic, or eroding popular confidence in the system—had their roots in other aspects of their country, and that unless peaceful but massive change was undertaken, the crisis would deepen and lead to foreign domination, increased misery, or revolution. How-ever, in contrast to revolutionaries, who pursue the stated goal of the toppling the ancien régime, great reformers frequently do not envision the extent and depth of changes they eventually promote. Many have assumed office before concluding their country faced a crisis, before having a comprehensive diagnosis of the problems, or before seeking or assuming the role of leaders of a great reform. For example, Franklin Roosevelt offered little indication in his 1932 presidential campaign that he envisioned the need for great reform.

Even though great reformers ultimately arrive at a pessimistic assessment of the current situation, they also have a basically optimistic assessment of the potential of purposeful political action within the existing political framework. Moreover, in contrast to revolutionaries, reformers usually believe that the inherited system had important aspects that were worth preserving.

Great reforms have usually occurred in a society mired in deep problems, but the problems frequently existed for some time, without bringing a reform movement to the fore. The Soviet Union before Gor-bachev and Turkey before Atatürk illustrate the point. Also, similar economic problems or external threats have persisted in other societies that did not undertake reforms. For example, it could be argued that Mexico for many years has needed reform, but the system persists without major change. The interesting questions concerning the origin of a great reform, therefore, are what prompts the perceptions of the political reformers, what galvanizes them to action, and what permits them to elicit a response. In this regard, the relationship between the political reformers and their brain trusters merits particular scrutiny, for the ideas that influence the leaders and that they turn into policy have frequently been perculating among intellectuals for some time. And the perception of the crisis that the reform leaders attain is not always precisely the same as the views of the reform-oriented intellectu-als. Richard Hofstader's discussion of the differences between the Pro-gressive thinkers of the early 1900s and Theodore Roosevelt and his pol-itical allies is germane here.[4] When, how, and with what effect the links are forged between the great reform political leaders and the commun-ity of reform-minded intellectuals are important questions in under-standing the origins of reform.

The historical instances of great reform also suggest, however, that the analytical focus cannot rest exclusively on the coming together of a reform coalition. A crucial difference among great reforms is the extent to which the perception of crisis is limited to the reformers or is more widely shared by other members of the elite and by significant portions of the populace. Peter the Great stands at one end of the spectrum and Franklin Roosevelt at the other. Peter the Great was far in front of the existing political elite and the populace, whereas Roosevelt headed a society in which there was widespread sense of crisis, even if there was no consensus on the diagnosis of the problem or the appropriate solution. Analysis of great reforms, therefore, must go beyond study of the objective conditions and illuminate the understanding that the reformers and their initial opponents have of societal conditions and of their political opportunities to alter those conditions.

The Chinese Case

In the Chinese case,[5] a crucial cause of the reforms was the effect upon Deng Xiaoping of his purge and banishment to rural Jiangxi province from 1966 to 1973 and the lessons absorbed by the hundreds of other officials during the Cultural Revolution and its aftermath (1966–1976). Their experiences during those years and especially their loss of privilege and their intimate contact with the populace impressed upon the entire leadership cohort who had been purged and then brought back to power from 1971 through 1978 that the regime they had helped to create in the 1940s and 1950s was suffering from a crisis of legitimacy. The purged leaders learned that the populace responded to commands more out of fear than respect for their leaders, and sweeping changes were needed to eliminate the cynicism, apathy, and alienation among the populace. Only rapid increases in the standard of living, a respite from continual political mobilization, and a restoration of order and tranquility could quell the growing discontent. This diagnosis propelled Deng and his associates to embark upon the changes of 1977–1978.

However, their specific reform program did not arise in their minds complete and fully developed. For some time, in fact, a number of policy communities had been quietly analyzing the deficiencies of a rigidly planned, nonmarket economy and of the isolation from Western technology.[6] Centered in the Institute of Economics in the Department of Philosophy and Social Sciences at the Chinese Academy of Sciences and extending to some universities, research bureaus in select ministries, and even party departments, clusters of intellectuals especially in the early and mid 1960s had begun to develop alternatives to both the Stalinist and Maoist approaches to development. Badly battered during the peak years of the Cultural Revolution (1966–1969), these policy communities began to reassemble in the early 1970s, and Deng turned to them in 1975, even before Mao's death, to draft three documents concerning policies in economics, science, and politics. They had also begun to plan for China's entry into the international economy. Then, early in 1978, well before the decisive December Central Committee plenum at which Deng and his allies first launched their rural reforms, Deng had solidified his ties with reform-oriented intellectuals by raising the slogan "Seek truth from facts" and by proclaiming himself in charge of logistics for the nation's scientists and technicians.

But not everyone among the leaders shared the Dengist diagnosis and prescriptions. In particular, many among officialdom had not only survived the Cultural Revolution, but benefited from it. The first political conflict of the post-Mao era pitted those who continued to have faith in the late Mao's approach to rule against those who had experienced its inadequacies and excesses. Interestingly, the first glimpse of the dispute between Deng and the beneficiaries of the Cultural Revolution came at the 1978 national conference on science and technology when Deng forged his links with reform-oriented intellectuals, while his opponents pledged to sustain Mao's policies toward the sciences.

Our purpose here is not to recount the origins of the Chinese reforms in detail. To do so would entail tracing how Deng, his associates, and many in the population became aware of China's declining agricultural performance, the growing inefficiencies in the industrial sector, the increasing gap in income and welfare between Chinese on the mainland and the residents of its East Asian peers (Japan, South Korea, Taiwan, and Hong Kong), the technological transformations underway in Japan and the West, and the growing military gap between the Soviet Union and China. Rather, our purpose here is to use the Chinese case to illustrate a broader point: Class analysis, local social history, an objective recounting of external threats, or the recitation of economic statistics—the staple (perhaps erroneously so) in explaining the origins of revolution—are not sufficient to explain the origins of great reforms. The New Deal was not brought into being by an aroused, unemployed proletariat, though the bonus marchers did have an effect. A discontented peasantry did not demand the dissolution of communes in China. Amorphous economic or social forces had to be perceived by and elicit a response from the reformers.

BELIEFS OF REFORMERS: CONSERVATIVE, PRAGMATIC, AND ECLECTIC

What generalizations can be made about the beliefs of great reformers? Richard Hofstader's *The Age of Reform*, a study of the beliefs of American reformers, provides one key to the analysis.[7] A contrast between reformers and revolutionaries provides a second key. Great reformers have usually been conservative (in the precise definition of the word) and pragmatic. Hofstader's classic work emphasizes that American political reformers have embarked upon their programs to preserve certain crucial and hallowed traditions of the American system. The biographies of other great reformers reveal that this insight is more generally applicable. In no instance did reformers initially envision their program to be a total break with the past; they called for a response to a perceived crisis because they believed the crisis might engulf them and in the process destroy something worth saving. To be sure, as the process of reform went forward, many in the reform coalition found less and less in the previous system worth preserving. But at the outset, the objective was to preserve some core features of the existing constitution. (Peter the Great is perhaps the exception, but had the Senate that he created ever challenged him, the reformist czar probably would have proven unwilling to weaken the power of his office and hence to tamper with authoritarian rule. And certainly he envisioned that his programs would strengthen Russia as nation-state.)

As the tragic suppression of dissent in June 1989 demonstrated, Deng Xiaoping did not see his reforms as a total departure from the past. He believed his goals—a strong, modern, and socialist China—were the same as Mao's goals. The Chinese reformers, including the purged Hu Yaobang and Zhao Ziyang, were committed to preserving the dominance of the Communist party and public ownership of the principal means of production. They jealously sought to guard Chinese sovereignty in world affairs. And with some personal variation, imprecision, and fluctuation in their vigilance, they all demanded that their populace not deviate from four principals: (1) adherence to Marxism-Leninism-Mao Zedong thought, (2) the leadership of the Communist party, (3) the socialist road; and (4) the dictatorship of the proletariat. In private conversations, even as he acknowledged Mao's mistakes, Deng Xiaoping from the outset convincingly talked about how he considered himself Mao's loyal disciple. Deng and certainly a number of others believed they were building upon the best of Maoist and Chinese traditions while jettisoning those past patterns that hindered the attainment of Mao's true objectives.

Hofstader and others also stress that reformers tend to see themselves as falling within an indigenous tradition of reform. The New Dealers saw themselves in the tradition of Andrew Jackson, Theodore Roosevelt, and Woodrow Wilson. Gorbachev looks back to Bukharin, the NEP, and Khrushchev, that is, the revisionists rather than the Stalinists in the party. Interestingly, some of Gorbachev's brain trusters see themselves as inheritors of a reformist tradition dating to Czarist times. Many of the Chinese reformers look upon earlier reform and restoration eras as historical precedents, and they seek lessons from these past successes and failures.

Most countries have their own distinctive traditions of reform, though the traditions appear stronger in some countries (as the United States, Britain, and Japan) than in others. One wonders whether countries in which the revolutionary impulse has been particularly evident (France and Russia, for example) possess social structures and cultures that make them somewhat rigid and prone to violence and hence that render them less amenable to successful reform and more vulnerable to revolution. Do some structures and cultures facilitate great reform?

Whatever the answer to that question, the inclination of reformers to harken back to indigenous reformist traditions sharply separates them from revolutionaries. Revolutionaries have partaken of a global political culture and tradition that can be traced to the French Revolution, bears a Marxist imprint, and has evolved from revolution to revolution. While the Mexican, Nazi, and Iranian Shi'ite revolutions are not in this chain, the French, Russian, Chinese, Cuban, and Vietnamese revolutions clearly are, and this tradition had an effect upon the decolonialization struggles in Africa and Asia in the 1960s and 1970s. Revolutionaries frequently have perceived themselves as part of a global community of political activists seeking through violence to liberate humanity from oppression and to transform totally their country's structure and values. As many analysts have pointed out, revolutionaries in reality also draw upon and reflect their nation's traditions, and even in consciously rejecting their nation's past, they are molded by it. Nonetheless, the contrast with great reformers is striking, for reformers until recently have not been conscious members of a global community or profession, and there is not much evolution of "reformist doctrine." (Such a tradition may now be in the process of formation within communist countries, however, beginning with Khrushchev and then going through the Yugoslavian, Hungarian, Gorbachev, Deng, Polish, East German, and Czech reforms.)

The deliberate drawing upon and preserving of national traditions of reform have important and often neglected implications for the study of reform. A proper illumination of the Deng or Gorbachev reforms involves understanding their relationship to previous indigenous reform efforts. In the Chinese case, at least, such careful analysis has yet to be done. It is likely to reveal that many of the ideas stimulating the reform effort come not only from the 1898 reforms and the May 4th reformers of 1919, but also from the policies of the Guomindang in the 1930s. Gorbachev's effort to retrieve the option of a socialist development path surrendered in the purge and subsequent disgrace of Bukharin appears to be an important aspect of his approach to reform. One senses similar linkages between Ataturk's reforms and early efforts to reform the decaying Ottoman Empire and between the restoration of Spanish democracy and the recurring tradition of reform in Spain under enlightened monarchical tutelage, most recently in the 1930s.

It would be erroneous, however, to conclude that great reformers seek only to return to a glorified past, the defining characteristic of restorationists, or to resist all influence from the outside. To the contrary, they do borrow from abroad, and as with Peter the Great and Meiji Japan, they often do so at a feverish pace. Indeed, one of the striking and recurring features of most reforms—Mexico under Cárdenas and Jacksonian democracy are at least two exceptions—is the desire of the reformers to open their countries to greater external intellectual influence. They tend to believe that intellectual isolation is a factor in bringing on the perceived crisis. But in contrast to revolution, the transfer of ideas from abroad tends to be eclectic and pragmatic. That which holds promise of working is imported. The leaders, bureaucrats, and intellectuals of Meiji Japan looked to Germany, France, Britain, and the United States. And Chinese under Deng have found inspiration in facets of Japan, South Korea, Taiwan, Eastern Europe, Germany, France, Britain, Brazil, Mexico, the United States, and the Soviet Union. China since 1978 has been on a worldwide idea importing spree, even as it seeks to preserve its cultural and political distinctiveness.

The eclecticism, of course, reflects the nonideological, nondogmatic character of most reformers. Yet most reforms do have a discernible thrust or orientation to them. In China under Deng this included the relaxation of state control over the economy, culture, and society (often characterized as a move from a totalitarian to authoritarian regime), an increased responsiveness of the state to popular opinion, and an opening to the outside world. But as with most great reforms, no blueprint guided the Deng reform, and a good deal of policy was formulated on an ad hoc basis. This inevitably led to inconsistencies in the beliefs and policies embraced by the reformers. The contradictions are inherent to the pragmatic, experimental character of the reforms. They are also the product of sometimes chaotic borrowing from incompatible models.

The messiness of reform doctrine was particularly evident, of course, in the New Deal programs, the first reform efforts of 1933–1934 under the NRA Blue Eagle; when these were declared unconstitutional, the efforts of the so-called second New Deal of the WPA, NLRB, and so on. In the Chinese case, too, one sees different intellectual influences in the rural reforms of 1978–1984 that harken back to China of the 1950s and possibly earlier and in the urban reforms beginning in 1984 that reveal the influence of Eastern European and East Asian countries.

The diverse intellectual currents upon which reformers draw generate two further observations on the role of intellectuals in reform and the cleavages around which reform politics frequently swirl. Reform intellectuals differ from revolutionary idealogues and polemicists not only in their pragmatism and desire to preserve aspects of their nation's traditions. They frequently include in their ranks lawyers, engineers, economists, and other technocrats who remain true to their professions and are capable of evaluating policy alternatives. The ranks of revolutionaries also draw from these professions, but the individuals frequently abandon their calling. Expertise and professionalism is valued in most great reforms, while fervor and mobilizational skills are esteemed in revolution. As a result, from Peter the Great to Bismarck, Meiji Japan, and Deng's China, strengthening the educational curriculum and reducing instruction in dogma were major aspects of the reform program.

The eclecticism and pragmatism of great reforms, however, also are the basis of many of the political struggles within reform movements. Reformers frequently divide over three issues. First, is the major source of inspiration to be derived from the past or from an alien experience? Not atypically, reforms are launched on conservative principles, but increasingly, the reforms draw upon external experience, leading to a cleavage between the conservatives and the outward looking leaders. This has certainly been the case in Deng's China. Second, disputes arise over how much and what of the past is core to the national identity, and how much and what from abroad can safely be disseminated without destroying the national essence. This issue, too, has been a salient and vexing one to China's reformers, as it was, for example, in Meiji Japan and the New Deal. Finally, reformers divide over the appropriate external model. Frequently, some in the reform coalition advocate importing ideas from a nation that others consider to be an ideological enemy. Some Chinese reformers find inspiration in the Soviet Union or Japan or the United States. Others consider that one or more of these nations pose deep dangers to China and assert that borrowing from them is subversive. Such deep and antagonistic fissures among Chinese reformers echo conflicts between conservative, red-baiting New Dealers and those who saw virtues in the Soviet effort to create a welfare state.

PROCESS OF REFORM: POLITICAL STRATEGIES FOR COALITION MANAGEMENT

The many tensions within the ranks of the reformers, as well as the inevitable opposition to the reform movement, make reform an exercise in political leadership. Partly for this reason, as Samuel Huntington has noted, the only thing more difficult than carrying out a revolution is implementing a successful reform.

In this section, again drawing primarily upon the Chinese case, we offer some general observations about the political choices and difficulties that reformers confront. Reformers face a series of choices they must make, either with or without a conscious design. Huntington emphasizes one in particular: whether to strike rapidly and across a broad front, which he labels "blitzkrieg" reform, as Roosevelt's hundred days, or to unfold the reform program in piecemeal and incremental fashion. Blitzkrieg reform catches the opponents off guard and takes maximum advantage of the broad coalition for reform that frequently exists in its early days. But it also risks rallying the opposition. Blitzkrieg reform occurs when the reformers fear their effort will easily stall; they may calculate that unless their reforms are undertaken comprehensively, the undone portion will subvert the whole effort. Some critics of Deng's piecemeal approach, for instance, argue that by failing to carry out sweeping price reform either in 1979–1980 or 1984–1986, the two major surges in his reform era, Deng may have imperiled his whole effort. According to this view, he did not break the back of his opposition when he was most able to do so. The rebuttal is that Deng was politically quite astute and sufficiently ruthless to achieve his goals when he could. Therefore, according to this reasoning, either he never had the overwhelming strength necessary to prevail over the vested interests who opposed price reform or he himself approached the issue with considerable caution.

The blitzkrieg approach is possible only in those rare cases when the reformers wield enough power to rout the opposition. Either the reformer has to be supreme within his own coalition or the perception of crisis must be widely held. Otherwise, it may be better to proceed step by step, identifying and fighting one or two opponents at a time. Perhaps even more important, blitzkrieg reform can occur only when the reformers have a blueprint or fairly detailed sense of their total reform package or are able (as in the early New Deal) to develop one rapidly. As we noted earlier, this is rarely the case.

Thus, most reforms are undertaken in piecemeal fashion not because the clever reformers are operating in a hostile environment where the perception of crisis does not match theirs and where they must divide and conquer to put their carefully considered plans into effect. Rather, piecemeal reform is typical because the reformer does not have a clear sense of the battlefronts that await him as he sallies forth. That, it seems, is the case not only with Deng and Gorbachev but even with the reformers who are often assumed to have the greatest sense of coherent purpose at the outset.

The Chinese case suggests therefore that the blitzkrieg versus piecemeal decision is not the only or even the most significant choice that reformers must make. Several others confront them. First, should the reformers move from the hard to the easy problems, or should they address the easy ones first and postpone the hard issues until later? The degree of difficulty is determined by the extent of the likely opposition, the ramifications of taking on the issue, the technical complexity of the issue, the clarity of choice, and so on. Deng's general strategy was quite evident, as Harry Harding in particular has noted, namely, to take on the easier issues and delay the tough ones. Peter the Great's strategy was different, attacking the central obstacles to reform in succession, with each reform revealing a new, more fundamental problem. He moved from military reform to tax reform to administrative reform to educational reform.

A second strategic choice involves priority to be given to reform at the high, intermediate, low, or primary levels of the political and social system. Does one begin by reforming national institutions? Or, does one focus upon the provinces? Or, does one start with local government? Or, does one target production units, the family, and so on? Deng has carried out a differentiated strategy. In some areas, such as military and agricultural reforms, he worked from the bottom up, while in other areas, such as fiscal reforms and industrial reforms, he has gone from the top down. What is not clear to outside observers is the criteria for deciding at which level of the hierarchy to launch a particular reform.

A third strategic choice involves establishing sectoral priorities. Does one begin with rural reform and then move to the urban areas, as in the Chinese case, or begin with urban reform, as Gorbachev is attempting? And, does one emphasize economic reforms at the outset and deter political reform, as has been Deng's preference, or does one, in the early stages, focus more on political than economic reform, as Gorbachev has done? Or, does one intertwine the two? If the political reforms precede economic reforms, then political instability may be the result. The populace will be able to make legitimate demands before they have begun to receive benefits from and acquire a stake in the economic reforms, but if the economic reforms race ahead of the political ones, instability may also result. Professional groups, entrepreneurs, managers, intellectuals, students, and possibly even industrial workers may begin to seek greater access to the policy process and to chafe under the restrictions of the unreformed political system. This is part of the explanation for the massive demonstrations in Beijing in 1989.

Finally, there are territorial or regional strategies to be settled. Does one make certain regions of the country pacesetters in the reform effort, as Guangdong in the Deng era, the Baltic States under Gorbachev, or St. Petersburg under Peter the Great? Does this introduce regional tensions? But if one seeks evenness in reform, does this constrain the regions whose interests most coincide with the orientation of the reform? And would this not deprive the reformers of locomotives for pulling the entire nation forward?

Out of the strategic decisions about pace, levels, sectors, regions, and the strength of the opposition comes what should be called the sequence of reform. The sequence in which a reform unfolds and particularly the consequences of the sequence are particularly neglected in thinking about the process of great reforms. What difference, if any, does it make if military reform precedes rather than follows rural reform, for example? What is the consequence of reforming the national level well before an effort is aimed at lower levels? In the Chinese case, that the rural reforms were among the earliest initiatives, along with the opening to the outside world, had an obvious and profound effect upon the total reform effort. The success of the rural reforms gave the reformers a firm base of support in the countryside as long as rural incomes continued to rise, but it also unleashed rapid rises in expectations for higher standards of living that the regime has not been able to meet. Perhaps equally important but less noticed were the consequences of one early Chinese reform—increasing the revenue base of provinces and municipalities—upon subsequent efforts to expand enterprise autonomy. Local officials became powerful and effective opponents of this subsequent reform because they feared loss of recently acquired sources of revenue. Again, our purpose is not to detail the Chinese case, but to use it for illustrative purposes. And what the case underscores is that in piecemeal reform, what gets changed early dramatically shapes the range and nature of subsequent choices available to the reformers. Yet, in the absence of a blueprint and usually with inadequate information, reformers make these early decisions without being able to assess the long-run ramifications.

The sequence of reforms is not the only strategic issue confronting reformers, however. Others entail how to manage the reform coalition and what to do with the opposition. These are classic issues confronting any set of leaders. Does one vanquish, isolate, pay off, or win over opponents? Does one fear or welcome ruptures in one's coalition? How does one distribute payoffs among one's coalition members? Here, too, the analyses of the historical cases do not say enough about the consequences of the strategic choices upon reform outcomes. But the case materials do indicate that a major challenge in most reforms—perhaps the foremost task—is for the leader to preserve a coalition that is strong enough to prevent retrogression and to permit further advance.

This challenge stems from the diverse origins of a reform coalition: People dreaming different dreams while sleeping in the same bed. The attempt to preserve a coalition has been one factor in causing the zig-zag pattern of the Chinese reforms. Repeatedly Deng and his top associates have launched initiatives, only to curtail them to placate malcontents in the reform coalition. For President Roosevelt, operating in an open and democratic society, the task was even more evident than in China, but FDR personally relished the commotion. In fact, in Roosevelt's case and quite possibly others (the evidence is frequently unclear on this point) the reform leader may deliberately foster tensions in his coalition in order to ensure that the issues percolate up to him for decision.

Until Deng's succession arrangements went awry in 1987–1989 and he ordered military forces to repress the Beijing demonstrations in June 1989, he had used other techniques for remaining the preeminent leader of his coalition and for controlling his opposition: fostering popular support, maintaining a political machine, cultivating foreign support, creating new institutions to replace those loaded with his opponents, packing key decision-making bodies with loyalists, and so on. These are the staple tactics of strong leaders and do not distinguish reformers from most politicians. What distinguishes successful reformers, however, is their adroitness in using them.

THE END OF REFORM: SUCCESSION, A NEW AGENDA, AND EXPANDED POLITICAL PARTICIPATION

When and how do great reforms end? And what are their outcomes? The most important conclusion from the historical cases is that the outcomes are usually different from the original intent of the reformers. In most instances the unintended consequences of great reform far outweigh the intended ones. The fit between the origins of the reform and its results is imperfect at best. Sixty years after the New Deal, for example, it is remembered not only for alleviating the suffering of the Great Depression but also for bringing big bureaucracy to the United States. The problems that brought on the reforms often persist, but the awareness of their existence diminishes. The perception of crisis passes.

These considerations prompt three ways of demarcating the end of an era of great reform. The most obvious way of defining the end of a great reform is the passing of the galvanizing leader. As we have noted, with some exceptions (the Meiji reforms, Britain in 1832 and the 1860s, and the transformation of the United States from confederation to federation), great reforms have been spearheaded by a single, extraordinary leader. And the record suggests that the momentum for reform rarely survives the leader. This is what makes the issue of succession to the great reform leader so important, for sustenance of the reform program frequently depends upon the acumen of the successor, who typically faces an effort to roll back the reforms. Indeed, the political challenge frequently arises in the waning years of the great reformer, as his opponents campaign for a successor willing to erode the reforms. In this sense, the problems that brought on reform no longer dominate the national debate. As the original reformers pass from the scene, typically the debate centers upon the reform program and the new problems its critics attribute to it.

A related way of identifying the end of a reform era is the loss of control by the reform leaders of their policy agenda. A reform ends when the reformers have to spend more time battling the unintended consequences brought on by their previous reform policies than they do initiating new reforms. (By this criterion Deng's great reform may have begun to run its course in 1986–1987.) Put another way, a great reform ends when the results of reform policies—whether beneficial and opening new opportunities or harmful and generating new problems—begin to dominate the leader's and populace's concerns.

A third way of demarcating the end of a reform period is the transformation of the ruling coalition. The coalition that great reform leaders assemble to design and implement their vision never endures. We have already identified the underlying issues that repeatedly cause fissures among the reformers, and the history of reform is full of instances in which initial proponents of reform end up among its most bitter foes. Meanwhile, new people surge to the top of the reform leadership, either promoted from within or recruited from the outside. Eventually, the reform coalition contains a substantial portion of supporters who were not there at the outset, while the opposition contains many disenchanted former reformers. This transformation usually proceeds gradually, though many reforms pass through a crisis when the coalition rapidly disintegrates, many desert the ship, and the leaders must rebuild a ruling coalition in favor of reform. If they fail to do so, they themselves may be driven from office, as occurred to the 1898 reformers in China and to Khrushchev. Or, they may become largely captives of conservatives, as possibly occurred to Deng Xiaoping in 1986–1989 and precluded a more flexible response by him to the Beijing demonstrations of 1989.

The transformation of the reform coalition is an important passage, for typically the revitalized coalition, if successfully created, brings beneficiaries into the elite. The beneficiaries have vested interests in the new order. The initial coalition had an interest in launching reforms; the transformed coalition has an interest in maintaining its benefits but not necessarily moving beyond the changes already wrought. Putting together a coalition that has the political clout to sustain the reform is therefore crucial in successfully moving from a reform to a postreform era.

Another crucial development for successful reform is the expansion of political participation so that the beneficiaries of the reform can politically defend their newly acquired interests. Broadening the base of recruitment into the bureaucracy and the military, forming new political parties, strengthening parliaments, and widening the electorate become the guarantee of reform. The British Reform Act of 1832 is the classic instance in which political participation was the first step to the economic reforms of the 1840s. And one can argue that the enhanced political role of trade unions and the enfranchisement of blacks were important measures for sustaining the New Deal program. The genius of Cárdenas's reform of the PRI in Mexico was its incorporation of all the pivotal sectors of Mexico in the 1930s: workers, peasants, the military, financiers and businesspeople, and bureaucrats. On the other hand, Peter the Great did not leave a coalition capable of defending his reforms. And the failure of Deng Xiaoping to welcome and include into his coalition the new urban middle class, the professionals, and the entrepreneurs that his economic reforms had generated imperiled all of his accomplishments. By rejecting their demands in 1989 and instead oppressing these sectors, Deng had no recourse but to turn to those conservative and antireform political bureaucracies whose power had waned during the changes of the previous decade: the public security forces, the Communist party propaganda and organization departments, the political department of the People's Liberation Army, and the central planners.

In sum, an era of successful great reform is followed by an era of consolidation and institutionalization of reform programs. The passing of the great reform leader, a change in the agenda of issues to which the leaders devote priority, and a transformation in the ruling coalition mark the transition from reform to postreform era. Inevitably, it seems, the ardor of the reform era is lost, and while the slogans remain, torpor, perhaps corruption, and some retrogression—if not abandonment of much of the reform program—take place. Great reforms leave an enduring mark through the new agenda of problems and opportunities they create, changed patterns of political participation, different patterns of interaction with the outside world, and altered boundaries between the state and the economy and the state and society. To leave a mark, however, great reformers eventually must expand political participation so that the beneficiaries of reform are at the ruling table to defend their gains and possibly to press for even greater change. Herein, one senses, is the supreme challenge confronting all the great reforms now underway in the communist world. Can they identify and institutionalize political access to those in their populace who are prepared to defend the reforms against conservative or even more radical forces? The answer is by no means obvious.

THE CONTEXT OF GREAT REFORMS

This chapter has identified some common aspects of great reforms. However, they also have varied greatly, not only in their origins, processes, and outcomes, but in the contexts in which they have occurred. They have occurred in different types of political systems (monarchical, communist, authoritarian, democratic). They have occurred in states at different levels of economic development (agrarian, developing, industrialized) and with different types of economic systems (traditional, market, command). They have occurred in states that are integrated into the international system of the time (the United States during the New Deal, Germany under Bismarck, Spain after Franco), partially involved (Britain in the 1830s), rather isolated from it (the United States under Andrew Jackson), or militarily, economically, or technologically threatened by it (Meiji Japan or China in 1978). They have occurred in states that are powerful and dominant in the international system (Britain in the 1860s) and weak and somewhat dependent (Turkey in the 1920s). They have occurred in international settings that are supportive (China since 1978), largely indifferent (the New Deal), and hostile (Mexico under Cárdenas).

CONCLUSION: A TYPOLOGY OF GREAT REFORMS

The variation in context and in the reformers' perceptions of the crises confronting them, largely explains the variation in the processes and outcomes of reforms. Drawing upon the literature in comparative politics on crises in political development (especially by Leonard Binder and Gabriel Almond) and on regime transitions (especially by Guillermo O'Donnell) and the analyses of economic development (especially by Karl Polanyi, Alexander Gerschenkron, and Mancur Olson), we offer a preliminary typology of reform that relates the outcomes of reform to its origins and context.[8]

Democratizing Reforms

Perceived legitimacy crises prompt efforts to broaden the base of support of the regime. Monarchical (Britain in 1832) and authoritarian (Spain in the 1970s) systems have all experienced such reforms. While economic difficulties may trigger the loss of popular support, the immediate problem that the reformers perceive is the growing discontent with the regime, and their solution is to undertake political reform, particularly by expanding political participation through creation or invigoration of parliament, expansion of the electorate, and development of either competitive or corporatist political parties (as in Mexico under Cárdenas). Another stimulus for democratizing or liberalizing reforms may be strategic. The reformers seek to alter the configuration of political institutions arrayed against them and to bring new participants into the policy process in order to strengthen their hand and undertake economic reform. This seems to be the Gorbachev approach.

No matter what the stimulus, democratizing reforms confront four major challenges, as the numerous conceptual and empirical studies of the transition to democracy stress. The first is how to discipline the agencies of authoritarian control and prevent them from torpedoing the reform. These include coercive bureaucracies (armed police, secret police, army), ideological bureaucracies (thought control agencies, such as the propaganda departments of Communist parties or religious institutions that enjoy special privileges and reinforce the political order), and the party apparatus in a single-party state. The second challenge of democratizing great reforms, to use Huntington's classic formulation, is to develop institutions rapidly enough to incorporate the increasing numbers of people who seek involvement in politics. The third is to maintain the unity of the country in the transition. Strong integrating institutions, as the monarchy in Spain in the mid 1970s and possibly the Catholic church in Poland in the 1980s, play pivotal roles in democratizing reforms. The fourth challenge is to develop friendly, or at least neutral, foreign relations to maintain an international environment conducive to democratic reform. A hostile external environment may provide the rationale to conservatives to reimpose discipline and control in order to rebuff the foreign challenge.

State-Building Reforms

The crisis involves a weakness of the state that has been revealed either through a sense of external military threat or economic backwardness. The remedy is to increase the power of the state. In traditional, agrarian economies of the preindustrialized era, as Polanyi argues, where the object was to enable commerce to prosper, the strengthening of the state required the development of the regulatory, monetary, and fiscal institutions to permit a market economy to flourish. The British reforms of the 1830s and early 1840s (especially the Corn Laws) and aspects of the American reforms of 1786–1788 and the Jackson era provide the prime examples. But reformers in countries embarking upon rapid industrialization after the initial wave, as Gerschenkron stresses, sought to enhance the power of the state not so much to create and regulate the marketplace as to increase the state's interventionist capacity: to become the agent of development itself. Thus, great reforms in late developing, traditional agrarian economies, primarily in the nineteenth and early twentieth centuries, expand the extractive capability of the state and employ the enhanced power of the state to foster industrialization, often with the purpose of increasing military capability. This remedy was particularly attractive in largely traditional economies, where markets for the factors of production (capital, labor, material goods, knowledge) had not yet been fully developed. The reformers wished their state, through its expanded capacity to command and coordinate, to accelerate economic development, instead of allowing the market to dictate the process. The reforms of Peter the Great, Alexander II, and to a limited extent Bismarck fit into this category.

Capitalist Crisis Reforms

Economic crisis in a market economy prompts efforts to expand the interventionist role of the state. The crisis involves the dislocations caused by industrialization and urbanization, such as unemployment, harsh working conditions, inadequate educational institutions, and exploitation of consumers. The response is greatly to increase the role of the state, to expand government bureaucracy, and to give the beneficiaries of these changes a greater voice in government. The British reforms of the late 1800s through the 1940s, the progressive movement in the United States, the New Deal, and many of Bismarck's measures are the instances of this type of great reform. The particular solutions in these cases were also congruent with the international economy of the time, with its strong protectionist proclivities that necessitated leaders to look within their states and colonial empire for the resources to deal with their problems.

Bureaucratic Economy Reforms

The 1970s and 1980s have witnessed great and lesser reforms in states with large state bureaucracies that regulate and manage the economy. These bureaucratically dominated economies arose in the course of revolution, the decolonialization process, hot and cold wars, or earlier reforms in response to a capitalist crisis. Drawing upon Mancur Olson's argument, the previous changes left countries with large state bureaucracies and overregulated marketplaces that eventually sapped their economic dynamism and innovative capacities. The common themes in such reforms are deregulation, privatization, divestiture of state enterprises, weakening of trade unions, and revitalization of the marketplace. The perceived solution to economic stagnation in large bureaucratic states is through the greater economic efficiency that competition in the marketplace yields. As with democratizing, state-building, and capitalist crisis reforms, the reforms of bureaucratically dominated economies are congruent with the international political economy of the era. That is to say, the loosening up of internal markets is perceived as an appropriate response of the 1980s to the emergence of an integrated and vibrant international economic system, the increase in world trade, and the availability and attractiveness of foreign capital and technology. And the international agencies that give a measure of coherence to this international economy—the International Monetary Fund, the World Bank, and the General Agreement on Tariffs and Trade—provide incentives to implement the market-oriented reforms that these agencies claim promote efficiency and growth.[9]

Multifaceted Reform

Several great reforms do not fit neatly into this typology, especially the Meiji reform, Turkey under Ataturk, and Mexico under Cárdenas. They involved responses both to economic and political crises, and their leaders had to reconcile and integrate the many dimensions of their reforms. As the previous section on the outcome of reform stressed, the Meiji, Ataturk, and Cárdenas reforms succeeded because their leaders passed the torch to successors who were committed to sustaining the reforms, they were able to manage the transformation from their initial coalition of support to a coalition including the beneficiaries of the reform, and they forged enduring participatory institutions. Gorbachev's and Deng's reforms are similar to the Meiji, Turkish, and Mexican cases in that the Soviet Union and China also face multifaceted crises that demand both economic and political reform. In contrast to the earlier cases, however, the demands for democratizing reform are more pressing, and the opportunity and need to integrate the economy into the international economy through market reform are greater. Further, the sheer size of China's population and the national diversity of the Soviet Union create problems for their governance that were not present in Japan, Turkey, or Mexico. Maintaining the unity of the Soviet Union and China in the midst of simultaneous economic and political reform is likely to be an even greater challenge than was the case in Meiji Japan, Kemalist Turkey, or Mexico.

Our cursory review of great reforms as a form of political change underscores the complexity of the tasks and the uncertainty of the outcomes in the transformations now underway in the Soviet Union and China.

POSTSCRIPT

This essay was written before the dramatic developments in Eastern Europe during 1989–1990. Events have unfolded too rapidly and too recently for full reflection on their nature and implications, and the outcome of these political, economic, and social changes are not yet known. Nevertheless, we would be remiss not to consider whether the changes in Eastern Europe can be incorporated into our framework.[10]

Some aspects are similar to other historical cases and therefore support our reasoning. For instance, these have been largely peaceful changes. With the notable exception of Romania, these unprecedented, and until recently unthinkable, developments have unfolded with remarkable restraint by both the besieged leaders and aroused masses. Some developments have also had unintended consequences. The leaders of East Germany's New Forum neither anticipated nor desired that their movement would lead to the disintegration of their nation and its absorption into a unified Germany. The irony of this is that the leaders of New Forum created the conditions for a new political system but had no influence on its final determination. They disappeared from the political stage almost as soon as the East German leaders they brought down.

The tendency of reformers to borrow from foreign countries has been referred to previously. The response of Eastern Europe's leaders to the mass movements in their countries exhibited a new level of learning from foreign experience. Whereas Chinese reforms borrowed successful elements of earlier East European reforms (particularly in Hungary), East European leaders learned from the failure of China's leaders to acquiesce to popular demands for change. When Egon Krenz, who was briefly First Party Secretary in East Germany, announced there would be "no Chinese solution" in his country, there was little choice but to concede to demands for political and economic liberalization.

These developments also have a cultural component consistent with our analysis. One of the immediate results has been the recapturing of a Central European identity and the reassertion of the nationality issue in international and, especially for Czechoslovakia, intranational relations. The proposed political and economic systems mark a return to the paths surrendered in the immediate aftermath of World War II.

Other aspects of change in Eastern Europe may necessitate revision of our framework. Previous great reforms were led by a single leader or group of leaders who perceived a crisis. Although they occasionally mobilized public support on behalf of their reform efforts, they did not respond directly to popular demands for change. In contrast, the recent events in Eastern Europe were peaceful movements initiated from below, which does not fit our perception of reform. They indicate that under specific circumstances public pressure may compel leaders, who are otherwise satisfied with the status quo and their positions within it, to consider changes to the existing political and economic order. Modern communication and transportation systems may facilitate the self-mobilization of concerned publics outside the control of the state. However, the political polarization that existed in these countries prior to the upheavals has more in common with revolution than reform.

Another new factor crucial to the changes in Eastern Europe, but not common to great reforms, was the decisive role of a foreign power. The whole sequence of events began with the abandonment of the Brezhnev Doctrine, which had deterred attempted challenges to the established order in these nations. After it became known that the Soviet Union would not intervene in their domestic affairs, the resulting process was similar to decolonialization: Once the previous elite, which was identified with the colonial power, proved vulnerable, new elites emerged and sought legitimacy in a popular mandate.

These developments in Eastern Europe do not fit neatly into the categories of either revolution or reform. They have elements in common with both, but also new elements unique to their own experience. They are likely to prove *sui generis*, unique, and unlikely to be repeated.

NOTES

*The authors did the research and bulk of the writing for this essay in 1988, when the Soviet Union and China were the pacesetters in economic and political reform in the communist world. The authors made marginal adjustments to the article in mid 1989, before the sweeping changes in Eastern Europe. We have added a postscript to the article that relates those developments to our analysis of great reforms. Our postscript notes that the various transformations in Eastern Europe share some but not all of the qualities we attribute to great reforms. They also partake of some aspects of great revolutions and of decolonialization experiences in earlier eras.

1. See Barrington Moore, Jr., *Social Origins of Dictatorship and Democracy: Lord and Peasant in the Making of the Modern World* (Boston: Beacon Press, 1966); Samuel P. Huntington, *Political Order in Changing Societies* (New Haven, Conn.: Yale University Press, 1968), esp. chap. 5; Theda Skocpol, *States and Social Revolutions: A Comparative Analysis of France, Russia, and China* (Cambridge: Cambridge University Press, 1979); Chalmers Johnson, *Revolutionary Change*, 2d ed. (Stanford, Calif.: Stanford University Press, 1982); Crane Brinton, *The Anatomy of Revolution*, rev. ed. (New York: Vintage Books, 1965).

2. See especially Gabriel Almond, Scott Flanagan, and Robert Mundt, eds., *Crisis, Choice, and Change: Historical Studies of Political Development* (Boston: Little Brown, 1973), esp. chaps. 1, 2; Huntington, *Political Order*, chap. 6; and Albert Hirschman, *Journeys*

Toward Progress (Garden City, N.Y.: Doubleday, 1965), esp. chap. 5.

3. The authors specifically read the following articles and monographs for this paper. A longer list could easily be generated to sustain a more learned and sophisticated discussion of great reform than this exploratory article provides. For Peter the Great: Vasily Klyuchevsky, *Peter the Great* (Boston: Beacon Press, 1984). For the 1830s British reforms: G. Bingham Powell, "Incremental Democratization, the British Reform Act of 1832," in Almond, Flanagan, and Mundt, *Crisis, Choice, and Change*, Chapter 3; Karl Polanyi, *The Great Transformation: The Political and Economic Origins of Our Time* (Boston: Beacon Press, 1957); E. L. Woodward, *The Age of Reform (1815–1870)* (Oxford: Oxford University Press, 1962); Asa Briggs, *The Age of Improvement (1783–1867)* (London: Longmans, 1979). For the New Deal: William Leuchtenberg, *Franklin Roosevelt and the New Deal* (New York: Harper & Row, 1963); Arthur Schlesinger, *The Age of Roosevelt* (Boston: Houghton Mifflin, 1957); James MacGregor Burns, *Roosevelt: The Lion and the Fox* (New York: Harcourt Brace, 1956). For Bismarck: Hajo Holborn, *A History of Modern Germany, 1840–1945* (Princeton, N.J.: Princeton University Press, 1969), chaps. 6 and 7. For Cárdenas: Wayne Cornelius, "Nation Building, Participation, and Distribution: The Politics of Social Reform under Cárdenas," in Almond, Flanagan, and Mundt, *Crisis, Choice, and Change*, chap. 7; Frank Brandenburg, *The Making of Modern Mexico* (Englewood Cliffs, N.J.: Prentice-Hall, 1964). For Meiji Japan: James White, "State Building and Modernization: The Meiji Restoration," in Almond, Flanagan, and Mundt, *Crisis, Choice, and Change*, chap. 8; William Lockwood, *The State and Economic Enterprise in Japan* (Princeton, N.J.: Princeton University Press, 1965); Thomas Smith, *Political Change and Industrial Development in Japan: Government Enterprise, 1868–1880* (Stanford, Calif.: Stanford University Press, 1965). For Turkey: Lord Kinross, *Atatürk* (New York: Morrow, 1965); Bernard Lewis, *The Emergence of Modern Turkey* (London: Oxford University Press, 1961); Dankwart Rustow, "Atatürk as Founder of a State," *Daedalus*, 97, no. 3 (Summer 1968): 793–828. For Spain: Donald Share, *The Making of Spanish Democracy* (New York: Praeger, 1986); Richard Gunther et al., *Spain after Franco: The Making of a Competitive Party System* (Berkeley: University of California Press, 19886). For the Soviet Union: Timothy Colton, *The Dilemma of Reform in the Soviet Union* (New York: Council on Foreign Relations, 1986); Ed A. Hewett, *Reforming the Soviet Economy* (Washington, D.C.: Brook-

ings Institution, 1988). For China: Harry Harding, *China's Second Revolution* (Washington, D.C.: Brookings Institution, 1987).

4. Richard Hofstader, *The Age of Reform* (New York: Vintage Press, 1955).

5. Harding, *China's Second Revolution*.

6. See Nina Halpern, "Making Economic Policy: The Influence of Economists," in the Joint Economic Committee of the Congress of the United States, *China's Economy Looks Toward the Year 2000*, vol. I (Washington, D.C.: Government Printing Office, 1986), 123–146; Cyril Lin, "The Reinstatement of Economics in China Today," *China Quarterly*, no. 85 (March 1981): 1–48.

7. Hofstader, *The Age of Reform*.

8. Leonard Binder, "Crises of Political Development," in Leonard Binder, James S. Coleman, Joseph L. Palombara, Lucian W. Pye, Sydney Verba, and Myron Werner, *Crises and Sequences in Political Development* (Princeton, N.J.: Princeton University Press, 1971); Almond, Flanagan, and Mundt, *Crisis, Choice, and Change,*, chaps. 1 and 2; Guillermo O'Donnell, Phillippe C. Schmitter, and Lawrence Whitehead, eds., *Transitions from Authoritarian Rule*, 4 vols. (Baltimore: Johns Hopkins University Press, 1986); Polanyi, *The Great Transformation*; Mancur Olson, *The Rise an Decline of Nations: Economic Growth, Stagflation, and Social Rigidities* (New Haven, Conn.: Yale University Press, 1982); Alexander Gerschenkron, *Economic Backwardness in Historical Perspective* (Cambridge, Mass.: Harvard University Press, 1962).

9. See Harold K. Jacobson and Michel Oksenberg, *China's Entry in the IMF, World Bank, and GATT: Toward an International Economic Order* (Ann Arbor: University of Michigan Press, 1990).

10. For a fuller discussion, see Timothy Garton Ash, "Eastern Europe: The Year of Truth," *New York Review of Books*, (February 15, 1990): 17–22.

Chapter
12

The Modernization of Socialism

Glasnost Versus *Perestroika?*

Klaus von Beyme

The modernization of socialism has been a continual process since Stalin's death and was not even completely interrupted in the period of agony of the Brezhnev era. An impetus for reform in many policy areas had developed even before *perestroika* was launched in 1985. *Perestroika* as a notion is not Gorbachev's invention. It was present in many debates before 1985 and was occasionally used as background for reform laws, such as the reform law on education in 1985.[1] In other socialist countries, notably in Hungary and Poland, the need for modernizing socialism had been debated and early initiatives, for reforms had been taken. These reform movements, though officially rejected in the Soviet Union, nonetheless had some impact on the thinking of Soviet elites.

In spite of this continuity of reform initiatives, nobody would say that *perestroika* is "nothing new under the sun." *Perestroika* deserves the term "great reform" much more than Khrushchev's reforms of 1956 to 1964. Gorbachev himself, to be sure, does not accept the term "great reform," preferring instead the term "revolution" and justifying that preference with quotations from Lenin. The great bourgeois revolution of 1789 needed to be completed by three more revolutions (1830, 1848, and 1871). Why not apply this insight to socialism?[2]

The effort to legitimize *perestroika* by quotations from Lenin shows that modernizing socialist systems are much more sensitive than modernizing autocracies about invoking their original (in this case revolutionary) legitimation. This is one of the reasons comparisons of *perestroika* with great reforms in monarchies, from Peter the Great to the Meiji movement in Japan, are not very telling. As long as autocratic reformers did not challenge monarchic legitimacy itself, autocratic reformers could challenge everything their predecessors had done: *Car tel est notre plaisir* was an accepted principle even among the more traditional monarchs.

Gorbachev emphasized the catchword revolution not only for reasons of historical legitimation. He also connected more systematic considerations with this choice of term. Reform in his perception was a slow process, whereas *perestroika* to him meant not only "transformation," but also the destruction of parts of some of the institutions and attitudes that had dominated the social system. Gorbachev remained silent about a third, more tactical reason for his preference for the term "revolution." For twenty years Soviet propaganda had been polemically attacking the concepts of "radical reform" and "active transformation" in Western Socialist and Social Democratic parties. How could Gorbachev overnight accept wholesale the very same notion? His choice of terminology thus is understandable. Even some Western scholars think that radical reform suffers from the stigma of being a kind of "second choice strategy."[3] Nevertheless, most Western experts continue to list *perestroika* correctly under the rubric of "radical reform."[4]

There is a second difference between *perestroika* and monarchical reform movements of the past. *Perestroika* is not the work of a great leader, as some analysts suggest.[5] The reform undercurrent in the party and large parts of the intelligentsia came first—and then found a leader. Gorbachev's personality, however, quickly became almost a kind of "independent variable." He pushed reform to extremes abhorred by many of his former supporters (especially those who, like Gromyko and Ligachev, accepted only the need for *perestroika* but remained hostile toward the idea of extensive *glasnost*). To characterize *perestroika* as a predominantly *political* reform, in contrast to Deng's *economic* reform in China, is hardly correct if we accept the intentions of the Soviet reformers. *Perestroika*, or restructuring, originally was the aim, and *glasnost*, or openness, was only an instrument to support this strategy. The process of *glasnost*, however, has continually enhanced its proponents' room for maneuver. Advocates of *glasnost* pushed for political reforms first, and the Soviet leadership accepted this pressure from below because economic and social reforms are less easy to implement. *Perestroika* as a concept remains oriented toward far-reaching economic and social change, even if the actual movement should eventually peter out into petty details of political reform.

Great reforms occupy a middle position between revolutionary grand designs and the piecemeal engineering of normal reforms. Great reforms in a complex society cannot be judged by the achievements of the *grand législateurs* of the past, from Moses to Solon. Oksenberg and Dickson criticize the eclecticism and even the "messiness of reform movements."[6] We should not, however, be overly demanding with regard to the coherence of the reform doctrine. Radical reformers in our own day cannot develop the holistic zeal of radicalism and impose a comprehensive view of a new society on the existing one at the very beginning of the transformation, while at the same time fighting all opposition to their goals from outside and from within the party.

Perestroika shows that in two respects this lack of coherence in the transformational device can have consequences that are not necessarily detrimental to the goal of reform. First, in contrast to the totalitarian phase of socialism under Stalin, a kind of piecemeal, pragmatic set of policies was developed only in the 1980s. In former times every goal had been attacked in great leaps through mass campaigns. (The Russians integrated the German word *Sturm*, "storm," into their language and created the term *shturmovshchina* for these mass campaigns.) Education and literacy in the early phase, health policy under Stalin, housing after World War II, and social welfare under Khrushchev were the aims of *shturmovshchinas*. But there was no really coherent perspective on major policy areas and no attention to the necessary choices of priorities. Only when social scientists discovered policy analysis in the 1980s was this perspective developed.

Indeed, despite the importance of economic debates before the 1980s, there was no explicitly economic policy; and, except for a general statement that everything was "political," the party had developed no detailed political strategies. In theory, socialism suffers from oversteering: The political is omnipresent in public propaganda. In practice, interventions by the state and by the party remained half-hearted and piecemeal. Political institutions were hardly seen in their own right and there was little differentiation with regard to the perception of policies. And even though everything was said to be determined by economic factors, there was no economic policy in the professional sense of that term.

Second, economic policy was fragmented because it was the responsibility of separate administrations, each in charge of its own branch of industry. Seventy-four out of ninety ministries and main administrations (*glavnye upravleniya*) were concerned with economic activities, and the priorities set by these administrations were subject to intensive lobbying and were not necessarily the outcome of coherent guidelines set by the party as a whole. Not until 1981 was "economic policy" in the technical sense of the term introduced as a kind of link between the long-term and short-term vistas of the goals of socialism. But the predominance of strategic thinking remained obvious: the terms economic strategies and economic policies were used almost as synonyms.

In contrast to the German Democratic Republic, the Soviet Union did not accept social policy as a coherent field of state activity until the 1980s. Books with titles referring to social policy published earlier were translations from Polish and German. Moreover, policy areas in their own right were more easily accepted in fields where the party did not claim control of all processes, like demographic, migration, and environmental policy. It is quite telling that these are the three areas where the loose talk about a nonpolitical notion of "revolution" first started in the Soviet debate. In the wake of the "demographic revolution," for instance, it had to be explained why the party was not able to guide every social development.

Only in the early 1980s did mainstream social scientists in the Soviet Union discover that effective steering requires a certain distance from the state and the party, on the one hand, and from the economy and society, on the other. Deregulation has gained importance in debates, especially in the field of social policy. Special institutions had to be developed, not just another "central administration." As Huntington already put it for modernizing societies in the 1960s, "in the total absence of social conflict, political institutions are unnecessary; in the total absence of social harmony, they are impossible."[7] The situation of the Soviet Union is somewhere between these extremes.

Within the Soviet social science intelligentsia, three trends were at work in creating a more complex view of society long before *perestroika* was officially announced. First, there was the discovery of policy analysis. Paradoxically, the ideological politicization of all spheres of life in Marxism-Leninism prevented a realistic exchange about politics. As a result, social scientists have only rarely developed concepts for the implementation of policy programs agreed upon by the party; still less is there an evaluation of outcomes. A plan regularly became a self-fulfilling prophecy; Russian authors called this the "Oedipus effect." Planners were inclined to believe that a plan was good because it was fulfilled, and they were hardly ever ready to consider whether the alternatives discussed before the plan's adoption would not have been better.[8] Recently, the weaknesses of such ex post facto evaluation have been discussed by Soviet scholars.[9]

Second, in response to the Western quality-of-life debate, the concept of the socialist way of life has evolved so that statistical indicators of goods and services must be supplemented by studies of satisfaction via subjective indicators based on surveys. In the recent literature Soviet scholars have emphasized that the socialist way of life is not an ideal but rather an empirical phenomenon. Idealization of this way of life is even considered detrimental because it all too easily arouses rising expectations.[10] Whereas policy analysts have discovered more and more structural deficiencies in the Soviet system, the official debate about improving the socialist way of life still largely concentrates on denouncing a lack of motivation that can be overcome by further mobilization.

A third intellectual trend that prepared for *perestroika* was the rediscovery of regional policies and of decentralization. In addition to functional differentiation and deregulation, territorial decentralization may be a necessary precondition for *perestroika*. After the failure of Khrushchev's *Sovnarkhozy* in 1965, the concentration of power in branch ministries increased. *Perestroika* has brought about serious attempts at regional and functional diversification—measures to which the older literature had paid only lip service.[11]

These three intellectual innovations since the late 1970s at first glance seem to have made the reform doctrine less consistent and "messier."[12] On the other hand, only such a diversification of theoretical tools could prepare for the development of a strategy complex enough to steer social processes efficiently. *Perestroika*, despite many inconsistencies, corrects its errors and failures much faster than former campaigns could. It aims to bring about comprehensive change and to eliminate contradictions and unintended consequences of the first steps toward reform. A glance at the contradictions in the prereform phase of modernization as reflected by the statistical data for central policy fields may highlight this observation for the whole group of socialist countries.[13]

Oksenberg and Dickson say that great reforms end when their unintended consequences get more of the attention of political leaders than their original aims. My counterhypothesis is that these by-products of reform, mainly in the field of *glasnost*, do not have only negative consequences. There is, however, a latent danger that the tail is wagging the dog, that is, that *glasnost* is working against *perestroika*. Both ideas will be developed in the next two sections.

DEFICIENCIES IN MODERNIZATION IN THE PERIOD BEFORE PERESTROIKA

Party and state in socialist countries have had to renounce their claims of steering all social processes. The failure to reach the planned goals was particularly striking in demographic policy. If we measure modernization and performance in terms of figures per capita, most socialist countries had a certain advantage over nonsocialist developing countries because birth rates increased more slowly, with the exception of Mongolia for a certain period. The medium-size growth of the Soviet Union's population is due to her developing areas in Transcaucasia and Central Asia. Even in Cuba the increase in population was cut down to half of its former size in a comparatively short time (see Table 12.1). In Poland the decline in population growth was least—a variance due to religion. Rumania was successful in stopping the decrease in the country's birthrate after 1966 by outlawing abortion. Hungary also experimented with abortion control, but not very successfully, since the application of contraceptives countervailed all efforts to increase birthrates. Positive methods for increasing birthrates have largely replaced the former repressive methods which are considered highly ineffective by Soviet demographers in light of the Rumanian experience.[14]

The interdependence of policies is recognized: Success in population policy depends entirely on success in other areas, such as housing policy. Material incentives such as child allowances have not proved to be effective; Soviet workers know that the additional income is not matched by any corresponding offer of goods. This applies also to allowances for young couples; high rates of marriage are counteracted by high rates of divorce. The Soviet Union in this respect is at the top of the rankings, a fact which Gorbachev denounced during his speech at the Twenty-seventh Party Congress in 1986. Moreover, some policies in socialist countries proved to be in conflict with one another. Goals in population policy conflicted with the goal of keeping as many women as possible in the workplace, at least in the German Democratic Republic (GDR) and the Soviet Union. The GDR found a better way around this dilemma than did other socialist states by promoting the establishment of preschool institutions. The fact that the GDR was on top of the list in this respect is due in part, however, to the fact that it maintained the highest rate of urbanization. Some results are the outcome of deliberate decisions of the socialist state; others are largely determined by other developmental factors such as per capita income and urbanization (see Tables 12.1 and 12.8).

The egalitarian impetus of socialist policies in the initial, redistributive phase did not take account of the indirect impact of other social policies. Social differences explained the variance of fertility much better than the allegedly important "socialist way of life." The number of children does not vary solely with the level of development in an area, but underdevelopment tends to reinforce certain disproportions. In Estonia, the most highly developed republic of the Soviet Union, those with the highest level of education had an average of 1.5 children per family, those with the lowest 1.64. In the least developed area of the Union, Tadzhikistan, the social differences were much more acute; the rates were 1.9 and 3.4, respectively.[15]

As in Western countries, there is a discussion on new combinations of policy areas. Recently, "demographication of social policy" has been

Table 12.1 DATA ON DEMOGRAPHY: BIRTHS, DEATH, AND POPULATION GROWTH

Country	Births per 10,000		Deaths per 10,000		Population growth per 10,000		Marriages per 10,000				Divorces per 10,000				Urbanization (% of urban population)			
	1940	1985	1940	1985	1940	1985	1970	1975	1980	1985	1970	1975	1980	1985	1970	1975	1980	1985
Bulgaria	22.2	13.2	13.4	12.0	8.8	1.2	8.6	8.6	7.9	7.4	1.2	1.3	1.5	1.6	53.0	58.0	62.5	64.9
Cuba	31.0	16.6	10.6	6.0	20.4	10.6	13.5	7.0	7.1	7.9	2.9	2.5	2.5	2.9	60.5	63.0	68.4	71.3
Czechoslovakia	20.6	14.9	14.0	11.8	6.6	2.7	8.8	9.5	7.7	7.7	1.7	2.2	2.2	2.5	62.3	65.7	72.6	74.3
German Democratic Republic	18.0	13.7	11.9	13.3	6.1	0.4	7.7	8.4	8.0	7.9	1.6	2.5	2.7	3.1	73.8	75.4	76.3	76.6
Hungary	20.0	12.2	14.3	13.8	6.1	0.4	9.3	9.9	7.5	6.9	2.2	2.5	2.6	2.7	49.9	51.7	55.1	56.8
Mongolia	26.1	37.0	21.8	11.1	4.3	25.9	3.1	6.6	5.6	6.6	0.1	0.1	0.3	0.4	45.7	47.5	51.1	51.8
Poland	24.6	18.2	13.9	10.2	10.7	8.0	8.5	9.7	8.6	7.2	1.1	1.2	1.2	1.3	52.3	55.7	58.7	60.2
Rumania	26.0	15.5	18.9	10.3	7.1	5.2	7.2	8.9	8.2	7.1	0.4	1.6	1.5	1.4	36.9	39.2	45.8	50.0
Soviet Union	31.2	19.4	18.0	10.6	13.2	8.8	9.7	10.7	10.3	9.8	2.6	3.1	3.5	3.4	56.9	60.7	63.4	65.6

Source: Narodnoe Khozyaystvo SSSR v 1986 g (Moscow: 1987), 626; Statisticheskiy Ezhegodnik stran-chlenov SEV Finansy i statistika (1986), 12.

widely discussed in the Soviet Union.[16] The mere notion indicates shifts in political priorities. Rather than stressing egalitarian goals for classes and groups of society, the emphasis of social concerns has shifted toward increasing the collective good via growth of the economy and the population. Even the demographic aspects of a society that grows older every year have recently been discussed, because of the alarming increase in the number of pensioners, along with the rising proportion of pensioners who can no longer be mobilized to continue in the workplace. Two-thirds of Soviet citizens entitled to a pension are said to be able to continue to work, but only one-third do so. The other third, according to surveys, speaks quite frankly about the reasons for not working any more.[17]

New structures of social incentives are discussed in order to balance the social policy concerns on the one hand and the needs of the labor market on the other. Some of the social problems of modernizing society have been created by the socialist bias in favor of urbanization. Marx, after all, suggested that one of the merits of the modern bourgeoisie was to "detach an important part of the population from the idiocy of rural life."[19]

Even the least developed COMECON country, Rumania, achieved a 50 percent urbanization rate, but was still overtaken by newcomers like Mongolia. After World War II, Poland integrated from Germany areas which were more urbanized on average than the previous Polish territory.[19] This original advantage might help to explain the slight advantage Poland still had over Hungary with respect to urbanization, which was not reflected in the overall ratio of Polish economic development compared to Hungary. Historical advantages also explain part of the variance in other cases. Czechoslovakia had reached almost the level of urbanization of the GDR, though her economic performance was much less favorable. The Soviet Union, with an urbanization rate of roughly two-thirds, is at the center of her bloc. But these results are nevertheless considerable because of large areas that were highly underdeveloped and thus started with low urban populations. Also, it is important to examine the quality of this urbanization. Without a socialist system Tashkent or Alma Ata today might well look like huge metropolises surrounded by miserable shanty towns, as is the case for São Paulo and Bombay. In the Soviet Union a sometimes brutal policy of controlled access to cities has made it possible to avoid such a result. Indeed, the Twenty-fifth and Twenty-sixth Party congresses had endorsed older resolutions for a freeze on the growth of the biggest cities.[20]

More recently, the rural population of the predominantly Islamic republics in the Soviet Union has been urged to move to towns rather than being prevented from doing so. Traditional psychological barriers—the reluctance to accept Western forms of huge agglomerations and work in big factories—have nevertheless dissuaded most underemployed people in the predominantly Islamic republics from migrating to the cities. When unemployed people migrated, they increasingly did not migrate in the direction favored by the planners. Brezhnev admitted at the Twenty-sixth Party Congress: "Until now people have preferred to move from the north to the south and from the east to the west, though a rational distribution of the productive forces requires migration in the opposite directions."[21]

Paradoxically, success in regional development policy so far has counteracted efforts to stimulate the economy. "Welfare imperialism" has made the regional differences in income so slight that the Islamic population in the south has little incentive to move into the north or east. A Turk from Anatolia can increase his income by a factor of ten if he migrates to West Germany's industrial Ruhr region. The incentive is far lower for a Soviet citizen speaking a Turkic language to move to the Far East, where he would earn 30 to 50 percent more, but also pay much higher prices for housing and clothing. Migration is encouraged but increasingly with less fervor because of its undesired collateral consequences such as lower fertility and higher rates of absenteeism due to illness and alienation in the new surroundings.[22]

Economic policy is at the center of modernization policy in any socialist society. In order to conceal the tendencies of declining economic growth, only index figures of growth are usually released. Table 12.2 shows that the Soviet Union's per capita growth rates of the national product lag behind leaders such as the GDR.[23]

Socialist planners showed decreasing satisfaction with growth figures of industrial output, shown in Table 12.2. They were expecting future growth from increasing labor productivity, yet growth remained below the level that the planners had expected. Socialist rhetoric for a long time asserted that socialism has a natural advantage over capitalism in increasing labor productivity because of advances in education, the absence of unemployment, and a higher consciousness due to the development of a socialist way of life. These ideological hopes were not fulfilled.[24] In recent years some specialists began to discuss whether or not too much security in the workplace is detrimental to the development of the economy. The indisputable success in educational policy, moreover, has not always enhanced labor productivity because the overqualification of many white collar workers causes increasing dissatisfaction with poorly paid, low-level jobs. Gorbachev, at the Twenty-seventh Party Congress, used the engineers to demonstrate certain negative developments in the vocational training structure.

The "scientific technical revolution," which allegedly mobilizes all skills, failed to have a positive impact on labor productivity. Gorbachev

Table 12.2 DATA ON SOCIALIST COUNTRIES ECONOMIC POLICY, 1970–1986

Country	Growth of National Income per Capita (1960=1)				Growth of Labor Productivity in manufacturing (1960=1)			Growth of capital investment (in %)		Material production		Nonproductive sphere		Production of (% of gross industrial products) — (A) Means of production, (B) Consumers goods								Cars per 10,000		
	1970	1980	1985	1986	1970	1980	1986	1976-1980	1981-1985	1976-1980	1981-1985	1976-1980	1981-1985	1970 A	1970 B	1975 A	1975 B	1980 A	1980 B	1985 A	1985 B	1970	1980	1985
Bulgaria	1.9	3.7	4.3	4.6	1.9	3.5	4.3	6.1	4.6	4.8	5.2	9.6	3.1	54.7	45.3	58.6	41.4	62.0	38.0	63.0	37.0	—	—	—
Cuba	—	—	—	—	—	—	—	3.7	9.6	4.4	9.9	1.3	8.4	—	—	—	n.a.	—	—	—	—	—	0.6	0.7
Czechoslovakia	1.5	2.1	2.3	2.4	1.5	2.5	2.9	2.8	−1.0	3.4	−0.6	1.2	−2.8	66.1	33.9	66.9	33.1	68.2	31.8	68.9	31.1	117	150	150
German Democratic Republic	1.5	2.5	3.1	3.3	1.8	2.9	3.6	3.4	−0.8	3.3	−1.1	4.1	0.1	64.3	35.7	65.5	34.5	66.4	33.6	66.6	33.4	88.4	128	154
Hungary	1.6	2.5	2.7	2.7	1.6	2.6	3.1	2.4	−3.1	2.4	−4.3	2.2	−0.8	65.1	34.9	64.7	35.3	64.5	35.5	62.6	37.4	3.1	0.1	0.1
Mongolia	—	—	—	—	1.7	2.7	3.5	10.5	8.3	12.4	7.7	7.1	9.5	52.6	47.4	49.5	50.5	58.3	41.7	55.5	44.5	—	—	—
Poland	1.6	2.3	2.4	2.4	1.6	2.8	3.2	−3.0	−2.5	−4.9	−3.5	2.8	−0.7	63.6	36.4	63.9	36.1	63.7	36.3	62.6	37.4	32.3	114	89.2
Rumania	2.0	4.5	5.4	5.8	2.1	3.9	4.9	8.5	−0.1	9.3	0.7	4.6	−4.6	70.4	29.6	72.2	27.8	74.3	25.7	74.6*	25.4*	28.9	54.0	n.a.
Soviet Union	1.8	2.6	3.0	3.1	1.7	2.6	3.2	3.3	3.5	3.5	3.1	2.5	4.6	73.4	26.6	73.7	26.3	73.8	26.2	74.8	25.2	—	n.a.	—

*Figure for 1984.

Source: *Nar. khoz.* (1985), 582, 657; *Nar. khoz. Za 70 let* (1987), 654; *Ezheg.* (1986), 64, 113, 140.

criticized some of the drawbacks of a narrow relationship between scientific activity and the state: "Many institutes remain the prolonged arm of the bureaucracy, and not infrequently they serve as advocates of interests of governmental departments. They are deeply involved in *schematicism* and paper production." But still there is no recognition of the necessity for more independence of science from the state agencies, though Gorbachev has clearly recognized that the social sciences, especially, have lost all critical capacity and have concentrated for a long time instead on "papers along the lines of toasts to good health."[25]

Next to the increased scientific input for improving factor productivity in the economy, capital investment is more openly discussed than in former times. Gorbachev showed no reluctance to accept the Western terms "investment policy" and "structural policy." The figures for the most recent planning periods show that capital investment in some countries did not grow but rather declined, most drastically in Rumania, which started limiting the nonproductive sector of the economy (see Table 12.2). Even Czechoslovakia showed a negative performance, and the GDR remained above a zero performance level by only a slight margin. The Soviet Union, because of its enormous lag in that field, has almost doubled its efforts in the nonproductive sphere. These index figures must, however, be compared with the data on the output shares for means of production and consumer commodities (A and B, respectively, in Table 12.2). In this sphere the Soviet Union showed an enormous lag compared to most of the socialist countries, except for Rumania. Still, in 1985 sector B remained at the level of one-quarter, compared to more than one-third in the GDR, Poland, and Hungary.

Data on income policy are given in units of national currency and are therefore difficult to compare; but even these figures may be utilized when, in Table 12.3, we compare relative wages in various branches of the economy. Only Rumania clearly favors the construction industry and Bulgaria the transport workers in the same way as the Soviet Union does. Commerce tends to be better off in the more highly developed countries such as East Germany and Hungary. Science, one of the fields considered most important during the Stalin era, no longer shows a uniform picture. In Poland, Hungary, and the Soviet Union, no special privileges exist in general (which does not mean that leading academy professors are not privileged!). For the GDR, even Soviet statisticians did not get the figures. Education, culture, and social security, including the health services, are everywhere at the bottom of the income hierarchy. It is not by chance that Gorbachev mentioned these fields; some of his announcements concerning the health sector in 1987 have been implemented.[26]

Success in the policy of distribution is not easy to measure by COMECON figures (see Table 12.4). The figures reported on savings

Table 12.3 DATA ON INCOME POLICY: WAGES IN SELECTED SECTORS IN RELATION TO AVERAGE IN INDUSTRY (=100), 1985

	Soviet Union	Bulgaria	Hungary	German Democratice Republic	Poland	Rumania	Czechoslovakia
Industry	100	100	100	100	100	100	100
Construction	112	110	105	101	98	116	106
Agriculture	86	88	97	94	89	97	97
Transport	105	107	101	108	86	104	108
Commerce	71	81	86	89	73	86	78
Municipal services	70	84	91	—	82	94	71
Science	96	112	97	—	96	108	108
Education, culture	69	87	93	—	74	99	83
Social security, health	63	87	91	—	70	95	87

Source: L. A. Gordon, "Sotsial'naya politika v sfere oplaty truda," *Sotsiologicheskie Issledeovaniya*, no. 4 (1987): 14.

are not enlightening. It is obvious that they were lowest in those socialist countries where commodities of good quality were most easily available, as in the GDR and Czechoslovakia. They were highest in Poland, but this was the result of an inflation-ridden currency rather than of efforts to save on the part of the population. More detailed are the figures on various products sold per capita. Again, however, the results hardly go beyond what specialists of the different countries would have guessed anyway: the GDR ranked first in consumption of potatoes and Cuba in uses of sugar. Cheap supply and national traditions explain this variance; the degree of wealth is hardly illustrated by these figures on food consumption. Meat consumption is still highly regarded by statisticians as a measure of living standards and has the advantage of being less dependent on national traditions, with the exception of the Far East where Vietnam's consumption of meat, contrary to experiences in the West, is still an indicator of development in the socialist camp. The GDR, Czechoslovakia, and Hungary are on top and rank above the Soviet Union.

Transnational comparisons of durable commodities are also not very indicative. Cars have not been promoted by most socialist countries. The opposite is true of television sets; for propaganda reasons they were subsidized in the initial phase and therefore were less useful as an indicator of development than was assumed by early comparisons in the style suggested by Lipset's *Political Man*.[27] Only modern color television sets are, at least in the Soviet Union, considered a politically neutral indicator of affluence, but the country's performance in this respect is fairly poor; only Bulgaria was behind the Soviet Union in her bloc. The indicator "private car" is not easily assessed for the whole bloc because the Soviet Union hides her production as well as her per capita consumption. Only in the most developed socialist countries, the GDR and Czechoslovakia, was there a correlation between the magnitude of automobile production and the ownership of private cars within the population. Bulgaria produces no automobiles but was relatively well equipped with private cars. In Poland the relationship is reversed: the country produced many more cars than the proportion of population in possession of a private car would suggest.

One of the main areas in which socialist countries suffered from permanent scarcity is housing. Following the enormous destruction of World War II, the Soviet Union under Khrushchev took a leading position in housing construction. Only after 1976 did the GDR focus its efforts on building new housing to replace that destroyed in the war. Its leaders most forcefully concentrated after World War II on building what they called the "economic-technical basis of socialism." This experiment had a high price in terms of human well-being, but in the long run it seems to have paid off because no other socialist country

Table 12.4 DATA ON DISTRIBUTION

Country	Growth of saving (1980 = 100)	Per capita consumption of meat (in kilos)			Consumption in durable consumer goods (items per 1000 of the population)								
					Refrigerators			Televisions			Cars		
	1985	1970	1980	1985	1970	1980	1985	1970	1980	1985	1970	1980	1985
Bulgaria	151	43.7	64.9	75.5	81	234	290	120	232	288	17	88	115
Cuba	n.a.	33.0	36.4	41.9	n.a.	70	108	53*	129	196	—	n.a.	—
Czechoslovakia	140	71.9	85.6	86.0	177	305	407	234	372	429	57	139	169
German Democratic Republic	125	66.1	89.5	96.2	215	423	538	276	408	460	60	148	188
Hungary	168	58.1	71.7	79.0	103	287	363	171	344	404	21	91	132
Mongolia	139	—	—	—		n.a.	—			—		n.a.	—
Poland	338	61.2	82.1	67.3	159*	272	313	240*	297	335	19*	53	66
Rumania	n.a.	—	—	—	—	n.a.	—	—	n.a.	—	—		—
Soviet Union	141	47.5	57.6	61.4	89	252	275	143	249	293	—	n.a.	—

*1975.

Source: Exheg. (1986), 51, 53, 55, 56.

achieved a similarly sound basis for developing its economy. In the 1980s housing was designated the top priority of social policy, and reconstruction of housing destroyed in World War II was to be completed by 1990 (in West Germany this was achieved between 1973 and 1975).[28] The GDR constructed, after the Soviet Union and Rumania, the smallest apartments in her camp. But these indicators for the size of the apartments have to be correlated with the average size of families in the countries; measured by this indicator the GDR can justify the small size of new flats.

There were also considerable differences within COMECON as far as the distribution of private building is concerned. Redistribution as a major goal of socialism in its initial phase did not affect private housing for use by one's own family. Housing remained, with the exception of the Soviet Union and the GDR, predominantly in private hands. The GDR, as the most highly urbanized country (see Table 12.1), again was at the bottom of the hierarchy of socialist countries; and the least developed countries on the Balkan peninsula were on the top. This suggests that the proportion of private ownership of housing tends to correlate positively with the proportion of the rural population. The GDR, however, restricted private building of houses for political reasons more than neighboring countries, and only after 1971 was this policy changed; still, the share of private building never was much above one-fifth (1981, 21.4 percent; 1984, 17.8 percent). Countries with low figures for housing generally have faced a problem not so much of private ownership, but rather of a minimum standard of privacy for each family in an apartment of its own. According to statistics in the Soviet Union, only 85 percent of the urban population have reached this level. Gorbachev promised to bring it to 100 percent by the year 2000.[29]

If one compares the number of newly built apartments and the number of marriages and divorces per year (see Tables 12.1 and 12.5), it becomes clear that the performance does not meet the needs of young couples, nor does it provide extra apartments for divorced couples. Housing scarcity and the strains of living with parents in a small flat contribute to the high rates of divorce and the low birthrate in the Soviet Union, as demographers frankly admit.[30] In the Soviet literature there already is some discussion that the psychological dependence of the younger generation that is reinforced by such living conditions does not serve to encourage the type of the "daring young worker" that Gorbachev is trying to movilize for *perestroika*.

The main virtues of socialist housing policy are that segregation of social and ethnic groups in the society is avoided and that rents are low. The former achievement is still highly thought of and is indeed a social advantage, which capitalist societies are unable to match. Low rents, however, are no longer considered an advantage in all cases. Gorbachev

Table 12.5 DATA ON HOUSING

Country	Average size of new apartments (square meters)	Apartments constructed per 1000 inhabitants					Share of private building in housing 1960–1961	Rural population (%) 1960–1961
		1955	1960	1970	1980	1985		
Bulgaria	64.6	n.a.	6.3	5.7	8.4	7.2	80.2	67.0
Cuba	—	—	—	—	21.0	74.0	n.a.	—
Czechoslovakia	69.5	3.9	5.6	7.6	8.4	6.7	35.3	42.5
German Democratic Republic	57.8	1.7	2.9	4.5	101.0	128.0	9.8	22.2
Hungary	62.7	3.2	4.2	7.3	8.3	6.8	70.8	60.3
Mongolia	—	—	—	—	30.0	38.0	n.a.	—
Poland	56.7	3.4	4.2	5.8	6.1	5.1	37.9	51.5
Rumania	47.5	n.a.	n.a.	7.3	8.9	4.6	71.8	67.2
Soviet Union	47.1	7.6	14	9.4	7.5	7.2	47.4	69.0

Source: Ezhegodnik (1986), 155; Trends in Housing Policies in ECE Countries (New York: United Nations, 1980), 60.

broached a touchy issue when he mentioned at the Twenty-seventh Party Congress that higher rents for the affluent and fairer distribution of apartments were inevitable. When expenditures for social services in various socialist states are analyzed, subsidies via the "housing funds" (Table 12.6) turn out to be highest in the GDR, Poland, and the Soviet Union.

The older traditions of various socialist countries have strongly influenced their performance in social policy. The more highly developed countries that had social allowances before entering the socialist stage, such as the GDR, Poland, and Hungary, have preserved more of the old insurance system. The Soviet Union, on the other hand, relies entirely on a state-organized fund with few possibilities for private efforts to improve one's situation in case of need. In all the socialist countries social allowances have been closely linked to work, which leads to a large group of underprivileged retired couple. Average retirement pensions compared to gross wages are low, with the exception of Rumania whose low minimum wages could hardly be lowered for the retirement age (see Table 12.6).

All the socialist states recognize the need to improve the situation of the retired. The Soviet Union has long chosen to reopen chances for agriculture on private plots and to promote the continuation of work upon reaching retirement age. Both measures, however, had other, ideologically undesired consequences, especially private agriculture with its leap back into "capitalist attitudes."

The promises for better care for old people are rarely followed by concrete measures. In the GDR, disappointment after the rhetoric at the party congress in 1976 was so widespread that concrete announcements for the increase of wages and pensions were made two months later. In the Soviet Union promises remained rather vague. Brezhnev announced an increase in retirement benefits "step by step." Gorbachev promised this "periodically," which introduced slightly more regularity into the rising expectations. Variable pensions and indexation are still not yet accepted, but are being discussed to prevent further groups from sinking below the minimum necessary for subsistence. For the first time, there is some admission that there is a certain degree of inflationary pressure on pensions.[31]

The coverage of groups under the social security systems is almost universal. Formerly underprivileged groups such as the *kolkhoz* farmers have been included in the system. The main problem today is instead the treatment of the privileged groups (in the bureaucracy, army, and security forces), which clamor for a completely new system. In all the socialist countries the proportion of pensioners is growing rapidly (see Table 12.6). The structure of what socialist countries call the "social funds of consumption" shows that the proportion of money spent on

Table 12.6 SOCIAL SECURITY AND HEALTH

| Country | Pensioners (thousands) | | | Average pension (in % of gross minimum wages) | | | | Structure of social consumption (%) | | | | | | | | |
| | | | | | | | | Pensions | | | Health and sports | | | Housing subsidies | | |
	1970	1980	1985	1960	1970	1980	1982	1970	1980	1985	1970	1980	1985	1970	1980	1985
Bulgaria	1,667	1,804	2,123	18.6	29.1	37.4	38.9	46.1	44.2	45.2	13.4	16.3	16.3	n.a.	0.8	0.9
Cuba	363	690	890	—	—	—	—	—	n.a.	—	—	—	—	—	—	—
Czechoslovakia	3,033	3,304	3,413	47.3	44.6	44.8	46.1	51.9	49.7	48.5	15.0	15.7	15.9	—	—	—
German Democratic Republic	—	n.a.	—	n.a.	24.0	30.8	29.6	41.5	37.1	31.3	15.3	17.9	18.8	7.1	11.5	16.6
Hungary	1,453	2,082	2,299	31.3	35.5	56.9	58.5	48.9	58.2	58.1	16.7	13.8	14.1	3.4	1.8	1.4
Mongolia	24.5	117	160	—	—	—	—	30.8	34.1	32.5	19.5	18.6	18.5	—	0.3	0.2
Poland	2,346	4,517	6,252	39.7	51.2	46.3	50.5	42.3	44.8	48.3	25.5	25.7	21.7	2.6	6.1	6.5
Rumania	1,117	1,606	1,948	n.a.	69.7	59.7	59.1	—	n.a.	—	15.6	n.a.	—	—	n.a.	—
Soviet Union	41,300	50,198	55,778	36.0	27.9	33.7	35.5	34.9	37.9	40.4	15.6	14.7	13.7	5.3	5.9	6.3

Source: Ezheg. (1986), 44, 414; Rocznik statystyczni, (1978), 471; (1984), 540.

279

pensions is increasing rapidly in some of those countries at the threshold of modernization, such as Poland and the Soviet Union. In the most developed countries, such as the GDR and Czechoslovakia, the proportion of money spent on retirement benefits was decreasing slightly. The proportion of funds spent on health was going down in some countries, such as the Soviet Union and Poland, but only in relative terms.

Comparative data on health policy in socialist countries are not very telling. Performance as measured by number of physicians and hospital beds per 10,000 of population is high, especially in the Soviet Union (see Table 12.7). However, the figures are particularly unsuited for transnational comparisons because of certain peculiarities of socialist health care systems. The ratio of doctors is high because nurses are rare, and doctors do a lot of work done in Western countries by nurses. This is especially true in the Soviet Union. (It is not by chance that 70 percent of all physicians are women.) Moreover, the duration of hospitalization tends to be long in the Soviet Union because bad housing conditions and huge distances inhibit ambulatory treatment. This also accounts for the high proportion of hospital beds and physicians.[32] Even if the figures were reliable, which is unlikely when we learn that Mongolia has a better performance than the GDR in the health sector, they do not reflect differences in quality. Relative performance can, however, be inferred from some of these figures, as in the case of Poland where health care performance declined and came close to that in a Third World socialist country such as Cuba.

Data on educational policy are normally the showpieces of the performance tests in socialist countries; yet most of the figures are useless unless we have figures on schooling per age cohort. Most socialist countries offer these figures only for the preschool age, with the exception of the Soviet Union since 1980, which did not keep up with the development achieved by most other socialist countries in this sphere, particularly the GDR, the leader in the camp (Table 12.8). But again explanation is necessary. Preschool attendance must be correlated with urbanization figures since in the countryside preschool institutions are less necessary to keep women integrated in the working process (see Table 12.1). Czechoslovakia deviates from the rule that most of the preschool institutions are to be found in the most urbanized countries. Rumania is another deviant case. Though least urbanized, it reports favorable figures. But once we learn that Rumania reports five times the number of students per 10,000 of the population, some doubts about the basis of this calculation are in order. Quality of the equipment is never reflected in these gross figures. *Perestroika* in the Soviet Union made it possible for deficiencies to come out into the open. It is remarkable that

Table 12.7   **DATA ON HEALTH POLICY**

Country	Physicians per 10,000			Hospital beds per 10,000		
	1970	1980	1985	1970	1980	1985
Bulgaria	22.2	30.0	35.1	77.1	90.8	94.2
Cuba	8.8	19.4	28.0	57.4	45.6	52.5
Czechoslovakia	23.1	32.4	36.0	99.9	99.8	102.0
German Democratic Republic	20.3	26.1	29.9	111.0	103.0	102.0
Hungary	22.0	28.1	31.5	78.6	84.2	90.2
Mongolia	17.9	21.9	24.0	94.3	108.0	111.0
Poland	19.3	22.5	24.3	74.0	71.6	69.7
Rumania	14.7	17.9	20.8	80.8	89.6	89.4
Soviet Union	27.4	37.5	42.0	109.0	125.0	130.0

Source: Ezheg. (1986), 411.

Gorbachev's rival, Ligachev, not suspected of too many sympathies for *perestroika*, went furthest in criticizing the qualitative deficiencies of the Soviet school system. All of a sudden horrifying figures were released: 30 percent lack running water, and 40 percent have no indoor toilets.[33] If we study investment figures in the educational system, the performance of the more developed countries has recently declined, whereas the developing countries, such as Mongolia and Cuba, are on the top of the performance list.

Outcome data on cultural policy tend to be the least useful of all the data in the statistical yearbooks of COMECON. We learn that the Soviet Union is way down in the ranking list in theater visits (see Table 12.8). If Vietnam is on top, it becomes clear that very different things are listed under the rubric of a theater visit. Only figures for cinema attendance seem to be comparable; high performance in this area, however, does not mean development. On the contrary, cinema attendance is highest in underdeveloped areas with no other distraction and a comparatively low number of television sets per capita or per family.

More interesting again are the trends over time. Socialist countries are proud of not distracting their people from cultural activities by mass circulation newspapers oriented toward sex and crime or by pornography in cinemas. However, they face the same problem as Western countries in declining theater and museum attendance. Even in Moscow, a city of top quality theater, the number of visitors from 1970 to 1985

Table 12.8   DATA ON EDUCATION AND CULTURE

Country	Students per 10,000			Children of preschool age in preschool institutions			Capital investment in science, culture, and arts (1980 = 100)	Theater visits per 100 per year			TV subscriptions per 10,000		
	1970–1971	1980–1981	1985–1986	1970	1980	1985		1970	1980	1985	1970	1980	1985
Bulgaria	186	120	112	40.9	50.8	48.5	104	63.7	72.3	67.3	1207	1861	1896
Cuba	84	250	300	12.1	20.6	21.6	110	14.0	15.4	14.6	—	n.a.	—
Czechoslovakia	199	216	168	34.9	49.6	56.4	66	66.2	57.0	54.6	2152	2808	2818
German Democratic Republic	112	103	98	50.4	78.9	83.6	90	71.9	62.6	60.2	2638	3424	3652
Hungary	174	195	183	37.1	59.5	67.1	69	54.1	52.6	57.0	1709	2582	2736
Mongolia	89	113	122	14.2	16.2	18.0	213	88.1	15.4	19.5	119	318	460
Poland	247	292	195	18.7	29.3	30.8	152	40.8	33.2	27.6	1293	2226	2535
Romania	76	454	550	18.5	42.6	44.9	47	40.8	41.0	51.7	733	1673	1707
Soviet Union	180	173	161	n.a.	43.2	n.a.	115	45.8	45.2	45.0	—	n.a.	—
Vietnam	—	—	—	—	—	—	246	n.a.	72.2	92.3	—	—	—

Source: Ezheg. (1986), 390, 394, 403, 408.

declined by roughly one-quarter. It is not yet the "rainbow press" that enters into competition with cultural institutions, but it is television, as in Western countries. Television, once used as an indicator to celebrate the progress of socialism, is much more carefully judged in recent years by Soviet scholars; increasingly, this indicator in the eyes of Soviet experts also points to the negative side of modernization.

The comparison of aggregate data in important policy areas has long invited scholars not to stop with a descriptive interpretation of these figures, but to look for the independent variable that explains modernization under socialist conditions. In the early modernization literature, urbanization, industrialization, and universal literacy were looked upon as the most important explanatory variables. Urbanization was achieved quickly; indeed, of all modern ideologies Marxism-Leninism exhibited the least resistance to modern urban life because of its bias in favor of the working class. Industrialization was, with the exception of the Chinese cultural revolution, a high-priority goal in all the socialist countries. Industrialization was fairly successful because of the creation of a regional market in which socialist countries, otherwise unable to compete in the world market, were able to sell their goods to a hegemonic power that was highly developed only in regard to arms production. This pattern of intrasocialist and COMECON trade, after an initial period of exploitation under Stalin, proved to be an advantage for the less developed socialist countries, even if calculations by Marrese and Vanous that the Soviet Union has supported the economies of her allies with 70 billion rubles over twenty years are still open to question. But there is little doubt that the Soviet Union, in order to promote shared goals, often paid political prices for the goods of her allies in order to promote collective goals.[34]

Universal literacy was achieved so quickly that it soon did not mean much because many intellectuals were overqualified and underemployed, which did not increase their labor productivity. Indicator studies show that the normal indicators for literacy rates, as developed by Pirages, offered no explanation of the capacity to modernize.[35] Poland was at the top of literacy rates, but it did not keep up with the needs for modernization. The GDR modernized economically but always ranked low on scales of literacy.

As additional functional prerequisites for modernization, the autonomy of subunits and the functional differentiation of institutions are frequently mentioned.[36] They were most necessary in socialist systems with ethnic cleavages. In Czechoslovakia early efforts in this direction failed after 1968. In Yugoslavia functional differentiation in some respects led to the worst of all possible worlds: a clumsy socialist party bureaucracy superimposed on a system where increasingly only the member republics of the federation functioned with some efficiency and an extreme decentralization of the economy. The GDR conferred some additional powers to the districts, but on the whole the system did not fare so badly even without decentralization by regions.[37]

The Soviet Union, as the largest country in the world, very much needed decentralization but failed to develop it after abolishing in 1965 the *Sovnarkhoz* system introduced by Khrushchev. Only *perestroika* for the first time promised a substantial step in this direction.

In the relevant literature on the socialist economies, no analysis on the basis of just one independent variable has led to satisfying results. Complex typologies encompassing various sets of indicators have led to complex clusters, some of them paradoxical at first glance. For example, the Soviet Union formed one group with the GDR and Bulgaria, which one might have expected only in the field of law and order issues. Czechoslovakia, ranking second for most indicators, was listed under "out of pattern."[38] Only the two other groups, comprising the remaining states on the Balkan peninsula (Albania and Yugoslavia) and a group formed by Hungary and Poland, corresponded to commonsense expectations.

The case of Czechoslovakia is interesting, however, for the study of deviance from the expected path of development. This country did not live up to what might have been expected of it as a part of the former Austro-Hungarian empire, with comparatively good starting conditions for development after World War II and an unusually low rate of wartime destruction among the countries in east-central Europe. The Czechoslovak experience raises question about the notion that COMECON fostered industrialization in the nations of the Socialist bloc. Indeed, for the more highly developed areas socialism and the division of labor within COMECON in the long run proved detrimental. This holds true not only for Czechoslovakia but also, if less obviously so, for the GDR, which performed well only in comparison to other socialist-bloc countries. Aggregate data obscure the fact that the southern parts of what became the German Democratic Republic were among the most developed areas in the German empire and that these lagged far behind in economic development when compared with the Federal Republic. Only with the Soviet *perestroika* and its repercussions in other socialist countries could criticism of all these contradictions among policies—formerly the almost exclusive domain of Western scholars—come to be voiced prominently within the Socialist countries. Even in those countries which claim to have had their *perestroika* in earlier modernization reforms, the influence of *glasnost* is increasingly felt. *Glasnost*, however, has a dynamics of its own, and it is not always beneficial for *perestroika*.

GLASNOST AND *PERESTROIKA*: TWO COUNTERVAILING POWERS OF MODERNIZATION?

Perestroika is aimed at a profound change of the economy and society. It made possible a discussion on the structural obstacles to modernization under socialism. Questions of modernization used to be dealt with from the assumption of the omnipresence of passivity and sabotage, the counterstrategy being to manipulate the motivation of the people. Structural deficiencies were hardly ever admitted. People were exchanged; sometimes tasks and responsibilities were redistributed; but in most reforms the mechanics of the system were left untouched.

Perestroika for the first time in Soviet history revolutionizes the whole system of institutions, at least theoretically. According to Gorbachev, there was too much "piecemeal engineering" in previous Soviet history. In social policy, for instance, privileges in the hands of a few and disadvantages for the many have accumulated to such an extent that the whole system of social security has to be reorganized.[39] New policy dimensions are also opened up. In order to play down the importance of classical human rights, the system had long emphasized social rights. Now the promises of the social constitution of 1977 are taken literally, and concrete demands are derived from its articles promising better social security and better housing.[40]

"Social justice," which once was denounced as another "Social Democratic euphemism" to embellish the dark realities in a class society, was put into the center of the debate by Gorbachev's speech during the Twenty-seventh Party Congress in 1986. This concept, which in the West too frequently has been dismissed as an empty formula, is filled with life and concrete demands by Soviet scholars. Soviet experts now are demanding institutional reforms. Deregulation and institutional autonomy for the social services are being debated with the aim of liberating the socialist state from being overburdened with too many responsibilities at once. Even private insurance schemes in competition with state insurance are no longer a taboo subject. Only decentralization to the extent that all responsibilities of the Union are handed over to the Union republics, a kind of Reaganite "new federalism," is not yet acceptable among Soviet experts. New policy areas open up when experts propose to hand over the whole complex of family and demographic policies to a new agency, which for the first time does not necessarily have to be just another state committee.[41] In legal policy everything is subject to possible reform. Administrative courts have already been created; an equivalent to a constitutional court, vehemently resisted until 1986, was due to be set up in 1990.[42]

Though political reform is envisioned only as an instrument for supporting the basic goal of economic and social reform, the first internal contradictions of radical reform already are visible. The basic problem is that *perestroika* and *glasnost* are less compatible than Gorbachev originally thought. But if Oksenberg and Dickson are right in claiming that the end of a great reform begins when the reformers "begin to spend much more time battling the unintended consequences brought on by their previous reform policies than they do initiating new reforms," then *perestroika* would already be in its final stage.

Gorbachev knew that there is a nationality problem in the Soviet Union. The plan of his great speech at the Twenty-seventh Party Congress gave this problem special prominence by taking it out of the sequence of the classification of the four social processes of homogenization (*sblizheniya* furthering *odnorodnost'*). But he hardly anticipated that in a short time secessionist movements might spring up which would discredit *perestroika* in the eyes of many conservative *apparatchiki*. Nevertheless, though Gorbachev and many of his followers are sometimes already completely absorbed in battling the unintended consequences, *perestroika* goes on. In some respects the unintended consequences are not just detrimental; rather they put pressure on the leadership for further reform. Perhaps Gorbachev had many far-reaching goals in mind, but he was careful not to confront the party with all of them at once. Unintended consequences open the way for reforms that Gorbachev might not have envisioned so soon. Judicial review hits the nerve of sovereignty of a Communist party. Nevertheless, with an increase in the potential for social and national conflicts it might turn out to be better to entrust the decision on touchy problems, such as the integration of Nagorno-Karabakh into Azerbaijan or the Estonian desire for a legislative veto, to a neutral body consisting of a few old wise men than to parliamentary bodies of the party. Without these dysfunctional conflicts set free by *glasnost*, many aspects of *perestroika* might have turned out to be more timid. Inconsistencies in the policy mix or policy mess (to use Oksenberg's terminology) have come out into the open and have to be tackled.

Though *perestroika* intends to give priority to economic and social reform, the outcome in the short run may be a dominance of *glasnost* over *perestroika*, or to put it more precisely, a temporary preoccupation with legal, institutional, and political reforms at the expense of the more far-reaching goals of *perestroika*.

The danger that *glasnost* benefits more from the great reform than economic *perestroika* is obvious with regard to economic reforms. The law on enterprises that was enacted in February 1987 and took effect in January 1988 has strengthened *glasnost* on the plant level. Codetermination, *glasnost* on the plant level, and the election of plant directors have attracted more attention than those parts of the law that were meant to enhance *perestroika*, such as its articles aimed at strengthening decentralization, *chozrazchet* (economic profitability), and self-financing. *Glasnost* is in danger of triumphing over *perestroika* and efficiency.

The dilemma of great reformers confronting the inertia of the system is that they cannot develop all their ideas for reform at once. Sometimes they start with trial balloons, knowing well that these are only partial reforms. Sometimes they accept policies that are not integral parts of the overall scheme so as to win over the more reluctant and conservative people. There is a rumor that Gorbachev became "Mineral Water Secretary" by launching an antialcohol campaign only in order to please the Ligachev faction. The campaign is about to peter out, and this may be taken as evidence of the fact that this reform is not one of Gorbachev's first priorities.

Some reforms are perceived by their opponents as policies that will weaken the party. In the long run, however, deregulation may strengthen the party, which could then concentrate on political guidelines, instead of taking the blame for any administrative failure that becomes public knowledge. The party's omnipresence in society becomes a distinct handicap once its omnipotence to steer all processes of society is withering away. Intentionally, the eclectic policy mix of the great reform of *perestroika* shows more consistency than was originally recognized. Still there is an implicit danger that the political movements and internal opposition will play havoc with the gradualism of the *perestroika* planners.

The conservative opposition is more and more worried by the unintended consequences of *perestroika*. Gorbachev was quite skillful in using fairly traditional methods, such as purging and elite rotation, to overcome resistance within the party apparatus. But large sections of the people, the party, and the working class are not yet won over and remain skeptical toward *perestroika*. Interview data collected in Estonian factories showed that the leading cadres have only slightly more confidence in *perestroika* than do the workers. The adherents of *perestroika* in the intelligentsia are afraid that new contradictions between *glasnost* and *perestroika* might emerge.[43] The average reaction to the inertia of the majority is also conventional: More mobilization is needed, though social scientists know from survey data that interest in the provision of additional social services is declining, as is the general interest in political and social questions, especially in the younger generation.[44] The search for one's personal identity is becoming more important, but it increasingly deviates from the officially accepted values of the system. Revised national identities among the non-Russian population, religion, and superstition are again spreading.[45] *Glasnost* revealed, moreover, that the unlimited social optimism, which is said to be a typical feature of the socialist way of life, is far less widespread than is assumed in official statements.

Socialism was able to control the public debate through censorship, at the price of undermining the credibility of the media. *Glasnost* makes the media more trustworthy, but at a cost previously unknown to socialist dictatorships: Permanent criticism in all the media now undermines trust in party and state institutions. Cautious critics of *glasnost* among Soviet writers call this the boomerang effect. Lenin is invoked for a true dialogue with the people that does not stop with giving a negative image to all the Soviet institutions.[46] Apparently, the realistic approach to criticism and plurality of opinions has to be learned and cannot just be taken for granted through *glasnost* for everybody. If *perestroika* is to succeed, citizens in socialist countries have to learn to live with frustrations and disappointments and to build the failures of rising expectations into their lives. One of the modest but important achievements of modern society is its tolerance for ambiguities—its willingness not to expect everything from some supreme authority, be it God or the state, without lapsing back into complete cynicism. Some societies learned this only after World War II, but in this respect most of the socialist systems lagged far behind. Only when *glasnost* and *perestroika*—political reform under populist pressure from below and substantial social reforms as the essence of *perestroika*—can be balanced in an equilibrium can great reform continue. If Gorbachev does not succeed in erecting boundaries to contain the unintended consequences of reform, so that the positive consequences outweigh the negative ones, *glasnost* will kill *perestroika*.

NOTES

1. *Narodnoe obrazovanie v SSS R. Sbornik normativnych aktov* (Moscow: Yurlit, 1987), 25.
2. M. Gorbachev, *Perestroika: The Second Russian Revolution* (New York: Norton, 1988), chap. 1.
3. C. Graf von Krockow, *Reform als politisches Prinzip* (Munich: Piper, 1976), 77 ff.
4. T. J. Colton, *The Dilemma of Reform in the Soviet Union* (New York: Council on Foreign Relations, 1986), 119.
5. Michel Oksenberg and Bruce Dickson, "The Origins, Processes, and Outcomes of Great Political Reform," Chapter 11 in this volume.
6. Ibid.
7. Samuel P. Huntington, *Political Order in Changing Societies* (New Haven: Yale University Press, 1968), 9.

8. A. N. Gendin, "Effekt Edipa i metodologicheskie problemy sotsial'nogo prognozirovaniya," *Voprosy filosofii*, no. 5 (1970): 80–89.

9. Andrea Stevenson Sanjian, "Constraints on Modernization: The Case of Administrative Theory in the USSR," *Comparative Politics* 18 (January 1986): 193–210.

10. V. I. Sas'yanenko, *Sovetskiy obraz zhizni* (Moscow: Politizdat, 1985), 3.

11. A. K. Belyi et al., eds., *Edinstvo ekonomicheskoi i sotsial'noi politiki razvitogo sotsialisticheskogo obshchestva* (Leningrad: Izdatel'stvo Leningradskogo universiteta 1985), 158.

12. Oksenberg and Dickson, "Origins, Process, and Outcomes."

13. Times are gone when a *pokazetel* in the Soviet Union and a *Kennziffer* in the GDR were said to be something completely different from a Western *indicator*. In Polish and Rumanian the term indicator was always accepted because there was no other native word for this. In the meantime even Soviet scholars use the terms almost synonymously. Cf. ISI AN SSSR, *Pokazately sotsial'nogo razvitiya Sovetskogo obshchestva* (Moscow: ISI, 1985), 37; G. Osipov, "Chelovecheskiy faktor uskoreniya," *Sotsiologicheskie issledovaniya*, no. 5 (1987): 13.

14. M. S. Bednyi, *Demograficheskie faktory zdorov'ya* (Moscow: Finansy i statistika, 1984), 105.

15. V. M. Moiseenko, ed., *Demograficheskie aspekty zanyatosti* (Moscow: Statistika, 1975), 37.

16. R. V. Ryabushkin, ed., *Demograficheskaya politika socialisticheskogo obshchestva* (Moscow: Nauka, 1986), 75.

17. V. D. Shapiro, *Sotsial'naya aktivnost'pozhilikh lyudei v SSSR* (Moscow: Nauka, 1983), 61.

18. Karl Marx and Friedrich Engles, *Werke*, vol. 4 (Berlin: Dietz Verlag, 1969), 466.

19. Cf. K. von Beyme, *Der Wiederaufbau: Architektur und Städtebau in beiden deutschen Staaten* (Munich: Piper, 1987), 153.

20. *Materialy XXV s'ezda KPSS* (Moscow: Politizdat, 1976), 223; *Materialy XXVI s'ezda KPSS* (Moscow: Politizdat, 1982), 138.

21. *Materialy XXVI s'ezda*, 54.

22. G. I. Kasperovich, *Migratsiya naseleniya v goroda i etnicheskie processy* (Minsk: Nauka i tekhnika, 1985), 15.

23. The Rumanian figures are difficult to explain and hardly believable. For a discussion see "Basket Two Compliance: East European Economic Statistical Quality," prepared for the Commission on Security and Cooperation in Europe, coordinated by the Congressional Research Service, May 1982, p. 4.

24. K. von Beyme, *Economics and Politics Within Socialism: A Comparative and Developmental Approach* (New York: Praeger, 1982), 173.

25. M. Gorbatschow [Gorbachev], *Die Rede* (Reinbek: Rowohlt, 1987), 52 ff.; *Materialy XXVII s'ezda KPSS* (Moscow: Politizdat, 1987), p. 28.

26. *Materialy XXVII s'ezda*, 46.

27. Seymour Martin Lipset, *Political Man: The Social Bases of Politics* (Garden City, N.Y.: Doubleday, 1960).

28. W. Junker, "Das Bauen hat in unserem Land eine klare Perspektive," *Architektur der DDR* (1980): 453.

29. *Materialy XXVII s'ezda*, 48; *Narodnoe khozyaystvo SSSR za 70 let* (Moscow: Finansy i statistika, 1987), 510 ff.

30. V. V. Elizarov, *Perspektivy issledovaniya semi* (Moscow: Mysl', 1987), 100; L. F. Filyukova, *Sovremennaya molodaya semya* (Minski: Nauka i tekhnika, 1986), 24.

31. M. L. Zakharov and E. G. Tuchkova, "O konceptii novogo zakona o pensionnom obespechenii trudyashchikhsya," *Sovetskoe gosudarstvo i pravo*, (1987): 68 ff.

32. C. R. Nechemias, "Welfare in the Soviet Union: Health Care, Housing, and Personal Consumption," in G. B. Smith, ed., *Public Policy and Administration in the Soviet Union* (New York: Praeger, 1980), 181.

33. "A Top Soviet Aide Calls for Change in the School System," *New York Times*, February 18, 1988.

34. Cf. K. von Beyme, "Economic Relations as an Instrument of Soviet Hegemony over Eastern Europe," in H. H. Hohmann et al., eds., *Economics and Politics in the USSR* (Boulder, Colo.: Westview Press, 1986), 224.

35. D. C. Pirages, "Socio-economic Development and Political Access in the Communist States," in J. F. Triska, ed., *Communist Party States* (Indianapolis, Ind.: Bobbs-Merrill, 1969), 261.

36. J. F. Triska and P. M. Johnson, "Political Development and Political Change," in C. Mesa-Lago and C. Beck, eds., *Comparative Socialist Systems* (Pittsburgh: University of Pittsburgh Center of International Studies, 1975), 250.

37. K. von Beyme, "Regionalpolitik in der DDR," in G.-J. Glässner, ed., *Die DDR in der Ära* Honecker: Festschrift *für* Hartmut Zimmermann (Berlin: Berlin-Verlag, 1988), 434–452.

38. W. A. Welsh, "Toward an Empirical Typology of Socialist Systems," in Mesa-Lago and Beck, *Comparative Socialist Systems*, 74 ff.

39. Yu. K. Tolskoy, "Problemy zhilishchnogo zakonodatel'stva," *Sovetskoe gosudarstvo i pravo*, no. 11 (1987): 90 ff.

40. "Aktual'nye problemy gosudarstvennogo strakhovaniya," Krugliy stol *Sovetskoe gosudarstvo i pravo*, no. 9 (1987): 65–70.
41. Yu. A. Korolev, "Pravovye aspekty zashchity semi gosudarstvom," *Sovetskoe gosudarstvo i pravo*, no. 5 (1983): 26.
42. V. Tumanov, "Guarantees for Constitutionality of Legislation in the USSR," in Ch. Landfried, ed., *Constitutional Review and Legislatures* (Baden-Baden: Nomos, 1988), 213–218; "Die Staatsorgane wehren sich: Die sowjetischen Juristen Wladimir Kudrjawzew and Waleriy Sawizki über die Perestroika im Rechtswesen," *Der Spiegel*, no. 4 (1988): 146–151.
43. M. N. Rutkevich, "Izmeneniya sotsial'noklassovoi strukture sovetskogo obshchestva i usloviya perestroiki," *Sotsiologicheskie issledovaniya*, no. 4 (1987): 34–47.
44. "Otnoshenie studentov k obshchestvennym naukam, *Sotsiologicheski issledovaniya*, no. 4 (1987): 20–24.
45. V. G. Nimirovskii and M. A. Manuilskiy, "Fantasticheskie predstavleniya kak element massovogo soznaniya," *Sotsiologicheskie issledovaniya*, no. 4 (1987): 70–75.
46. Yu. A. Kovalev, " 'Negative' v presse i 'effekt bumeranga'," *Sotsiologicheskie issledovaniya*, no. 5 (1987), 80 ff.

Chapter

13

The Revolt of Islam and Its Roots

Nikki R. Keddie

The revolution led by the Ayatollah Ruhallah Khomeini in Iran in 1979, for all its appearance of traditionalism in such matters as dress and morality, was in fact an unparalled event within the world of Islam. One sign of this nontraditionalism was Khomeini's 1987 decree that his own rulings could and should supersede Islamic law when necessary.[1] A Shi'i clerical-populist interpretation of Islam, having roots in past practices, was carried to radically new lengths in Khomeini's Iran. It is useful in understanding the Khomeini movement and its influence abroad to consider both earlier Islamic revolts and contemporary Islamist movements and to see how Khomeini's Islam is different from or similar to them.

The contrast between Shi'ism and Sunnism goes only part way in explaining the special features of Khomeinism. While it is true that early Shi'ism was often rebellious, this was not, until the late nineteenth century, true of the Twelver line of Shi'ism to which Iran adheres. Twelver Shi'ism for a long time adapted and accommodated to existing governments.[2] Rebellious movements in Islam in the eighteenth and nineteenth century were almost exclusively Sunni and nearly always tied to Sunni Sufi (or mystical) orders. The only similar movement that occurred in the Shi'i world was the mid nineteenth-century Babi movement in Iran, which explicitly broke with Shi'ism and its clergy and provoked a united clerical and governmental campaign to suppress it.

More important than Shi'ism as a belief system encouraging revolt was the centuries-long development of the Iranian clergy into a powerful, hierarchical, financially strong body, with a position largely independent of the government. Economic, political, and doctrinal forces account for this development, which helped pit leading clerics against the government in a major protest movement in 1891–1892 and in Iran's constitutional revolution of 1905–1911. The clerical organization was not effectively broken up by the Pahlavi shahs (1925–1979) and reemerged with a new mass populist militancy in 1963 and again in the 1978–1979 revolution.

ISLAMIC REVOLTS IN THE PAST

The ties of Khomeini's movement to Shi'i organization and ideas have been traced by various authors, including myself. It is also instructive to look at the relation of recent movements to past Islamic revolts. The most important of these revolts was the one that founded Islam itself and the first Islamic state, first in the town of Medina and then throughout Arabia in the seventh century. It was, in part, an ideological and political revolt against the regime of Mecca's wealthy tribal leaders. Although different interpretations have been made of this event, the most satisfactory one is that of Montgomery Watt and Maxime Rodinson, who see the Hejaz, on the western Arabian coast, as ready, chiefly owing to the rise of urban trade and the decline of tribalism, for the foundation of its first true state. Islam furnished the ideology, structure, and much of the law for that emerging state.[3] As in many of the later revolts, women took an active part in the struggles that led to the rise of Islam, but the effects of Islam on the position of women were mixed at best—increased inheritance rights on the one hand, but growing segregation and unequal marriage rights on the other.

The next major revolts in the Muslim world, beginning in the first century of Islam, were characterized by sectarian ideology, whether Kharijite or Shi'i, and often represented either people who wanted to return to tribal ways or members of recently urbanized and displaced classes, often newly converted to Islam. These revolts were concentrated in periods of socioeconomic change. While such sectarian rebels generally unified their religion, politics, and leadership (for the Shi'a in the person of the infallible imam), religion, politics, and leadership were far less unified among the Sunni majority. It is commonly said that religion and politics have always been united in Islam, but this is untrue. The formation of the ulama in the first Islamic centuries created a religious class that had considerable independence of the state, and rulers were generally about as active in religious matters as they were in the West. The Twelver Shi'i view that the infant twelfth imam was hidden and would return as the mahdi (or messiah) at the end of time seems to have been adopted largely in order to limit themselves to the religious sphere and take themselves out of politics. This they did by removing the imam and his political claims and by stressing their loyalty to the Sunni Abbasid caliph. The later interpretation of the Twelver imam mahdi as an immediate oppositional inspiration came after a long and complex evolution, which is only one of many proofs that is not static and cannot be interpreted simplistically.[4]

EIGHTEENTH- AND NINETEENTH-CENTURY MOVEMENTS

In the eighteenth and nineteenth centuries there were a number of Islamic revolts or jihad ("holy war") movements. They preceded European conquest but nonetheless were partly caused by relations, especially trade relations, with Europe. These precolonial revolts tended to occur on the periphery of the Muslim world, from Senegal to Sumatra. Because of their scattering in different regions, they have rarely been studied together. The most important occurred (1) in West Africa, including Senegambia, Nigeria, and Mali, where a series of movements lasted over a century, (2) among the Wahhabis of Arabia, (3) in West Sumatra, and (4) in South Asia, where some movements began before the British conquest of their area.

These movements thus occurred over a widespread area, but happened in a relatively short time period, after some centuries in which militant Islamic revolts were rare.[5] Certain common factors may account for their simultaneity. First, the impact of Western trade and the rise of internal trade strengthened the trading classes, increased stratification, and made the situation ripe for state formation. In West Africa and Sumatra there is something like the re-creation of the situation in Arabia in Muhammad's time, when the rise of trade created the need for a stronger state with a new ideology. Revolts in West Africa closely followed the path of the spread of the slave trade.

Second, during this period dynastic empires declined—of the Safavids in Iran, the Ottomans in Turkey, and the Moghuls in India. Although most revolts did not take place within the borders of the empires, the decline of central empires can create conditions for the setting up of new states and movements outside their borders, as in the original revolt of Islam.

Third, the eighteenth century saw the spread of more orthodox, learned, and organized Sufism (usually translated as Islamic mysticism), now often called neo-Sufism. It is significant that several leaders of precolonial revolts and all the leaders of nineteenth-century anticolonial revolts were leaders of Sufi orders that were rather orthodox in orientation.

Fourth, internal socioeconomic change, which, according to some scholars, included an eighteenth-century movement toward worldwide population growth, could have had disruptive effects. This has been alleged for Arabia. In the Sudan, where the Mahdist movement of the 1880s had similar features, the suppression of the slave trade produced economic dislocation.

Fifth, the eighteenth-century development of Islamic learning and of travel over long distances to acquire it (studied especially by John Voll[6]) seems to have influenced many leaders and to have spread ideas to many different regions. The leaders of Sumatra's Padri movement and Osman dan Fodio of Nigeria had both traveled to Mecca, and other movement leaders had also traveled in search of learning.

Sixth, most precolonial Islamic revolts and nearly all colonial revolts drew their main support from tribal peoples, who were often the best equipped and trained to carry on warfare.

Though some of these movements were ephemeral, those of the Wahhabis in Arabia (after 1736), the Mahdi in Sudan (1883–1885), and Osman dan Fodio in Nigeria set up important states, while the Padris in Sumatra were defeated only after decades by the Dutch, who used the movement as an excuse to conquer its territory.

The next great wave of jihad movements was triggered mainly by Western conquest, as with Sayyid Ahmad Brelwi and the Fara'izis in South Asia, Abdel Qadir and others in Algeria (1840–1846), and Shamyl in the Caucasus (1834–1859). These movements did not, however, occur randomly throughout areas of Western conquest, but were concentrated in areas distant from central governments, often with largely tribal populations. Their leaders were either local heads of major mainstream Sufi orders or disciples of major Islamic reformers.

Postconquest movements had major similarities to preconquest ones, although Western conquest or partial conquest (Algeria, the Caucasus) and socioeconomic dislocations caused by conquest were a major new causative factor. The ideological counterpart to opposition and economic intrusion was opposition to the conquest of believers by unbelievers. In the "Wahhabi" movement of Sayyid Ahmad Brelwi and his successors and its rural Bengali Fara'izi offshoot, the socioeconomic dislocations were especially important. The later Senussi movement against the Italians in Libya is similar in its anticonquest, antiunbeliever orientation and its connection with a Sufi order and its leader. It occurred much later than other postcolonial movements because the Italian conquest did not come until the twentieth century.

The early Shi'i movements tended to be mahdist-messianic and often heterodox or "extremist" in ideology. This is one pole of Islamic rebellious ideology and is found also in movements not mentioned above, including the rise of the Safavids in fifteenth- and sixteenth-century Iran and Anatolia. Most of the eighteenth- and nineteenth-century movements noted above fit into another tradition that of the "Wahhabis," who were puritanical and literal in their interpretation of the Quran. These traditions overlap in that messianists are sometimes puritanical, as were the Sudanese Mahdi, and purists can be messianic, as are the followers of Khomeini in today's Iran.

The militance and relative clarity of injunctions regarding morality and gender separation that characterized early Islam provided a continuing model for these and similar movements. It is striking how much unconnected militant movements use the same early Islamic models; insistence on women's veiling, for example, is found in the Wahhabis and in Wahhabi-type movements like the Padris. Such gender separation was not only the result of copying early Islam, but also arose from the role of these movements, including the African ones, in state formation with its accompanying stratification of classes and genders.

Charismatic leadership has characterized all these movements, but, as usual, the charismatic leader appeared just at the time when other conditions were ripe for militant revolt. As the high point of Muhammad's career was the Prophet's hijra (or flight) from Mecca to Medina in 622, so the leaders often imitated Muhammad in having their own hijra and in other ways.

ISLAMIC REFORMISM SINCE THE LATE NINETEENTH CENTURY

Islamic reformism today appears to be in eclipse, but it was for many decades, from the late nineteenth century until after World War II, the major intellectual trend in the Muslim world, and it may still regain its creativity and influence.[7] Although this is a chapter about Islamic militance, it should not be forgotten that militance has almost always been a minority trend in the Muslim world as a whole and remains so today. Many educated people continue to believe in some form of Islamic reform, even though it may not be their primary belief. The main trend in Islamic reform, which may be said to have begun in the mid nineteenth century with Young Ottomans like Namik Kemal (although the Arab world stresses later Arabs like Muhammad 'Abduh), was to interpret Islam in accord with the needs of the modern world. Although Islam had its own rationalist and reforming traditions, what was mainly done was to interpret Quranic and early Islamic injunctions in ways that made them more in accord with Western liberalism on a whole range of matters from parliaments and constitutions to nationalism and women's rights. When women began to organize for their rights in the early twentieth century, their ideology was often both feminist and Islamic-modernist.

If the modernist effort in the end was repudiated by many, including those who took more secular or leftist positions, it was not so much because the effort was intellectually weak—it was no weaker than similar efforts in other cultures. The repudiation of modernism came more because many Muslims were more inclined than other people to reject the West and its ways, largely due to centuries-old hostility to Christian or Western infidels, and to the new obstacle of Israel. Also, liberal or secular rulers who were associated with Islamic reformist ideas were not very successful, and the rejection of their rule and the reformist ideas and institutions that accompanied it often meant rejection of the reformist ideology. Today, among educated Muslims, as revealed largely in private conversations, the perhaps most prevalent strain of thought is a kind of radical-sounding anti-Western or anticolonial Third Worldism, which is reflected in quite different schools of Islamism, nationalism, and leftism. Islamic reformism enters more as an apologetic element allied to Third Worldism than as a positive ideology.

Third Worldism is essentially a belief that all the important problems of the Third World arise from Western colonialism and neocolonialism, which is often supplemented by a view of constant interference by the West in the Third World to control even relatively minor events and personalities. On the left it is generally related to some form of dependency theory, as exemplified by the works of Samir Amin and André Gunder Frank.[8] But it can also be part of a nationalist or Islamist view. One of the most vocal defenders that I have heard of the view that Western machinations caused everything that went wrong in the Third World was a Moroccan royalist nationalist. Modern Islamic revivalism fits especially well with Third Worldism, as it can present itself as a more authentic and indigenous alternative to Westernism than is liberal secular nationalism.[9] Third Worldism contains large elements of reality, usually mixed with exaggerations.

A man with roots in Islamic modernism who was also a pioneer in modern Islamist militance and a kind of proto-Third Worldism was Sayyid Jamal ad-Din "al-Afghani" (1839–1897), significantly of Iranian Shi'i birth and upbringing, who sensed the potential of militant Islamic identification as a wellspring of political action in the modern world. Afghani responded to prevailing moods as much as he directed them. Until the early 1880s his writings and talks were nearly all in the liberal and local nationalist vein with a strong dose of Islamic modernism and especially of hostility to British colonialism, the feature that stayed with him throughout his career. With the growth of Islamic identification in the Muslim world, coming especially after the Russo-Turkish war of 1877–1878, and Western occupation of Tunisia in 1881 and Egypt in

1882, Afghani joined with others who took up the cause of pan-Islamic unity against the menacing West.[10]

Reformist pan-Islamism, like Islamic modernism, was pioneered as an intellectual and reformist cause by the Young Ottomans and especially Namik Kemal, but once again, as with Islamic modernism, those who wrote in Arabic had more influence. Afghani, whose words were published in Arabic by Muhammad 'Abduh and other disciples, was particularly influential because he tied pan-Islamism to a strong stand against British encroachments in Muslim lands. Indeed, this anti-imperialist, proto-Third-Worldist approach may be said to be the most important element in Afghani's thought. It was an element that had increasing resonance after his death, and it is no accident that Afghani is the only important writer and speaker who was popular with liberal and nationalist thinkers and still retains his popularity with today's Islamists.

The failures of Islamic modernism and of secular nationalism were primarily failures of political and economic practice. The world failure is relative; in noncolonized countries like Turkey and Iran what is usually called secualr rule, with a strong nationalist element, got a strong start soon after World War I and had a number of notable successes. (In the United States the word secular tends to mean that state and church operate relatively freely in different spheres, whereas Atatürk, Reza Shah, and similar leaders in a number of countries did not dare let religious institutions operate freely, but instituted as much control over their activities by the state as they thought feasible.) A problem faced by regimes in Turkey and Iran and by the secular regimes of Nasser in Egypt and Bourguiba in Tunisia was that they did not meet the problems and discontents of the masses or the traditional petty bourgeoisie, who were precisely the people most tied to Islam and least convinced of the benefits of Westernized secularism. In other words, these rulers did not meet the felt economic and cultural needs of the masses, although Atatürk, given his personal role as leader of a victorious war against the West and the pre-1920 history of secularizing reforms in Turkey, had the greatest success. In large measure the successes of Islamism in the 1970s and 1980s occurred in reaction to failures of secular nationalist governments, such as those in Iran, Egypt, Turkey, and Tunisia.

ISLAM OR IRAN: WHICH ENCOURAGES REVOLUTION?

Although there is a tendency among recent writers to compare Iran's Islamic revolution with Islamist movements in other countries, with the implication that they too are likely to become more revolutionary or at least to take over governments, there are unique features of Iran's revolution that are rooted in Iranian history and are not duplicated anywhere else. Not so much Twelver Shi'ism as such, which began as a politically quietist movement without a clergy, but the evolution of Shi'ism and politics in Iran help explain Iran's revolutionary history. There are also other Iranian factors that help explain why Iran has had two major revolutions, in 1905–1911 and 1978–1979, important uprisings such as the Tobacco Movement of 1891–1892, uprisings after World War I and World War II, the Mosaddeq movement in the 1950s, and the Khomeinist movement of 1963.

These movements have made Iran the most revolutionary country in the Muslim world, comparable probably only to China on a world scale. Among the non-Islamic factors helping to explain this are Iran's position, like China, as a prize fought over by major powers, which helped destabilize both. In both countries there were heavy and divided Western interest, penetration, and even control without outright Western colonial rule. There are many differences between Iran and China, but, like China, Iran has had a strong sense of premodern national or cultural identity, combined with a strong rejection of foreigners. In Iran's case this rejection was strengthened by the greater insistence of Shi'ism than of Sunnism that unbelievers were unclean, reinforcing notions about the impurity of outsiders that go back to pre-Islamic times. Compared to other heavily penetrated Muslim countries of the Middle East, Iran also had a powerful Muslim merchant class, which was ready to compete with Western merchants and which influenced strongly both of Iran's revolutions.

Iranian Shi'ism was brought in as the state religion by the Safavids in 1501, and they favored forcible conversion to Shi'ism, partly because their Ottoman and Uzbek enemies in Turkey and central Asia were Sunni. Whereas the early Safavids largely controlled the religious hierarchy, this hierarchy became increasingly independent and wealthy over time. It made use of the institution of the mujtahid, which predated the Safavids but now became more important. Mujtahids, based on their religious and legal learning, were empowered to lay down interpretations of doctrine. According to what became the dominant school of thought, all believers had to follow a living mujtahid in doctrinal matters. Sunni ulama had no such powers. By the nineteenth century the school of thought that accorded this role to mujtahids became victorious in Iran.

At the same time, other developments strengthened clerical power. One was direct clerical collection of religious taxes, which in Sunni countries came to be mediated or taken over by the state. Another was the creation of a more hierarchical structure than in Sunni countries, with the top clerics from the 1720s to the 1920s living in Ottoman Iraq, away from the control of Iran's government, somewhat like the premodern Catholic church. In the nineteenth century some clerics began to be active in movements they saw as primarily directed against giving

Iran to unbelievers: the small but effective movement against the notorious all-encompassing Reuter concession (granted by the shah in 1872 for railway building, mining, and other "internal improvements"); a successful mass movement against a tobacco monopoly concession to a British subject in 1891–1892; and the constitutional revolution of 1905–1911, directed against a dynasty that had been too compliant to foreigners and not protective of the abode of Islam. Recent revisionist Iranian scholars, moved in part by hostility to Khomeini, have denied or played down the clerical role in these past movements. But, however much one may say that revolutionary thought and activity was initiated by merchants and intellectuals who used clerics because of their mass appeal, the very facts that the clerics were at a minimum willing to be so used and to speak out against rulers and were needed if the movement were to have mass appeal differentiates Iran in this respect from all other Muslim countries.

This Iranian and Iranian Shi'i background must be kept in mind in looking at the 1979 revolution and comparing it to Islamist movements elsewhere. The Khomeinists built upon the existing clerical and hierarchical structure in setting up a clerical organization that both entered politics and helped meet the felt needs of the urban masses even before the revolution.

Although the effects on the clerical structure of the years of the Pahlavi shahs have not been well studied, it seems that the structure itself was not weakened and may even have been tightened with the growth of the city of Qom as a top clerical center and the development there of educational and propaganda institutions. The idea of having a clerical leader as an oppositional political leader did not appear suddenly and without background in Iran, as it would have in most Sunni countries; clerical leaders and their decrees were involved in politics in the 1891 tobacco movement, in the 1905 constitutional revolution, largely but not always on the conservative side under Mosaddeq, and in the early 1960s. Although the Khomeinist phenomenon was a new one in Iran (none of the earlier clerics had spoken of Islamic rule, for example), it was not nearly as novel as it would have been in most Muslim countries. In those countries the idea of one or a few recognized religious leaders with the power to make statements on law, religion, and politics that all should follow would be without precedent.

Although the Shi'is of the world have followed Khomeini more than Sunnis have, it should be stressed that Iran's relatively tight hierarchy and its consequences for leadership are essentially novel for most Shi'is, too. Many Shi'is abroad have a general allegiance to Khomeini, but few non-Iranians, in practice, have the habit of following a single clerical leader on doctrinal matters. Many, as among the educated middle-class Pakistani Shi'is, insist that they do follow such leaders, but almost none that I interviewed could name any specific matter in which they did so.[11] The ulama are relatively unimportant in Pakistan and in many other Shi'i areas. To be sure, it is easier to mobilize Shi'is than Sunnis around a doctrine that can be presented with much justification as an international Shi'i doctrine, especially when it is embodied in a successful and charismatic leader like Khomeini, but this trend is a recent development under the impact of Khomeinism, rather than being an intrinsic feature of Shi'ism everywhere.[12] Non-Iranian adherence to top Shi'i leaders is, in practice, more tied to religious taxes or to Khomeini than it is to long-standing doctrines.

PAST ISLAM AND CONTEMPORARY ISLAM

Three actual or potential influences from past Islamic trends on contemporary Islamism, including the Khomeinist revolution, have been discussed above: first, precolonial and colonial militant jihad movements, directed in the precolonial period against indigenous rulers found insufficiently Islamic and in the colonial period against Western conquerors; second, Islamic modernists and related pan-Islamic militants; third, Shi'i political tradition as it evolved in Iran since 1500. What is the relation of these influences to contemporary militance and revolution?

What is most immediately striking about the eighteenth- and nineteenth-century jihad movements is how little relation they have to contemporary movements. Contemporary Islamism duplicates neither their tribal following nor their Sufi ties. And whereas the early movements tended to be on the peripheries of Islam, recent movements concentrate in the central areas that have experienced Westernized rule. The only modern Islamism with evident ties to the past is in the Sudan.

Nonetheless, these early movements have something to tell us that is relevant to contemporary Islamism. Both aim at overthrowing states found insufficiently Islamic and at installing Islamic states. Both stress what are seen as central Islamic themes, including veiling and regulating women and legislating various areas of individual morality. In addition, both are tied to the Western social and economic impact, in its economic disruptions and in threatening social customs ranging from the early regulation of slavery to the family. Finally, what stands out in viewing the whole range of movements from the eighteenth century to now is that, while they require appropriate socioeconomic and political circumstances in order to make their appearance, their vocabularies have a remarkable similarity that is not based on circumstances so much as on common knowledge of the Quran and Islamic traditions.

One recurrent way the movements meet a crisis, especially one associated with a Western or Westernizing disruptive threat, is to appeal to the eternal verities of the Quran, especially its regulation of women's status and moral issues like drinking and gambling. Not only are such appeals made frequently, but in rebellious or revolutionary situations they are generally accompanied by the idea that a return to true Islam and its rules will introduce a utopian society of equality and justice. Following Quranic rules is expected greatly to improve everyone's position. The eighteenth- and nineteenth-century movements show us the strength of basic Islamic themes, especially as defenses against unbelieving intrusions.

The second influence on contemporary Islamism, which generally followed the jihad movements in time, was that of Islamic reformism. Although the major reformists, except the borderline militant Afghani, are in bad repute with the Islamists, it is nonetheless true that it was the reformists who started the modern trend, used as much by today's Islamists as by anyone else, of picking and choosing from among early Islamic sources and then interpreting them to fit their own needs. Such choosing was known in premodern times, but not on such a vast scale. One may note that this habit is even more common in Islam than in other traditions, largely because the Quran is believed to be the literal word of God, so that there is not, say, a school of Quranic interpretation that talks of possible variance in its texts or refuses to accept some of the Quran's contents. What must be done is to work with the existing text. The most radical Muslim treatments of the Quran I have seen are by an Egyptian scholar and by a group of Sudanese called the Republican Brothers, who say that the legalistic Medinan suras of the Quran were intended for Muhammad's time only.[13]

Islamists interpret the texts almost as much as the modernists did, often using similar means. Tunisian Islamists, for example, including their biggest organization, the Islamic Tendency Movement (MTI), now calling themselves al-Nahda, had an original program that shows throughout the influence of Western reformism and radicalism, down to calling for "from each according to his ability, to each according to his work."[14] Radical or leftist Islamists, such as Ali Shariati, interpreted texts more radically than did most Islamic modernists, as in Shariati's reading of the Cain and Abel story in terms of class struggle.[15]

It is hard to avoid the conclusion, for which more evidence could be given, that what many Islamists most dislike about modernists is not so much the fact that they reinterpret the Quran and early Islam, but rather that they were often associated with the West and with a kind of upper middle class liberalism that did not meet the needs of the urban and rural masses and traditional bourgeoisie. Muhammad 'Abduh is rejected largely because of his association with the British government in Egypt; Afghani is acceptable because of his lifelong hostility to British rule in Muslim lands. Naturally, the Islamists have different interpretations of Islam than the modernists. Because they have reinstated some customs deemed Islamic, notably with regard to women and morality (including adding to the ways of circumventing the Quranic prohibition on interest), they are often seen as returning to early Islam. In fact, however, they are citizens of the modern world, making outstanding use, for example, of its means of communication and propaganda and calling for state and military structures that are fully contemporary. Islamism, like other fundamentalisms, can only be understood as a twentieth-century phenomenon.

It is the third past phenomenon, the evolution of modern political Shi'ism, that is clearly the most directly tied to an Islamist movement. It must be realized, however, that this evolution was essentially an Iranian phenomenon and that, partly as a result of this past history of political Shi'ism, Iran has had a unique development of Islamic revolution. As of today it seems unlikely that Iran's recent history of a mass revolution with clerical leadership will be emulated in any non-Shi'i country, and even in countries with a large Shi'i population it seems doubtful. Shi'i evolution was far from being the only cause of the Iranian revolution, and other causes have been analyzed elsewhere.[16] Briefly, one may note the widespread feeling that the Shah was a puppet of the United States and Great Britain, revulsion against his attempts to impose non-Islamic Western ways at high speed and against his attacks on the bazaar and religious classes, and socioeconomic disruptions including a growing income distribution gap. Most of these phenomena have been found in other oil-rich Middle Eastern countries, however, and it seems possible that the factor of Shi'i culture and organization helped tip the balance toward successful revolution.[17]

Once the revolution occurred it is not surprising that Shi'i populations in the Gulf, Lebanon, and Pakistan identified more with Khomeini than did Sunnis. As most of these populations are minorities, however, it is unlikely that they can mount successful revolutions, although they can campaign and have frightened their own governments into concessions.

In the Sunni world the influence of Khomeinism has declined since the first years of the Iranian revolution, especially now that the Iranians are often seen as anti-Arab and were unable to sustain their Gulf war victories. Among Islamist groups Khomeinism still has an appeal, but most of these groups seem to recognize that they cannot hope to follow the Iranian pattern of revolutionary organization.

PATTERNS OF MILITANT ISLAM

Outside Iran, there is no Islamic country today that appears to be on the verge of Islamist revolution, although such things may change very quickly. It is not even the case today that all Muslim countries have strong Islamist movements. In 1983-1986 I traveled widely in the

Muslim world and found that the countries visited were about evenly divided among those that had strong Islamist movements and those that did not.[18] In an article published in 1988 I wrote:

> The profile of countries with strong Islamist movements nearly always includes the following. The country should have had one or more nationalist governments which tried to unify the country by relying more on national than Islamic ideology. It should have experienced rapid economic development and dislocations, which have brought rapid urbanisation and visibly differential treatment for the urban poor and the urban rich. Although not all such countries have oil income, virtually all have profited from oil economies at least at second hand, and oil income has hastened the urbanisation and income gaps, corruption, and visible wealth for the few that have made many responsive to the Islamists' call for equity, simplicity, and honesty. In addition, countries ripe for Islamism have experienced a longer and more radical break with an Islamically-orientated past government and society than is true of a country like [North] Yemen. Most have experienced a heavy Western impact and control and Western and secularly orientated governments.[19]

Although this was written without reference to Algeria, it exactly fits Algeria, where Islamists won a majority in the June 1990 elections.

If, on the one hand, Iran is unique for reasons given earlier, on the other hand it can be grouped with the countries decribed by that profile. These countries include, among those I visited, Egypt, Tunisia, Nigeria, and Malaysia. The latter two have a slightly different Islamic profile, in that there are very large and economically advanced non-Muslim minorities and Islam and Islamism are means of increasing the power of the Muslims. All these examples reinforce the notion that Islamism is a contemporary force, designed in part to help bring the Muslim masses into politics armed with ideological tools efficient for mass mobilization and for combating the class-limited attempts of governments to imitate the West, usually under the banner of nationalism.

Both in Iran and elsewhere the class origins and position of Islamist leaders support the above social analysis. In Iran both Khomeini and his close followers in government tend to have rural or small town backgrounds, in contrast to the other great ayatollahs and other religious and political opponents of Khomeini, who tend to have a higher class background. A similar difference is often found among Islamists outside Iran. A typical Islamist activist in nearly all Muslim countries is a science or technology student or ex-student of rural background—a person likely both to be alienated by wealthy urbanites and to have the intellectual tools to combat the status quo and to enlist others in this struggle.[20]

Although Islamists have taken over no governments since the Iranian revolution, they have had an impact in many Muslim countries. Intellectual discussions lean more to Islamic themes than they did before. In Egypt the widespread appeal to authenticity or heritage has a strong Islamic component. When the Coptic secularist Louis Awad wrote critically of Afghani, many Egyptians of various views, including Islamists, entered the fray against him in a well-known controversy.[21]

Most dramatic has been the impact of Islamism on gender relations. Women's dress has become more covered nearly everywhere. In Cairo, where twenty years ago women widely wore Western clothing, they now wear a variety of headcoverings and "modest dress." Efforts to repeal modern legislation affecting women have succeeded in Iran and Sudan, but have been largely stopped elsewhere, including Pakistan and Egypt, where women and their allies have been active against such legislative moves. The election of Benazir Bhutto represented a new trend, although she was unable before she was ousted in 1990 to fulfill her promise to repeal measures prejudicial to women which did get through under Zia al-Haqq. Struggles are now mostly defensive rather than for new laws or rights. It must be realized that Islamists include many women who, along with their male counterparts, argue that women should be "separate but equal."[22] Most Islamists do not imagine they can return to the past regarding women but accept woman suffrage and women in parts of the labor force, for example. For some women, Islamist activity is their first entry into public life, and for some literalists Islam promises more rights than they now have.

Women's status and dress have been very visible symbols of Islamism, just as the Westernization of women's position was a visible symbol for Atatürk and the Pahlavis. In both cases the question of whether one wished to approach the West or be distant from it was crucial, although many other factors were and are involved.

For the present, it might be best to stop focusing on the apocalyptic question of whether Islamist revolutions are likely to succeed soon and to look rather at what Islamism has already meant in practice both in Muslim countries and, now, among Muslims in the West.[23] Instead of revolutionary change it is possible to imagine that the Iranian state will continue to become more like other states, while several Muslim states may see a continued growth of Islamist influences in their society, so that the gap between Iran and certain other societies may shrink. At the same time, secular nationalism and various forms of leftism are far from dead and might well experience a revival, perhaps in new form, in several countries. In addition, like past trends, Islamism, once it gets power or even influence, usually brings disillusionment—as has already happened to many in Iran—so that the trend to Islamism is not to be seen as a permanent one, even in countries calling themselves Islamic.

In this regard, Pakistan is most instructive. There, in 1985 and 1986, I met hardly anyone who identified as a supporter of the Zia government and met few who favored Islamic politics. The very existence of a not very popular state calling itself Islamic discouraged Islamic politics and encouraged secularism, and this could happen even where Islamic government was more popular to begin with than it was in Pakistan. The election of Benazir Bhutto in 1989 shows the vulnerability of Islamism in Pakistan, where Islamist calls against the election of a woman had little effect.

Just as the eighteenth- and nineteenth-century trends discussed above were not permanent, so today's intellectual and political spectrum will surely continue to change.

NOTES

This article summarizes some of the results of research done in several Muslim and non-Muslim countries since 1981. In the summers of 1983 and 1984, in all of 1985, and in the fall of 1986, I traveled to West and North Africa, Egypt, North Yemen, Tunisia, Pakistan, Indonesia, and Malaysia. In all these countries I interviewed many educated Muslim men and women with varying views. Some of my research has been presented in conference papers on particular topics and some has been published in articles. The material presented here may appear at greater length in the future in a book on militant Islam, past and present.

1. See Maziar Behrooz, "Elite Factionalism in the Islamic Republic of Iran and Khomeini's New Decrees (1987–88)," supplementary paper at a conference on Iran, the United States, and the USSR, University of Californis at Los Angeles, April 1988 (updated version forthcoming in *Middle Eastern Studies*), and Said Arjomand's unpublished paper on Khomeini's decree.

2. See the editor's introduction and the chapters by W. Montgomery Watt and Juan R. I. Cole in Nikki R. Keddie, ed., *Religion and Politics in Iran: Shi'ism from Quietism to Revolution* (New Haven, Conn.: Yale University Press, 1983) and the editors' introduction to Juan R. I. Cole and Nikki R. Keddie, eds., *Shi'ism and Social Protest* (New Haven, Conn.: Yale University Press, 1986).

3. W. Montgomery Watt, *Muhammad at Mecca* (Oxford: Clarendon Press, 1953); Watt, *Muhammad at Medina* (Oxford: Clarendon Press, 1956); Maxime Rodinson, *Mohammed* (London: Allen Lane, 1971). These views have been challenged by Patricia Crone and others.

4. See the works cited in note 2 and Moojan Momen, *An Introduction to Shi'i Islam* (New Haven, Conn.: Yale University Press, 1985).

5. On these eighteenth- and nineteenth-century movements, see Nehemia Levtzion's article in N. Levtzion and John O. Voll, eds., *Eighteenth Century Renewal and Reform in Islam* (Syracuse, N.Y.: Syracuse University Press, 1987); William Roff's article in William Roff, ed., *Islam and the Political Economy of Meaning: Comparative Studies of Muslim Discourses* (Berkeley: University of California Press, 1987); Nikki R. Keddie, "Militant Islamic Revivalism in the Eighteenth and Nineteenth Centuries: Comparative Reflections," unpublished conference paper.

6. John O. Voll, *Islam: Continuity and Change in the Modern World* (Boulder, Colo.: Westview Press, 1982); and Levtzion and Voll, *Eighteenth Century Renewal and Reform.*

7. See the classic work by Albert Hourani, *Arabic Thought in the Liberal Age (1792–1939)* (London: Oxford University Press, 1970).

8. Samir Amin, *Neocolonialism in West Africa* (New York: Monthly Review Press, 1973); André Gunder Frank, *Capitalism and Underdevelopment in Latin America* (New York: Monthly Review Press, 1968).

9. See Nikki R. Keddie, "Islamic Revival as Third Worldism," in *Le Cuisinier et le philosophe: Hommage a Maxime Rodinson*, ed. Jean-Pierre Digard (Paris: Maisonneuve et Larose, 1982).

10. See Nikki R. Keddie, *An Islamic Response to Imperialism* (Berkeley: University of California Press, 1983); and *Sayyid Jamal ad-Din "al-Afghani": A Political Biography* (Berkeley: University of California Press, 1972).

11. My interviews on this point concentrated on educated Shi'i men and women in Lahore, Karachi, and Islamabad and took place in 1985 and 1986.

12. On Shi'i movements throughout the world, see Cole and Keddie, *Shi'ism and Social Protest*; Martin Kramer, ed., *Shi'ism, Resistance, and Revolution* (Boulder, Colo.: Westview Press, 1987).

13. For the doctrines of the interesting, original, and underappreciated Sudanese Republican Brothers, see especially Mahmoud Mohamed Taha, *The Second Message of Islam*, trans. Abdullahi Ahmed An-Na'im. The similar views of an elderly Egyptian scholar I heard only orally.

14. This is in the original, 1981 program of the Tunisian Islamic Tendency Movement, reprinted, along with interviews of leading Islamists, in Nikki R. Keddie, "The Islamist Movement in Tunisia," *The Maghreb Review* 11, no. 1 (January–February 1986): 26–39. Since his release from prison in May 1988, Rashed Ghannoushi, the leader of the movement, has been even more conciliatory in his interpretations of Islam. After praising democracy, liberty, and tolerance, he said that Tunisia's Personal Status Code (formerly

opposed by his organization) had its spiritual foundations in Islam and "it is a valuable code to promote family relations." (*Al-Sabah*, Tunis, July 17, 1988.)

15. Ali Shariati, *Islam shenasi*, 2 (Tehran: Entesharat-e Qalam, 1362/ 1983–1984), 291–294. See also Ervand Abrahamian, "'Ali Shari'ati: Ideologue of the Iranian Revolution," in Edmund Burke III and Ira M. Lapidus, eds., *Islam, Politics, and Social Movements* (Berkeley: University of California Press, 1988).

16. See especially Nikki R. Keddie, *Roots of Revolution* (New Haven, Conn.: Yale University Press, 1981), and "Iranian Revolutions in Comparative Perspective," *American Historical Review* (June 1983): 579–598. Among the authors who have written about this are E. Abrahamian, S. Arjomand, S. Bakhash, and F. Halliday.

17. Henry Munson, Jr., *Islam and Revolution in the Middle East* (New Haven, Conn.: Yale University Press, 1988) makes interesting comparisons of similar features found in prerevolutionary Iran and other countries that did not have revolutions. He gives more weight to perceptions of Carter's human rights program than I would.

18. The countries considered were North Yemen, Syria, Pakistan, Indonesia, Senegal, Nigeria, Malaysia, Tunisia, and Egypt.

19. Nikki R. Keddie, "Ideology, Society and the State in Post-Colonial Muslim Societies," in Fred Halliday and Hamza Alavi, eds., *State and Ideology in the Middle East and Pakistan* (London: Macmillan, 1988), 17.

20. This profile was found in nearly all the countries I visited and is also widespread in the literature.

21. Rudi Matthee, "Jamal Al-Din Al-Afghani and the Egyptian National Debate," *International Journal of Middle East Studies* 21, no. 2 (May 1989): 151–169.

22. This phrase I have taken from U.S. constitutional history, but it applies well to gender arguments in the Muslim world. As with blacks in the United States, separate in practice means unequal. See Nikki R. Keddie and Beth Baron, eds., *Shifting Boundaries: Women and Gender in Middle Eastern History* (New Haven, Conn.: Yale University Press, 1991) Introduction.

23. On Islamism among migrants to France, see Gilles Kepel, *Les banlieues de l'Islam: naissance d'une religion en France* (Paris: Editions du seuil, 1987). Among the many other books on Islamism, see especially Gilles Kepel, *Muslim Extremism in Egypt: The Prophet and Pharaoh*, trans. Jon Rothschild (Berkeley: University of California Press, 1985); and Emmanuel Sivan, *Radical Islam: Medieval Theology and Modern Politics* (New Haven, Conn.: Yale University Press, 1985).

Chapter
14

How Consequential Are Revolutions?

The Latin American Experience

Susan Eckstein

Much is known about the conditions under which revolutions occur. Little, however, is known about the effects of revolution and what accounts for them. Advocates and opponents of revolutions alike presume that the upheavals usher in major change. But in what ways do societies develop differently after revolutions than before, and do societies that have had revolutions develop differently from societies that have never undergone cataclysmic changes?

This chapter offers some answers to these questions. First, some ways in which revolutions might be expected to modify the course of a country's development are hypothesized. Then, the explanatory power of the hypotheses is examined in light of twentieth-century Latin American experiences. By limiting the cases to the twentieth century and, in the main, to the period after World War II, "world time," or forces affecting all nations, can be "controlled for." By limiting the cases to Latin America, cultural and historical forces influencing continental options can similarly be "controlled" for. That is, the selection of cases holds critical factors constant that the wide-ranging comparisons dominating the literature do not.[1]

The hypotheses listed below do not include all factors that might possibly affect revolutionary outcomes. They nonetheless address factors that there is reason to believe—from the literature on revolutions and development—are particularly consequential. The factors considered do not operate independently of each other. To the extent that they are important, they shape outcomes of revolutions at different stages of the political process.

Hypothesis I: Postrevolutionary developments are shaped by the *productive capacities* and *trade vulnerability* of countries at the time of the upheavals and by *geopolitical dynamics* that may operate somewhat independently of economic strength.

Hypothesis II: Postrevolutionary developments are shaped by the class base of the insurrection.

Hypothesis III: Postrevolutionary developments are shaped by the *dominant mode of production* instituted and the *form of property ownership* associated with it.

Hypothesis IV: Postrevolutionary developments are affected by the *time lapse* since the upheaval.

Hypothesis V. Countries with regimes rooted in *revolution* develop differently from *nonrevolutionary* societies.

For reasons of space, the intellectual rationale for postulating each hypothesis is not presented here.[2]

The countries with revolutions to be examined are Mexico (1910), Bolivia (1952), Cuba (1959), Peru (1968), and Nicaragua (1979). These are the five countries in twentieth-century Latin America that experienced regime changes through extralegal means in which control of the state shifted to a new social class or socioeconomic group committed to economic modernization and the welfare of the "popular" sectors and where the New Order entailed a modification of class relations in at least some sector of the society. Accordingly, the countries meet the structural definition of revolution, centered on state-class changes, that I use.

The types of revolutions that the countries experienced differed in important respects. Peru had a revolution "from above" in that the extralegal takeover and the initiation of the social transformation were organized and led by high-level state functionaries with negligible mass participation. Peru's "revolution" was initiated in 1968 by General Velasco Alvarado, a top-ranking army officer. After assuming power by a coup d'état, he used the powers of the state to restructure the economy and society. The other countries experienced revolutions "from below," that is, the extralegal usurpation of state power had not only middle class support, but also peasant and worker support.

The types of political economies instituted after the revolutions also varied, somewhat independently of the social bases of the movements that led to the collapse of the old regimes. The nationalization of the Cuban economy wiped out the capitalist class and most of the independent petty bourgeoisie. In the other countries state ownership expanded after the upheavals and social relations of production changed in certain rural regions, but in none of them did class relations change to the extent that they did in Cuba. Nicaragua, like Cuba, was committed to socialist organizational and ideological principles under the Sandinistas, but the Central American country was a "mixed" economy (and their successors are dismantling the state sector).

The revolutions occurred in countries with different productive capacities and with different trade linkages to the world economy. For revolutionary-based regimes, in principle, the larger, more diverse, and more complex the economies they "inherit" and the less dependent they are on trade in a commodity commanding weak earnings in international markets, the greater will be their means to develop their economies and societies. Such structural factors as productive resources and global linkages are likely to shape options that new regimes have independently of the class base of the state-class transformations or the type of political economy instituted. Mexico was one of the most economically advanced Latin American countries in 1910 when its ancien régime collapsed. However, it probably then was still, in Immanuel Wallerstein's terminology, a "peripheral" country within the world economy.[3] By the time of the other twentieth-century Latin American revolutions, though, it had developed to the point of being a "semiperipheral" country, or what others would call "semi-industrial" or "newly industrial." Bolivia and Nicaragua, by contrast, were peripheral, trade-dependent societies when their revolutions took place. Peru and Cuba are more difficult to categorize. They had peripheral and semiperipheral characteristics when their state-class transformations occurred; their economies were more developed than Bolivia's and Nicaragua's, but not as large as Mexico's. Moreover, Cuba had a very trade-dependent economy.

The resource base and world economy theses thus lead us to expect different postrevolutionary development patterns in Mexico when compared to Bolivia and Nicaragua. It also leads us to expect postrevolutionary developments in Cuba and Peru to be fairly similar, somewhere "in between" the other countries. In Wallerstein's scheme, position in the world economy is of greater consequence than domestic class relations, property relations, and ideology in shaping government options.

Yet, if the class base of upheavals affects subsequent societal developments, independently of the productive base and trade linkages of regimes, as postulated in Hypothesis II, peasants and workers in the four countries experiencing revolutions from below—Mexico, Bolivia, Cuba, and Nicaragua—should have enjoyed benefits that their Peruvian counterparts did not. Peru, as noted above, is the only one of the countries to have had a revolution from above.

If (contrary to Wallerstein) the main form of economic ownership is of greater consequence than the productive base or the class base of the state-class transformations, then Mexico, Bolivia, and Peru should develop in ways that Cuba and, to a lesser extent, Nicaragua do not. Cuba, as already indicated, is the only country to have socialized most of its economy; Sandinista Nicaragua had a mixed economy, though its leadership and social base were committed to socialist economic and political principles. If the time lapse since the upheaval is important, the impact of revolution should be most apparent in Mexico and least apparent in Nicaragua.

Finally, there is reason to believe that revolutionary regimes, irrespective of their class base or dominant mode of production, are more concerned with development and distribution than the regimes they displace and are more concerned with such matters than governments with no revolutionary history. Revolutionary regimes are apt to try to improve the productive capacities of their economies, in part to increase resources available for the groups that helped "make" the revolutions. They should succeed if institutions impeding production are destroyed and removed from the control of groups with parochial and conservative economic interests in the course of the upheavals.

If forces rooted in revolution influence country developments in ways that nonrevolutionary forces do not, it will be apparent from changes in the regional rankings of all societies experiencing state-class transformations since their respective prerevolutionary periods. On quantifiable indicators the performance of the societies that have had state-class transformations can be ranked and traced over time relative to that of other countries in the region. If the revolutionary states register change, but the rankings of the countries remain unchanged, either revolutionary and evolutionary forces can have similar effects or the changes in the postrevolutionary societies reflect forces not specifically rooted in the sociopolitical transformations. In either case revolutions do not have a markedly distinguishable impact on the aspects of societal development under consideration.

Table 14.1 summarizes different patterning among the countries that would support each of the hypotheses under consideration, given the different histories and productive bases of the countries. The case studies involve (1) revolutions from above and below; (2) revolutions instituting capitalist and socialist modes of production based, respectively, on private and state (or cooperative) ownership of the economy; and (3) revolutions occurring in countries at different levels of economic development and differently integrated into the world economy. While only tentative empirical generalizations can be drawn from the experiences of five countries, comparisons with nonrevolutionary societies add to our ability to "tease out" how sociopolitical transformations modify the growth and distributional potentials of countries. The countries are

Table 14.1   SUMMARY OF CHANGES IN REGIONAL RANKINGS SINCE EACH REVOLUTION

	Mexico	Bolivia	Cuba	Nicaragua	Peru
Hypothesis I: Productive capacity, trade vulnerability, and geopolitical dynamics					
Most developed (semiperipheral)	X				
Intermediately developed (peripheral and semiperipheral characteristics)			X		X
Least developed (peripheral)		X		X	
Hypothesis II: Class base					
Revolution from above					X
Revolution from below	X	X	X	X	
Hypothesis III: Dominant mode of production and form of ownership					
Capitalist	X	X			X
Mixed				X	
Socialist			X		
Hypothesis IV: Time lapse					
Long	X				
Medium		X	X		X
Short				X	

compared on measures of economic modernization and national autarky (country growth and diversification, trade vulnerability, and foreign indebtedness) and measures of social welfare (land distribution and health standards).

ECONOMIC EXPANSION AND DIVERSIFICATION

Since World War II Latin American countries have been concerned not only with expanding but also with diversifying their economies. Domestic industrialization, it came to be believed, would make the countries less vulnerable to, and less dependent on, adverse foreign market conditions than their previous trade-oriented economies. Industrialization also came to be viewed as a sign of modernity. When import-substitution industrialization created a balance of payments crisis, owing to the neglect of exports to offset the costs of needed industrial inputs, Latin American countries modified their economic priorities. They remained committed to industrialization, but tried to generate foreign exchange by exporting industrial products as well as other goods and services.

In principle, the larger and more diversified a country's economic base, the higher the living standards of its people can be and the more influence a government can wield in the international as well as domestic arena. Gross national production data, in the aggregate, and by sector, provide a basis for evaluating how successful countries have been at expanding and diversifying their productive capacities.

Four of the five countries expanded their economic base since removing old regime "fetters." The improvements are reflected in both GDP and GDP per capita data, through the mid 1980s (Table 14.2). Only Nicaragua experienced a decline on both measures. It should be remembered that Nicaragua's revolution was the most recent of the five. During a comparable period following the fall of the Porfirio Diaz dictatorship, for example, the Mexican economy was still in turmoil. With the Sandinista electoral defeat in 1990 the economy may improve, owing to a more favorable international environment.

The factors accounting for Nicaragua's difficulties under the Sandinista regime were numerous. They can be traced to the weak economic base on which the Sandinistas had to build, limited external support at the same time that the United States acted to destabilize the economy, and problems rooted in a "mixed" economy. Business was reluctant to invest, given the precarious state of the economy and fears of nationalization, and the state sector was plagued by bureaucratic problems and the politicization of entrepreneurial activity. Workers left skilled, productive jobs for more lucrative black market activity. Meanwhile, the anti-Sandinista contras, financed and trained by the United States, disrupted production and forced the Sandinistas to institute a draft that exacerbated labor shortages and diverted scarce resources from social and productive investments to military concerns. Approximately 40 percent of the national budget purportedly went to military activity. The ousting of the Sandinistas in 1990 may usher in economic improvements, especially because the United States wants the Violeta Barrios de Chamorro government to succeed.

Although the four other countries experiencing revolutions can claim improvements in their productive capacities in the aggregate and on a per capita basis, their economic performances are not impressive compared with those of other countries in the region. Cuba is the only one to have improved its regional GDP ranking, and its ranking improved only by one place; and Cuba and Bolivia are the only countries to have improved their regional GDP per capita ranking. Moreover, the improvements in Cuba and Bolivia are not sufficiently great to conclude, with confidence, that either country has benefited on these measures from revolution. The improvements may merely be a function of national differences in currency conversions (artificial official exchange rates) and in bases of national product compilations. Indeed, Cuba's economic performance has been the subject of great dispute.[4]

Bolivia's economic performance is indeed unimpressive from a regional perspective, given how much foreign assistance it received during the first decade of the new regime. It received more per capita economic assistance from bilateral (United States) and multilateral sources than any other Latin American country. Although the United States government does not typically finance revolutions, once it recognized the noncommunist bent of the MNR (National Revolutionary Movement) leadership, it offered extensive aid to the fledgling government.

Cuba's economic performance might also seem unimpressive given the amount of Soviet aid it has received. It has received, in most years under Castro, significant sugar and nickel price subsidies as well as technological transfers and development and balance-of-payments aid. Official Western sources, however, overestimate the sugar subsidy (by comparing Soviet prices with world market prices, rather than with the subsidized prices at which most Western sugar is traded, and by using official peso-dollar exchange rates) and they underestimate the costs of the "tied" nature of Soviet aid (that is, the high cost and poor quality of Soviet imports that must be purchased with the rubles received for Cuban exports). A full assessment of Soviet aid must also take into account the opportunities thereby forgone, namely, the consequent loss of aid from and trade with the United States.

More than the improved GDP and GDP per capita ranking of Cuba, and, in the mid 1980s, the GDP per capita ranking of Bolivia, the most significant change revealed in Table 14.2 is the plunge in Peru's GDP per capita ranking. Peru ranked eighth in Latin America on the measure before Velasco's "elite revolution;" by 1986 it had dropped to fifteenth. The rise in support for guerrilla movements in Peru in the 1980s has undoubtedly been fueled by the deterioration in living standards. Peru's problems were compounded in the late 1980s by a cut-off of new foreign loans; the IMF prevented the country from gaining access to new lines of credit as punishment for the government's refusal, under President Alan García, to allocate more than 10 percent of export earnings to repay foreign loans.

The aggregate economic growth that has occurred in four of the countries with revolutionary histories has been linked, in part, to industrialization (Table 14.3). Data on value added in manufacturing and on

Table 14.2 GDP (GROSS DOMESTIC PRODUCT) AND GDP PER CAPITA (MILLIONS OF 1980 DOLLARS) AND LATIN AMERICAN (LA) RANKING ON EACH MEASURE

	Mexico	LA rank	Bolivia	LA rank	Cuba	LA rank	Nicaragua	LA rank	Peru	LA rank
					GDP[a]					
1950	18,821.4	2	1,127.0	12	4,815	9	626.3	20	4,854.4	7
1955	26,341.6	1	1,209.4	12	5,555	9	932.8	20	6,525.9	7
1960	34,994.9	2	1,260.0	14	6,235	8	1,044.4	16	8,393.9	6
1965	49,354.1	1	1,477.4	14	7,190	8	1,687.5	18	11,131.7	7
1970	68,928.7	2	2,048.6	14	7,414	8	2,036.3	15	13,716.9	6
1975	90,853.2	2	2,720.7	14	10,810	8	2,667.5	18	17,896.7	6
1980	130,613.7	2	3,183.0	17	14,159	8	2,219.4	19	18,358.0	6
1985	141,554.2	2	2,824.7	14	22,549[d]	—	2,291.0	19	17,943.6	8

316

GDP Per Capita[a]

Year										
1950	710.8	5	372.3	17	836	9	582.2	19	604.5	10
1955	811.7	5	357.8	19	871	10	750.1	14[b]	732.0	9
1960	907.1	5	382.5	19	887	6	694.9	11	808.3	8
1965	1,096.9	5	346.5	19	921	10	1,026.4	12	952.2	8
1970	1,306.1	6	477.0	19	867	12	1,067.3	8	1,013.9	9
1975	1,461.0	3	554.4	18	1,158	8	1,188.9	16	1,164.7	11
1980	1,863.0	4	568.4	19	1,455	9	916.3	16	1,100.7	12
1986[c]	1,640.2	5	414.8	16	2,199[d,e]	—	770.3	18	1,001.6	15

[a]Information for all twenty countries for all years, except Cuba 1985. In ranking countries on GDP per capita in 1986, Cuba is assumed to have the same rank as in 1980. The rankings of countries for 1950, 1955, 1960, 1965, and 1975 are based on GDP data in 1970 dollars and for 1985 and 1986 on data in 1986 dollars (except in the case of Cuba).

[b]Tied with one other country.

[c]Preliminary.

[d]Constant 1981 pesos; peso conversion is based on 1981 year-end official exchange rate. The 1985 data estimate the Gross Social Product (larger than market-economy GDP estimates).

[e]Economic data for 1985; population data for mid 1986.

Sources: Claes Brundenius, *Measuring Economic Growth and Income Distribution in Revolutionary Cuba*, Research Policy Studies, Discussion Paper 130 (Lund, Sweden: Research Policy Institute, Lund University, 1979), 14; Brundenius, *Revolutionary Cuba: The Challenge of Economic Growth and Equity* (Boulder, Colo.: Westview Press, 1984), 39, 145; Inter-American Development Bank (IDB), *Economic and Social Progress in Latin America* (Washington, D.C.: IDB, 1983), 345, (1987), 426; James Wilkie and Stephen Haber, *Statistical Abstract of Latin America*, vol. 21 (Los Angeles: University of California, Latin American Center, 1981), 274–277; Susan Eckstein, "Revolutions and the Restructuring of Local Economies: The Latin American Experience," *Comparative Politics*, July 1985, 474; Economist Intelligence Unit (EIU) *Country Profile, Cuba* (1987–1988): 5, 8; James Wilkie and David Lorey, *Statistical Abstract of Latin America*, vol. 25 (Los Angeles: University of California, Latin American Center, 1987), 748.

317

Table 14.3 MANUFACTURING: TOTAL VALUE, SHARE OF GDP, AND METAL AND MACHINE INDUSTRIES AS PERCENT OF TOTAL MANUFACTURING PRODUCTION, AND LATIN AMERICAN (LA) RANKING ON EACH MEASURE

	Mexico	LA rank	Bolivia	LA rank	Cuba	LA rank	Nicaragua	LA rank	Peru	LA rank
	Total Value of Manufacturing (in millions of 1980 $ U.S.)[a,b]									
1950	4,153.1	3	172.8	14	—	—	62.6	17	729.0	7
1955	5,515.8	3	222.5	14	1,166.4[c]	6	102.6	16	980.0	8
1960	7,124.5	2	160.0	14	3,286.2[c,d]	4	145.4	17	2,170.1	7
1965	10,334.9	2	211.4	16	3,575.4[c]	4	303.7	13	2,228.8	7
1970	16,827.9	2	296.4	17	4,619.0[c]	4	416.3	14	3,822.8	6
1975	22,667.0	2	411.5	17	7,052.0[c]	4	554.6	15	5,037.5	6
1980	32,532.1	2	507.3	17	8,425.4[c]	4	556.8	16	4,529.3	6
1985	34,735.0	2	302.5	17	12,793.3[c,e]	3	580.8	15	3,897.8	8
	Manufacturing as Percent of GDP/GSP									
1950	21	2[f]	15	13[g]	—	—	10	16[f]	15	13[g]
1955	21	3[f]	18	9	21	3[g]	11	15	15	6[c]
1960	19	2[g]	14	14[g]	45[h]	1	16	9[f]	18	6[f]
1965	21	4	15	13[g]	43[h]	1	18	7[f]	20	5[g]
1970	23	4	13	19	47	1	19	7	21	5
1975	24	3	14	17[f]	40	1	19	7[f]	23	4[g]
1980	25	4	15	18	41	1	26	3	25	5
1985	25	4	10	19	44	1	25	2	22	6

Metal and Machine Industries as Percent of Total Manufacturing Production[i]

Year										
1960	12.6	5	—	—	5.2	12[c]	2.0	17	—	—
1965	17.8	4	—	—	4.7	15[g]	6.1	9	—	—
1970	20.0	4	20	1.2	6.4	15[g]	6.9	13[g]	6.8	14
1975	21.1	2	19	2.3	13.2	7	8.1	12	17.1	4
1980	21.3	4	19	3.6	8.8	12	4.2	17	10.8	9
1984	17.3	4	20	1.3	9.8	7	4.6	14	7.9	12

[a] Value added by manufacturing for 1960, 1970, 1975, 1980, and 1985. Estimates for 1950, 1955, and 1965 are calculated on basis of manufacturing as percent of GDP (in constant 1980 $).

[b] Latin American ranking: data for 16 countries for 1950, 17 countries for 1955, and 20 countries for all other years. Countries without data for a given year are assumed to have the same ranking as in the succeeding year with data.

[c] Includes mining and electricity; 1981 prices.

[d] 1961.

[e] Estimates based on first eleven months of 1985.

[f] Tied in rank with two other countries.

[g] Tied in rank with one other country.

[h] Includes mining, petroleum, and quarrying.

[i] Latin American ranking: data for 15 countries for 1960, 14 countries for 1965, 17 countries for 1975, and 20 countries for 1970, 1980, and 1984. Countries without data for a given year are assumed to have the same ranking as in the succeeding year with data.

Sources: James Wilkie and Peter Reich, *Statistical Abstract of Latin America*, vol. 19 (Los Angeles: University of California, Latin American Center, 1978), 247–248, (1980), 258; Brundenius, *Measuring Economic Growth*, 6–7; Brundenius, *Revolutionary Cuba*, 39, 145; Brundenius, "Development and Prospects of Capital Goods Production in Revolutionary Cuba," in Andrew Zimbalist, ed., *Cuba's Socialist Economy: Toward the 1990s* (Bounder, Colo.: Lynne Rienner, 1987), 100; Carmelo Mesa-Lago, *The Economy of Socialist Cuba: A Two-Decade Appraisal* (Albuquerque: University of New Mexico Press, 1981), 56; United Nations, Economic Commission on Latin America (UN-ECLA), *Statistical Yearbook for Latin America, 1979* (New York: United Nations, 1981), 76, and *Economic Survey of Latin America and the Caribbean, 1985* (Santiago, Chile: UN-ECLA, 1987), 222, 239; *Statistical Yearbook for Latin America and the Caribbean* (New York: United Nations, 1987); IDB, *Economic and Social Progress* (1981), 405, (1983), 349, (1987), 43, 50; World Bank (WB), *World Development Report (WDR)* (New York: Oxford University Press, 1987), 214.

industry's share of the national product both indicate that the countries with revolutionary histories forged ahead with import-substitution industrialization, at least until the 1980s. In the 1980s austerity policies, implemented also under pressure from the IMF, adversely affected industry. Industry suffered in the 1980s especially in Bolivia and Peru.

The accomplishments of revolution on this measure of economic performance, however, prove in the long run to be little better than on GDP from a comparative perspective. In the short run revolutions seem to have done more to stimulate industry, in good part because new regime redistributive policies (discussed below) fostered demand-based growth at the same time that investment, trade, and exchange rate policies favored industry over agriculture. Cuba again is the only one of the five countries with revolutionary histories to have its regional value added ranking improve between the period immediately preceding the state-class transformation and the mid 1980s. Bolivia's and Peru's rankings have actually declined over the years while Nicaragua's stayed the same. Peru's had improved under Velasco's revolutionary military junta; however, when Velasco and then a more conservative military government were succeeded by democratically elected governments in the 1980s, the country's industrial performance took a nosedive relative to that of other countries in the region.

Bolivia also experienced what might be considered an industrial boomlet—in the context of the country's history as an export-oriented mining enclave—during the first few years of revolutionary rule. The MNR government stimulated industrial production by instituting protective tariffs, selectively allotting access to scarce foreign exchange (largely on the basis of political patronage), and by broadening the domestic market for manufactures with a land reform. Yet before the MNR was ousted by a conservative military coup in 1964, industrial production fell. The country's regional ranking in industrial output never recuperated to that of the prerevolutionary and early revolutionary periods, even when industrial output picked up.

The deterioration in Bolivia's industrial performance came with an IMF stabilization program, backed by the United States, in 1956. The program benefited the export sector but forced the government to terminate tariffs that protected local industry; under the circumstances fledgling firms could no longer withstand foreign competition. The military governments, which ruled most years between 1964 and the 1980s, allied with the trade-oriented elite; they accordingly backed the types of policies encouraged by the stabilization program. When the military returned to the barracks in the 1980s, industry did not revive, initially (under President Siles Zuazo) because of domestic unrest and economic chaos and subsequently (under President Paz Estenssoro) because the civilian government's political base differed little from that of the previous military governments. Thus, the industrial marginalization of Bolivia results from a combination of global and domestic political and economic forces.

Our first two industrial indicators together suggest that revolution had its greatest impact on economic diversification in Cuba. Mexico also registered impressive industrial gains, and the country ranks among those in the region with the highest degree of industrialization. Moreover, postrevolutionary Mexican governments pioneered in legislation to carve out a role for domestic capital, both private and public, and the country experienced in the 1950s one of the highest industrial growth rates in the world. However, were comparative data available for the turn of the century, before Porfirio Díaz's dictatorship collapsed, we would undoubtedly see that Mexico already ranked among the most industrial countries in the region. It also took Mexico some twenty-five years after the fall of the ancien régime before its industry "took off."

The improved postrevolutionary regional ranking of only Cuba on the two measures of industrialization suggests that the state and societal restructuring associated with socialism may allow more rapid economic diversification than capitalism. Nicaragua's ranking on industrial output was the same in 1985 as in the decade before, and its ranking on industry's GDP contribution rose during the same 10 year period. The improvements appear to give added evidence that socialism allows governments to intervene in ways that boost industrialization. However, Nicaragua's industrial performance had barely recuperated by the mid 1980s from the damages caused by the civil war, and it had expanded much more under Somoza than under the Sandinistas (thanks in part to the Central American Common Market, then in effect). Moreover, by the late 1980s the economy in general, including industry, was in disarray.

As impressive as Cuban industrial expansion may be, island manufacturing output continues to pale in comparison to Mexico's and that of such other semiperipheral countries such as Brazil. Yet Cuban industrialization under Castro is noteworthy, especially given the typical U.S. portrayal of Cuba as a "basket case" and a monoproduct export economy.

Cuba's impressive industrial performance is partly a function of the changes under Castro in the bases of national product calculations.[5] Comparative assessments of Cuba's performance are made difficult by problems of artificial exchange rates, valuation of industrial activity, and inclusion of mining in aggregate industrial data. Because no uniform pre- and postrevolutionary measure exists for assessing either the national product or industry's contribution to the national product, and because no consensus exists among economists concerning Cuba's general economic performance, data on changes in output within the industrial sector are more revealing.

The metal and machine sector in particular reflects a nation's ability to develop modern industry with "forward linkage" potential, that is, to stimulate other economic (including other industrial) activity and minimize dependence on foreign capital inputs for light industry. Four of the five countries under study expanded this sector's contribution to manufacturing output between the latest prerevolutionary and latest postrevolutionary year with data. However, the contribution of the sector tapered off in most of the countries in the 1980s, undoubtedly because the sector was adversely affected by the debt crises and austerity policies implemented to address the debt crises. Debt-ridden countries were forced to constrict imports needed for production in the sector. In the 1980s the sector's role in industrial output expanded only in Cuba and Nicaragua, and in both countries its contribution then was less than in the mid 1970s. On this indicator of industry as well, Nicaragua has yet to recuperate to levels attained under Somoza.

Despite the increased presence of the metal and machine sectors until the economic crises of the 1980s, comparative data suggest that revolutions do not spur this industrial activity more than evolutionary forces. Only Mexico, Cuba, and Peru improved their regional ranking on the measure of industrialization. The two countries with especially dynamic metal and machine sectors from a regional vantage point were Peru, under Velasco's revolutionary military government, and Cuba. One reason Peruvian industry improved under Velasco (especially between 1968 and 1972) is that its metal and machine sector expanded. Although the regime met considerable resistance, above all from multinational corporations, to aspects of its industrial reforms, its anti-Oligarchy policies encouraged investment in industry.

In Cuba the metal and machine sector expanded dramatically in the first half of the 1970s, to the point that available data indicate that the island's regional ranking rose from fifteenth to seventh in a five-year period. The impressive jump was a by-product of heavy state emphasis on investment (versus consumption) in the late 1960s. But it also resulted, paradoxical as it may seem, from the impact of high world market sugar prices in the 1970s. Despite Cuba's COMECON trade links, economic opportunities continue to be affected by global market conditions. Castro "seized the opportunity" that favorable world market conditions permitted during the early 1970s. The government invested the surplus and Western financing to which it gained access at the time, in capital-intensive industry. However, for reasons to be explained, the borrowing that spurred industrialization contributed to a debt crisis in the late 1970s.

Cuban industrialization, of course, cannot be attributed merely to clever use of a "market opening." Cuban industry also benefited from Soviet (and, to a lesser extent, other COMECON) aid. According to available information, approximately three-fourths of Soviet technical and economic assistance for development during the first thirteen years of Castro's rule went to industry, and programs that the Soviets assisted in the early 1980s accounted for 10 percent of total Cuban industrial production.[6] The Soviets have assisted the most technologically sophisticated sectors, including steel, machine building, sheet metal, and electric power. They have drawn upon a variant of their own economic development model, which historically emphasized heavy over light industry, in their dealings with Cuba.

Foreign assistance per se does not distinguish Cuba from other countries in the region. Industry in other Latin American countries also benefited from foreign assistance, though the form of capital assistance differed. The market economies were heavily dependent on foreign direct investment until the mid 1970s, and then on bank capital. Initially light industry and only recently basic industries received major foreign funding. In the market economies, foreign assistance, especially from private sources, has hinged primarily on profit considerations, with profits often repatriated. In Cuba, by contrast, profits generated by Soviet-assisted firms did not leave the country, and the Soviets did not necessarily base their aid on profit considerations.

Foreign direct investment was probably greater in Cuba than in all but one other Latin American country before Castro took power. Consequently, the island undoubtedly would have industrialized had the revolution not occurred. Yet there is no reason to believe that Cuba's regional ranking in industrialization in general and in metal and machine production in particular would have improved to the extent that it did in the absence of the sociopolitical transformation. The capitalist countries in the region where industry is concentrated have larger internal markets than Cuba; much of the impetus for industrialization in Latin America until recently has been rooted in domestic demand.

REDUCTION OF TRADE VULNERABILITY

International trade is one of the most important elements of the world economic system, and trade is one of the foremost mechanisms contributing to Third World vulnerability to external forces. The composition of exports and the export–national product ratio reflect the extent of trade vulnerability. The greater the diversity of exports, the less prey a country is to international price fluctuations of any single item; and the more a country diversifies from the commodity to the industrial export market, the more stable its export earnings and the more favorable its terms of trade are likely to be. While a country's import capacity will depend on its export earnings, as the role of exports in the national product declines, a country will be less adversely affected by unfavorable global conditions.

Revolutions in no predictable way affect a country's capacity to reduce trade dependence on a single export item (Table 14.4). Mexico and, to a lesser extent, Nicaragua have become more dependent on the export of a single product, and Bolivia, Cuba, and Peru less so. Moreover, although Bolivia and Cuba are now less dependent on a single export item than at the time of the collapse of their old regimes, they remain, since their prerevolutionary days, among the most monoproduct in the region. From a regional vantage point it even appears that all five countries have been adversely affected by revolution: the regional ranking in mono-product export dependence of the five countries rose after the upheavals. This finding is striking given the concern revolutionary regimes have had with global vulnerability. The increased trade vulnerability of the countries experiencing revolutions is also reflected in the data on industrial exports. Although four of the five countries expanded industry's role in exports (Bolivia and Cuba only minimally), the regional ranking of four of the countries on the trade measure deteriorated.

Mexico, with one of Latin America's most diversified export profiles in the 1950s, by 1980 was one of the most monoproduct. The shift came with the discovery of large new oil fields. The postrevolutionary state played a leading role in developing the petroleum industry, having nationalized it in the 1930s, as the new regime consolidated. However, it also benefited from high world market prices that coincided with its oil reserve discoveries. The profitability of oil led to the neglect of other exports. Consequently, when the price of oil in international markets fell in the mid 1980s, Mexico was faced with a foreign exchange crisis and less competitive alternative exports than in previous decades. Indicative of the neglect of other exports, Mexico dropped from producing 30 percent of the region's capital goods exports in 1970 to only 15 percent in the early 1980s.[7] Mexico's semiperipheral status has not made it immune to monoproduct export concentration and the adverse economic effects of downturns in world commodity prices.

One of the major moves of the Bolivian revolutionary government, upon assuming power, was to nationalize the main tin mines, to destroy the economic and political base of the prerevolutionary tin-based oligarchy. Since then tin's role in exports has declined markedly. However, this occurred more because of depleted reserves and the collapse of the world tin market than because of successful export diversification (at least of legal exports, which official statistics record).[8] The discovery of oil fields boosted petroleum exports later in the decade, but the depletion of those reserves left the government, by the 1980s, primarily dependent on natural gas exports and a limited market for the commodity.

Although data suggest that Cuba, like Bolivia, reduced its monoproduct export dependence, the decline is also partly attributable to low world market prices for its main tradable commodity as distinct from export diversification. The low level of export diversification reflects Cuba's inability to find markets for nonsugar products, owing largely to global geopolitical dynamics and, surprising as it may seem, to Soviet trade policy. Cuba should not be blamed to the extent that it typically is in the United States for its continued monoproduct export dependence; it is, in the main, the victim of forces beyond its control. Both Western and Soviet bloc countries have been resistant to buying industrial goods from Cuba, though for somewhat different reasons. To the extent that COMECON countries have imported industrial goods, they have preferred the higher quality of Western manufactures. Cuba's trade problem will be compounded with the collapse of the Communist regimes in Eastern Europe, although by the end of the 1980s Cuba began to serve as a *maquiladora* for the Soviets, assembling electronic products for their market. The United States, the main consumer of Latin American industrial exports, refuses to trade with Cuba for political reasons.

The greater success of most other Latin American countries in expanding their industrial exports and Cuba's inability to move into the industrial export market reflect not only superpower trade policies, but also multinational corporation global strategies. Faced with balance of payment crises and debt crises, Latin American governments have offered tax and other incentives to attract foreign investors to their export sectors. Though the Castro government has tried to do so as well, its efforts have proved to no avail.[9]

In the West Cuba has had difficulty finding buyers not only for manufactured goods but also for its expanded nickel industry. The United States refuses to purchase the mineral from Cuba, and its refusal to purchase industrial goods that contain Cuban nickel from other countries makes the Cuban product unattractive to nations seeking to sell nickel-based goods to the United States.

Cuba's inability to diversify exports thus shows how global dynamics constrict the possibilities of revolutionary regimes to restructure their economies. Domestic changes in ownership and control of production and economic priorities may be of little consequence when world powers do not cooperate. Cuba's commitment to socialism has marginalized the island from Western export options.

Nonetheless, at the same time that revolutions have had no uniformly positive effect on export diversification, they appear to help countries reduce the role of exports in the economy (as reflected in

Table 14.4 EXPORTS AND LATIN AMERICAN (LA) RANKING ON EACH MEASURE

	Mexico	LA rank	Bolivia[a]	LA rank	Cuba	LA rank	Nicaragua	LA rank	Peru	LA rank
				Main Export as Percent of Total Exports[b]						
1950	—	—	—	—	89.2	—	—	—	—	—
1955	29.2	17	66.5	8[c]	79.6	4	38.7	16	25.1	19
1960	20.7	19	81.3	2	79.4	3	30.6	16	21.9	18
1965	18.9	20	84.9	3	86.2	2	44.4	13	23.3	19
1970	8.8	20	56.8	5[c]	76.8	2	19.2	19	28.0	16
1975	15.8	19	38.7	8	89.1	2	25.4	14	22.5	15
1980–1982[d]	70.4	2	37.3[i]	9	82.7	1	31.2	11	16.6	18
1984–1986[j]	52.6	7	55.5	5	73.9[e]	2	34.1	11	15.7	18
				Exports and Nonfinancial Services as Percent GDP[f,g]						
1950	14.1	13	—	—	31.9	2	30.2	3[c]	20.4	8[c]
1955	16.7	12	—	—	26.7	4	27.4	3	20.1	9
1960	10.3	18	12.9	16	22.9[h]	6	23.6	5	23.7	4
1965	9.3	18	17.3	9	16.7	11	30.3	3	18.0	8
1970	8.2	18	20.0	8	25.0	5[c]	27.5	3	19.7	9
1975	7.7	18	21.1	11	33.2	3[c]	28.8	7	12.4	17
1979–1981[d]	9.1	18	16.5	15	27.9	4	30.0	4	17.6	13
1984–1986	12.5	18	28.9	5	21.8[e]	9	17.8	13	17.0	14
				Exports of Manufactures as Percent of FOB Value of Total Exports of Goods[i]						
1960	12.6	2	.1	17[c]	—	—	5.6	4[c]	.8	15

1965	15.9	2	.7	18[c]	4.0	13	4.9	10	.8	16[c]
1970	27.0	3	.5	18	—	—	15.6	5	1.4	14
1975	36.4	1	.6	19	—	—	14.9	9	3.8	13
1980	11.3	12	1.9	18	2.9	17	13.8	10	16.7	9
1984–1985	20.6	6	.6	19	4.2[j,e]	17	8.3	13	13.4	11

[a]Exports would assume greater importance, especially in the 1970s and 1980s, if illegal coca and cocaine exports were included in official statistics. Data on export concentration refer to legal exports only.

[b]Latin American ranking: information for all 20 countries for all years.

[c]Tied with one other country.

[d]For Cuba, 1980 data.

[e]Preliminary.

[f]National product in current GDP or GNP prices for all countries besides Cuba. In Cuba national product calculations are based on GNP estimates in current prices for 1950 and 1955 and on GMP estimates in current prices for all subsequent years except 1985. Since GMP is a conservative estimate of GDP, Cuba's export–national product ratio is higher than it would be if GDP estimates were used. Cuban 1985 calculations are based on GSP estimates, which are larger than GMP estimates; however, GSP, like GMP, excludes important services, such as education, health, and other government services.

[g]Latin American ranking: information for 17 countries for 1950, 19 countries for 1955, and all 20 countries for other years. Countries without data for a given year are assumed to have the same ranking as in the succeeding year with data. The higher the country rank, the higher the export–national product ratio. The Cuban data refer exclusively to the value of commodity exports; data on other countries refer also to the value of nonfinancial services.

[h]1961.

[i]Latin American ranking: information for 18 countries for 1960, 1970, and 1975; for 19 countries for 1965 and 1980; and for 17 countries for 1984–1985. Countries without data for a given year are assumed to have the same ranking as in the most proximate year with data.

[j]Unspecified exports, that is, not exclusively manufactured goods.

Sources: WB, World Tables (Baltimore: Johns Hopkins University Press, 1980), 34–211; WB, WDR (1980), 124–125, (1987), 222–223; WB, World Atlas (Washington, D.C.: WB, 1980); Wilkie and Reich, Statistical Abstract (1980); Wilkie and Haber, Statistical Abstract (1981), 424; Wilkie and Lorey, Statistical Abstract (Los Angeles: University of California, Latin American Center, 1987), 412; William LeoGrande, "Cuban Dependency: A Comparison of Pre-Revolutionary and Post-Revolutionary Cuban International Economic Relation," Cuban Studies 9 (July 1979): 6, 7, 9; Mesa-Lago, Economy of Socialist Cuba 34, 79, 81, UN-ECLA, Economic Survey of Latin America, 1963 (New York: UN, 1965), 268, 273; UN-ECLA, Statistical Yearbook for Latin America, 1979 (New York: UN, 1981), 77, and UN-ECLA, Economic Survey (1987), 232; UN-ECLA, Statistical Yearbook (1987), 108; IDB, Economic and Social Progress (1983), 108, 116, (1986), 394, 396 (1987), 121, 129; Brundenius, Revolutionary Cuba, 75; Brundenius, "Development and Prospects," 101; Banco Nacional de Cuba (BNC), Informe economico (Havana: BNC, 1982), 15, 31.

export–national product ratios). Bolivia is the only postrevolutionary society to have exports increase their weight in the economy (at least since 1960), and the only one of the five countries that did not reduce its regional export–national product ranking. The improvement in the export–national product rankings of the other four countries may reflect a distinctive nationalist and developmental bent of revolutions and the capacity of postrevolutionary states to influence production for the domestic market if not for export. Yet no revolution has significantly modified the historical advantage that large countries have: Their economies are large relative to their export sector.

As Latin American countries have accumulated uncontrollable foreign debts in the latter 1970s and 1980s, the emphasis on import substitution created new economic problems. As a consequence, one of the accomplishments of revolution has proved to be a liability.

FOREIGN PUBLIC DEBT

Third World countries rely on foreign capital to supplement and compensate for meager domestic investment funds. Their access to foreign bank capital expanded in the mid 1970s when Western banks accumulated large new reserves (petrodollars, following the rise in world oil prices). The banks willingly lent to them because their repayment capacity seemed good. They had to repay the loans in hard currency. Because of a commodity boom at the time, they were in a strong position to earn foreign exchange.

Time has shown that foreign borrowing may be a mixed blessing. Repayment obligations can compel borrowers to subordinate production for domestic consumption to production for export. Loan repayments can drain a country of scarce foreign reserves, and large debt-service payments necessarily reduce the surplus available for domestic capital formation. Moreover, creditors have come to make additional loans to debt-ridden countries contingent on economic restructuring, including implementation of policies that cut deeply into lower class living standards, a reduction of the role of the state in the economy, and trade "liberalization" (tariff reductions), which has increased the vulnerability of countries to global market conditions beyond their control. In essence, foreign banks, in collaboration with the IMF, have imposed policies that are the antithesis of what revolutionary regimes sought to accomplish when coming to power.

Adverse effects of foreign borrowing are reflected in the size and growth of the public debt, the debt-export ratio, and, especially, the debt service–export ratio. Since the debt must he repaid in convertible currency, the debt service–export ratio is perhaps the best indicator of the weight of the debt on the economy. The greater export earnings are, the greater a country's capacity to generate the revenue to repay outstanding loans and thereby keep interest payments on the unpaid debt from accumulating. Moreover, the lower export earnings are, the larger the fraction of those earnings that must be used for debt obligations and the smaller the fraction available for financing imports that stimulate domestic production, the initial rationale for borrowing.

Since banks channeled much of their funding through Third World governments,[10] and since revolutionary regimes typically expand the role of the state in the economy, there is reason to believe that governments rooted in state-class transformations would be especially likely to turn to the new source of investment funding when it opened up. While the nationalist bent of revolutions might make foreign financing unattractive, bank capital was assumed, in the mid 1970s, to give Third World governments greater control over investments than direct investment by subsidiaries of multinational corporations. Moreover, multinational corporations concentrated their overseas investments, especially in industry, in only the largest Third World economies with the greatest domestic market potential. The smaller economies with limited domestic funds could therefore not press ahead with import substitution as much as they wanted without foreign bank capital.

All five countries indeed borrowed heavily from abroad in the mid 1970s, when foreign banks made new lines of credit available. The extent of borrowing varied primarily with size of the economy, not with the need or scarcity of domestic capital sources. However, state ability to repay borrowed money has depended very much on the performance of the export sector. Countries accumulated ever larger debts as the value of commodity exports plunged with the world recession in the late 1970s and as interest rates soared, both of which were factors beyond their control. The range of increase in the debts of the countries under study varied between 733 percent (in Bolivia) and 3534 percent (in Nicaragua) between 1970 (before heavy overseas borrowing) and 1985 (Table 14.5). Along with the rapid rise in the money owed to foreign banks, the countries' debt-export and debt service–export ratios rose. Having emphasized import substitution, the countries were not in a good position to absorb the costs of foreign borrowing when global economic conditions turned against them.

Of course, the postrevolutionary governments were not the only governments in Latin America to borrow from abroad when the funding became available. Indeed, they were not uniformly more likely than other governments to drive their economies into debt. Several countries in the region with no revolutionary history developed even greater debt problems than the countries under study. As a consequence, the regional size-debt ranking of only one of the five countries, Nicaragua,

Table 14.5 CUMULATIVE OUTSTANDING HARD CURRENCY FOREIGN PUBLIC DEBT: AMOUNT, AMOUNT IN RELATION TO THE FOB VALUE OF HARD CURRENCY EXPORT EARNINGS (DEBT–EXPORT RATIO) DEBT SERVICE–EXPORT RATIO, AND LATIN AMERICAN (LA) RANKING ON EACH MEASURE

	Mexico	LA rank	Bolivia	LA rank	Cuba	LA rank	Nicaragua	LA rank	Peru	LA rank
	Amount[a]									
1970	3,245.0	1	477.0[b]	8	291.0	9	155.0[b]	14	856.0[b]	6
1975	11,533.0[b]	2	797.0[b]	9	1,338.0	7	598.0[b]	12	3,021.0[b]	5
1980	57,141.6	2	2,699.4	12	4,536.8	9	2,196.6	13	9,988.4	6
1985	97,429.3	2	3,971.3	13	3,566.4[c]	15	5,633.1	9	13,688.0	7
Percent increase (1970–1985)	2,902		733		1,126		3,534		1,499	
	Debt–Export Ratio[d,e]									
1975	279	4	182	7	117	11	133	10	370	1
1980	216	6	262	5	273	4	369	1	207	7
1985	353	9	528	2	484	3	1,460	1	375	8
1987[c]	377	8	767	2	—	—	1,968	1	445	5

Debt Service–Export Ratio[f]

1970	24	2	11	10	—	—	11	8[g]	12	7
1975	26	4	15	7	9	13	13	8	26	3
1980	33	3	26	5	19	8	15	11	33	4
1985	37	2	29	7	33[c]	4	14	15	8	17

[a] Disbursed public debt.

[b] Debt with maturity of one or more years.

[c] Preliminary; data for all countries besides Cuba. For 1987 Cuba's LA ranking is assumed to be the same as in 1985.

[d] Total disbursed debt data for all countries in 1980 and 1985 and for most countries in 1975. The data for the other countries in 1975 refer only to disbursed medium and long-term debt, not to short-term debt.

[e] Data for all countries for 1975, 1980, and 1985 and for 19 countries for 1987.

[f] Data for 20 countries for 1975, 1980, and 1985 and for 19 countries for 1970. The country without data for 1970 is assumed to have the same rank as in the nearest year with data.

[g] Tied with one other country.

Sources: IDB, *Economic and Social Progress* (1981), 437, (1987), 428, 463, 471; UN-ECLA, *Statistical Yearbook* (1987), 714; UN-ECLA, *Economic Survey* (1987), 57, 235, 239, 240; U.S. Congress, Joint Economic Committee, *Cuba Faces the Economic Realities of the 1980s*, 97th Cong., 2d sess., March 22 (Washington, D.C.: U.S. Government Printing Office, 1982), 82; Wilkie and Lorey, Statistical Yearbook, 647, 748; WB, WDR (1987), 220, 238–239; BNC, *Informe economico*, 47.

deteriorated under the new regimes, and the debt service–export ratio ranking of only two of the countries, Cuba and Bolivia, deteriorated. Yet Cuba was the only Latin American country to reduce the total amount owed foreign banks between 1980 and 1985. (Its debt, however, dramatically rose after 1985.[11])

A deterioration in Bolivia's, Cuba's, and Nicaragua's regional debt–export ratio rankings between the mid 1970s and late 1980s suggests that debt-based growth is a particularly problematic economic strategy for socialist and peripheral Third World countries (whether or not they are socialist). For economic and political reasons such countries have difficulty competing in foreign export markets. Bolivia's problems are compounded by the high cost of transporting its products to foreign markets; it is a mountainous, land-locked country.[12]

The socialist countries suffer from political discrimination. Nicaragua's ability to generate hard currency exports with which to repay its foreign debt deteriorated under the Sandinistas, largely because of U.S. efforts to "destabilize" the regime. Nicaragua's export sector was adversely affected by a general softening of world market prices for the commodities it exports, unfavorable climatic conditions, divestment by remaining large farmers, and mismanagement in the cooperative and state sectors. However, U.S.-backed contra activity and the U.S. trade embargo also had a major adverse effect on the country's export earnings. Nicaragua had the highest debt-export ratio in the region in 1987; in 1975, under Somoza, nine other Latin American countries had higher debt-export ratios. The impoverished Sandinista government, however, withheld debt service payments to the point that the country had one of the lowest debt service–export ratios in the region.

Table 14.5, by contrast, shows that Mexico has done an impressive job, from a regional vantage point, in addressing its debt crisis. It had the second largest foreign debt in the region in the mid 1980s. Nonetheless, between 1970 and the mid 1980s it dropped from having the largest debt, and its debt-export regional ranking improved. The attention given in the United States to Mexico's debt crisis therefore reflects the interests of U.S. banks, with their large investments in the country, more than fiscal irresponsibility of our neighbor to the south (in comparison to other Third World countries).

That debtor governments need not be so subservient to foreign banks as Mexico is exemplified by Peru. Peru's regional ranking in the size of its debt has remained more or less the same since 1970, as the reins of government shifted from Velasco's elite-led revolution to a conservative military junta to democratically elected governments. However, the governments in the 1980s limited debt-service payments to the point that the country's regional debt service–export ratio dropped from fourth to seventeenth place between 1980 and 1985. President Alan García, who initially sought to establish himself as a populist nationalist, widely publicized his intent to restrict payments to 10 percent of export earnings. However, his predecessor, Belaunde Terry, had already held back payments to multilateral banks.

Castro has been more reluctant to defy the banks. He has argued for a debtors' cartel and for a moratorium on debt repayments. Yet he has not dared, without the support of other countries, to act on the policies he preaches. His reluctance to do so reflects the precarious status of a publicly committed Third World socialist state in a capitalist world economy.

Unlike most other Latin American countries, Cuba's foreign debt is not confined to Western banks and governments; the island is also heavily indebted to the Soviet Union. Western sources have exaggerated the size of the Cuban debt to the Soviet Union, though it is unclear by how much. Most Soviet funding is trade-linked (although, as noted above, most funding earmarked for domestic development goes to industry). The tied nature of the aid, in the form of export credits, renders almost indeterminable the net benefit of Soviet loans. Cuba must purchase Soviet goods with Soviet financing. Since Soviet products are often inferior to and more costly than comparable Western goods, Cuba's ties to the Soviet Union drive up the island's import bill. Thus, the superpower contributes to the debt burden that its loans mitigate.

Precisely because of Soviet credit restrictions, Cuba drew on Western sources of capital when they became available in the mid 1970s. Western financing lacks the concessionary qualities of Soviet credits, but it allows the island to acquire goods and technology unavailable from the Soviet bloc.

SOCIAL WELFARE

Revolutions should be judged not only by their aggregate economic performance but also by their effect on people's well-being. Revolutions might improve the living standards of previously deprived groups whether or not they expand and diversify production and restructure global aid and trade relations. They might have such an effect because of the social welfare values that guide insurrectional movements and the allocative powers of states. The measures of social welfare to be examined are land distribution and health welfare. These measures tap some of the more important aspects of well-being, for reasons to be discussed.[13]

Land Distribution

In societies where much of the population remains involved in agriculture, landownership constitutes an important component of social welfare. Landowners can exercise control over production on their property and appropriate the surplus produced. In contrast to landless rural laborers, tenant farmers, and sharecroppers, the owners of land typically need not sell their labor, pay rent, or share what they produce. Since social and economic standing depends in part on the size of holdings, land distribution patterns will be examined.

Landownership was highly concentrated before all five revolutions. Mexico had the highest Gini index value of land concentration on the continent (.96), even twenty years after the demise of the Porfirio Díaz dictatorship.[14] Bolivia had the second highest index of land concentration (.84) on the eve of its revolution, and Peru scored only slightly lower (.88) in 1950. Cuba and Nicaragua were among the Latin American countries with least land concentration (Gini coefficients of .79 and .76, respectively), although land was inequitably distributed there too by world standards.[15]

Given how inequitably land was distributed and the importance of land to rural livelihood, it is not surprising that all five new regimes announced land reforms shortly after assuming power. The land reforms transformed rural class relations, encouraged more efficient land use, and ushered in more equitable land distributions.[16] They reduced, in particular, the number of large private farmers.

Between the latest prerevolutionary and the latest postrevolutionary year for which there are data, the private land area in large farms changed most in Cuba, least in Bolivia (Table 14.6). Privately held land in independent farms of 1000 or more hectares dropped from 92 to 65 percent in Bolivia, from 69 to 42 percent in Peru, and from 82 (in 1923, after the breakdown of the ancien régime, but before widespread land distribution) to 32 percent in Mexico. Land area in privately held farms of 340 or more hectares dropped in Nicaragua from 36 to 10 percent between 1970 and 1987.[17] In Cuba most holdings over 67 hectares have been outlawed since 1963. Consequently, by the late 1960s only about 5 percent of the land in private farms remained in units over 67 hectares, and by 1981 only about 9 percent of the arable land on the island remained in private hands.[18]

At the same time that large landholders lost some or all of their property, sharecroppers, tenant farmers, and squatters gained property rights, often to small parcels that they previously held in usufruct. The land reform beneficiaries could, as a consequence of the reforms, appropriate the full product of their labor, even if the land they tilled was no greater than under the old order. However, the reforms accordingly did not resolve the problem of *minifundismo*. *Minifundismo* becomes an increasingly serious problem when successive generations subdivide the land tilled into ever smaller parcels.

Although the five revolutions ushered in land reforms, the new regime land allocations cannot be specifically traced either to the social base of the transformations or to the dominant mode of production instituted. Rural laborers did not necessarily gain more land or acquire

Table 14.6   **LAND DISTRIBUTION BEFORE AND AFTER REVOLUTION**

Country and size of units (hectares)	1923	1950	1960	1967	1970
			Percentage of Farm Units		
Bolivia					
Less than 5.0		59.3		56.6	(14.0)[a]
5.0–99.9		25.7		41.4	(6.0)
100.0–999.9		7.2		1.6	(1.0)
1,000 and over		6.3		0.4	(1.0)
Mexico					
Less than 5.0	59.0	72.6	65.9		(18.0)[a]
5.0–99.9	32.0	21.2	26.0		(11.0)
100.0–999.9	7.0	4.7	6.4		(2.0)
1,000 and over	2.0	1.5	1.6		(0.3)
Cuba					
Less than 5.0		20.1[b]		47.4 (less than 6.7 ha)[d]	
5.0–99.9		71.9		51.7 (6.7–67.0 ha)	
100.0 and over		8.0		0.9 (over 67.0 ha)	
Nicaragua					
Less than 5.0			50.8[f]		
5.0–99.9			44.3		
100.0–999.9			4.4		
1,000 and over			0.6		
Peru					
Less than 5.0			83.4[c]		(66.0)[a]
5.0–99.9			15.3		(12.0)
100.0–999.9			1.1		(0.8)
1,000 and over			0.2		(0.1)

Table 14.6   *Continued*

Country and size of units (hectares)	1923	1950	1960	1967	1970	1987
			Percentage of Land Area			
Bolivia						
Less than 5.0		0.2			(0.2)[a]	
5.0–99.9		1.5			(1.0)	
100.0–999.9		6.4			(3.0)	
1,000 and over		91.9			(65.0)	
Mexico						
Less than 5.0	0.8	0.9	0.8		(0.7)[a]	
5.0–99.9	5.0	5.5	5.7		(6.0)	
100.0–999.9	12.0	14.1	15.3		(15.0)	
1,000 and over	82.0	79.4	78.4		(32.0)	
Cuba						
Less than 5.0		1.0[b]		14.9 (less than 6.7 ha)[d]		
5.0–99.9		28.7		80.0 (6.7–67.0 ha)		
100.0 and over		71.0		5.1 (over 67.0 ha)		
Nicaragua						
Less than 5.0		3.5[f]				
Less than 7.0[g]				2.0[e]	1.9	
5.0–99.9		37.8				
7.0–33.9				15.0	7.8	
34.0–339.9				46.0	44.3	
100.0–999.9		28.3				
340 and over				36.0	10.0	
1,000 and over		30.5				
Peru						
Less than 5.0		5.8[c]		(6.0)[a]		
5.0–99.9		10.3		(10.0)		
100.0–999.9		14.6		(11.0)		
1000 and over		69.2		(42.0)		

[a] 1970 data refer exclusively to the private sector. Land reform beneficiaries accounted for 78, 69, and 21 percent of the farm units and 31, 46, and 31 percent of the land in farms in Bolivia, Mexico, and Peru, respectively. The Peruvian data are for 1973.

[b] Data for 1945.

^cData for 1961.

^dThe 1967 data exclude Havana and Oriente provinces and refer only to the private sector.

^eData for 1978.

^fData for 1963.

^gData for 1987 refer to the private (individually owned) sector. In 1987, 61 percent of the land area was individually owned, and 36 percent belonged to cooperatives (10 percent in credit-service cooperatives, 13 percent in Sandinista cooperatives, and 13 percent in state-owned farms).

Sources: WB, *Land Reform in Latin America: Bolivia, Chile, Mexico, Peru, and Venezuela*, Staff Working Paper 275 (Washington, D.C.: WB, 1978), 21, 23, 30; Sergio Aranda, *La revolución agraria en Cuba* (Mexico, DF: Siglo XXI, 1968) 138, 162; Jose Illán, *Cuba: Facts and Figures of an Economy in Ruin*, trans. George Wehby (Miami: Editorial ATP, 1964), 151; Bolivia, Ministerio de Asuntos Campesinos y Agropecuarios (MACA), *Diagnostico del Sector Agropecuario* (La Paz: MACA, 1974), 459; Central American Education Fund (CAEF), *Central American Report* (Cambridge, Mass.: CAEF, 1988), 7.

property rights sooner, and large landowners did not necessarily lose more property in the four countries experiencing revolutions from below than in Peru's revolution from above. Also, land distribution in none of the five countries was dictated entirely by the dominant mode of economic organization instituted under the new regime.

Land was redistributed much more rapidly in Bolivia than in Mexico. It took Mexico thirty years to allot land to as large a percentage of farm families as Bolivia did in three years. Bolivian redistribution occurred more rapidly because *latifundistas* there were weaker and less able to resist pressure from below than in Mexico. Bolivian *latifundistas* contributed little to the economy; they produced less for export and less for the domestic market than their Mexican counterparts.

After creating a propertied peasantry, however, postrevolutionary Bolivian governments built up a new agrarian capitalist class. In agriculture the capitalist class had been insignificant before 1952. Postrevolutionary governments created the new class by alloting enormous land tracts to market-oriented settlers in the sparsely populated lowlands. The large land allocations account for the highly inequitable distribution of land in contemporary Bolivia. Many of the new agrarian elite are old *latifundistas* in new clothes. The newly created class has been heavily dependent on subsidized state financing, and its members have relied on the state to bail them out when market conditions made their highly speculative operations unprofitable.[19] The shift from alloting small holdings to distribution of large holdings reflects the change in the class base of the ruling coalition that followed the 1956 U.S.-backed IMF stabilization program. In Mexico postrevolutionary governments also came to favor agrarian capitalists over peasants, but less through land allocations than through credit and infrastructural subsidies.

Cuba, in turn, has had two agrarian reforms. As in Mexico and Bolivia, the first reform, in 1959, addressed peasant concerns. It extended property rights to sharecroppers, tenant farmers, squatters, and some rural wage workers, though it allowed farmers to maintain up to 402 hectares. Unlike Mexico and Bolivia, however, Cuba transformed large capital-intensive holdings into cooperative and then state farms. The second reform, in 1963, reduced the maximum size of holdings to 67 hectares unless exceptionally productive. Economic as well as political concerns influenced the two reforms. In expropriating the large farms the government gained control over domestically generated surplus and it prevented foreign profit remittances (by owners of foreign-owned estates). In distributing land to the tillers, Castro solidified his rural social base. The second reform also reflects the regime's anticapitalist bias. Had the government been primarily concerned with output maximization, it would not have implemented the reform. Productivity on the state farms established with the first reform proved to be lower than on private holdings.[20]

Many of the remaining private farmers (approximately 20 percent of the farm population) are beneficiaries of the first reform law; they have come to include some of the wealthiest families in Castro's Cuba.[21] Ironically, the small farm–peasant stratum does better, relative to other socioeconomic groups, in Cuba than in the countries where private property and capitalist organizing principles dominate all economic sectors. The private farm sector has been tolerated for both political and economic reasons.

In Nicaragua the Sandinista government confiscated large holdings, involving about 22 percent of the arable land, soon after assuming power. It took over all property owned by Somoza, his family, and his military officers and followers, as well as property of delinquent taxpayers, lands obtained illegally from the public domain, and uncultivated lands. As in Cuba, state farms were designed at least as much to preserve economies of scale in the agro-export sector as to hasten a socialist transformation. Most of the confiscated farms had been large capital-intensive enterprises. Yet, consistent with its commitment to socialism, the Sandinista government took steps to improve the living conditions of the new state sector workers. Small health units, schools, and housing projects were established, and small stores were opened where basic necessities were sold at regulated prices.

Except with regard to holdings of the former governing class, the Sandinistas respected private property. However, they encouraged cooperatives in the remaining private sector by offering members access to subsidized credit and other state resources. Cooperatives were believed to allow for economies of scale as well as production organized according to socialist nonindividualistic principles. Yet the land restructuring gave rise to new economic problems. As a consequence, the government promulgated a law in January 1986 that allowed for the confiscation of property worked inefficiently and for the break up of state farms.[22] Between 1986 and 1988 half the land in the state sector was distributed either to workers on the farms or to landless laborers. The Sandinistas subdivided and privatized state properties even though they remained committed to socialism, because state farms were plagued with labor difficulties and bureaucratic inefficiencies. Also, the privatization apparently was aimed at solidifying Sandinista support in regions threatened by the *contras*.

In Peru the Velasco administration transformed agrarian property relations in part of the rural economy as rapidly as in Bolivia, Cuba, and Nicaragua. Within a year it turned the largest and economically most important estates into agrarian cooperatives, and it expropriated all farms not managed directly by their owners. Former landowners could not maintain any portion of their property (in Mexico former landowners were entitled to a portion of their holdings). The experience of Peru accordingly demonstrates that a land reform can in certain respects be more sweeping in a capitalist country with a revolution from above than in one undergoing revolution from below. A larger percentage of farmland may have been redistributed in Peru in four years than in Mexico, Bolivia, or Nicaragua since their upheavals;[23] also, a smaller percentage of private farm units remained in holdings over 1000 hectares in Peru than in Mexico or Bolivia after their reforms (I know of no Nicaraguan data on the portion of farm units in different size holdings).

In terms of the portion of the rural population benefiting from the reform, however, Peru's revolution from above appears less impressive. A smaller percentage of agricultural families benefited from the Peruvian than either the Mexican or Bolivian reforms. Probably two-thirds of Peru's rural inhabitants did not take part in the land distribution program. The smaller number of beneficiaries in Peru reflects national differences in the organization of production before the upheavals, more than redistributive limits of revolutions from above. Before the revolutions a much larger percentage of farm families were employed by large estates (over 1000 hectares) in Mexico and Bolivia than in Peru, and workers on such estates were the main beneficiaries of the land reform programs in the three countries.

The measures implemented by Velasco also demonstrate that the dominant mode of production does not in itself dictate agrarian property relations. In transforming large estates into cooperatives, the Peruvian land reform resembled Cuba's and Nicaragua's more than Mexico's or Bolivia's, even though the new regime in Peru, as in Mexico and Bolivia, was always committed to a market economy.

Yet, the Peruvian, like the Nicaraguan land reform, proved to be reversible. In Peru the democratically elected governments of the 1980s broke up rural cooperatives. By 1988 about half the cooperatives established under Velasco were farmed individually.[24] The parcelization has not, however, involved a return to the status quo ante: Estate peons of the pre-Velasco period now are individual landholders, and the old oligarchy has not reclaimed former estates. The demolition of cooperatives had both economic and political roots, just as cooperativization had had. The populist military president Velasco transformed large, privately held estates into cooperatives partly to consolidate a rural social base among the laboring classes while preserving economies of scale, whereas the democratically elected Belaunde Terry allied with individual propertied interests (as he had when he was president before the Velasco coup). By the time of Belaunde's regime in the 1980s, moreover, many cooperatives had proved to be unprofitable.

While the experiences of the five countries suggest that revolutions—irrespective of their class origins or the political economy to which they give rise—usher in land reforms favoring at least some segment of the peasantry, most other countries in the region also promulgated agrarian reforms as of the 1960s. The reform decrees in the nonrevolutionary societies convey the impression that secular trends, and not merely revolutionary forces, worked against agrarian elites in favor of rural laborers. However, implementation of the decrees differed markedly in the countries that have and have not had revolutions. According to available data, the proportion of the farm population receiving land and the proportion of the farmland redistributed as a result of land reform programs were greatest in the countries experiencing revolutions. In the other countries large landowners more successfully resisted pressure for land redistribution. The land reforms in the nonrevolutionary countries were put on the books to avert revolution (with U.S. support, to prevent "other Cubas"). Before 1959 Latin American governments implemented land reforms only when pressured from below by agrarian rebellions.

Although revolutionary and nonrevolutionary countries differ in the extent to which they have implemented land reforms, no one factor accounts for land distribution patterns in the countries experiencing state-class transformations. Governments after revolution have had to accommodate to economic exigencies inherited from the prerevolutionary economies, and they have modified their policies over the years when their political bases and economic concerns shifted.

Health Welfare

Health welfare is reflected in infant mortality and life expectancy rates, although per capita statistics on the two measures unfortunately do not permit analyses of health conditions among diverse socioeconomic groups. We will have to assume that as the two rates improve, health welfare standards among all socioeconomic groups improve, even though we do not know the extent to which this is so.

According to Table 14.7, revolutions appear to have a positive effect on both measures, especially on life expectancy rates. The populace in all five countries in 1985 lived, on average, more years than before the state-class transformations; and the infant mortality rate dropped in all but one of the countries, Peru. In Peru the infant mortality rate declined considerably under Velasco. Yet under both the more conservative military junta of the late 1970s and Belaunde Terry's democratic government in the 1980s children's chances of surviving the first, most precarious year of life deteriorated, to levels of the 1950s.

While health conditions improved in four of the countries, the improvements were not significantly greater than in other countries in the region. Latin American countries in general have been upgrading their health welfare standards in recent decades. Data on the regional ranking of the countries on the two health measures suggest that the only hypothesized factor shaping outcomes of revolution is the dominant mode of production. Cuba, Nicaragua, and Mexico have improved their regional rankings on the two measures since their active upheavals, but Bolivia and Peru have not.[25]

Cuba has the lowest infant mortality and highest life expectancy rate in the region. Its impressive health record (even by First World standards) reflects the allocative possibilities and priorities of a socialist government. However, it also results from Castro's particular commitment to health welfare, and the prerevolutionary social base on which he had to build. The island had the lowest infant death rate and the third highest life expectancy rate in Latin America under Batista.

That socialism may have a positive effect on health welfare is suggested also by the Nicaraguan experience. Nicaragua ranked eighteenth among Latin American countries in infant deaths per capita in 1978, the last year of Somoza's rule;[26] by 1985 the country's regional ranking improved by three places. And its regional life expectancy ranking improved by one place under the new regime. The Sandinistas, like the Cubans, made health care a national priority; they even benefited from Cuban (as well as Western European, UNICEF, and other international agency) medical aid in their efforts. Despite the economic problems the Sandinistas faced and the enormous portion of the national budget that they had to allocate to defense to fight the U.S.- financed contras, their allocative policies lowered mortality rates among the young and old, more than secular trends would lead one to expect. The Sandinista government initiated preventive medical care programs (including large-scale vaccination campaigns against infectious diseases), expanded training of physicians and other medical personnel, and encouraged

Table 14.7 INFANT MORTALITY AND LIFE EXPECTANCY RATES AND LATIN AMERICAN (LA) RANKING ON EACH MEASURE

	Mexico	LA rank	Bolivia	LA rank	Cuba	LA rank	Nicaragua	LA rank	Peru	LA rank
					Infant Mortality[a]					
1945–1949	105	12	123	16	39	1	102	10	109	13
1950–1954	92	11	99	13	—	—	77	7	100	14
1960	74	9	167	19	35	1	70	7	92	13
1965	61	9	77	13	38	1	52	7	91	15
1970	69	12	154	20	36	3	122	18	65	10
1975	53	12	147	20	27	2	103	18	65	18
1980	60	11	138	20	20	1	97	17	105	18
1985	50	10	117	19	16	1	69	15	94	18

Life Expectancy

1950–1955	52	9	40	19	59	3[b]	43	16	44	15
1960	57	7	43	20	64	3	47	17	48	15
1965	60	7	44	20	67	2	49	18	50	15
1970	61	8[b]	46	20	70	1	52	18	53	15
1975	63	9	48	20	71[c]	1	54	18	56	17
1980	65	8	50	20	74[d]	1	56	18	58	17
1985	67	8	53	20	77	1	59	17[b]	59	17[b]

[a] Number of deaths of infants of less than one year per thousand live births. The higher the country rank, the lower the infant mortality rate. Data for 19 countries for 1945–1949, for 17 countries for 1950–1954, and for all 20 countries for succeeding years. Countries without data are assumed to have the same rank as in the next most proximate year with data.

[b] Tied with one other country in rank.

[c] 1970–1975.

[d] 1980–1981.

Sources: Wilkie and Haber, *Statistical Abstract* (1981), 108; Wilkie and Lorey, *Statistical Abstract* (1987), 120; WB, *WDR* (1982), 150–51, (1987), 258–259; WB, *World Tables* (1980), 451, (1984), 5, 11, 13, 39, 67.

newly created mass organizations to participate in health programs even when budget allocations for the health sector were kept at about the level of Somoza's.[27] The Somoza regime had used its monies differently; it concentrated on curative hospital care for the urban middle class.

The improvements in health welfare in Cuba and Nicaragua, relative to those in other countries in the region, imply that health welfare is not determined by country wealth alone. Cuba's infant mortality rate is lower and its life expectancy rate is higher than that of Mexico and other countries with larger national and per capita national products. Resource allocations, not resources per se, prove to have a major bearing on the life chances of the young and old. Allocations vary with the values of the governing class and the organization of production. When the state owns "the means of production" it has more discretionary power than when the economy remains predominantly in private hands.

CONCLUSION

The comparison of social and economic developments in the Latin American countries that have and have not had revolutions in the twentieth century advances our understanding of how and why sociopolitical transformations are of consequence. The analysis compared (1) pre- and postrevolutionary trends within each country that experienced a state-class transformation; (2) the impact of revolutions that had different class origins, that instituted different political economies, and that had different productive bases; and (3) developments in societies that did and did not undergo revolutions.

Table 14.8 shows whether the rank of the five Latin American countries that experienced revolutionary upheavals improved, fell, or remained unchanged on specific indicators of economic and social development since the collapse of the old regimes. Examination of the pattern of country ranks on such measures since the prerevolutionary period is believed to be the best way to differentiate revolutionary as distinct from evolutionary tendencies.

Revolutions seem to have no consistent effect on the economic dimensions under study, except negatively in Bolivia. Bolivia's ranking improved on only one economic indicator, the size of its total debt. (Its improved GDP per capita ranking in the 1980s may well reflect changes in the official peso-dollar exchange rate at the time.) In general, the better off the economy before revolution, the greater its accomplishments after revolution; and, conversely, the worse off and more trade-vulnerable the economy beforehand, the fewer the revolutionary accomplishments. Prerevolutionary conditions, in essence, structure the

Table 14.8 SUMMARY OF CHANGES IN REGIONAL RANKINGS SINCE EACH REVOLUTION

	Mexico	Bolivia	Cuba	Nicaragua	Peru
GDP	No change[a]	Deteriorated	Improved	Deteriorated	Deteriorated
GDP per capita	No change[a]	Improved	Improved	Deteriorated	Deteriorated
Value of manufacturing output	Improved[a]	Deteriorated	Improved	No change	Deteriorated
Manufacturing as percent of GNP	Deteriorated[a]	Deteriorated	Improved	Improved	Deteriorated
Metal and machine industries as percent of total manufacturing output	Improved[a]	No change[a]	Improved[a]	Deteriorated	Improved[a]
Export product diversification	Deteriorated[a]	Deteriorated[a]	Deteriorated	Deteriorated	Deteriorated
Exports as percent of GDP	Improved[a]	Deteriorated[a]	Improved	Improved	Improved
Manufacturing exports as percent of total exports	Deteriorated[a]	Deteriorated[a]	Deteriorated[a]	Deteriorated	Improved
Size of debt	Improved[a]	Improved[a]	Improved[a]	Deteriorated	Improved[a]
Debt-export ratio	Improved[a]	Deteriorated[a]	Deteriorated[a]	Deteriorated	Improved[a]
Debt service–export ratio	No change[a]	Deteriorated[a]	Deteriorated[a]	Improved	Improved[a]
Reduction in infant mortality rate	Improved[a]	Deteriorated	No change	Improved	Deteriorated
Life expectancy rate	Improved[a]	Deteriorated	Improved	Improved	Deteriorated
Land distribution: reduction in large holdings	Improved[a]	Improved	Improved	Improved	Improved

[a] Information only for postrevolutionary period.

economic possibilities of revolution, although they do not in themselves determine subsequent economic developments.

The impact of revolutions on different aspects of the economy seems to vary. With respect to the productive capacity of countries, revolutionary regimes fared poorly, from a comparative perspective. More often than not countries that experienced sociopolitical transformations (except Cuba) showed no improvement in their regional ranking on GDP and GDP per capita. Of course, there is the possibility that they would have done even worse in the absence of revolution, for state-class transformations typically are stirred by economic difficulties (at least for the groups that rebel).

The countries with revolutionary histories did better in fostering industry than total aggregate output. All countries except Bolivia improved their regional ranking on at least one indicator of industrialization.

The revolutionary countries also did better at lowering their export vulnerability, though only by reducing the role of exports in the economy, not by reducing monoproduct export dependence. The high cost of import substitution has typically made their industrial exports uncompetitive; however, politically motivated U.S. trade policy has also limited the export options of the socialist-leaning countries, and the oil bonanza did more than the "deepening" of import substitution to make Mexican industry ever less competitive in international markets (at least through the mid 1980s).

The regional ranking of four of the five revolutionary countries on money owed foreign banks improved between 1970 and the mid 1980s. However, only two of the countries improved their Latin American debt service–export ranking and their improvement reflected regime willingness to stand up to the banks and resist meeting debt obligations more than success at raising foreign exchange for loan repayments.

Nicaragua's as well as Bolivia's poor economic performance, from a regional vantage point, suggests the limits of revolution in peripheral countries. Bolivia did poorly despite foreign assistance, Nicaragua in its absence. Nicaragua's foreign assistance, from Soviet and Western-bloc countries, paled in comparison to that which Bolivia received under the MNR. Moreover, the Nicaraguan economy suffered from the country's being under siege by a hostile foreign power.

The fact that Nicaragua did not do worse than Bolivia suggests that socialism, in a supportive or neutral global context, may allow greater possibilities for economically marginal countries than capitalism. However, the domestic state-class transformation in itself has not been sufficient to usher in major economic improvements.

Although we analyzed fewer social welfare than economic measures, the data indicate that the dominant mode of production and ruling ideology matter here. Mexico's improved ranking on our health welfare indicators suggests that the productive base of countries is also of consequence. However, the improvements in Cuba and Nicaragua, with much smaller economies, imply that resource allocations influence health conditions independently of country wealth. Socialist states, our study indicates, are more inclined than capitalist states to allocate monies in ways that lower infant mortality and improve life expectancy rates. Were there cross-national data on health welfare standards among diverse socioeconomic groups, we probably would find, moreover, that the greatest improvements among urban and rural poor occurred in the two countries committed to socialism. Governments in the two countries made a deliberate effort to improve health care among underprivileged groups.

Land distribution, by contrast, improved in all countries experiencing revolutions, whether or not they ushered in socialist transformations. Countries with revolutionary histories have redistributed land to an extent that other countries in the region have not. State commitment to socialism or capitalism has a less decisive impact on land ownership patterns than one might expect. Were it decisive, Nicaragua's land reform would have been more sweeping and Peru's less so.

It may be, as our data indicate, that the gains from socialism are social more than economic. However, the economic potential of socialism has not been fully "tested" either in Cuba or in Nicaragua. The United States has used its hegemonic influence to constrict the economic capacities of socialist countries in the Western hemisphere. It has done so by containing trade, investment, loan, and aid options, on which all Third World countries remain highly dependent, and, at times, by supporting counterinsurgency movements. Soviet aid and trade have been insufficient to offset the constrictive impact of U.S. foreign policy, above all in Nicaragua but even in Cuba. Soviet goods have often been inferior to their Western equivalents, and superpower politics have denied recipients of Soviet aid access to the U.S. market.

Should United States Latin American policy change, revolutions ushering in socialist transformations might prove to be economically more impressive. The difficulties that have led Eastern European countries and China to initiate market reforms, however, suggest that statist economies generate certain problems that market economies resolve better.

In sum, the Latin American experience suggests a need for new theorizing about revolution. First, our study reveals that global geopolitical and economic forces shape outcomes of revolutions much more than theories of revolution that focus on revolutionary leadership, ideology, and modes of production lead one to believe, the nationalism of the movements notwithstanding. Second, the prerevolutionary heritage structures new regime options no matter how hard the revolutionary leadership seeks to break with the past. Third, revolutions, especially but not exclusively socialist ones, typically benefit segments of the laboring classes, even when their macroeconomic performance proves unexceptional. The redistributive impact of revolutions tends to be greatest when new regimes first consolidate power, whatever the social origins of the societal transformation and whatever the mode of production to which the upheaval gives rise. The driving force behind revolutionary movements, to correct past injustices, is partially though inadequately addressed in all societies experiencing sociopolitical transformations. The urban and rural poor have fared better, relative to other socioeconomic groups, under socialism than capitalism, but socialism per se has proven to be no panacea.

NOTES

I have benefited in writing this essay from discussions with Shane Hunt about statistical data and from financial support from the Social Science Research Council. I am also grateful to Forrest Colburn and Kenneth Erickson for comments on an earlier version of this essay.

1. Crane Brinton, *The Anatomy of a Revolution* (New York: Vintage Books, 1960); Barrington Moore, Jr., *Social Origins of Dictatorship and Democracy: Lord and Peasant in the Making of the Modern World* (Boston: Beacon Press, 1966); and Theda Skocpol, *States and Social Revolutions: A Comparative Analysis of France, Russia, and China* (Cambridge: Cambridge University Press, 1979), for example, base their arguments on revolutions that span many centuries and revolutions occurring in countries with very different economic bases. Jeffery Paige, *Agrarian Revolution: Social Movements and Export Agriculture in the Underdeveloped World* (New York: Free Press, 1975), and Eric Wolf, *Peasant Wars of the Twentieth Century* (New York: Harper & Row, 1969), by contrast, focus on the twentieth century, but on countries with very different histories and cultures.

2. See Susan Eckstein, "The Impact of Revolution on Social Welfare in Latin America," *Theory and Society* 11 (1982): 43–94.

3. Immanuel Wallerstein, *The Capitalist World Economy* (Cambridge: Cambridge University Press, 1980), especially "The Rise and Future Demise of the World Capitalist System: Concepts for Comparative Analysis," "Dependence in an Interdependent World: The Limited Possibilities of Transformation Within the Capitalist World-Economy," and "Semiperipheral Countries and the Contemporary World Crisis."

4. See the debate between Claes Brundenius and Andrew Zimbalist on one side and Jorge Pérez-López and Carmelo Mesa-Lago on the other, in *Comparative Economic Studies* (Spring, Fall, and Winter 1985). The data cited in Table 14.3 on the value of Cuban industrial output represents the more positive assessment of the island's economic performance.

5. Industry's importance is exaggerated because (1) Cuban gross material product (GMP) and gross social product (GSP) estimates exclude information on the social services, which have expanded dramatically under Castro, and, if included in economic calculations, would reduce industry's share of the national product; (2) complete data on the contribution of different sectors to the national product are available only for GSP estimates, and since GSP calculations involve double counting, they overestimate the value of industrial output as measured by market economy value-added compilations; and (3) postrevolutionary pricing policy overvalues industrial output and undervalues agricultural output, although Cuba is not the only country in the region to have such a pricing bias.

6. Cole Blasier, "COMECON in Cuban Development," in Cole Blasier and Carmelo Mesa-Lago, eds., *Cuba in the World* (Pittsburgh: University of Pittsburgh Press, 1979), 230, 239; U.S. Congress, Joint Economic Committee, *Cuba Faces the Economic Realities of the 1980s* 97th Cong., 2d sess., March 22 (Washington, D.C.: U.S. Government Printing Office, 1982), 10. Aid to the sugar industry is probably included in the industrial figure.

7. James Wilkie and David Lorey, *Statistical Abstract of Latin America*, vol. 25 (Los Angeles: University of California, Latin American Center, 1987), 449.

8. As the legal export economy collapsed, the illegal export economy expanded. Bolivia now is a major coca and cocaine exporter, coca being a crop that Indians in the highlands have long grown for their own consumption.

9. It promulgated a foreign investment code in the early 1980s. In so doing the government reversed its initial nationalist and statist economic emphasis. The government attracted more foreign capital to the tourist than the industrial sector.

10. Banks did so because large loans to governments were easy to administer and because they assumed they could hold governments responsible for loan repayments.

11. Cuba's debt rose steeply in the late 1980s largely because the dollar fell in value. The island mainly receives dollars for its hard currency exports, while its hard currency loans are not in dollars (the U.S. government prohibits U.S. banks from lending to Cuba). Cuba's

hard currency debt was also adversely affected by a drop in world market sugar and petroleum prices, the island's main foreign exchange export items at the time.

12. The importance of Bolivia's distance from markets, however, should not be exaggerated. Bolivia profits from illegal coca trade despite the distance, and such landlocked countries as Switzerland rank among the richest economies in the world.

13. For a discussion of the impact of revolutions on income distribution see Eckstein, "Impact of Revolution," 67–79. Since the distribution of wealth has become more concentrated among top income earners in recent years, with the implementation of austerity policies, while available national income data are by now very dated, income distribution is not examined here.

14. World Bank, *Land Reform in Latin America: Bolivia, Chile, Mexico, Peru and Venezuela*, World Bank Staff Working Paper no. 275 (Washington, D.C.: World Bank, 1978), 2.

15. The Nicaraguan data are for 1950, before the expansion of cotton, sugarcane, and beef contributed to increased land hoarding. The Somoza family was heavily involved in the expansion of these agro-exports.

16. For a more detailed discussion of the impact of land reforms in Mexico, Bolivia, Cuba, and Peru, see Eckstein, "Impact of Revolution," 52–67.

17. Central American Educational Fund, *Central America Report* (Cambridge, Mass.: CAEF, 1988), 7.

18. *New York Times*, January 25, 1981, E9. Moreover, by the late 1980s approximately half of all privately held land was cooperatively farmed.

19. Susan Eckstein, "Transformation of a 'Revolution from Below': Bolivia and International Capital," *Comparative Studies in Society and History* 25, no. 1 (January 1983): 105–135.

20. Andres Bianchi, "Agriculture," in Dudley Seers, ed., *Cuba: The Economic and Social Revolution* (Chapel Hill: University of North Carolina Press, 1964); Donald Bray and Timothy Harding, "Cuba," in Ronald Chilcote and Joel Edelstein, eds., *Latin America: The Struggle with Dependency and Beyond* (New York: Wiley, 1974), 635.

21. In the 1960s private farmers with incomes of 10,000, 15,000, or 20,000 pesos a year were not uncommon. In comparison, cabinet ministers earned 8,400 pesos a year and technicians and other specialists in industry a high of about 10,000 a year. In the early 1980s, when private commerce was permitted in the cities, a farmer who worked one hectare of land allegedly made as much as 50,000 pesos a year. A peso is roughly equivalent to a dollar. See Leo Huberman

and Paul Sweezy, *Socialism in Cuba* (New York: Monthly Review Press, 1969); *Granma Weekly Review* February 6, 1986, 2.

22. Central American Educational Fund, *Central America Report*, 7.
23. Eckstein, "Impact of Revolution," 58.
24. *New York Times*, December 11, 1988, 24.
25. Cuba, more accurately, has retained its regional ranking as the country with the lowest infant mortality rate, since the prerevolutionary period.
26. Wilkie and Lorey, *Statistical Abstract*, 120.
27. Thomas Bossert, "Health Care in Revolutionary Nicaragua," in Thomas Walker, ed., *Nicaragua in Revolution* (New York: Praeger, 1982).

POLICY MAKING IN INDUSTRIAL WELFARE STATES

Chapter
15

Explaining Democratic Welfare States

Supply, Demand, and Context

Douglas E. Ashford

Commenting on the transition from tradition to modernity among developing countries some years ago, Clifford Geertz noted that social science seemed confined to interest theories, which obliterated the social realities of traditional societies, or strain theories, which violated their cultural richness.[1] While we surely have little need of another label for the historical and political transformation of liberal into welfare states, the purpose of this chapter is to suggest that comparative analyses of welfare states pose a similar choice. There is, first, the understandable concern with methodological and quantitative refinement even at the price of putting aside some crucially important historical and institutional realities. Secondly, there is the no less misleading but often more forceful argument that welfare states can be compared only in terms of a dynamic, if not overdetermined, model of history or society. Methodological preoccupations can mislead by emphasizing only those characteristics of welfare states that are readily measurable, and abstract theorists may ignore contradictory historical events and political experience. Welfare "realities" exclude unique experience, and welfare "theory" treats differences in political norms and values as superfluous.

When the two strands of comparative inquiry meet,[2] there is a mutual accommodation that suggests that the intellectual and epistemological roots of highly abstract theory and methodological precision are not all that different. For example, the grand theories of social class, either Marxist or conservative, desperately need orderly evidence that the chosen attributes of class not only exist but can be correlated with social differences and welfare state performance.[3] Methodological purists are often quite aware of the limitations of their own results[4] but more often than not become deferential before the theorists who provide broad salience and contextual meaning for highly complex calculations. With no less selectivity, the grand socioeconomic theories of welfare state growth need compelling evidence that their key assumptions are correct. Because this essay will argue that closer examination of contextual realities within each democracy is an essential preliminary step in comparing welfare states, as well as many other complex experiences of modern democracies, it is worth exploring why the methodologists and theorists so often find themselves in agreement.

When imputing universal causal relationships to history or politics, the grand theorists necessarily evoke external circumstances such as class conflict, labor mobilization, and market imperfections that presumably operate toward the same end in all democracies. That these relationships exist in all modern democracies is obvious; how they are imbedded in the particular historical and political experience of a country is not. There are, for example, perfectly respectable theories of welfare state development based on contrasting patterns of industrial development,[5] urbanization,[6] and social class.[7] Both neoliberals and neo-Marxists can present persuasive explanations of welfare states rooted in political economy truths.[8] Those who see the welfare state as primarily demand driven, either for Keynesian or Marxist reasons, have their own macro-level theories.[9] Those who favor supply-based or performance theories can present equally strong theories on both the left and the right.[10] While the Marxists tend to await the collapse of liberal welfare states because distributive politics must eventually fail,[11] the neoliberals and the neoconservatives expect democracy to be crushed by the cost of an unproductive economy or the fiscal foolhardiness of apologists of capitalism.[12] For nearly all of these differences one can produce both detailed evidence and elaborate microeconomic models as well as fervently argued theoretical positions. The thread running through all of this research is that socioeconomic realities can be studied independently from particular patterns of institutional change and democratic decision making.

Apart from the occasional comparative study arguing ideas have consequences,[13] the response-reaction mode of analysis presupposes that our main interest should be welfare states as objects, that is, we should focus on the empirically identifiable body of activities existing apart and separate from political situations. For both liberals and Marxists, such an assumption is a *sine qua non* for methodological purists and a conceptual convenience for abstract theorists. Both neoliberals and neo-Marxists suffer a fatal epistemological blow if ethnic and religious links, irrational social solidarities, and unwieldy political loyalties are seriously accepted. But the possiblity that ideas sometimes transcend individual rationality has not been dispelled by Mancur Olson or Jon Elster.[14] The mixture of greed, affection, and relief woven into the fabric of welfare states threatens the methodological simplifications of both liberals and Marxists. On closer examination, we shall see that the platitudinous notion that welfare states are only another form of market intervention[15] bruises liberal sensitivities as easily as working class faithlessness torments Marxists.

If we are to have valid, persuasive, and possibly even popularly comprehensible notions of what welfare states are, theoretical and methodological adjustments are needed that can accommodate the differentiated political meanings of welfare states. Though an ambitious standard for social science, Gertrude Himmelfarb has magnificently illustrated how the British welfare state was a response to the rising labor movement and other radical demands of Victorian Britain[16] which penetrated cultural, historical and even artistic Victorian life. Clearly, we cannot all labor in the same vineyard, but to confine our comparative efforts to the available hypothetical constructs and to adhere to rigid empirical constraints is to forcefully and, perhaps in J. A. G. Pocock's sense,[17] to brutally foreshorten our understanding of an immensely intricate political and historical transformation of democratic governance. Subjective understanding does not necessarily mean that the laborious efforts to achieve higher objective standards must be abandoned, nor does it necessarily mean that abstract social and economic models are obsolescent. On the contrary, more concern with the subjective aspects of welfare states might help us to discriminate among conflicting hypotheses and to assess the confidence to place in the fragmentary and disconnected statistical images of welfare state activities.

There are many formulations of contextual knowledge and how it is used,[18] but perhaps it will suffice for present purposes to note that many complex interactions represent highly subjective accumulations of tradition, experience, and history as well as momentary expressions of socioeconomic realities as arbitrarily defined by hypothetical constructs. Essentially, contextual inquiry says that equal care must be taken in assigning meaning (validity) as in correctly and persuasively manipulating evidence (reliability). Contextual understanding requires a simultaneous concern with the subjective expression of concepts through time and history[19] and the alleged empirical relationships the concepts expose. The problem is quite familiar to linguistics, aesthetics, ethics, and history.[20] The methodological problem is fairly obvious. Contextual description unavoidably overlaps the evidence that enters into conventional hypothetical formulations, thereby leaving any contextual or structural explanation open to the charge of circularity. While the logic of contextual explanation need not detain us here, it is important to note, first, that the possible circularity need not bias a conventional empirical explanation of the same phenomenon and, second, that the contextual analysis may as easily add as detract from the persuasiveness of an empirical explanation.

An instructive illustration might be the relationship of labor movements and the working class to the emergence and development of welfare states. Clearly, a reasonable hypothesis is that objective characteristics of labor movements such as their size, organization, and strength are positively related to the expansion of welfare states and perhaps ultimately to a social democratic formulation for government. There are highly quantified comparisons of how worker behavior as represented in strikes relates to social policies and programs.[21] The difficulties with these comparisons are not their internal methodologies or even the occasional stretching of our historical credibility,[22] but that important contextual questions may be left unanswered. For comparative purposes there are untreated questions about the meaning of strikes in both social and political terms; the scale, productivity, and ingenuity of industry; and the historical clarity of the public-private distinction. Justifiable or not, the hard knocks now being suffered by the British welfare state are in no small measure a product of disastrous public rather than private sector strikes under the previous Labour government. In contrast, equally or even stronger French public sector unions accept (even plan ahead) disruptive strikes. Contemporary labor movements present fundamentally different strategies to achieve social justice. The French CFDT (Confédération Française Démocratique du Travail), for example, has a localized, participatory vision of labor power that seems to embarrass the Socialist party; the British TUC (Trades Union Congress) still operates on an almsot Victorian image of labor power where labor barons dominate a highly centralized Labour party; and the Swedish LO (Confederation of Labor Unions) virtually dictates social policy by operating large chunks of Swedish government. These are historical and political nuances of labor movements that cannot be ignored if we wish to understand how labor may or may not combine with political forces to achieve welfare state objectives.

Overzealous efforts to make welfare states into objects instead of probing for their subjective variations and differences lead to an unbalanced and at times distorted treatment of union politics. The British TUC, for example, was one of the most powerful labor movements in Europe in the 1920s but refused to support child allowances, a major redistributive social reform.[23] Driven by Fabian compulsion to rationalize British society, William Beveridge infuriated powerful TUC leaders, including Ernest Bevin, by insisting that workmen's compensation be treated as any other disability.[24] The outrage of French unions over the arbitrary reduction of their representation on social security boards (*caisses*) in 1967 can be traced to the earliest social policy debates in 1898 on workmen's compensation where French unions insisted that they be equal partners in managing social security funds.[25] For grand theory, neo-Marxist, neoliberal, or neoconservative, the complications of policy making are secondary and often simplified. All this is not to say that methodological or theoretical objectivity cannot clarify how welfare states behave, but only that objects viewed in contextually exclusive ways may blind us to the intricacy of complex decisions and values. The intellectual cost is high, possibly even damaging, because comparison of welfare states may become a professional niche rather than an effort to understand how social and political values are redefined through time. The laboriously assembled body of comparative knowledge often sheds little light on classical problems of democratic governance and sometimes underestimates democratic capabilities. Some of these problems and their relevance to welfare state comparison can be specified rather easily.

THE POLITICAL MEANINGS OF WELFARE

There is no question that welfare objectives display similar economic and social characteristics across countries and societies,[26] but the pursuit of welfare also takes on peculiar meanings in the historical and philosophical development of each democracy. A basic source for such meanings is the juxtaposition of ideas that enabled democratic government to emerge from various forms of royal absolutism, territorial fragmentation, and the remnants of great European empires. The underlying premise of democratic governance was that individual rationality, unfettered by religious and other particularistic claims on human loyalties, could more ably select leaders and more effectively restrict absolute authority than earlier regimes. To be sure, in both the Catholic and Protestant traditions the idea of charity predates democracy. In this respect, the French phrase *l'état providence* is more accurate than the English phrase *welfare state*, which implies that welfare begins with the modern state. One of the most admired of welfare states, Sweden, rarely applied that phrase. In the 1930s the shared concept of the Swedish social democratic welfare state was that of "folk society." The heavy emphasis on localized, participatory welfare contradicts more recent interpretations that assume the nationalization of social services was a natural consequence of Swedish politics.[27] While it is widely recognized that the amazingly early advances of welfare in Germany were the work of an autocratic emperor acting through a wily chancellor, many accounts say little about the political consequences of undemocratic social reforms on German political development.[28]

The political realities of the development of welfare states are not simply the objective use and abuse of welfare for political purposes. Grand theory and comparative statistics are both seriously circumscribed because providing welfare had very different meanings in democratic theory itself. Until Margaret Thatcher's monarchical habits few welfare state comparisons would heed Pocock's brilliant analysis of the seventeenth-century democratic compromise which helped preserve the concept of monarchical power. The "Anglicization of the republic" provided England with a "paradigm of custom, grace and fortune" that effectively rejected republicanism.[29] Contrary to common philosophical experience of the emergent democracies, there was no need to "invent" people and so no need to consider social, economic, or even spiritual rights apart from the remarkably stable pattern of aristocratic rule that prevailed in Britain until 1911.[30] The two main nineteenth-century advocates of republican reform, Sir Charles Dilke and Charles Bradlaugh, were both struck down for the most offensive of Victorian sins, adultery, while their great political leader, Joseph Chamberlain, like so many British leaders, was seduced by political ambition and abandoned his radical Birmingham program.[31] Thus, there never was a need to link the British welfare state to democracy.

The paradox is that what until recently seemed the paragon of welfare states was never a very democratic welfare state. In 1911 a young Winston Churchill, still a Liberal, pouted that Lloyd George had stolen the "political plums" in social welfare, and after World War I Lloyd George displayed his political cynicism by abandoning the array of reforms assembled by his own political agent, Addison, in the Ministry of Reconstruction.[32] The effort to finally terminate the Poor Laws under the Local Government Act of 1929 was repeatedly delayed by Treasury maneuvering, some of which was later continued by the chancellor, Neville Chamberlain, who had proposed the 1929 law as Minister of Health. Beveridge was eager to find ways to avoid parliamentary debate of his plan. In his arrogant concern for the plan, he committed the cardinal Whitehall sin of publicly agitating for legislation and was forever banned from Whitehall corridors.[33] Aneurin Bevan was no doubt a leftwing Labour activist, but faced with determined resistance from the Royal College of Surgeons, he not only adopted their life-style but promised "to stuff their mouths with gold."[34] The generally high performance of the National Health Service notwithstanding, it was organized to exclude consumer and patient participation, carefully preserved the high status of "consultants" (specialists), gave complete control of medical education to the profession, and assured that preventive medicine and other less glamorous forms of medical care would be downgraded.[35]

Were one considering political ideas rather than objective realities, republicanism would surely be the essential dividing line, making Britain and Germany exceptions rather than leaders among welfare states. Despite the slow progress of the French welfare state, in the revolutionary debates, vagrancy (*mendacité*) was frequently pointed out as a blot on the republic. The Declaration of the Rights of Man contained clear provision for protecting citizens from social and economic risks. The revolution horrified many European statesmen, but the French commitment to social reform never relaxed over the nineteenth century, including the ill-fated *ateliers* of the Second Republic and state-supported mutual insurance under the Second Empire. One critical scene in the transition from monarchial to radical republicanism in the Third Republic was the abolition of the traditional local *bureaux de bienfaisance*, associated with conservative Catholicism, and the creation of the *bureaux d'assistance publique*, state-supervised and state-supported social assistance agencies.[36] However meager the results, Robert Waldeck-Rousseau labored over the problem of how contractual protection might be extended to unions, and the independent socialist Alexandre Millerand laid the foundations for labor participation.[37] The principles that became central to French social welfare nearly a century later were missing in British political thought.

In the context of the early definition and redefinition of democratic principles, welfare state objectives are more controversial for their subjective implications for family, religion, community, and race than for the material, social, and economic commitments of governments. The subjective nature of welfare activities and policies regularly appears in partisan party politics. For purposes of aggregated comparison, it is possible to assess partisanship by objective standards,[38] but such measures rarely place social welfare in the context of internal party developments, political pressures, or long-term problems of developing coherent, disciplined parties. Until the 1930s Labour party disinterest in social reform had more to do with its pacificist tradition than any Marxist failures.[39] The various schisms of French socialism at the turn of the century forced Jean Jaurès to qualify his support for parliamentary democracy, but then as now factions coalesced to vote for the major social and educational reforms of the radical republicans.[40] In brief, across countries politicization of welfare did not progress at the same pace among parties with the similar traditions and doctrines or under similar electoral hurdles. A simplified measure of left and right in either quantitative or theoretical terms may easily distort the meaning of welfare politics in democratic processes.

The natural inclination to see advocacy of welfare state reforms as progressive has very likely produced an unfortunate, and possibly inaccurate, perception about social reform. First, in the 1930s there was a sombering regularity in fascist exploitation of social reform in all the democracies. This is not to raise a red herring, but to underscore the extent to which social reform is value-neutral in partisan politics, if not in relation to abstract moral and humane values. In Britain Sir Oswald Moseley's black shirts were organized after the brilliant, young politician had his massive program of social spending rejected by a sanguine J. Ramsay MacDonald.[41] France was more fascinated by Benito Mussolini's corporatist fascism. Two important prewar leaders of the then-noncommunist CGT (Confédération générale du travail) were affected, Michel Déat, who created a middleclass brand of national socialism and René Belin, Vichy's Minister of Labor, who found the total mobilization of wartime consistent with national socialism.[42] A totally and permanently mobilized society is one form of tyranny and for a moment the war made a social order without democratic politics seem attractive. While never approaching fascist fanaticism, the intense moral indignation found in Richard Titmuss's account of social life during the war[43] is readily converted into intolerance of any form of opposition to social reform. Only recently has the purity of the Swedish social democratic vision been smudged by accounts of the wartime fascist movement in Sweden.[44] Even Franklin Roosevelt's social reforms were in part propelled by his fears that the populism of Huey Long and the extravagance of Francis Townsend might blur the Democratic party's social image.[45]

In the case of social policy lightly generalizing about the intricacies of partisan calculations can be misleading. Theda Skocpol's frequent invocation of Civil War pensions as a building block of the American welfare state is no doubt correct in terms of enlarging the federal commitment in quantitative terms,[46] but it was also politically advantageous for the Republican party. But the link between veterans' pensions and later events is tenuous, while partisan justification was easy as mass warfare became a natural consequence of mass democracy. The institutionalization of welfare states placed huge segments of governmental activity beyond partisan consideration, but intended and unintended effects should not be confused. In the same vein, Aneurin Bevan's optimistic estimates of the cost of the National Health Service regularly produced deficits that contributed to the corrosive feud between Hugh Gaitskell and Bevan and eventually destroyed the credibility of the Labour Party and produced thirteen years of Tory rule.[47]

Likewise, the Cold War, the sabotage of French factories by the CGT in 1947, and the occupation of Czechoslovakia in 1948 destroyed the postwar consensus on social policy of the French left, but the resurgent center and right parties did not dismantle the French welfare state. They used the precedent of privileged pension coverage to create a second level pension for professionals, the self-employed, and *cadres* (roughly, white-collar workers). Over the next thirty years, these huge, self-financing funds produced inequalities in retirement income which under a socialist government in 1983 made possible a scheme for retirement on state pensions at 60 years.[48] In 1939 amendments to the social security system in the Unisted States responded to business and banking fears that the huge social funds might one day disrupt the capital market,[49] but supporting the myth that U.S. wage-earners indeed pay for their pensions required generous contributions from general revenues that far exceed those made in more redistributive European social security systems. The point of all these examples is that nationalizing social welfare does not necessarily simplify partisan politics. Partisan opportunities are not readily predicted and partisan decisions about social reform do not always have the desired effects.

The institutionalization of welfare at the national level is now taken for granted, but this was not so a hundred years ago nor does it appear essential to future welfare state growth. Though generally omitted from most historical and political accounts of welfare states, the elevation of societal responsibilities from local to national governments was integral to the nationalization of welfare.[50] In Britain, where local democracy has been virtually abolished by Margaret Thatcher,[51] local poor relief was once the main source of social support. The story of nineteenth-century social reform in Britain is encapsulated by futile struggle to differentiate the "deserving" and "undeserving" poor without enlarging the local tax burden of the landed aristocracy.[52] Local subordination to national designs, however poorly conceived, created a "culture of poverty" that plagues British policy makers to the present. The Unemployment Act of 1935 and the Beveridge proposals of 1942 cannot be understood without realizing the suspicion with which national politicians and policy makers viewed localities.[53] The same fears influenced the nationalization of hospitals in 1948 for the ironical reason that over the nineteenth century locally supported hospitals had been given the most unrewarding and routine public health tasks which doctors and nationalizers were eager to dismantle.[54] The result is that, compared to Germany, France, and the consumer-based social services of Sweden, for many years British localities provided elaborate local social services, but had virtually no voice in national social policy making.

Few democracies can avoid the underlying conflict between the spatial and functional aspects of social policies with major modification of democratic practices.[55] Germany has a long tradition of strong local services in the old trading cities, now Social Democratic strongholds. The elaborate peak organizations for sickness insurance are in part a solution to overcome territorial fragmentation.[56] Though rarely debated in a highly consensual Swedish society, regional agencies are key actors in distributing services, and localities in fact collect two-thirds of income taxes.[57] Though not all the left wished for, decentralization of education and social assistance were the key elements in Francois Mitterrand's decentralization of French local government. Although often used to distinguish American social security from Europe, circumventing territorial fragmentation in the form of localized parties and racial discrimination in the South were critical elements in Roosevelt's success in 1935. The immense burst of social services in the 1960s and 1970s can be partly accounted for by both Democratic and Republican desires to enlist the support of cities and states for other reforms. Federalism sets America apart, but under some circumstances, territorial fragmentation accelerates the growth of social services.[58]

If the development and comparison of welfare states is seen through the subjective lens of democratic traditions and constraints, we acquire perspective on the politics of welfare that is not provided by abstract theorists and statistical manipulators. Contextual analysis shows how social and economic objectives were reconciled with democratic institutions and at times helped shape democratic institutions. Intricate patterns of intergovernmental negotiation, bureaucratic struggle, and constitutional limitation are the context for welfare state politics and policy making. Indeed, the major achievement of democratic welfare states may not be social and economic, but the political achievement of the successful integration of such massive changes within existing democratic institutions and practices. From a comparative political perspective, the objective success of welfare states may be their least interesting accomplishment.

THE POLITICAL BOUNDARIES OF WELFARE STATES

Political science has been willing to let large-scale socioeconomic theories, Marxist and entrepreneurial, define the political boundaries of welfare state developments. The price is not only that these disciplines then define what democratic politics is, but that pessimistic and overly constrained views prevail in considering welfare state futures. A belief in the rational capabilities of citizens is an assumption of democratic political life. One of the major oversights of grand theory has been to overlook the intimate connection between individual rational capabilities and protecting citizens against unreasonable risks. In this sense, law, order, and welfare are alike. A host of external conditions ranging from nuclear waste to mental handicap are now included in the category of unreasonable risk. Forty years ago Britain's leading economist of the left, Colin Clark, estimated that once governments took more than 25 percent of national income, the state would collapse.[59] Thirty years later the conservative economist Milton Friedman opted for 60 percent of GNP.[60] There is a long social science tradition of seeing welfare as outside the state. Contrary to recent efforts to bring the state "back in," a realistic assessment of the political limitations of welfare states may require more precise consideration of how democratic states are constituted and their normative links to the past. The democratic welfare states operate in a socioeconomic context, but they also work within the institutional, constitutional, and political boundaries of each country's historical experience.

If social policies are treated as the primary object of modern democratic governance, and sometimes rather hastily translated into objective phenomena for social science purposes, our understanding of normative and contextual meanings is neglected. Renewed awareness of the interaction of state and society has greatly enhanced comparative welfare state studies, but the formulations remain predominantly socioeconomic and leave little room for historical, diversity and institutional complexity. For example, having made the provocative assertion that the growth of welfare states blurs the distinction between state and government, Martin Rein and Lee Rainwater rest their argument on the difference between the common law foundations of Anglo-Saxon governments and the Roman law foundations of most continental governments.[61] But we are not given the contextual, historical, or philosophical differences in these legal principles as they affect the formulation, implementation, and evaluation of social policies. Their assumption that common law implies checks and balances goes unexamined. Common law has not prevented Britain from becoming one of the most highly centralized of welfare states. As Thatcher holds compulsory sales of public housing, decides to put school districts under direct grants, and creates a mysterious "Social Fund" from which local governments must borrow to meet social assistance needs, one wonders where the checks and balances are.[62] The presumed centralizing effect of Roman law, it is suggested, produces a more unified and energetic attack on welfare state problems, yet France had no state-sponsored unemployment insurance until 1958 (under a conservative regime), and Germany tolerates an unbelievably intricate system of territorial and local agencies that are fully woven together into a typically German peak organization.[63]

In a more promising contextual mode of analysis, a recent study of the development of the welfare state in the United States acknowledges that the common neo-Marxist frameworks for social policy analysis, business hegemony (welfare capitalism), and working class weakness do not fit the case. Four pages later we read that American "state formation" includes three elements, economic development, urbanization, and liberal values, all distinctly social phenomena that might be driving forces of either pluralist or Marxist versions of any democratic state.[64] Major contextual questions are left unanswered. Although it is common to see the United States as an "outlier" in grand designs of welfare states,[65] poverty assistance in the United States follows the European pattern and American unions like European unions were skeptical supporters of welfare state policies.[66] Like independent variables, contextual arguments are arbitrarily selected, but they should, first, not strain historical credibility and, second, deal even-handedly in drawing comparisons. Having been led to believe we are offered a distinctly "statist" explanation, the peculiar political conditions that delayed welfare state development in the United States in the early twentieth century are all negative and with little elaboration of similar negative political features arresting welfare state development in other democracies. We are eventually left with the macrosociological conclusion that the United States progresses toward welfare state objectives with "big bangs."[67]

This criticism may seem unfair since many recent studies take pains to note that policies are reflexive and cumulative in ways that are poorly understood. But the favored structural relationships claim a face validity that is never examined and often rests on a selective use of history. Contextual analysis is one way of assuring ourselves that such claims are correct. To give some simple illustrations, the early industrial labor barons such as Samuel Gompers, Ferdinand Lassalle, and Tom Mann were all skeptical of social assistance but for very different reasons. Gompers seemed to think, probably correctly, that federal government would not be likely to come to the aid of workers until they acquired political clout. Mann and the British labor leaders were champions of industry and accepted much of the evangelical thinking that inspired the Edwardian liberals. Lassalle was on good terms with the chancellor, Otto von Bismarck, and approved of state socialism.[68]

Moreover, the relationship between the labor movements and the nascent socialist parties was different in each country. The French socialists suspected their militantly Marxist German comrades and displayed distinct anarchist tendencies. The early Labour party ignored the TUC's main social demand in its alliance with the liberals in 1906. American socialism languished so that labor leaders had to be tough-minded to survive. Thus, a broadly correct structural phenomenon—the weakness of labor movements and the delay of welfare and social reforms—rests on very different political and social circumstances. The persistence of welfare capitalism abstractly derives from labor weakness, but one must also explain labor neglect of children, resistance to family allowances, disinterest in women workers, fear of minority and colonial labor competition, and so forth. The subjective side of labor's interests and policies is not alike in all countries. To generalize from a vague "weakness" argument without showing how such weakness affected policies risks confusion of political causation and political history.

In some respects the breakdown of pluralist explanations of welfare (the assertion that all organized interests get a piece of the action) and the Marxist explanation (the assertion that labor conflict and capitalist fears produce welfare concessions) both falter on the similar complex issue of private and public sector interactions within democratic welfare states. There are both neoliberal and neo-Marxist accounts of how privately provided welfare produces negative results.[69] Private sponsorship and private means were often resistant to change, and less generous, but historically business behavior was often remarkably similar to labor behavior. More interesting perhaps, workers and owners needed to learn about social and economic complexities of highly complex industrial societies. But the political and cultural roots for the industrial transformation were substantially different in different countries, in part because capitalism itself incorporates important contextual differences and in part because governments took different positions demarcating the public and private spheres. Public-private boundaries have never been sharply defined in French politics.[70] Unions, including the communist CGT, helped break up the centralized social security system that Pierre Laroque planned for France in 1945 in order to protect their pension privileges.[71] American federalism bears the stamp of agrarian power as much as industrial power well into the 1930s. Roosevelt's social reforms are incomplete without seeing both the political subtlety and immense social effect of cheap electricity for rural areas. But the greatest confusion may be the implied claim that public provision is somehow preferable to private provision. Rein and Rainwater, for example, admit that "sectoral blurring" occurs, but interpret this to mean an inescapable tension between welfare and markets.[72]

The aggregate statistical studies of the growth of welfare never promised to shed light on the role of the state, though at times they arrive at mind-boggling comparisons, [73] but the efforts to revive the state as an important actor have reached few new conclusions about democratic states as such. In socioeconomic terms states remain the creatures of social forces, social class, and social needs, responding and reacting to presumably similar social and economic conditions as best they can. Causes seem to run in one direction and states always seem to be catching up with history. There are at least three important remedies for such a bias which help establish the autonomy of the state and, in doing so, help us better understand the democratic context of welfare states.

POLICY MAKING, POLITICS, AND WELFARE

First, a number of essential characteristics of democratic states are conceptually independent of welfare and social objectives. Legal traditions and instruments are one example. English common law was the keystone of seventeenth-century parliamentary democracy in Britain and its individualist framework heavily influenced interpretations of poverty, the organization of social justice, and eventually the entire administration of social assistance.[74] Both political and legal controversies over social justice in France centered on how citizens might act collectively without impairing the popular will.[75] The constitutional fragmentation of American political power is self-evident and no doubt accounts for the ingenious myths and convoluted strategies used to make New Deal social legislation palatable to Congress and to the public. From its beginning American social assistance and welfare confronted intergovernmental complexities that exceed by far the formal demands placed on other reforming democracies.[76] The constitutional and legal hurdles to the construction of an interventionist state are perhaps the most neglected aspect of welfare state comparisons.

Second, there are enormous differences in the administrative practices and procedures brought to bear on social needs and social programs. Even so powerful a Whitehall baron as Sir Robert Morant could not get the government to pay high-level social administrators salaries equivalent to Treasury and Home Office officials. Possibly the most enduring administrative creation of the French radical republicans was the *établissement public* in 1901, a legal fiction to rationalize the pursuit of collective goals within the framework of an unrelentingly individualist state.[77] The startling uniformity of the Swedish welfare state would be impossible without a governmental structure that leaves the major segments of social policy entirely in the hands of civil servants with the assurance that they will operate under near total publicity. How the "consumerism" of Swedish social democracy requires years, sometimes decades, of consultation to achieve basic reforms often eludes studies of Swedish welfare.[78] An examination of the postwar French welfare state suggests that in the absence of the highly elitist, centralized legal bureaucracy it would be hard to imagine progress after the war.[79] Thus, the transformation of state structures and procedures in order to intensify action on social and economic programs meant changing basic administrative habits and radical reconstruction of intergovernmental links, nearly all of which took place in the administrative context.

Third, many objective comparisons treat lightly the diverse forms of electoral participation, party organization, political mobilization of demands, and participant evaluation of social programs. We read little about programs the public dislikes or proposals that communities reject. Surely a fundamental element in the dispersion of social programs in the United States is the highly localized nature of American parties and elections. Indeed, the "big bang" notion of how American welfare proceeds may obscure how minor inroads to favor the blind, the disabled, and dependent mothers provided springboards for future expansion. The interesting political explanation is not why so little was done over long intervals, but how federal and local politics voluntarily exploited the handholds on social reform that the federal government offered.[80] Likewise for Britain, the extraordinarily centralizing effects of British electoral and party practices have a direct bearing on the ease with which the British welfare state took shape and, incidentally, the ease with which it is now being dismantled.[81] Nor is it easy to understand how France surged ahead of Germany as a social provider in merely one decade if one does not take into account Gaullist determination to modernize France and later Socialist determination to unite the left in French politics, if only momentarily. For those fascinated by the external conditions, the internal political conditions only seem to count when welfare states take hard knocks.

Lastly, note should be made of the methodological importance of comparative policy studies in understanding the political obstacles to future welfare state growth. The macrosociological and macroeconomic theories rarely look at how governments behave across policy areas, in part because the outputs are often difficult to measure in standard terms and in part because of the functional bias. There is much to be learned about British democracy, and quite possibly about its economy and society as well, from seeing that the political formulas for organizing the National Health Service, nationalizing basic industries, reorganizing manpower programs in the Manpower Services Commission, providing grants to universities, and even organizing the higher civil service are similar. In all instances the formulas minimize participation, insulate officials from parliamentary accountability, give ministers extraordinary discretionary powers, and, for constitutional reasons, severely foreclose opportunities to appeal authoritative decisions.[82] In examining only one policy area, the almost unavoidable error is to treat general political features as peculiar causes. Without seeing, for example, that the sporadic progress of American social security is not unlike the sporadic progress of racial justice, public transportation, and public housing, the possibility of identifying contextual truths is minimized.

Essentially, unless one frames hypotheses that acknowledge the possible autonomy of the state and politics, it is unlikely that politics will be shown to have significant impact on our lives. To be sure, welfare states arose because social and economic forces were unleashed by industrialization, urbanization, and labor mobilization, but there were also compelling political features of these complex events. Welfare states, including the social democratic experiments, were made possible by democratic governments' working through accountable bureaucracies, using free electoral processes, and enjoying public confidence that individual rights and reason are reconcilable and by allowing for the diverse historical experience of each democracy. If such political considerations are excluded or, worse, included capriciously, welfare state meanings are distorted. Welfare is no doubt a shared object of states and societies, but the objectives of states are not confined to social welfare. New social aims would never have arisen without the ingenuity of democratic leadership, the stimuli of new ideas in both the public and private minds, and the patient elaboration of policy solutions within the framework of each country's democratic tradition. The political context of welfare states does not always conform to objective concepts, but the subjective setting for democratic government can be ignored only at our peril. Successful democracies are not totally preoccupied with social and economic policies and few think they should be. Comparison of welfare states can also make us more alert to the subjective roots of democratic politics.

NOTES

1. Clifford Geertz, "Ideology as a Cultural System" in David Apter, ed., *Ideology and Discontent* (New York: Basic Books, 1964), 47–76.
2. The most ambitious effort to bring the two strands together is Peter Flora and Jens Alber, "Modernization, Democratization, and the Development of Welfare States in Western Europe," in P. Flora and A. Heidenheimer, eds., *The Development of Welfare States in Europe and America* (New Brunswick, N.J.: Transaction Books, 1981), 37–80.
3. Among the many quantitative studies bearing on welfare state development and growth, see Harold Wilensky, *The Welfare State and Equality: Structural and Ideological Roots of Public Expenditure* (Berkeley: University of California Press, 1975); Frank Gould and Barbara Howeth, "Public Spending and Social Policy: The United Kingdom 1950–1977," *Journal of Social Policy* 9 (July 1980): 337–357; David Cameron, "The Expansion of the Domestic Economy," *American Political Science Review* 72 (1978):1213–1261; Phillips Cutright, "Political Structure, Economic Development and National Social Security Programs," *American Political Science Review* 70 (1965): 537–550; Christopher Hewitt, "The Effect of Political Democracy and Social Democracy on Equality in Industrial Societies," *American Sociological Review* 42 (1977): 450–464.
4. On the whole, economists seem to be more explicit about the limits of their data. See, for example, Frederick L. Pryor, *Public Expenditures in Communist and Capitalist Nations* (New Haven, Conn.: Yale University Press, 1968). The reverse side of this problem is the oddly market-based appeal of two Hungarians for more liberal

social security policies in Ivan Szelenyi and Robert Manchin, "Social Policy Under State Socialism: Market Redistribution and Social Inequalities in East Europe Socialist Societies," in Martin Rein, Gösta Esping-Andersen, and Lee Rainwater, eds., *Stagnation and Renewal in Social Policy: The Rise and Fall of Policy Regimes* (New York: Sharpe, 1987), 102–142.

5. Karl Polanyi, *The Great Transformation: The Political and Economic Origins of Our Time* (Boston, Mass.: Beacon Press, 1957).

6. Gaston Rimlinger, *Welfare Policy and Industrialization in Europe, America, and Russia* (New York: Wiley, 1971).

7. Walter Korpi, *The Democratic Class Struggle* (London: Routledge and Kegan Paul, 1983).

8. Ian Gough, *The Political Economy of the Welfare State* (London: Macmillan, 1979); Thomas Wilson and Dorothy J. Wilson, *The Political Economy of the Welfare State* (London: Allen and Unwin, 1982).

9. Gösta Esping-Andersen, *Politics Against Markets: The Social Democratic Road to Power* (Princeton, N.J.: Princeton University Press, 1985); Carolyn L. Weaver, *The Crisis in Social Security: Economic and Political Origins* (Durham, N.C.: Duke University Press, 1982).

10. Fred Hirsch, *The Social Limits to Growth* (London: Routledge and Kegan Paul, 1977); Roger A. Freeman, *The Growth of American Government: A Morphology of the Welfare State* (Stanford, Calif.: Hoover Institution, 1975); and Neil Gilbert, *Capitalism and the Welfare State, Dilemmas of Social Benevolence* (New Haven, Conn.: Yale University Press, 1983).

11. Michael Shalev, "The Social Democratic Model and Beyond: Two 'Generations' of Comparative Research on the Welfare State," in Richard F. Tomasson, ed., *Comparative Social Research: The Welfare State, 1883–1983* (Greenwich, Conn.: 1983, JAI Press), 315–352. Though often cited as a representative bibliographic essay, the Shalev article is primarily a critique of the demand model with little attention to producer models.

12. R. Bacon and W. Eltis, *Britain's Economic Problem: Too Few Producers* (London: Macmillan, 1976); Richard Rose and Guy Peters, *Can Governments Go Bankrupt?* (New York: Basic Books, 1978); Charles Lewis Taylor, ed., *Why Governments Grow: Measuring Public Size* (Beverly Hills, Calif.: Sage Publications, 1983).

13. Although there are now diverse critiques of the limits of the Swedish model, Francis G. Castles, *The Social Democratic Image of Society* (London: Routledge and Kegan Paul, 1978), was among the first to suggest there may be limits to the application of Swedish socialism. The peculiar historical conditions favoring Swedish social

democracy are now more widely recognized: a tiny intellectual elite, modernization during depression conditions, export-led agriculture as well as industry, survival of World War II intact, and so forth (Thorsten Nybom, "The Swedish Social Democratic State: A Tradition of Peaceful Resolution," 1988, mimeographed).

14. For both a neoliberal and a neo-Marxist interpretation of market failure see Mancur Olson, *The Logic of Collective Action: Public Goods and the Theory of Groups*, rev. ed. (Cambridge, Mass.: Harvard University Press, 1971); and Jon Elster, *Ulysses and the Sirens* (Cambridge: Cambridge University Press, 1979). Neither study has much to say about such common political imperfections in demands as ethnicity, religion, nationalism, and family.

15. Asa Briggs, "The Welfare State in Historical Perspective," *Archives Européennes de Sociologie* 2 (1961): 221–258.

16. Gertrude Himmelfarb, *The Idea of Poverty* (New York: Vintage Books, 1985).

17. J. A. G. Pocock, *Politics, Language and Time: Essays on Political Thought and History* (New York: Atheneum, 1971).

18. Among numerous books see John Dunn, *Rethinking Political Theory* (Cambridge: Cambridge University Press, 1985), especially chaps. 7, 8, 9; Paul Rabinow and William M. Sullivan, eds., *Interpretive Social Science: A Reader* (Berkeley: University of California Press, 1979); Roger Trigg, *Understanding Social Science* (Oxford: Blackwell, 1985); Ernest Gellner, *Relativism and Social Science* (Cambridge: Cambridge University Press, 1985).

19. There are endless illustrations in the welfare state literature where analytical language imperceptibly acquires objective confidence. For example, Gösta Esping-Andersen's enthusiasm for consumer-driven welfare states becomes "Conservative or liberal reformism did indeed occasionally lure workers away from the correct path," in "De-commodification and Solidarity," in Rein, Esping-Anderson, and Rainwater, *Stagnation and Renewal* , 81; or Ann Shola Orloff's bland claim about the American "underdeveloped state bureaucracy" in "The Political Origins of America's Belated Welfare State," in Margaret Weir, Ann Orloff, and Theda Skocpol, eds., *The Politics of Social Policy in the United States* (Princeton, N.J.: Princeton University Press, 1988), 59.

20. For a historiographical selection, see Patrick Gardiner, ed., *The Philosophy of History* (Oxford: Oxford University Press, 1972); Gertrude Himmelfarb, *The New History and the Old: Critical Essays and Reappraisals* (Cambridge, Mass.: Harvard University Press, 1987). From the perspective of analytical philosophy, Peter Winch, *The Idea of a Social Science and Its Relation to Philosophy* (London: Routledge and Kegan Paul, 1958). From a cultural perspec-

tive, Clifford Geertz, *The Interpretation of Cultures* (New York: Basic Books, 1973). For a fascinating account of the subjectivity of political science, Stefan Collini, Donald Winch, and John Borrow, *The Noble Science of Politics: A Study in Nineteenth Century Intellectual History* (Cambridge: Cambridge University Press, 1983).

21. Among many, see, for example, Morris Beck, "Public Sector Growth: A Real Perspective," *Public Finance* 34 (1979): 313–355; Wayne W. Snyder, "Measuring the Stabilizing Effects of Social Security Programs in seven Countries, 1955–65," *National Tax Journal* 23 (1970): 263–273; David Cameron, "The Expansion of the Political Economy: A Comparative Analysis," *American Political Science Review* 72 (1978): 1243–1261; Cutright, "Political Structure."

22. For example, Orloff's contention in "The Political Origins," 56, that Gompers was really similar to many more demanding European union leaders, or Skocpol's unqualified acceptance of Labour party solidarity behind the welfare state in "The Limits of the New Deal System," Weir, Orloff, and Skocpol, *Politics of Social Policy*, are rather misleading historical generalizations.

23. On TUC conservativism on social issues between the wars see Douglas E. Ashford, *The Emergence of the Welfare States* (Oxford: Blackwell, 1986), 211–216, 253–254. For a full account, Elizabeth Rathbone, *The Disinherited Family* (London: Allen and Unwin, 1924).

24. See Jose Harris, *William Beveridge: A Biography* (Oxford: Clarendon Press, 1977), 399–402.

25. See Ashford, *Emergence of the Welfare States*, 189–194. For a full account, E. Levasseur, *Questions ourvrières et industrièlles en France sous la Troisième République* (Paris: Rousseau, 1907).

26. For an application of convergence ideas to the American welfare state see Gary Freeman and Paul Adams, "Ideology and Analysis in American Social Security Policymaking," *Journal of Social Policy* 12 (1983): 75–95.

27. Among recent revisions, see Peter Aimer, "The Strategy of Gradualism and the Swedish Wage-Earner Funds," *West European Politics* 8 (1985): 43–55; Diane Sainbury, "Scandinavian Party Politics Reexamined: Social Democracy in Decline?" *West European Politics* 7 (1984): 67–102. Perhaps the most important revisionist study by a Swede is Gunnar Hechscher, *The Welfare State and Beyond* (Minneapolis: University of Minnesota, 1984). See also Gunnell Gustafsson, "Swedish Social Security and Welfare," 1985, mimeographed.

28. G. V. Rimlinger's essay, "Social Policy under German Fascism," in Rein, Esping-Andersen, and Rainwater, *Stagnation and Renewal*, 59–77, is an important historical contribution but oddly divorced

from the heavily bureaucratic and heirarchical history of German social policy.

29. J. A. G. Pocock, *The Machiavellian Moment: Florentine Political Thought and Atlantic Republic Tradition* (Princeton, N.J.: Princeton University Press, 1975), 401.

30. In a noteworthy but rather heterogeneous collection of essays trying to define temporal boundaries, Charles Maier, ed., *Changing Boundaries of the Political* (Cambridge: Cambridge University Press, 1987), has almost nothing to say about Britain where political boundaries are best defined. Compare with Ian Harden and Norman Lewis, *The Noble Lie* (London: Hutchinson, 1987); and Tom Nairn, *The Enchanted Glass: Britain and its Monarchy* (London: Radius, 1988).

31. On the rejection of republicanism in Britain, see Willard Wolfe, *From Radicalism to Socialism: Men and Ideas in the Formation of Fabian Socialist Doctrines, 1881–1915* (New Haven, Conn.: Yale University Press, 1975); Edward Royle, *Radicals, Secularists and Representatives: Popular Freethought in Britain, 1866–1915* (Manchester: Manchester University Press, 1980).

32. On Lloyd George's cynical use of social reform, see Robert J. Scaly, *The Origins of the Lloyd George Coalition: The Politics of Social Imperialism, 1900–1918* (Princeton, N.J.: Princeton University Press, 1975); on the main victim, see Kenneth and Jane Morgan, *Portrait of a Progressive: The Political Career of Christopher Viscount Addison* (Oxford: Clarendon Press, 1980).

33. Jose Harris, *William Beveridge*, 434–441.

34. Poor costing and budget forecasting for NHS helped produce the Labour party crisis of 1951 and the party's demise of thirteen years. See John Campbell, *Nye Bevan and the Mirage of British Socialism* (London: Weidenfeld and Nicolson, 1987), 180 ff.

35. See John E. Pater, *The Making of the National Health Service* (London: King Edward's Hospital Fund, 1981); and the remarkably insightful work of Daniel M. Fox, *Health Policies, Health Politics: The British and American Experience, 1911–1965* (Princeton, N.J.: Princeton University Press, 1986).

36. See Ashford, *Emergence of the Welfare States*, 131–139.

37. See Pierre Sorlin, *Waldeck-Rousseau* (Paris: Colin, 1966); Martin Derfler, *Alexandre Millerand: The Socialist Years* (The Hague: Mouton, 1977).

38. Hewitt, "The Effect of Political Democracy and Social Democracy."

39. The best account is David Marquand, *Ramsey MacDonald* (London: Jonathan Cape, 1977).

40. On the critical intellectual role of Jaurès, see Daniel Lindenberg and André Meyer, *Lucien Herr: Le socialisme et son destin* (Paris: Calmann-Lévy, 1977).

41. See the remarkably evenhanded account by Robert Skidelsky, *Sir Robert Moseley* (New York: Holt, Rinehart and Winston, 1975).

42. On the role of disillusioned socialists in Vichy, see Philippe Bauchard, *Les Technocrates et le pouvoir: X-crise, CGT, Clubs* (Paris: Arthaud, 1966), 113–141.

43. See his official social history of the war, Richard Titmuss, *Problems of Social Policy* (London: HMSO, 1950).

44. Ulf Lindstrom, *Fascism in Scandinavia, 1920–40* (Stockholm: Almqvist and Wiksell, 1985).

45. See W. Andrew Achenbaum, *Social Security: Visions and Revisions* (Cambridge: Cambridge University Press for the Twentieth Century Fund, 1987), 19–37; on the interlocking nature of welfare programs in the United States, Lester M. Salamon, *Welfare: The Elusive Consensus* (New York: Praeger, 1978), 64–101. Compare with Theda Skocpol's account of the "belated progress toward a European-style welfare state" in her essay "America's Incomplete Welfare State: The Limits of the New Deal Reforms and the Origins of the Present Crisis," in Rein, Esping-Andersen, and Rainwater, *Stagnation and Renewal*, 35–58.

46. First appearing in Theda Skocpol and John Ikenberry, "The Political Formation of the American Welfare State in Historical and Comparative Perspective," in Tomasson, *Comparative Social Research*, 87–150.

47. Britain is perhaps the best illustration of the political costs of social policy debate. The most balanced account of its relations to the decline of the Labour party in the 1950s is Philip Williams, *Hugh Gaitskell* (London: Jonathan Cape, 1978).

48. Douglas E. Ashford, "The French Socialists Discover the Welfare State," to appear in G. Ross and J. Hollifield, eds., *In Search of Socialist France*.

49. The enormous effects of the 1939 amendments on providing general revenues for social security pensions were wholly unanticipated. See Bruno Stein, "Funding Social Security on a Current Basis: The 1939 Policy Change in the United States," in Douglas Ashford and E. W. Kelley, eds., *Nationalizing Social Security in Europe and America* (Greenwich, Conn.: JAI Press, 1986), 105–126.

50. On the local impediments to nationalizing welfare, see Ashford, *The Emergence of the Welfare States*, 121–143.

51. Oddly enough, British local social policy has come full circle. In 1929 localities were supposed to terminate Poor Law Boards in

favor of grant-supported local relief administered by Local Assistance Boards. Under the financial crunch of the depression, these became nationalized Unemployment Assistance Boards and in 1956 the Supplementary Benefits Commission. Now Thatcher has created the "Social Fund" from which localities must borrow social assistance funds. See Patricia Ruggles and Michael O'Higgins, "Retrenchment and the New Right: A Comparative Analysis of the Impacts of the Thatcher and Reagan Administrations," in Rein, Esping-Andersen, and Rainwater, *Stagnation and Renewal*, 160–190.

52. Douglas E. Ashford, "A Victorian Drama: The Fiscal Subordination of Local Government," in D. Ashford, ed., *Financing Urban Government in the Welfare State* (London: Nethuen, 1980), 71–96.

53. The discussions of the cabinet committee on reconstruction reflects the unanimous feeling of ministers concerned with postwar social policy that local authorities should be excluded from health, land use, and employment policies. See Ashford, *Emergence of the Welfare States*, 264–281.

54. As Rudolf Klein argues in *The Politics of the National Health Service* (London: Longmans, 1983), it is more accurate to speak of the nationalization of hospitals than the nationalization of the health professions, medical education, or medical research.

55. It is not coincidental that one of the most advanced European welfare states, Holland, has also virtually abolished partisan local government by appointing mayors and making local identification almost impossible in national election.

56. Deborah Stone, *The Limits of Professional Power: National Health Care in the Federal Republic of Germany* (Chicago: University of Chicago Press, 1980).

57. On the conflict between decentralization of services and economic recovery, see Agne Gustafsson, *Decentralization in Sweden* (Stockholm: Swedish Institute, 1984).

58. For example, in nineteenth-century America the federal system enhanced the development of poor relief decades before the federal government acted. See Michael B. Katz, *In the Shadow of the Poorhouse* (New York: Basic Books, 1986).

59. Colin Clark, "Public Finance and Changes in the Value of Money," *Economic Journal* 55 (1945): 371–389.

60. Milton Friedman, "The Line We Dare Not Cross: The Fragility of Freedom at 60 Percent," *Encounter*, November 1976, 8–14.

61. Martin Rein and Lee Rainwater, "The Public/Private Mix," in M. Rein and L. Rainwater, eds., *Public/Private Interplay in Social Protection: A Comparative Study* (New York: Sharpe, 1986), 3. Compare with the subtle and informed view of the common law and

social security by Anthony Ogus, "Great Britain," in P. Kohler and Hans Zacher, eds., *The Evolution of Social Insurance, 1881–1981* (London: Pinter; New York: St. Martin's Press, 1982), 150–264; or such monumental studies of the judicial foundations of social justice as W. Friedmann, *Law in a Changing Society* (London: Stevens, 1959).

62. See Michael O'Higgins, "Inequality, Redistribution and Recession: The British Experience, 1976–1982," *British Journal of Social Policy* 14 (1985): 279–307.

63. Christa Altensetter, "German Social Security Programs: An Interpretation of Their Development, 1883–1985," in Ashford and Kelley, *Nationalizing Social Security*, 73–97.

64. Margaret Weir, Ann Shola Orloff, and Theda Skocpol, "Understanding American Social Politics", in Weir, Orloff, and Skocpol, *Politics of Social Policy*, 9–13. Yet the same authors point to numerous parallel developments such as the appearance of "new liberals" in the United States and Britain (p. 12); the similarity of the poor relief in the United States and Europe (p. 49); the similarity in the spread of worker compensation laws (p. 53); the fear that excessive reliance on the "dole" would have debilitating effects on the population (p. 73); the indifference of unions toward tax code reforms (p. 131).

65. For reasons noted above, the neoradicals tend to agree with the statistical studies done in the 1960s and 1970s. A contextual analysis would suggest that even statistical concepts must be closely examined to see to what extent urbanization, industrialization, and growth were indeed similar or dissimilar across countries before making such abstract variables the foundation for a state formation theory. Compare this with the much more cautious approach of historians such as Raymond Grew, ed., *Crises of Political Development Europe and the United States* (Princeton, N.J.: Princeton University Press, 1978).

66. Except for Sweden trade unions have a relatively undistinguished record in relation to social reform and social security in all the democracies but for very different reasons. French unions labored under the spell of anarchists; British unions distrusted elitist Labour party leaders; Weimar unions wanted more direct representation in industry, etc. See Kenneth D. Brown, *Labour and Unemployment, 1900–1914* (London: Rowman and Littlefield, 1971); Georges Lefranc, *Histoire du travail et des travailleurs* (Paris: Flammarion, 1957); John A. Moses, *Trade Unions in Germany from Bismarck to Hitler* (Totowa, N.J.: Barnes & Noble, 1982).

67. Skocpol and Ikenberry, "Political Formation of the American Welfare State," acknowledge the origin of the "big bang" metaphor in

Christopher Leman, "Patterns of Policy Development: Social Security in the United States and Canada," *Public Policy* 25 (1977): 261–291, but Leman was comparing systems with remarkably similar structural features in their constitutions, territorial organization, historical development, and even cultural heterogeneity.

68. Again, the simple working class argument does not do justice to the lure of political power in each system. John Burns, head of the Local Government Board in the Lib-Lab government of 1906, renowned for organizing the London match girls, staunchly defended punitive Poor Laws before the 1909 Royal Commission. He never used the board for the social reform, leaving the way open for Lloyd George at the Treasury and Churchill at the Board of Trade. See Ashford, *Emergence of Welfare States*, 121–132. Léon Jouhaux's uninspired leadership of the interwar, noncommunist CGT made the communist union takeover much easier in 1945. See Bernard Georges and Denise Tintaut, *Léon Jouhaux: Cinquantes années de syndicalism*, 2 vols. (Paris: Presses Univérsitaires de France, 1962).

69. The neo-Marxist thread that runs through the welfare capitalism argument is not completely misleading, but its applications often only note the negative effects of business-driven social reform and simply skip over the internal uncertainties growing social awareness often caused within business circles. See, for example, Beth Stevens, "Blurring Boundaries: How the Federal Government Has Influenced Welfare Benefits in the Private Sector," in Weir, Orloff, and Skocpol, *The Politics of Social Policy*, 123–148.

70. Richard Kuisel, *Capitalism and the State in Modern France* (London: Cambridge University Press, 1981).

71. Henri Galant, *Histoire politique de la securité sociale en France, 1945–1952* (Paris: Colin, 1955); Douglas E. Ashford, *The Boundaries of the Welfare States*, forthcoming.

72. Martin Rein and Lee Rainwater, "The Future of the Public/Private Mix," in Rein and Rainwater, *Public/Private Interplay*, 203. For Charles Maier, "The Politics of Time," in Maier, *Changing Boundaries of the Political*, 156, all the demarcations of time are attributed to socioeconomic aspects of bourgeois society.

73. Market public spending and socialist public spending are compared by Frederick Pryor, *Public Expenditures in Communist and Capitalist Nations* (New Haven, Conn.: Yale University Press, 1968). Comparisons can be perplexing. See Szelenyi and Manchin, "Social Policy under State Socialism," 102–139, which thoroughly excoriates market redistribution and concludes with an account of a private Hungarian welfare group that works better than state agencies.

74. Most macrolevel and statistical research omits consideration of the instrumentalities and procedures generated by welfare state development. For example, the French law on associations of 1901 was regarded as a major republic innovation to enable groups, associations, and volunteers to participate in social activites. The invigoration of associational acivity became a central feature of socialist social policy in 1981. See Journal Official, Conseil Economique et Social, *La place et le rôle du secteur associatif dans le développement du rôle du secteur associatif dans le développement de la politique d'action éducation sanitaire et social* (Rapport Théry), session de 1986, 26 juillet 1986. Likewise, the sharp boundaries between public and private pensions in Britain are primarily due to the rigid interpretation of trust under the common law. On the complications of creating an integrated pension plan, see Treasury and Civil Service Subcommittee, *The Structure of Personal Income Taxation and Income Support*, London, Parliamentary Papers, H.C. 331, session 1981–1982.

75. The best account of the wide-ranging intellectual implications of adjusting to welfare politics in France is William Logue, *From Philosophy to Sociology: The Evolution of French Liberalism, 1870–1914* (Dekalb, Ill.: Northern Illinois University Press, 1983). In fact, as argued by Pierre Rosanvallon, *Le Moment Guizot* (Paris: Gallimard, 1985), it is doubtful if political or economic liberalism was taken seriously in France after the Restoration period.

76. Katz, *In the Shadow of the Poorhouse*, 217–229. Leaders of the American charity movement were well known to the British Charitable Organization Society and participated in the 1901 World Exposition in Paris with European welfare reformers.

77. Contrary to the Crozier model of French policy and politics, there is such an abundance of associational life in France that the Conseil d'État gave up its effort to count them some years ago. For a sample listing see Conseil National de la Vie Associative (a Socialist innovation), *Bilan de le vie associative en 1982* (Paris: Documentation Française, 1985).

78. As a socioeconomic theory of the welfare state Esping-Andersen's ideas about "decommodification" are notable, but even his *Politics Against Markets* tells us little about how we are to reconcile our multiple roles as consumers, patients, parents, workers, students, and so forth under nonmarket conditions without the same market imperfections that often blemish competitive markets.

79. All the democracies encountered the low status assigned to social policy and social work within government. Both the survival and limitations of the French social security system have much to do with the leadership provided by the Conseil d'État and in particular

Pierre Laroque's work. See Ashford, *The Boundaries of the Welfare States*, forthcoming.

80. Historical studies such as Katz's *In the Shadow of the Poorhouse* and Achenbaum's *Social Security: Visions and Revisions* are generally more sensitive to the intergovernmental complexities, as are such policy-oriented books as Salamon's *Welfare*.

81. For a sobering account, see Margarite A. Sieghart, *Government by Decree: A Comparative Study of the History of the Ordinance in England and French Law* (London: Stevens, 1950). An even more provocative historical account is A. P. Thornton, *The Tradition of Authority: Paternalism in British History* (London: Allen and Unwin, 1965).

82. Though meant as an attack on the monarchy, Tom Nairn's *The Enchanted Glass* is really an impassioned account of what historical and constitutional scholars have long known but failed to see clearly. Compare with W. H. Greenleaf, *The British Political Tradition* (London: Methuen, 1983 and 1988); and Peter Smith, *A Social History of English Law* (London: Stevens, 1975).

Chapter

16

The Policy Community Approach to Industrial Policy

Jack Hayward

The salient characteristic of the industrial policy process should not be regarded as either state-centered or dispersed decision throughout a myriad of specific markets. Industrial policy communities are based on the functional interdependence between a fragmented public administration and its sponsored private subgovernments. The symmetrical expansion of public and private organizations in the nineteenth and twentieth centuries led to a recognition of the need to engage in a continuing collaboration between them. In traditional state-centered political systems such an emerging partnership involved an acceptance of the partial autonomy of business and professional organizations that could not simply be reduced to the subordinate status of civil service functionaries. In less authoritarian systems there was an acceptance that private activities had to accept public regulation, exchanging a measure of protection for acquiescence in state supervision, for the effective pursuit of business and professional purposes in an interdependent industrial environment.

The fragmentation of the public industrial authorities and the partial cohesions that develop between the private sector authorities destroy both the monolithic singularity of the state and the unstructured pluralism of society. What emerges is a structured pluralism of both the public and private authorities that need to collaborate to avoid mutually damaging conflicts. A centralized administration internalizes the variety of the society that it seeks to regulate rather than eliminating social differences by reducing them to a standardized uniformity. What appears to be uniform conceals the differential resistance of social forces to central control, as well as their capacity to shape and steer the public authorities into serving their private purposes. A dualistic view of the state versus society distorts realities in that it ignores the extistence of a complex network of sectoral clientelistic relationships between relatively autonomous "segments of the state," particular subgovernments or public agencies, on the one hand, and the societal sectional interest groups whose activities they seek to regulate on the other. What can be observed are stable interorganizational links between public and private actors in the policy process, whose informal relationships are the key to the way in which formal arrangements work in practice.

The proposed policy research strategy seeks to assist directly in the empirical investigation of industrial policy. It falls into five parts. First, the discussion of symmetrical sectorization focuses upon the industrial policy subsystems that have developed out of the associated processes of functional specialization and "sectorization" both of organized interests and public administration. Sectorization refers to the perception of decision making and implementation as taking place within specific, discrete, empirically identifiable sectors, forming stable segments of a more complex, abstract whole. Second, regulatory norms and legitimizing rhetoric are contrasted with the behavioral realities in matters of economic policy making generally and industrial policy in particular. The research strategy considers in turn the normative policy reference points, the policy objectives, and the mediating or leading agents capable of spreading the norms and achieving their practical application. Third, a contrast is drawn between a more integrated policy communities approach and a less integrated policy networks approach, and an attempt is made to clarify the conceptual confusion which has developed. Fourth, alternative explanations based on the view that industrial policy is dominated either by a few major market-oriented firms or by a state-oriented bureaucratic elite are criticized. Fifth, in considering a research agenda for the 1990s, we examine whether a policy community approach, which focuses upon the activities of policy makers without ignoring policy outcomes, might be useful in cross-sectoral and cross-national research.

THE REINTEGRATION OF DISINTEGRATED DECISION

The spuriously singular terms "government," "industry," and "policy" predispose one to regard industrial policy decision as integrated. In fact, they are usually piecemeal expedients, an improvised amalgam of ad hoc instruments and inconsistent objectives, intended to influence firms to behave in ways that would not have spontaneously occurred in a market context.[1] The conception of "two sides of industry" oversimplifies both of them, as well as the industrial policy that links them, by neglecting the complex of stable linkages that have developed between subgovernments and industrial sectors.

The process of functional specialization was institutionalized by the establishment of compartmentalized, vertical divisions within each ministry or government department. The administrative culture that was associated with this structure did not merely lead to "departmentalism." Each bureaucratic segment of the ministry developed its own traditions, practices, loyalties, and clientele, so that a symmetrical sectorization occurred between the "sponsored" interests and the "sponsoring" subdivisions of the ministry. Here, the French sense of the word *corporatisme*, as the myopic and exclusive pursuit of short-term, sectional interests, should be combined with the farsighted and comprehensive pursuit of the long-term, general interest attributed to members of the state-trained *grands corps*. What united the societal advocates of a particular policy with the segment of the state administration officially responsible for this particular matter was their specialized concern with a specific policy issue. Despite the claim that public officials served the public interest, concentration upon their shared concern in the outcomes of the particular policy with the private interests meant that their vision was usually as circumscribed as that of their unofficial partners. However, their superior claim to legitimate authority imparted a status to the shared expertise and social interaction with unofficial policy professionals that it would not otherwise have had. The extent to which a relatively closed policy community may emerge from this bilateral conjunction of two *corporatismes*, rather than either a looser, more dispersed multilateral policy network or a policy monopoly by a dominant actor capable of imposing nonnegotiable decisions, will be discussed later.

What this process of sectorization suggests is that the disintegration of decisions among "numerous relatively narrow and self-contained policy-making systems" should lead analysis to be focused upon the policy outputs.[2] The presumption, originally argued by Lowi and more recently developed by Gary Freeman, is that policy determines politics because outputs are less the result of choices made by policy actors than the functional necessities of particular policy problems. Consequently, a subsystems policy perspective would suggest starting with a policy problem, before working back to the public and private actors who cluster in relatively autonomous groups around the particular policy program, who will need to mobilize the necessary political and financial support to implement the politics concerned. Freeman argues that "the logic of subsystem policies leads us to expect that policy communities will develop around particular programmes, ministries, or policies.[3]

The attempt to cope with the incapacity of an ambitious macro-corporatism to deal adequately with the specific problems of sectorization has lead to attempts to stretch it. This exercise has involved the development of "mesocorporatism" and "microcorporatism" to account for decisions at the sectoral and firm level. However, the difficulty in finding actual examples confirms the suspicion that these concepts seem rather remote from reality. While Cawson has pursued the search for sectoral corporatism energetically, he is hard put to it to identify a good example outside the dairy industry, although agriculture generally is regarded as more susceptible to corporatist arrangements than manufacturing industry.[4] Discussion of the government's relations with particular firms will be postponed until we consider unilateral domination.

REGULATORY NORMS, LEGITIMIZING RHETORIC, AND BEHAVIORAL REALITIES

If sectorization is the structural basis of policy making, then regulatory norms and the legitimizing rhetoric which tends to accompany the norms provide its cultural basis. The values and beliefs form the normative framework within which policy is initiated, formulated, elaborated, implemented, and evaluated. They set the shifting but nevertheless enduring standards that shape the working of the policy process. Specific industrial policies as behavioral realities need to be seen as undertaken within a framework of norms that may give priority to preserving socioeconomic stability over promoting modernization or favor preserving national firms by protectionism instead of exposing them to international competition. When these metapolitical norms change, they affect the way in which specific policies are pursued as well as the substance of the policies themselves. While the changing rhetoric has only a belated and partial impact upon behavioral realities, it legitimizes some industrial activities and delegitimizes others. If this normative dimension is neglected, both the industrial policies of particular countries and national comparisons will be misconceived. To allow us to understand the relationship between industrial norms, rhetoric, and realities, we must first ask where these norms come from.

In Western Europe the Roman Catholic church traditionally provided the general norms that governed behavior. It was not the sole normative guide; urban development led to the emergence of regulatory guilds which provided "sectoral," professional, general guiding beliefs. (Such "corporations" are rarely invoked in neocorporatist theories, although they could provide such theories with historical roots.) In late twentieth-century capitalist and liberal democratic societies, churches seldom play their earlier comprehensive normative role. When they attempt to do so, they are usually treated by political actors with either indifference or hostility. They are told to "mind their own business," religious norms being confined to a limited, other-worldly aspect of social life. In communist societies attempts to subordinate behavior to overarching ideological norms have proved even less successful. Only in parts of the Middle East, with the revival of Muslim fundamentalism, have religious norms of the Koran been reasserted with fanatical fervor.

Without an accepted religious or ideological set of norms governing political behavior, we have to fall back upon a procedural code or logic that provides the implicit framework within which public issues are analyzed and assessed. As Charles Anderson has put it, "Policy making is not simply problem-solving. It is also a matter of setting up and defining problems in the first place."[5] I have elsewhere referred to these metapolitical norms as "the relatively stable set of semi-absolutes that constitute the normative framework . . . by which actual policy practice is categorized and judged."[6] Dyson has written of a "higher-order normative code" which "forms part of the thought processes of policy-makers as a shared way of looking at, and responding to, problems."[7] Similarly, Sharpe, in the context of discussing professional and policy communities at the subnational level, has used the concept of "operating ideology."[8]

If we are to grasp how the policy norms play this crucial role, both at the general and sectoral levels, it would be useful to consider an example. In postwar France, the metapolitical norm that has shaped industrial policy has been modernization, which displaced the previous commitment to stability. This was a result of changed circumstances. By the mid twentieth century, the consciousness of economic backwardness and the need to modernize the political system to make it capable of steering France in its desperate race to catch up and surpass its rivals was translated into the dramatic demographic, economic, and political transformation of the country. A new international political and economic context, an incapacity to prevent this new world from intruding into French economic, political, and cultural life, and the legacy of defeat and decolonization meant that there was a major shift in France's dominant metapolitical norms. In place of the preservation of stability, modernization became the general policy reference point of a techno-bureaucratic elite that had its political, business, trade union, and farm union allies. Associated with the mobilizing norm of modernization was the substitution of competitiveness for protectionism, as part of a partial sacrifice of national political will to the necessary constraints of the international market. In the process an earlier emphasis on "small is beautiful" gave way to the need to create national and later multi-national champion firms capable of operating on an international scale. The subsidiary metapolitical norm of solidarity meant that industrial decline had to be managed with a modicum of good order, in terms of the treatment of the displaced, particularly when the industries concerned had a high symbolic status and the firms involved were household names.[9] Legitimation of industrial change had to be by reference to norms whose acceptability would allow painful adjustments to be made with a minimum of discord. The values of community are useful in facilitating the trouble-free dismantling of protective barriers against competitiveness. The 1970s retreat from Keynesianism in favor of monetarism represents a similar change in norms in advanced industrial societies, generally but differentially.

The regulatory norms may also take the practical form of "rules of the game" among those who share in policy activity. Rhodes and Wright have discussed these limitations upon discretionary action (generalizing from the earlier emphasis by Heclo and Wildavsky in their study of the British public expenditure community) upon "the networks of reciprocal trust" that provide the basis of mutual confidence in the British expenditure community.[10] In addition to mutuality, Wright specifies as other rules of the unwritten constitution of policy networks in Britain a willingness to consult informally, the acceptable use of state intervention, and so forth,[11] secrecy and confidentiality being pushed to obsessive lengths to protect the mutual concessions made by those who bargain from premature revelation while negotiations are proceeding. Some of the rules are observed selectively, a good subject for cross-sectoral and cross-national research. In Britain the "leak" is the counterpart of the rule of secrecy, so that behavioral reality will be at a greater or lesser remove from the rhetoric of confidentiality and the norm of reciprocal trust at different times and in relation to different issues.

However important the relationships between policy actors are in the capacity to formulate and implement specific industrial policies, the very general metapolitical norms must be translated into achievable objectives. A major difficulty here is that just as sectorization has separated the policy actors into specialized subsystems, so there are a variety of separate but interdependent policy objectives; for example, industrial policy as such will at times be secondary to exchange rate, energy, employment, or research policies. Before we consider the problem of managing many autonomous but interdependent policy actors, each pursuing their own priorities, often without a mediator or leader capable of bringing about a consistent policy, it is necessary to explore the range of objectives pursued. Kirschen and his economist associates distinguished between primary and subsidiary objectives of economic policy (though he called them "pure" and "quasi" objectives, respectively), the former being ends in themselves and the latter being indirect and instrumental ways of attaining the primary objectives.[12] To put industrial policy and its train of industrial policies in their broader, interdependent context, let us consider these general objectives of economic policy. The seven primary objectives are: full employment, price stability, increased production, promotion or protection of firms or industries, redistribution of income, increased leisure, and reduction of regional disparities. The seven subsidiary objectives are: a favorable balance of payments, secure supplies of essential energy and raw materials, increased international trade and mobility, increased competition, technological modernization, increased investment, and changed pattern of consumption.

From after World War II until the 1970s, full employment—a slippery concept, as is unemployment—was a prime objective of short-term macroeconomic policy. Like price stability, it became a deliberate goal of public policy only when the "automatic" classic economic mechanisms could not be relied upon and Keynesian demand management policies were adopted to correct short-term deflationary phases of the business cycle. The currently more fashionable monetarist policies have an equally short-term preoccupation with the inflationary consequences of the postwar concern to achieve high and sustained rates of economic growth. An attempt was made to show that rates of unemployment and inflation were inversely related, an example of the kind of macroeconomic explanation of how changes in economic variables are related to each other. This Phillips curve explanation has now been discredited by monetarist critics. It was based upon a trade-off between the rate of inflation and the level of unemployment, which could not account for the coexistence of hyperinflation and persistent mass unemployment, whereas Keynesians had assumed constant price levels and believed that fiscal policy could provide short-term adjustment to avoid both price stability and mass unemployment.[13]

There are five longer-term economic policy objectives, broadly related to increasing economic growth and redistributing the wealth created in terms of income, working hours, and regional allotment. Increasing production and the protection or promotion of specific firms or industries are clearly industrial policies aimed at increasing economic growth and reinforcing or redeploying the industrial structure. However, these policies aimed at increasing wealth have to compete with policies intended to redistribute wealth. Income policies may have anti-inflationary as well as redistributive purposes, while the increase in leisure by the reduction of the working day, week, year or life has significant effects on economic growth as well as redistribution. Social justice objectives may also compete with the objective of territorial justice, the reduction of regional disparities being one aspect of regional policies, which have an impact upon industrial policies.

The seven subsidiary economic policy objectives can be divided into three categories. First, two intermediate objectives relate to the need to protect a country's capacity to make purchases abroad. It is necessary to achieve a favorable balance of payments and maintain adequate reserves of gold and foreign exchange. It is also indispensable to secure supplies of essential energy and primary products, as the 1973 oil crisis demonstrated dramatically. Second, in market economies, two subsidiary objectives aim at promoting an optimum allocation of resources. They are increasing international trade and the mobility of goods, services, labor, and capital on the one hand and increasing domestic competition by the prevention of the emergence of monopolies and cartels on the other. Third, three subsidiary objectives are concerned with changing the economic structure, a purpose that was originally characteristic of communist command economies but was increasingly adopted in market economies. They are the deliberate promotion of a shift from agriculture to industry and from industry to services, with an emphasis on technologically advanced activities; selective increase in investment; and a change in the pattern of consumption, that is, a change in the balance between collective and private consumption. It is not necessary to stress the difficulties involved in interpreting, still less reconciling in practice, all these objectives, which form the focus of the complex process of interaction from which policies eventually emerge.

When it comes to national comparisons of actual achievements with the objectives fixed, Kirschen and his associates found that in the 1960s the countries with the most ambitious annual economic policy targets were (in decreasing order) West Germany, France, and Italy, while the United States and especially the United Kingdom had the least ambitious annual targets. As far as medium-term economic policy targets were concerned, the Netherlands and France emerged as the most ambitious and West Germany, Italy, and the United Kingdom as the least ambitious. We should be clear that the achievement ratios do not measure policy success in any normative sense. They merely provide an "index of realism" on the part of the policy makers.[14] The retreat from comprehensive attempts at medium-term national economic planning, both in capitalist countries such as France (and Britain and Italy, where it can hardly be said to have been tried) and in the communist countries of Eastern Europe and the Soviet Union, indicates realism of a different kind. The increasing inability of governments to achieve impressive economic policy targets calculated to arouse public enthusiasm has discouraged them from setting such targets.

As far as the short-term objectives of full employment, price stability, and balance of payments equilibrium in the 1960s are concerned, West Germany's performance was good, France's average, and the United Kingdom's poor. On the medium-term objective of economic growth (involving increases in production, investment, and employment) France achieved a high rate of growth, Italy and the Netherlands did better than average, West Germany did below average, and the

United States and United Kingdom performed worst of all. France's relatively good performance on growth compared to the short-term objectives may have reflected her priorities, a willingness to sacrifice price stability, for example, to medium-term expansion, while West Germany's priorities were the reverse. However, as France increasingly entered the EEC and the world market in the 1960s, her capacity to sacrifice the short-term to the medium-term came under increasing constraint. This was reflected in the French Fifth Plan (1966–1970) highly sensitive early warning indicators attached to the antiinflationary policy objectives of price stability and balance of payments equilibrium and the rather insensitive indicators for the antideflationary policy objectives of increasing productive investment and restraining unemployment. Increasingly, such macroeconomic indicators came to be measured not in absolute terms but relative to the performance of France's competitors in the EEC and OECD, as was the case in the Ninth Plan (1984–1988).

Wright has set out the three policy norms fixed by Britain's Department of Industry in 1983, which were subdivided into fourteen major aims and a hundred and fifty precise policy objectives.

> For example, one of the 14 main aims was "the systematic use of public purchasing to promote innovation and meet international standards." Further analysis of this policy norm in operation would indicate the particular "standards" currently set: how much and what kind of public purchasing policy, in what circumstances and under what conditions. The public purchasing processes would be regulated in general terms by those standards, and the policy issues and problems which arose would be concerned with the making and carrying out of policy within those standards. It would also be about trying to extend or contract those standards.[15]

Such official policy guidelines were those set by the ministry and we shall later consider the way in which such official norms have to be adapted to fit in with the exigencies of dealings within policy networks, policy communities, and a policy monopoly by a dominant actor.

The major contrast within public administration is between the "horizontal" ministries—particularly the Finance Ministry responsible for protecting the general interest from the depredations of sectional interests—and the "vertical" ministries, which often work in conjunction with the special interests that they sponsor. The latter, working within their associated policy networks, communities, and dominant actors, exercise disintegrative pressures upon overall public policy. The outcome of the annual bargaining process measures the ability of the finance minister and the department to count upon the prime minister's or president's backing to enforce a measure of constraint and coordination upon the demands of the official and unofficial spokespersons of those with designs upon the public purse. It also allows one to observe the rhetorical invocation of public interest regulatory norms and procedures for imposing budgetary limits. The need to mobilize allies within and outside the processes of public decision making and implementation is a major incentive to develop policy networks and communities. However, before we consider these features of the industrial policy process, it is necessary to consider the innovative agents whose role is to impart an impetus and impress a legitimacy upon the sectoral realities.

This function of sectoral leadership may be performed either by modernizing elite agents within the administration or by changing agents from among the organized interests. Usually, it is a matter of inducing incremental changes within the existing normative framework; occasionally it is the values themselves that are being changed. In the French case those who have usually performed this function are the specialist *corps* who, to preserve or extend their positions of power and policy influence, may colonize a policy sector, both within and outside government, by the process of *pantouflage* or mobility between top positions. Such technocratic leadership was important in the early postwar years when a new conception of industrial development had to be spread among public policy makers.

At the general level, no one *corps* was able to assume leadership, so the gospel of the "industrial imperative" was spread by an innovative alliance of planners, members of the finance inspectorate, and mining engineers recruited respectively through the *École Nationale d'Administration* and the *École Polytechnique*, with allies from among their fellow *corps* members attached to ministers' *cabinets*, sympathetic businesspeople, and economic journalists. The itinerary of Lionel Stoléru, the author in 1969 of *L'Impératif Industriel*,[16] is indicative of the capacity of such modernizing agents to form part of an interlocking policy directorate that transcends political divergences. He was a product of *Polytechnique* and the *Corps des Mines*, served in the Planning Commissariat, was a member of Finance Minister Giscard d'Estaing's *cabinet*, became a minister during Giscard's presidency, and in 1988 provisionally ended up as minister in charge of planning in Michel Rocard's Socialist government.

Other examples are provided by Jobert and Muller. In applying the notion of what they call policy mediators, they show how the telecommunications engineers of the French Post Office's General Direction of Telecommunications (DGT) played the key role in using the rhetoric of the high tech "information society" to legitimize the modernization of the French telephone system, before using the notion of a "cultural imperative" to develop a much wider ranging cable plan. They also indicate how the earlier modernization of French agriculture owed a great deal to the leadership of the Young Farmers leaders of the CNJA, in alliance with an innovative minister of agriculture.[17] Such examples show how the inertial hold of both bureaucratic and interest organizations can be broken and new policy norms can be translated into behavioral realities.

POLICY COMMUNITIES AND INDUSTRIAL POLICIES

Although it was two American political scientists, Heclo and Wildavsky, who first related the notions of policy and community in their 1974 study of *The Private Government of Public Money*, their insight subsequently evoked most interest among British scholars, perhaps because the book was devoted to a study of the British "expenditure community," but also thanks to their being accustomed to a club approach to decision making. Although it appeared in the same year as Schmitter's essay "Still the Century of Corporatism?" it took longer to prompt others to follow up its suggestive study of a specific policy process, whose key notion was that "Community is the cohesive and orienting bond underlying any particular issue."[18] Before it caught on, it required the appearance in 1978 of an essay by Hugh Heclo on "Issue Networks and the Executive Establishment" in American politics, which eschewed the concept of policy community in favor of a contrast between and partial transition from closed subgovernments, or "iron triangles," to open issue networks. This iron triangle consisted of an administrative agency, its associated interest group(s), and the appropriate congressional committee(s).

> Iron triangles and subgovernments suggest a stable set of participants coalesced to control fairly narrow public programs which are in the direct economic interest of each party to the alliance. Issue networks are almost the reverse image in each respect. Participants move in and out of the networks constantly. Rather than groups united in dominance over a program, no one, as far as one can tell, is in control of the policies and issues.[19]

Subsequent research in the United States has suggested that in recent decades there has been a decline in the prevalence of iron triangle subgovernments and structured pluralism in favor of the looser and unstructured pluralism of issue networks. Outsiders erupt much more readily and unpredictably into the policy arena, which is more permeable than a closed policy community. Conflict rather than consensus arises from the neglected importance of political partisanship, while appreciation of the interdependence of policy issues and the significance of the side effects of isolated policy activity breaks down the compartmentalization presupposed by sectoral subgovernment.[20] The notion of sectoral policy networks has been used in attempting to distinguish "strong" from "weak" states in the sphere of comparative industrial policy, initially by Katzenstein and more recently by Atkinson and Coleman.[21] However, as Ezra Suleiman has shown in a recent French case study, an apparently "strong" state may be in a paralyzing sector symbiosis with organized private interests that are capable of manipulating the various public actors—political, bureaucratic, and financial—with which they have dealings.[22] For a focus upon policy communities, we must turn to European scholars who are accustomed to a more tightly structured pluralism than is usually found in North America.

From a British perspective, Jordan did not see the Heclo distinction as involving a duality so much as opposite ends of a continuum in which the differences concerned who was part of the policy process.

> Thus issue networks are not discretely different arrangements from iron triangles, but are iron triangles with a greatly increased group population, with a further disaggregation of power, with less predictable participants, with reduced cohesion and homogeneity caused by the mobilization of value changing groups, which in turn leads to the reduced capacity to "close" a decision.[23]

He and Richardson developed the notion of a policy community as sharing characteristics in common with both iron triangles and issue networks.

In applying the concept of policy community to Britain, Richardson and Jordan dropped the parliamentary side of the iron triangle. They argued that policy outcomes owed most to "the *policy community* of departments and groups."[24] Within this bilateral conception of government departments and their client groups, the former were designated by Jordan as the senior partners. "The virtue of the term 'community' in describing how policy is made is that community implies a shared implicit authority. Not all parties are equal: the government department is an actor with special resources (legitimacy, prior knowledge, staff) not available to all the other actors."[25] Jordan and Richardson repeatedly stress the departmentalism of British government, acting in policy association with an inner core clientele.

> In practice, it is realistic to think of each policy sector as consisting of several, interrelated, policy communities . . . there is usually an inner core of groups and individuals who really count in any one issue. The existence of these cores is a strong force preventing disintegration of policy communities and sectors into the ill-defined issue networks suggested by Heclo.[26]

However, empirical reality simply cannot be fitted into the straitjacket of corporatism's requirements of highly aggregated, regulated, and institutionalized interests, by adapting it until it looses any precise identity.

In 1979, the same year as Richardson and Jordan proposed the concept of policy community for the purpose of analysis and not merely as a metaphor for policy subsystem, Hogwood applied it, together with that of policy network, directly to the study of British industrial policy. Faced with the multiplicity of organizations involved in industrial policy, Hogwood argued that industrial policy organizations could be regarded as an "industrial policy network." He stressed the role of a "shared policy language" but admitted that the "industrial policy community is clearly a much more dispersed and fragmented community than the expenditure community described by Heclo and Wildavsky," which was confined to Whitehall.[27] This idea was quickly picked up by Wyn Grant in his descriptive treatment of the industrial policy community in Britain, although, like his British predecessors, he accorded almost without argument a priority to Whitehall as the nucleus of the policy communities. "The place of interest groups and firms in the industrial policy community must be considered, although clearly the core of the community is to be found in central government departments."[28]

In the book he edited on *Policy Styles in Western Europe*, Richardson recognized that sectorization of policy making might undermine the attempt to attribute a single policy style to a particular country because different policy communities within the same country would have different policy styles.[29] He could have added, in the wake of Lowi, that the same policy community in two countries might have more in common than different policy communities in the same country. Dyson's chapter on West Germany in Richardson's book applied the policy community concept to the nuclear energy and industrial policy sector in ways that revealed that a ministry-centered approach would be quite misguided. In the case of nuclear energy policy, he showed how, with the commissioning of the first German commercial reactor in 1967–1968, what had been a "small, exclusive and relatively closed policy community of professionals" was forced to adapt under pressure from citizen action groups and political parties. Until then, "The policy community was clearly defined and divided roughly into two opposed groupings: on the one hand, the reactor construction industry, the German Atom Commission and the Federal Ministry of Atomic Affairs, and on the other, the Federal Economics Ministry, the Federal Finance Ministry and the electricity supply companies."[30]

The politicization of the nuclear energy issue in the wake of citizen action group demonstrations, especially after 1973, blocked the German production of nuclear energy at a time when in France the energy policy community, led by the nationalized electricity corporation (EDF) in conjunction with the Atomic Energy Commissariat, was developing with presidential support and despite the Finance Ministry's resistance, a massively ambitious electronuclear energy investment program.[31] By contrast with West Germany, the French nuclear energy policy community demonstrated an enviable control over the membership and access to the policy community, over its agenda of policy issues, the identification of problems, the elaboration of solutions to them, mobilizing consent, and controlling policy implementation. Only in the mid 1980s was a modest cutback in the electronuclear program made because the supply had outrun demand. On industrial policy more generally, the contrast with France is stark. Dyson also shows how difficult it has been for industrial policy to acquire official recognition in West Germany as a sector, to the point that there is no industry ministry. Although a Research and Technology Ministry was established, it was denied any influence over industrial structure policy, the Economics Ministry protecting market self-regulation from state intervention. Insofar as it exists, industrial policy is subordinated to financial policy, over which the Bundesbank exercises uncontested leadership.[32]

More recently, the policy community approach has been elaborated and applied by Rhodes outside the economic-industrial policy sectors to cover the "organizational networks based on the major functional divisions of government" but constituted more broadly by "professional-bureaucratic complexes" with stable memberships, characterized by "vertical interdependence" and horizontal insulation and competition with other function-specific networks.[33] Rhodes argues that the rival concepts of corporatism and network are inadequate to the task of explaining particular policy processes, which involve investigating how they relate to policy content. "If corporatism presents a too rigid metaphor, then issue network is too unstructured: the metaphor of policy communities is an attempt to bridge the gap."[34]

Rhodes helpfully directs attention toward the need to explain policy messes arising from the noncorrespondence of policy systems and policy problems.

It is possible to identify three major forms of non-correspondence. First, the policy system can be overstructured: that is, the policy community is tightly compartmentalized. Consequently, complex policy problems are simplified to the extent that they have few or none of the intended effects but generate a series of side effects within the policy area such that the most undesired outcomes are attained and the problem becomes ever more intractable for future policy decisions which will, in all probability, simply repeat the cycle. Second, the policy system can be under-structured: that is, the policy spans a number of discrete policy communities but there is no articulation between these communities. Consequently, policy messes are generated both by problem simplification within each community and by problem interdependence between the communities. Finally, the policy system can be de-structured: that is, there is no set of interlocking organizations and consequently there is no coherent policy but a series of discrete reactions to particular events.[35]

The main problems with Rhodes's approach are that he retains the earlier emphasis upon the divisions of the central ministries as the nuclei of policy communities and treats policy networks as a looser form of community instead of confining them to the linkages between policy communities, these linkages often being the vital factor in determining success or failure in outcomes rather than intracommunity relations. Heclo had argued that "the growth of specialized policy networks tends to perform the same useful services that it was once hoped a disciplined national party system would perform," but Rhodes, who regards the intergovernmental, professional, and producer networks as looser forms of community, does not see party and network as substitutes. He considers that "the fluctuating relationship between party and policy community is central to understanding the policy process. . . . Both party and policy community can, by turns, initiate and frustrate. Both can act to integrate government action or they can sustain governmental fragmentation."[36]

To conclude this review of attempts to impart greater conceptual precision to the terminology used, Wright defines a "policy function" as constituting discrete areas of government activity in which a "policy universe" of actors have an interest, and a "policy community" as "a group of actors or potential actors drawn from the policy universe whose community membership is defined by a common *policy focus*," identified by product, service, technology, market, and so forth in the industrial sector.[37] Wright proposes that "policy network" should be used to designate the transactions within and between policy communities. He argues that this has several advantages. Members of a policy community who are excluded from stable policy networks can be identified, while a policy network may draw its members from several policy communities. In this way, cross-sector and cross-national comparisons can be made at the level of policy subsystems.

In my own work on French industrial patriotism and economic intervention, I have used the notion of a policy community to identify a network of clustered "insiders" engaged in an interactive process to attain their policy aims. While they do not share common objectives in terms of means or ends, they are sufficiently committed to their established, closed policy processes to accept some sacrifice of their short-term particular interests. What imparts some semblance of unity to a collection of piecemeal expedients, dignified with the spuriously singular appellation of "industrial policy," is an underlying set of cultural or sub-cultural norms.[38] Through successive case studies of trade unions as policy community outsiders, the steel policy community, as well as local and regional economic policy communities, the functional and territorial subsystem dimensions of this form of structured pluralism are examined. Before considering whether this is a sound policy research strategy, we must examine an alternative view that rejects the whole sectorization approach and with it the various policy community and mesocorporatist approaches that have followed from it as applied to industrial policy.

BUSINESS OR BUREAUCRATIC UNILATERAL DOMINATION

Without getting drawn into abstruse arguments about the "relative autonomy of the state" from capitalist firms, in contrast to the collusive interdependence between firms and government, which is presupposed by the policy community approach, it is necessary to consider a powerful counterargument that reduces industrial policies to industrialists' policies. It is not sectoral *corporatismes* that are important, still less macrocorporatism, but corporations, the industrial firms that take industrial decisions. Furthermore, let us consider this approach as formulated in relation to a country that is agreed to have an activist state, France. After a study of the French Government's energy policy, Feigenbaum concluded that it is firms—public or private, French or foreign—that are autonomous from the French state, which has been "captured" by companies that are "the main repositories of expertise and active promoters of policies that administrators are all too inclined to accept."[39] This line of argument has been generalized by Bauer and Cohen on the basis of numerous case studies of French government-industry relations. They have explored "the paradox of the state's fantastic potential power and its actual intervention that usually only sanctions the results of the trial of strength between private industrial groups."[40] The latter, by playing upon the internal divisions of the public administration, can use their industrial influence to steer public resources toward their objectives, converting the state into their financier, client, and commercial traveler.

Because they rely solely upon sectoral information, the public authorities find it difficult to formulate a policy other than that acceptable to the industrialists. What Bauer and Cohen write of the state's arm's length relationship with individual firms in the case of France is true of most advanced industrial market economies.

> Is it not remarkable that in all official documents describing indus-
> trial activity, the situation of particular firms is never mentioned?
> Is it not surprising that the competitive rules of the game and the
> industrialists plans are never taken into account when ministries
> prepare analyses and plans? Senior civil servants treat "sectors" as a
> fact, identifying a statistical category with an economic unit.[41]

The government may help to create national champions, capable of
standing up to foreign firms in the competitive international market,
but in the process it loses any capacity it may have had to influence their
behavior. Thereafter, the firms can play off each part of a fragmented
public administration against the others, which have their own objectives, ensuring that the fragments conform to the industrialists' strategy
rather than the reverse.

The reason the public authorities do not get to grips with the industrial reality of individual firms is that the appeal to legitimizing "general
interest" norms prevents them from concerning themselves directly with
private interests. As a result, they are condemned to deal officially with
the respectable representatives of the general interests of industry at the
peak national level or through their functional trade associations and
territorial chambers of commerce.[42] However, these bodies are
ineffective at playing the role of intermediaries with and leaders of
industrial communities, acting as agents of both business and the state,
because those who take the decisions are the firms. By negotiating regulatory norms indirectly through such nominally representative organizations, public authorities either forgo the ability to exercise a direct
influence over events or in practice have to bypass these bodies. They
surreptitiously hide their actual activities behind formal recourse to the
public pretense of a sectoral plan symbolically demonstrating the
supremacy of the public interest over the private interests.

Cohen and Bauer distinguish three types of relationship underlying
the French pretence of being the heroic architect of ambitious industrial
development rather than the humdrum registrar of modest industrial
regulation. It all depends upon who, if anyone, has industrial power in
a specific instance. Where the government is confronted by powerful
firms in an industrial area, such as the electronics firm Thomson, the
firms can impose their own strategy upon the public authorities, even
when the authorities have recourse to financial pressure or to nationalization. Government industrial policy is reduced to underwriting
schemes devised by others, taking the risks while the firms take the
profits. When the government faces firms that have lost their industrial
power and are in effect bankrupt, such as the firms of France's machine
tools industry (or Britain's for that matter), successive plans fail to
merge the many "lame ducks" into a few "winners." No new industrial

power is constituted or reconstituted by an amalgamation of impotences. Lastly, where no powerful industrial firm exists, the government may decide to take a direct hand through hybrid public sector bodies, such as the DGT in the case of telecommunications, which we referred to earlier. There have been other spectacular instances in the oil, nuclear, space, aerospace, and armaments industries.[43] However, once it has succeeded in creating a powerful industrial actor, the government finds itself in the first type of situation described. It can support a powerful firm but it cannot share its power.[44] It is therefore reduced in microeconomic matters to a regulatory role.

At the level of macroindustrial policy, a similar process occurred on a grand scale, with the Planning Commissariat assisting in the emergence of major firms which then treated it with contempt. The leadership it lost as the innovating agent of industrial modernization allowed the Finance Ministry to reemerge in its traditional regulatory role, providing public resources for the massive investment programs of powerful industrial actors such as *Electricité de France*. Rather than sectorization, what such an approach suggests is the concentration of monopoly industrial power in the hands of a few industrial firms, each in its own sector, who go through the motions of negotiation but are capable of imposing their leadership. In place of the assertion of state *volontarisme*, we have here the proclamation of each major corporation's unilateral domination within its own subsystem.

In my own work on French industrial policy, I have sought to combine the theoretical insight and empirical findings of both the policy community approach and the industrialists' policies approach. I have argued that industrial policy is "usually a symbolic, unitary fiction to cover a multitude of piecemeal, improvisatory and portentous claims by governments to be pursuing a comprehensive and consistent medium and long-term industrial strategy," so "it should not be surprising that it frequently amounts to an industrialists' policy" to whom industrial affairs have been subcontracted.[45] However, whereas a focus upon the firms wholly disintegrated the notion of industrial policies, it is necessary to acquire a broader view, if only because of the interdependencies between firms that may dominate their industrial subsystem but are dependent within the industrial system.

In attempting to make the concept of structured pluralism more precise and more usable in cross-sectoral and cross-national comparison, I have suggested the model of a hexagon of clustered pluralist power. The model focuses attention upon the elites of insider actors who engage in concerted politics, with relapses into endemic conflict or domination by one of the actors in the policy process. The six clusters are the leaders of the partisan executive who take the political decisions covering industry with the help of policy advisers; the leaders of the senior civil service and judiciary responsible for the administration, adjudication, and enforcement of industrial decisions; the heads of the public financial and industrial corporations responsible for public industrial management; the leaders of the private financial and industrial corporations, trade associations, and peak organizations; the labor market leaders of trade unions and professional organizations; and lastly, the parliamentary and party leaders, the prominent elite, and mass media pundits in industrial matters concerned with communication, mobilization, and legitimation. In matters of industrial policy, the presupposition is that there is a convergence of assumptions and purposes between two types of partners: the leaders of the major public and private, national or multinational enterprises, sometimes with their associated but subsidiary representative organizations on the one hand and the elected or selected state officials who manage the ministries, public enterprises, and banks on the other hand. The relationship of enduring partnership—sometimes reinforced by an exchange of members—may give rise to a macroindustrial policy community, superimposed upon specialized, sectoral subcommunities, with more or less institutionalized memberships. Not only do the mass of outsiders include most of those who ought in some measure to shape public policy in an industrial democracy—the workers and the consumers. Those who are supposed to have a say according to liberal democracy—the voters and their representatives—only make an occasional intrusion into the policy process.

In a study of industrial patriotism and economic intervention in France, I applied this approach to one functional and two territorial policy communities: the steel industry and the Lille and Valenciennes areas. Both the industrial and the territorial cases were observed at a time of economic decline (late 1970s and early 1980s) when it might be supposed that the policy partners would be most inclined acrimoniously to part company. In practice, what was observed was a retreat in good order rather than a rout, thanks to the continued collaboration in adversity of the major policy actors. There were, however, major casualties. In the case of the steel policy community the onset of the industrial crisis led to an increasingly important role for the French steel trade association, the successor of the notorious *Comité des Forges*. To it fell the task of uniting the rival actors in each of the private and public sectors—the two major firms (USINOR and SACILOR) and the Finance and Industry Ministries—before bringing them together in support of industrial plans having the backing of all the insiders. However, once the crisis had led to the de facto bankruptcy of the steel firms, nationalization—first covert and then overt—meant that the policy community had in effect been replaced by de facto state domination, prior to the resurgence of a reconstructed state monopoly enterprise.

In the case of the local industrial policy communities, it was not possible to withdraw, an option open, however painful, to an industrial firm. Steel firms might migrate from Lorraine to coastal installations or simply go out of business altogether. Local political and industrial representative bodies are unreservedly committed to their territorial community. Disengagement is not an option, because they have nowhere to which they can retreat. The policy partners from both the representative and bureaucratic public sector—notably the leaders of the local authorities and the chambers of commerce—see their fate as inseparable from the survival and regeneration within the existing locality of its industrial activities, whereas the local firms and banks do not. I concluded that in conditions of industrial crisis, more or less footloose firms—particularly when they are subsidiaries of large national or multinational enterprises—can, with or without compunction, disengage on the basis of pecuniary calculation. Even employees can take the option of "exit" when "voice" has failed. Local public administrators and semi-public bankers can continue their career elsewhere in the country. Only the local representative bodies are irretrievably committed to "loyalty." The fight to stem local economic decline must ultimately depend mainly upon the capacity and will of the democratically elected representatives of the local political community, rather than on those members of the industrial policy community to whom retreat offers an easier way out.[46] The increasing industrial role of local authorities, not merely in France, in the 1980s has confirmed this assessment.

Such an analysis identifies the actual participants in the process at the international, national, regional, and local level, seeking to show the contrast between the legitimizing rhetoric and regulatory norms and the behavioral realities, considering policy failures and successes. Nevertheless, it suffers from being focused upon a single country. Firms are usually better able to work within the international market economy than states, so that an analysis that sees industrial policy communities in national terms, with the state actors playing the role of nucleus of the community, misconceives industrial reality. It would amount in practice to accepting that the overt activities of policy communities, where they exist, amount to underwriting decisions over which they have little influence and confining themselves to dealing with their side effects. Their more fundamental, latent function would be to legitimize the decisions taken by firms, making them acceptable to the public as part of a broader system of regulatory norms, which may require legislation as well as the financial and political support at the national or international level. From time to time, modernizing elites may be able to change significantly the normative framework within which industrialists act, as well as changing the personnel who manage industrial enterprises. Thereafter, the new overall industrial policy system will settle down to work with its new values and leading actors.

THE RESEARCH AGENDA

Industrial policy has suffered from being approached separately either from the side of the government ministries that officially formulate public policy or from the side of organized interests that represent the main industrial actors. The main virtue of the policy community approach is that it avoids such one-sided approaches. It starts from the fact of policy sectorization and considers the way in which the structured pluralism of both public and private actors interrelate. The public authorities are not treated as capable of unilaterally controlling access to the policy-making arena. They cannot fix the normative rules of the game on their own. They do not decide the agenda, timing, or scope of policy decisions. Nor are the public authorities the puppet of "outside" interests that unilaterally impose access, set the rules, initiate and manage the agenda of policy issues from problem identification to implementation and evaluation.

Empirical investigation so far suggests that in matters of industrial policy, the policy community approach, based upon symmetrical policy sectorization, usually fits the facts better than do rival approaches. It is capable of identifying a limited number of actors involved in the continuous collaboration of devising and carrying out specific industrial policies. Despite their conflicting interests, the members of a policy community share values and purposes to a sufficient extent to allow them to continue working together. Their relationships are sufficiently stable and amicable to institutionalize and integrate what would otherwise become improvisatory and adversarial attempts to deal with each policy problem as it arises. Preservation of the policy community becomes an end in itself, not simply because the actors are inclined to be self-absorbed. Policy output is more likely to be evaluated as successful if consensus is achieved by those involved in the process of policy input. The efficient secret of policy success is perceived as being achieved by a strategy of collusive interdependence.

Nevertheless, there are problems with the policy community approach that may prove to be insuperable. Given the particularizing, almost anthropological research strategy adopted, shunning the grand generalizations that were fashionable in earlier attempts at comparative research, one may despair at ever providing the kind of ambitious explanations after which many hanker. The interdependence between policy sectors suggests the need to attain a more comprehensive kind of coordination than is presupposed by the fragmented universe of policy communities, subcommunities, and networks. If the communities provide only a partial account of the policy process because of their narrow and introverted focus, they may also have other severe limitations. Are they concerned with the normative and legitimizing aspects of industrial policy, while other—notably industrial firms—make the actual policy decisions? Once again, only further cross-sectoral and cross-national research can help us to answer such questions.

While the policy community approach is flexible enough to treat much of the relevant data, it badly needs to be tightened up and specified in ways that will become clearer as comparative research uses it. While it is still much too broad gauge, a research strategy has been suggested by Gary Freeman. He puts forward two testable propositions of such a research strategy. Policy-making goals and outcomes in a country will vary significantly between sectors; policy-making goals and outcomes in a particular sector will tend to be similar as between countries. "The policy sector approach, in sum, predicts *differentiation* within individual countries across sectors and *convergence* across nations within sectors."[47] As there are few comparisons of different industrial policies within the same country and the same industrial policy in different countries, there is immense scope for testing the propositions Freeman has advanced.

That the policy community approach can be useful in this connection is suggested in the case of a set of comparative studies of recent changes in communications policies in Western Europe. Dyson sets the scene by showing that "Communications policy in Western Europe had traditionally been characterized by discrete, closed and exclusive 'policy communities' in telecommunications and broadcasting. Now, under the stimulus of deregulation and attacks on monopoly, each began to be crowded and destabilized by new entrants."[48] European collaboration, organized by the European Commission and Europe's leading information technology companies, led to a new policy community at a supranational level, the European Strategic Programme for Research and Development in Information Technology (ESPRIT) in 1982.

> The ESPRIT programme has seen the emergence of a core of key decision-makers comprising representatives from Western Europe's 12 largest computer companies, officials from the European Commission and national civil servants, whose continued contact with each other has developed into and reinforced a relatively closed and privatized world that reflects a consensus on the problems to be addressed and the strategies to be adopted.[49]

While ESPRIT is the most advanced version of the phenomenon, there appears to be a movement toward a policy community style of industrial collaboration within the European Community that would provide a good context for further investigation. An advantage of this policy approach is that it can easily transcend the limitations of state-centered approaches because policy communities do not respect national frontiers.

The policy community approach is likely to be less appropriate or even inappropriate in communist or Third World political systems, having emerged in the context of structured pluralism. It would be interesting to put this to the test. However, it would seem relevant to global industrial policy and research in this direction would be well worth undertaking.[50] It is also far from being appropriate to all policy areas because the lack of clear policy focus or the looseness of the relationships between the actors will mean that what is present is at best a policy network. Here, again, only further comparative work of a cross-industrial nature will enable us to establish the necessary typologies. Nor is the existence of a policy community independent of changing circumstances. As industrial structures are altered and new conjunctures emerge, the conditions for the emergence, consolidation, survival, or disintegration of a policy community will transform the industrial policy universe. New policy configurations will emerge and old ones recede. To integrate such dynamic perspectives with cross-national and cross-sectoral research seems for the present inordinately ambitious, but it should remain a longer-term objective.

Other approaches, such as the mesocorporatist, state-centered, or firm-centered, will continue to be used to study industrial policies. In the case of particular countries, such as Austria and Sweden, labor movements play a prominent role in industrial policy making although they have virtually been ignored in this chapter. The neocorporatist approach may even fit an occasional country like Austria reasonably well.[51] However, this chapter has tried to show that the policy community approach has a breadth and flexibility that enables it to provide a useful framework for analysis of such policies in terms of their meta-political norms as well as their political-industrial practice. By embracing both the objectives and actions of industrial policy makers, as well as the outcomes of their activities, the policy community approach neither assumes that policy determines politics nor that politics determines policy.[52] To the extent that policy issues can be kept out of the public eye and be treated as relatively uncontroversial, specialized issues of concern primarily to specialists, policy issues may not only take priority over politics, but may be depoliticized. Otherwise, politics will reintroduce wider normative and practical concerns that put industrial policy in its subsidiary, instrumental place, with outsiders intruding into the habitual preserves of the partners who share industrial power or the leaders that seek to monopolize it.

NOTES

1. Jack Hayward, *The State and the Market Economy. Industrial Patriotism and Economic Intervention in France* (Brighton: Wheatsheaf Books, 1986), 8.

2. Gary P. Freeman, "National Styles and Policy Sectors: Explaining Structural Variation," *Journal of Public Policy* 5 (October 1985): 485.

3. Ibid., 484. See also Theodore J. Lowi, "American Business, Public Policy, Case Studies, and Political Theory," *World Politics* 16 (1964): 677–715.

4. Alan Cawson, *Corporatism and Political Theory* (Oxford: Oxford University Press, 1986), chap. 6; A. Cawson, ed., *Organized Interests and the State: Studies in Meso-Corporatism* (Newbury Park, Calif.: Sage, 1985). See also John T. S. Keeler, "Corporatism and Official Union Hegemony: The Case of French Agricultural Syndicalism," in Suzanne Berger, ed., *Organizing Interests in Western Europe: Pluralism, Corporatism, and the Transformation of Politics* (New York: Cambridge University Press, 1981), chap. 7; John T. S. Keeler, *The Politics of Neo-Corporatism in France: Farmers, the State, and Agricultural Policymaking in The Fifth Republic* (New York: Oxford University Press, 1987).

5. Charles W. Anderson, "The Logic of Public Problems: Evaluation in Comparative Policy Research," in Douglas E. Ashford, ed., *Comparing Public Policies. New Concepts and Methods* (Beverley Hills, Calif.: Sage, 1978) 20, cf. 23.

6. Jack Hayward, "Mobilizing Private Interests in the Service of Public Ambitions," in Jeremy Richardson, ed., *Policy Styles in Western Europe* (London: 1982), 111–112.

7. Kenneth Dyson, "West Germany: The Search for a Rationalist Consensus," in Richardson, *Policy Styles*, 19.

8. L. J. Sharpe, "Central Coordination and the Policy Network," *Political Studies* 33, no. 3 (September 1985), 371.

9. Bruno Jobert and Pierre Muller, *L'État en Action* (Paris: Presses Universitaires de France, 1987), 63–69. See also John Gaffney, ed., *France and Modernization* (Aldershot: Avebury, 1988), esp. chap. 3; Hayward, *State and the Market Economy* chaps. 5, 6.

10. Hugh Heclo and Aaron Wildavsky, *The Private Government of Public Money: Community and Policy in British Political Administration* (Berkeley: University of California Press, 1974), 16, cf. 14–15.

11. Maurice Wright, "Policy Community, Policy Network and Comparative Industrial Policies," *Political Studies* 36, no. 4 (December 1988); cf. R. A. W. Rhodes, *The National World of Local Government* (London: Allen & Unwin, 1986), 19.

12. E. S. Kirschen, ed., *Economic Policies Compared* (Amsterdam: North Holland Publishing Co., 1974), vol. 1, 18–27.

13. James E. Alt and K. Alec Chrystal, *Political Economics* (Berkeley, Calif.: University of California Press, 1986), 63–66; Charles

Andrain, *Politics and Economic Policy in Western Democracies* (Boston, Mass.: Duxbury Press, 1980), 142–144, 151–152.

14. Kirschen, *Economic Policies Compared* I, 51, cf. 198–200.

15. Wright, "Policy Community," 600.

16. Lionel Stoléru, *L'Impératif Industriel* (Paris: Seuil, 1969).

17. Jobert and Muller, *L'État en Action,* 71–78, chap. 4. See also Keeler, *The Politics of Neo-Corporatism in France*, chap. 2.

18. Heclo and Wildavsky, *Private Government*.

19. Hugh Heclo, "Issue Networks and the Executive Establishment," in Anthony King, ed., *The New American Political System* (Washington, D.C.: American Enterprise Institute, 1978), 102, cf. 103–106.

20. See Thomas L. Gais et al., "Interest Groups, Iron Triangles and Representative Institutions in American National Government," *British Journal of Political Science* 14, no. 2 (April 1984), 163–166; Robert H. Salisbury et al., "Iron Triangles: Similarities and Differences Among the Legs," paper presented at the American Political Science Association Conference, 1985, 28.

21. Peter J. Katzenstein, ed., *Between Power and Plenty: Foreign Economic Policies of Advanced Industrial States* (Madison, Wisc.: University of Wisconsin Press, 1977), conclusion; Michael M. Atkinson and William D. Coleman, "Strong States and Weak States: Sectoral Policy Networks in Advanced Capitalist Economies," *British Journal of Political Science* 19 (1989): 47–67.

22. Ezra N. Suleiman, *Private Power and Centralization in France. The Notaries and the State* (Princeton, N.J.: Princeton University Press, 1987), esp. 17–25.

23. A. Grant Jordan, "Iron Triangles, Woolly Corporatism and Elastic Images of the Policy Process," *Journal of Public Policy* 1, no. 1, (February 1981): 103.

24. Jeremy J. Richardson and A. Grant Jordan, *Governing Under Pressure: The Policy Process in a Post-Parliamentary Democracy* (Oxford: Robertson, 1979), 74; see Table 3.1 on p. 44 for examples of policy communities.

25. Jordan, "Iron Triangles," 106.

26. A. Grant Jordan and Jeremy Richardson, *British Politics and the Policy Process* (London: Allen & Unwin, 1987), 175, cf. 123, 174–176.

27. Brian W. Hogwood, "Analyzing Industrial Policy: A Multi-Perspective Approach," *Public Administration Bulletin*, no. 29 (April 1979), 37. It is worth noting that Hogwood and Richardson are currently colleagues at the University of Strathclyde, but their community of ideas developed when they were both at the University of Keele, as for a time was Jordan. For more recent comments on policy communities by Hogwood, see his *From Crisis to Compla-*

cency? Shaping Public Policy in Britain (Oxford: Clarendon Press/ New York: Oxford University Press, 1987), 18–22, 54–55.

28. Wyn Grant, *The Political Economy of Industrial Policy* (London/ Boston: Butterworths, 1983), 27.

29. Richardson, *Policy Styles*, 3. See also the chapter on Britain by Jordan and Richardson, which claims: "One should see tripartism not as a type of policy-making discrete from policy communities, but policy communities developed to a very formal degree with exceptionally clear acceptance of the group veto power" (96–97; cf. 94–95).

30. Kenneth Dyson, chap. 2 in Richardson, *Policy Styles*, 26.

31. Ibid, 27–30; Hayward, *State and the Market Economy*, 36–37. See also N. J. D. Lucas, *Energy in France: Planning, Politics and Policy* (London: Europa Publications, 1979), 23–27, 32–33, 56–58, 139–153, 186–187.

32. Dyson, 34–41. More generally see Andrew Cox, *The State, Finance, and Industry. A Comparative Analysis of Post-War Trends in Six Advanced Industrial Economies* (Brighton, Sussex: Wheatsheaf, 1986).

33. Rhodes, *National World of Local Government*, 22–23, 389.

34. Ibid., 25, cf. 28.

35. Ibid., 28–29.

36. Heclo, "Issue Networks," 117; Rhodes, *National World of Local Government*, 389.

37. Wright, "Policy Community." For an application of his approach, see Maurice Wright, "City Rules O.K.? Policy Community, Policy Network and Takeover Bids," *Public Administration* 66 (Winter 1988): 389–410.

38. Hayward, *State and the Market Economy*, 7–8.

39. Harvey B. Feigenbaum, *The Politics of Public Enterprise. Oil and the French State* (Princeton, N.J.: Princeton University Press, 1985), 94, cf. 173.

40. Michel Bauer and Elie Cohen, *Qui gouverne les groupes industriels? Essai sur l'exercice du pouvoir du et dans le groupe industriel* (Paris: Senil, 1981), 103 cf. 97, 102, 107, 113.

41. Elie Cohen and Michel Bauer, *Les Grandes Manoeuvres Industrielles* (Paris: P. Belford, 1985), 139.

42. Jack Hayward, "Employer Associations and the State in France and Britain," in Steven J. Warnecke and Ezra N. Suleiman, eds., *Industrial Policies in Western Europe* (New York: Praeger, 1975). Chapter 5 presents an overly sanguine picture of the role of such associations.

43. On the key role of the French Defence Ministry's engineer-technocrat dominated General Delegation for Armament in leading

the security policy community in an industrial direction see Edward A. Kolodziej, *Making and Marketing Arms: The French Experience and Its implications for the Industrial System* (Princeton, N.J.: Princeton University Press, 1987), esp. p. 3.

44. Cohen and Bauer, *Les Grandes Manoeuvres Industrielles*, 282–286.
45. Hayward, *State and the Market Economy*, 230.
46. Ibid., 149. More generally see Jean Bouinot, *L'Action Économique des Grandes Villes en France et à l'Etranger* (Paris: Economica, 1987).
47. Freeman, "National Styles," 486, cf. 485.
48. Kenneth Dyson, "West European States and the Communication Revolution" in the special issue of *West European Politics* 9, no. 4 (October 1986): 14. See also Stephen Wilks and Maurice Wright, eds., *Comparative Government-Industry Relations* (Oxford: Clarendo/New York: Oxford University Press, 1987), heralding a series of case studies that are due to follow.
49. Claire Shearman, "European Collaboration in Computing and Telecommunications: A Policy Approach," *West European Politics* 9, no. 4 (October 1986): 157, cf. 150, 158, 161.
50. See Nina P. Halpern, "Policy Communities in a Leninist State: The Case of the Chinese Economic Policy Community" in *Governance* 2, no. 1 (January 1989), a special issue on policy communities which also discusses Japan, France, and Yugoslavia.
51. See Peter J. Katzenstein, *Corporatism and Change: Austria, Switzerland, and the Politics of Industry* (Ithaca, N.Y.: Cornell University Press, 1984); Andrew Martin, in Peter Gourevitch et al., *Unions and Economic Crisis: Britain, West Germany and Sweden* (London/Boston: Allen & Unwin, 1984).
52. Freeman, op. cit. pp. 469–70.

Chapter

17

Japan and Sweden

Polarities of "Responsible Capitalism"

T. J. Pempel

Probably no two countries among the capitalist democracies are more dissimilar than Japan and Sweden. Japan is crowded, with a population of 120 million; Sweden, although slightly larger in area, is sparse, with only 8.3 million. Though both have relatively homogeneous populations, Japan's is an oriental culture centered on Buddhism, Shinto, and Confucianism; Sweden's culture is occidental and Lutheran. The Japanese GNP is the second largest in the capitalist world, equal to about 50 percent that of the United States. Sweden's is far smaller, equal to only 3 percent that of the United States and only 16 percent that of West Germany. Although both Sweden and Japan were late industrializers, Japan followed a path that led to authoritarianism and empire for the first half of this century. Sweden moved quickly toward parliamentary democracy and maintained a long-standing policy of neutrality, compromised though it may have appeared to some by German transshipments during World War II. Sweden has continued its neutrality to the present, whereas Japan has a close bilateral security treaty with the United States that permits numerous American military bases on its soil.

The contrasts between the two countries could be elaborated, and there can be little doubt about the wide array of their differences. One of the most analytically interesting of these many differences involves their contrasting approaches to political economy. It is the argument of this paper that the two countries represent radically different end points of what is politically possible in business-labor interactions under capitalist democracies and that a comparison of the countries' approaches offers insights into the general problems of comparative capitalism and comparative democracy.

Nowhere are the differences between Sweden and Japan greater than in the broad nexus of public policies the two countries have pursued in economics and social welfare. For most students of comparative politics, Sweden is the quintessential "social welfare state" with a "big state apparatus," and a fifty-year history of relatively peaceful relations between business and labor. Social welfare benefits have long been universalistic, comprehensive, and institutionalized. The government's budget represents approximately 60 percent of the nation's GNP, the highest figure in the Organization for Economic Cooperation and Development (OECD). Taxation rates are the highest in the world. All major political parties share a commitment to full employment and the public sector has been a key sponge in that policy. Most Swedish women work and at jobs and salaries that, if no fully equal to those of men, are much farther along the road to equality than in almost any other capitalist country. Only 6.5 percent of Swedes continue to work after the age of 65; a national pension scheme, supplemented for many by private plans and savings, makes such work unnecessary. For approximately forty years Sweden has had one of the lowest strike rates in the industrialized world.

Japan in contrast is often portrayed in the West as the embodiment of the "economic animal." Its government is among the smallest in the industrialized world and it has consistently implemented policies to remain so.[1] Whereas Sweden has the largest state expenditures as a percent of GNP, Japan has the smallest. The Japanese government spends heavily on certain politically sensitive areas related to social welfare, notably agriculture, public works, and health; and it did flirt with widening the scope and coverage of its medical and pension programs in the late 1970s. Yet by any comparative account it is still a "welfare laggard,"[2] and Japanese officials still treat the social welfare state as emblematic of what they call "the European disease." Though Japanese women work before marriage and after children, most hold only low paying, low prestige jobs. Sexual discrimination in the workplace was taken as a given by most employers, at least until the passage of Japan's equal employment law in 1986.[3] The elderly continue to work, with more than 26 percent of those over age 65 still active in the work force, most because of economic necessity. Although labor-management conflicts in the 1980s are at a national and world low, Japan's history from the 1950s into the mid 1970s was characterized by medium to high levels of strikes in international terms, and confrontation rather than conciliation was the operative norm in relations between organized business and organized labor.[4]

One single statistic sums up the contrast between Sweden and Japan: total hours worked per year. The Swedish worker averages 1596; the Japanese worker logs 2061, in effect, putting in an extra ten weeks per year of normal hours.

In short, Sweden's policies seem to be those of a benign, somewhat paternalistic social-democracy. Japan's seem to be those of an extremely competitive, social-costs-be-damned version of labor market capitalism that looks in many respects more like Marx and Engels' portrait of a capitalist society than any other in the capitalist world today.

The many striking contrasts between Japan and Sweden are countered by two important similarities. First, the economies of both countries have performed rather well in the world economy. This was certainly the case for the first two decades or so following World War II when both countries had moderate to high rates of growth in GNP, low unemployment, and expanding shares of world trade. Yet as part of the long boom and the "politics of productivity" that marked the capitalist world economies following the war, their successes were not unusual.[5] More remarkable comparatively, despite many complaints within each country to the contrary, were their economic performances in the fifteen years since the early 1970s. Japan was by far the more impressive, ranking first since 1973 among the twenty-four OECD countries in its "crisis performance index," a mixture of low unemployment, high growth, and low inflation. But Sweden ranks high, being in sixth place behind only Japan, Norway, Austria, Switzerland, and West Germany.[6] In particular, Japan and Sweden are similar in that they have both managed to maintain exceptionally good performance records for low unemployment and expanding total employment during the entire period.[7]

The second area of striking similarity between the two countries is that both had exceptionally long periods of government dominated by a single political party. For Sweden this meant forty-four years of uninterrupted rule (from 1932 to 1976) by the Social Democratic party (SAP) and its return to power after a six-year interregnum by a shifting "bourgeois coalition." By 1990 the SAP had governed the country for fifty-two out of the previous fifty-eight years. This constitutes the longest socialist rule in the history of pluralist democracy. Many would even suggest that the policies of the intervening government were so close to those of the Social Democrats that indeed even out of office, the SAP controlled Sweden's political agenda.[8]

In Japan the Liberal Democratic party and its predecessors controlled all the prime ministerships and all but a handful of cabinet posts from 1948 into the 1990s, making this the longest uninterrupted conservative rule in any democracy. Indeed, if one discounts the ten-month parenthesis of an ineffective socialist coalition government in 1947–1948 (under the watchful and none-too-tolerant U.S. Occupation), one could easily argue that Japan has had over a hundred years of uninterrupted conservative governance.[9]

It is largely as a result of this long-term political dominance by these two political parties of dramatically different preferences, I would argue, that the two countries have been able to institutionalize their radically different approaches to the management of capitalism. Politics and the public policies that followed long-term single-party rule have been the key ingredients in allowing the two countries to set themselves up at the polar opposites of "social welfare state" and "economic animal."

At the same time there is a paradox in the character of each one's political approach to managing their national economies. Despite the strength of business in the conservative coalition that has dominated Japanese politics, and despite the defeat of organized labor and its systematic exclusion from political power for virtually the entire history of the country, Japanese government policies, particularly since the 1960s, have been far less draconian toward organized labor and average working class citizens than has been the case in countries with much stronger political lefts, such as the Netherlands, Denmark, New Zealand, France, England, and West Germany.[10] Despite the well-documented "fudging" on Japan's official unemployment statistics,[11] there is little question that Japanese unemployment is low by international standards, that total employment has expanded, and that in times of economic downturn Japanese firms have tended to reduce total hours worked, encourage early retirements and internal transfers, increase reliance on part-time help, and take other comparable action rather than to pursue a policy of large-scale worker layoffs.[12]

Furthermore, on the Gini index of income equality, Japan ranks among the most egalitarian countries in the world. In most of Japan's largest corporations the gap in wages between the highest and the lowest paid individuals is far narrower than in most other countries. And on a host of indicators related to health care, education, housing, and the absence of a semipermanent underclass, Japan also stands in a surprisingly positive comparative position for a country with such an explicitly "pro-business" regime.[13]

Additionally, labor-management conflict as measured in terms of numbers of strikes and hours lost to strikes, while relatively high until the early 1970s, has dropped off to among the lowest within the OECD.[14] In this regard the Japanese case poses a striking anomaly to the association of long-term left wing rule and/or corporatist patterns of interest intermediation between labor and business with benefits to the working class and conversely associates long-term conservative rule and the absense of corporatism with conflict and lack of working class benefits.[15]

It is also worth noting that in contrast to the common image of a "pro-business" government, many Japanese businesses, especially big businesses, do not fare particularly well. In almost no major industrial field does a single company or two control the bulk of sales; more typically, four, five, or more compete with one another.[16] Intrafirm competition is often ruthless and bankruptcies typically top 1500 per month. The country's top one hundred firms account for only 26 percent of retail trade, compared to 41 percent in the United States and 45 percent in West Germany. Many businesses do quite well in Japan, but it is rarely because they are politically insulated from the discipline of the market, at lest in terms of domestic market competition.

Government in Sweden has been far less hostile toward business, and particularly big business, than might be expected under social democratic rule. In contrast to countries far less nominally socialist, such as England, Italy, and France, Sweden has witnessed far lower levels of nationalization of industry; 87 percent of industry remains under private control. Although nominal rates of corporate taxes are high in Sweden, the effective rates are quite low, largely because the national system of investment reserves encourages companies to set aside in special funds vast proportions of annual profits for future investment.[17] The government provides major financing for private research and development. Plant level autonomy by management remains high. Management remains quite independent of state control. Capital is highly concentrated, with only 2 percent of the nation's stockholders owning nearly two-thirds of the total stock.[18] Furthermore, the Swedish stockmarket has proven to be one of the world's most profitable, with a 52 percent rise in the Affarsvarlden index for the year 1988.[19] Such performances led one major economics journal to dub the country "Europe's Japan."[20] The conservative financial journal *Euromoney* in 1984, surveying senior international bankers to nominate the world's most innovative and successful borrower, found that 80 percent named the Kingdom of Sweden.[21] In March 1976 *Fortune* summed up the overall situation succinctly in an article on the Swedish corporate giant Electrolux (which makes, among other things, vacuum cleaners). The article was entitled "How Electrolux Cleans Up in Socialist Sweden."[22]

Perhaps no single fact better illustrates the business orientations of the Social Democrats than the party's first action on returning to power in 1982: a 16 percent devaluation of the Swedish kroner, which provided a massive subsidy to business aimed at aiding the country's exporters. In Sweden, big finance and big business remain highly profitable and quite autonomous.[23]

The somewhat favorable situation of business in Sweden has been more frequently remarked on than the relatively good situation of Japanese labor. Indeed for many analysts, that business should do well is in fact the essence of capitalism, and the Swedish case is not taken to be surprising.[24] But within the broader context of comparative capitalist democracies, the Swedish situation is indeed striking, for it appears that in many ways, Swedish business does far better, despite a long-standing government of the left, than business in countries with far stronger pro-business political parties. Thus, for any student of comparative political democracies, the central paradox posed by a comparison of the political economies of Japan and Sweden is threefold: Why have the conservatives in Japan and the Social Democrats in Sweden had such long-term rules? Secondly, why, despite such long-term rule by conservative and social democratic parties, do Japanese labor and Swedish business do so well? And finally, why have the economies of both countries done so well compared to other industrial democracies?

The answers to these puzzles, I will argue, are interrelated and rest heavily on answering two key questions. The first is the historical question, "Who got the farmers?" (and its equally important corollary, "How do you get rid of them once they are no longer politically useful?"). The second is the internationally relevant question, "How has the domestic economy interacted with the world economy?" On the first question Japan and Sweden are polar opposites; on the second they are in many ways similar.

BUSINESS, LABOR, AGRICULTURE, AND THE STATE

Both Japan and Sweden were late industrializers, with many of the consequences for concentrated financial and industrial structures laid out so well by Alexander Gerschenkron.[25] But the Swedish state, unlike that in most other industrialized countries, by virtue of its neutrality in both world wars, was never given the belligerent's impetus toward an active and aggressive role in the suppression of labor and in the total mobilization of most economic resources.[26] Instead, it remained far more politically liberal and took a much smaller role in the organization of industrial production, relying instead on company monopolies. Agriculture was organized around commercial family farming, the peasantry was relatively independent, and, as industrialization proceeded quickly, the country witnessed a simultaneously rapid diminution in the number of people employed in agriculture. As early as 1910 only 17 percent of the Swedish population was in agriculture with most of them working on small family farms.[27] Moreover, a climate of political liberalism, early mass suffrage, few juridical and police impediments to labor union organization, and an industrial structure that relied heavily on mass production using relatively unskilled labor combined to make Sweden ripe for politically powerful and highly centralized labor union organizations.[28] The Social Democratic party (SAP) was formed as early as 1889; ten years later the unions were confederated into the Confederation of Labor Unions (LO); as early as 1920, some 21 percent of the work force were union members.

By the 1920s political conflict and economic competition between business and labor in Sweden were viciously zero-sum, seeming "to validate the classical prediction of class polarization."[29] Following their electoral defeat in 1928, the Social Democrats shifted to a strategy of pragmatic reformism that led to increased voter mobilization and eventually to their taking office in 1932 as a minority government. Once in office, they formed their famous Red-Green coalition with the Agrarian party, a bargain predicated on deficit-financed unemployment insurance for the workers and price supports for the farmers. Although this coalition between organized labor and the farmers eventually unraveled in the 1950s over the issue of mandatory pensions, it proved sufficiently strong electorally to keep the SAP in power for the first twenty-odd years of their rule. Equally importantly, it prevented the formation of a business-farmer bloc that has at different times been so critical to conservative control in Germany, Australia, New Zealand, Italy, and other countries.

In Japan industrialization began in the last quarter of the nineteenth century with neither a history of nonelite support for political tolerance and diversity such as was found in Sweden. The Meiji constitution was modeled on that of Bismarck's Prussia. Huge armaments expenditures and overseas expansion quickly became guiding national goals. It was the government that formed and ran the country's major early industries, and when these were sold off in the 1890s it was to the large financial and industrial combinations known as zaibatsu.[30] This forged tight links among the state bureaucracy, the zaibatsu, and the military. The agricultural work force remained numerous, with nearly 50 percent of the population still engaged in agriculture as late as the end of World War II. In the prewar period most of these were tenant farmers or small holders, heavily subject to the local influences of a numerically small but politically powerful landlord class. Through a series of trade-offs based on local patronage and parliamentary representation, these large local landowners were brought into the conservative fold, resulting in their inclusion in the dominant coalition that governed Japan through World War II.[31] Thus in Japan, unlike Sweden, business initially got the farmers. Moreover, as a result of the tremendous mobilizational efforts associated with the war, Japan's national bureaucracy came to assume a legitimate and extensive role in both macro- and microeconomic intervention.[32]

Meanwhile, in contrast particularly to the robust situation of Swedish labor, Japanese labor had little chance to grab a share of power in the prewar period. Universal male suffrage did not come until 1925 and then it was accompanied by the so-called Peace Preservation Law that curtailed numerous civil liberties and made organization by the political left even more difficult than it had been in prior years, when it was certainly far from easy.[33] At the height of its organizational strength, the labor movement enrolled no more than 8 percent of the work force. The politically harassed and internally fragmented socialist parties could garner only 10 percent of the vote in their best showing (1936 and 1937).

Japanese labor received a bolt of new energy with the end of the war, the purge of many political leaders on the right, land reform, demilitarization, strong support from many in the U.S. Occupation, new legislation, public disdain for the political right and prewar authoritarianism, a changing industrial structure, and a host of other factors. By the early 1950s approximately 50 percent of the work force was unionized; the Japan Socialist party actually headed a coalition government in 1947. When the Occupation ended, the Communist party was weak, dispirited, and politically marginalized. By 1955 with the consolidation of the two wings of the Japan Socialist party (JSP) and the consolidation of the conservatives as the Liberal Democratic party, many pundits were predicting the emergence of a two-party system in Japan, a system that would eventually and inevitably, through the exigencies of demographic change, fall into the hands of the JSP.[34]

Instead, Japanese labor was subjected to a barrage of attacks from both government and business during the 1950s and 1960s that limited its ability to penetrate into smaller industries and that kept its success in the larger private firms tightly tied to an acceptance of managerial goals and prerogatives, most especially firm profitability. At the national level and among public sector unions, both labor and the JSP clung to a decreasingly appealing ideology of class confrontation even though Japan's economy and absolute wages and living standards soared. Equally impolitic, the party embraced the foreign policy goal of "unarmed neutrality," at least implicitly hostile to Japan's close military and economic ties to the United States and favorable to Japan's historical enemy, the Soviet Union.[35] Meanwhile, the resurgent conservatives continued to court the rural sector, by then largely independent landowners due to the Occupation-induced land reform. The farm bloc was cohesively organized into a comprehensive national system of agricultural cooperatives that enrolled nearly 100 percent of the nation's farm families.

To hold onto the farmers, the conservatives relied heavily on technological assistance, massive farm subsidies, rural development, and patronage projects, along with ideological appeals to Japan's "traditional" values and the importance of the countryside.

If Japanese labor ever had any serious intentions to build an Asian equivalent of Sweden's Red-Green coalition (and there is little evidence to suggest it did, with the possible exception of the Rōnōtō efforts in the early 1950s), Japan's conservative business sector, both big and small, industrial and financial, more than obviated any chance to do so. These business-agriculture ties have been critical to the continued conservative electoral dominance in Japan and to the strength of the conservative, antilabor coalition that has consequently been virtually unchallenged as the semipermanent government.

JAPAN, SWEDEN, AND THE WORLD ECONOMY

Stephen Krasner has suggested that the economies of the world can be divided into "makers, shakers, and takers." A small number of powerful countries *make* the broad rules under which world commerce and finance function; a somewhat larger number of less significant countries are still sufficiently powerful to *shake* this system periodically; most countries must simply learn to *take* what the others dish out. At the end of World War II both Sweden and Japan were essentially takers. Japan's economic stature has increased tremendously since then and many might argue that by the late 1980s it was strong enough to be a rule maker. But for much of their contemporary history, Sweden and Japan were alike in that their best national option was to attempt to deal in flexible ways with the rapidly changing world economy. In different ways both have been highly dependent on their export industries. Both have therefore pursued what might be thought of as policies of "positive adjustment" to structural changes in the world economy. They rarely resisted long-term economic changes if resistance would be detrimental to their domestic industries; instead, through a series of policy measures government and business collaborated to adjust rapidly and positively to changing markets and to minimize the domestic dislocations such adjustments entailed. A compelling illustration of this point is the fact that Sweden and Japan respectively rank number one and number two in the per capita installation of industrial robots. The politics and economics behind such adjustments, however, differed in many ways.

Sweden's interaction with the world economy has been based on a strategy of what Peter Katzenstein labeled "democratic corporatism." Similar to the other small states of Europe, business and labor in Sweden have found it imperative to cooperate closely with one another as a consequence of their country's international economic vulnerability.[36] Too much internal conflict between the two would render the nation's industries ineffective in international competition. As Andrew

Martin has stated the problem, the "juxtaposition of a capitalist economy and a powerful labor movement renders the country especially vulnerable to distributive conflict between capital and labor. It places a high premium on managing that conflict so that foreign demand is not jeopardized."[37]

Following the formation of the Red-Green alliance and the ascent of the Social Democrats to power in 1932, industrial peace was secured in an agreement between the peak associations of business and labor— the famous "historical compromise" between business and labor at Saltsjöbaden in 1938. The cooperation between business and labor achieved at Saltsjöbaden provided the basis for subsequent accommodations between the two that came eventually to involve a trade-off in which business accepted the Social Democratic government, higher welfare costs, an expanding fiscal policy, and higher labor costs in exchange for labor peace, maintenance of private ownership and managerial control in the property and capital markets, and openness to the world economy.[38] Such cooperation was predicated on policies designed to make and keep Swedish industry internationally competitive, while sharing the burdens of industrial adjustment among the state, business, and labor. With time and the expansion of social welfare services, organized labor became increasingly willing to sacrifice some income from plant level bargaining for an increased social wage from the government.

An important component in this compromise was the Rehn-Meidner policy, which was elaborated during the 1950s. Briefly stated, wages for the bulk of organized Swedish labor were established annually on the basis of maintaining international competitiveness for Swedish firms as a whole and maintaining relative equality in wages for comparable jobs. A major consequence of this policy was to put a wage squeeze on Sweden's least efficient and internationally noncompetitive firms, while providing an implicit subsidy in the form of "lower than market wages" for the most productive and efficient firms. In this way firms were encouraged to modernize plants, invest in research and development, rationalize production, and strive for ever higher levels of efficiency and better shares of world markets. Those that failed to do so, for whatever reasons, essentially were compelled to shut down. Thus when one speaks of "business doing well" in Sweden, one is speaking only of those businesses that accept and function effectively under international market discipline; those that do not are guaranteed little assistance from either government or successful businesses.

The well-established policies of "full employment" required that government provide job retraining, economic assistance, and relocational allowances for workers displaced from decreasingly competitive firms.[39] Because labor has been so strong in the political arena, it has been able to pursue a strategy that encourages internationally competitive industry at the expense of less competitive businesses (at home and abroad) with the full knowledge that domestic labor will not pay an unduly high proportion of the adjustment costs for an internationally successful Swedish economy.

This combination of policies, in turn, has encouraged the concentration of private ownership in the search for national champions, firms large and efficient enough to compete effectively in world markets. The result has been a steady expansion of industrial concentration. Thus, in the twenty-five years from 1945 to 1969, some 3500 enterprises were merged, with half of these mergers occurring after 1965. From 1970 to 1976, an additional 3700 mergers took place.[40] Industry in Sweden today is approximately 40 percent more concentrated than in the larger industrialized countries.[41]

Critical to the successful implementation of these closely related policies designed to keep Swedish industry competitive and to provide widespread benefits for organized labor was a high degree of insulation of Swedish industry from foreign investors, particularly equity holders. Sweden's economy is relatively open to a wide range of foreign imports and open in the large outward movement of niche-oriented export goods. One-third of Sweden's GNP is accounted for by foreign sales. In contrast, it is rather closed to foreign capital.

Perhaps three-fifths of the Stockholm bourse's capitalization is in the hands of corporate owners or managers. Two-fifths alone is controlled directly or indirectly by the Wallenberg family. Only about one-fifth takes the form of unrestricted shares that foreigners can own, and these shares have few or no voting rights.[42] This is accomplished by dividing stock shares into two classes, with different voting strengths. For example, SKF, Sweden's tenth largest company, has 12.3 million unrestricted A shares, 10.2 million unrestricted B shares, and 4.5 million restricted B shares. The voting power of B shares is one-thousandth the value of A shares, and foreigners may buy only B shares. Leveraged buyouts and company breakups, such as those that have dominated much of American stock market activity in recent years, are thus unheard of in Sweden.

Also in the interests of preventing unwanted foreign takeovers, the financial markets are tightly controlled. In the words of one Swedish financier, "When it comes to international banking, Sweden might as well be Albania."[43] As late as 1984 Sweden remained the only country in Western Europe to bar foreign banks from operating within its borders.[44]

In short, Sweden was able to pursue export-oriented policies that encouraged Swedish producers to adapt continually in style, price, and productivity. Their reward for doing so was labor costs below world market levels and the ability to salt away profits for future investment and further adjustments up the technological gradient. Labor was able to accept such policies because levels of overall economic growth remained relatively high and because it could supplement cash wages with a social welfare wage delivered by the state. This collaborative strategy between Swedish business and labor worked in large measure because Swedish national elites from business, labor, and the state could agree on and could deliver on mutual commitments without fear of losing national control of the combined policy to foreign transnationals or corporate raiders.

A somewhat analogous mercantilism prevailed in Japan for a long period from the end of the war until the mid 1960s. Until the liberalization of tariffs starting in the mid 1960s and accelerating in the 1970s, and until the liberalization of the financial markets in 1980, there were a series of barriers to both foreign imports and, more importantly, to direct capital investment. In this respect Japan's domestic resources, like Sweden's, were developed by and for Japanese corporations. As noted, these corporations were for the most part highly competitive with one another, particularly within the Japanese market.

Japan's firms are a mixture of pygmies and giants. The rather small number of giants are among the largest and best capitalized in the world.[45] Standing well below the giants are the numerous small and medium-sized firms, many of which are linked through subcontracting arrangements or retail distribution to the larger manufacturers.[46] Competition at home among these many firms was until the early 1980s largely an intramural battle from which non-Japanese players were essentially excluded. This competition in the home markets allowed many Japanese firms to develop products and expertise that served them well once they chose to move into international markets. And until the early 1970s, when Japanese firms began a rapid expansion of direct investment overseas, moving into international markets meant, for the most part, exporting goods, not capital or plants. Government industrial policies, financial policies, fiscal policies, and (the virtually nonexistent) social welfare policies all dovetailed to support this system, providing rapid growth and increased success in world markets.[47] But as Daniel Okimoto and others have pointed out, the overarching direction of such government policies was "market conformity."[48] For Michele Schmiegelow, the appropriate term was "positive adjustment."[49] According to Ronald Dore, structural adjustment was possible due to a series of "flexible rigidities."[50] And Richard Samuels reminds us that relations between business and government historically were based less on state direction of the private sector and far more on "reciprocal consent."[51] The central point that emerges from all of these studies is that international market considerations and opportunities, a high degree of business autonomy, a good measure of state support, and a hothouse national economy well-insulated from the cold winds of foreign capital and non-Japanese management all were key ingredients in the economic policies that prevailed in Japan for the first three decades or so of the postwar period.[52]

Important, too, was the fact that the high level of economic growth enjoyed by Japan from the start of the Korean War until at least the early 1970s was widely perceived as benefiting all Japanese, not just a relatively few. Land reform had made the rural sector far more egalitarian than it had been in prewar Japan. Government assistance to the rural areas kept most rural incomes parallel to those in urban areas.[53] Massive postwar inflation wiped out most family fortunes, eliminating another visible class gap. As industry prospered, profits were rapidly plowed back into further expansion by moderately paid managers rather than flaunted in bouts of conspicuous consumption by exuberant entrepreneurs.

Educational opportunities were also quite egalitarian and job opportunities were far more closely related to the level and source of one's education than to one's family background. The rapidly expanding economy created a tight labor market; there were almost always far more jobs available than there were workers to fill them. Moreover, the relatively large number of family-owned firms also served as the ultimate sponge for the unemployed; the laid-off factory worker or the cousin unable to find work in the city could typically fall back on "job creation" in the family shop or firm. Such occupational discrimination as existed within Japan's dual labor market, particularly toward women, the elderly, and the young, tended to have its effects within families rather than on one family and not another. This, too, blurred income inequalities, statistics for which were almost always based on family, not individual, income.

Between 1955 and 1970 Japanese productivity rose 3.6 times and GNP jumped roughly 10 times. Real wages rose only 2.3 times, a lag greater than in most other industrialized countries.[54] Nonetheless, the widespread public perception was one of increased growth, wealth, and opportunity, of improved health and living standards, and of relative equity in the distribution of gains from the recovering economy. To whatever extent the benefits of Japan's growth were in fact unequally distributed, class polarization and advantage were both objectively and subjectively far less extreme than in much of Western Europe.

Such overall perceptions of equal opportunity and relatively unhoned lines between classes made the task of organizing a labor movement along horizontal class lines extremely difficult in Japan. Historical legacy and overt political and business efforts also conspired against organized labor and such a basis for organization. As noted above, organized labor faced massive obstacles in its efforts to organize during the prewar period, some of them self-inflicted, many of them the result of state and business actions, all of them resulting in an overall weakness at both the factory level and the political level.

While there were surely some government and business officials who believed differently, one of the overriding concerns for many in both of these arenas was to avoid the large and politically disruptive union movements that had already become part of the political landscape in Western Europe and North America. As Gordon has demonstrated so clearly, "By the end of the 1920s, managers had contrived to banish almost all strong, independent unions from major shipyards, machine factories, and steel mills."[55] Many others felt a benign paternalism toward workers was a far wiser long-run strategy than outright confrontation.[56]

Furthermore, the economics of securing a skilled labor force impelled many businesses to collaborate within industries to constrict labor mobility from firm to firm and thereby ensure their retention of skilled workers at less than market prices. The result was the development of what has come to be known as Japan's system of "permanent employment." Under this system large companies would hire unskilled workers upon their entry into the work force, provide them with on-the-job training designed specifically for company equipment and procedures, rotate them through a series of jobs within the company, and keep them employed during periods of economic slowdown, perhaps shifting them to alternative jobs within the company, even when doing so was economically inefficient in the short run.

Flexibility over what would otherwise be high, fixed wage bills was ensured by the bonus system, under which company profitability (or the lack of it) would be reflected in the wage packet. Twice a year, bonuses amounting to several months pay would be given to the workers if profits warranted; if they did not, the bonus was adjusted accordingly.

It is important to realize that while this system was carried over into many areas of employment in the postwar period, it was not a comprehensive scheme. Only about 30 percent of Japan's workers today function under some such system. It is they who are most frequently unionized, but typically they are organized into "enterprise unions," which bond the fortune of the worker to that of the firm, rather than to that of a class. Many workers are employed in small firms or family shops in which there is no permanent employment system. Many enjoy far less absolute job security as subcontractors, part-timers, contract workers, or self-employed workers. Almost none are unionized; almost all are subject to far greater labor market discipline than their counterparts in the larger firms.

The reality of Japanese business-labor relations is quite different from the current cartoon of Japan's workers that so delights the foreign business manager—happy chaps who sing the company song, do fifteen minutes of group calisthenics before moving on to jobs they perform with zero defects and absolute flexibility to managerial demands, cheerfully surrendering vacation time and putting in voluntary overtime, all the while making helpful suggestions for improvement of production quality.[57]

To the extent that there is any validity to this picture, it exists largely as a result of the historical defeat of organized labor in Japan. The late 1940s, 1950s, and early 1960s were marked by a number of long strikes, violent confrontations, worker efforts to gain control over factory production, and the rhetoric of unending class conflict. Labor initially confronted a reversal in U.S. occupation policy that removed many labor rights.[58] Subsequently, it confronted a hostile business community with access to the major resources of the state. Massive strikes at the Miike Coal Mine and at the Nissan Auto Company were broken, leaving organized labor fundamentally crippled[59] and removing, at least to the early 1990s, any serious challenges to managerial prerogatives or to the linking of the fate of workers with that of their company through Japan's now pervasive system of enterprise unionism.[60]

Shalev aptly described the logic of the "settlement" that ended the major labor struggles of this period.

> It is clearly materially worthwhile for the permanent/unionized workforce to join efforts to improve the competitive position of the enterprise—especially since these efforts are supported by ramified forms of social control over would-be free riders. The benefits for employers have included low turnover costs, a high probability of enjoying the fruits of investments in worker training, little or no disruption to production or challenge to managerial authority by unions, and the ability to mitigate the fixed costs of a permanent workforce by flexible job assignments and the elastic utilization of temporary and subcontracted labor."[61]

The relatively weakened position of organized labor in Japan was exacerbated as a result of the economic difficulties faced by most Japanese companies with the quadrupling of world oil prices in 1973–1974. Rapidly rising prices throughout the country initially led labor to demand correspondingly large wage hikes. They succeeded in 1974, but starting in 1975 they agreed to what Shinkawa, Kume, and others have seen as a "de facto incomes policy." Under its terms private sector labor agreed to moderate future wage demands in exchange for business guarantees of continued job security and government guarantees of low taxes and antiinflationary policies, at least for the core (unionized) employees in larger firms.[62] This policy had numerous important effects. First, it allowed Japanese business to adjust rapidly to the rise in oil prices as annual wage hikes quickly dropped from 32.9 percent in 1974 to 5 to 6 percent in 1978–1980.[63] Second, it provided an effective and rapid stop to possible wage-price inflation. Third, it provided an implicit commitment by business to limiting layoffs. Fourth, it forged even closer ties between blue-collar workers in the private sector and the firms for which they worked. Finally, as will be discussed below, it opened up the possibilities for these workers to move politically closer to the conservative LDP.[64]

It is interesting to note the parallels between these agreements in Japan and the so-called Haga agreements in Sweden at about the same time. There, a reduction in taxes on workers' incomes was to give them a higher disposable income while employers would hold down wages but make higher contributions to the social insurance system. Government and business would share the costs of lower taxes and higher social benefits. Labor would agree to lower wage hikes.[65] In fact, however, wages proved difficult to hold down and wage drift soon undercut much of the agreement.

Nonetheless, it is also important to recognize that if organized labor in Japan is politically weak and quite possibly historically defeated, workers as a whole and Japanese citizens more broadly have fared tolerably well as individuals under Japan's conservative rule. Japan's "creative conservatism" has been sufficiently flexible to make broad accommodations to citizen equality and to job security, among other things, in ways that would have been mind boggling in Reagan's America or in Thatcher's Britain.[66]

The cumulative picture that emerges from these two portraits is of economic strategies that were radically different at their roots, but remarkably similar in their attempts to adjust rapidly to world markets in ways that secured benefits for the national economy. While supporters of the "free market system" might be tempted to label both countries "free riders," they rather appear to have been "smart riders." Both proved to be "clever shakers" rather then "blind takers" of the rules of the free trade system. Both astutely pursued policies designed to advance national economic well-being in ways hardly in conformity with the original expectations of the system's rule makers.[67]

But it is also fruitful to underscore the fact that the national benefits that were enjoyed were not denied to the alleged political or class "enemies" of the ruling coalitions. Segments of Swedish business have unquestionably fared better under the Social Democrats than have most components of Japanese labor under the Liberal Democrats. But that should not be surprising in a capitalist economy. What is more striking is the extent to which each ruling party appears to have been far more accommodating to its alleged opponent than have less dominant business or labor parties in other industrialized countries (at least once the ruling party has established its relative indomitability).

INTERNATIONAL CHALLENGE AND PARTY RECOMPOSITION

The previous analysis is too static. Sweden and Japan look too perfect and too blessed with permanently clever economic strategies. In fact, each has undergone substantial changes as a result of two different types of shifts, shifts in the international economy and in their domestic demographics. These have necessitated changes not only in the composition of the dominant parties in each country, but in each nation's economic strategies as well.

Essentially, high growth throughout the world economy during the 1950s and 1960s allowed the Swedish and Japanese "settlements" to continue relatively unchallenged. High total profitability in the economies of each nation made it politically easy to continue policies that were economically irrational. For Japan this meant such things as irrational import restrictions and costly price supports that rewarded farmers and small businesses in a successful effort to keep them as supporters of the conservative voting bloc. For Sweden, it meant such things as rapidly expanding public employment and wage hikes that often outstripped productivity. Such positive-sum games were possible because elements of international isolation allowed each country to export to the world economy many of the costs of its domestic political and economic strategies. This in turn kept domestic politics positive-sum as well. Broad ideological conflicts over distributional principles could, with time, be shelved in the face of a rapidly expanding economic pie. Or more importantly, widespread public consensus could be generated over the policies that lay behind them: wage solidarity and full employment in Sweden; high economic growth in Japan.

This situation changed dramatically with the massive shifts in the world economy arising from the breakdown of Bretton Woods and the OPEC oil shocks of the early 1970s. Japan faced accelerating pressures from its trading partners to liberalize its import and investment policies. Both countries confronted the need to reexamine how best to remain internationally competitive in the face of new international rules on monetary, trade, and investment policies.

Domestic sociostructural changes also challenged the links between long-term, single-party dominance and each country's strategy of political economy. In both countries the economic and electoral significance of the agricultural vote diminished with increased industrialization. So, too, did total industrial employment. The middle classes expanded proportionally, in the Swedish case being particularly reflected in the big jump in citizens working in the private service sector and the public sector.[68] Thus, between 1970 and 1983 public sector employment rose from 26 percent to 36 percent of Sweden's total; the total number of public

employees increased by about 70 percent. In Japan increased urbanization and white collarization combined to create what Murakami has
called "Japan's new middle mass," a group economically and politically
quite different from the earlier support groups of the LDP.[69]

In short, in neither country could the politics or the economics of
one-party dominance continue unchanged. Each dominant party confronted parallel and interrelated needs to adjust support bases and
economic strategies. For the Social Democrats the first such major coali-
tional shift was accomplished with the dropping of ties to the Agriculture party, and the solidification of ties between the hitherto blue-collar
party and the emerging white-collar workers. This shift took place in
the period 1957–1959 over the development of the SAP's system of
earnings-related second-tier pensions (ATP).[70] Once accomplished, the
shift provided the SAP with a revitalized electoral base from which to
pursue its agenda of increased social benefits and the Rehn model of
positive-sum industrial and labor market policy. This, in turn, served
the economy so well during the late 1950s and more especially through
the 1960s that a nonpartisan consensus emerged as to its utility.

For the LDP in Japan the original electoral base of the party served
it well into the mid 1970s. But by then even the bizarrely gerryman-
dered districts that wildly overrepresented the rural electorate could not
insulate the party from the specter of electoral defeat. Nor could the
party continue to insulate the domestic economy from import and
investment competition. Indeed, even if its trading partners had been
willing to allow it to do so, many of the party's major business supporters would not. Large numbers of Japan's corporations realized that they
had become orchids too big for a hothouse and they were anxious to
benefit from overseas investment and the opening of Japan's markets. It
was no longer economically tolerable to continue policies aimed at pla-
cating weaker coalition partners, most notably agriculture and smaller
businesses, that would impede such moves.

Efforts by Japan's conservatives to bolster their electoral and coalition base, and to do so by forging a new relationship with the international economy, have been going on for less than a decade. They are far
more inchoate than the rather tangible moves by the Social Democrats
to replace farmers with white-collar workers through the pension plan.
Rather, the LDP has been engaged in a fitful process of attracting new
supporters from urban white-collar workers, blue-collar workers in
internationally competitive firms, and the younger generation. At the
same time, although it is not overtly rejecting its core supporters in
farming and small- and medium-sized industry, it is subjecting them to
unalloyed competition from far more efficient foreign producers.

The electoral results of 1979 through 1986 suggest great success in
handling this delicate transition.[71] The election of 1989 shows its pit-

falls. Certainly the macrolevel economic performance of Japan during the 1980s suggests that the country is adjusting to its new relationship to the world economy in an exceptionally successful manner, likely to minimize internal political conflicts, except as these affect previous core support groups in farming and small, declining businesses. But the political firestorm by these groups in 1989 shows that the political costs of external adjustment may be high. The resolution of this tension will unquestionably have a great influence on the future of the LDP, Japanese economics, and domestic politics. It remains to be seen whether the LDP can successfully make the kind of shifts that the SAP made in the late 1950s, shifts that could well generate another "virtuous cycle" of electoral success and the consequent ability to carry out socioeconomic policies that result in still further electoral success and in which the opposition parties continue to suffer from "the enervating impact of permanent opposition."[72] The LDP's victory in the 1990 Lower House elections suggests that they might well do so. A seemingly equally plausible possibility would be the loss of the LDP's electoral core or the bifurcation of the LDP (more likely into two intraparty wings at war with one another than into two new parties).

The situation in Sweden for the SAP is less sanguine. There is widespread agreement that the nonsocialist governments of 1976 to 1982 did an extremely poor job of managing the national economy, relying as they did on massive subsidies for declining industries and doing little to improve Sweden's international competitiveness.

> Sweden's economy by the early 1980s seemed to be drifting toward permanent decline. Exports lagged, production and investment remained weak, and borrowing to cover deficits was reaching record levels that made interest on the national debt the largest category of state spending. Structural adjustments to the harsher international economic climate were slow in coming and obviously were not going to be as painless as policymakers in the early 1970s had hoped.[73]

When the SAP returned to power in 1982, it took a number of measures to increase Sweden's international competitiveness including the 16 percent devaluation mentioned earlier, budget constraints on public spending, a consumption tax increase, a reduction in subsidies to lame-duck industries such as textiles, and a shutting down of Sweden's no longer efficient shipyards in Malmo and Uddevalla and the public mine at Kiruna.[74] Pleasing as such actions were to many in the business community, they posed a central difficulty for LO and the SAP.

Andrew Martin summarized the dilemma:

> Full employment, higher living standards and greater social justice [have] to be won in the face of stiffer international competition,

driven by fundamental, accelerating technological and economic change. Now, as before, there is no way to achieve these goals except through continual adaptation of industry to the forces of change. Insulating industry against them can only bring illusory security, merely making the adaptation harder when it can no longer be postponed. Even if industry continues to be exposed to these international forces, however, its response cannot be expected to be adequate nor consistent with equality, security and, ultimately, democracy if "economic forces are given free play."[75]

The stickiest problem has been with wage solidarity. Many of the country's industries are showing improved productivity and are highly successful in world markets; workers in such industries are demanding a share in such success through higher wages. But productivity in the public sector has remained relatively low. As a result high wage increases require expanded government expenditures counterproductive to long-term economic growth. This issue was most severely confronted by the metalworkers' defection from the centralized wage agreements and by the general strike by public sector workers in 1985. The metalworkers demanded and got a high wage package and greater wage spread for its members. The public sector successfully demanded a wage hike equal to that of private sector employees, despite a worsening budget picture for the government. Both cases provided undeniable evidence of the heightened tensions within the socialist coalition. These tensions had become even more acute both within the SAP and within the labor movement by the early 1990s, and wage solidarity proved impossible to sustain. It remains to be seen whether these tensions can be resolved in a positive-sum way such as was achieved by the policies begun in the 1930s and reformulated in the 1950s. If they are not continued, long-term rule by Social Democrats along with their strategies for continued growth, high employment, and extensive social benefits would seem destined for dramatic changes. The government's resignation in February 1990 and its subsequent need to rely on the Liberals for economic reforms offers perhaps a vision of the Swedish future.

CONCLUSIONS AND FUTURE QUESTIONS

This two-country comparison offers several suggestions concerning studies of comparative industrial societies. Most obviously, it suggests that there is more than one way to "organize capitalism." But more importantly, it also points to the obvious difficulties of an unrefined perspective that bifurcates a nation's socioeconomics too crisply into "labor" and "capital." The Swedish and Japanese examples make it clear that internal divisions within both groups, combined with the historical importance of agriculture, necessitate a more fine-grained analysis. This is particularly so as economies become more complexly oriented toward the service sector and as public sector workers become an increasingly important component of a nation's total labor force. The dualism of Japan's labor market is increasingly well recognized; it is almost certainly mirrored in many other countries. Far less well understood is the dualism of capital in both Japan and Sweden, particularly as this is manifested in tensions between large, sophisticated, and internationally competitive firms on the one hand and smaller, less sophisticated, and less competitive firms on the other, as well as between such key groups as industry and the service sector. Surely, such divisions of capital have been, and will continue to be, salient in the political economies of most capitalist democracies.

A second suggestion offered by the two-country comparison is the importance of political institutions, especially political parties. For a variety of reasons, political parties have lost favor as "independent variables" in explaining policy differences among countries.[76] The Japanese and Swedish cases reemphasize the importance of the interplay among broad socioeconomic blocs, electoral competition, and political parties. Parties still play a critical role in the resolution of socioeconomic conflicts within countries. Their role may be most visible in one-party dominant democracies such as Sweden and Japan, but parties are also significant in reaching socioeconomic compromises in the small democracies.[77]

A third area of observation concerns the interconnections between the world economy and domestic politics. In the Japanese and Swedish cases, it was clear that the relationship was dynamic and interactive. Domestic political choices depended on opportunities afforded by the international arena. Changes in these opportunities forced alterations in long-standing and domestically desirable policies. Only by successfully adapting domestic choices to the changing world economy in positive-sum ways could the governments of Sweden and Japan remain in office.[78]

This relationship underscores another, namely, the link between policy and politics. The Swedish and Japanese cases demonstrate convincingly how governments can and do use public policies to reward supporters and to punish opponents. But it also shows how long-term rule by a single party with relatively consistent policy orientations allows that party to create a positive cyle in which policy successes lead to further electoral successes which allow for further institutionalization of the party's policy agenda.[79] Moreover, this cycle can lead to the continual marginalization of opposition parties and to the broad public acceptance of a specific orientation toward public policies. What was once controversial thus becomes widely accepted as "common sense." This was certainly the case with Swedish full employment, the social welfare state, and wage solidarity; it also held true for Japanese high economic growth policies, the security alliance with the United States, and (until recently) agricultural protectionism.

One final observation should be made. The Swedish and the Japanese cases make it rather clear that a stark and easily perceptible division of rewards and benefits may not be in the best political interests of a ruling party. To the extent that the SAP and the LDP have enjoyed long periods of governmental hegemony, it has been because each has been rather flexible in its willingness to jettison old allies and replace them with new, and because it has been soft in its treatment of its ideological opponents.

Such flexibility and softness were not always employed. Indeed in the 1930s and on many occasions thereafter, Swedish labor and the SAP had to make clear to Swedish business who ran the government, and business acceptance of this fact was a prerequisite for any subsequent softness by the Social Democrats toward business and the SAF. Similarly, Japanese business and government became more magnanimous toward Japanese workers only after they had delivered a death blow to radical and political unionism and had institutionalized the ideological goals of close ties with the United States, limits on social welfare, and a strong privately based economy. Yet once such messages had been delivered to their opponents, both dominant parties, and the coalitions behind them, remained dominant by flexibility, rather than rigidity.[80]

These thoughts are perforce sketchy. But they suggest the utility within comparative politics of reexamining several long-standing truisms and directions of research. Thus, while Sweden and Japan may not appear initially to belong in the same category, whatever that category might be, in fact, they offer interesting possibilities for examining the polarities of responsible capitalism.

NOTES

Earlier versions of this paper were presented at the Centrum for Stillahavsasien-studier at the University of Stockholm and at the Joint Centre on Modern East Asia at the University of Toronto. I would like to thank the many participants in both seminars, as well as those at the conference on Comparative Political Dynamics for helpful comments. My thinking for this analysis was greatly stimulated by the workshops and papers that led to *Uncommon Democracies*, a volume I edited which was published by Cornell University Press in 1990. In addition, Kent Calder, David Collier, Jonas Pontusson, and Göran Therborn offered a number of specific comments that have influenced my analysis.

  1. Comparing numbers of government employees as a proportion of the total population, or of the labor force, shows Japan to be one-

third or more smaller than almost all the other major industrialized democracies (e.g., 9 percent of the labor force versus 14 to 20 percent elsewhere). Under the rubric "administrative reform," Japan has undertaken several major programs to reduce, or to hold constant, the size of its national bureaucracy. See T. J. Pempel, *Policy and Politics in Japan: Creative Conservatism* (Philadelphia: Temple University Press, 1982), chap. 7; Shumpei Kumon, "Japan Faces Its Future: The Political-Economics of Administrative Reform," *Journal of Japanese Studies* 10, no. 1 (Winter 1984).

2. An early comparative treatment can be found in Harold Wilensky, *The Welfare State and Equality: Structural and Ideological Roots of Public Expenditure* (Berkeley: University of California Press, 1975). More recent data confirm the picture. See OECD, *Social Expenditure 1960–1990* (Paris: OECD, 1985).

3. Women's salaries, for example, are approximately one-half those of men in Japan. Until recently most managerial and professional career tracks were effectively closed to women. On the bill, see Frank Upham, *Law and Society in Japan* (Cambridge, Mass.: Harvard University Press, 1987). It is worth noting, for example, that several Japanese companies in the United States, when faced with equal rights complaints from American female employees, attempted to argue that they should be exempt from U.S. laws in such matters and allowed to "do things the Japanese way." They lost.

4. Walter Korpi and Michael Shalev, "Strikes, Power and Politics in the Western Nations, 1900–1976," in Maurice Zeitlin, ed., *Political Power and Social Theory*, vol. 1 (Greenwich, Conn.: JAI Press, 1980), 301–334. Michael Shalev, "Strikes and the Crisis: Industrial Conflict and Unemployment in the Western Nations," *Economic and Industrial Democracy* 4 (1983): 417–460.

5. The average annual growth rate of GNP between 1950 and 1973 ranged from a low of 3.9 percent for the United States to a high of 9.8 percent for Japan, with most of Western Europe around 5 percent. Interdependence in world trade and finance expanded enormously. Unemployment levels and inflation levels were extremely low throughout the OECD countries. See, for example, Philip Armstrong, Andrew Glyn, and John Harrison, *Capitalism Since World War II: The Making and Breakup of the Great Boom* (London: Fontana, 1984); David Cameron, "The Expansion of the Public Economy: A Comparative Analysis," *American Political Science Review* 72 (1978): 1243–1261; Cameron, "Social Democracy, Corporatism, Labour Quiescence and the Representation of Economic Interest in Advanced Capitalist Society," in John H. Goldthorpe, ed., *Order and Conflict in Contemporary Capitalism* (Oxford: Oxford University Press, 1984), 143–178; Robert Keohane, *After*

Hegemony: Cooperation and Discord in the World Political Economy (Princeton, N.J.: Princeton University Press, 1984); Charles Maier, "The Politics of Productivity," in Peter J. Katzenstein, ed., *Between Power and Plenty: Foreign Economic Policies of Advanced Industrial States* (Madison: University of Wisconsin Press, 1978), 23–50.

6. This data is based on Francis G. Castles, "Neocorporatism and the 'Happiness Index,' or What the Trade Unions Get for Their Cooperation," *European Journal of Political Research* 15 (1987): 381–393.

7. Göran Therborn, *Why Some Peoples Are More Unemployed Than Others* (London: Vesco, 1986). Therborn finds that only Austria, Switzerland, and Norway compare to Japan and Sweden as full employment countries since the economic crises of 1973 and then 1980. It is possible that New Zealand might fit the picture as well, although it was not included in Therborn's study.

8. One good example of this argument is found in Francis G. Castles, *The Social Democratic Image of Society* (London: Routledge and Kegan Paul, 1978). See also Gösta Esping-Andersen, *Politics Against Markets* (Princeton, N.J.: Princeton University Press, 1985), although he also makes an important case for Sweden's being at something of a political crossroads, and also Esping-Andersen, "Single-Party Dominance in Sweden: The Saga of Social Democracy," and Jonas Pontusson, "Conditions of Labor Party Hegemony: A Comparison of Sweden and Britain," both in T. J. Pempel, ed., *Uncommon Democracies: The One-Party Dominant Regimes* (Ithaca, N.Y.: Cornell University Press, 1990).

9. The defeat of the LDP in the Upper House elections of July 1989 may force some modifications in this pattern of dominance, but with the LDP's victory in the 1990 Lower House election, conservative control remained intact.

10. See Therborn, *Why Some Peoples*; also Manfred G. Schmidt, "The Welfare State and the Economy in Periods of Economic Crisis: A Comparative Study of Twenty-Three OECD Nations," *European Journal of Political Research* 2 (1983): 1–26; Philippe C. Schmitter, "Interest Intermediation and Regime Governability in Contemporary Western Europe and North America," in Suzanne Berger, ed., *Organizing Interests in Western Europe: Pluralism, Corporatism, and the Transformation of Politics* (New York, Cambridge University Press, 1981).

11. The best single study of this point is Angelica Ernst, *Japans unvollkommene Vollbeschäftigung: Beschäftigungsprobleme und Beschäftigungspolitik* (Hamburg: Institut für Asienkunde, 1980). An abbreviated English version of Ernst's analysis can be found in a

review of her book by Barbara Malony in *Pacific Affairs* 56, no. 4 (Winter 1984): 753–755.

12. For example, Kazutoshi Koshiro, "Development of Collective Bargaining in Postwar Japan," in Taishiro Shirai, ed., *Contemporary Industrial Relations in Japan* (Madison: University of Wisconsin Press, 1983), 247. See also Ronald Dore, *Flexible Rigidities* (Stanford, Calif.: Stanford University Press, 1986), esp. chap. 5; Haruo Shimada, *The Japanese Employment System* (Tokyo: Japan Institute of Labor, 1980), esp. 22–27. It is important to realize that these measures have a dual character. On the one hand, they do ensure employment for a relatively large portion of a company's core work force. At the same time, they reinforce the dual character of the Japanese labor market as well as the dependence of individuals in the core work force on the benevolence of the firm, resulting in what Goldthorpe has called "the fundamental division and effective depoliticization of the working class." John H. Goldthorpe, "The End of Convergence: Corporatist and Dualist Tendencies in Modern Western Societies," in Goldthorpe, ed., *Order and Conflict*, 340. See also Michael Shalev, "Class Conflict, Corporatism and Comparison: A Japanese Enigma" unpublished paper, Hebrew University of Jerusalem, November 1988.

13. This point is expanded at length in T. J. Pempel, "Creative Conservatism under Challenge," in Francis G. Castles, ed., *The Comparative History of Public Policy* (London: Polity Press, 1989). See also Malcolm Sawyer, *Income Distribution in OECD Countries* (Paris: OECD, 1976); Sidney Verba et al., *Elites and the Idea of Equality: A Comparison of Japan, Sweden, and the United States* (Cambridge, Mass.: Harvard University Press, 1987), and Martin Bronfenbrenner and Yasukichi Yasuba, "Economic Welfare," in Kozo Yamamura and Yasukichi Yasuba, eds., *The Political Economy of Japan*, vol. 1 (Stanford, Calif.: Stanford University Press, 1987).

14. OECD, *Economic Survey* (Paris: OECD, annual); ILO, *Yearbook of Labor Statistics* (Geneva: ILO, annual); Kazuo Koike, "Human Resource Development and Labor-Management Relations," in Yamamura and Yasuba, eds., *Political Economy of Japan*, 292.

15. For example, see John D. Stevens, *The Transition from Capitalism to Socialism* (London: Macmillan, 1979); Walter Korpi, *The Working Class in Welfare Capitalism* (London: Routledge and Kegan Paul, 1978); Cameron, "Social Democracy," and "Expansion of the Public Economy"; Schmitter, "Interest Intermediation and Regime Governability"; Francis G. Castles, *The Impct of Parties* (Beverly Hills, Calif.: Sage, 1982). A particularly good review of these views is found in Michael Shalev, "The Social Democratic Model and Beyond: Two 'Generations' of Comparative Research on the Welfare State," *Comparative Social Research* 6 (1983): 315–351. Shalev

attempts to unravel the Japanese paradox presented to such interpretations in "Class Conflict, Corporatism and Comparison." My views on "Japanese corporatism" are explored in T. J. Pempel and Keiichi Tsunekawa, "Corporatism without Labor: The Japanese Anomaly?" in Philippe C. Schmitter and Gerhard Lehmbruch, eds., *Trends Toward Corporatist Intermediation* (Beverly Hills, Calif.: Sage, 1979). One useful Japanese perspective on this question is Tsujinaka Yutaka, "Rōdō Dantai: Kyūchi ni tatsu 'Rōdō' no Seisaku Kettei [Labor Organizations: Policy Making by a Labor in Dilemma]," in Nakano Minoru, ed., *Nihonkei Seisaku Kettei no Henyō [Changes in Japanese Style Policy Making]* (Tokyo: Toyo Keizai Shimbunsha, 1986), 267–300. It is worth noting that current research by Tsujinaka on a concept he calls "osmotic corporatism" argues that some forms of corporatism involve absorptions of a weak labor movement into far less than equal bargaining processes.

16. Kokuseisha, *Nihon Kokuseizue [The Conditions of Japan in Graphs]* (Tokyo: Yano, 1984), 348.

17. Jonas Pontusson, "Comparative Political Economy of Advanced Capitalist States: Sweden and France," *Kapitalistate* 10 (1983): 52; Sven Steinmo, "Political Institutions and Tax Policy in the United States, Sweden, and Britain," *World Politics* 41, no. 4 (July 1989): 504–508, 516–523.

18. Joachim Israel, "Swedish Socialism and Big Business," *Acta Sociologica* 21, no. 4 (1978): 346.

19. "Taking Stock Home," *The Economist*, May 28, 1988, 76, showed a 34 percent gain for the first six months of 1988. The final issue of *The Economist*, December 24, 1988-January 6, 1989, 130, showed the gain of 52 percent for the year.

20. *Far Eastern Economic Review*, May 26, 1988, 64.

21. "Borrower of the Year: The Kingdom of Sweden," *Euromoney*, October 1984, 32–39.

22. As cited in Israel, "Swedish Socialism and Big Business," 341.

23. A quite different viewpoint is put forward by the Swedish Employers' Confederation. See, for example, their 1984 convention publication, *A Creative Sweden: People and Enterprise*, Document no. 1095 (Gothenburg: SAF 1984).

24. A classical statement can be found in James O'Connor, *The Fiscal Crisis of the State* (New York: St. Martins Press, 1973). See also Claus Offe, *Disorganized Capitalism* (Cambridge, Mass.: MIT Press, 1985); Adam Przeworski, *Capitalism and Social Democracy* (Cambridge: Cambridge University Press, 1985).

25. *Economic Backwardness in Historical Perspective* (Cambridge, Mass.: Harvard University Press, 1962).

26. On this relationship, see Charles Tilly, "Reflections on the History

of European State-Making," in Charles Tilley, ed., *The Formation of National States in Western Europe* (Princeton, N.J.: Princeton University Press, 1973), esp. 73–76.

27. Esping-Andersen, *Politics Against Markets*, 48–52.

28. Esping-Andersen, *Politics Against Markets*, passim but esp. chaps. 2, 3. See also Korpi, *The Working Class in Welfare Capitalism*, chaps. 3, 4; Timothy Tilton, "The Social Origins of Liberal Democracy: The Swedish Case," *American Political Science Review* 68 (1974).

29. Esping-Andersen, *Politics Against Markets*, 51.

30. Thomas C. Smith, *Political Change and Industrial Development in Japan* (Stanford, Calif.: Stanford University Press, 1965). It is worth pointing out in this context that the history of business-state relations in Japan, while generally congenial during this period, was marked by a number of conflicts resulting from business anxiety to resist government regulation, and bureaucratic efforts to expand their control. This was particularly true in the energy sector. See Richard J. Samuels, *The Business of the Japanese State* (Ithaca, N.Y.: Cornell University Press, 1987). On the role of the government bureaucracy, see Chalmers Johnson, *MITI and the Japanese Miracle* (Stanford, Calif.: Stanford University Press, 1982).

31. This argument is made in greater detail in Pempel, *Policy and Politics in Japan.*

32. This point is especially well made in Johnson, *MITI and the Japanese Miracle.*

33. Ōkochi Kazuo, *Nihon no Rōdō Kumiai* [*Japanese Labor Unions*] (Tokyo: Tōyō Keizai Shimposha, 1954); Hyōdō Tsutomu, *Nihon ni okeru Rōshi Kankei no Tenkai* [*The Evolution of Labor-Capital Relations in Japan*] (Tokyo, Tōyō Daigaku Shuppankai, 1971); Andrew Gordon, *The Evolution of Labor Relations in Japan* (Cambridge, Mass.: Harvard University Press, 1985); Sheldon Garon, *The State and Labor in Modern Japan* (Berkeley: University of California Press, 1987).

34. Ishida Hirohide, "Hoshu Seitō no Bijon [Vision of a Conservative Party]," *Chūō Kōron* 78, no. 1 (January 1963): 88–97.

35. Those less familiar with Japanese history should be reminded that the Russo-Japanese War (1903–1905) was the culmination of years of confrontation over rights to Korea and Manchuria and that Japan wrested a number of territories from Russia as a result of that war; that the Russian Revolution was seen by Japan's conservative elite as making the Soviet Union not only a geographical but also an ideological enemy; that near the end of World War II, Japanese political leaders were seeking to use the "good offices" of the Soviet Union, with which they had a nonaggression pact, to find a face-

saving means of surrendering to the Americans; that the Soviets in turn were seeking to prolong the war so as to declare war on Japan in accord with the Yalta Agreement; and that almost immediately after the bombing of Hiroshima, they did so, occupying among other places, several small islands to the north of Japan to which Japan still lays claim.

36. Peter J. Katzenstein, *Small States in World Markets* (Ithaca, N.Y.: Cornell University Press, 1985).

37. Andrew Martin, "Wages, Profits, and Investment in Sweden," in Leon N. Lindberg and Charles S. Maier, eds., *The Politics of Inflation and Economic Stagnation* (Washington, D.C.: Brookings Institution, 1985), 403.

38. Katzenstein, *Small States in World Markets*, 141; Esping-Andersen, *Politics Against Markets*, 62; Walter Korpi, *The Democratic Class Struggle* (London: Routledge and Kegan Paul, 1983), 46–52; Peter Gourevitch, *Politics in Hard Times* (Ithaca, N.Y.: Cornell University Press, 1986), chap. 4.

39. A high proportion of Swedish monies for labor policy are used for retraining measures rather than for unemployment insurance. Rudolf Meidner, "Sweden: Approaching the Limits of Active Labour Market Policy," in K. Gerlach et al., *Public Policies to Combat Unemployment in a Period of Economic Stagnation* (Frankfurt: Campus Verlag, 1984), 249–250.

40. Israel, "Swedish Socialism and Big Business," 348.

41. Katzenstein, *Small States in World Markets*, 113–115.

42. "Taking Stock Home," 76.

43. As quoted in *Business Week*, June 4, 1984, 41.

44. Ibid. This was changed by new legislation in 1985.

45. For example, some 94 of its firms are capitalized at over $5 billion, compared to 81 in the United States, 18 in Britain, and 12 in West Germany. *The Economist*, November 14, 1987. In addition, Japan has 152 companies in the Fortune International 500; it has the world's six largest trading companies and the ten largest banks.

46. An excellent survey of these smaller firms is found in Hugh T. Patrick and Thomas P. Rohlen, "Small-Scale Family Enterprises," in Yamamura and Yasuba, *Political Economy of Japan*, 331–384.

47. The literature on this subject is immense, and my description is a gloss over a number of more complex topics. I have elaborated on many of these points in T. J. Pempel, "Japanese Foreign Economic Policy: The Domestic Bases for International Behavior," in Katzenstein, *Between Power and Plenty*, 139–190, and also in *Policy and Politics in Japan*. See also Chalmers Johnson, *MITI and the Japanese Miracle*; Hugh T. Patrick and Henry Rosovsky, eds., *Asia's New Giant* (Washington, D.C.: Brookings Institution, 1976).

48. Daniel I. Okimoto, *Between MITI and the Market: Japanese Industrial Policy for High Technology* (Stanford, Calif.: Stanford University Press, 1989).

49. Michele Schmiegelow, "Cutting across Doctrines: Positive Adjustment in Japan," *International Organization* 2, no. 39 (Spring 1985): 261–296.

50. Dore, *Flexible Rigidities*.

51. Samuels, *Business of the Japanese State*.

52. Often overlooked in current debates over the relative "openness" or "closedness" of the Japanese marketplace to foreign goods is the fact that these preliberalization policies afforded many Japanese firms time, space, and freedom from foreign competition in home markets to develop the kinds of corporate structures, markets, products, and product reputations that enable them today to withstand foreign competition even on a relatively "even playing field." This point is developed in T. J. Pempel, "The Unbundling of 'Japan, Inc.': The Changing Dynamics of Japanese Policy Formation," *Journal of Japanese Studies* 13, no. 2 (1987): 271–306.

53. Michael Donnelly, "Conflict over Government Authority and Markets: Japan's Rice Economy," in Ellis Krauss et al., eds., *Conflict in Japan* (Honolulu: University of Hawaii Press, 1984), 350–354.

54. Pempel, "Japanese Foreign Economic Policy," 172.

55. Gordon, *Evolution of Labor Relations in Japan*, 125.

56. Byron K. Marshall, *Capitalism and Nationalism in Prewar Japan* (Stanford, Calif.: Stanford University Press, 1967).

57. It is difficult to separate the reality from the caricature. See the opening chapter of Ronald Dore, *British Factory; Japanese Factory: The Origins of National Diversity in Industrial Relations* (Berkeley: University of California Press, 1973) for an astute sociologist's observations of work and workers in comparable factories in Japan and Britain. Dore's subtle portrait of the Japanese work day describes a number of elements that are presented in oversimplified and exaggerated form in the cartoons of contemporary Western media.

58. Takemae Eiji and Amakawa Akira, *Nihon no Senryō Hisshi* [*Secret Documents of the Japanese Occupation*], vol. 1 (Tokyo: Asahi Shimbunsha, 1977).

59. Benjamin Martin, "Japanese Mining Labor: The Miike Strike," *Far Eastern Survey* 30, no. 2 (February 1961): 26–30; George Frantz, "Government and Declining Industry: The Japanese Coal Mining Industry" unpublished, Cornell University; Satoshi Kamata, *Japan in the Passing Lane* (New York, Pantheon, 1982).

60. Japanese unionization rates were around 50 percent in the early 1950s and have declined steadily to below 30 percent today. There are some 75,000 autonomous enterprise unions today, and few are

affiliated with a national federation. The largest federation, Sohyo, enrolled only about 33 percent of the union members; the second largest, Domei, an additional 16 percent. In 1987 a new federation, known by the acronym Rengo, emerged. By 1989 it had absorbed Domei, Sohyo, and most of the other national federations. This was the first time most Japanese unions were in a single organization since the 1950s. Predictions on the future of this new federation range from the painfully pessimistic views of many disappointed radicals at labor's latest capitulation to capital to the starry-eyed optimism of many liberal business leaders who view Rengo as a uniquely Japanese solution to the division between business and labor.

61. Shalev, "Class Conflict, Corporatism and Comparison," 13–14.

62. Shinkawa Toshimitsu, "Senkyuhyaku Nanajugonen Shunto to Keizai Kiki Kanri [The 1975 Spring Offense and the Economic Crisis Management]," in Ōtake Hideo, ed., *Nihon Seiji no Shoten* [*Problems in Japanese Politics*] (Tokyo: Sanichi Shobō, 1984); Ikuo Kume, "Changing Relations Among the Government, Labor and Business in Japan after the Oil Crisis," *International Organization* 42, no. 4 (Autumn 1988): 659–687.

63. Taishiro Shirai, "A Theory of Enterprise Unionism," in Shirai, ed., *Contemporary Industrial Relations in Japan* (Madison: University of Wisconsin Press, 1983), 133.

64. It is probable that "Rengo," which in 1990 unified public and private sector unions in one federation committed to "economic unionism," has its real roots in this 1975 agreement. See Tsujinaka Yutaka, "Rōdōkai no Saihen to Hachijurokunen Taisei no Imi [The Significance of the Reorganization of Labor Relations and the 1986 System]," *Leviathan* 1 (1987): 47–72.

65. Hugh Heclo and Henrik Madsen, *Policy and Politics in Sweden: Principled Pragmatism* (Philadelphia: Temple University Press, 1987), 58–59.

66. A clear contrast can be found in Joel Krieger, *Reagan, Thatcher and the Politics of Decline* (Oxford: Oxford University Press, 1985).

67. The Japanese and Swedish successes may also be of great interest to students of the political economics of Third World nation states anxious to devise national strategies to cope with unfavorable world economic systems. My thanks to Kenneth Erickson for pointing this out to me.

68. R. Henning, "Sweden: Political Interference with Business," in M.P.C.M. Van Schendelen and R. J. Jackson, eds., *The Politicisation of Business in Western Europe* (London: Croom Helm, 1987), 20; Bo Jangenas, *The Swedish Approach to Labor Market Policy* (Stockholm: The Swedish Institute, 1985), 28–29.

69. Yasusuke Murakami, "The Age of New Middle Mass Politics: The Case of Japan," *Journal of Japanese Studies* 8, no. 1 (Winter 1982).

70. This story is well told in Gösta Esping-Andersen, "Single Party Dominance in Sweden: The Saga of Social Democracy," in T. J. Pempel, *Uncommon Democracies.*

71. See, for example, Gerald L. Curtis, *The Japanese Way of Politics* (New York, Columbia University Press, 1988). Sato Seizaburo and Matsuzaki Tetsuhisa, *Jiminto-Seiken* [LDP Power] (Tokyo: Chūō Kōronsha, 1986); Miyake Ichiro, ed., *Seito Shiji no Bunseki* [Analysis of Political Party Support] (Tokyo: Sokobunsha, 1985).

72. Curtis, *Japanese Way of Politics,* 123.

73. Heclo and Madsen, *Policy and Politics in Sweden,* 62.

74. Ibid., 72–73.

75. In Peter Gourevitch et al., *Unions and Economic Crisis: Britain, West Germany and Sweden* (London: Allen and Unwin, 1984), 231.

76. As just a brief overview, consider the recent importance given to corporatism, single issue movements, socioeconomics and class conflict, the state, and so forth.

77. Katzenstein, *Small States in World Markets.*

78. The interaction between the domestic and international levels is explored in an interesting way in Robert Putnam, "Diplomacy and Domestic Politics: The Logic of Two-Level Games," *International Organization* 42, no. 3 (Summer 1988): 427–460.

79. This point is explored at greater length in the contributions to T. J. Pempel, *Uncommon Democracies.* See especially the essays by Gösta Esping-Andersen, Michael Shalev, and Sydney Tarrow. It is also elaborated in Castles, *Social Democratic Image.*

80. Sidney Tarrow, "One Party Dominance in Italy: 'The Softer They Rise, the Slower They Fall,'" in Pempel, *Uncommon Democracies.*

THE CHALLENGE FOR COMPARATIVE POLITICS

Chapter
18

Global Research Perspectives

Paradigms, Concepts, and Data in a Changing World

Kenneth Paul Erickson and Dankwart A. Rustow

In the three decades since the 1960s the world has changed in unexpected and dramatic ways. In the socialist world, Mikhail Gorbachev's reforms of Soviet economic, social, and political institutions, his adroit support for reform in Eastern Europe, and his government's pledge not to intervene there have precipitated rapid changes in institutions and policy throughout that region. In the industrial capitalist world, the European Community's integration of markets, scheduled for 1992, is expected to lead to closer political coordination among its members, to more intensive patterns of economic interaction with the United States and Japan, and perhaps to formal association with transformed Eastern European countries. In Latin America and East Asia, many longstanding authoritarian military regimes have given way to new democracies. In much of Central America, on the other hand, tighter integration into the world economy did not raise living standards and support democracy but instead intensified poverty, spawned revolutionary processes, and precipitated foreign intervention.[1] In South Africa, the erosion of apartheid and the enhanced worldwide prestige of the African National Congress and Nelson Mandela have created opportunities for dramatic social and political change. In the rest of Africa, however, the high hopes of the newly independent nations of the 1960s for political democracy and rising living standards have given way to the harsh realities of instability, authoritarian rule, and economic crisis.

PARADIGMS AND THE ANALYSIS OF POLITICAL SYSTEMS

For scholars gathering data and developing concepts to interpret this changing world, these dynamic transformations pose hazards as well as opportunities, but they certainly guarantee that the field of comparative politics will remain one of the most intellectually lively and challenging academic disciplines.

Thomas S. Kuhn, analyzing creativity in the physical sciences, observed that work of the scientific community in any given field is oriented by a common paradigm, that is, by a coherent tradition of research that includes theories, concepts, and research agendas. Members of a scientific community validate the paradigm in the course of their research, and they perpetuate it as they prepare their students to enter the community. Only when phenomena under study cease to conform to the expectations fostered by the dominant paradigm, Kuhn observed, does this paradigm give way to another one in what he described as a scientific revolution.[2]

The political world, of course, contains the most varied of cases and does not lend itself to replication and testing under laboratory conditions. These circumstances, combined with the normative aspect of political science, have prevented any single paradigm, in Kuhn's scientific sense, from holding sway in most fields of political analysis.

Using the term more loosely, however, in the sense of "an implicit though fairly general agreement on what to do and how to proceed in the field," David B. Truman identified and was highly critical of the key features of the paradigm that dominated American political science from the 1880s through the 1930s: "an almost total neglect of theory" and a conception of science that identified it principally with empiricist fact-gathering and descriptive studies; "a strongly parochial preoccupation with things American that stunted the development of an effective comparative method; . . . an unconcern with political systems as such, including the American system, which amounted in most cases to taking their properties for granted;" and "an unexamined and mostly implicit conception of political change and development that was blandly optimistic and unreflectively reformist."[3]

That paradigm collapsed in the face of dramatic changes in the world during the interwar period. Such processes as the Russian Revolution, the rise of Nazism and fascism, and the Great Depression led many to recognize the need for a systematic, theoretical, and truly comparative study of political systems. An alternative already existed in the approaches usually identified with the "Chicago school" of social scientists in the 1920s. This broader conception was reinforced by the arrival of refugee social scientists from Europe and by the exchange that occurred when many academic political scientists and social scientists in other disciplines worked together in Washington during the New Deal and World War II.

By the 1950s and through the 1960s, therefore, a new dominant paradigm developed as the expansion of political scientists' research interests to the Third World led them to interpret politics as experiences of universal processes of modernization and development.[4] The very terms "modernization" and "development" conveyed a fundamental optimism about humankind's capacity for individual and collective self-improvement, an optimism grounded in and perpetuated by liberal philosophy from the Enlightenment onward.[5] And, for many observers during the first two postwar decades, an apparent advance in the human condition seemed to justify such optimism. Indeed, European colonialism was giving way to independent new nations in Asia, Africa, and the Caribbean; democratic civilian rule was replacing dictatorship in Latin America; and rapid economic growth almost everywhere offered the promise of substantially improved material conditions of life.

But from the left and the right came a few dissenting voices from this optimistic liberal consensus. Samuel P. Huntington, one of the conservative critics, contended that the mainstream modernization and development theories of political scientists had been unduly influenced by other social sciences. These scholars, in their political analyses, had come to take as independent variables the subject matter of economists, sociologists, psychologists, and anthropologists. Huntington instead called upon political scientists to return to analysis of expressly political institutions and processes and to consider them as independent variables. He predicted that, while such indicators of modernization as urbanization, literacy, and economic output were likely to rise in the contemporary world, their rise would not by itself bring about an enduring, irreversible increase in political stability and in the effectiveness of national political institutions. Unless political analysts and statesmen understood the primacy of political institutions, he argued, the outcome of the modernization processes then underway was at least as likely to be political decay, instability, and arbitrary authoritarianism as it was to be an optimistically interpreted development.[6]

There was a strong dose of economic determinism in both liberal and Marxist analyses of the 1950s and 1960s, for both schools predicted that desired social and political modernization would follow almost automatically in the wake of economic development. Liberal analyses of W. W. Rostow and Seymour Martin Lipset, for example, indicated that economic development would bring about political democracy.[7] Such determinist reasoning provided the intellectual foundation of the foremost foreign assistance program of the era—the Alliance for Progress. The architects of the alliance called for the vast sum of 100 billion dollars of investment capital, both domestic and foreign, which they expected ultimately to transform, modernize, and develop the economies and, through them, the societies and polities of the Latin American countries.

This economic process was expected to strengthen an industrial and commercial bourgeoisie, expand the middle class, and create a large skilled, urban working class. Together these modern sectors would outweigh politically the landed oligarchy and other interests that liberal U.S. analysts associated with exploitative traditional rule. Political elites, elected by and responsive to these growing modern sectors, would enact socioeconomic reforms to improve the welfare of the masses, expanding access to education, health care, housing, and sanitation. And the modern working class would, through strengthened trade unions in now favorable market conditions, bargain at the workplace to obtain better pay. Thus, the distribution of income, wealth, services, and political power would become more egalitarian.

Subsequent events partly bore out these optimistic expectations. Despite a slow start, Latin America did achieve notable economic growth and social modernization in the 1960s. Average GDP increased annually at 5.9 percent; industry, utilities, and other modern sectors significantly increased their share of overall economic activity; urban population increased from one-half to two-thirds of total population; and school attendance and literacy increased markedly.[8] For some observers, it seemed that the economic determinist scenario was proceeding as expected.

Yet in perhaps the most crucial regard, the reality turned out to be quite different from the expectation. As the decade wore on, Latin American societies not only did not become more egalitarian or equitable, but markedly less so. Most remarkably, and absolutely contrary to the predictions of liberal developmentalists, this trend was most acute in precisely those countries with the highest rates of growth, such as Brazil and Mexico. And far from consolidating democratic rule and broadening participation in the polity, economic growth seemed to correlate with, and perhaps even to cause, the collapse of egalitarian democracies and their replacement by repressive authoritarian regimes whose policies sharply aggravated inequitable income distribution.

Does this experience put to rest the arguments based on economic determinism? Conversely, does the recent shift toward democratization revive or vindicate them? David Apter, another exception among the leading specialists on Third World politics in the 1960s, advanced an argument in his *Politics of Modernization* (1965) that attributed both processes, that is, the breakdown of democratic regimes and their later revival, to economic variables. The level of economic development, he believed, so structured the options available to governing elites in modernizing nations that they were more likely to choose authoritarian institutions at one time and democratic institutions at a later time. Thus, he proposed concepts that foreshadowed and helped explain both the tidal wave of authoritarianism in Third World areas after the mid 1960s and the transition away from authoritarianism in the 1980s.[9]

Apter claimed that all political systems rely on two basic functional requisites as they seek to implement policy—information (including voluntary cooperation) and coercion—and that they combine them in roughly inverse proportions. He assumed that the principal policy goal of all Third World countries was economic development, and he argued that different stages of economic development require different mixes of the two. In the early stages of economic development, coercion could mobilize resources for costly industrial and infrastructural investment, whereas investments by individuals in a poor society would be unlikely to generate sufficient resources for such projects. Also, without a strong government, a nation could not expect to bargain from strength with potential foreign investors. Apter thus predicted for Latin America that "as modernizing processes become transformed into industrialization processes, we may expect to see an increase in the power and number of mobilization [that is, authoritarian] systems. . . . More explicitly, if the Alliance for Progress is a great success in Latin America, it is likely to result in the creation of more mobilization systems. . . ."[10]

Conversely, later stages of economic development should foster a transition from authoritarian to more democratic political regimes. Successful industrialization policies ultimately create societies of such economic and social complexity that authoritarian coercion then hobbles or impedes the continued economic development that legitimizes such political systems. The government thus finds it necessary to reduce coercion and allow independent flows of information to guide economic activity and growth. Apter argued that an authoritarian system that has successfully promoted industrialization would need "to confront its own successes, . . . to decentralize authority and increase its economic efficiency," and he thought Khrushchev's market reforms in the Soviet Union might presage such a process there.[11] His perception was premature, but the logic seems borne out by more recent events in Latin America, Asia, the Soviet Union, and Eastern Europe. Apter did not predict specific paths to such reform. Indeed, as Michel Oksenberg and Bruce Dickson indicate earlier (Chapter 11), such prediction cannot be reliably made about great reform movements, because they lack the kind of ideology that supplies a generally predictable plan to most revolutionary movements. Great reforms therefore develop a particular logic of their own, responding to the weight of the social forces in contention. Comparative analysis of such movements, along the lines proposed by Oksenberg and Dickson, can help the profession better understand the process and delineate its likely paths.

With the exceptions noted, the dominant interpretive frameworks of unilinear modernization and development had difficulty accounting for the breakdown of democratic regimes, the advance of authoritarianism, and economic crisis. By the late 1960s for the Third World and the mid 1970s for the industrial West, therefore, scholars began testing other frameworks such as dependency, a concept that took into account external influence within Third World nations;[12] corporatism and other approaches that consider the state as a major political actor and independent variable for analysis;[13] political economy, that examines empirically and normatively the relationships between political and economic phenomena; and policy studies that focus on the output of government programs and the actual allocation of resources.[14]

POLITICAL REALITIES AND PARADIGM BREAKDOWN

No matter how important and desirable the achievement of a dominant paradigm may be to scientists, Kuhn notes that "the road to a firm research consensus is extraordinarily arduous" and that some scientific fields or subfields go for long periods in a "preparadigmatic" state.[15] There is every reason to believe that most subfields of political science, including nearly all in comparative politics, will long remain in such a preparadigmatic state. Unlike the physical sciences, which are empirical in nature, the discipline of political science has traditionally combined empirical, descriptive research with normative concerns. In the physical sciences there is a "time-honored philosophical theorem: 'Is' cannot imply 'ought.'"[16] By contrast, from the time of the ancient Greeks through the eighteenth- and nineteenth-century political economists, the field we now call political science was fused with moral philosophy, and its leading thinkers devoted their energies to bringing the "is" and the "ought" together, that is, to searching for institutions and practices that would improve humankind's condition.

In the era between World War II and the oil shock of 1973, when cheap, abundant Third World petroleum reserves fueled rapidly rising living standards throughout the industrial world, most political scientists in the United States believed that the "is" already embodied the "ought," at least in the democratic industrial welfare states that would serve, for the rest of the world, as the end point of a universal development process.[17] No need existed for further debate, therefore, over the most appropriate political, economic, or social institutions; political science could now proceed as a mature, purely empirical, heavily quantitative "value free" discipline. So completely, it was believed, had the prosperous capitalist economies of these nations made socialist ideologies anachronistic symbols of a now bygone age that Daniel Bell could title his book *The End of Ideology*.[18] Reflecting from the perspective of the 1980s, one analyst wryly summed up the scientific or behavioralist view of modern politics:

> . . . steady economic growth and affluence were taken for granted as stabilizing elements in the politics of advanced capitalist democracies. Much of the new "behavioral" political science was devoted to exploring the sociological and psychological roots of partisan voting and similar activities. Political outcomes were assumed to reflect these constraints together with the benign interplay and competition among pluralistic interest groups representing all sectors of society. . . . The "welfare state" and "mixed economy" were assumed to have eliminated most of the historic ideological class conflicts over fundamental political values.[19]

For scholars working on the Third World, the situation just described was simply disconnected from and irrelevant to political reality. Gabriel Almond, who more than any other individual had inspired, exhorted, and led comparative political analysts to study the Third World, expressed alarm that the profession's drive toward formal and methodological rigor could lead us to "pick our problems by their amenability to these methods, reducing the rest of the human situation to non-problems in the scientific sense." Steeped in history and very much a product of the liberal Enlightenment, he warned of "gross distortions which occur when we lose contact with the roots of our profession."[20]

Sustained postwar prosperity drove this process in the industrial West. The world economic crisis triggered by the oil shock of 1973 ended the era for citizens and political scientists alike, precipitating, in Kuhn's words, "the common awareness that something has gone wrong."[21] By calling into question the premise of the end of ideology, the crisis reawakened political scientists to normative issues. Classical political economy in the nineteenth century explicitly combined normative and empirical concerns, and the revival of political economy in the 1970s has drawn upon the two principal schools of thought of that era, liberalism for the public-choice school and socialism for Marxist writers.[22]

PARADIGM BREAKDOWN AND THE ENRICHMENT OF COMPARATIVE POLITICS

The shortcomings of the dominant modernization-and-development per-spective in no way diminish the achievement of comparativists and in opening Western eyes to Third World political realities in the 1950s and 1960s. Knowledge is cumulative, and the findings of that earlier work have provided important building blocks for the research that followed. The very inability of liberal, pluralist models to explain fully the nature of political systems in the Third World and, later, in the advanced industrial Western countries led comparativists to explore concepts and hypotheses from alternative intellectual traditions.

One such tradition was Marxism. During the 1960s, Marxist analysis occupied a minor place in comparative politics. Scholars in the Marxist tradition focused on class variables or on histories of communist or revolutionary movements, but few challenged the dominant liberal paradigm. Like the liberal developmentalists, Marxist analysts also expected history to follow universal patterns of modernization.[23] Indeed, in the 1950s and early 1960s most communists in Third World countries followed the Moscow line, applying universal development models abstracted from the European experience. Brazilian and Indian Communist party leaders, for example, accepted the Comintern's argu-ment that in the Third World, the bourgeois revolution must precede the ultimate proletarian revolution. Party members, therefore, were directed to support their respective national bourgeoisies in their drive to industrialize.[24]

Marxism helped shape the dependency analyses that comparativists turned to in the late 1960s and 1970s, and its tendency to conceive of the political and economic worlds as *systems* illuminated significant blind spots originating in the structure of the political science profession as well as in the liberal, pluralist tradition. The traditional division of pol-itical science in the United States into the subfields of comparative poli-tics and international relations had created a blind spot in the zone where the two subfields met. Most researchers wrote exclusively in one or the other subfield, and they failed to trace international political rela-tionships or events down to their ultimate impact upon the social and public policies—and thus upon the people—of the dependent states.

Liberal ideology reinforced this blind spot, because of its concern with the individual, whose freedom it seeks to safeguard and promote. Its biases led political scientists to focus on political actors, groups, or states *as individuals*. Liberal scholars therefore tended to break down global systems such as capitalism into their component parts, instead of analyzing them *as systems*. Marxists, on the other hand, consider capi-talism to be a world system and thus are drawn by the analytic logic of their ideology to probe the links from dominant capitalist countries to dependent ones.[25] The emergence of the dependency approach, initially developed in Latin American Marxist circles, thus helped North American liberals look into one of their blind spots.

Another alternative tradition was corporatism, which focused on the institutional arrangements by which the state structures the political participation of interest groups and social sectors and thus constrains their autonomy. Corporatist political thought represents a major branch of conservative Western philosophy, with roots running back to Aristotle and St. Thomas Aquinas; but its adoption and advocacy by the fascist countries that were defeated in World War II discredited it in the eyes of many and led most specialists in political theory and comparative politics to consider it a topic of historical curiosity with no contemporary vitality or applicability. With the breakdown of the liberal developmentalist perspective, however, a new generation of comparative analysts in the late 1960s and 1970s highlighted the important role of corporatist institutions and practices in contemporary Latin America and Europe. Howard J. Wiarda, who in this volume (Chapter 3) reassesses sympathetically the development-modernization literature, has described elsewhere how his earlier disillusionment with its teachings led him to the corporatist model. When he first went to do field research in Latin America, armed with the conceptual apparatus of the dominant paradigm, he was faced with a harsh learning experience: In large measure the political reality in his subject countries failed to conform to the expectations created by developmentalism. However, there in the field—in Latin American philosophy, institutions, laws, and culture—he discovered clearly articulated corporatist thought that made predictable the practices he was observing. A corporatist model derived from these sources provided him with a far better guide to political behavior and patterns than did developmentalism.[26]

Comparative politics has been greatly enriched by the addition of these perspectives, for they have created new levels of awareness for analysts and added new concepts and tools to their repertoires. Initially, of course, liberalism, Marxism, and corporatism were political ideologies, that is, calls to action. When converted into paradigms for political research, however, each tradition emphasizes its own distinctive variables and sociopolitical dynamics, so that the comparativist who draws insight from them in combination can avoid the blind spots of any one taken alone.

RESEARCH AGENDAS FOR THE 1990S

Ronald H. Chilcote, surveying here both Marxist and liberal approaches to political analysis (Chapter 5), finds that the profession is now returning to classical questions of political science; we are not rejecting those earlier analytic models but rather putting them in perspective. Comparative politics, like political science in general, is no longer searching for a universal theory or paradigm that explains the totality of political behavior and processes. Rather, the profession is more modestly seeking concepts and tools that explain aspects of such behavior and processes. The essays in this volume illustrate a number of such conceptual and research efforts and signal topics for the research agenda of the 1990s and the turn of the century. David Collier, for example, optimistically demonstrates in Chapter 2 that conceptual innovations in the basic sets of tools for comparativists—the comparative method and the case study, experimental, and statistical approaches—now provide us with a considerably more powerful set of tools for carrying out research, testing propositions, and developing concepts.

One thread running through these essays is the need for comparative analysis to be grounded in historical knowledge, not only of the country or countries of one's focus, but, for the purposes of true comparison, of other areas as well. The assumption that the capitalist industrial world had achieved a permanently self-sustaining prosperity, for example, betrays a hubris untempered by historical knowledge of the rise and fall of civilizations. S. N. Eisenstadt, calling attention to the "civilizational" dimension of political development (Chapter 4), emphasizes that history does not run everywhere along the same track and that a society's structure of conflict, rooted in basic cultural experience and values, shapes its broad pattern of political development. Such an approach helps us understand why Japan, for example, has not modernized through revolution but rather under the symbolism of great reform. Metin Heper (Chapter 9), applying a historical approach drawn from Eisenstadt's earlier work, explains different patterns of democratization in light of the specific colonial and institutional legacies of the countries involved.

Regional comparison may give some new life to older stages-of-development theories. Edmond J. Keller (Chapter 7) and Henry Bienen and Jeffrey Herbst (Chapter 10) suggest that Africa, the poorest and least economically developed continent, is also in a different phase of political development. Analysts of Africa, like those of Latin America or Eastern Europe in earlier eras, find rulers struggling to increase their state's capabilities and treating democratization as an impediment. Indeed, Keller finds it helpful to draw upon concepts associated with the recent authoritarian past in Latin America, such as corporatism, to help interpret the African context.

The exciting political news from almost every part of the world in recent years may tempt scholars, understandably, to immerse themselves more deeply into their own particular area specialties to follow history-making events. Still, the more dynamic those events, the more perspective we need in order to understand them. The reforms under Mikhail Gorbachev in the 1980s invite comparison with those under

Nikita Khrushchev in the late 1950s and early 1960s, as do the differing Soviet responses to the Prague spring in 1968 and the Eastern European reform movements in 1989 and 1990. The application of Oksenberg and Dickson's framework (Chapter 11) for tracing the trajectory of great reform movements will supply concepts and hypotheses for dozens of research projects in the coming years. In sum, the more unprecedented the changes in any country or region, the more the student of politics must turn to comparable events in other times and places to fully appreciate the significance of the changes.

Political change or regime transition has always intrigued observers. The course of great revolutions has been charted by political analysts from Aristotle to the present, with Crane Brinton's comparative *Anatomy of Revolution* (first published in 1938) standing as a modern landmark in the genre.[27] By contrast, the policy output of revolutions, that is, their impact upon the lives of citizens, has received relatively little empirical treatment, and Susan Eckstein here (Chapter 14) presents a model for scholars to apply elsewhere. She compares five Latin American revolutionary regimes on criteria of income distribution, land tenure patterns, infant mortality, life expectancy, industrialization, and economic dependency; compares results of revolution from above and from below; and compares revolutionary and nonrevolutionary countries in the region. Similarly, Klaus von Beyme (Chapter 12) assesses the actual impact of government policy in the Soviet Union and Eastern Europe upon each country's social structure and economic performance in recent decades.

Regime transitions from authoritarian rule toward democracy in the 1980s seized the attention of the public as well as specialists in comparative politics. Metin Heper, as already mentioned, seeks indicators for the success of contemporary democratization in the different historical legacies of his subject countries. Comparing transitions over several decades in Latin America, Terry Karl (Chapter 8) derives a set of alternative paths to democratization, and she also raises normative implications of democratization by pact. Critics of the burgeoning literature on democratization argue that it focuses almost exclusively on elite roles in the transitions, and they call for new research on the expressly political institutions and processes that weave citizens into the body politic. As Daniel H. Levine suggests, "Such studies would have to consider changes in social structure and cultural norms that help create and nurture new groups, and that shape their links to the state and other dominant institutions."[28] In this way researchers can shed instructive light on the success or failure of the consolidation of democratic institutions.

The time is now ripe for scholars to broaden the comparison to include Asian countries such as South Korea, Pakistan, and the Philippines.[29] Indeed, the world has changed so dramatically in recent years that the comparison must extend to Eastern Europe as well. Recent history has refuted in a dramatic way the controversial claim that won for Jeane Kirkpatrick the U.S. ambassadorship to the United Nations. Her distinction between totalitarian and authoritarian regimes caught then-candidate Reagan's attention, for it argued that communist political systems could never democratize while authoritarian regimes could, thus justifying U.S. support for such authoritarian allies as the Shah of Iran and Anastasio Somoza of Nicaragua.[30]

The excitement generated by redemocratization may obscure the successful endurance of some long-time Third World democracies, such as India. Comparative analysis of the ways that these democracies have coped with crises may also hold lessons for comparativists. Myron Weiner's observation on the British legacy deserves attention: "But why the British, almost alone among the former colonial rulers, successfully transplanted their institutions to some countries while other imperial powers were less successful is one of the most interesting questions for comparative analysis."[31] India, the democracy with the largest electorate in the world, has produced a rich store of studies on the electoral process.[32]

As we pay closer attention to the economic performance of governments, we see that much of the day-to-day politics in both democracies and authoritarian systems involves the interplay of rival economic forces. Jack Hayward (Chapter 16) moves analysis beyond a simple model of political demand and governmental response to one of a policy community, composed of politicians, administrators, and business and labor representatives. T. J. Pempel (Chapter 17) makes an innovative comparison of such seemingly different countries as Japan and Sweden, demonstrating how political stability and the long-term dominance of each polity by one party—labor-based in Sweden and capital-based in Japan—resulted from each ruling party's willingness to base policy outputs upon compromise with its economic opponents. Douglas E. Ashford's comparative examination of four apparently similar European welfare-state systems (Chapter 15) reveals how different were the political motivations and processes that led to their establishment.

Socioeconomic actors have long been subjects for study by liberal analysts, and Marxists have generally applied class analysis to these groups. Ronald H. Chilcote (Chapter 5) indicates the ways in which contemporary politics blurs some of the distinctions between the two traditions. Ecological politics, feminism, and the accommodative evolution of sectors of the working class itself, for example, have led Marxists in industrial capitalist societies to seek new forms of organization and of political analysis. Field work by comparativists can illuminate this process. For the Third World, Irving Leonard Markovitz has coordinated a project to demonstrate the utility of class analysis not only in describing

the reality of power and of policy in Africa, but also in suggesting remedial measures to the tragedy of drought in the Sahel.[33] David G. Becker
(Chapter 6) calls for a nondeterministic class analysis, and he urges
comparativists to carry out more microlevel studies of factories, neighborhood associations, trade unions, bourgeois organizations, and political parties. Once a number of such case studies have been completed,
scholars can follow the lead of J. Samuel Valenzuela, who comparatively analyzed case material from eight countries on three continents,
delineated various roles of organized labor during democratization, and
suggested the implications of each for the labor movement itself, for
union members, and for the process of democratization.[34]

Newly democratizing countries now lend themselves to voting and
mass opinion surveys that had been prohibited or irrelevant under
authoritarian rule. In the framework of this chapter, it is worth noting
that such research constitutes perhaps the only subfield in comparative
politics that does have an established paradigm, in Kuhn's strict sense of
the term. Cross-national research in this new context can test the validity of concepts and hypotheses generated in industrial democracies.
Ronald Inglehart's most recent study on political culture, for example,
uses data from over twenty countries on five continents to test
hypotheses on the emergence of "postmaterialist" values and their
impact on patterns of economic and political behavior.[35] Finally, comparativists would do well to apply to the newly democratic regimes
Susan Eckstein's model for comparing and evaluating regime performance.

In an era when President Gorbachev astonished the world by
declaring that "the moral values that religion generated and embodied
for centuries can help in the work of renewal in our country, too,"[36] it
seems that no one can any longer ignore the political significance of religious forces. From the leader of the communist superpower, this
declaration marks the illumination of a blindspot for many Marxist
analysts. Fred Halliday's otherwise perceptive class analysis of the
Shah's regime in Iran, for example, paid scant attention to the role of
Islam and thus could not prepare readers for the fundamentalist revolution that followed.[37] Nikki R. Keddie's analysis (Chapter 13) of historical and cultural forces in the Islamic world, on the other hand, does
illuminate this issue, and her comparative treatment demonstrates that
the role of Islamic fundamentalism in Iranian history is so distinctive
that similar revolutions are quite unlikely in other Islamic nations.

In countries around the globe in the late 1960s and 1970s, authoritarian rule restricted political participation and forced opposition
activity underground. Much of it then came to be expressed through
religious organizations, and the volume and quality of scholarly and

journalistic studies of the phenomenon now provide analysts of the comparative political aspects of religion with a rich store of data, concepts, and hypotheses.[38]

There are truly global forces and processes at work in the world today, and one challenge for comparativists is to analyze them systematically. The dependency perspective sheds light on processes once assumed by specialists in comparative politics to belong in the domain of their colleagues in international relations. Continuing acceleration of world trade, European economic integration, increasing foreign investment in nearly all economies, the surge of the Japanese and German economies, and the rise of newly industrial countries make it clear that international economic competition will take place less among natural resources than among human skills of inventiveness and organization. This constitutes a clear invitation for comparative research on the political economy of international competitiveness, research that should combine institutional, historical, and cultural tools. Another issue, global in nature but until recently ignored by comparativists, is the international drug trade and its impact on both supplying and consuming states and their peoples.[39]

A polemical literature exists on topics such as whether revolution has been exported into a given country, for example, into Nicaragua by Soviet or Cuban agents. Sober research generally finds that revolution cannot be effectively exported and that such movements are indigenous.[40] The current wave of transitions from authoritarianism toward democratization in Latin America, Eastern Europe, and parts of Asia should allow comparativists to assess the degree to which such processes arise from "contagious" influences or examples from other countries, or whether they are simply common responses to similar domestic conditions. One researcher has begun exploring the process by which neoconservative ideology, which was generated in the United States and England, came to be implemented in Latin American authoritarian regimes even before the Reagan and Thatcher governments had a chance to apply it in its countries of origin.[41]

The focus of our energies in comparative politics seems to shift between broad conceptualization and narrow data gathering. Surely the most exciting periods are those when new concepts are formulated and new data are gathered in response to dramatic changes in the world. Given the unprecedented changes taking place in the world today, we can expect a burst of new ideas and concepts to test over the coming years. One political scientist in the Bush administration wrote a much publicized article in 1989 announcing that communism is now dead, and this event marks the end of history.[42] Comparativists would do well to recall the lessons of the "end of ideology" and of the paradigm of that era. The agenda for comparing political institutions and forces across decades and continents in no way commits us to any notion of history as mere repetition. Indeed, one could rewrite the old saw, in light of recent events: *Plus ça change, plus ce* n'est pas *la même chose.*

In sum, it is the task of the student of comparative politics to analyze current processes of political change by placing them in an international, socioeconomic, and historical perspective that will highlight both similarities and unique aspects of those processes. As we broaden our reach and sharpen our hypotheses, we may hope, in the spirit of the Enlightenment, that our work will become increasingly relevant to policy makers and implementers who have the means to improve the lives of citizens. As the comparative study of politics rises to the challenge of our times, we hope that it will enter a new phase of relevance not only for political analysts in the auditorium, but also for political actors on the very stage of politics.

NOTES

The authors gratefully acknowledge the very helpful comments and suggestions offered on this chapter by Sumit Ganguly and Irving Leonard Markovitz, though we accept responsibility for errors of commission or omission that may remain.

1. See, for example, the comparative analysis in Morris J. Blachman, William M. LeoGrande, and Kenneth E. Sharpe, eds., *Confronting Revolution: Security Through Diplomacy in Central America* (New York: Pantheon, 1986); Forrest D. Colburn, *Post-Revolutionary Nicaragua: State, Class and the Dilemmas of Agrarian Policy* (Berkeley: University of California Press, 1986); Tommie Sue Montgomery, *Revolution in El Salvador: Origins and Evolution* (Boulder, Colo.: Westview Press, 1982).

2. Thomas S. Kuhn, *The Structure of Scientific Revolutions*, 2d ed. (Chicago: University of Chicago Press, 1970), esp. 10–15, 176–181. The scientific communities to which Kuhn refers are for the most part subfields of any given discipline.

3. David B. Truman, "Disillusion and Regeneration: The Quest for a Discipline," *American Political Science Review* 40, no. 4 (December 1965): 866. This was Truman's presidential address to the APSA convention that year.

4. See, for example, Gabriel Almond and James S. Coleman, eds., *The Politics of the Developing Areas* (Princeton, N.J.: Princeton University Press, 1960); Edward Shils, *Political Development and the New States* (The Hague: Mouton, 1962); David E. Apter, *The Politics of Modernization* (Chicago: University of Chicago Press, 1965); and Dankwart A. Rustow, *A World of Nations: Problems of Political*

Modernization (Washington, D.C.: Brookings Institution, 1967); and other sources cited in Chapter 3.

5. Gabriel Almond acknowledges his intellectual debt to the Enlightenment in his collected essays, *Political Development: Essays in Heuristic Theory* (Boston: Little, Brown, 1970). His abundant optimism and faith in human nature are clear throughout these essays, and he notes that the founding generation of modern comparative political analysts was inspired and motivated by "the missionary and 'Peace Corps' mood that swept the students and intellectuals of this country during the 1950s and early 1960s" (p. 21).

6. Samuel P. Huntington, "Political Development and Political Decay," *World Politics* 17, no. 3 (1965): 386–430. That Huntington's values owe much to classical conservative thought can be seen in the following definition of the public interest, which he proposes as an alternative to liberal, Marxist, and other formulations: "The public interest . . . is whatever strengthens governmental institutions" (p. 412).

7. Walt W. Rostow, *The Stages of Economic Growth: A Non-Communist Manifest* (Cambridge: Cambridge University Press, 1960); Seymour Martin Lipset, *Political Man: The Social Bases of Politics*, 2d ed. (Baltimore: Johns Hopkins University Press, 1981).

8. See the tables in Kevin J. Middlebrook and Carlos Rico, "The United States and Latin America in the 1980s: Change, Complexity, and Contending Perspectives," in Middlebrook and Rico, eds., *The United States and Latin America in the 1980s* (Pittsburgh: University of Pittsburgh Press, 1986), 10–17, 54–57.

9. David Apter, *Politics of Modernization*, esp. 223–265, 305, 390, and 427–428. Apter later expanded on these concepts in *Choice and the Politics of Allocation: A Developmental Theory* (New Haven, Conn.: Yale University Press, 1971).

10. Apter, *Politics of Modernization*, 252–253.

11. Ibid., 305; see also 427–428.

12. For a discussion of the logic of the dependency approach and a rich case study employing it, see Peter Evans, *Dependent Development: The Alliance of Multinational, State, and Local Capital in Brazil* (Princeton, N.J.: Princeton University Press, 1979). On the new approaches generally in this period, see Ronald H. Chilcote, *Theories of Comparative Politics: The Search for a Paradigm* (Boulder, Colo: Westview Press, 1981); Howard J. Wiarda, ed., *New Directions in Comparative Politics* (Boulder, Colo: Westview Press, 1985); and Myron Weiner and Samuel P. Huntington, eds., *Understanding Political Development* (Boston: Little, Brown, 1987).

13. See, for example, Philippe C. Schmitter, "Still the Century of Corporatism?" *The Review of Politics* 36, no. 1 (January 1974): 85–131, and other essays in this special issue on corporatism; Alfred Stepan, *The State and Society: Peru in Comparative Perspective* (Princeton, N.J.: Princeton University Press, 1978); and Peter B. Evans, Dietrich Rueschemeyer, and Theda Skocpol, eds., *Bringing the State Back In* (Cambridge: Cambridge University Press, 1985); Philippe C. Schmitter, ed., *Corporatism and Policy-Making in Contemporary Western-Europe*, special issue of *Comparative Political Studies* 10, no. 1 (April 1977).

14. Stuart S. Nagel, *Public Policy: Goals, Means, and Methods* (New York: St. Martin's Press, 1984), and the voluminous conceptual discussions and research reports in the *Policy Studies Journal* whose board Nagel coordinates.

15. Kuhn, *Structure of Scientific Revolutions*, 15.

16. Ibid., 207.

17. See, for example, Robert E. Lane, "The Politics of Consensus in an Age of Affluence," *American Political Science Review* 59, no. 4 (December 1965): 874–895.

18. Daniel Bell, *The End of Ideology: On the Exhaustion of Political Ideas in the Fifties*, rev. ed. (New York: Free Press, 1962).

19. Norman J. Vig, "Introduction: Political Science and Political Economy," in Norman J. Vig and Steven E. Schier, eds., *Political Economy in Western Democracies* (New York: Holmes and Meier, 1985), 3–4, 5.

20. Almond, *Political Development*, 24. Albert O. Hirschman also argued that insensitive and rigid application of "scientific" methods led political scientists to understand less rather than more about the subjects they were treating, in "The Search for Paradigms as a Hindrance to Understanding," *World Politics* 22, no. 3 (April 1970): 329–343.

21. Kuhn, *Structure of Scientific Revolutions* 181.

22. See Vig and Schier for examples of contemporary scholarship in political economy. On the institutions that scholars in the social sciences have developed to support such research, such as the Conference Group on the Political Economy of Advanced Industrial Societies, formed by political scientists, and the Union for Radical Political Economy, formed by economists, see Edward J. Harpham and Alan Stone, "The Study of Political Economy," in Harpham and Stone, eds., *The Political Economy of Public Policy* (Beverly Hills, Calif.: Sage, 1982), 11–25.

23. For a perceptive analysis showing the common components and characteristics of liberal and Marxist developmentalist theory, see

Geisa Maria Rocha, "Brazil's Dilemma: Dependency, Debt, and Democracy," Ph.D. dissertation, City University of New York, 1989, 1–83.

24. Ronald H. Chilcote, *The Brazilian Communist Party: Conflict and Consensus, 1922–1972* (New York: Oxford University Press, 1974), 64–75; Bhabani Sen Gupta, *Communism in Indian Politics* (New York: Oxford University Press, 1972).

25. See Immanuel Wallerstein, *The Modern World-System*, 2 vols. (New York: Academic Press, 1974–80).

26. Howard J. Wiarda, "The Making of a Latin Americanist: A Note on Corporatism and Its Sociology of Knowledge," Chapter 1 of his *Corporatism and National Development in Latin America* (Boulder, Colo.: Westview Press, 1981), 3–10. Wiarda's experiences are representative of those of many of his colleagues in that first postdevelopmentalist generation.

27. Crane Brinton, *The Anatomy of Revolution*, rev. ed. (New York: Vintage Books, 1952).

28. Daniel H. Levine, "Paradigm Lost: Dependence to Democracy," *World Politics* 40, no. 3 (April 1988): 389. See also Karen Remmer, "New Wine or Old Bottlenecks? The Study of Latin American Democracy," *Comparative Politics*, forthcoming, July 1991.

29. See an important first step in the ambitious four-volume study by Larry Diamond, Juan J. Linz, and Seymour Martin Lipset, eds., *Democracy in Developing Countries* (Boulder, Colo.: Lynne Rienner Publisher, 1988–90).

30. See the lead essay (first published in 1979) in Jeane J. Kirkpatrick, *Dictatorship and Double Standards: Rationalism and Reason in Politics* (New York: Simon & Schuster, 1983).

31. Myron Weiner, "Political Change: Asia, Africa, and the Middle East," in Weiner and Huntington, *Understanding Political Development* 38. See also Myron Weiner and Ergun Özbudun, eds., *Competitive Elections in Developing Countries* (Durham, N.C.: Duke University Press, 1987).

32. The most recent of them is David Butler, Ashok Lahiri, and Prannoy Roy, *India Decides: Elections, 1952–1989* (New Delhi, Living Media India: 1989).

33. Irving Leonard Markovitz, ed., *Studies in Power and Class in Africa* (New York: Oxford University Press, 1987).

34. J. Samuel Valenzuela, "Labor Movements in Transitions to Democracy: A Framework for Analysis," *Comparative Politics* 22, no. 4 (July 1989): 445–472.

35. For paradigm studies of elections and voter behavior, see Angus Campbell et al., *The American Voter* (New York: Wiley, 1960); Russell J. Dalton, *Citizen Politics in Western Democracies: Public*

Opinion and Political Parties in the United States, Great Britain, West Germany, and France (Chatham, N.J.: Chatham House, 1988); Asher Arian, *Politics in Israel: The Second Generation*, 2d ed. (Chatham, N.J.: Chatham House, 1989). On political culture, see Ronald Inglehart, *Culture Shift in Advanced Industrial Society* (Princeton, N.J.: Princeton University Press, 1990), and the bibliography therein.

36. Quoted on the eve of his audience with the Pope. *New York Times*, December 1, 1989.

37. Fred Halliday, *Iran: Dictatorship and Development*, 2d ed. (Harmondsworth: Penguin Books, 1979).

38. Daniel H. Levine, "Religion and Politics in Comparative and Historical Perspective," *Comparative Politics* 19, no. 1 (October 1986): 95. See also Daniel H. Levine, ed., *Religion and Political Conflict in Latin America* (Chapel Hill: University of North Carolina, 1986).

39. Douglas A. Chalmers sets the agenda for a comparative research seminar on this topic at Columbia University in "Changing the Language on Drug Trafficking," unpublished, Institute of Latin American and Iberian Studies, Columbia University, November 1989.

40. For an assessment of the alleged Soviet and Cuban roles in the Nicaraguan revolution see William M. LeoGrande, "Cuba," and Cole Blasier, "The Soviet Union," in Blachman, LeoGrande, and Sharpe, *Confronting Revolution*, 229–255, 256–270.

41. See Hector Schamis, "Reconceptualizing Latin American Authoritarianism in the 1970s: From Bureaucratic-Authoritarianism to Neoconservatism," *Comparative Politics*, forthcoming, 1991.

42. Francis Fukuyama, "The End of History?" *The National Interest*, Summer 1989.

Selected Bibliography

GENERAL CONCEPTS, COMPARATIVE METHOD, THE STATE

Almond, Gabriel A. *A Discipline Divided: Schools and Sects in Political Science*. Newbury Park, Calif.: Sage, 1989.

Almond, Gabriel A., Scott Flanagan, Robert Mundt, eds. *Crisis, Choice, and Change: Historical Studies of Political Development*. Boston: Little, Brown, 1973.

Almond, Gabriel A., and G. Bingham Powell. *Comparative Politics Today: A World View*. 4th ed. Glenview, Ill.: Scott, Foresman, 1988.

Almond, Gabriel A., and Sidney Verba. *The Civic Culture*. Princeton, N.J.: Princeton University Press, 1963.

Apter, David E., ed. *Ideology and Discontent*. New York: Basic Books, 1964.

Ashford, Douglas E., ed. *Comparing Public Policies: New Concepts and Methods*. Beverly Hills, Calif.: Sage, 1978.

Badie, Bertrand, and Pierre Birnbaum. *The Sociology of the State*. Chicago: University of Chicago Press, 1983.

Bell, Daniel. *The End of Ideology: On the Exhaustion of Political Ideas in the Fifties*. Rev. ed. New York: Free Press, 1962.

Benjamin, Roger, and Stephen L. Elkin, eds. *The Democratic State*. Lawrence: University Press of Kansas, 1985.

Block, Fred. *Revising State Theory: Essays in Politics and Postindustrialism*. Philadelphia: Temple University Press, 1988.

Blondel, Jean. *Political Leadership: Towards a General Analysis*. Newbury Park, Calif.: Sage, 1987.

Bobbio, Norberto. *The Future of Democracy*. Minneapolis: University of Minnesota Press, 1987.

Brinton, Crane. *The Anatomy of Revolution*. Rev. ed. New York: Vintage Books, 1965.

Cameron, David. "The Expansion of the Political Economy: A Comparative Analysis." *American Political Science Review* 72 (1978): 1243–1261.

Carnoy, Martin. *The State and Political Theory*. Princeton, N. J.: Princeton University Press, 1984.

Castles, Francis, ed. *The Comparative History of Public Policy*. London: Polity Press, 1989.

Chilcote, Ronald H. *Theories of Comparative Politics: The Search for a Paradigm*. Boulder, Colo.: Westview Press, 1981.

Clapham, Christopher, ed. *Private Patronage and Public Power: Political Clientelism in the Modern State*. London: Frances Pinter, 1982.

Dahl, Robert A. *Polyarchy: Participation and Opposition*. New Haven, Conn.: Yale University Press, 1971.

Downs, Anthony. *An Economic Theory of Democracy*. New York: Harper & Row, 1957.

Duverger, Maurice. *Political Parties*. 3rd ed. London: Methuen, 1969.

Eckstein, Harry. "Case Studies and Theory in Political Science." *Handbook of Political Science* 7 (1975): 79–137.

Eisenstadt, S. N., ed. *The Origins and Diversity of Axial-Age Civilizations*. Albany, N.Y.: SUNY Press, 1986.

Eisenstadt, S. N. *Revolution and the Transformation of Societies*. New York: Free Press, 1978.

Eisenstadt, S. N. *A Sociological Approach to Comparative Civilizations: The Development and Directions of a Research Program*. Jerusalem: The Hebrew University, 1986.

Evans, Peter B., Dietrich Rueschemeyer, and Theda Skocpol, eds. *Bringing the State Back In*. Cambridge: Cambridge University Press, 1985.

Gramsci, Antonio. *The Modern Prince and Other Writings*. New York: New York University Press, 1957.

Huntington, Samuel P. "Will More Countries Become Democratic?" *Political Science Quarterly* 99 (1984): 194–210.

Johnson, Chalmers. *Revolutionary Change*. 2d ed. Stanford, Calif.: Stanford University Press, 1982.

Jordan, Bill. *The State: Authority and Autonomy*. Oxford: Basil Blackwell, 1985.

Kennedy, Paul. *The Rise and Fall of the Great Powers: Economic Change and Military Conflict from 1500 to 2000*. New York: Random House, 1988.

Krasner, Stephen D. "Approaches to the State: Alternative Conceptions and Historical Dynamics." *Comparative Politics* 16 (1984): 223–246.

Kuhn, Thomas S. *The Structure of Scientific Revolutions.* 2d ed. Chicago: University of Chicago Press, 1970.

Laclau, Ernesto, and Chantal Mouffe. *Hegemony and Socialist Strategy: Towards a Radical Democratic Politics.* London: Verso, 1985.

Lijphart, Arend. *Democracies: Patterns of Majoritarian and Consensus Government in Twenty-One Countries.* New Haven, Conn.: Yale University Press, 1984.

Linz, Juan J., and Alfred Stepan, eds. *The Breakdown of Democratic Regimes.* 4 vols. Baltimore: Johns Hopkins University Press, 1978.

Lipset, Seymour Martin. *Political Man: The Social Bases of Politics.* 2d ed. Baltimore: Johns Hopkins University Press, 1981.

Loewenberg, Gerhard, and Samuel C. Patterson. *Comparing Legislatures.* Boston: Little, Brown, 1979.

Macridis, Roy C. *Contemporary Political Ideologies.* 4th ed. Glenview, Ill.: Scott, Foresman, 1989.

Macridis, Roy C. *Modern Political Regimes: Patterns and Institutions.* Boston: Little, Brown, 1986.

Magdoff, Harry. *The Age of Imperialism.* New York: Monthly Review Press, 1969.

Mayer, Lawrence C. *Redefining Comparative Politics: Promise Versus Performance.* Newbury Park, Calif.: Sage, 1989.

Moore, Barrington, Jr. *Social Origins of Dictatorship and Democracy: Lord and Peasant in the Making of the Modern World.* Boston: Beacon Press, 1966.

Nordlinger, Eric A. *On the Autonomy of the Democratic State.* Cambridge, Mass.: Harvard University Press, 1981.

Olson, Mancur. *The Logic of Collective Action: Public Goods and the Theory of Groups.* Rev. ed. Cambridge, Mass.: Harvard University Press, 1971.

Pateman, Carole. *Participation and Democratic Theory.* Cambridge: Cambridge University Press, 1970.

Perlmutter, Amos. *Modern Authoritarianism: A Comparative Institutional Analysis.* New Haven, Conn.: Yale University Press, 1981.

Popper, Karl R. *Conjectures and Refutations: The Growth of Scientific Knowledge.* New York: Harper & Row, 1968.

Poulantzas, Nicos. *Crisis of the Dictatorships.* London: New Left Books, 1976.

Poulantzas, Nicos. *State, Power, Socialism*. London: New Left Books, 1978.

Powell, G. Bingham. *Comparing Democracies: Power, Stability, and Violence*. Cambridge, Mass.: Harvard University Press, 1982.

Przeworski, Adam, and Henry Teune. *The Logic of Comparative Social Inquiry*. New York: Wiley, 1970.

Rabinow, Paul, and William M. Sullivan, eds. *Interpretive Social Science: A Reader*. Berkeley: University of California Press, 1979.

Rae, Douglas W. *The Political Consequences of Electoral Laws*. New Haven, Conn.: Yale University Press, 1967.

Ragin, Charles C. *The Comparative Method: Moving Beyond Qualitative and Quantitative Strategies*. Berkeley: University of California Press, 1987.

Rustow, Dankwart A. "Transitions to Democracy: Toward a Dynamic Model." *Comparative Politics* 2 (1970): 337–364.

Sartori, Giovanni. *Parties and Party Systems*. New York: Cambridge University Press, 1976.

Sartori, Giovanni. *Theory of Democracy Revisited*. 2 vols. Chatham, N.J.: Chatham House, 1987.

Sartori, Giovanni, ed. *Social Science Concepts: A Systematic Analysis*. Newbury Park, Calif.: Sage, 1985.

Schumpeter, Joseph A. *Capitalism, Socialism and Democracy*. 2d ed. New York: Harper & Row, 1947.

Skocpol, Theda. *States and Social Revolutions: A Comparative Analysis of France, Russia, and China*. Cambridge: Cambridge University Press, 1979.

Skocpol, Theda, ed. *Vision and Method in Historical Sociology*. New York: Cambridge University Press, 1984.

Tilly, Charles. *Big Structures, Large Processes, Huge Comparisons*. New York: Russell Sage, 1984.

Vallier, Ivan, ed. *Comparative Methods in Sociology: Essays on Trends and Applications*. Berkeley: University of California Press, 1971.

Verba, Sidney, et al. *Elites and the Idea of Equality: A Comparison of Japan, Sweden, and the United States*. Cambridge, Mass.: Harvard University Press, 1987.

Weber, Max. *From Max Weber: Essays in Sociology*. Ed. H. H. Gerth and C. W. Mills. New York: Oxford University Press, 1958.

Wiarda, Howard J., ed. *New Directions in Comparative Politics*. 2d ed. Boulder, Colo.: Westview Press, 1990.

Willner, Ann Ruth. *The Spellbinders: Charismatic Political Leadership*. New Haven, Conn.: Yale University Press, 1984.

POLITICAL DEVELOPMENT

Almond, Gabriel A. *Political Development: Essays in Heuristic Theory*. Boston: Little, Brown, 1970.

Almond, Gabriel A., and James S. Coleman, eds. *The Politics of the Developing Areas*. Princeton, N.J.: Princeton University Press, 1960.

Apter, David E. *The Politics of Modernization*. Chicago: University of Chicago Press, 1965.

Apter, David E. *Rethinking Development: Modernization, Dependency, and Postmodern Politics*. Newbury Park, Calif.: Sage, 1987.

Becker, David G. *The New Bourgeoisie and the Limits of Dependency*. Princeton, N.J.: Princeton University Press, 1983.

Binder, Leonard, et al. *Crises and Sequences in Political Development*. Princeton, N.J.: Princeton University Press, 1971.

Black, Cyril E. *The Dynamics of Modernization: A Study in Comparative History*. New York: Harper & Row, 1966.

Chilcote, Ronald H. *Theories of Development and Underdevelopment*. Boulder, Colo.: Westview Press, 1984.

Diamond, Larry, Juan J. Linz, and Seymour Martin Lipset, eds. *Democracy in Developing Countries*. 4 vols. Boulder, Colo.: Lynne Rienner, 1988–1990.

Finkle, Jason L., and Richard W. Gable, eds. *Political Development and Social Change*. 2d ed. New York: Wiley, 1971.

Huntington, Samuel P. *Political Order in Changing Societies*. New Haven, Conn.: Yale University Press, 1968.

Lipset, Seymour Martin. *The First New Nation: The United States in Historical and Comparative Perspective*. New York: Basic Books, 1963.

Migdal, Joel S. *Strong Societies and Weak States: State-Society Relations and State Capabilities in the Third World*. Princeton, N.J.: Princeton University Press, 1988.

O'Donnell, Guillermo, Philippe C. Schmitter, and Lawrence Whitehead, eds. *Transitions from Authoritarian Rule: Prospects for Democracy*. 4 vols. Baltimore: Johns Hopkins University Press, 1986.

Oxaal, Ivar, et al., eds. *Beyond the Sociology of Development*. London: Routledge and Kegan Paul, 1975.

Pye, Lucian W., and Sidney Verba, eds. *Political Culture and Political Development*. Princeton, N.J.: Princeton University Press, 1965.

Rostow, Walt W. *The Stages of Economic Growth: A Non-Communist Manifesto*. Cambridge: Cambridge University Press, 1960.

Rudolph, Lloyd I., and Susanne Hoeber Rudolph. *The Modernity of Tradition*. Chicago: University of Chicago Press, 1967.

Rustow, Dankwart A. *A World of Nations: Problems of Political Modernization*. Washington, D.C.: Brookings Institution, 1967.

Shils, Edward. *Political Development and the New States*. The Hague: Mouton, 1962.

Trimberger, Ellen K. *Revolution from Above: Military Bureaucrats in Japan, Turkey, Egypt, and Peru*. New Brunswick, N.J.: Transaction Books, 1978.

Weiner, Myron, and Samuel P. Huntington, eds. *Understanding Political Development*. Boston: Little, Brown, 1987.

POLITICAL ECONOMY

Becker, David G., et al. *Postimperialism: International Capitalism and Development in the Late Twentieth Century*. Boulder, Colo.: Lynne Rienner, 1987.

Bennet, Jon, and Susan George. *The Hunger Machine: The Politics of Food*. New York: Basic Blackwell, 1987.

Burawoy, Michael. *The Politics of Production: Factory Regimes Under Capitalism and Socialism*. London: Verso, 1985.

Cawson, Alan. *Corporatism and Political Theory*. Oxford: Oxford University Press, 1986.

Cawson, Alan, ed. *Organized Interests and the State: Studies in Meso-Corporatism*. Newbury Park, Calif.: Sage, 1985.

Esping-Andersen, Gösta. *Politics Against Markets: The Social Democratic Road to Power*. Princeton, N.J.: Princeton University Press, 1985.

Feigenbaum, Harvey B. *The Politics of Public Enterprise: Oil and the French State*. Princeton, N.J.: Princeton University Press, 1985.

Gerschenkron, Alexander. *Economic Backwardness in Historical Perspective*. Cambridge, Mass.: Harvard University Press, 1962.

Gilbert, Neil. *Capitalism and the Welfare State: Dilemmas of Social Benevolence.* New Haven, Conn.: Yale University Press, 1983.

Goldthorpe, John H., ed. *Order and Conflict in Contemporary Capitalism.* Oxford: Oxford University Press, 1984.

Goodman, David, and Michael Redclift. *From Peasant to Proletarian: Capitalist Development and Agrarian Transitions.* New York: St. Martin's Press, 1982.

Gough, Ian. *The Political Economy of the Welfare State.* London: Macmillan, 1979.

Harpham, Edward J., and Alan Stone, eds. *The Political Economy of Public Policy.* Beverly Hills, Calif.: Sage, 1982.

Hayward, Jack. *The State and the Market Economy: Industrial Patriotism and Economic Intervention in France.* Brighton, England: Wheatsheaf Books, 1986.

Heclo, Hugh, and Aaron Wildavsky. *The Private Government of Public Money: Community and Policy in British Political Administration.* Berkeley: University of California Press, 1974.

Jackman, Robert W. "The Politics of Economic Growth, Once Again." *Journal of Politics* 51 (1989): 646–661.

Jacobson, Harold K., and Michel Oksenberg. *China's Entry into the IMF, World Bank, and GATT: Toward an International Economic Order.* Ann Arbor: University of Michigan Press, 1990.

Katzenstein, Peter J. *Corporatism and Change: Austria, Switzerland, and the Politics of Industry.* Ithaca, N.Y.: Carnell University Press, 1984.

Keeler, John T. S. *The Politics of Neo-Corporatism in France: Farmers, the State, and Agricultural Policymaking in the Fifth Republic.* New York: Oxford University Press, 1987.

Keohane, Robert. *After Hegemony: Cooperation and Discord in the World Political Economy.* Princeton, N.J.: Princeton University Press, 1984.

Kolodziej, Edward A. *Making and Marketing Arms: The French Experience and Its Implications for the Industrial System.* Princeton, N.J.: Princeton University Press, 1987.

Lange, Peter, and Geoffrey Garrett. "The Politics of Growth Reconsidered." *Journal of Politics* 49 (1987): 257–274.

Lehmbruch, Gerhard, and Philippe C. Schmitter, eds. *Patterns of Corporatist Intermediation.* Beverly Hills, Calif.: Sage, 1982.

Lindblom, Charles. *Politics and Markets.* New York: Basic Books, 1977.

Lowi, Theodore J. "American Business, Public Policy, Case Studies, and Political Theory." *World Politics* 16 (1964): 677–715.

Moran, Theodore H. *Multinational Corporations and the Politics of Dependence*. Princeton, N.J.: Princeton University Press, 1974.

O'Connor, James. *Accumulation Crisis*. Oxford: Basil Blackwell, 1984.

Offe, Claus. *Disorganized Capitalism*. Cambridge, Mass.: MIT Press, 1985.

Olson, Mancur. *The Rise and Decline of Nations: Economic Growth, Stagflation, and Social Rigidities*. New Haven, Conn.: Yale University Press, 1982.

Paige, Jeffrey. *Agrarian Revolution: Social Movements and Export Agriculture in the Underdeveloped World*. New York: Free Press, 1975.

Polanyi, Karl. *The Great Transformation: The Political and Economic Origins of Our Time*. Boston: Beacon Press, 1957.

Poulantzas, Nicos. *Classes in Contemporary Capitalism*. Trans. David Fernbach. London: New Left Books, 1975.

Pryor, Frederick L. *Public Expenditures in Communist and Capitalist Nations*. New Haven, Conn.: Yale University Press, 1968.

Przeworski, Adam. *Capitalism and Social Democracy*. Cambridge: Cambridge University Press, 1985.

Resnick, Stephen, and Richard D. Wolff. *Knowledge and Class: A Marxian Critique of Political Economy*. Chicago: University of Chicago Press, 1987.

Ross, George, et al. *Unions and Economic Crisis: Britain, West Germany and Sweden*. London: Allen and Unwin, 1984.

Schmitter, Philippe C., ed. *Corporatism and Policy-Making in Contemporary Western-Europe*. Special issue of *Comparative Political Studies* 10, no. 1 (April 1977).

Staniland, Martin. *What Is Political Economy?* New Haven, Conn.: Yale University Press, 1985.

Stevens, John D. *The Transition from Capitalism to Socialism*. London: Macmillan, 1979.

Vig, Norman J., and Steven E. Schier, eds. *Political Economy in Western Democracies*. New York: Holmes and Meier, 1985.

Wallerstein, Immanuel. *The Capitalist World Economy*. Cambridge: Cambridge University Press, 1980.

Wallerstein, Immanuel. *The Modern World-System*. 2 vols. New York: Academic Press, 1974–1980.

Wallerstein, Immanuel. *The Politics of the World Economy*. New York: Cambridge University Press, 1984.

INDUSTRIAL COUNTRIES: WESTERN EUROPE, NORTH AMERICA, JAPAN

Aberbach, Joel D., et al. *Bureaucrats and Politicians in Western Democracies*. Cambridge, Mass.: Harvard University Press, 1981.

Ashford, Douglas E. *The Emergence of the Welfare States*. Oxford: Blackwell, 1986.

Ashford, Douglas E., and E. W. Kelley, eds. *Nationalizing Social Security in Europe and America*. Greenwich, Conn.: JAI Press, 1986.

Berger, Suzanne, ed. *Organizing Interests in Western Europe: Pluralism, Corporatism, and the Transformation of Politics*. New York: Cambridge University Press, 1981.

Bracher, Karl D. *The German Dictatorship: The Origin, Structure and Effects of National Socialism*. New York: Praeger, 1970.

Brown, Bernard E., ed. *Eurocommunism and Eurosocialism: The Left Confronts Modernity*. New York: Irvington, 1978.

Castles, Francis G. *The Social Democratic Image of Society*. London: Routledge, 1978.

Crozier, Michel. *The Bureaucratic Phenomenon*. Chicago: University of Chicago Press, 1964.

Crozier, Michel, et al. *The Crisis of Democracy: Report on the Governability of Democracies to the Trilateral Commission*. New York: New York University Press, 1975.

Dalton, Russell J. *Citizen Politics in Western Democracies: Public Opinion and Political Parties in the United States, Great Britain, West Germany, and France*. Chatham, N.J.: Chatham House, 1988.

De Tocqueville, Alexis. *The Old Regime and the French Revolution*. Garden City, N.Y.: Doubleday, Anchor Books, 1955.

Dogan, Mattei. *Comparing Pluralist Democracies: Strains on Legitimacy*. Boulder, Colo.: Westview Press, 1988.

Esping-Andersen, Gösta, and Lee Rainwater, eds. *Stagnation and Renewal: The Rise and Fall of Social Policy Regimes*. Armonk, N.Y.: Sharpe, 1987.

Flora, Peter, and Arnold Heidenheimer, eds. *The Development of Welfare States in Europe and America*. New Brunswick, N.J.: Transaction Books, 1981.

Fox, Daniel M. *Health Policies, Health Politics: The British and American Experience, 1911–1965*. Princeton, N.J.: Princeton University Press, 1986.

Garon, Sheldon. *The State and Labor in Modern Japan*. Berkeley: University of California Press, 1987.

Gourevitch, Peter, et al. *Unions and Economic Crisis: Britain, West Germany and Sweden*. London: Allen and Unwin, 1984.

Gunther, Richard, et al. *Spain After Franco: The Making of a Competitive Party System*. Berkeley: University of California Press, 1986.

Heclo, Hugh, and Henrik Madsen. *Policy and Politics in Sweden: Principled Pragmatism*. Philadelphia: Temple University Press, 1987.

Heidenheimer, Arnold J., et al. *Comparative Public Policy: The Politics of Social Choice in Europe and America*. 2d ed. New York: St. Martin's Press, 1983.

Hewitt, Christopher. "The Effect of Political Democracy and Social Democracy on Equality in Industrial Societies." *American Sociological Review* 42 (1977): 450–464.

Inglehart, Ronald. *Culture Shift in Advanced Industrial Society*. Princeton, N.J.: Princeton University Press, 1990.

Johnson, Chalmers. *MITI and the Japanese Miracle*. Stanford, Calif.: Stanford University Press, 1982.

Kahler, Miles. *Decolonization in Britain and France: The Domestic Consequences of International Relations*. Princeton, N.J.: Princeton University Press, 1984.

Katzenstein, Peter. *Small States in World Markets: Industrial Policy in Europe*. Ithaca, N.Y.: Cornell University Press, 1985.

Korpi, Walter. *The Democratic Class Struggle*. London: Routledge and Kegan Paul, 1983.

Krieger, Joel. *Reagan, Thatcher, and the Politics of Decline*. Oxford: Oxford University Press, 1985.

Nagel, Stuart S. *Public Policy: Goals, Means, and Methods*. New York: St. Martin's Press, 1984.

Nordlinger, Eric A. *On the Autonomy of the Democratic State*. Cambridge, Mass.: Harvard University Press, 1981.

Pempel, T. J. *Policy and Politics in Japan: Creative Conservatism*. Philadelphia: Temple University Press, 1982.

Pempel, T. J., ed. *Uncommon Democracies: The One-Party Dominant Regimes*. Ithaca, N.Y.: Cornell University Press, 1990.

Rimlinger, Gaston. *Welfare Policy and Industrialization in Europe, America, and Russia*. New York: Wiley, 1971.

Rose, Richard, and Guy Peters. *Can Governments Go Bankrupt?* New York: Basic Books, 1978.

Samuels, Richard J. *The Business of the Japanese State.* Ithaca, N.Y.: Cornell University Press, 1987.

Schmitter, Philippe C., and Wolfgang Streek, eds. *Private Interest Government: Beyond Market and State.* Beverly Hills, Calif.: Sage, 1985.

Share, Donald. *The Making of Spanish Democracy.* New York: Praeger, 1986.

Suleiman, Ezra N. *Private Power and Centralization in France: The Notaries and the State.* Princeton, N.J.: Princeton University Press, 1987.

Taylor, Charles Lewis, ed. *Why Governments Grow: Measuring Public Size.* Beverly Hills, Calif.: Sage, 1983.

Tilly, Charles, ed. *The Formation of National States in Western Europe.* Princeton, N.J.: Princeton University Press, 1975.

Tomasson, Richard F., ed. *Comparative Social Research: The Welfare State 1883–1983.* Greenwich, Conn.: JAI Press, 1983.

Van Schendelen, M. P. C. M., and R. J. Jackson, eds. *The Politicisation of Business in Western Europe.* London: Croom Helm, 1987.

Weir, Margaret, Ann Orloff, and Theda Skocpol, eds. *The Politics of Social Policy in the United States.* Princeton, N.J. Princeton University Press, 1988.

Wilensky, Harold. *The Welfare State and Equality: Structural and Ideological Roots of Public Expenditure.* Berkeley: University of California Press, 1975.

Wilson, Thomas, and Dorothy J. Wilson. *The Political Economy of the Welfare State.* London: Allen and Unwin, 1982.

Wolfe, Willard. *From Radicalism to Socialism: Men and Ideas in the Formation of Fabian Socialist Doctrines, 1881–1915.* New Haven, Conn.: Yale University Press, 1975.

COMMUNIST AND FORMERLY COMMUNIST COUNTRIES: EASTERN EUROPE, SOVIET UNION, CHINA

Barry, Donald D., and Carol Barner-Barry. *Contemporary Soviet Politics: An Introduction.* 3rd ed. Englewood Cliffs, N.J.: Prentice-Hall, 1987.

Bialer, Seweryn. *Politics, Society, and Nationality in Gorbachev's Soviet Union*. Boulder, Colo.: Westview Press, 1988.

Bialer, Seweryn. *The Soviet Paradox: External Expansion, Internal Decline*. New York: Random House, 1987.

Bialer, Seweryn. *Stalin's Successors: Leadership, Stability, and Change in the Soviet Union*. New York: Cambridge University Press, 1980.

Brown, Archie, ed. *Political Culture and Communist Studies*. Armonk, N.Y.: Sharpe, 1984.

Brzezinski, Zbigniew. *The Grand Failure: Communism's Terminal Crisis*. New York: Scribner, 1989.

Colton, Timothy J. *The Dilemma of Reform in the Soviet Union*. Rev. ed. New York: Council on Foreign Relations, 1986.

Fischer-Galati, Stephen. *The Communist Parties of Eastern Central Europe*. New York: Columbia University Press, 1979.

Griffith, William E. *Central and Eastern Europe: The Opening Curtain?* Boulder, Colo.: Westview Press, 1989.

Harding, Harry. *China's Second Revolution*. Washington, D.C.: Brookings Institution, 1987.

Hewett, Ed A. *Reforming the Soviet Economy*. Washington, D.C.: Brookings Institutions, 1988.

Hough, Jerry F. *Russia and the West: Gorbachev and the Politics of Reform*. New York: Simon & Schuster, 1988.

Janos, Andrew C., ed. *Authoritarian Politics in Communist Europe: Uniformity and Diversity in One-Party States*. Berkeley: University of California Institute for International Studies, 1976.

Kittrie, Nicholas N., and Ivan Volgyes. *The Uncertain Future: Gorbachev's "Eastern Bloc."* New York: Paragon House, 1989.

Lewin, Moshe. *The Gorbachev Phenomenon: A Historical Interpretation*. Berkeley: University of California Press, 1988.

Medvedev, Roy. *Let History Judge: The Origins and Consequences of Stalinism*. Rev. ed. New York: Columbia University Press, 1989.

Moore, Barrington, Jr. *Soviet Politics: The Dilemma of Power*. New York: Harper Torchbook, 1967.

Motyl, Alexander. *Will the Non-Russians Rebel? State, Ethnicity, and Stability in the USSR*. Ithaca, N.Y.: Cornell University Press, 1987.

Pye, Lucian W. *The Dynamics of Chinese Politics*. Cambridge, Mass.: Oelgeschlager, Gunn & Hain, 1981.

Rakowska-Harmstone, Teresa. *Communism in Eastern Europe*. Bloomington: Indiana University Press, 1984.

Rothschild, Joseph. *Return to Diversity: A Political History of East Central Europe.* New York: Oxford University Press, 1989.

Shapiro, Leonard. *The Communist Party of the Soviet Union.* 2d ed. New York: Vintage Books, 1971.

Shmelyev, Nikolai, and Vladimir Popov. *The Turning Point: Revitalizing the Soviet Economy.* Garden City, N.Y.: Doubleday, 1989.

Smith, Tony. *Thinking Like a Communist: The State and Legitimacy in the Soviet Union, China, and Cuba.* New York: Norton, 1987.

Terry, Sarah M. *Soviet Policy in Eastern Europe.* New Haven, Conn.: Yale University Press, 1984.

Tucker, Robert C. *Political Culture and Leadership in Soviet Russia.* New York: Norton, 1987.

Tucker, Robert C. *The Soviet Political Mind: Stalinism and Post-Stalin Change.* New York: Norton, 1972.

Von Beyme, Klaus. *Economics and Politics Within Socialism: A Comparative and Developmental Approach.* New York: Praeger, 1982.

Walker, Martin. *The Waking Giant: Gorbachev's Russia.* New York: Pantheon, 1988.

White, Stephen, et al. *Communist Political Systems: An Introduction.* 2d ed. New York: St. Martin's Press, 1987.

White, Stephen, and Daniel Nelson. *Communist Politics: A Reader.* New York: New York University Press, 1986.

DEVELOPING COUNTRIES: ASIA, AFRICA, LATIN AMERICA

Amin, Samir. *Accumulation on a World Scale.* New York: Monthly Review Press, 1974.

Arian, Asher. *Politics in Israel: The Second Generation,* 2d ed. Chatham, N.J.: Chatham House, 1989.

Baloyra, Enrique A., ed. *Comparing New Democracies: Transition and Consolidation in Mediterranean Europe and the Southern Cone.* Boulder, Colo.: Westview Press, 1987.

Biersteker, Thomas J. *Multinationals, The State, and Control of the Nigerian Economy.* Princeton, N.J.: Princeton University Press, 1987.

Booth, John, and Mitchell Seligson, eds. *Elections and Democracy in Central America.* Chapel Hill: University of North Carolina Press, 1989.

Bozzoli, Belinda, ed. *Class, Community and Conflict: South African Perspectives*. Athens: Ohio University Press, 1987.

Burke, Edmund, III, and Ira M. Lapidus, eds. *Islam, Politics, and Social Movements*. Berkeley: University of California Press, 1988.

Butler, David, Ashok Lahiri, and Prannoy Roy. *India Decides: Elections, 1952–1989*. New Delhi: Living Media India, 1989.

Callaghy, Thomas M. *The State-Society Struggle: Zaire in Comparative Perspective*. New York: Columbia University Press, 1984.

Cardoso, Fernando Henrique, and Enzo Faletto, *Dependency and Development in Latin America*. Trans. Marjorie Mattingly Urquidi. Berkeley: University of California Press, 1979.

Cole, Juan R., and Nikki R. Keddie, eds. *Shi'ism and Social Protest*. New Haven, Conn.: Yale University Press, 1986.

Collier, David, ed. *The New Authoritarianism in Latin America*. Princeton, N.J.: Princeton University Press, 1979.

Collier, Ruth Berins, and David Collier. *Shaping the Political Arena: Critical Junctures, the Labor Movement, and Regime Dynamics in Latin America*. Princeton, N.J.: Princeton University Press, 1991.

Coquery-Vidrovitch, Catherine. *Africa: Endurance and Change South of the Sahara*. Berkeley: University of California Press, 1988.

Crummey, Donald, ed. *Banditry, Rebellion and Social Protest in Africa*. Portsmouth, N.H.: Heinemann, 1986.

Domínguez, Jorge I. *Cuba: Order and Revolution*. Cambridge, Mass.: Harvard University Press, 1978.

Drake, Paul W., and Eduardo Silva, eds. *Elections and Democratization in Latin America, 1980–1985*. San Diego: Center for Iberian and Latin American Studies, University of California, 1986.

Ergas, Zaki, ed. *The African State in Transition*. Basingstoke: Macmillan, 1987.

Erickson, Kenneth Paul, *The Brazilian Corporative State and Working-class Politics*. Berkeley: University of California Press, 1977.

Evans, Peter, *Dependent Development: The Alliance of Multinational, State, and Local Capital in Brazil*. Princeton, N.J. Princeton University Press, 1979.

Fagen, Richard R., Carmen Diana Deere, and José Luis Carragio, eds. *Transition and Development*. New York: Monthly Review Press, 1986.

Falola, Toyin, ed. *Britain and Nigeria: Exploitation or Development?* London: Zed Press, 1987.

Fatton, Robert, Jr. "Bringing the Ruling Class Back In: Class, State, and Hegemony in Africa." *Comparative Politics* 20, no. 3 (April 1988): 253–264.

Fatton, Robert, Jr. *The Making of a Liberal Democracy: Senegal's Passive Revolution 1975–1985.* Boulder, Colo.: Lynne Rienner, 1987.

Feit, Edward. "Military Coups and Political Development: Some Lessons from Ghana and Nigeria." *World Politics* 20 (1968): 179–193.

Frank, André Gunder. *Capitalism and Underdevelopment in Latin America.* Rev. ed. New York: Monthly Review Press, 1969.

Geertz, Clifford. *Religion, Politics and History in India.* The Hague: Mouton, 1970.

Gendzier, Irene L. *Managing Political Change: Social Scientists and the Third World.* Boulder, Colo.: Westview Press, 1985.

Giorgis, Dawit Wolde. *Red Tears: War, Famine and Revolution in Ethiopia.* Trenton, N.J.: Red Sea Press, 1989.

Greenberg, Stanley B. *Legitimating the Illegitimate: States, Markets, and Resistance in South Africa.* Berkeley: University of California Press, 1987.

Gutteridge, William. *Military Regimes in Africa.* London: Methuen, 1975.

Halliday, Fred, and Hamza Alavi, eds. *State and Ideology in the Middle East and Pakistan.* London: Macmillan, 1988.

Heper, Metin. *The State Tradition in Turkey.* Walkington, England: Eothen Press, 1985.

Heper, Metin, and Ahmet Evin, eds. *State, Democracy and the Military: Turkey in the 1980s.* Berlin: de Gruyter, 1988.

Higgenson, John. *A Working Class in the Making: Belgian Colonial Labor Policy, Private Enterprise and the African Mineworker.* Madison: University of Wisconsin Press, 1989.

Howard, Rhoda E. *Human Rights in Commonwealth Africa.* Totowa, N.J.: Rowman and Littlefield, 1986.

Iliffe, John. *The African Poor: A History.* New York: Cambridge University Press, 1989.

Isaacman, Allen, and Barbara Isaacman. *Mozambique: From Colonization to Revolution.* Boulder, Colo.: Westview Press, 1983.

Jackson, Robert H., and Carl G. Rosberg, Jr. *Personal Rule in Black Africa.* Berkeley: University of California Press, 1982.

Jonas, Suzanne, and Nancy Stein, eds. *Democracy in Latin America.* New York: Bergin and Garvey, 1990.

Joseph, Richard A. *Democracy and Prebendal Politics in Nigeria: The Rise and Fall of the Second Republic*. Cambridge: Cambridge University Press, 1987.

Karl, Terry Lynn. *The Paradox of Plenty: Oil Booms and Petro-States*. Berkeley: University of California Press, 1991.

Keddie, Nikki R., ed. *Religion and Politics in Iran: Shi'ism from Quietism to Revolution*. New Haven, Conn.: Yale University Press, 1983.

Keller, Edmond J. *Revolutionary Ethiopia: From Empire to People's Republic*. Bloomington: Indiana University Press, 1989.

Keller, Edmond J., and Donald Rothchild, eds. *Afro-Marxist Regimes: Ideology and Public Policy*. Boulder, Colo: Lynne Rienner, 1987.

Kennedy, Paul. *African Capitalism: The Struggle for Ascendancy*. New York: Cambridge University Press, 1988.

Kitching, Gavin. *Class and Economic Change in Kenya*. New Haven, Conn.: Yale University Press, 1980.

Lan, David. *Guns and Rain: Guerrillas and Spirit Mediums in Zimbabwe*. Berkeley: University of California Press, 1985.

Libby, Ronald T. *The Politics of Economic Power in Southern Africa*. Princeton, N.J.: Princeton University Press, 1987.

Markakis, John. *National and Class Conflict in the Horn of Africa*. Cambridge: Cambridge University Press, 1987.

Markovitz, Irving Leonard, ed. *Studies in Power and Class in Africa*. New York: Oxford University Press, 1987.

Mittleman, James. *Underdevelopment and the Transition to Socialism: Mozambique and Tanzania*. New York: Academic Press, 1981.

Munson, Henry, Jr. *Islam and Revolution in the Middle East*. New Haven, Conn.: Yale University Press, 1988.

Newbury, Catherine. *The Cohesion of Oppression: Clientship and Ethnicity in Rwanda, 1860–1960*. New York: Columbia University Press, 1988.

O'Brien, Philip, and Paul Cammack, eds. *Generals in Retreat: The Crisis of Military Rule in Latin America*. Manchester: Manchester University Press, 1985.

Oyugi, Walter O., et al. *Democratic Theory and Practice in Africa*. Portsmouth, N.H.: Heinemann, 1988.

Ranger, Terence. *Peasant Consciousness and Guerrilla War in Zimbabwe*. Berkeley: University of California Press, 1985.

Roff, William, ed. *Islam and the Political Economy of Meaning: Com-*

parative Studies of Muslim Discourses. Berkeley: University of California Press, 1987.

Roquié, Alain. *The Military and the State in Latin America*. Berkeley: University of California Press, 1987.

Rothchild, Donald, and Naomi Chazan, eds. *The Precarious Balance: State and Society in Africa*. Boulder, Colo.: Westview Press, 1988.

Rothchild, Donald, and Victor Olorunsola, eds. *State Versus Ethnic Claims: African Policy Dilemmas*. Boulder, Colo.: Westview Press, 1983.

Russell, Diana E. H. *Lives of Courage: Women for a New South Africa*. New York: Basic Books, 1989.

Scott, James. *Weapons of the Weak: Everyday Forms of Peasant Rebellion*. New Haven, Conn.: Yale University Press, 1985.

Sivan, Emmanuel. *Radical Islam: Medieval Theology and Modern Politics*. New Haven, Conn.: Yale University Press, 1985.

Sklar, Richard L. *Corporate Power in an African State: The Political Impact of Multinational Mining Companies in Zambia*. Berkeley: University of California Press, 1975.

Stallings, Barbara. *Class Conflict and Economic Development in Chile, 1958–1973*. Stanford, Calif.: Stanford University Press, 1978.

Stepan, Alfred. *Rethinking Military Politics: Brazil and the Southern Cone*. Princeton, N.J.: Princeton University Press, 1988.

Stepan, Alfred. *The State and Society: Peru in Comparative Perspective*. Princeton, N.J.: Princeton University Press, 1978.

Stepan, Alfred, ed. *Democratizing Brazil: Problems of Transition and Consolidation*. New York: Columbia University Press, 1989.

Waterbury, John. *The Egypt of Nasser and Sadat: The Political Economy of Two Regimes*. Princeton, N.J.: Princeton University Press, 1983.

Welch, Claude. *No Farewell to Arms: Military Disengagement in Africa and Latin America*. Boulder, Colo.: Westview Press, 1987.

Wiarda, Howard J. *Corporatism and National Development in Latin America*. Boulder, Colo.: Westview Press, 1981.

Wiarda, Howard J., ed. *Politics and Social Change in Latin America: The Distinct Tradition*. 2d ed. Amherst: University of Massachusetts Press, 1982.

Wolf, Eric. *Peasant Wars of the Twentieth Century*. New York: Harper & Row, 1969.

Young, Crawford. *Ideology and Development in Africa*. New Haven, Conn.: Yale University Press, 1982.

Young, Crawford, and Thomas Turner. *The Rise and Decline of the Zairian State*. Madison: *University of Wisconsin Press, 1985*.

Zartman, I. William. *Ripe for Resolution: Conflict and Intervention in Africa*. Rev. ed. New York: Oxford University Press, 1989.

Index